Library of the History of Psychology Theories

Series Editor
Robert W. Rieber
Fordham University
New York, NY
USA

For further volumes:
http://www.springer.com/series/6927

Eugene Taylor

The Mystery of Personality

A History of Psychodynamic Theories

 Springer

Eugene Taylor
Saybrook Graduate School and
    Research Center
747 Front St
San Francisco, CA
94111
USA
etaylor@igc.org

ISBN 978-0-387-98103-1   e-ISBN 978-0-387-98104-8
DOI 10.1007/978-0-387-98104-8
Springer Dordrecht Heidelberg London New York

Library of Congress Control Number: 2009927014

Printed on acid-free paper

Springer is part of Springer Science+Business Media (www.springer.com)

"Every man is. . .
like all other men,
like some other men,
like no other man."

Henry A. Murray, MD, PhD (1893–1988)

Acknowledgments

Readers, I hope, will forgive me at the outset for any inordinate focus on materials in the English language and particularly my focus on dynamic theories of personality in the history of American psychology, although I have also referred to British and European sources and even touched lightly on the classical psychologies of Asia. My formal acknowledgments are gratefully extended to Mrs. Bay James Baker, literary executor of the William James Estate, for permission to refer to unpublished material in the James papers at Harvard; to Harley Holden, director emeritus at the Harvard University Archives; and to the Trustees of the Ella Lyman Cabot Trust for allowing me to establish a stewardship over the papers of Gordon Willard Allport from 1979 to 1985, which permitted me to create an index for the files and to complete the index of correspondence begun by Mrs. Kay Bruner; to Dr. Gardner Murphy for first introducing me to Anthony Sutich back in 1969; and to Dr. Lois Murphy for the chance to assist her on her biography of her husband 20 years later; to Mrs. Geraldine Stevens, for bequeathing to me before she left Harvard the 10,000 piece combined collection she had assembled alphabetically of other authors' reprints belonging to Edwin G. Boring, Gordon Willard Allport, and Stanley Smith Stevens; to Dr. Caroline Fish Chandler Murray for the many kindnesses she extended to me during the years I worked for her husband, the late Henry A. Murray. Through Harry I met everyone who was still alive who had been connected to his era in psychology, including Erik and Joan Erikson, Sol Rosenzweig, Robert White, Sylvan Tomkins, Nevitt Sanford, and others. Acknowledgments also go to Ms. Analize Katz, former librarian in the Department of Psychology in William James Hall; she preceded Mr. Richard Kaufman, who also granted me unrestricted access to his library's holdings; and to the late Paul Roazan for wise counsel on certain points of psychoanalytic lore. Acknowledgements also to the medical historian, John Burnham, for directing my attention to the Swiss influence on American psychology and psychiatry. I owe a particular debt to the late Henri Ellenberger for his keen support of my early work reconstructing the American scene in dynamic psychiatry, which he had so admirably chronicled from the perspective of events in Europe; to Sonu Shamdasani, PhD, reader in Jung History at the University of London and editor of the new translations of Jung through the Philemon Foundation for many endnotes and editorial comments; to Richard Wolfe, then Joseph Garland Librarian in the Boston Medical Library and Archivist at Harvard

Medical School, now Distinguished Scholar in Residence at the College of Physicians, Philadelphia, and Elin Wolfe, co-author of the Walter B. Cannon biography, who both sheltered an errant scholar back in the beginning who had come from Divinity and then entered the history of psychiatry; their circle included Benjamin White, MD, primary author of the Stanley Cobb biography; the late Mark Altschule, MD, pathologist and historian of medicine at Harvard Medical School; and Sanford Gifford, MD, archivist of the Boston Psychoanalytic Society and Institute, among others. The late Eric Carlson, MD, at Payne Whitney/New York Hospital, was an avid supporter, as was the late Ernest Hilgard. The late Rollo May was particularly helpful in clarifying points having to do with the history of existential-humanistic psychology; as were the late Anthony Sutich, and also Miles Vich, successor to Sutich as editor of the *Journal of Transpersonal Psychology*; to Natalie Rogers, PhD, for invaluable material on her father, the late Carl Rogers, and herself, now being developed by Sue Ann Herron; and to the late Francis O. Schmitt, molecular biologist and University Professor at MIT for drawing my attention to the relation between my historical work and certain humanistic implications of the neuroscience revolution in which he participated as a founder of the Neuroscience Research Program. I am indebted also to Herbert Benson, MD, for the many hours I was able to review his work as Visiting Historian in the Mind/Body Medical Institute from 2000 to 2002. One of the greatest in my personal pantheon of intellectual mentors was my friend and confidant, the late Sheldon White. And a special tribute goes to the existential-humanistic, transpersonal, and phenomenological faculty at the original PhD program in humanistic psychology, now operating under the name of Saybrook Graduate School: among them, Maureen O'Hara, Arthur Bohart, Jeannie Achterberg, Stan Krippner, Tom Greening, David Lukoff, Alan Combs, Amedeo Giorgi, Ruth Richards, Donald Rothberg, Kirk Schneider, and others. Jim Anderson provided important materials on Henry A. Murray, while Nicole Barenbaum graciously read over the chapter on personality theory at Harvard, and Teresa Iverson the chapters on Jung and Adler. Thomas J. Martinez contributed on Binzwanger.

Ward Williamson assisted with the collection of sources and Susan Gordon, newly minted Saybrook PhD, peroically assisted me with the endnotes and the final draft of the manuscript, while Robert Rieber served as a series editor, of which the present volume is one of eleven, produced through the good offices of, Sharon Panulla, Executive Editor at Springer.

Contents

Chapter 1
The Trinity of Affinity: Personality, Consciousness, and Psychotherapeutics

One could say that three of the most dreaded plagues in the history of scientific psychology have been conceptions of personality, models of the unconscious, and systems of psychotherapy. They have proven more than a mere inconvenience; they have encroached so much into the domain of the orderly, the logical, and the rational that to the experimentalist they have come to represent a veritable disease. Worse, all three converge in what has come to be referred to as dynamic theories of personality. If the experimentalists actually believe that such concepts even refer to anything real, which most of them do not, the history of such theories has been the perpetual bane of scientific psychology because they represent domains of human experience that are not readily amenable to precise measurement, prediction, and control. Yet, they not only refuse to go away but also have tended to dominate the definition of psychology in popular culture, condemning scientific psychology to the oblivion of the specialized peer reviewed journals and the university laboratories, reductionistic science being perceived as generally tackling insignificant problems with impeccable methods.

Dynamic theories of personality have always encroached on the experimental sciences in a variety of ways. Random examples include Freud's insistence that psychoanalysis was a science independent of neurology, psychiatry, and psychology; Jung's word association experiments around 1900, which were believed to measure unconscious complexes; Wolfgang Pauli's application of Jung's theory of the archetypes to problems in quantum physics in the 1920s; the experimental analysis of psychoanalytic concepts in the 1930s; the experimental depth psychology of the gestaltist, Werner Wolff, or the attempted fusion of learning theory and psychoanalysis in the 1950s; or the effort today to fuse psychoanalysis with neural Darwinism. One could say the scientist–practitioner model, the so-called Boulder model, is another preeminent example, except that even there the reductionistic epistemology that has gripped psychology for the past 100 years has always been promoted as the primary and more important orienting attitude underlying clinical practice.

Thus, historians of psychology have placed dynamic theories of personality as a minor and relatively unintegrated idiom in the history of mainstream psychology, a scientific discipline, despite the fact that psychotherapy, its most visible product, is probably the primary activity of most psychologists and psychiatrists as those disciplines are defined in the West.

E. Taylor, *The Mystery of Personality*, Library of the History of Psychology Theories, DOI 10.1007/978-0-387-98104-8_1, © Springer Science+Business Media, LLC 2009

To understand this conundrum, in its broadest and most eclectic sense, psychology must be considered both an art and a science, instead of the present situation where reductionistic science is elevated to an undeserved status as the ideal, while the interior phenomenological life of the person, the domain of meaning, and the problem of the personal equation in science, which are preeminently problems of psychology, are completely ignored. Historically and epistemologically, psychology is defined as having its roots as an academic discipline in the methods of the natural sciences, while it remains situated within the social sciences. But practically, in the clinic, where the therapist must deal with the mystery of the person in front of them and adapt the data of research wherever feasible to the more pragmatic criteria of what works, here, psychology becomes more an art, dominated by intuitive norms that may or may not be informed by reductionistic science.

From a scientific standpoint, however, for this reason the academy and the clinic are not considered equal. Following the German metaphor of hard science, what the clinician calls an art, which is actually an endeavor in its own right, the academic refers to somewhat pejoratively as applied science, that is, a lower order subsidiary of the so-called empirical and measurement-oriented sciences. Ideally, the scientific myth goes, nothing is allowed in the clinic that was not first verified in the laboratory. It is a dictum that remains largely unspoken, since it rarely ever happens in reality, yet it is at the root of the unity in science movement among the experimentalists who control theory building and who find psychology always so untidy; it can be seen in new trends toward evidence-based practice, and it is the implied epistemology behind the construction of the licensure exams and insurance re-imbursement for clinicians.

Thus, psychology exists as a discipline defined by a split between its experimental and clinical traditions. Some experts still believe that it is an integrated science to the extent that the clinical subsumes itself under the experimental, so that the field is united by a single reductionistic epistemology. Others see the experimental and clinical traditions as separate lineages, each with their own famous figures, methods, and epistemologies that define personality and consciousness in radically different ways.

However, the attempt by individuals to fathom their own personal reality and formulate an adaptive language of self and others to their experience must be considered yet a third venue defining psychology. Curiously, experimentalists reject this view that defines psychology as self-knowledge in favor of defining psychology as a science, the purpose of which is the manipulation, prediction, and control of behavior. Scientists believe that only they deal with the real and that they have no metaphysics. They think that first person accounts of personal experience are like unreliable hallucinations. Meanwhile, every system of thought, including reductionistic science, has metaphysical underpinnings. Yet the reductionists claim that only they possess the superior source of knowledge. As a result, dynamic theories of personality have made little incursion into the experimentalists' venue. This also means that Freud never really had the impact on psychology and psychiatry that people think that he had, where the core of these endeavors is defined in both disciplines as laboratory-oriented research.

The historical reality is that other kinds of psychology have flourished outside the laboratory mentality, creating a situation where there is more than one definition of psychology in common currency. The fact that dynamic theories of the unconscious have developed independently in the clinical and more experiential spheres, but not in the laboratory, is a case in point. Logically, then, if there is more than one definition of psychology in common currency, then there must be more than one history of psychology. This is the vantage point taken in the present volume.

The Hypothesis of the Three Streams

Figure 1.1 illustrates the hypothesis of the three streams. Academic laboratory psychology has its own history, which is actually independent of the history of clinical psychology, and these two streams stand in relation to a third stream, the history of a tradition of folk psychology that is primarily experiential in orientation. The experimental tradition, based on an epistemology of scientific reductionism, has dominated the laboratory within the academy and attempted to confine a definition of psychology primarily to what can be measured, although there have been important exceptions.[1] Deriving its roots more from German experimental laboratory methods and English mental testing, this lineage is exemplified by Boring's *History of Experimental Psychology* (1929, 1950).[2] In contrast to this lineage is the clinical stream; by definition more person-centered but still partly under the sway of the experimentalists' epistemology, where dynamic theories of personality have tended to flourish, conceptions of the unconscious have multiplied, and definitions of personality have been more diverse. This stream is best exemplified by works such as Henri Ellenberger's *Discovery of the Unconscious* (1970).[3] Finally, there is the experiential stream, a lineage of psychospiritual anthropologies indigenous to popular culture, developed by individuals for purposes of understanding their own lifetime journey toward self-realization. This line is best exemplified by my brief study, *Shadow Culture: Psychology and Spirituality in America* (1999).[4] For purposes of the present volume, we may say that dynamic theories of personality have developed within the second and third streams, but always been subjected to the criticism of psychologists in the first stream, who have, by and large, but with a few very distinguished exceptions, no dynamic theories linking personality and consciousness of their own.

A second observation is that models of psychotherapy and consciousness, particularly in the past 50 years, have flourished in the counterculture to such an extent that they constitute a veritable revolution out in culture at large that is wider and deeper and more pervasive than that recognized by the theories and practices of the academy and the professions. This revolution is particularly obvious at the interface where clinical services meet consumer demand. There, an ideological war is being waged between greater scientific control of what goes on in the therapeutic hour and expectations of the client that the therapist is prepared to address via the depth and breadth of the client's own personal experience. However, depending on economics, education, and worldview, the licensed therapist is confronted with multicultural

Experimental	Clinical	Experiential
1860s Era of Religion and Moral Philosophy	Era of the Physician and Minister	Literary Psychology of the Transcendentalists
1880s Physiological Psychology, German psychophysics, and English Mental Testing	The French Experimental Psychology of the Subconscious and Psychical Research	Era of Spiritualism and Mental Healing
1890s The Functionalism of William James	The Era of Experimental Psychopathology	Christian Science, New Thought and the World Parliament of Religions
1900s The Era of the ìSchools" including Gestalt Psychology	The Era of Psychotherapeutics and the Emmanuel Movement Jung precedes Freud	The Depth psychologies of Freud and Jung flourish among the artists and psychics
1910s Behaviorism takes Control of the academic laboratories	Era of Military psychology and mass Testing	Jung, Freud, and Bergson define popular psychospiritual consciousness; Buchmanites organize into the Oxford Group
1920s Era of Tests and Measurements and advances in inferential analysis	Tests and Measurements	Era of Psychics, Swamis, Marx, and Radical Sexual Politics
1930s Age of Theory Begins: Era of Learning Theory versus The Macro-Personality Theorists	Era of Psychoanalytic Ego Psychology Psychosomatic Medicine, and Pastoral Counseling	Radicalization of Social psychology Era of the Surrealists and existentialists; AA is founded
1940s Era of Military Psychology	Emergence of Scientist-Practitioner Model	Era of Huxley, Merton and Watts begins
1950s Neo-Behavioristic Era of Modeling begins: Humanistic Psychology emerges as an Academic Endeavor	Humanistic, Existential, and Phenomenological Therapies Dominate Clinical Psychology	Era of Suzuki, Zen and the Beat Generation
1960s Cognitive Psychology takes over the academic laboratories	Psychedelics, the Community Health Movement, and Client-Centered Therapy challenge psychoanalysis	Human Potential Mvt. Arises, Era of psychedelics begins, Radicalization of depth psychology accelerates. Bodywork and group encounter become the rage
1970s Cognitive Science expands	Medicalization and over-regulation dominates clinical psychology; Clinicians take control of the American Psychological Assn.	Maslow and Sutich launch Transpersonal Psychology, Absorbs Existential and Humanistic psychology; Gender politics and meditation emerge as new forms of psychotherapy.
1980s Era of Artificial intelligence, information processing Models; Scientists bolt From APA and form the Amer. Psychological Society	Licensing requirements tighten Psychologist win class action suit Against the MD psychoanalysts; Homosexuality depathologized Behavioral Medicine develops	Shamanism, spirituality and health become linked. Multiculturalism emerges Mind/body medicine develops
1990s Neuroimaging introduced	Evidenced based practice and psychopharmacology introduced Cognitive therapy colonizes spirituality	Noetic Sciences, Holistic Medicine, Ecopsychology, and entheogens emerge in psychotherapy
2000 Positive Psychology launched and Brain neuroscience expands	Race, Class and Gender become a new focus; Only cognitive and behavioral and psychoanalytic therapies permitted for licensure	Complementary and Alternative therapies, Mind/body medicine, and Socially engaged spirituality emerge

Fig. 1.1 A history of American psychology in three streams

differences, new experiments with gender identity, exposure to non-Western therapies such as meditation and alternative medicine, or questions about spirituality that science and the professions are not presently prepared to meet. In this sense, the focus has shifted from the reality of the unconscious and dynamic theories of personality to much more sophisticated conceptions of personality and consciousness coming from non-Western influences, which represent both a radicalization of depth psychology and a portal through which Western cultural consciousness might pass in its inevitable encounter with worldviews different from its own. Dynamic theories of personality represent a bridge into that domain.

Dynamic Theories of Personality and Their Histories

The great historian of experimental psychology, Edwin G. Boring, once wrote that everyone in Titchener's lab understood that to know the history behind a fact was what differentiated the scholar from the mere experimentalist. Boring, of course, was a special case, as he was a trained experimentalist, but remembered mainly for his groundbreaking work, *A History of Experimental Psychology*. He struggled with the relationship between historical scholarship and scientific experimentation throughout his entire career, torn between the extreme physicalist and deterministic lineage with which he chose to most closely identify and more whimsical conceptions, such as the *zeitgeist*—the consciousness or spirit of the times, which he could not prove, but which explained exactly the kind of synchronicity, readiness, and emergence of novelty that marked events and personalities simultaneously occurring in different places in the history of science.

Historiography in psychology since Boring's time has continued to proceed by fits and starts and has not yet actually achieved its maturity. This is due in no small part to Boring's overemphasis on the German experimental laboratory tradition and his erroneous equation of that lineage with experimental psychology in the United States as the only scientific psychology to be considered legitimate. Most historiography of psychology since then continues to be an elaboration on this one, overly simplistic theme. Lightner Witmer, for instance, is widely considered to be the "father" of clinical psychology in the United States, largely because his students, who were not historians, later erroneously claimed he had coined the term "clinical psychology."[5] Witmer was certainly of the so-called proper lineage, having been a student of Wundt, but the historical problem this claim leaves unresolved is that Witmer was violently against a dynamic psychology of the unconscious and engaged in no form of psychotherapeutics himself. Yet clinical psychologists and psychiatrists have always been primarily identified as practitioners of psychotherapeutic methods which, until the advent of the cognitive behavioral therapies, have been based on dynamic theories of personality.

Another example is the attempt to draft a history of clinical psychology. Reisman (1966),[6] not a trained historian, followed closely Boring's earlier history, emphasizing the German laboratory tradition. Although he brought in English and French influences and crossed over occasionally into clinical psychiatry, his tendency was uncritically to mix events that could plausibly be related to what we might call clinical psychology today with a history of psychology as an academic experimental science. His facts are wrong in many places, his dates incorrect, and his knowledge of the historical literature of the different periods slim. The result is a more seamless story than actually occurred, especially since many of the real issues argued in different historical periods went unrecognized.

There are numerous works, known and unknown, that have reviewed dynamic theories of personality from one vantage point or another. Gregory Zilboorg's *A History of Medical Psychology* (1941) and Franz Alexander and Sheldon Selesnicks's *History of Psychiatry* (1966) have a particularly psychoanalytic slant.[7] Dieter Wyss's *Depth Psychology: A Critical History* begins as if there was nothing before Freud, but gives a particularly detailed look at the systems after psychoanalysis, including the Jungian and the existential.[8] Histories of psychoanalysis in the United States abound, particularly those by John Burnham, Nathan G. Hale Jr., and works by Jacques Quen and Erik Carlson.[9] A new genre has emerged with books such as Frank Sulloway's *Freud: Biologist of the Mind*, Jeffrey Masson's *The Assault on Truth: Freud's Suppression of the Seduction Theory* (1984), and John Kerr's *A Most Dangerous Method*, but these are largely historical studies encompassing a specific theme.[10] An important representation of the new Freud scholarship is Andre Haynal and Ernst Falzader's *One Hundred Years of Psychoanalysis.*[11]

Some of the standard histories of psychotherapy include Donald K. Freedheim's *History of Psychotherapy a Century of Change* (1992), which simply made: up what the history of the subject before 1900 must have been like; Jan Ehrenwald's *The History of Psychotherapy: From Healing Magic to Encounter* (1976), and Phillip Rief's *Triumph of the Therapeutic* (1966), all of which are popular and not serious historical studies.[12] More general histories of clinical psychology and psychiatry also touch upon dynamic theories of personality.[13]

There are also idiosyncratic period pieces, well known in their own time but quite forgotten today. Examples include The History of Psychotherapy. I. The Psychotherapy of Drugs; The History of Psychotherapy. II: Psychotherapy by Means of Miraculous; and The History of Psychotherapy. III: The History of Psychotherapy IV. These were written by Jean Camus and Philippe Pagniez, translated from the French by Frederick Peterson and Evelyn Garrigue in 1908–1909. There is also William Lovell Northridge's *Modern Theories of the Unconscious* (1924) and Pierre Janet's, two volume *Psychological Healing* (1925).[14]

The key figure most influential in the present era regarding the history of dynamic theories of personality was the late Henri Ellenberger. Ellenberger wrote extensively on what he interchangeably called the history of dynamic psychiatry, dynamic psychology, or dynamic psychotherapy. His most well-known and groundbreaking work was *The Discovery of the Unconscious*, but he virtually founded a new school of historiography in psychology and psychiatry even before that with numerous shorter studies on figures such as Hermann Rorschach and Pierre Janet.[15] Prior to his work, dynamic psychotherapy was considered erroneously to have originated with Freud. The histories of modern psychotherapy almost all begin with Charcot and the rehabilitation of hypnosis as a diagnostic and therapeutic tool for understanding the psychoneuroses in France in the early 1880s, but the story would then always jump to Freud and the Clark University Conference in 1909, as if nothing of any consequence went on in between. Ellenberger showed decisively that, in addition to Breuer and Freud in Vienna, a dynamic psychology of the subconscious flourished in France and elsewhere long before Freud came on the scene. Such a psychology focused largely around first Charcot and Bernheim, Pierre Janet and what Binet had called the French Experimental Psychology of the Subconscious and figures such as August Forel, Eugen Bleuler, Carl Jung, and Paul DuBois in Switzerland. Subsequently, scholars following Ellenberger's work have defined a 40-year period before the founding of the psychoanalytic institutes in the 1920s in which Freud played but a small part. This earlier era was dominated by developments in scientific psychotherapy along a French-Swiss-English-and-American psychotherapeutic axis, in which a tremendous amount of cross-communication was taking place among a community of physicians, philosophers, ethicists, psychologists, psychical researchers, and social service workers. The center of gravity of these discussions between 1880 and 1920 was Paris, Cambridge, England, Geneva, and Boston, until it was displaced by the advent of psychoanalysis as an international movement in the West. The focus of scientific psychotherapy then shifted to Vienna, Berlin, London, New York, and Washington, DC in the 1920s and then went on to have an important history as a psychoanalytic enterprise from then on.

Jung and Adler must be considered independently, however. Their respective systems rested on completely different epistemological foundations, and their models of the unconscious were different from Freud's. It must also be understood that we now live in a post-Freudian era, where Freud, who was not accurately interpreted in his own time, has yet to be accurately understood today.

A word must also be said for the centrality of the person in different histories of the dynamic theories. The rational impulse is to criticize an all too exclusive focus on the interior life of the individual, leaving out or considering as quite peripheral both the developmental trajectory of the person over the life span and the social forces impinging from the external environment that mould and shape personality. Neither of these omissions is real from a phenomenological standpoint. The interior life of the person is not just one more category on the rationalists' laundry list of how individuality is to be defined. The interior point of view is just that—the perception of one's self from the standpoint of one's self at the center of the experience. But the literature on the developmental trajectory of the person is vast and the rational critic looks at the psychodynamic focus and demands an allegedly more balanced view. Introductory textbooks in psychology, the least up-to-date sourcebooks on new developments, in this regard, traditionally cite only the developmental models of Freud, Piaget, Erikson, and Kohlberg. Freud looked at the psychosexual stages of the developing child from birth to adolescence. Piaget looked at the cognitive tasks achieved in the early years. Erikson focused on identity through the stages of the entire life span, while Kohlberg focused on the stages of moral development. Possibly the most important idea to come out of psychoanalysis was the developmental hypothesis. This notion posited that elements of personality may fixate at certain early stages of life, while the rest of personality continues to evolve to adulthood. Therapy involves uncovering the fixation, making it conscious, and integrating it into the larger on-going worldview of the person.

While these are significant models they remain incomplete; they give the impression that not much has happened in the area of development beyond a simple, rational progression of events. What development does not yet mean is the expansion and contraction of consciousness at any point along the evolutionary scale, giving development a new meaning of maturity, discernment, or widened and deepened consciousness in the immediate moment at any point along the developmental scale. A 12 year old can in this way be more self-actualized than an old man, wise beyond their years, just as an older person can be wise from building resilience to a lifetime of events. But development is still confined to identifiable stages in the linear progression of time from birth to death.

We have an equally compelling case that can be made for external social forces defining personality, which must also be taken into account. But the psychodynamic point of view resists the idea that personality is shaped largely by external social forces. Meanwhile, psychodynamically oriented social theories, while not absent, are also not the rule. Social psychology in France in the 1890s also flourished, but was understood according to the ideas of the French Experimental Psychology of the Subconscious and was therefore based on the dissociation model of consciousness. American psychologists such as Boris Sidis and transplants such as William MacDougall generated social theories of the group mind in the United States from the 1890s to the nineteen-teens. Psychoanalysis itself went through a social phase beginning in the 1930s with the development of ego psychology, and the reinterpretation of the Neo-Freudians, but the theory still stayed within the bounds of the Freudian unconscious and the further one got away from the primary teachings of Freud, the more the theory was judged as indefinite. Hence, the social dimension was not ignored so much as it was interpreted as an extension of the personal inward experience of the individual. However, rather than some reconciliation, the battle between interior phenomenological control and external social control only became more acute as the decades passed. And to this day, no middle ground has seemed possible.

The Meaning of the Word "Dynamic"

Consideration must also be given at the outset with regard to the meaning of the word dynamic, which in the case of a history of dynamic theories of personality plays the role of an adjective to the noun "theories." As a general rubric, it refers to the transformation of energy from one state into another. Typically, in the 19th century, dynamic was equated with such terms as dynamogenic, referring to the tendency or potential to change, as well as the impulse to act.[16] William James equated it with ideomotor activity, where ideas lead to behaviors, such as in the case of the harnessing of the will or the activation of a movement through intentionality, or the compulsive act of the neurotic, who, as soon as he or she thought of the idea it had to be acted out. Freud and Jung associated the term dynamic with depth psychology, referring to the transformation of psychic energy into a variety of forms. A traumatic experience or extended intrapsychic conflict could be converted into a subconscious image, which in turn could be expressed as a dream symbol or an actual physical symptom. It was the transmutation of psychic energy from one form into another, but always implying a certain valence or force capable of having concrete effects.

At the same time, however, we may also consider yet another meaning of the term dynamic—the Gestalt theory of Kurt Lewin. Historians of psychology would not at first associate the experimental laboratory tradition of Gestalt psychology with dynamic theories of personality, but Kurt Lewin, who worked with Wertheimer, Koffka, and Köhler at the Psychological Institute in Berlin, in fact, had a book by that title.[17] Overtly, Lewin had no depth psychology, although his experimental work on personality dealt with ideas similar to Freudian repression, while many of his disciples went on to pioneer in the scientific measurement of psychoanalytic concepts. Rather, the term dynamic in Lewin's system referred to the way one might use it in physics—as a change in matter from one state to another. But he used it in the sense of force fields of energy, in which ideas and actions are connected. Lewin attempted to formulate problems of personality in terms of the life space. Behavior was always a function of the person plus the environment in the totality of the immediate problem under consideration.

To capture this wholistic picture, Lewin reverted to mathematical concepts, trying to define a geometry of space and time appropriate for psychology. He called his system a topological psychology, and his primary methodology he called action research. While psychologists remain primarily Aristotelian in their thinking, we will have to turn to a more Galilean mode of thinking to fathom the relationship between the Lewin's force fields and the more psychodynamic conceptions of the unconscious that prevailed in personality theory on which he had an influence.

The Conflation of Self, Ego, and Personality

For Kant, the self, which he called the transcendental ego, is necessary in order for there to be a unified self-consciousness. The self synthesizes sensations according to the categories of the understanding. Nothing can be known of this self because it is a condition of knowledge, not an object as such. By taking this position, he was able to focus on mathematics and the sciences according to the rational ordering of sense data alone while still protecting the domain of religion and intuition.

According to Baldwin's *Dictionary of Philosophy and Psychology*,[18] there are two selves: the subjective and the objective. The subjective self is the subjective of the individual's self-consciousness, while the objective self is the object of that same individual's self-consciousness. Lehrman adds that the self is "that subject whose activity is the subject's object."[19] Considered simply as the subject of experience, the primary self is unreflective and primitive. In reflective consciousness, the self is both subject and object—that is, the subject reflecting upon itself. James calls this the "me," as opposed to the "I" of the subjective self. Royce and others extended the notion of the self to include the other—that the ego, the analytic, and synthesizing function of personality, are defined in terms of a perception of difference between the subject and other human beings. One's definition of one's self thus grows in relation to imitation, suggestion, and internalization.

The psychological sense of personal identity was not only defined by late 19th-century psychologists as a definition of the self as conscious. The presumption also was that the sense of personal identity was totally absent in lower animals, least developed in primitives, and more so in the adult than the child. It was also malleable, in that its evolution toward perfection through its moral and esthetic cultivation would lead to the highest levels of self-realization possible for humans to experience.

The essential problem with self-identity, however, is that it is not totally in possession of a full awareness of itself. This is because the consciousness that is seeking itself is also the one that finds itself, so that self-affirmation of one's complete unity is always provisional, thus never complete. One may believe one has attained such a state, for instance, but it may be obvious to others that the person has attained no such condition. The problem with the construct, Baldwin's *Dictionary* maintains, is the value and meaning of the category. One view is that personality is a function of the physiological substrate—that is, the more permanent organization in the brain which stands for conscious personality. Another view is that it is a function of sensory and motor phenomena and is therefore an epiphenomenon of one's physiology.

Mary Whiton Calkins (1863–1930) was allegedly the first to propose a theory of the self in the context of the new scientific psychology,[20] although James, Royce, and Dewey had already proclaimed that the self was at the center of their respective systems. Calkins had been an ardent student of both James and Royce at Harvard, so that her theory was built on a similar epistemological foundation. She went to great lengths to show that the sense of self could be measured in the context of the new experimental psychology, using concrete examples from published investigations in English, French, and German.[21] Studies in perception and imagination often involved the subject's reports of self-reference, in addition to studies in memory, where the subject was responding not to the objective similarity of the objects to be recalled and compared but to the subject's own internal sense of the familiar. Further, she declared the distinction between controlled introspection in the laboratory and casual introspection in real life to be a false dichotomy and maintained that the reason psychologists did not attempt such measurements was an artifact of not only their methods but also their prejudices, in much the same way that James defined "the psychologist's fallacy"—the tendency for the investigator to confuse his own state of mind for that of his subject's. She did not infer a theoretical existence of the self, but rather appealed to direct observation and measurement to construct her system, the implications of which paralleled James's radical empiricism and his emphasis on the phenomenology of immediate experience in *The Varieties of Religious Experience* (1902a).[22]

For Freud, the self or I, which he called *ich* or the ego of personality, remains in contact with the world through perception and cognition and is responsible for analysis and synthesis, but it also serves the executive function, mediating between the demands of the outward environment and the internal structures of the id and the superego. The ego, in other words, also has an unconscious aspect. Jung, on the other hand, considered personality development to be dominated by the ego until consciousness awakened to the reality of its own unconscious dimensions and began a dialogue, actually often a confrontation, in which a more mature side of personality finally emerged. During this process, which he called individuation, the center of personality shifts from the half conscious ego to the fully awakened self. A distinction between the ego and the self is thus clearly delineated and the self is centered in a greater reality than that which has been known by the ego. The ego may only mediate between the external material reality and the internal milieu, but even Freud said essentially that the unconscious was infinite. The self may be one's sense of personal identity within one's self or in dynamic relationship with others, but neither of these are closed systems. Just because trait theorists remain atomistic does not mean that traits do not add up to something greater than the sum of their parts.

Thus, concepts of the self, the ego, and the personality are not interchangeable in the history of dynamic theories of personality, or, in fact, in any theory. It was as if they are presumed to be the same, yet there is a separate literature for each. So, one must always inquire as to the meaning of a term in the theorist's system. At the same time, it is possible to infer the underlying epistemology held by any given theorist by the way such terms are used.

This suggests that there may be some as yet unexamined relationship between attitudes toward consciousness and one's conception of personality.[23] In general, we might say that the more reductionistic and positivist in orientation is the physician or psychologist, the more personality is likely to be defined exclusively in terms of traits or disorders defined by traits, if given legitimacy at all. But the more phenomenological the therapist or researcher, the more their definition of personality becomes a dynamic theory of human experience, and the greater tendency that psychotherapeutics and a theory of the unconscious are employed. But toward such more phenomenological and experiential theories, the basic question remains with regard to their legitimacy, whether in one discipline or the other; namely, "Are they scientific?" At the same time, the basic question asked by more phenomenological interpreters is "how true to human experience?" are their theories and "do they actually help the person to live?"

I would go so far, in this regard, to postulate three separate epistemologies in science that define one's attitude toward consciousness and therefore condition one's definition of personality. These are the positivistic laboratory-oriented reductionists, the psychodynamic theorists who largely follow Freud, and the more phenomenological, or transcendent wing of the existential-humanistic tradition (see Fig. 1.2)

Positivist epistemology assumes that consciousness is identical to awareness and that reality is defined solely by what we can see, hear, feel, taste, touch, and smell, all of which occur against the backdrop of a single unchanging field. What you see is what you get. There is no unseen hand behind the world of appearances. The thought is the thinker. Consciousness ranges across a spectrum from coma to hyper-excitability. Personality in this sense is be defined by the measurement of individual traits, both genetically endowed and subsequently learned, the sum of which is called personality, which can be known through the measurement of bodily functions, thoughts, and behaviors.

The Positivistic Assumption:
Consciousness is defined as solely what is in the field of the everyday rational waking state, in contrast to states of coma, sleep, or hyperexcitability. Consciousness is equal to awareness. There is no such thing as an unconscious. The thinker is the thought. Manipulation of the person's articulated thoughts and observable behavior is believed to be all that is needed to change personality.

The Psychodynamic Assumption:
Consciousness is defined as a field of awareness in the everyday waking rational state, but is largely controlled by a vast interior and more primitive domain of the unconscious. Consciousness is also used to refer to the ability of consciousness to bring accessible parts of the unconscious into the field of waking rational awareness, thus leading to a change of personality, based on resolution of unconscious conflicts.

The Transcendent Assumption:
Consciousness is considered either a plurality of states or a single, universal and integral field. Waking consciousness is only one state of consciousness among many others, ranging from the psychopathic to the transcendent. The function of the waking rational state is preservation of the biological organism, which is the primary vehicle for the experience of these other states of consciousness. Awareness and consciousness are not considered the same, as inferior or superior states can control the waking condition without waking rational consciousness being aware of it. Waking consciousness can be transformed through the experience of higher, more expanded transcendent states of awareness and the development of intuitive insight.

Fig. 1.2 Epistemologies of consciousness underlying models of personality in the history of psychology

Psychodynamic epistemology, in agreement with the positivist's approach, admits the reality of the waking state of rational consciousness, in which the person remains attached to material reality through the senses in a perpetual state of adjustment. However, its defining characteristic is that it also postulates the existence of the unconscious, which exists as a vast interior domain essentially controlling the content of the waking rational state, but is inferior to it from an evolutionary standpoint. Personality in this sense is a function of unconscious, largely instinctual drives that have been made over through relatively fixed developmental stages and reshaped through waking rational consciousness to allow the organism to adapt to the external physical environment and to social pressures within one's culture.

A transcendent epistemology acknowledges the waking state and emphasizes the reality of the unconscious, but defines its scope as wider and deeper and higher than the psychodynamic. The unconscious, if it is even appropriate to call it that, since the term itself seems implicitly to privilege waking consciousness, is comprised of an essentially unlimited number of altered states of consciousness, acknowledging both the psychopathic and the transcendent. The psychopathic is well known in abnormal psychology, but the transcendent only appears in the religious literature. It refers to the experience of expanded awareness and the development of a lasting state of higher consciousness. Such states may come about through an instantaneous vision of a noetic sort, carrying a sense of wisdom, power, and authority for all aftertime, or gradually, through the application of techniques designed to foster intuitive insight over long periods. Personality in this sense may be said to contain a growth-oriented dimension missing in the other two epistemologies. This transcendent dimension exists in addition to a primitive dimension in the unconscious. They are the two poles on a continuum, which passes somewhere in the middle through the waking rational state, whose function is primarily adaptation of the biological organism to the physical and social environment.

The implications of these three models are important for laying out the history of dynamic theories of personality, because they account for many of the differences between internalist versus externalist histories and also account for much of the criticism leveled against a given theory. The critic is almost always of a totally different mindset, as the experimentalist Elizabeth Loftus is the great critic of the false memory syndrome, or Witmer, a school psychologist, the vilifier of psychotherapeutics. In other words, one must always inquire into the epistemology of consciousness of any given interlocutor in order to understand the implicit model of personality being fielded in any given discussion, especially when it comes to the use of language bound to the waking rational state that is employed to describe states of consciousness beyond itself.

Notes

1. The functionalist arch from William James, through the macropersonality theorists such as Gardner and Lois Murphy, Gordon Allport, and Henry Murray, to the early humanistic psychologists such as Maslow, Rogers, and May, would be a case in point. See Taylor, E. I. (1992). *The case for a uniquely American Jamesian tradition in psychology.* In M. E. Donnelly (Ed.), *Reinterpreting the legacy of William James* (pp. 3–28). Washington, DC: American Psychological Association. Similarly, the developmental models of Piaget, Erikson, and Kohlberg would be another.
2. Boring, E. G. (1929). *A history of experimental psychology.* New York, London: The Century Company; Boring, E. G. (1950). *A history of experimental psychology* (2nd ed.). New York: Appleton-Century-Crofts.
3. Ellenberger, H. (1970). *The discovery of the unconscious: The history and evolution of dynamic psychiatry.* New York: Basic Books.
4. Taylor, E. I. (1999). *Shadow culture: Psychology and spirituality in America.* Washington, DC: Counterpoint.
5. In 1896, Witmer only mentioned "the clinical method." By 1898 there was already a *Journal of Psychology Clinical and Applied* in France, but it was tied to psychotherapeutics, which represented a lineage that Witmer himself rejected as unscientific. See Butler, RA (1983). French contributions to the origin of clinical psychology. Paper presented at the annual meeting of the American Psychological Association. Also, Taylor, E. I.(2000). Psychotherapeutics and the problematic origins of clinical psychology in America. *American Psychologist, 55:9,* 1029–1033.
6. Reisman, J. M. (1966). *The development of clinical psychology.* New York: Appleton-Century-Crofts.
7. Zilboorg, G., & Henry, G. W. (1941). *A history of medical psychology.* New York: W. W. Norton; Alexander, F., & Selesnick, S. T. (1966). *The history of psychiatry: An evaluation of psychiatric thought and practice from prehistoric times to the present.* New York: Harper & Row.
8. Wyss, D. (1966). *Depth psychology: A critical history, development, problems, crises.* New York: W. W. Norton.

9. Burnham, J. C. (1967). *Psychoanalysis and American medicine: 1894–1918: Medicine, science, and culture*. New York: International Universities Press; Hale, N. G. (1971a). *Freud and the Americans: The beginnings of psychoanalysis in the United States, 1876–1917*. New York: Oxford University Press; Hale, N. G. (1995). *The rise and crisis of psychoanalysis in America: Freud and the Americans, 1917–1985* (2 Vols.). New York: Oxford University Press; Quen, J. M., & Carlson, E. T. (1878). (Eds.). *American psychoanalysis: Origins and development: The Adolf Meyer seminars*. New York: Brunner/Mazel.

10. Sulloway, F. J. (1979). *Freud, biologist of the mind: Beyond the psychoanalytic legend*. New York: Basic Books; Gelfand, T., & Kerr, J. (Eds.). (1992). *Freud and the history of psychoanalysis*. Hillsdale, NJ: Analytic Press; Masson, J. M. (1984). *The assault on truth: Freud's suppression of the seduction theory*. New York: Farrar, Straus and Giroux; Kerr, J. (1993). *A most dangerous method: The story of Jung, Freud, and Sabina Spielrein*. New York: A. A. Knopf.

11. Haynal, A., & Falzader, E. (Eds.). (1994). *One hundred years of psychoanalysis: Contributions to the history of psychoanalysis*. London: H. Karnac Books.

12. Freedheim, D. K. (Ed.). (1992). *History of psychotherapy: A century of change*. Washington, DC: American Psychological Association; Ehrenwald, J. (Ed.). (1976). *The History of psychotherapy: From healing magic to encounter*. New York: Jason Aronson Inc.; Aronson, J., & Rieff, P. (1966). *The triumph of the therapeutic: Uses of faith after Freud*. New York: Harper & Row.

13. Routh, D. K. (1994). *Clinical psychology since 1917: Science, practice, and organization*. New York: Plenum Press; Reisman, J. M. (1976). *A history of clinical psychology*. New York: Irvington; Reisman, J. M. (1991). *A history of clinical psychology* (2nd ed.). New York: Hemisphere Publishing; Walker, C. E. (Ed.). (1991). *The history of clinical psychology in autobiography*. Pacific Grove, CA: Brooks/Cole Publishing Company; Berrios, G. E., & Porter, R. (Eds.). (1995). *A history of clinical psychiatry: The origin and history of psychiatric disorders*. London, New Brunswick, NJ: Athlone Press; Somerset, NJ: Transaction Publishers.

14. Camus, J., & Pagniez, P. (1908–1909a). The history of psychotherapy. I. The psychotherapy of drugs (W. B. Parker, Ed., F. Peterson & E. Garrigue, Trans.). *Psychotherapy: A course of reading in sound psychology, sound medicine and sound religion, 1*(3), 64–71; Camus, J., & Pagniez, P. (1908–1909b). The history of psychotherapy. II. Psychotherapy by means of miraculous. In W. B. Parker (Ed.) (F. Peterson & E. Garrigue, Trans.), *Psychotherapy: A course of reading in sound psychology, sound medicine and sound religion, 1*(4), 54–64; Camus, J., & Pagniez, P. (1908–1909c). The history of psychotherapy. III. The history of psychotherapy IV. In W. B. Parker (Ed.) (F. Peterson & E. Garrigue, Trans.), *Psychotherapy: A course of reading in sound psychology, sound medicine and sound religion, 3*(1), 50–59; Northridge, W. L. (1924). *Modern theories of the unconscious*. London: Kegan Paul, Trench, Trubner and Company; Janet, P. (1925). *Psychological healing: A historical and clinical study* (2 vols.). (E. Paul & C. Paul, Trans.). New York: The Macmillan Company.

15. Micale, M. (Ed.). (1993). *Beyond the Unconscious: Essays of Henri F. Ellenberger in the history of psychiatry* (F. Dubor & M. S. Micale, Trans.). Princeton, NJ: Princeton University Press.

16. See also, Madison, B. (Ed.). (1916). *Studies in social and general psychology from the University of Illinois*. Princeton, NJ, Lancaster, PA: Psychological Review Company.

17. Lewin, K. (1934). *A dynamic theory of personality: Selected papers* (D. K. Adams & K. E. Zener, Trans.). New York, London: McGraw-Hill; See also Marrow, A. J. (1969). *The practical theorist: The life and work of Kurt Lewin*. New York: Basic Books.

18. Baldwin, J. M. (Ed.). (1901/1960). *Dictionary of philosophy and psychology* (3 Vols.). Gloucester, MA: Peter Smith.

19. Baldwin, 1901/1960, 2, p. 507.

20. Strunk, O., Jr. (1972). The self-psychology of Mary Whiton Calkins. *Journal of the History of the Behavioral Sciences, 8*(2), 196–203.

21. Calkins, M. W. (1915). The self in scientific psychology. *American Journal of Psychology, 26,* 495–524. Article retrieved October 1, 2007, from http://psychclassics.yorku.ca/Calkins/self.htm

22. By 1895 she had completed all requirements for the PhD in psychology at Harvard, even to the point of passing the oral exam, but President Eliot refused her the degree on the advice of the Overseers because Harvard did not grant doctorates to women. See Furumoto, L. (1979). Mary Whiton Calkins (1863–1930): Fourteenth president of the American Psychological Association. *Journal of the History of the History of Behavioral Sciences, 15*(4), 346–356; James, W. (1902a). *The varieties of religious experience: A study of human nature.* New York: Longmans, Green, and Company.

23. Wade, N. (2005). *Perception and illusion: Historical perspectives.* New York: Springer Science.

Chapter 2
Charcot's Axis

The modern history of dynamic theories of personality in Western science begins with Jean-Martin Charcot in 1881.[1] True, the Christian church had long before appropriated the idea of personality as a way to define the soul and to compare it to the personality of Jesus. True, mesmerism could be construed as a dynamic theory of consciousness, but it was generally rejected by the scientific establishment of the times. True, by the early 1830s the phrenologists had devised a map of characteristics defining the person according to bumps on their head which the homeopathic phreno-magnetists then fused in their system with techniques for entering altered consciousness by way of parlor entertainments such as mesmerism.[2] The founder of homeopathy, Samuel Hahnemann, had even included a chapter on mesmerism as an appendix to his *Organon of Medicine*.[3] The result was a map of personality, a technique for getting below the surface of consciousness, and a total psychophysical system of mind/body healing to go along with it. And true, Emerson lectured on scientific subjects to the Boston Society of Natural History just after stepping down from his Unitarian pulpit at the First and Second Church; and true, the New England transcendentalists had articulated an intuitive, spiritual psychology of character development. Within that intuitive psychology, everything one needed to know about psychosomatic medicine could be found in Hawthorne's *The Scarlet Letter* (1850) or his friend Herman Melville's *Moby Dick* (1851). It was Melville, who when reviewing Emerson, opened with "I love all men who dive," while Emerson also wrote a book on personality types, *Representative Men* (1850).[4] There is also a sophisticated and complete classification of personality, thoroughly dynamic in orientation, though based on phrenology, that can be found in James Freeman Clarke's *Self-culture* (1880).

But these were not science, according to modern historians of science. Charcot, however, was science through and through. A wealthy, sophisticated, world-class neurologist who had treated kings and queens, Charcot was a major contributor to our understanding of aphasia, and a skilled laboratory man and clinician who oversaw 2000 inmates at the Salpêtrière, a mental asylum in the heart of Paris for women only. It was Charcot who, in 1882, rehabilitated hypnosis before the French Academy of Sciences, after three previous scientific commissions had debunked it under the names of mesmerism and animal magnetism.[5]

E. Taylor, *The Mystery of Personality*, Library of the History of Psychology Theories, DOI 10.1007/978-0-387-98104-8_2, © Springer Science+Business Media, LLC 2009

Forget that Charles Richet, experimental physiologist in Charcot's inner circle, had started it all by allowing the hypnotist Burq into the Salpêtrière to first introduce hypnosis to the patients; forget that hypnosis was still the primary tool of the spiritualists for their regimes of mental healing; forget that, until Charcot, no French, German, Italian, or Russian medical scientist in their right mind would have considered hypnosis to be in any way more than mere charlatanism.[6]

Instead, Charcot's tack was to present hypnosis as a true physiological phenomenon having distinct and identifiable neurological stages. He called them lethargy, catalepsy, and somnambulism and he could command the attention of large professional audiences at his weekly lectures at the hospital while he demonstrated these stages in his patients. One was the infamous Blanche Whitman, though it was later shown that the women were coached. Hypnosis was a state, Charcot claimed, of extreme hypersuggestibility brought on by mental pathology, which disappeared once the patient got well. The response of the academy was not enthusiastic, but neither did they condemn him, so the idea that hypnosis might be genuine went through.

Charcot had first made a name for himself in anatomical pathology and the demonstration of the tabetic arthopathies. He went on to a delineation of amyotrophic lateral sclerosis (Charcot's disease), locomotor ataxia, cerebral and medullar localizations, and aphasia. He launched several medical journals and he transformed the Salpêtrière from a backwater warehouse to a first-rate facility for research and teaching. In his later career, however, he became known primarily for his identification of hysteria, hypnotism, dual personality, catalepsy, and somnambulism. He differentiated hysteria from epilepsy and identified the full-blown hysterical crisis as *grand hystérie*. He investigated the traumatic paralyses, differentiating true neurological conditions growing out of organic causes from those caused by psychological factors associated with hysteria. Hysterical paralyses could be induced through post-hypnotic suggestion under hypnosis and also banished under hypnosis by the same means. He called them "dynamic paralyses"—hysterical, post-traumatic, and hypnotic, in contrast to paralyses which had an organic origin in lesions of the nervous system.[7]

Charcot had also been interested in the type problem. Studying cases of aphasia, he noted problems with memory associated with specific kinds of representation, which he categorized as auditive, visual, motor, or indifferent. William James took note of this classification scheme in his *Principles of Psychology* (1890a),[8] while Charcot's primary spokesperson, Alfred Binet, developed them as distinct personality types, to which Théodule Ribot added an affective type. This model was widely taken up at the time.[9]

Charcot's circle included a number of distinguished personages. Among his students there had been Gilles de la Tourette, later investigator of Tourette's syndrome, Paul Richer, Charcot's disciple who had assisted him in identifying *grand hystérie*[10] and in the investigation of psychogenesis—that symptoms of hysteria could be the reenactment of portions of the original traumatic experience.[11]

Charles Richet was a noted research physiologist and later winner of the Nobel Prize who rediscovered the earlier magnetists such as Antoine de Puységur and showed contemporary investigators that most of what they had discovered was already known to French doctors 40 years earlier. An early investigator of what we call today parapsychology, he introduced Charcot to hypnosis in 1878. Among other things he wrote a sensational novel of dual personality, *Sister Marthe*, under the pseudonym of Charles d'Ephere, the story of a would-be nun whom a young doctor hypnotized to cure her hysteric symptoms. He encountered an alternate personality instead, who became as if another person—lively and vivacious, who fell in love with him. The young doctor naturally fell in love with her. But on the night of their elopement she changed back to the original personality, went on to take her vows as a nun, and died shortly thereafter.[12]

Joseph Babinski was an old schoolmate of Binet, who had assisted Charcot with the hysteric Blanche Wittman in Brouillet's famous painting. He retained the neurological portion of Charcot's legacy and continued to be suspicious of the more purely psychological parts. Later he turned against Charcot's star pupil, Pierre Janet.

Alfred Tissié was another member of Charcot's circle. He was later known as the father of French sport psychology. Tissié wrote on dreams and also studied cases of extreme exertion, such as the state of bicyclists immediately after long-distance marathons.[13] He also wrote on alien voyagers, a study of people who enter fugue states for long periods. His best-known case was that of Albert, a soldier who, when commanded to turn left 1 day, kept on walking in a straight line all the way across Europe, with no knowledge of who he was or what he had done.[14]

Théodore Ribot[15] was a renowned physiologist who first introduced then most recent developments in English and German psychology into France. Today he is called the father of French psychology. He wrote on disorders of memory, introduced the concept of retrograde amnesia—that brain damage effects recent more than distant memories—and anhedonia, pathological loss of interest in objects of pleasure.[16] He was an early correspondent of William James, whose psychology of the emotions influenced Ribot's essays on memory and personality. In the early 1880s, Ribot was a major figure in Charcot's circle. He chaired several of the more important International Congresses of Experimental Psychology in which French dissociation psychology was featured.

Julian Ochorowicz[17] was a Polish physician who was a member who had summarized in print Pierre Janet's first paper before Charcot's Society for Physiological Psychology in 1885. He had an interest in psychical research.[18] While a lecturer at the University of Lemberg, he had discovered the mediumship of Mlle. Stanislawa Tomczyk, of Wisla, Poland, a woman who had been one of his patients. In the state of hypnotic sleep she revealed an alternate personality, Little Stasia, who would converse with Ochorowicz without the knowledge of the primary personality of Mlle. Tomczyk. Through Little Stasia, Ochorowicz recorded his observations on double consciousness.

Charles Féré studied such topics as moral choice in infants and was interested in the sexual perversions emanating from an original psychological trauma.[19] He began his career with an interest in the neurology of movement, criminal degeneracy, and hereditary psychopathology in the family. During this period he also assisted Charcot in the differentiation of epilepsy from hysteria. Thereafter, he co-authored a survey of animal magnetism with Alfred Binet, and wrote, himself, on the pathology of the emotions.[20]

Eugene Azam, professor of surgery at the Bordeaux Medical School and another associate of Charcot's, was interested in the relation between sleep and hypnosis in his search to understand the difference between reason and madness. In 1858, he began his study of the celebrated case of Félida X, who demonstrated the phenomenon of dual personality. Félida had lost her father when she was very young and grew up in relatively normal circumstances, but with persistent headaches and neuralgias. At one point she fell into syncope and awakened a different person, before sullen and taciturn, but now a gay, vivacious, and elated personality. From then on, she alternated regularly between her old primary state and the newer secondary one. To these she later added a newer state of extreme fright and terrible hallucinations. Azam studied her for over 30 years and was able to document a developmental picture of her disorder. He published on this case and related subjects in *Hypnotism, Double Consciousness, and Alternations of Personality*, which appeared with a preface by Charcot in 1887.[21]

Alfred Binet was a biologist with a PhD. Long before he got into mental testing of the feebleminded in French schools, he had originally written on such topics as the psychic life of microorganisms. He became Charcot's chief spokesperson for the physiological explanation of hypnosis and hysteria and, with Charles Féré, a distinguished investigator of dissociation and multiple personality. Binet's career plummeted, however, after Charcot's theories waned and he experienced a number of setbacks in his own professional development that cast him into obscurity. All this was before he took up the study of intelligence, beginning with an investigation of his own two children. In 1889 he did produce a book-length study, *Multiple Personality*, an edition of which has been found in the library of William James.[22]

Possibly the most enduring of Charcot's pupils was Pierre Janet, professor at the College de France and accomplished psychopathologist, all the more curious because, according to Ellenberger, Janet had only a small following among professionals during his early career and his most ardent audiences he continued to find in the United States, not France.[23] Janet brought forward the famous case of Léonie, the subject of his doctoral dissertation in philosophy, before apprenticing himself to Charcot, under whom he studied for the MD degree while working at the Salpêtrière. Janet's career began with two influential works, *Psychological Automatisms* (1889) and *The Mental State of Hystericals* (1893), before he wrote major works on hysteria, psychasthenia, and the obsessions. He, and many others, believed that he held priority over Freud for defining psychogenesis based on subconscious fixed ideas and their remediation.

The distinguished nature of Charcot's international reputation drew attention to the phenomenon of hypnosis, but, according to Ellenberger, the real impetus for international attention afforded to dynamic theories of personality occurred as a result of an ideological war that soon developed between Charcot's circle and the so-called Nancy School around Hippolyte Bernheim. Shortly after Charcot read his paper on hypnosis before the French Academy of Sciences, Bernheim, a professor at the Medical School at Nancy, attacked Charcot's position by claiming that hypnosis was neither a pathological condition nor a physical one, but a psychological phenomenon that was based on suggestion alone and characteristic of the normal personality. In fact, the same changes that could be achieved under hypnosis could be effected by suggestion in the waking state, making hypnotism itself superfluous. Moreover, Bernheim and his followers emphasized that many cures could be effected of maladies brought to the physician by his patients, including such organic diseases of the nervous system as rheumatism, gastrointestinal diseases, and menstrual ailments. Ellenberger even asserts that Bernheim's followers were the ones who first coined the term "psychotherapeutics."[24]

It is hardly ever the case that the provinces are able to trump the Parisian point of view, but in this instance, the little school at Nancy won the day and established a point of view with regard to dynamic theories of the subconscious that prevails to this day, namely, that one does not have to acknowledge the reality of alternate states of consciousness different from the waking state to study trance consciousness. This is likely one source for the debate between trait versus state theorists in contemporary hypnotherapy, a debate which has degenerated into patent but superficial rationalizations to placate the trait theorists.

There were only a few men who constituted the Nancy School's point of view: Ambroise Auguste Liébeault, Hippolyte Bernheim, Henri Beaunis, and Jules Liégeois. The Nancy school of thought originated with A. A. Liébeault, a country doctor who practiced in a small village near Nancy and was successful enough to have made himself a small fortune practicing regular medicine. In medical school he had found an old book on magnetism and, self-taught, began a separate practice treating patients by psychological means alone. He kept these patients completely separate from his regular practice, treating 40 patients a day in an old shed, and, in fact, did not charge them, taking only voluntary contributions. He treated all disorders, whether psychological or organic, by the same method, which he called induced sleep.

Eventually, in 1868, Liébeault published a book on his researches, *Sleep and Analogous States*, in which he described hypnosis as a conscious focus on sleep and the rapport that developed between patient and physician as the logical extension of that intention. The local physicians considered the book the work of a quack and a fool. Ellenberger notes that few copies of the book were sold, some in France and Switzerland and a few in Russia.[25] William James purchased a copy as a young medical student at Harvard and read it while abroad at the baths at Bad Nauheim instead of attending lectures by Wundt and Helmholtz, contrary to the chain of events presented by the historians of experimental psychology. James then wrote a provocative review of Liébeault, which he published in *The Nation*.[26] It took Bernheim another 12 years to discover Liébeault, become his disciple, and draw his methods into the medical school curriculum. Liébeault then became quite famous.

Ellenberger notes that Bernheim was the real center of the Nancy point of view, however. Already known for his medical work on typhoid fever and pulmonary diseases, Bernheim had secured a position at Nancy after he was forced from his medical school position at Strasbourg in 1871 when it was annexed by the Germans. He began using Liébeault's method in 1882 on peasants, industrial workers, and old soldiers, but with less success on the wealthier classes. Nevertheless, he was so successful that he published *Suggestive Therapeutics* in 1886 to wide acclaim.[27]

Henri Etienne Beaunis, a forensic medical expert at Nancy and colleague from Strasbourg, had written on pathological anatomy of the nervous system before turning his attention to the physiology and psychology of provoked sleep. Liégeois was a lawyer interested in hypnosis and criminal responsibility. At one point he gave a dramatic demonstration, where he had hypnotized his subjects and provided them with the means to commit a pseudo-murder, which they did, implying that hypnosis could be used to control a person and to force them into acts that were illegal.

Bernheim's followers, on the other hand, were legion. There was Albert Moll in Berlin, author of *Das Doppel-Ich* (1890), *The Double Ego*, Baron von Schrenk-Notzing in Germany, Krafft-Ebing in Vienna, Vladimir Bechterev in Russia, Milne Bramwell in England, G. Stanley Hall, Morton Prince and to some extent Boris Sidis in the United States, Otto Wetterstrand in Sweden, Frederick van Eeden and A. W. van Renterghem in the Netherlands, August Forel in Switzerland, and, of course, Sigmund Freud. Charcot died in 1893 and in a certain sense his school of interpretation had already gone into eclipse by then, but was carried on in a new form in the United States, in the so-called Boston School of Psychopathology, where Janet found his own greatest following.

Accompanying these developments in France was the founding of the Society for Psychical Research in England in 1882. In 1884, the American Society for Psychical Research was founded in the United States. Spiritualism had suddenly sprung up in 1846 with the advent of the Fox sisters, though it had been around for millennia before that. The claim that the sisters could communicate with a departed spirit who had previously died in their home was judged by the popular press as absolutely genuine. It inflamed a movement that quickly spread across the United States and soon reached international proportions in the West. Allan Kardec, a French spiritualist, for instance, was a significant influence on the spread of spiritualism to Brazil. Millions came to believe that we had scientifically established communication with the dead and séances were regularly conducted accordingly. A huge underground network of newspapers and venues for public lectures sprang up, particularly in the United States. Itinerate vendors of all sorts proliferated. Elixirs, methods for altering consciousness, psychic healings, and advice for everything from marriage to personal transformation became the vogue, now mixed with the more established communications emanating from the Christian church and the halls of orthodox science. In the United States, as reductionistic science came under increasing scrutiny for its narrowness, atomistic focus, and materialistic orientation, a virtual second Great Awakening was occurring in the Midwest, in which membership in the major Christian denominations as well as spiritualist circles swelled. Spiritualism and mental healing, Christian revivalism, and orthodox science became rivals for control of the same set of living symbols in the mental and spiritual life of the individual.

Sitting in the audience at the Salpêtrière in the summer of 1882 was the American physician and psychologist William James.[28] James was well known to the French, as his psychological essays, published in American and British journals had been translated into French by Renouvier, Delboeuf, and Pillion, editors of *Revue Philosophique*, for a decade. Delboeuf had introduced James to Théodule Ribot, which later developed into an important correspondence linking French and American developments in experimental psychopathology.

To put the matter in a larger historical perspective, neurology and dynamic psychology were becoming more and more intertwined. In 1873, the New York neurologist George Miller Beard had addressed the American Neurological Association on "The Potency of Definite Expectation in the Cause and Cure of Disease."[29] Physicians use psychology all the time in their practice, Beard declared. Why not harness its uses in medicine more systematically? His proposal was received with hostility, however, and the derision heaped upon Beard was quelled only when it was determined by cooler heads among the members present that science just did not know enough about the emotions.

Nine years later, in 1884, William James brought the study of the emotions out of philosophy and into physiology with his controversial paper, "What is an Emotion?" (1884).[30] He had only meant, he said, to make the point that emotions were physiological and therefore amenable to the methods of science, not merely ideal philosophical categories of the mind, as was commonly held. This and other theories similar to his, such as that of the Danish physician, Walter Lange, established that the emotions were a legitimate topic of study in a scientific context. The scientific study of the emotions was soon to proliferate. Letters and footnote references show that James's essay influenced a series of papers by Ribot on "Diseases of the Will," "Diseases of Attention," and "The Psychology of the Emotions," culminating in "Diseases of Personality" in 1888, thus linking advances in physiology in the United States and France.[31] The emotions were linked not only to cognitions but to the subconscious. A study of their pathology became a vital part of dynamic theories of consciousness, revealing the hidden springs of thoughts and actions. And out of these investigations, the field of motivation was born.

Meanwhile, another link in this chain was being forged by the psychical researchers. In 1882, The Society for Psychical Research was first founded in England around a distinguished coterie of Cambridge and Oxford men who spanned the sciences, humanities, and the clergy. Its purpose was to apply the methods of science to test the outrageous claims of the spiritualists and mental healers. At the same time, their remarkable success in attracting a large number of members was also partly fueled by the extraordinarily zealous and hyper-rational response among scientists to the Darwinian hypothesis, verging on an atheism that the educated English class found intolerable, even in such distinguished lights as Julian Huxley.

While numerous luminaries signed up to support a more moderate view of science, the actual players in the Society were a tight group of investigators with varied backgrounds. Sir Arthur Balfour, Henry Sidgwick, Alfred Russel Wallace, and Sir William Crookes carried the banner for science. The actual day-to-day running of the organization fell to Frederick William Henry Myers, a classicist with an extensive knowledge of contemporary science whose métier was the investigation of mediums. There was also Edmund Gurney, who organized many of the studies of hypnosis, replicating the results of what Binet (1890) had dubbed the French

Experimental Psychology of the Subconscious.[32] There was also Frank Podmore, who was interested in the study of apparitions, hallucinations, and other phenomena of mental imagery. Investigating the possibility of clairvoyance, telepathy, and telekinesis excited them. But the real phenomenon they set out to prove or disprove turned out to be the question of life after death. It was also the question upon which the ultimate fate of the British group foundered for lack of ever finding definitive proof.

Nevertheless, their efforts drew large audiences interested in resolving the conflicts that had arisen between science and religion in an era when science was on the ascendant. Phantasms of the living, visions communicated over long distances at the moment of death, the ability to move objects without touching them, and such topics as the influence of one person's thoughts on another, made their investigations preeminently psychological. Thus, investigators in the United States, such as William James, already drawn to the researches of the French psychopathologists, turned as well to the psychical researchers in Britain. James had lectured on the self and the stream of consciousness to the "Scratch Eight," when in London in 1882. In attendance when James lectured was F. W. H. Myers, with whom James was to establish a lifelong friendship and who would prove to be a lynchpin linking dynamic theories of personality in England, Europe, and America.

Frederick William Henry Myers (1843–1901), classicist, poet, and psychical researcher, was a Fellow and College Lecturer at Trinity College from 1865 to 1869; Inspector of Schools from 1862 to 1901; and founding member of the Society for Psychical Research in 1882. He was the son of an Anglican minister. While his background was in literature and poetry, his knowledge of the sciences was extensive, and he played a crucial role in abstracting advances in dynamic theories of personality from the French and German literature so they might reach a larger English-speaking audience. With Edmund Gurney, Frank Podmore, and others, Myers replicated the hypnotic researches of the French in the hope of not only finding out more about the interior life but also producing evidence for life after death. Thus, his own study of séances and mediums was also extensive.

As the French physicians had discovered, all the symptoms of hysteria could be induced under hypnosis. Myers and his colleagues also discovered that all the phenomena of mediumship could similarly be reproduced in the hypnotic trance. He now had a means to open the door to the interior life of the person, and the scope of what he found there astonished him. He consumed all the known information of the day on these subjects and began to formulate his own theories about the nature of personality and states of consciousness possible to experience. This work culminated in his posthumously published *Human Personality and Its Survival of Bodily Death* (1903).[33]

The mediumistic séance was the living laboratory of experiments for the psychical researchers. Séances had sprung up everywhere, in which a circle of sensitive and sympathetic individuals joined hands and attempted to call forth one of the departed spirits. Usually, one would allegedly return through the personality of someone sitting at the table that had recently lost a loved one. That person became the medium for the dead spirit, who was called the control. Through the medium, who would pass off into a trance, others in the group were able to communicate through the control with additional spirits and learn more details of the afterlife.

While entranced, the medium, if a woman, might speak like a man. Similarly, a man might take on the aura of a woman. Married women, who were usually not permitted to speak in pubic except through their husbands, would now be permitted to address sometimes audiences of thousands, giving communications from beyond the grave while entranced.[34] It was also not infrequent that those who discovered they possessed mediumistic powers to thereafter also demonstrate other capacities for such abilities as clairvoyant visions and telepathic communication. In this regard, mediums held the same status as subjects prone to hysteria and multiple personality. Both mediums and hysterics were considered viable means for investigators to enter the subconscious.

Hypnosis was the main avenue of exploration. Different levels of trance could be demonstrated, suggesting successively deeper strata of personality. Through suggestion, the subject could have parts of his body made anesthetic, or perhaps paralytic. Hysterical blindness could be induced or suggested away. Through post-hypnotic suggestion, the subject could be made to perform acts at a later time. And when entranced during the interval, it was found that at the subconscious level, the patient was counting the days and the hours until the appointed time. But in waking consciousness, the subject denied any such knowledge that a suggestion of any kind had been made. The only exception was that, at the precise moment the act was to be carried out, the waking state of the subject would disappear, and the trance state reappears, during which time the suggested act would be performed, without the later memory of the subject for the act. As well, another post-hypnotic suggestion could also be implanted at this time, so the subject would perform some other unconscious act at some even later date.

Myers had also been experimenting with the technique of automatic writing, which took different forms.[35] He had long known of writers who could pass off into a lightly distracted state and write continuously, only half-conscious of what they wrote. Automatic writing, however, was a more systematic version of this phenomenon, in which the hypnotized subject could be made to sit at a table with a screen between his head and his hand, which held a pencil over a piece of paper, and write automatically from deeper and more profound springs of intelligence from within. The hypnotist could speak to the subject, or else speak to the hand, which the subject could not see, and get two different versions of the same story. A subject in a light trance might be asked about some incident involving a plausible explanation, which the hand would then contradict through a written statement when asked about the same incident. The hand behind the screen would remain immobile while the subject talked to the investigator, but when the investigator talked to the hand, the subject's head would fall to the side and his eyes would close, as he seemed to pass into a deeper trance as long as the hand was writing. Thus, different states of consciousness holding different sets of memories emerged as a defining characteristic of personality.

Crystal gazing was yet another means that Myers and the psychical researchers used to tap into interior states of consciousness. The image reminds us of the circus magician looking into the crystal ball, but neurological records at the Massachusetts General Hospital show that the method of crystal gazing was used there as early as the 1880s to induce a dissociated state of consciousness in hysteric patients.[36] Thoreau did this when he sat by Walden Pond meditating on the reflection of the setting sun on the water, after which he would write about insights that resulted from his trance reverie in nature. James Jackson Putnam, MD, would induce the trance state in his patients by getting them to do relaxed breathing while gazing at a source of light reflected off the surface of a common glass of water. Myers called this the subliminal region and soon came to champion, as his colleague William James also did, what he called a subliminal psychology.[37]

Myers was convinced that not only do we live perpetually ignorant of these interior states of consciousness, but that the majority of who we are can be found there. Others may think we are only whom we appear to be in the external world, but within is a vast interior life which actually determines who we are and how we then shape our outward personality, which may show little of what is actually within. Myers called the layer immediately beyond the waking state the hypnotic stratum and identified it as both highly susceptible to suggestion and also the source of our interior imaginative productions. Normal psychology stops here and declares all that is beyond cognitive thought is mere fantasy, but Myers believed that there were potentially different levels, or strata of the person, each level containing knowledge and memories which may or may not be known to the other levels. The condition most in the dark about these other states was particularly our own daily habitual state of waking awareness.

The deeper we went, the more ideas became images, which then took on a numinous character, sometimes creating visions of mythic proportions. To the insane, such visions come unbidden and are known as unwanted hallucinations. To the physician they are mere fantasy. To the psychic, the medium, and the religious adept, they are welcomed as signs of a higher spiritual state of consciousness beyond the normal everyday waking one. Myers called this visionary capacity mythopoesis, referring to not only the creative capacity of our imagination, but to the manner in which representations from a universal source deeply within each of us finds expression through the life of the individual personality. This included the mythic, numinous, and energic power of our inner symbolic life, as well as the image laden domain of the person allegedly suffering from mental illness.

Hysteria, Myers maintained, was a disease of the hypnotic stratum, while instances of telepathy, clairvoyance, and telekinesis gave us a clue to the growth-oriented dimension of personality. The disintegration of personality he referred to as the dissolutive dimension of the subliminal, while the visions of ecstasy, spiritual epiphanies, and psychic occurrences he called evolutive—indications of where mankind as a whole could evolve into in the future.

We are thus an ultimate plurality of selves in Myers's scheme, capable of experiencing states of consciousness that range from the psychopathic to the transcendent. Waking consciousness occurs probably somewhere in the middle—its function being primarily the biological survival of the physical organism, so that we could experience those other states of consciousness beyond waking, which, as yet unknown, somewhere had their appropriate fields of application and adaptation.

Myers developed these ideas in a series of essays first published in the *Proceedings of the Society for Psychical Research* (British) (*JSPR*) beginning in 1884. During this same period, he traveled to Paris and visited Charcot at the Salpêtrière and to Nancy, where he met with Bernheim and Liébeault. On his return, he and his brother, A. T. Myers, along with Edmund Gurney and Frank Podmore, attempted to replicate the findings of the French investigators and to report their results in the *JSPR*, copies of which were immediately distributed to British and American audiences.

Of particular importance was his essay "Human Personality in Light of Hypnotic Suggestion" (1886). There, Myers emphasized the possibility of a supernormal dimension to personality development. Experimental psychology in its strictest sense, Myers said, at least acknowledges normal and abnormal functioning, both mental and physical, of all kinds. Spontaneous states included sleep and dreams, somnambulism, trance, hysteria, automatism, alternating consciousness, epilepsy, insanity, death, and dissolution. Induced states included narcotism, hypnotic catalepsy, hypnotic somnambulism, and the like, which M. Beaunis had called "psychical vivisection." These topics are generally disregarded by scientists who focus on the rational ordering of sense data alone as the only acceptable method for conducting empirical science.

Following Reid's common sense philosophy, Myers characterized the normal view of personality as one of personal identity, which

> Implies the continued existence of that indivisible thing which I call myself. Whatever this self may be, it is something which thinks, and deliberates, and resolves, and acts, and suffers. I am not thought, I am not action. I am not feeling: I am something that thinks, and acts, and suffers. My thoughts and actions and feelings change every moment: they have no continued [effect], but a successive existence; but that *self* or *I*, to which they belong, is permanent, and has the same relation to all the succeeding thoughts, actions, and feelings which I call mine. . . . [38]

A central will, continuous memory, and homogenous character represent the three key elements of the theory of personality at that time put forth by psychophysical inquiry, he said. Yet hypnotism, when employed as a tool in experimental psychology, can show through post-hypnotic suggestion that the will can be held in abeyance and also preprogrammed from without, that memories are not continuous but state dependent, and that the self may actually exist within us as fragments, each being a part of the greater whole. Personality, in other words, is neither definite, permanent, nor stationary, but is, rather, shifting, illusory, and modifiable.

Myers went on to examine cases where the hypnotic trance could not be considered abnormal, such as its successful use in problems of alcohol and nicotine addiction and recovery from a variety of functional disturbances of the nervous system. He presented in the end, what William James was later to call "Myers's problem," the fact that waking consciousness confuses the psychopathic and the transcendent, because both ends of the psychic spectrum present themselves to waking rational consciousness through the self-same channels. How to differentiate them is the question, for each one of us ought to want to move, both individually and collectively, from the lower, dissolutive states to the higher evolutive levels.

By 1886, Myers had proceeded sufficiently in his own investigations to outline his psychology of the subliminal. He began with the first of a series of seminal articles with the subject of automatic writing in the *JSPR*. But his major publication that same year was Gurney, Myers, and Podmore's *Phantasms of the Living* (1886).[39] The book is ostensibly about telepathy, apparitions, and phantasms of all kinds, meaning not just visual, but auditory, tactile, and even purely ideational and emotional impressions. In other words, this is a contribution to the early scientific study of mental imagery. The cases they collected were purely anecdotal, but soon gave way to the first international census on hallucinations, the first truly scientific attempt in experimental psychology to collect data on a single subject of study on a mass scale.[40]

Meanwhile, the American Society for Psychical Research (ASPR) was first convened in 1884 and officially launched in 1885 as an independent but parallel organization to the British group. G. Stanley Hall, William James, and Josiah Royce were among the founding vice presidents of the ASPR. Simon Newcomb, Director of the Smithsonian Institution, was its first president. Originally they convened in the prestigious rooms of the American Academy of Arts and Sciences, where they organized investigating committees devoted to experimental psychology, hypnotism, apparitions, thought transference, etc. These committees were made up of a distinguished coterie of scientists and professors, mainly from Harvard and MIT.

The astronomers wanted to test for evidence of thought transference and launched an extensive study to gauge the extent of this alleged faculty in the general population at large. The committee on hypnotism under William James operated mainly out of the Harvard Psychological Laboratory and replicated most of the major phenomena identified by the French Experimental Psychology of the Subconscious and the British psychical researchers. The committee on mediumship went out and took verbatim transcripts of séances. The committees investigated any claim brought before them. Their aim was not to prove the existence of life after death, but they did hope to establish what they termed "consistent laws of mental action."[41]

Possibly the single most important accomplishment of the ASPR was to verify the efficacy of crystal gazing, automatic writing, and light hypnosis and to recommend that these were the most effective techniques for understanding and inducing dissociative states of consciousness. In some cases they also provided a therapeutic intervention for the alleviation of symptoms of hysteria or neurasthenia. As a result, these techniques were taken up in the newly opened outpatient clinics at local medical centers such as the Massachusetts General Hospital, the Adams Nervine Asylum, and the Boston City Hospital in the treatment of the ambulatory psychoneuroses, beginning in the mid-1880s. By the 1890s, functional disorders of the nervous system with no known organic origin were combined with psychotherapeutic treatments and presented alongside the theories of biological insanity in an altogether new field called experimental psychopathology. William James taught such a course at Harvard at the graduate level from 1893 to 1898, and Adolf Meyer taught a similar course at Clark University after 1897 as Chief Pathologist at the Worcester State Hospital, while Morton Prince taught similar courses at Tufts after 1898.[42]

James's major contribution from this earlier period was the discovery of the medium, Mrs. Leonora Piper. Born in 1857 into a working class family, Leonora Piper sustained a blow to her head at age 8 and at the same time experienced a voice telling her that her Aunt Sarah was still with her. The aunt had, in fact, died a distance away at that very moment. The girl continued to have similar experiences throughout her otherwise normal childhood. She married at age 22, after which she went to visit J. R. Cocke, a blind clairvoyant medium, who entranced the young girl in an attempt to heal her of these episodes. Cocke drew her into one of his group séances, and she began to receive a communication from the spirit of a dead son of a judge who was in the same circle. She wrote the message down and gave it to the judge. Thereafter, when word got around of the episode, she was inundated with people who wanted sittings.

She withdrew from these overtures, but did agree at one point to an appointment with the mother of William James's wife, Alice Howe Gibbons James. Mrs. Gibbons was favorably impressed and convinced William James to visit Mrs. Piper as well. James was so astounded at the information Mrs. Piper was able to impart that he arranged an extended study of her abilities, including the scheduling of all her sittings for an 18-month period. She seemed to have either secret information and was a fake or had real supernormal abilities, which James wanted to investigate.

While Mrs. Piper had several later temporary controls, among then an Indian girl named Chlorine, a Commodore Vanderbilt, Longfellow, Loretta Pencini, J. Sebastian Bach, and an actress, a Mrs. Siddons, a so-called Dr. Phenuit appeared as her spirit control while James was studying her trances. Phenuit was later replaced by the spirit of the recently departed George Pelham. He reigned for some time, but was himself eventually replaced by The Imperator, a triumvirate of three apparently distinct personalities.

The investigation of Mrs. Piper was taken over by Richard Hodgson when he arrived to become the officiating secretary of the ASPR in 1886. He continued to study her trances until his death in 1905, whereupon Mrs. Piper began receiving communications from him from beyond the grave, which James was forced to investigate, with inconclusive results.[43] While he was alive, Hodgson arranged for Mrs. Piper to go to London to be tested by the psychical researchers there. Her fame preceded her and she grew even more well known afterward.

The significance of her case for James was that the evidence suggested she had genuine powers and was not a fake. Moreover, she was a healthy mother of two children and could not be labeled pathological. She became his famous "white crow," proving that all crows are not black. The medium was no humbug. Rather, his point was that scientific prejudice against the phenomena of mediumship was all that was preventing it from being studied.

Janet's Case of Léonie

The years from 1882 to 1889 constituted the first phase of Janet's theories. During this time Janet taught at the Lyceum at La Havre, an industrial center outside Paris. This allowed him to visit his family often, where he sometimes saw patients with his brother, who was studying medicine and who had a keen interest in psychology and hypnosis. While at Le Havre, it is known that Janet devoted much of his spare time to volunteer work at La Havre Hospital and to psychiatric researches of his own. Looking for a topic for his thesis in pursuit of a *doctorate es-lettres,* he was led to a patient, Léonie, a hysteric woman who reputedly could be hypnotized from a distance. His extensive experiments on her showed that she was very highly suggestible and could display all the usual signs of being easily hypnotized. The results of these studies were first presented in a paper Janet wrote that was delivered in Paris by his uncle, Paul Janet, November 30, 1885, at the *Société de Psychologie Physiologique,* which had been convened by Charcot.[44]

This paper created a sensation, and delegations from both Charcot's group of psychopathologists in Paris and psychical researchers in England converged on La Havre to make their own examination of the patient. F. W. H. Myers, his brother, and Henry Sidgwick came from England, and Charles Richet, the physiologist, brought Ochorowicz and Marillier from Paris. It was a historic meeting for several reasons. Not the least of these, Janet came to the attention of Charcot. Janet also became familiar with the psychical researchers. He remained skeptical of their agenda, however, and afterward vowed to stay focused on the psychological and medical phenomena of hypnosis and suggestibility.

Janet's experiments with suggestion at-a-distance, published in the *Revue Philosophique* between 1886 and 1889, culminated in his PhD thesis, *L'automatisme Psychologique.* They confirmed Charcot's previous findings that in psychopathology patients of this kind were more highly suggestible, that physical symptoms can be controlled, being either induced or banished away by a suggestion implanted while entranced, and that the origin of a particular hysteric symptom is often found in a previous traumatic experience.

Moreover, the persistent state of consciousness the patients found themselves in caused a certain monoideism for the therapist, such that the therapist's personality assumed an inordinate influence over all others in the psychic life of the patient. Janet considered this phenomenon a form of "negative hallucination," where the patient, through a decision made subconsciously, became anesthetic to all other sensory impressions, while those impressions coming from the therapist were pathologically heightened. The hypnotizer could speak to the patient in low tones and be heard by her across the room in a crowd of people. Over time, Janet found the patient could show dramatic improvements in the treatment of her symptoms and then suddenly relapse, due largely to an uncontrollable urge to return to the hypnotic state and a pathological need for more contact with the therapist, whom, it turns out, she had been thinking about subconsciously all the time. This phenomenon, which had been long known to the old magnetizers, was called hypnotic rapport.[45] Janet recognized it as the basis for successful treatment, since it had to be invoked before it could be worked through. He also noted its erotic element.

L'automatisme Psychologique (1889a)[46] was on psychological and motor automatisms. These encompassed behaviors such as writing, sleeping, walking, talking, and hallucinating below the level of conscious awareness, activities which nevertheless Janet believed always held some primitive element of consciousness and, hence, were as much psychological as motoric. Total automatisms, such as catalepsy, extended to the person as a whole, but partial automatisms implied that only a segment of personality was split off from the rest, such as with obsessions, fixed ideas, hallucinations, and feelings of possession. In either case, the organism functions without awareness or control by the ego. Janet considered these behaviors to be inferior forms of human activity, but they were nevertheless not only partly conscious but tied to immediate acts. Thus he was able to explain compulsions, post-hypnotic suggestion, hypersuggestibility in some subjects, and more.[47]

The method Janet developed, which he called psychological analysis, began with a detailed investigation of the life history of the patient, followed by an attempt at a synthesis of the parts. He first discovered that every time a symptom had been banished a new one appeared, representing an even older trauma. As Myers had pointed out, personality seemed to be made of deeper and deeper strata of memories.[48]

The 1889 Congress of Experimental Psychology

L'automatisme Psychologique (1889a), Janet's dissertation for the PhD in philosophy, broke new ground because it applied the budding principles of psychodynamic psychology to psychotic patients. Moreover, Janet's patient population was entirely separate from that of Charcot's at la Salpêtrière, so his results were not contaminated by the tremendous forces of suggestion in what Ellenberger described as "that hothouse environment." He also departed from the classical traits of the prevailing psychology, which employed concepts such as the will, the affections, and reason. Instead, he forged a new theory of personality based on levels of instinctual and subconscious activity. His dissertation was awarded publicly in Paris in 1889 at the First International Congress of Physiological Psychology.

The Congress, it turned out, was an event of historic importance for the development of the new dynamic psychology of the subconscious. Originally organized by Charcot's circle, delegates from all over Europe, England, and the United States were invited to discuss the newest developments in the new science.[49] Representatives from Austria, Brazil, Belgium, Chile, England, Germany, Holland, Italy, Mexico, Romania, Russia, Finland, Poland, Salvador, Sweden, Switzerland, and the United States took part. F. W. H Myers, A. T. Myers, and Henry Sidgwick came from England, among others. William James, Joseph Jastrow, Boris Sidis, and Morton Prince came from the United States. Bernheim, Liégois, Binet, Janet, Richet, and Ribot were there from France as well as Déjerine. Delboeuf came from Belgium, Forel from Zurich, Caesar Lombroso and G. Ferrari came from Italy, and Münsterberg and Schrenk-Notzing came from Germany. Unfortunately, most of the other invitees from Germany boycotted the meeting. Although it was originally organized by Charcot, who could not make it for medical reasons, Magnan, Richet, and Ribot, as members of the executive committee, convened the meeting instead. The discussions were quite lively, but in the on-going rivalry between the Salpêtrière and the Nancy schools, the Nancy group dominated the discussions, which centered on hypnosis and suggestibility. Clearly, the explanation that the Nancy group put forward—that the phenomena of hypnosis were a function of normal suggestibility rather than a symptom of pathology, as Charcot had claimed—was firmly established as a result of the meetings.

Nevertheless, Janet's work was highlighted and thereafter served to bring together international opinion that fueled further development of a so-called French-Swiss-English-and-American psychotherapeutic axis. It should also be mentioned that lurking around the meetings of his own accord as an auditor, but remaining in the background, was a young Viennese neurologist who had come into town to consult with Bernheim about a patient. The neurologist was Sigmund Freud.

James on "Person and Personality"

James is always remembered for having written on the tender and tough-minded types in the first chapter of his *Pragmatism* (1907). He was there talking about different types of philosophers and made the point that the differences between their theories was always one of temperament. The tender-minded were rationalistic and operated according to theories. They were intellectualistic, idealist, optimistic, religious, free-willist, monistic, and dogmatical. The tough-minded were empiricists, relying on facts; they tended to be sensationalistic, materialistic, pessimistic, irreligious, fatalistic, pluralistic, and skeptical.

Next to that discussion, James is always remembered for his definition of the self in his *Principles of Psychology* (1890a).[50] He said there that there is, first of all, the me and the I, who I am in the experience of the first person, and the I as an objectified entity. Of this objectified entity, we have biological, social, and spiritual sides to the self, which may actually be independent from each other. He also gave a number of examples of multiple personality throughout the text, that is, the possibility of multiple states of consciousness within us. He affirmed this position in his article "The Hidden Self," which appeared the same year in *Scribner's Magazine*.[51] There he introduced the work of Janet and Binet on psychogenesis and multiple personality, citing numerous cases presented by each investigator. In 1894 he was the first to mention the work of Breuer and Freud to the American psychological public, when he reviewed their "Preliminary Communication on the Nature of Hysterical Phenomena," noting that it was corroboration for Janet's "already old findings."[52]

Throughout the 1890s James continued to interpret the psychological literature on dynamic theories of the subconscious to American audiences, generally favoring the advances of the so-called French Experimental Psychology of the Subconscious, the investigations of Théodore Flournoy in Switzerland, and those of the British psychical researchers. He refuted the so-called searchlight view of consciousness put forward by the German investigators, who by their very conceptualization of the problem privileged waking rational consciousness as the evolutionary state superior to any that might exist below the surface. He also continued to challenge the American psychologists on the scientific study of the emotions as a way to get them to see that everything is not just a study of cognition alone and that an emotion is not just an ideal category in the mind. He also repeatedly attacked the brass instrument psychologists who haunted the laboratories and asserted that only by the rational ordering of sense data could all of reality be known.

What James had in mind instead was a radically different epistemology for experimental science that was much more phenomenologically oriented, which he eventually dubbed radical empiricism.[53] For this, however, he was rejected by psychologists as a mere philosopher and a has-been. After all, psychology had at last established itself as a laboratory science and the philosophers had just been metaphorically banished from the newly founded American Psychological Association and encouraged to start their own national organization. James was made to look like a throw back to the days when psychology was dominated by philosophy, a chant repeated particularly by newly minted psychologists returning from Germany. His days as a psychologist they believed, as reductionistic psychologists continue to believe today, ended with *The Principles of Psychology* in 1890.

James, however, was not to be deterred. He set about pioneering in a variety of new fields that he considered legitimate science, among them, besides experimental psychopathology and psychical research, philosophical psychology, and the psychology of religion. Meanwhile, he continued to clarify the meaning of the person in psychology.

James himself published on the meaning of "person and personality" in *Johnson's Universal Cyclopedia,* which remained in print between 1893 and 1898.[54] He began his entry by deriving the word person through Old French, but originally from the Latin *persona*, meaning a theater mask, the part one has, as in a play, personage, or person, which he took to be a loan word from Greek for mask, or face. Its presumed etymology comes from *per*, meaning through, and *sonare*, sound, meaning sound, or "to speak."

Insofar as usage is concerned, he said, personality came to denote a man's corporal appearance rather than his inner attributes. Later the word came to represent relationships with others, as in *personage*, and still later it came to refer to a spiritual function. So James said, "In common parlance today 'person' means an individual man in his typical completeness as uniting a human body with a free and rational soul."[55] This, he assured his mainly Christian readers, excludes pure spirits, the souls of the departed awaiting resurrection, idiots, maniacs, and animals other than humans.

In psychology the term referred, James said, to personal identity, either as the ultimate principle at the core of man or a subsidiary derived from other principles. He then turned to Hindu philosophy, where he contrasted the Samkhya from the Vedanta on the subject. "Absolute plurality or independent finite souls," James compared to the doctrine that "there exists only one self, the supreme Brahman, with whom all particular selves (Atman) are really coincidental, but (until they are redeemed by knowledge) dwell in the illusion of finite personality through not distinguishing themselves from the organisms with which they are severally conjoined."[56] This distinction is crucial, because it indicates a relatively sophisticated understanding of the difference in the varying Hindu systems with particular reference to the uniqueness of the Samkhya, which can be construed as non-Vedic in origin. Samkhya was committed to a dualism in which pure consciousness and lifeless matter both exist as ultimately real but separate forces. This is one potential source for both his doctrine of noetic pluralism and his conception of radical empiricism as pure experience in the immediate moment, before the differentiation of subject and object.[57]

Having established the doctrine of the Samkhya, James then proceeded to give a description in the Vedanta system. That is, how, after the disintegration of the physical body after death, the subtle body, with the senses, active powers, including consciousness and will, the breath, and the person's *karma*, or "moral worth acquired," form principles of individuality, which enter future bodies, and through an indefinite series of transmigrations keep up one's finite personal life. He commented that the Theosophists' doctrine of personality is almost wholly constructed on the Vedanta system.[58] He then concluded with reference to other conceptions of the person from different religious traditions and finished with a discussion of then recent scientific studies in the French, German, and English literature on multiple personality.

James on Multiple Personality in the Lectures on *Exceptional Mental States*

His own major contribution to similar developments in the United States was the effect his work had on the development of what came to be called the Boston School of Psychopathology, which flourished between 1884, the year the American Society for Psychical Research first convened, and 1918, the year James Jackson Putnam died. The so-called Boston "school," which actually refers to an attitude toward personality and consciousness rather than a specific facility or institution, was made up of a loose-knit group of investigators with various backgrounds in medicine, psychiatry, psychology, philosophy, ethics, social work, and nursing. The first generation was defined by the activities to establish, first, mental science, and then experimental psychopathology at Harvard, Clark, and Tufts. William James, James Jackson Putnam, and Henry Pickering Bowditch, Josiah Royce, Richard Cabot, Joseph Hersey Pratt, Elwood Worcester, Morton Prince, Adolf Meyer, and Edward Cowles were among the early players. G. Stanley Hall came out of this group but soon stood apart from them with his own agenda. A similar situation obtained with the German émigré, Hugo Münsterberg, who opposed hypnosis and dynamic theories from the moment he arrived at Harvard to teach experimental psychology in 1892. The next generation of their students or junior colleagues included figures such as William Healy, Boris Sidis, Gertrude Stein, Ida Cannon, Isador Coriat, William Parker, Harry Linenthal, and L. Eugene Emerson, among others.

The true era of applied psychotherapeutics occurred after 1896, however, when there was an explosion of interest in personality, consciousness, and psychotherapeutics both nationally and internationally. In the United States, Boston became the Mecca for the new cures. Clinical trials on various psychotherapeutic regimes began at the Massachusetts General Hospital (MGH) in 1903, group psychotherapy for the treatment of tuberculosis was initiated at the Emmanuel Church in the Back Bay in 1904; the Department of Social Services was founded at the MGH in 1905 and the first school of social work in the United States was launched at Simmons College that same year. The Emmanuel Movement was first launched in 1906, which combined then known advances in scientific psychotherapy with the Christian teachings of character formation, and brought physicians and ministers together. Soon, it became international in scope. In addition to a major era launching the field of the psychology of religion, the Emmanuel Movement can also be considered as chapter one of the clinical pastoral education movement that re-emerged in the 1920s around Rev. Anton Boisen and the physician, Helen Flanders Dunbar.

A major event identifying the emergence of the Boston School of Psychopathology was William James's 1896 Lowell Lectures on Exceptional Mental States.[59] They were eight lectures delivered in late October in the Lowell Institute building in the Back Bay to a public audience under the auspices of the Lowell Institute. Since 1838, The Lowell Lectures had been paying a handsome sum for a just a short lecture series to Harvard and MIT professors only if they were able to make their field of specialization intelligible to the common working man and woman. James's titles were "Dreams and Hypnotism," "Automatism," "Hysteria," "Multiple Personality," "Demoniacal Possession," "Witchcraft," "Degeneration," and "Genius." The first four lectures established James' understanding of then known advances in a dynamic psychology of the subliminal, while the second four described the workings of the subconscious in the social sphere. Of particular interest for the present discussion is James's lecture on "Multiple Personality."

He began by reviewing the three major types of alienation from one's self—fugue states, where the person's consciousness passes from one state to another with no memory for the previous one; epileptic cases, where there are convulsive fits, contractions, and anesthesias of the hysterical crises, which pass off when the subject returns to waking consciousness; and psychopathic cases characterized by dreamy states, hallucinations, and morbid insanity, but which occur while fully awake. To these he added a fourth type—mediumship.

He reviewed a variety of cases, beginning with alternating personalities, proceeding to cases of multiple selves. He noted in detail Tissié's case of Albert, highlighted in Tissié's *Les Aliénés Voyageurs* (1887). He discussed Raymond and Janet's case of "P," and one of his own, the case of "Miss O.," Mitchell's case of Mary Reynolds, which he had previously cited in *The Principles of Psychology* (1890), along with the example of the Rev. Ansel Bourne. He cited the case of Mollie Fancher, "The Brooklyn Enigma," which demonstrated five different personalities. James's copy of the printed version of the case, by A. H Dailey, contains the only letter extant written to James from Pierre Janet.[60] James then introduced the physician, Osgood Mason's case of "Number One, Twooey, and The Boy," reviewed Azam's case of Felida X., and then Janet's case of Léonie and her several selves.

He reviewed Janet's explanation of multiple personality as split off fragments of the waking state, which operate in the subconscious according to laws of their own, until they gather enough memories and psychic energy to present themselves by bursting forth into consciousness as an apparently different and independent personality. From there he turned to F. W. H. Myers's theory that at any given time, each one of us has in the subliminal region, parallel personalities to the one our friends know that habitually shows itself in the waking state. These parallel personalities are ready to surge forth at any moment, given the right circumstances, some more malevolent, some more transcendent. James cited cases such as Mrs. Sarah Underwood and her "spirit control," and the case of Laurancy Venuum, the "Watseka Wonder," whose body was allegedly inhabited by that of her dead neighbor's daughter, Mary Roff.

Personality Transformation in *The Varieties of Religious Experience*

With these non-pathological examples in the lectures on *Exceptional Mental States* (1896), James posited a growth-oriented dimension to personality and the possibility that we could evolve into a higher, better, more discerning type of individual. It was a theme he brought into a more precise clarity in *The Varieties of Religious Experience*.[61] By religion, he told his audience there, he did not mean to refer to the specific denominations or the institutional church, made up of the priesthood and the texts. Rather, he equated religion with spiritual experiences within the individual. Further, he suggested that exploration of the personal subconscious was the doorway to opening the person up to ultimately transforming experiences of a mystical nature, and he proposed that the truths of such experiences be tested in terms of their fruits for life; in other words, in their ability to improve the moral and esthetic quality of a person's daily living. Psychological science confirms this view, James said there, in light of work by F. W. H. Myers, Pierre Janet, Morton Prince, Boris Sidis, and "Breuer and Freud"—In Boston, Freud was always considered the junior pupil of Breuer, up until 1915, according to James Jackson Putnam.[62]

The transcendent experience, he maintained, was the vehicle for the ultimate transformation of personality. Veritably, James implied, it was possibly the source of the discursive intellect itself. The change in who the individual was, precipitated by the transcendent experience, remained just as profound as the change that the railroad worker Phineas Gage had undergone in 1848 when an explosion had driven a bar through his skull and he had afterward lived a relatively normal life to tell about it, but as a completely changed person. The one means was wholly psychological and not pathological, while the other was wholly physical, but the results were the same. It was possible to achieve a radical transformation of personality by psychological means alone and *The Varieties* was full of such examples.

The Swiss psychiatrist, Carl Gustav Jung, understood this when he later counseled Rowland Hazard that there was nothing in medicine or psychiatry that could cure him of his alcoholism. Jung suggested instead that Hazard seek out some spiritual community that would foster the experience of transcendence as the only means to change his behavior and cure his addiction.[63] Hazard went out and saved Ebby Thatcher, who then took James's *Varieties of Religious Experience* to Bill Wilson in the hospital. Bill Wilson came to understand this same point when, after what he called a white light experience, read James's *Varieties,* and later said that James was the source of the first three of the Twelve Steps of Alcoholics Anonymous.[64]

Along with James, other figures in the Boston School of Psychopathology who were considered experts on the subject of multiple personality included Boris Sidis and Morton Prince. As a young man, Sidis had escaped from political persecution in Russia and landed penniless in the United States. By sheer resourcefulness he made his way to Boston and worked his way into Harvard as an undergraduate. Befriended by William James from the beginning, Sidis went on to take a PhD under James in experimental psychopathology for a dissertation on crowd psychology, which was later published with a preface by James as *The Psychology of Suggestion* (1898).[65]

According to the historian Starch, Sidis's work, among other influences, made a major contribution to the continued development of crowd psychology in France during that period.[66] While Charcot and Bernheim were busy in the 1880s arguing for a dynamic psychiatry within the individual, Gabriel Tarde and Gustave Le Bon were developing the new dynamic concepts of the subconscious and applying them to an understanding of social phenomena by the early 1890s. Sidis's work further fueled the dynamic interpretation of the period and extended the dissociation hypothesis well into the 20th century. Actually, James had left the development of a dynamic theory of the subconscious in the social sphere unfinished after he delivered his 1896 Lowell lectures, which he never returned to publish. Instead, the dynamic theories found a significant place in various chapters of *The Varieties of Religious Experience* in 1902 and contributed to the development of the psychology of religion. James even went so far as to call for the development of a cross-cultural comparative psychology of mystical states of consciousness in 1902, suggesting an international scope for his dynamic theories of personality, while at the same time proposing that this was possibly psychology's most important contribution to the religious sphere.

James also bequeathed those theories to Sidis as one of the next generation of investigators to develop them. Sidis went on to the New York Psychiatric Institute, where he taught techniques of psychotherapy to budding young physicians such as William Alanson White. Sidis began publishing on dissociation and multiple personality and presented his own case of alternating personality, the Rev. Hannah. He soon returned to Boston to take an MD under James Jackson Putnam at Harvard Medical School in 1904. While there, he did an extensive study of sleep and concluded that the hypnotic trance was a special case of an alternate hypnoid condition which he hypothesized was once the dominant state of consciousness in humans.

Over evolutionary time, deep sleep and waking consciousness became differentiated from the more primitive hypnoid condition, but it was possible to enter into it
again through different means by dissociating consciousness. His important contribution of the period was his article "The Psychotherapeutic Value of the Hypnoidal
State."[67]

Prince on Ms. Beauchamp

Morton Prince (Harvard Medical School Class of 1879), began his career as an
eye, a ear, a nose, and a throat man, but soon changed his field of specialization
to diseases of the nervous system. He became an ardent spokesperson for developments in French psychopathology and even took his mother abroad for a consultation with Charcot. Influenced at first by John Hughlings Jackson and Pierre Janet,
Prince began his study of multiple personality in the 1890s, soon adding the work
of Ivan Pavlov to his theories. In charge of what came to be the Department of
Neurology at the Boston City Hospital, Prince was also a Professor of Neurology
at Tufts Medical School. He is best remembered for the case of Sally Beauchamp,
a multiple whom he treated successfully and later reported about in *Dissociation
of a Personality* (1906).[68] Among other contributions, he was founder and editor
of *The Journal of Abnormal Psychology* in 1906, the main organ of the Boston
School of Psychopathology. He was also elected first President of the American Psychopathological Association, which sought to represent psychotherapeutics in psychology, psychiatry, and neurology from an eclectic standpoint. Toward the end of
his career, in 1926, after James, Putnam, Bowditch, and others had long passed from
the scene; Prince endowed the Harvard Psychological Clinic, eventually empower-
ing the career and accomplishments of yet an even younger generation of investigators around Henry A. Murray.

Flournoy on Hélène Smith

In this regard, a major player in the history of dynamic theories of personality, and
a central figure in the French-Swiss-English-and-American psychotherapeutic axis
in the late 19th century, was Théodore Flournoy, Professor of Experimental Psychology at the University of Geneva.[69] Flournoy was born on August 13, 1854, 2
years before Freud. In 1878 he received his MD from the University of Strasbourg.
He then went to Leipzig where he studied experimental psychology with Wilhelm
Wundt for 2 years and even founded the first laboratory of experimental psychology
in Switzerland. But he was no Wundtian and soon found himself interested in the
new dynamic psychology of the subliminal according to Myers and Janet. Beginning in the late 1880s, he established ties that would lead to a lifelong friendship
with William James, who believed that both of them propounded a truly functional
psychology, "the only true psychology worthy of the name," as James once put it.[70]

Flournoy soon discovered Hélène Smith, a case of multiple personality who claimed to speak numerous foreign languages while entranced, including French, Chinese, and Sanskrit. When pressed too closely about the actual content of these languages over the years that she was studied, she reverted to Martian, which later drew the attention of the linguists, since they believed it was the first example of a complete artificial language they had ever seen.

Flournoy's account of Ms. Smith, published in 1899 under the title *From India to the Planet Mars*, drew widespread attention to the new dynamic psychology of the subconscious. His work became a key addition to the other paradigm cases of mediumship and multiple personality that defined the era, such as Mrs. Piper, developed by William James; Rev. Hannah, developed by Boris Sidis; Sally Beauchamp, developed by Morton Prince; and Lucy Goodrich Freer, Stanton Moses, and other cases developed by F. W. H. Myers. Others, such as the young C. G. Jung, contributed the case of Hélène Preiswerk. Whereas physiological psychology in the 1860s defined its subject matter using the frog, and behaviorists from the 1920s onward would later substitute the white rat, for a 40-year period between 1880 and 1920, researchers, such as James, Flournoy, and Sidis, sought to establish a cross-cultural comparative psychology of subconscious states, based on the single case study of either a medium or a case of multiple personality.[71]

Flournoy was particularly interested in the phenomenon of what he called cryptomnesia, the accrual of information or experiences long forgotten which emerge into consciousness at a much later time and appear as if new material that was original to the experiencer, apparently underived from any outside source. Flournoy did not subscribe to the spiritualist hypothesis of entities trying to communicate with us from beyond the grave, and cryptomnesia, he believed, was the more likely explanation for much of the productions of the mediums he studied. Nor did he believe that there was a life after death and that science could know it. Rather, he felt that scientific study of mediumship had at least demonstrated that human beings were capable of developing supernormal capacities, that is, penetrating into dimensions of experience beyond the normal everyday waking state in which exceptional abilities could be demonstrated and that these abilities could be developed by individuals in varying degrees.

Jung on Hélène Preiswerk

Carl Gustav II Jung, so known to his family because he had been named after his grandfather who had been a physician, was born in Kesswil, Switzerland in July 1875 and raised outside Zurich. His father, a minister, was a *seelesorg*, appointed at a local asylum, and had a library of psychiatric texts, while his mother, who came from a well-to-do Swiss family, was prone to visions and promoted the reality of spiritualistic phenomena among her extensive family members, many of whom showed a similar gift of psychic second sight. One was Hélène Preiswerk, or Helly, as she was called, daughter of her sister.

Jung's decision to become a physician pushed him in the direction of the medical sciences, but in 1898, when he was considering what specialty to enter, he was drawn to psychiatry because he thought it would address some of the burning questions he had been pondering about the dynamics of human consciousness, to which he had already been exposed.[72] The true question for Jung was to become, "where did personality get its motivational force?"[73]

At first, he was somewhat hesitant, as psychiatry seemed to be in the grip of the lesion theory of disease, where all mental symptoms were believed to have an underlying organic cause, and all mental disorders were quickly being reduced to Kraepelin's new psychiatric classification, which later became the foundation for the DSM. The only sources for a truly dynamic psychology of personality he found in Passavant, DuPrel, Swedenborg, and others, 18th- and 19th-century authors dealing with the interior life of the mind and especially in Swedenborg's case, not only psychopathology but also the spiritual transformation of consciousness.[74] *Dreams of a Spirit Seer* (1899),[75] Kant's attack on Swedenborg, first published in 1766, was particularly influential in Jung's thinking. Then Jung read Richard von Krafft-Ebing's *Psychopathia Sexualis* (1892)[76] just before his state examination granting medical certification in 1900. Led by these influences, Jung committed himself to the course in psychiatry.

Immediately after passing his exam, Jung reported to the Burghölzli, the cantonal psychiatric hospital associated with the University of Zurich, to become an assistant to Eugen Bleuler (1857–1939). Bleuler practiced *Anstaltspsychiatrie*, institutionalized treatment characterized by a close relationship between patient and physician. Thus, the entire regime at the hospital was over regulated with regard to daily examinations and reports. Every physician was expected to know everything about every patient. Inmates also participated in the governance of the hospital. The psychotherapeutic treatment of the psychoses became Bleuler's specialty, in which he emphasized not only contact, but the establishment of rapport, in delivery of therapy to patients who had experienced a complete break with reality. Bleuler had studied with Charcot and Magnan in Paris and Bernard von Gudden in Munich and developed the approach called *affektiver*, rapport, or emotional connection to the schizophrenic patient. But Bleuler was chiefly known as a student of August Forel, the former superintendent. A world-class myrmecologist and brain neuropathologist, Forel had, during his tenure before Bleuler, established the Burghölzli as a world-class institution and at the same time participated as a major player introducing Swiss psychiatry into American psychotherapeutic circles.

In his new position, Jung spent his first 6 months without going out once. He was introduced to the association experiments of Wundt and Galton, and the recently published *Interpretation of Dreams* (1900)[77] by Freud, although he paid scant attention to Freud's ideas at the time. He was more interested in séances and mediumistic trances and to his surprise was encouraged by Bleuler, who was also interested in the subject. Out of this interest, Jung began to summarize a year of séances he had held with cousin Helly, which became the core of his dissertation, *On the Psychology and Pathology of so-called Occult Phenomena* (1902).[78]

Jung began this dissertation with a summary of research on the topic by William James, before he turned to Charcot, Flournoy, and Bleuler. He then presented Hélène Preiswerk as his single case study. His position was that psychic powers are perfectly normal accompaniments of certain states of consciousness and do not derive from the supernatural. He believed the investigation of the séance would be transformative for experimental psychology, as it would lead to the development of a more mature psychology of the unconscious. It was approved by the medical faculty in 1901 and published in 1902.

The Young Roberto Assagioli

In the late 19th century, Italian psychiatry had been dominated by such theories as that of Cesare Lombroso, the criminal anthropologist who had made a name for himself by comparing the size of skulls of different types and cultures. Generally, the Italians looked to the Germans for their definition of psychiatry, until the Italian courts woke them up from their slumber. One year a man was tried for inciting a mob to riot in which someone had been murdered. Brought to trial, the man's lawyers argued that recent advances in French crowd psychology had scientifically proven that one loses one's identity in the hyper-suggestible environment of the crowd, whose uncontrolled madness can become infectious. Personal identity dissolves and the individuals all become fused into a vortex defined by the fickle changes of the crowd itself. Their client, in fact, was not responsible for his actions. The court agreed, which sent the Italian psychiatric community scrambling to absorb the new work on French psychopathology.

Various individuals were already involved in such researchers, however. Enrico Morselli, Professor of Psychiatry at the University of Turin, had studied the trances of the stage hypnotist, Donato, and written a work on hypnosis defending him. Morselli was also an enthusiastic supporter of Flournoy's researches into Hélène Smith. Santi de Sanctis, another Italian psychiatrist, had been studying sleep and dreams and was favorably reviewed in the American literature by William James. Guilio Cesare Ferrari, psychiatrist and asylum superintendent who had at one point examined Helen Keller, was also favorably disposed toward developments in the French-Swiss-English-and-American psychotherapeutic axis. Ferrari, along with Giovanni Papini, Vailati, and others were members of the Italian pragmatist circle and were involved after 1900 in translating William James's works into Italian. Ferrari was also editor of *Revista di Applicata Psicologia*. In 1909 he published a remarkable article on the psychology of forced ideas by the young medical student, Roberto Assagioli, later to become known a half a century later within the American psychotherapeutic counterculture for his psychology of the will and his system of personality development, which he called psychosynthesis.[79] The seeds of Assagioli's system, which not only included a dynamic theory of self-actualization but also drew on indigenous non-Western psychologies, were already planted at this earlier period.

In his article for Ferrari, entitled "La Psichologia Della Ideé-forze e la Psicagogia," Assagioli began his comments with a quote from the *Dhammapada*, a Theravada Buddhist text enjoining rules for the life of the monk seeking enlightenment, that is, release from suffering through meditation and non-attachment. He began by chastising contemporary psychiatry for being so primitive in its state of development with regard to problems of consciousness. He reviewed Alfred Fouillee's concept of forced ideas as one of the prevailing contemporary theories that might have some substance, and he also pointed out the works of such Western physicians as the Swiss psychiatrist, Paul Dubois of Bern, who had then recently promoted the idea of self-knowledge as a central focus of psychotherapy. He reviewed Janet's *Psychological Automatisms* and mentioned works on meditation and the psychology of the will as viable topics that should be explored. He then launched into a discussion of yoga and the psychology of concentration. He referred to Breuer and Freud, but cited only Italian interpretations of their work, never referring to Freud's writings directly. He then referred to William James's work, just then becoming more well known in Italian through the translations of Papini and others, and he particularly recommended the psychology of Vedanta and Samkhya in Hindu philosophy as well as teachings of the Buddhists. Analogous literature, Assagioli said, can be found in the literature in Christian religious mysticism, and the American New Thought Movement, which laid out a detailed psychology of intuition, spiritual visions, and mystical consciousness. Modern psychiatry must take these claims of higher consciousness seriously and recognize that there is a spiritual dimension to personality that the epistemology of reductionistic science cannot fathom because of the limits of its own presuppositions about the nature of reality. He ended the article with an extensive annotated bibliography, expanding on the works of the authors cited with additional citations of authors from the French-Swiss-English-and-American psychotherapeutic axis, and various authors on East-West spirituality and the American New Thought Movement. All this, Assagioli broached in 1909.

To whit, in the closing decades of the 19th century, while German experimentalists around Wilhelm Wundt were preoccupied with measuring reaction times and sensory thresholds in the laboratories, and the English, following Francis Galton, were turning toward mental testing, the French, following Charcot, Janet, and Ribot and also Bernheim, came to be identified with the investigation of hysteria, hypnotism, dual personality, catalepsy, and somnambulism. The pathology of the emotions led investigators to formulate new scientific methods for studying the subconscious springs of human actions, out of which the field of motivation was born. It would not be long before the budding subdisciplines of personality, abnormal, clinical, and social psychology would emerge as significant counterpoints to an over-rigid emphasis on laboratory methods, paper-and-pencil tests, and the emergence of reductionistic trait theory as the only allegedly legitimate forms of psychological science, especially in the American universities.

Ellenberger notes that by 1900 four different aspects of the unconscious had been demonstrated: (1) its conservative function, the capacity of storing a number of memories and perceptions; (2) its dissolutive function, the tendency for dissociation and automatic actions; (3) its creative function, and (4) its mythopoetic function, the capacity to produce "mythopoetic subliminal romances."[80]

To this I would add the assumption that investigators acknowledged a growth-oriented dimension to personality—meaning a spiritual aspect to personality generic to each person—and that this evolutive wing of our higher nature lays in potentia until tapped through a variety of means, ranging from contemplative reflection and the moral life to the more irregular routes of creative illness, the deliberate induction of altered states of consciousness, spontaneous mystical awakening, or the systematic pursuit of techniques designed to foster spiritual insight, whether pursued within the context of organized religion or outside of it.

These ideas developed in a climate of scientific inquiry defined by a more liberal underlying epistemology within the French-Swiss-English-and-American psychotherapeutic axis 125 years ago than that afforded by similar thinking in mainstream cognitive behaviorism and trait theory today. Preeminently, the reconstruction of this axis is the articulation of Charcot's school of thought regarding trance states, tempered with a more eclectic and expansive definition of personality and consciousness informed by other French and German theorists, British and American psychical researchers, and influential American psychopathologists. Figure 2.1

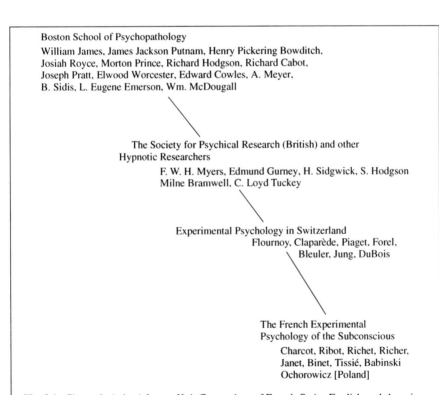

Boston School of Psychopathology
William James, James Jackson Putnam, Henry Pickering Bowditch,
Josiah Royce, Morton Prince, Richard Hodgson, Richard Cabot,
Joseph Pratt, Elwood Worcester, Edward Cowles, A. Meyer,
B. Sidis, L. Eugene Emerson, Wm. McDougall

The Society for Psychical Research (British) and other
Hypnotic Researchers
F. W. H. Myers, Edmund Gurney, H. Sidgwick, S. Hodgson
Milne Bramwell, C. Loyd Tuckey

Experimental Psychology in Switzerland
Flournoy, Claparède, Piaget, Forel,
Bleuler, Jung, DuBois

The French Experimental
Psychology of the Subconscious
Charcot, Ribot, Richet, Richer,
Janet, Binet, Tissié, Babinski
Ochorowicz [Poland]

Fig. 2.1 Charcot's Axis: A Loose-Knit Consortium of French-Swiss-English-and-American Psychotherapeutic Investigators (1882–1920)

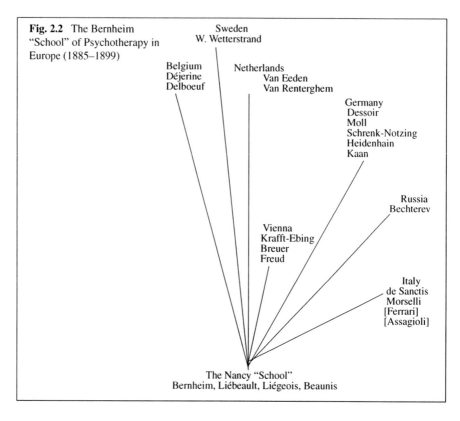

Fig. 2.2 The Bernheim "School" of Psychotherapy in Europe (1885–1899)

depicts this state of affairs from approximately the early 1880s to the beginning of the 1920s. Figure 2.2 suggests at least the early decades of approximately the same time period but looking toward Europe, before the advent of psychoanalysis. There was certainly communication between these different cohorts, but nothing like the interrelationships exhibited by the French-Swiss-English-and-American psychotherapeutic axis. If anything, we could say the European investigators represented more the attitude of Bernheim and the Nancy School. There were certainly numerous interconnections. Assagioli was influenced by both Freud and Jung, for instance, but in the end his psychology looked more like Jung's than Freud's. Sidis subscribed to both schools, but was more clearly allied with James and Janet. This was also Freud's period of "glorious isolation."[81] Richard von Krafft-Ebing was the foremost personality in Viennese psychiatry in this early period.

Morton Prince remarked at the end of his own career in the late 1920s that "psychoanalysis flooded the field and left the rest of us like clams submerged at high water." The essential historical question, then, is, why did psychoanalysis seem to take over so rapidly and so completely as to obscure this vibrant period that produced so many dynamic psychologies of the subconscious? Ellenberger himself remarked on this in an interview in 1964, when he pointed out that of all the developing sciences in the late 19th century, only the spectacular advances in depth psychology failed to become assimilated into the general flow of knowledge about science in the 20th century. Psychoanalysis, in fact, was the only dynamic language of inner experience allowed entry into the ultra positivistic scientific era that followed in the United States, and even then only grudgingly.

What, then, was this theory that so captivated modern popular culture in the West that literally took control of clinical teaching in psychology and psychiatry for half a century and acted as the persistent gadfly to the reductionistic scientists who considered it so unscientific in the experimental laboratory tradition in both professions?

Notes

1. Well into the Middle Ages, the Greek physician, Hippocrates (426BC–377 BC) was best known for his references to the system of temperaments or humors, known as choleric, melancholic, sanguine, and phlegmatic. Personality in this system was equated with the predominance of different kinds of bodily fluids. Choleric was represented by yellow bile from the liver and was correlated with the passionate type; Sanguine, blood from the heart, meaning someone who was eager and optimistic; Melancholic, black bile from the kidneys, referring to a type that was reticent and doleful; and Phlegmatic, phlegm from the lungs, referring to types that were calm. A perfect balance of the humors defined the normal personality, although it was also believed that one predominated over the other and determined the primary direction of the individual.
2. Taylor (1999).
3. Hahnemann, S. (1810). *Organon der rationellen Heilkunde*. Dresden, Germany: Arnold; First English edition; Hahnemann, S. (1901). *Organon of medicine* (R. E. Dudgeon, Trans.). Philadelphia: Boericke & Tafel.
4. Hawthorne, N. (1850). *The scarlet letter*. Boston: Ticknor, Reed, and Fields; Melville, H. (1851). *Moby Dick*. New York: Harper and Brothers; Clarke, J. F. (1882) *Self-culture: Physical, intellectual, moral, and spiritual*. Boston: James R. Osgood; Emerson, R. W. (1850). *Representative men*. London: John Chapman.
5. Ellenberger (1970) notes that in the 1820s, physicians such as Noizet, Deleuze, Bertrand, Despine, Dupotet, and others had tried in vein to influence the academy on the beneficial effects of mesmerism (p. 76).
6. James Braid, the Scottish physician who coined the term hypnosis, was an exception. Mesmerism and hypnosis were debunked generally throughout mainstream European and Anglo-American medicine. An examination of every issue of the *American Journal of Insanity*, for instance, through the entire decade of the 1880s did not mention anything about a psychogenic revolution going on in French neurology around hypnosis and referred only two or three times to anything in Germany, mainly having to do with stage hypnotism. Actually, a previous generation of both French and German investigators, not all of them physicians, had attempted to study the phenomena of mesmerism. Ellenberger (1970) notes that in Germany these included "Gmelin, Kluge, the brothers Hufeland, Kaiser, Nasse, Passavant, and Wolfart" (p. 77). Carl Alexander Ferdinand Kluge, in his *Versuch einer Darstellung des animalischen magnetismus als Heilmittel* (Berlin, 1811, pp. 102–108, as cited in Ellenberger, 1970, p. 78), for instance, distinguished six degrees of the magnetic state: (1) the waking state; (2) half-sleep; (3) "inner darkness," meaning sleep proper with insensibility; (4) "inner clarity," meaning consciousness within one's own body, extrasensory perception, and vision through the epigastrium; (5) "self-contemplation," meaning the subject's ability to perceive with great accuracy the interior of his own body and that of those whom he is put into rapport; (6) "universal clarity," meaning the removal of veils of time and space, where the subject perceives things hidden in the past, the future, or remote distances.
7. For more sources on Charcot see Micale on Charcot's 30 cases of male hysteria. Micale, M. S. (1990). Charcot and the idea of hysteria in the male: Gender, mental science, and medical diagnostics in late 19th-century France. *Medical History 34*, 363–411; Also Micale's *Diagnostic*

discriminations: Jean-Martin Charcot and the nineteenth-century idea of masculine hysterical neurosis (Doctoral Dissertation, Yale University, 1987). (Dissertation Abstracts UMI No. ATT8729120)
  8. James, W. (1890a). The principles of psychology (2 Vols.). New York: Henry Holt and Company.
  9. Discussed in Shamdasani, S. (2003). Jung and the making of modern psychology. London: Cambridge University Press, p. 41.
 10. Richter, P. (1881). Etudes cliniques sur l'hystéro-épilepsie ou grande hystérie. Paris: Delahaye et Lecrosnier.
 11. For a spirited defense of Charcot's theories see Gilles de la Tourette, G. (1891). Traité clinique et thérapeutique de l'hysterie d'apres l'ensignement de la Salpetriere. Paris: Librairie Plon, Nourrit et Cie.
 12. Giles de la Tourette, 1891, p. 166.
 13. Tissié, P. (1890). Les rêves: Physiologie et pathologie. Paris: Ancienne Librairie German Baillière, p. 214.
 14. Tissié, P. (1887). Les aliénés voyageurs:Essai médico-psychologique. Paris, Doin.
 15. Nicolas, S., & Murray, D. J. (1999). Théodule Ribot (1839–1916), Founder of French psychology: A biographical introduction. History of Psychology, 2(4), 277–301.
 16. Routh, D. K. (2004, August). The challenges of writing a history of international clinical psychology. Paper presented at the meeting of the International Society of Clinical Psychology in Beijing, China. Retrieved July 11, 2007 from http://htpprints.yorku.ca/archive/00000222/01/Beijing.htm
 17. Ochorowicz, J. (1887). De la suggestion mentale. Paris: Doin.
 18. Ochorowicz, J. (1891). Mental suggestion (J. Fitzgerald, Trans.). New York: Humboldt Publishing Company.
 19. Féré, C. (1899a). L'instinct sexuel: Évolution et dissolution. Paris: Félix Alcan.
 20. Féré, C. (1892). La pathologie des emotions: Études physiologiques et cliniques. Paris: F. Alcan. See also Féré, C. (1899b). The pathology of emotions:Physiological and clinical studies. (R. Park, Trans.). London: University Press.
 21. Azam, E. (1887). Hypnotisme, double conscience, et altérations de la personnalité. Paris: J. B. Baillière et Fils.
 22. Binet, A. (1892). Les altérations de la personnalité. Ancienne library. Germer Baillière et Cie. Paris: Félix Alcan.
 23. Ellenberger, H. F. (1978). Pierre Janet and his American friends. In G. E. Gifford, Jr. (Ed.), Psychoanalysis, psychotherapy, and the New England medical scene, 1894–1944 (pp. 63–72). New York: Science History Publications.
 24. The Jung scholar Sonu Shamdasani disputes this point, Shamdasani, Jung and the making of modern psychology, p. 87.
 25. Ellenberger, 1978, p. 87.
 26. James, W. (1868). Moral medication. Review of Liébeault's Du sommeil des états analogues, considérés surtout au point de vue de l'action du moral sur le physique. The Nation, 7(159), 50–52.
 27. Bernheim, H. (1889). Suggestive therapeutics:A treatise on the nature and uses of hypnotism (C. A. Herter, Trans.). New York, London: G. P. Putnam's Sons.
 28. Allen, G. W. (1967). William James: A biography. New York: Viking.
 29. Beard, G. M. (1873). The influence of the mind in the causation and cure of disease and the potency of expectation. Journal of Nervous and Mental Diseases, 3, 430–431.
 30. James, W. (1884). What is an emotion? Mind, 9(34), 188–205.
 31. The full correspondence between James and Ribot has yet to be collected in one place.
 32. Binet, A. (1890). On double consciousness. Chicago: Open Court.
 33. Myers, F. W. H. (1903). Human personality and its survival of bodily death. New York: Longmans, Green, and Company.
 34. Braude, A. (1989). Radical spirits: Spiritualism and women's rights in nineteenth-century America. Boston: Beacon Press.
 35. Shamdasani, S. (1993, Spring). Automatic writing and the discovery of the unconscious. Journal of Archetype and Culture, 54, 100–131.
 36. Taylor, E. I. (1988). On the first use of psychoanalysis at the Massachusetts General Hospital, 1903–1908. Journal of the History of Medicine and Allied Sciences, 43(4), 447–471.
 37. James, W. (1902b) Frederick Myers's services to psychology. Proceedings of the Society for Psychical Research, 17, 13–23.

38. Myers, F. W. H. (1886). Human personality in the light of hypnotic suggestion. *Proceedings of the Society for Psychical Research*, *4*, 1–24.
39. Gurney, E., Myers, F. W. H., & Podmore, F. (1886). *Phantasms of the living*. London: Rooms of the Society for Psychical Research; Trübner and Company.
40. Remarking on his year at Harvard in 1892–1893, James Angell wrote "I enjoyed a peculiarly intimate contact with James by virtue of his turning over to me for study and digest the great mass of documentary material, which had come to him in connection with the effort of the American Society for Psychical Research to secure exhaustive and reliable information regarding abnormal psychic experiences of normal individuals—especially so-called veridical hallucinations." Angell, J. R. (1961). James Rowland Angell. In C. Murchison (Ed.), *A history of psychology in autobiography* (Vol. 3., pp. 1–38). New York: Russell and Russell.
41. Taylor, E. I. (1985a). Psychotherapy, Harvard, and the American Society for Psychical Research, 1884–1889. *Proceedings of the 28th Annual Convention of the Parapsychological Association*. Tufts University, Medford, Massachusetts, August 15, 319–346.
42. Taylor, E. I. (1983). *William James on exceptional mental states*. New York: Charles Scribner's Sons.
43. James, W. (1909). Report on Mrs. Piper's Hodgson-Control. *Proceedings of the Society for Psychical Research*, *23*, 2–121.
44. Janet, P. (1885). Notes sur quelque phénomènes de somnambulisme. *Bulletins de la Société de Psychologie physiologique*, *2*, 70–80.
45. The Jungian analyst John Haule maintains that the theory of the transference originated not with Freud, but with Janet. Haule, J. R. (1986). Pierre Janet and dissociation: The first transference theory and its origins in hypnosis. *American Journal of Clinical Hypnosis*, *29*(2), 86–94.
46. Janet, P. (1889a). *L'automatisme psychologique. Essai de psychologie expérimentale sur les formes inférieures de l'activité humaine*. Paris: Ancienne Librairie Germer Ballière.
47. Following the prevailing notion on the will propounded by Ribot, and the theory of Fouillée on "idée-force," Janet came to believe that it is the natural tendency of an idea to develop into an act. James, among others, called it "ideomotor activity"—the automatic discharge of a thought into its consequences.
48. By 1892, Janet reported that he had manifested such forgotten memories in dreams, automatic writing, distractions, and by a method he called automatic talking, in which the patient was encouraged to talk aloud at random. Before 1890, Janet was also aware of the often symbolic nature of the presenting symptom—the fits of terror which were traced back to the patient's reaction to a terror filled event; a rash on the hysteric patient's face derived from a memory where as a young girl the hysteric had to sleep in the same bed with an older woman whose face bore a disgusting eruption. He also recognized the developmental component in the patient's recovery—that traumatic experiences from the past were usually accompanied by immature behavior and that relief from these symptoms allowed a more fully functioning and mature person to emerge.

   In his medical dissertation under Charcot, *The Mental State of Hystericals* (1893), Janet summarized the cases he had been working on in the wards. Focusing on hysteria, he distinguished between two levels of symptoms, accidents, and stigmata. The accidents were contingent on circumstances and depended on the existence of fixed ideas, while the stigmata were a function of a single basic disturbance that caused an extreme narrowing of the patient's field of consciousness. Hysteria was not purely neurological, nor was the patient pretending. It was, rather, psychogenic—of psychological origin, based upon a morbid physiological condition.

   These conclusions allowed Janet to expand on his original conceptions of the psyche. At the lowest level were primitive emotional reactions and useless muscular movements. Next came the functions of imagination—memory, reasoning, fantasy, and daydreaming. Above that is the level of interested activity, which included habits and actions that were indifferent and automatic. The highest level of synthesis was that of voluntary action and attention. This is the level of what he called presentification, the capacity for grasping reality to the maximum.

   By the end of the 1890s Janet had shifted his focus from the study of hysteric patients to other forms of neuroses. He developed a synthetic theory in *Neurosis and Fixed Ideas* (1898) and *Obsessions and Psychasthenia* (1903) in which hysteria and psychasthenia became the two primary forms of neurosis. By 1913, his work was publicly being subjected to systematic deconstruction by the psychoanalysts-turned historians who marginalized all his earlier work, giving credit for the psychogenic hypothesis exclusively to Freud. In the 1920s, Janet fell under the influence of the developmental psychologist, James Mark Baldwin, who was living as an American ex-patriot in Paris at the time. Janet's theories took a decidedly developmental turn, as he began to theorize about personality across the life span. He also presented lectures on the psychology of religion during this same period. A renaissance of his work occurred in the 1930s when his ideas were taken up by Elton Mayo at the Harvard Business School, and he was invited in 1936 to the Harvard Tercentenary to receive an honorary doctorate, along with Jung and Piaget. Then, after his death in 1946, at that time a forgotten figure, his ideas were resurrected again in the 1970s around the neo-dissociation theorists who were interested in the historical antecedents of post-traumatic stress disorder, dissociation, and traumatic shock. These included figures such as the psychiatrists Bessel van der Kolk and Onno van der Hart, psychoanalysts such as John Nemiah, and even the aging Ernest Hilgard in psychology, whose work on hypnosis had led him back to Janet's writings. [Janet, P. (1893). *Contribution à l'étude des accidents mentaux chez les hystériques.* Paris: Rueff et Cie; Janet, P. (1889b). *Névroses et idées fixes* (2 vols.). Paris: Alcan; Janet, P. (1903). *Les obsessions et la psychasthénie* (2 vols.). Paris: Alcan.]

49. Myers, A. T. (1890). International congress of experimental psychology. *Proceedings of the Society for Psychical Research, 6*, 171–182.
50. See Leary, D. (1990). William James on the self and personality: Clearing the ground for subsequent theorists, researchers, and practitioners. In M. G. Johnson, & T. B. Henley (Eds.), *Reflections on "The Principles of Psychology": William James after a century* (pp. 101–137). Hillsdale, NJ, England: Lawrence Erlbaum Associates, Inc.; Coon, D. (2000). Salvaging the self in a world without soul: William James's *Principles of Psychology. History of Psychology, 3*(2), 83–103.
51. James, W. (1890b). The hidden self. *Scribner's Magazine, 7,* 361–73.
52. James, W. (1894). Review of Breuer and Freud's "Preliminary communication on the nature of hysterical phenomenae." *Psychological Review, 1,* 199.
53. James, W. (1897). Preface. In *The will to believe.* New York: Henry Holt.
54. James, W. (1893). Person and personality. *Johnson's universal cyclopedia.* In F. H. Burkhardt, F. Bowers, & I. K. Skrupskelis (Eds.). (1975), *Works of William James. Essays in psychology* (pp. 315–321). Cambridge, MA: Harvard University Press.
55. Burkhardt, Bowers, & Skrupskelis, 1975, p. 315.
56. Burkhardt, Bowers, & Skrupskelis, 1975, p. 316.
57. In the Samkhya, all individuals are not subsumed under the same *purusha.* Rather, each person exists as a light unto him or herself. See also, Taylor, E. I. (2008). William James on pure experience and Samadhi in Samkhya Yoga. In K. R. Rao (Ed.), *Handbook of Indian psychology.* Delhi, India: Cambridge University Press Ltd.
58. James had been a member of the Theosophical Society in Boston since 1888, read their literature, and commented regularly upon it, particularly in *The Varieties of Religious Experience* (1902a).The local lodge of which he was a member was run by the American branch under Katherine Tingley and William Q. Judge, who had separated from the International Society by then. The current theosophical society dates its beginnings from the 1920s, when Katherine Tingley died in an auto accident and Annie Besant brought the Boston Lodge back under the wing of the International Society, dating its inception from that period. Acknowledgments to Sylvia Cranston for providing me with documentation for James's membership in the earlier Theosophical Society.
59. Taylor (1983).
60. Letter dated June 8, 1895 in which Janet comments on the Fancher case—Rare Books, Countway Library of Medicine, Harvard. See also Walsh, A. A. (1978). "Mollie Fancher: The Brooklyn enigma." *New Port Magazine, 1,* 2 (Salve Regina College); and *Proceedings of the Society for Psychical Research [British], 14,* 396 (1899).
61. James (1902a).
62. Putnam, J. J. (1915). *Human motives.* Boston: Little, Brown, and Company.
63. Bluhm, A. C. (2006). Verification of C. G. Jung's analysis of Rowland Hazard and the history of Alcoholics Anonymous. *History of Psychology, 9*(4), 313–324.
64. T. Powers (personal communication, March, 1989). Also, Taylor, E. I. (2001–2002). *The Varieties* and its influence. In *William James and the spiritual roots of American pragmatism.* Lectures on the Centenary of James's *Varieties of Religious Experience* for the Swedenborg Society at Harvard.
65. Sidis, B. (1898). *The psychology of suggestion: A research into the subconscious nature of man and society* (Preface by William James). New York: D. Appleton & Company.

66. Karpf, F. B. (1932). *American social psychology: Its origins, development, and European background*. New York, London: McGraw-Hill Book Company.
67. Sidis, B. (1909a). *An experimental study of sleep (from the Physiological Laboratory of the Harvard Medical School and Sidis Laboratory)*. Boston: Badger. Also Sidis, B. (1909b). Studies in psychology: The psychotherapeutic value of the hypnoidal state. *Boston Medical and Surgical Journal, 161,* 242–247; 287–292; 323–327; 356–360.
68. Prince, M. (1906). *The dissociation of a personality*. New York: Longmans, Green & Company.
69. Shamdasani, S. (1994). Encountering Hélène: Théodore Flournoy and the genesis of subliminal psychology. In S. Shamdasani (Ed.), *From India to the planet Mars: A case of multiple personality with imaginary languages*, (pp xi–li). Princeton, NJ: Princeton University Press. (Original work published 1899)
70. LeClair, R. C. (Ed.). (1966). *The letters of William James and Théodore Flournoy*. Madison, WI: University of Wisconsin Press.
71. A differentiation needs to be made at the outset between the experimentalists' view of a case study, which can be a single subject or a cohort of subjects taken by itself, and the meaning of the case study in personality theory, which conveys more of a clinical understanding regarding the assessment of a single patient. For examples more compatible with the experimentalists view that are adapted to general research designs, see Yin, R.K. (2003). *Case study research: Design and methods*. Thousand Oaks, CA: Sage. For a clinical example focusing on a single person, see Kreuter, E. A. (2006). *Victim vulnerability: An existential-humanistic interpretation of a single case study*. New York: Nova Science Publishers.
72. At one point a 70-year-old walnut dining table had cracked in his house inexplicably in a way that could not be ascribed to any physical defect in the wood. Then a few weeks later, a loud noise had been heard and it was found that a hefty bread knife in a sideboard drawer had been inexplicably broken into three even pieces with no visible marks on the blade. These events sent Jung into the spiritist literature for an explanation. Even though he found such material weird and questionable, they at least seemed to treat such events as "objective psychic phenomena." See Bair, D. (2003). *Jung: A biography*. Boston: Little, Brown and Company, p. 43.
73. Bair, 2003, p. 45.
74. Taylor, E. I. (2007). Jung on Swedenborg redivivus. *Jung History, 4*. Ardmore, PA: Philemon Foundation.
75. Kant, I. (1899). *Dreams of a spirit-seer, illustrated by dreams of metaphysics*. London: S. Sonnenschein & Company; New York: The Macmillan Company.
76. Krafft-Ebing, R. v., & Chaddock, C. G. (1892). *Psychopathia sexualis*. Philadelphia: F. A. Davis Company.
77. Freud, S. (1900). The interpretation of dreams. In J. Strachey (Ed. & Trans.), *The standard edition of the complete psychological work of Sigmund Freud* (Vols. 4–5, pp. 1–622). London: Hogarth Press.
78. Jung, C. G. (1901). *On the psychology and pathology of so-called occult phenomenae*. Medical Dissertation, University of Zurich (*Collected Works, Vol.1*, 1902).
79. Assagioli, R. (1909). La psicologia della ideé-forze e la psicagogia. *Revista di Psicologia Applicata, 5*(1), 371–393.
80. Ellenberger did not exactly agree with Jung that the unconscious was also a source of imagery that had never been conscious in the psychic life of the person.
81. And while Freud later claimed that "Charcot was my master," Charcot did not remember him in that way. Bernheim was Freud's next incarnation after Charcot. Freud later developed psychoanalysis as an alternative to therapeutic suggestion, an endeavor of Bernheim's, not Charcot's. In any event, it is my impression that Freud's relation to Charcot was overplayed by Freud himself and then further amplified by Freud's followers.

Chapter 3
Freud's Shibboleth: Psychoanalysis

[Freud]... himself, after all, had discovered the roots of
scientific investigation in children's sexual curiosity.
Peter Gay[1]

Freud's story begins at the Institute of Ernest Brücke, professor of physiology at
the University of Vienna.[2] In Brücke's laboratory, Freud spent 6 years, 1876–1882.
There, in addition to being introduced to reductionistic physiology and publishing
a few neurological papers, he first met Josef Breuer. He also studied with the phenomenologist, Franz Brentano, and translated some of his works. Freud received
the MD in 1881. The years 1882–1893 became his period of clinical training. He
published a single experimental study, the effects of cocaine on muscular strength in
1885. He prescribed the drug for his patients, took it frequently himself, and introduced it to his medical colleagues until one of them died of it through the deleterious
effect of the cocaine on a preexisting medical condition. But in all this, Freud never
mastered the methodology of the experimental laboratory.

Instead, Freud's conception of science became clinically oriented toward the
treatment of patients, which proceeded under Theodore Meynert. He had a brief
encounter with Charcot, where he audited his lectures and translated two of his
works. Here, the history of psychoanalysis as the psychoanalysts tell it, quoting
Freud himself, was that Freud always considered himself a student of Charcot and
Charcot his master. Charcot, however, returned no such recognition. Freud, in fact,
although he identified himself briefly as an ardent Francophile, was probably closer
to Bernheim, whose work he also translated. It was the occasion of consulting with
Bernheim that brought Freud to Paris in the first place, where he attended the International Congress in 1889 as an auditor.

Meanwhile, Freud continued in private practice with Breuer, who introduced him
to the patient, Anna O., neé Bertha Pappenheim. Apparently, by talking out her
problems, her symptoms were relieved, a process which she, herself, called "the
talking cure." Freud took the case over from Breuer, mulled over the implications
of her venting, noted a sexual component, and hatched the idea of repression—
that there was a censor at work normally preventing traumatic memories from
coming to the surface, probably related to the patient's sexual experiences. These
memories could be intentionally liberated by various means, hypnosis being the

E. Taylor, *The Mystery of Personality*, Library of the History of Psychology Theories,
DOI 10.1007/978-0-387-98104-8_3, © Springer Science+Business Media, LLC 2009

primary medical vehicle of the era, which at first Freud employed. Freud claimed remarkable success with Anna O., but, it turns out, that was not the complete story.[3]

In 1893 Breuer and Freud published the results of their researches with hysteric patients in the *Neurologische Centralblatt*, in an article entitled "Preliminary Communication on the Nature of Hysterical Phenomena."[4] F. W. H. Myers published a note on it right away in the psychical research literature and in 1894 William James summarized it in the inaugural issue of *Psychological Review*, the first introduction of Freud's work to the American psychological public, according to the later historians of psychoanalysis.[5] Breuer and Freud followed in 1895 with their collaborative work, *Studies in Hysteria*, which reproduced the 1893 "Preliminary Communication," had theoretical sections by Breuer and by Freud, respectively, and presented a collection of their cases, mainly Freud's.

Their main point was to highlight the cathartic cure of hysterical symptoms by the release of repressed memories, usually of sexual origin. While they did cite some of the French literature, their interpretation was decidedly slanted toward German sources. The document hinted at priority for the psychogenic hypothesis— that psychological causes can create physical symptoms—despite the fact that the year before, William James, citing Pierre Janet as the originator of this doctrine, had praised Breuer and Freud for corroborating Janet's "already old findings." The controversy would continue, first Freud and then his followers claiming priority, then Janet asserting himself. But after 1913, the Freudians, just starting to come into their own, finally prevailed, sweeping Janet's claims to the side.

Even before 1895, Freud began to have his own ideas about the origins of the neuroses and started pulling away from Breuer, eventually to develop a system, which sometime after 1896 he called psychoanalysis. What he meant by that can be variously defined. His father had died in 1896 and he went into a period of creative illness, in which he engaged in an intensive process of self-analysis, particularly the analysis of his own dreams, having earlier elaborated on the technique of free association as a replacement for hypnosis. Psychoanalysis, in this sense was the unique product of his own psyche, underived, which he developed into a language and system unique to himself. He did this, he believed, according to the dictates of objective science and believed thereafter that psychoanalysis was also a science, equivalent to but entirely a separate science from neurology, psychology, and psychiatry. Thus began another great controversy, namely whether or not psychoanalysis was a legitimate science, since part of it seemed to be anchored in biology and Darwinism, yet the other part seemed wholly and idiosyncratically confined to Freud's own psyche and there never has been a way to tell which was which.[6]

During this time, Freud wrote but did not publish his "Project for a Scientific Psychology" (1895).[7] In it, he attempted to move from a neurologically based understanding of mental events to a theory of psychogenesis in which he conceptualized the effects of unconscious conflicts arising from the defenses of the ego. The unpublished document was preserved by his new collaborator, Wilhelm Fleiss, an eye, ear, nose, and throat man who introduced Freud to the ideas of the inherent bisexuality of all human beings and the notion that nasal tissue was erectile in nature. He also became his sounding board, at least until Freud began to gather a small group of auditors around him after 1904.

Much has been made of "The Project," most of it erroneous or based on false assumptions, mostly because writers focus exclusively on Freud and have no clue about the previous contextual history of the psychogenic hypotheses. Suffice it to say that in "The Project," Freud had attempted to correlate mind states with brain states by subjecting psychogenesis to a critical interpretation according to the current state of neurophysiology at the time. It was a brilliant move, but it failed utterly, since not that much was actually known about the neurophysiology and neurochemistry of the brain and nervous system. He abandoned "The Project" precisely because neurophysiology had yet to catch up to what was rapidly becoming known clinically about the influence of the mind upon the body, which far outstripped scientific corroboration in the laboratory or by autopsy, yet showed decisive psychological effects. He was forced to reassert the scientific basis of psychoanalysis, yet return to the method of symbolism, which he had been employing to uncover the unconscious meaning of the person's internal images presented in dreams as well as free associations.

It was not until 1899, or rather 1900, that psychoanalysis first became public, with publication in German of Freud's *Interpretation of Dreams*.[8] In it, Freud first reviewed the prevailing scientific literature on dreams, before turning to an elucidation of his method for interpreting them, with examples. He finished off with a general psychology of the dream process.

Dreams, he declared, were the royal road to the unconscious. The dream, Freud said, is made up of unfinished or unresolved thoughts generated during the day, which fuse in the dream world with memories derived from early childhood. These dream images are thrown together through association and contiguity, which the dreamer feels compelled to fit into the dream upon awakening as if actually related; hence, the story line with fantastic elements juxtaposed onto one another.

The book's thesis is that a wish and its fulfillment lay behind every dream but in disguised form. Every dream is a compromise between the wish and the resistance to its expression. He differentiated secondary from primary process thinking in this regard—what the overt dream was as told by the dreamer, as opposed to its real underlying meaning, which was buried in the dreamer's unconscious and could be called forth by the new method of free association. In this regard, Freud declared dreams and psychoneurotic symptoms as similar, both having their origin in earliest infancy.

This can be demonstrated by an examination of the Oedipal phase of the child's development, which basically determined by age 5 or 6 the nature of the child's adjustment to his parents, his or her sexual orientation, and the extent to which he would grow up to become either a maladjusted neurotic plagued by distorted sexual fantasies and their concomitant behaviors or a functioning, relatively adjusted member of society, able to have stable, healthy human relationships.

The theory was based on the play *Oedipus Rex* by Sophocles, where the hero, unbeknownst to himself, grows up to slay his father and marry his own mother. Freud believed that at a certain early moment in the life of the child, the boy develops the urge to sleep with his mother and destroy the father, so he can take his place in the marital bed. In the normally adjusted family, the father rises to the occasion and reasserts his place as the head of the family, with whom the boy, fearing castration, simultaneously acquiesces to and identifies with. In that new position, he has found his rightful place as heir to the father, but destined to find a mate who will probably resemble his mother, if he cannot actually have his mother as the object of his infantile yearning.

Distortions of this process, however, are unending. If the father refuses or cannot assert himself, for instance, the son triumphs and identifies instead with the mother, thus emasculating the father. This distorts the boy's future quest for a mate, and hence a stable family, as well as proper same-sex identification with his own future children, since symbolically, at that tender age, he takes on his own mother as an absolute object of sexual identification and never achieves same-sex identification through the father with other males that would allow him properly to enter the world of masculinity. At the same time, the father may even triumph, but the child never gets over the primitive wish to kill him. To the extent that he unsuccessfully represses, then sublimates this wish, their relationship becomes combative, which then generalizes to other males, and so on. The key to understanding the Oedipus myth, Freud suggested, was that all relationships stem from adjustment with the parents, especially during this crucial early period, and that maladjustments in this relationship may prefigure in dreams and neurotic symptoms in behavior and one's relationships for the rest of the person's life.

"Irma's Injection" was Freud's central specimen dream. Irma had been one of Freud's patients, a woman who was also quite involved with Freud and his family. Doctor and patient had reached a temporary impasse because while her hysterical symptoms had disappeared, her somatic ones persisted. Freud felt this was because she would not accept his interpretation, partly because of her own resistances and partly due to the weakening of Freud's authority because of his overinvolvement with the patient's emotional life. They agreed to suspend analysis for the summer.

Later Freud encountered a close colleague who had just spent time with the woman and her family and the colleague indicated she was better but not quite well, to which Freud found he had an annoying reaction. That night he wrote up the case and upon going to sleep had a dream. Irma came into a large hall where guests were being greeted and Freud pulled her aside and reproached her for not following his advice on how to rid herself of the somatic symptoms. She complained instead of excruciating pains in her throat and abdomen. It occurred to Freud that possibly he had missed something organic. Various physicians suddenly appeared in the dream and examined her again, suggesting a real infection, possibly from a dirty needle, Freud thought, that one of them had used to give her an injection. There were more details to the dream, on which Freud then free associated in his text to demonstrate that the dream was an unfinished thought in waking life mixed up with his own personal concerns from his past.

But the outcome in waking life was quite different. Her somatic symptoms, which had persisted after Freud had cured the hysteria, were due not to her refusal to accept Freud's explanation of the psychogenic and sexual origin of her symptoms, as he had thought, but to gauze that Fleiss had accidentally left in her nasal cavity from a recent minor operation. The gauze, it turned out, had caused an actual infection.

The dream of Irma's injection was a centerpiece of the book. Freud used it as a means to show the reader the associations linked to each phase of the dream symbols, revealing the structure of the mind as stratified into levels—what was conscious, what was preconscious, and what was unconscious. He linked many parts to incomplete thought chains of the previous, but immediate period related to a recent illness of his own wife, to the injection associated with von Fleischl-Marxow's death from cocaine, and his guilt over that episode, and these events in turn revealed the extent to which the dream was related to the fulfillment of outcomes he had wished for in his own life.

Ernest Jones noted in his biography of Freud a half century later that 600 copies of *The Interpretation of Dreams* were printed and it took 8 years to sell them. Some 123 copies sold in the first 6 weeks and then 228 in the next 2 years. After 18 months Freud lamented that no reviews had yet appeared in any scientific periodical, although there had been a few in popular magazines here and there.[9] It is also true, however, that, later, the work went into numerous editions between 1913 and 1938, had been translated into eight languages, and remains in print today.

Eventually, when the book was finally reviewed, it was variously hailed as both good and evil. When they learned about it, Puritans, Calvinists, Catholics, and fundamentalists everywhere were shocked at the idea that children would have such thoughts about their parents, let alone thoughts about sexuality at all at that young age. Most of them probably did not even read the book. Bleuler at the Burghölzli in Zurich read it as soon as it was published and Jung was exposed to it not long after. Both began to incorporate Freud's theories into their treatment of the insane there at the asylum right away. Freud's followers declared that it had answered the riddle of the sphinx—what is man?—and unlocked the door to the secrets of our humanity.

The Interpretation of Dreams also marked the end of Freud's communications with Fleiss. He was soon replaced in 1902 by a young coterie of admirers who gathered around Freud to discuss psychoanalysis, called the Wednesday Psychological Society, a circle of younger men around a central father figure. It would later develop into the Vienna Psychoanalytic Society. Alfred Adler, Wilhelm Stekel, Max Kahane, and Rudolf Reiter were among the first. By 1906 there were 17 members, including Paul Federn, Isadore Sadger, Max Graf, Victor Tausk, David Bach, Eduard Hitschmann, Hugo Heller, and Fritz Wittels. Hans Sachs joined in 1910. Otto Rank was also a member. Jung had joined in 1907, Jones after the Clark Conference in 1909. As well, Karl Abraham, Max Eitingon, Sandor Ferenczi, A. A. Brill, Ludwig Binswanger, Oskar Pfister, and Otto Gross appeared at different times; it is interesting to note that these men all came to Freud through the Burghölzli. At the same time, according to the prevailing legend, Wilhelm Stekel was the first to "defect," then Adler, then Jung, and others.

We may conjecture at this point on the tremendous impact this work must have had on those who became so devoted to Freud's theories that many would commit their careers to the defense of psychoanalysis and write books that may have been polemic here and there but always essentially in tune with Freud's original presuppositions about the unconscious. Enthralled, entranced, fascinated, absorbed into the spell of Freud's own unconscious are the terms that come to mind, yet all the while maintaining that psychoanalysis was a science. Meanwhile, to those outside the bubble, it all looked like a cult.

Despite the lack of reviews, Freud kept on writing. In 1900 he began treating the case of Dora, which he published as a "Fragment of an Analysis of a Case of Hysteria."[10] Examining the subsequent impact of Freud's ideas on culture at large, Eli Zaretsky maintains that with Dora, Freud moved from a discussion of men versus women to a condition of ambivalence about gender opposites as they presented themselves in the unconscious.[11] The effect this had on Freud's theory was that gender was no longer confined merely to sexuality as an object choice but now had to do more with the larger sphere of masculinity and femininity in personality development. It was then not a great stretch in the way his work was subsequently interpreted to extend these considerations to the choice of one's lifestyle in the world to the so-called homosexual way of life. Dora was a case in point.

Dora was an 18-year-old Jewish student and ardent feminist who had sworn off marriage at the time and had been suffering from a recurrent depression, a condition from age 8, for which she had received at one point electrotherapeutic treatments, but to no avail. Her father, a former patient of Freud's who had been treated for both tuberculosis and syphilis, brought her to be treated for hysteric symptoms, including a persistent cough. As a young girl, the father had encouraged the daughter to engage in a relationship with a much older man, so the father could involve himself with the man's wife, whom the daughter was actually more attracted to herself. Although the analysis was prematurely terminated after a short time, Freud was able to divine that the origin of the girl's persistent cough was a fixed idea she had on the experience of oral sex her father was having with the older man's wife, a nongenital and generalized sexual excitement that the girl was acting out through her own mouth. The girl was also physically attracted to both the man and his wife, a condition of ambivalence, since she could not choose one over the other, which Freud labeled bisexuality.[12]

The solution to her hysterical symptoms, Freud concluded, was not that she could not choose between them; the conflict arose from not choosing. The case pointed to other examples of sexual ambivalence as a source of hysteric symptoms and also an explanation for the approach-avoidance behavior at the beginning of normal sexual encounters. It also ended Freud's adherence to a black-and-white doctrine of men versus women and the penchant to define these categories by a set of fixed traits. Masculinity and femininity became, rather, a range of possibilities within individual identity. A bundle of contradictions himself, Freud continued to emphasize male development in the Oedipus complex in his writings, however, only addressing slightly the Electra complex (the Oedipus myth, but in women) and did not write directly on the subject of female sexuality until the 1920s.

After *The Interpretation of Dreams* in 1900, Freud also followed in quick succession with *The Psychopathology of Everyday Life* (1901), *Jokes and Their Relation to the Unconscious* (1905a), and *Three Essays on the Theory of Sexuality* (1905b).[13] The first two applied Freud's theories to slips of the tongue, momentarily forgotten names, and the kinds of phenomena seen in normal everyday waking life. Our outward behavior, over which we believe we have so much control, is actually dominated by vast unconscious forces; the normal and the pathological are on a continuum and not that far apart; humor serves the same function as sexual foreplay.

Three Essays on the Theory of Sexuality was all about sex and the libido, what was at the core of our psychic energy. The first essay reviewed the perversions, the second childhood sexuality, and the third what happens at puberty. Freud separated first the object from the aim. Most men and women prefer each other, some prefer the same sex, and others prefer animals and objects. The perversions are biological experiments leading through evolution to the normal sex act. Therefore, they are universal dispositions of the sexual instinct in all human beings, which can be seen in childhood and later, in the face of normal adult sexual development, with its single aim of reproduction. The perversions show themselves in the form of developmental inhibition and sexual infantilism.

The child first awakens to the erotogenic zones: the mouth, the anus, and the reproductive organs. In the child, the period of ages 2–5 is one of efflorescence, going through oral, anal, and genital phases. The child's behavior is first characterized by autoeroticism, but then followed by a period of latency, in which direct sexual experience is held off as the sexual instinct is distributed throughout patterns of relationships with others and the establishment of personal habits related to repression and reaction formation which mold the later personality. Disruption at this phase, such as through seduction, can make the child further uneducable, sexually and emotionally, in adult life. Otherwise, in normal development, pleasure, excitement, and self-stimulation give way to the actual discharge of sexual products, which then culminate in a revival of adjustments made during the previous Oedipus phase coming forth at the beginning of adolescence, where there is the awakening of strong distinctions made between the genders. This, because of the incest taboo, in turn, leads to the search for a mate outside the family, courtship, marriage, reproduction, and a repetition of the Oedipus cycle with the new offspring.

Fixation can occur at any point along the way and be incorporated into personality makeup accordingly. Repression, the automatic blocking out of contents from conscious awareness, and sublimation, the diversion of sexual energy into more socially acceptable channels, are both processes at work in psychopathy, bringing about a regression to previous, earlier phases of personality development. At the same time, incomplete adaptation, particularly at the crucial developmental periods as the child passes through the oral, anal, genital, and then phallic phases, can produce fixation of parts of personality at that stage, while other parts of personality continue to develop. The adult then exhibits oral fixations, or possibly becomes anal retentive, or its opposite, or exhibits genital compulsions, where one's sexual organs can become the center of one's personality, as in the permanent display of breast implants or the flaunting of the size of one's reproductive apparatus.

Three Essays on the Theory of Sexuality was a seminal text in Freud's corpus, second only to *The Interpretation of Dreams* as far as the importance he gave to it. Successful navigation of these developmental phases was always only approximate, however, so every adult struggles in some way with neurotic symptoms from the past. One could call it the normal neurosis, as far as Freud's budding conception of personality was concerned. The only problem was that Freud spent the first part of his career as a psychoanalyst talking about the unconscious and psychopathology and only in the second part did he begin to broach a psychology of the ego and therefore of the normal personality. As Otto Fenichel later pointed out in 1946, psychoanalytic characterology remained in its infant stage until only much later, when enough had been written about the normal personality to even broach such an all-encompassing system of classification.[14] But the way in which Freud's theories have often been presented suggests that such a characterology was already in place from an early date, when it was not.

Freud did elaborate on some aspects of the psychosexual stages and character development in 1908 in a paper on anal eroticism.[15] He had already noted in his clinical practice that excrement, money, and obsessional neuroses were somehow linked. He came to understand that some types of patients experienced pleasure at retaining their feces and display this through traits of orderliness, stinginess, and obstinacy.[16] One of his more distinguished biographers, Peter Gay, notes that character in psychoanalytic theory meant a stable configuration of traits. But the problem is that this refers to a cluster of fixations, not something inherent and unchanging in the individual. Personality in this sense is the organization of inner conflicts, not their resolution. They are for Freud the building blocks of the ego, however.

Freud expanded this idea much farther in a paper a few years later on "Formulation of the Two Principles of Mental Functioning." It was all about primary and secondary process thinking. Primary process thinking is controlled by the pleasure principle, largely under the sway of the unconscious. Development proceeds by its modulation through the secondary process, the reality principle. The many combinations of these forces shape the kind of person we become in each individual case as the secondary process becomes stronger through maturation and socialization. The two principles continue to co-exist, often in conflict, however.

Meanwhile, the psychoanalytic movement was going through its own growing pains. One example is the claim that they were unfairly persecuted or opposed when in fact that was not always the case. Contradicting this view, Ellenberger notes that in 1907 the First International Congress of Psychiatry and Neurology was held in Amsterdam, September 2–7. Numerous dynamic theories were critiqued,[17] Freud's included, but it was not a major attack as the Freudians had claimed. Most were more interested in a discussion of their own theories, not psychoanalysis. There, Janet gave the main report at the session on theories of hysteria. Subconscious fixed ideas and a narrowing of the field of consciousness resulting from mental dissociation was his model. He thought hysteria belonged to a wider group of depressions. Aschaffenburg said Freud and Jung focused so much on sexuality that their patients naturally did the same, not the other way around. Jung gave Janet credit for the theoretical foundation of psychoanalysis. Dupré, Auguste Marie, and Sollier gave their own theories. Janet gave Breuer and Freud credit for their novel cases, but believed everyone knew there was an occasional sexual component, except these few cases were not the basis for an iron-clad theory of sexual origin. At one point, Janet was heard to call psychoanalysis a "mauvaise plaisanterie," or "practical joke."[18]

DuBois, van Renterghem, and others also presented. At the time, Ernest Jones characterized the discussion as one of violent polemics, which Ellenberger later disputed.

By 1908, psychotherapeutics was flourishing throughout Europe, the Netherlands, Britain, and the United States. The most noted psychotherapist internationally was not Bernheim, or Freud, but Paul DuBois of Bern, Switzerland. His rational theory of moral reasoning stressed self-knowledge and a spiritual component of personality and drew widespread attention. Meanwhile, an informal gathering at Salzburg, Austria, April 26, drew 42 participants and was later dubbed the first International Congress of Psychoanalysis. Six papers were presented, one by Freud. Freud and Bleuler also launched a new journal devoted to psychoanalysis, with Jung as editor. In the United States, the Emmanuel Movement, blending Protestant Christianity with psychotherapy, was in full swing. William Parker, a former student of William James, even launched a home study course on psychotherapy.

In 1909, the Sixth International Congress of Psychology was held in Geneva, chaired by Claparède, Piaget's teacher. The main theme was the subconscious. The keynote address was given by Janet.[19] A conference on psychotherapeutics was also held that same year at New Haven, Connecticut, sponsored by the American Therapeutic Society, primarily a group of physicians who normally dealt only with physical medicine. It was chaired by Frederick Henry Gerrish, a physician from Maine interested in the new work on the subconscious. The speakers, including James Jackson Putnam, Morton Prince, and Tom Williams, more accurately represented the state of psychotherapy at the time as international, eclectic, and interdisciplinary. Only Ernest Jones, even though he was not yet a member of Freud's circle, rang a note of elitist specialization, saying one can only do psychotherapy, by which he exclusively referred to Freud and meant psychoanalysis, after long training.

So, many professionals were not opposed to psychoanalysis; they simply did not know of or were ignoring it. But then in September 1909, the Twentieth Anniversary conference commemorating the founding of Clark University was held in Worcester, Massachusetts. Herbert Spencer Jennings was the featured speaker; Adolf Meyer spoke on the psychotherapeutic treatment of schizophrenia. A special session was also held where Freud and Jung spoke and were awarded honorary doctorates. Freud's lecture, however, was not the most important event of the congress. Interviews that appeared in the New York and Boston newspapers had been prearranged by Hall. In other words, the reporters did not flock to the conference to report on Freud. Only a handful of invited guests knew who he was, and his talks to a wide audience would have been of limited interest. They would not have been readily comprehended except by college-educated professionals, since he delivered them in German. He opened by saying how the event was so meaningful to him, since this was the "first official recognition" of his work, a point Ellenberger thought odd, since his ideas had been adopted by Eugen Bleuler at the Burghölzli 10 years earlier.

Psychoanalytic historians usually present the Clark Conference as the first international recognition of the movement. There was an amusing episode to report in this regard. After the conference was over, Ernest Jones reported that William James came up to him and putting his arm around his shoulder said, "The future of psychology belongs to your work." Afterward, the psychoanalysts always believed that James was referring to psychoanalysis as the future of psychology, when James had actually said the same thing to F. W. H. Myers and the psychical researchers and also to Anagarika Dharmapala and the Buddhist meditators. Nevertheless, later psychologists, embellishing even further on Jones, got it turned around and reported that James had uttered those words not to Jones, but to Freud himself.[20]

So-Called Defectors, the First Turn Toward Ego Psychology and the Death Instinct

After the Clark Conference, an entirely new set of circumstances arose for Freud, especially around increased marginalization by the professions, while at the same time the exaggerated absorption of his ideas into popular culture occurred. On the one hand, everything Freud had written the Russians had translated between 1909 and 1914.[21] On the other, this was the era of a psychoanalytic hiatus in the United States as far as psychology and psychiatry were concerned, as only a handful of professionals followed Freud's ideas. Behaviorism had recently risen to dominate academic psychology, followed by mental testing, while in academic, scientific psychiatry, spectacular advances in brain neurophysiology and the beginning of major advances in psychopharmacology dominated. Personality was conceived as the study of a person's moral character. Clinical psychiatry was considered Meyerian, led by the students of Adolf Meyer who had passed through Johns Hopkins. At the same time, Benjamin Beit-Hallami maintains that the so-called religious psychotherapies, which Freud had decried in one of his newspaper interviews at the Clark Conference, were the primary cultural forms, along with the artists and writers that preserved psychoanalysis until the founding of the psychoanalytic institutes in the 1920s.

During this period Freud was continually bedeviled by political instability within his own circle that took valuable time away from his writing. Eventually, however, it would also begin to dictate what he was writing about.

Psychoanalysis and archeology Freud naturally related since both excavate successive layers below the surface, an idea upon which *Totem and Taboo* was meant to elaborate. At the same time, however, Freud intended it, he told Abraham, to cut off from psychoanalysis everything that was "Aryan-religious" in his attempt to outdo Jung, who had just left the fold.[22] *Totem and Taboo* (1912–1913)[23] was made up of four interrelated essays: The first was on the horror of incest, from primitive religions to modern culture; the second on the infantile return to totemism in the neuroses; the third on the relation of animism to magical thinking; and the fourth linked totemism to the incest taboo by identifying it with the father and therefore the Oedipus complex. Men are related to their gods as they are to their fathers. Freud considered the work an analytic reconstruction, not a mere guess. His analysis made it clear that civilized consciousness passes through three stages of thought: the animistic, the religious, and the scientific.

In 1914, Freud produced his controversial paper "On Narcissism."[24] It was controversial because it was partly an answer to both Adler and Jung, who had left Freud's circle by then, so it was reactive to begin with. Second, it marked a major shift in emphasis from a focus on the Id to the beginning of a psychology of the ego. Its very production caused Freud headaches and intestinal disturbance. Narcissism meant the infatuation of the person with himself, specifically with his own genital organs. Freud now maintained it was a necessary stage between autoeroticism and normal object love. Narcissism can be a neurotic perversion but it is also a characteristic of schizophrenics who have withdrawn from reality. It can also be found in children as well as primitive cultures. In this sense, it is not a perversion but, as Freud said, "the libidinal complement to the egotism of the self-preservation drive."[25] Parents show self-love when they see their own traits in their children. Lovers express it in how they present themselves to their partners or try to make them over into beings like themselves. Vanity would be a word to cover such types in the general population, possibly more prone in women than men, Freud had hinted. It can even become an ego ideal, when socialization demands attention away from self toward others, which proceeds by the attempt to find one's own traits in others. Its pathological manifestation is the delusion of being watched, while in the normal ego ideal it is associated with superego functioning, which is the guardian of the ego ideal. Its difficulty for orthodox psychoanalysts was that it implicated sexual instincts with the ego that classically had been normally confined to the unconscious.

Also in 1914, Freud must have sensed the end of an era and determined it was time to codify it by penning his version of events. He did so with his essay "On the History of the Psycho-analytic Movement" (1914b).[26] It was also a way to characterize Adler and Jung so there would be no mistake about their newly diminished role in the development of psychoanalysis.

In the early 1920s, Freud produced "Beyond the Pleasure Principle" (1920a) on eros and the death instinct, "Group Psychology and the Analysis of the Ego" (1921), and "The Ego and the Id" (1923).[27] Peter Gay describes these as Freud's structural essays—the writings on metapsychology. The stress was now on aggression and death.

"Beyond the Pleasure Principle" announced that in addition to *eros*, the entangling of sex and love in the creation of culture, there was *thanatos*, the death instinct. World War I had convinced Freud that evil was indeed a part of basic human nature in both men and women, for which his theory had also to account. The mind itself was a battlefield between *eros* and *thanatos*. While all mental events conspire toward the pleasure principle, the pleasure principle is also modulated by the reality principle. But then there is the incessant reenacting of situations that are disturbing to us, the compulsion to repeat a painful experience, the repetition of the same calamity in different situations over and over. These were but smaller manifestation of the larger ones, such as the urge to make war, a fascination with the dark side, even a cultivation of pain. It was, Freud came to assess, a drive toward annihilation, in contrast to the drive toward creation, which had guided his theories up to that time. He labeled it the death instinct.

"Group Psychology and the Analysis of the Ego" was Freud's psychoanalytic interpretation on the social psychology of the masses and the relation of the individual to the community. His thesis was that in every aspect of one's interior life, the other exists as object, ideal, helper, or adversary, and while the laws of the individual and the laws of the crowd appear at first as totally different systems, from a psychoanalytic viewpoint they are actually one and the same. True, groups have laws of their own. They are more intolerant, irrational, immoral, heartless, and inhibited than the individual. But they add nothing to our knowledge of psychology that cannot already be found in the individual except in an exaggerated state.[28] Their power and consequently cohesiveness were held together by diffused sexual emotions, the same passions that unite families. But particularly in more anonymous groups, they tend to be more neutral as mere emotional attachments. Nevertheless, erotic bonds are what bind people in a group in terms of loyalty to other members and fealty to whoever is the leader. As one feels more emotionally secure, one's guard drops to the collectively lowest common denominator, and personal inhibitions are relaxed. The power of the group dissipates as these bonds are weakened; panic being a sign of increased but unconscious group cohesion, not the lack of it.[29] Such sublimated erotic alliances account for strong group cohesion and also account for the repressed hatred for outsiders that develops with increased group identification. Where love is the self-consciously avowed motive, hatred is often the repressed feeling sequestered in the unconscious.

But psychologists interpreting psychoanalysis like to point to the doctrine of the id, ego, and superego as Freud's conception of the basic structure of personality. He did not articulate this model until the publication of *The Ego and the Id*, although parts of it lay strewn throughout his works before then.[30] In this work, Freud attempted to weave his model of consciousness; that is, waking consciousness (what he abbreviated as cns), the preconscious (pcs), and the unconscious proper (ucs), with first, the ego and the id, and then the superego. The ego, which grew out of the id, was the executive function, extending libido out into the world to cathect with objects. It operated according to the reality principle—that pain and compromise are sometimes necessary to express the longings of the id. The id, which represents the unconscious proper, is the vast interior inner world of the most basic and primitive instincts, whose material is all completely repressed. It operates unrestrictedly as the pleasure principle and presents its wishes to the ego as demands for immediate gratification, which the ego has to modulate.

The superego is an outgrowth of the ego, which has introjected social standards of right and wrong and developed a repertoire of emotions around shame, guilt, and remorse that serve the purposes of reestablishing harmonious adjustment with the environment. The development of the superego is the appearance of conscience, but also much more, as it expresses the entire repertoire of the person's beliefs and values. These three systems play off on one another depending on the person's level of libido, biological endowment, and past history.[31]

The Future of an Illusion (1927a)[32] was an attempt to protect psychoanalysis from the priests. Freud professed that he had been a devout atheist all his life and this was his chance to link his ideas about personal religion and neurosis under one heading. Both obsessives and religious types performed rituals, both practice renunciation, and both are used to protect from and ward off the vicissitudes of the world. His conclusion was that religion was a universal obsessional neurosis as neurosis was a religion.[33] Hence, he believed, religion originates in the drives, which manifest themselves particularly in the appetites, vicissitudes, and helplessness of early childhood. In this context, we become what our parents were. We usually follow their gods and those of the clan and the tribe. But this does not change the circumstance that religion is based not on reality but on a wish for the way things ought to be. But they remain wishes, nonetheless, based on our earliest childhood illusions.

Civilization and Its Discontents,[34] which appeared in 1930, carried on from previous discussions; Freud maintained that we are inherently dissatisfied with culture. We resist it because it suppresses our most instinctual urges, at the same time that it acts as a panacea from the larger problems of destruction by natural forces, unfulfilled relationships, and our inevitable physical decline. In it, we feed the senses as substitute gratification and intoxicate ourselves into insensitivity. Religion he gave as a primary example. Work was another. Neither leads to happiness, however, or an answer to the big questions. For this, we hate civilization.

These works he saw as a reflection of dynamic tensions between the id, ego, and superego within the individual except now played out on a wider stage. Collectively they were attempts to move psychoanalysis more into the sphere of normal ego development and then to demonstrate the efficacy of psychoanalytic concepts for understanding culture at large. They were also a means to keep Freud occupied in the midst of continued political turmoil within his own ranks.

In 1923, the young Wilhelm Reich had published *The Impulsive Character*, later expanded into *Character Analysis*.[35] Reich linked the different forms of resistance to the stages of infantile sexuality. Ferenczi and Rank answered with their jointly authored *Development of Psychoanalysis* (1924), presenting the heretical idea that the relationship in therapy, not insight alone, was the locus of cure.[36] The same year, Rank also published *The Trauma of Birth*.[37] For it, he was ejected from the inner circle. His first heresy was that the bond between the mother and the child was preeminent, whereas Freud had laid greater emphasis on the father. Second, the root of neurosis was not the sex drive, but the trauma of birth, that is, the more existential attempt to overcome the trauma of existence between two dark voids, the one of birth and the one of death. In between, we are faced simultaneously with meaningless existence and the urge to create ourselves. Failure to face this dilemma, which is the unending human condition, throws the person into a neurosis because they have given up the process of creation in despair. The neurotic is essentially, Rank would later say, a failed artist.

Freud answered Rank in 1924 with a long letter that circulated in the psychoanalytic community describing their similarities and differences.[38] Rank himself was on a triumphant tour of the United States.[39] He attempted to defend himself against Freud's criticisms, recanted his own theory, was forgiven by Freud, but then recanted his recantation. He left for Paris in 1926, severing all ties to the secret committee that had formed around Freud when Jung had defected in 1912. By 1930, he said, he no longer called himself a psychoanalyst.

Rank would go on to develop these ideas and to place the locus of cure in the therapeutic relationship itself, not, as Freud maintained, on the therapist's interpretation of the patient's Oedipal adjustments, which were believed to lead to a lifting of repression through insight. For Freud, the therapist was the uninvolved scientist. For Rank, he was there to affirm the creative life of the patient through the therapeutic relationship. Rank's psychology focused more on the therapist and the phenomenology of what went on between patient and therapist. He identified, for instance, the Promethean complex. Prometheus was punished because he was the mortal who had stolen fire from the Gods, thus giving men their power, so that they believed that they were gods. The Prometheus complex was what beset parents in their role to shape the ego of the child and to make the offspring like themselves. It is also the indifferent attitude of the Freudian therapist, who remolds the patient in the direction of his interpretations. Overcoming this complex allows the inferior in the relationship to achieve independence and growth.

Growth in this sense, however, for Rank, in the end meant transcendence and individuation, not merely adjustment to external social norms. The patient needed to affirm their need for love and belongingness, which they attained in successful therapy, but at the same time, they needed to end therapy, break away, and be reborn into their own person. Life was this constant balance between belonging and breaking away, love and will, union with others in love and separation through growth and individuation, until the final rebirth back into the void at death.

The more sinister development in 1924, however, was that in April; Freud was diagnosed with nasal cancer. Eventually, he had to be fitted for a painful prosthesis in order to separate the nasal and mouth cavities, which had to be removed each night. He also continued to smoke 20 cigars a day up to the time he died 16 years later, in 1939. Nevertheless, after the diagnosis, he continued to work, to write, and to see patients. But the immediate group of his followers had dispersed. Rank was soon gone. Abraham died in 1925. Eitingon went to Palestine, and Sachs drifted to the periphery and eventually went to the United States. The committee itself was dissolved in 1924. A year later, it was briefly taken over by Anna Freud, Lou Andreas Salomé, Marie Bonaparte, and Loe Kann.[40] But this reconstituted committee dissolved by 1926. The committee, which was to have been Freud's successor, was then effectively replaced by the much larger and more diffuse international movement. This led to the creation of a network of institutes that operated outside the universities, but that become nonetheless more heavily medicalized. Psychoanalysts in the United States, against Freud's own more favorable position, had essentially rejected lay analysis, at the same time that America more and more appeared to become the new center of analytic activity. In 1925 the American Psychoanalytic Association first required a medical degree for every analyst, at a time when Freud had just published "The Question of Lay Analysis" (1926).[41] Vienna, Berlin, Budapest, and London continued to hold sway as long as Freud was alive. Nevertheless, the march toward increased professionalization, a new theoretical focus on the ego, and the mother–infant and mother–daughter relationships and female sexuality, became the new driving forces.

The Berlin Institute, run by Abraham, Eitingon, and Simmel, remained the center of European orthodoxy. Supported by government funds and recognized by the medical community, it focused on ego psychology. Graduates included Otto Fenichel, Käthe Friedländer, Edith Jacobson, George Gëro, Erich Fromm, Franz Alexander, Karen Horney, Sándor Rádo, Melanie Klein, Theodore Reik, Therese Benedek, Helene Deutsch, and Edward and James Strachey.[42]

Psychoanalysis also invaded the universities during the interwar years: Ferenczi taught at the University of Budapest and Max Eitingon at Hebrew University in Jerusalem. Franz Alexander taught part-time at the University of Chicago, while Stanley Cobb and Henry Murray, both power brokers in their own domain, introduced psychoanalysis at Harvard. This was also the era of "experimental psychoanalysis," when the question of whether or not psychoanalysis was really a science was put to the test.

Zaretsky notes that besides Vienna, Budapest, Berlin, London, Holland, Switzerland, and Russia, societies had been formed in Paris, Calcutta, Japan, the United States, Jerusalem, South Africa, and Scandinavia.[43] It was a mark of the spread of modernism. Generally, however, in places such as the Philippines and New Zealand, psychoanalysis was also to become associated with the spread of colonialism.[44] In 1924 the first collected works of Freud were initiated by Ortega y Gasset. Mexico, Brazil, Peru, and Argentina also by then had reading groups. Charlotte Bühler in Vienna, anti-Freudian though she was, taught Réne Spitz, Else Fraenkel, Marie Jahoda, Rudolf Ekstein, Bruno Bettelheim, and Edith Weisskopf. Piaget, a member of one of the Geneva psychoanalytic societies, aborted his analysis with Sabina Spielrein.

The 1930s was tumultuous, being simultaneously one of accolades and decline. In 1927 Freud's essay on "Fetishism,"[45] the transfer of one's sexual libido to particular objects, soon drew the attention of surrealists such as Salvador Dali, in what can only be called Dali's phase of extreme paranoid delusions, the phase for which his works are best known. In response to Freud's ideas about the sexual origin of the fetish, Dali began to incorporate realistic objects into his paintings that apparently had no artistic or aesthetic function with regard to the content of the painting itself. He even rendered a picture of Freud at their meeting and later said of that period, "Freud was my father," suggesting that Freud's ideas had loomed large in his interior life. For his part, Freud was charmed at their meeting in 1932 but failed to grasp what the surrealists were really up to with regard to a critique of Western cultural consciousness. Dali would go on to depict the surrealistic horrors of the Spanish uprising, before taking up a mystical interpretation of quantum theory. In that later phase he said, "Freud was my father. Now it is Heisenberg."[46]

The attempt to maintain purity of ideas within the psychoanalytic ranks prevailed as long as Freud was still alive. Vienna, Berlin, and New York remained the bastions of Freudian orthodoxy. In 1933 Wilhelm Reich, the really bad boy of psychoanalysis, published *The Mass Psychology of Fascism*,[47] a scathing political critique from a dynamic perspective. It was only slightly less radical than his books on the sexual revolution. Finally, in 1934 Reich was thrown out of the international psychoanalytic movement for his radicalism, while in 1937 Anna Freud's *Ego Psychology and the Mechanisms of Defence*[48] appeared. She was her father's daughter, meaning that no son had stepped forward to carry on the legacy. From an early age, it was Anna who became Freud's most devoted follower and eventually heir apparent. Her father had pioneered in putting forth his ideas about the unconscious. Anna effectively put the stamp of approval on Freud's new emphasis after 1914, applying psychoanalysis to the normal personality.

Alongside Anna's emphasis on the ego, Melanie Klein proposed her version of object relations theory, which focused on attachment bonding with the mother.[49] Freud had argued for autonomy in articulating the Oedipus complex. Anna and Melanie opted to emphasize relationships. Another new interpretation also sprang on the scene in 1934, Jacques Lacan and his theory of linguistic mirroring.[50] A third was Ferenczi, who emphasized passive receptivity, not activity, as the force behind development. Imre Hermann, Alice and Michael Balint, and Heinz Kohut followed his line.[51]

Freud's other well-known works during this period included *Civilization and Its Discontents* (1930), "Female Sexuality" (1931), "Analysis Terminable and Interminable" (1937a), and *Moses and Monotheism* (1939).[52] His mother also died in 1931. In January 1933, Hitler came to power in Germany. On May 10, Freud's books were burned in Berlin. Sixty-five members were reduced to 15 at the institute. The number of students dropped from 222 in 1931 to 34 in 1934.[53] In 1936 the German Psychoanalytic Society joined the Goring Institute but finally dissolved in 1938. In 1937 Horney's *Neurotic Personality of Our Time*[54] was published, and in 1939, John Dollard's *Frustration and Aggression* and Abram Kardiner's *Individual and His Society* both appeared, further diffusing Freud's ideas.[55]

Feud's last major work was *Moses and Monotheism*. The work was composed of three essays, each longer than the other, in which Freud explored the mystery of Jewishness and the problem of self-hatred. To the question "Who was Moses?," Freud's answer, in the form of what he himself described as kind of "historical novel," was that Moses, Israelite leader and Hebrew lawgiver, was an Egyptian.[56] Christian and Jewish scholars of religion have by and large ignored Freud on the matter, but the issue is by no means settled as far as the historical question is concerned. This highlights the speculative nature of the document, which suggests a more important angle of interpretation; namely to what extent was Freud's Moses autobiographical? We know that Freud identified with Moses as someone who was a leader, was misunderstood, and was vilified as well as praised, all of which paled next to his central role in the birth of Israel. Freud saw himself as a Moses of the mind. After 1907, for instance, to Lou Andreas Salome, he characterized himself as Moses and Jung his Joshua who would enter the promised land of a transformed psychiatry, where he could never go.[57] At the same time, Freud placed himself in the lineage of Judaism while professing himself an atheist. One wonders the extent to which it is possible to separate one's Jewishness by simply ignoring the religious side of its history and still claiming the rest. We know from an analysis of Freud's artifact collection that the majority of figures were Egyptian and Greco-Roman, with a few Oriental pieces mixed in, suggesting a stronger identification with the mythic origins of European and Germanic culture than any self-conscious association with the religion and culture of the Semites. Science, rather, was Freud's ultimate concern. David Bakan, however, has convincingly argued for a greater influence of the Jewish mystical tradition on Freud's thinking than Freud himself was possibly aware.[58]

Freud's Flight

November 7, 1938, had been *Kristallnacht*, the night 7000 Jewish stores were destroyed and 50,000 Jews were sent to concentration camps. In March, gangs of brown shirts invaded Freud's home and publisher's office and raided his safe. Later, Anna Freud was arrested by the Gestapo, but released later that day. Extensive preparations were made behind the scenes to obtain the right papers and to pay large sums of money. The Freud family was not able to leave for England until May 1938, but finally Freud arrived safely with the last of his family. In June 1939, Freud was in pain, his prosthesis unmanageable, his cancer suppurating. He had come to London, he said, to protect his Anna and to die in freedom. He passed away on September 23, 1939.

Freud's Influence

In 1952, Franz Alexander described the diffusion of psychoanalysis into a variety of scientific disciplines. The statement was somewhat hagiographic, in that he believed Freud was the first to "discover" the unconscious, and Alexander also ignored all forms of depth psychology except psychoanalysis. The penetration of psychoanalysis into psychiatry began with William Alanson White, Smith Ely Jelliffe, and Adolf Meyer, he said, forgetting the neuropsychiatry of James J. Putnam. By the 1950s, Alexander continued, six areas of psychoanalytic influence could be identified: clinical psychiatry proper, by which he meant the subfields of psychopathology and psychotherapy; the borderline between psychiatry and anthropology, where personality is studied across different cultures, which has led to the development of social psychiatry; in experimental psychology, which could refer to the experimental analysis of psychoanalytic concepts by Sears, Murray, Rosenzweig, and others (Alexander said that he was specifically referring to the Thematic Apperception Test and the Rorschach); in animal psychology, where learning theorists in the tradition of Pavlov (such as Dollard and Miller) had investigated frustration and aggression; in medicine, by which he meant the new subfield of psychosomatic medicine; and particularly in child psychiatry, where psychoanalysis had probably had its greatest influence.

The outgrowth of this "scientific cross-fertilization," Alexander called "dynamic psychiatry." Dynamic psychiatry, he said, "is liquidating" the isolation of psychoanalysis, maintaining that as a therapy it was being reunited with medicine and as a body of theory accepted as "basic science" in both psychiatry and the social sciences.[59]

This, of course, was a fantasy in Alexander's own head, based upon his hope for the fulfillment of a wish. His characterization of the diffusion of psychoanalysis into just those specific branches of the medical and social sciences he named seems accurate, but each one of those disciplines was clearly split on their opposition to psychoanalysis. Also, it is probably more accurate to say that between roughly 1933 and the early 1960s, psychoanalysis dominated clinical teaching in psychology and psychiatry, while psychobiology predominated in scientific psychiatry and behaviorism controlled the prevailing definition of psychology in the laboratories of the universities. Freud may have had a tremendous impact on modern culture, but it was chiefly through literature, the arts, and the soft side of anthropology, sociology, and psychology, which themselves had to fight continuously for legitimacy within the sphere of mainstream science, if even recognized there at all. At the same time, Freud's ideas were disseminated through his closest disciples, the Freudians, but also through a new iteration of psychoanalysis promulgated by the Neo-Freudians, before being radicalized in the psychotherapeutic counterculture. In this way, his ideas gained wide currency in the culture at large and disciplines in the so-called soft side of the academy.

Notes

1. Gay, P. (1988). *Freud: A life for our time*. New York: Norton, p. 531.
2. See Holt, R. R. (1989). *Freud reappraised*. New York: The Guilford Press and also Fancher, R. (1973). *Psychoanalytic psychology: The development of Freud's thought*. New York: Norton, for what I do not cover here.
3. Ellenberger, H. (1993). The story of Anna O. A critical review with new data. In M. Micale (Ed.), *Beyond the unconscious: Essays of Henri F. Ellenberger in the history of psychiatry* (pp. 254–272). Princeton, NJ: Princeton University Press.
4. Breuer, J., & Freud, S. (1893). Studies on hysteria. On the psychical mechanism of hysterical phenomena: Preliminary communication. *The standard edition of the complete psychological works of Sigmund Freud* (Vol. 2, 1–18). London: Hogarth Press.
5. This is, of course, not completely true. Freud had defended Charcot's physiological explanation of hysteria before the Viennese Medical Society in 1886 and the session was briefly outlined in the *American Journal of Insanity* for 1888. Also, Freud was Breuer's second author and junior pupil, so one must always say "Breuer and Freud," not "Freud" alone before 1896 when talking about Freud's contribution to psychotherapeutics.
6. See, for instance, Pumpian-Mindlin, E., Hilgard, E. R., & Kubie, L. S. (1952). *Psychoanalysis as science: The Hixon Lectures on the scientific status of psychoanalysis*. Stanford, CA: Stanford University Press.
7. Freud, S. (1895). Project for a scientific psychology. In J. Strachey (Ed. & Trans.), *The standard edition of the complete psychological works of Sigmund Freud* (Vol. 1, pp. 281–392). London: Hogarth Press.
8. Freud (1900).
9. Jones, E. (1953). *The life and work of Sigmund Freud: The formative years and the great discoveries, 1856–1900* (Vol. 1, p. 360). New York: Basic Books.
10. Freud, S. (1905/1901). Fragment of an analysis of a case of hysteria. In J. Strachey (Ed. & Trans.), *The standard edition of the complete psychological works of Sigmund Freud* (Vol. 7, pp. 1–122). London: Hogarth Press.
11. Zaretsky, E. (2004). *Secrets of the soul: A social and cultural history of psychoanalysis*. New York: Alfred A. Knopf.
12. Zaretsky, 2004, pp. 53–54.

13. Freud, S. (1901). The psychopathology of everyday life. In J. Strachey (Ed. & Trans.), *The standard edition of the complete psychological works of Sigmund Freud* (Vol. 6, pp. 1–291). London: Hogarth Press; Freud, S. (1905a). Jokes and their relation to the unconscious. In J. Strachey (Ed. & Trans.), *The standard edition of the complete psychological works of Sigmund Freud* (Vol. 8, pp. 1–237). London: Hogarth Press; Freud, S. (1905b). Three essays on the theory of sexuality. In J. Strachey (Ed. & Trans.), *The standard edition of the complete psychological works of Sigmund Freud* (Vol. 7, pp. 123–231). London: Hogarth Press.

14. Gay, 1988, p. 336.

15. Freud, S. (1908). Character and anal eroticism. In J. Strachey (Ed. & Trans.), *The standard edition of the complete psychological works of Sigmund Freud* (Vol. 9, pp. 167–176). London: Hogarth Press.

16. Gay, 1988, p. 336.

17. De Bussy, J. H. (1908).Théories modernes sur la genèse de l'hystérie. *Compte rendu des Travaux du Premier Congrès International de Psychiatrie, de Neurologie, de Psychologie et de l'Assistance aux aliénés*. Amsterdam, September 2–7, 1907, pp. 264–270.

18. Ellenberger, 1970, pp. 797, 875.

19. Compare with Ellenberger, 1970, p. 800; Claparède, E. (Ed.). (1910). Vle Congrès International de Psychologie, 1909 Rapports et Comptes-Rendus. Geneva: Kündig.

20. Along with Gardner, H. (1985). *The mind's new science: A history of the cognitive revolution*. New York: Basic Books; Ross Stagner also mistakenly maintained that James had said to Freud, "the future of psychology belongs to your work." Stagner, R. (1988). *A history of psychological theories*. New York: Macmillan, p. 297.

21. Zaretsky, 2004, p. 87.

22. Gay, 1988, p. 326.

23. Freud, S. (1912–1913). Totem and taboo. In J. Strachey (Ed. & Trans.), *The standard edition of the complete psychological works of Sigmund Freud* (Vol. 13, pp. 1–161). London: Hogarth Press.

24. Freud, S. (1914a). On narcissism: An introduction. In J. Strachey (Ed. & Trans.), *The standard edition of the complete psychological works of Sigmund Freud* (Vol. 14, pp. 67–104). London: Hogarth Press.

25. Gay, 1988, p. 340.

26. Freud, S. (1914b). On the history of the psycho-analytic movement. In J. Strachey (Ed. & Trans.), *The standard edition of the complete psychological works of Sigmund Freud* (Vol. 14, pp. 1–66). London: Hogarth Press.

27. Freud, S. (1920a). Beyond the pleasure principle. In J. Strachey (Ed. & Trans.), *The standard edition of the complete psychological works of Sigmund Freud* (Vol. 18, pp. 1–64). London: Hogarth Press; Freud, S. (1921). Group psychology and the analysis of the ego. In J. Strachey (Ed. & Trans.), *The standard edition of the complete psychological works of Sigmund Freud* (Vol. 18, pp. 65–144). London: Hogarth Press; Freud, S. (1923). The ego and the id. In J. Strachey (Ed. & Trans.), *The standard edition of the complete psychological works of Sigmund Freud* (Vol. 19, pp. 1–59). London: Hogarth Press.

28. Gay, 1988, pp. 404–405.

29. Gay, 1988, p. 406.

30. Freud (1923).

31. Parenthetically, Freud also wrote about the type problem as a way to understand personality development. In 1931 he wrote on libidinal types and characterized different personalities in terms of the distribution of their libido. This led him on the basis of his clinical experience to the tripartite classification of erotic, narcissistic, and obsessional types. The erotic type is focused on love and being loved, dominated by the id, and is expressed differently depending on whether it is strong or weak. The obsessional is dominated by the superego. They suffer from the anxiety of conscience, tend to be conservative, and according to Freud are "the upholders of civilization." The narcissistic types can only be described in the negative. Erotic needs of the id and the moral conscience of the superego are given up for sheer self-preservation. Lots of ego aggression is available, there is a proneness to activity, and they may be identified as a result by others as leaders.
    While these Freud onsidered pure types, it is the mixed types that are more the norm. The erotic-narcissistic type is the most common, while erotic-obsessional and narcissistic-obsessional are seen frequently in therapy. There is no perfect combination of all three types, only dual combinations getting together to strengthen themselves at the expense of the third. There are pathological types

but in the neuroses they do not differ that much from the norm except in exaggerated ways. Freud, S. (1956/1931). Miscellaneous papers: Libidinal types. In J. Strachey (Ed.), *Collected papers* (Vol. 5, pp. 247–251). London: Hogarth Press.

32. Freud, S. (1927a). The future of an illusion. In J. Strachey (Ed. & Trans.), *The standard edition of the complete psychological works of Sigmund Freud* (Vol. 21, pp. 1–56). London: Hogarth Press.

33. Gay, 1988, p. 526.

34. Freud, S. (1930). Civilization and its discontents. In J. Strachey (Ed. & Trans.), *The standard edition of the complete psychological works of Sigmund Freud* (Vol. 21, pp. 57–146). London: Hogarth Press.

35. Reich, W. (1925). *Der triebhafte Charakter: Éire psychoanalytische studie zur pathologie des ich* [Character-analysis; principles and technique for psychoanalysts in practice and in training] Leipzig: Internationaler Psychoanalytischer Verlag. See also, Reich, W. (1945). *Character-analysis: Principles and technique for psychoanalysts in practice and in training* (T. P. Wolfe, Trans.) (2nd ed.). New York: Orgone Institute Press.

36. Ferenczi, S., & Rank, O. (1924). *Entwicklungsziele der Psychoanalyse zur Wechselbeziehung von Theorie und Praxis* [The development of psychoanalysis]. Neue Arbeiten zur ärztlichen Psychoanalyse, Heft 1. Wien: Internationaler Psychoanalytischer Verlag.

37. Rank, O. (1924). *Das trauma der geburt und seine* [*The trauma of birth*]. Leipzig: Internationaler Psychoanalytischer Verlag.

38. Zaretsky, 2004, p. 174.

39. Rank, O. (1996). In R. Kramer, & R. May (Eds.), *A psychology of difference: The American lectures.* Princeton, NJ: Princeton University Press.

40. Zaretsky, 2004, p. 176.

41. Freud, S. (1926). The question of lay analysis. In J. Strachey (Ed. & Trans.), *The standard edition of the complete psychological works of Sigmund Freud* (Vol. 20, pp. 177–250). London: Hogarth Press.

42. Zaretsky, 2004, p. 180.

43. Zaretsky, 2004, p. 183.

44. Zaretsky, 2004, pp. 189–190.

45. Freud, S. (1927b). Fetishism. In J. Strachey (Ed. & Trans.), *The standard edition of the complete psychological works of Sigmund Freud* (Vol. 20, pp. 147–158). London: Hogarth Press.

46. His quantum mysticism was soon replaced by a profound period of interest in Catholicism, when he was permitted by the Pope to join the church, during which time he brought a mystical surrealism to religious themes such as the crucifixion and the resurrection in his paintings. He followed this with a period of his own spiritual revelations, before a final phase of paranormal, psychedelic-like art, sometimes working in non-traditional media. From "Dali": Exhibit at the Philadelphia Museum, of Art, May, 2005.

47. Reich, W. (1933). *Die massenpsychologie des faschimus* [*The mass psychology of fascism*]. 2 Auflage, Sexpol Verlag; See also first English edition: Reich, W. (1946). *The mass psychology of fascism* (T. P. Wolfe, Trans.). New York: Orgone Institute Press.

48. Freud, A. (1937). *The ego and the mechanisms of defence.* The International Psycho-analytical Library, No. 30. London: Hogarth Press.

49. Klein, M. (1932a). *Die psychoanalyse des kindes* [*The psycho-analysis of children*]. Vienna: Internationaler Psychoanalytischer Verlag. Also published in English in 1932 by International Psycho-analytical Library, No. 22. London: Hogarth Press.

50. Lacan, J. (1968). *The language of the self* (A Wilden, Trans.). Baltimore, MD: John Hopkins University Press.

51. Zaretsky, 2004, p. 182.

52. Freud (1930); Freud, S. (1931). Female sexuality. In J. Strachey (Ed. & Trans.), *The standard edition of the complete psychological works of Sigmund Freud* (Vol. 21, pp. 221–246). London: Hogarth Press; Freud, S. (1937a). Analysis terminable and interminable. In J. Strachey (Ed. & Trans.), *The standard edition of the complete psychological works of Sigmund Freud* (Vol. 23, pp. 209–254). London: Hogarth Press; Freud, S. (1939). Moses and monotheism: Three essays. In J. Strachey (Ed. & Trans.), *The standard edition of the complete psychological works of Sigmund Freud* (Vol. 23, pp. 1–138). London: Hogarth Press.

53. Zaretsky, 2004, p. 226.

54. Horney, K. (1937). *The neurotic personality of our time.* New York: W. W. Norton & Company.
55. Dollard, J. (1939). *Frustration and aggression.* New Haven: Yale University Press; Kardiner, A. & Linton, R. (1939). *The individual and his society: The psychodynamics of primitive social organization.* New York: Columbia University.
56. Gay, 1988, p. 605.
57. Gay, 1988, p. 605.
58. Bakan, D. (1958). *Sigmund Freud and the Jewish mystical tradition.* Princeton, NJ: Princeton University Press.
59. Alexander, F., & Ross, H. (Eds.). (1952). *Dynamic psychiatry.* Chicago: University of Chicago Press, pp. vi–vii.

Chapter 4
The Freudians

As long as Freud was in Vienna he remained surrounded by a devoted circle that reached out into a wider network of close disciples. There was Alexander in Berlin, Ferenczi in Budapest, and Jones in England, who was later joined by Melanie Klein. Then there was Freud, himself, and his daughter, Anna Freud with him in Vienna. Meanwhile, Marie Bonaparte, among others, championed psychoanalysis in France, before Lacan. The empire was far flung, but the greatest concentration of analysts eventually was found in the United States, where major centers sprang up, mainly around New York, Boston, Washington DC, Chicago, and eventually Los Angeles. An all-too-brief survey of only a selection of these Freudians will suffice to show that several even made major modifications of Freud's theories, but almost all to a great extent stayed within the structure of personality defined by Freud.

The origin of this orthodoxy can be traced back to a series of events beginning in 1902, when Freud first gathered what he believed were his earliest disciples around him as a sounding board for his ideas. "A number of physicians gathered around me with the declared intention of learning, practicing, and disseminating psychoanalysis."[1] They met in Freud's waiting room.

Constituting the original group, Freud sent postcards to Wilhelm Stekel, a physician and analysand, Max Kahane, who had also translated a volume of Charcot's work into German, Alfred Adler, a practicing physician interested in social causes, and Rudolf Reitler, whom Freud analyzed and then crowned "the world's second analyst" in 1902. The group grew to 19 by 1906, when they retained a paid secretary—Otto Rank. It formally became the Vienna Psychoanalytic Society in 1908.

By 1912, Stekel and Adler "had defected," and Jung was in his last days as "heir apparent," though neither Adler nor Jung ever claimed they were a "student" of Freud. This was always the Freudians' view, however. To prevent further deviancies, Jones proposed a Secret Committee while visiting Vienna in the fall of 1912. Ernest Jones, Otto Rank, Sandor Ferenczi, Hans Sachs, Karl Abraham, and Max Eitingon became members. Freud commemorated the event by distributing intaglios that were turned into rings they all wore, pledging not to deviate from his teachings. The group took a great weight off of Freud's shoulders, he said to them, knowing now that the future of psychoanalysis had been vouchsafed to such a loyal group. They proved to have their most important influence just after World War I. Meanwhile, Americans flocking to Vienna to seek an analysis with Freud, especially those who constituted the foundation of the New York Institute, carried this sense of orthodoxy with them back to America.

The influence of the group waned into the 1920s, dissolving in 1924. After a brief interlude when an attempt was made to reconstitute it under Anna Freud and the women of psychoanalysis, its function was replaced by the network of independent free-standing psychoanalytic institutes devoted to training. So it was the early years that were clearly the most vibrant.

Ferenczi in Budapest

Sándor Ferenczi became one of Freud's most devoted disciples, and as such developed a circle in Budapest rivaling Berlin and Vienna. Sándor Radó, Margaret Mahler, Michael Balint, Alice Balint, and Franz Alexander, all passed through his scene before moving elsewhere.

Ferenczi was born in Hungary, July 7, 1873, and raised in an open-minded middle class Jewish family as 1 of 10 children. His father was a book dealer, whose shop attracted a wide variety of intellectuals, including poets, writers, and artists. Ferenczi himself graduated from the University of Vienna Medical School in 1894, where he fell under the influence of Richard von Krafft-Ebing and his theories relating to sexual psychopathology. Early on, during his postdoctoral years Ferenczi worked in charity hospitals and also developed an interest in non-ordinary states of consciousness. In this vein, he became an expert in hypnosis, somnambulism, automatic writing, and the investigation of mediums and spiritualists. He was already a well-published author by the time he met Freud in 1908.[2] Thereafter, he committed himself to Freud's teachings and remained loyal almost to the end, when they had a falling out over theoretical issues.[3] Ferenczi became focused on the transference/countertransference relationship and began to emphasize the intersubjective nature of the therapeutic relationship. He also put great emphasis on the mother–child bond in contrast to Freud's all consuming focus on the father and he de-emphasized the patient's fantasy of the traumatic experience in favor of a focus on actual trauma. At the same time, Ferenczi was concerned that the therapist was also in need of assistance overcoming his or her own neuroses and so recommended the didactic teaching analysis, following Jung, in which the therapist himself became the patient to prepare for treatment of his own patients.[4] He followed Rank's idea that birth trauma determined all that subsequently occurred to the person and underlay all neuroses. But more than merely the urge to return to the safety of the womb, Ferenczi believed that regression was the organism's way of returning to the aqueous environment out of which human beings originally evolved.[5]

Rank and His Circle

Billed as Freud's longest and most devoted disciple and then his harshest critic, Otto Rank was born in Vienna and earned the PhD from the University of Vienna in 1912 when he was 28. Rather than medicine, he trained in philosophy and the humanities and through these subjects widened the scope of psychoanalysis considerably. He earned a living as secretary of the Vienna Psychoanalytic Society; was managing editor of the two most important analytic journals, *Internationale Zeitschrift für Psychoanalyse* and *Imago*; and was also director of Freud's publishing house. In addition, he was acting secretary in the International Psychoanalytical Association.

Rank's disciples believed that his theories promoted an active and egalitarian psychotherapy focused on the here and now, the actual relationship between the patient and the therapist, and the power of consciousness to harness the resources of the will. Past history, the nature of the transference, wish fulfillment, and a focus on the unconscious were Freud's concerns, not Rank's. Nevertheless, his reading of Sigmund Freud's *The Interpretation of Dreams* inspired him to write *Der Künstler* (1907; "The Artist"),[6] an attempt to explain art by using psychoanalytic principles, which he extended to the idea that the neurotic was essentially a failed artist. He followed with *The Myth of the Birth of the Hero* (1909),[7] which dealt with myths using the hero motif from different cultures, but without reference to a collective unconscious. *The Incest Motif in Poetry and Saga* followed in 1912, which was his own analysis of the Oedipus complex in poetry and myth.[8] He contributed two chapters to later editions of *The Interpretation of Dreams* on myths and legend, his major work was on birth trauma. But *The Trauma of Birth* (1924),[9] which defined the act of being born as the prototype for all traumatic experiences during life that follow, precipitated the break with Freud after 18 years of discipleship. Rank's major deviation from Freud was his focus on separation anxiety, a concept which Freud could not abide. Rank traveled to the United States and then went to Paris in 1926. He moved to the United States permanently in 1935, where he died at age 55 in 1939.

During the 1930s Rank developed a concept of the will as the guiding force in personality development. The will could guide the instincts in ways not acceptable to Freud's theory. He also developed his own ideas about life and death. The life instinct leads us to become competent individuals who seek to live in freedom, and the death instinct draws us toward identification with family, community, and social relationships in general as a natural protection from separation anxiety, and the final major event, our own annihilation.[10]

Ernest Becker, author of *The Denial of Death*, was influenced by Rank.[11] Paul Goodman, co-founder of Gestalt Therapy with Fritz and Laura Perls, borrowed Rank's ideas on the importance of the immediate moment for the Gestalt emphasis on the here and now. Anaïs Nin was analyzed by Rank and later wrote about their affair. Carl Rogers was profoundly affected by Rank's ideas concerning the intersubjective bond in the therapist–patient relationship. He invited Rank to lecture and followed further developments of Rankian thought through the work of Jessie Taft and other Rankians. Rollo May and Irvin Yalom were both influenced by the profoundly existential nature of Rank's ideas. The transpersonal psychiatrist Stanislav Grof adapted Rank's ideas about birth trauma to his theory of rebirthing and the awakening of systems of condensed experience.

Anna Freud, the Devoted Daughter

Foremost, of course, there was Anna Freud, analyzed by her own father. By default, she became heir apparent to the Freudian ethos, in the absence of any of Freud's sons taking up the banner of their father. She was born December 3, 1895, Freud's youngest child,[12] she attended the Cottage Lyceum in Vienna in 1912. Remembered as Freud's favorite, she received, however, no education higher than the lyceum. Freud began an analysis with her in 1918, which lasted for 4 years. In 1923, at the age of 28, she began a private practice with children and also began lecturing on child psychoanalysis and involved herself as the secretary of the International Psychoanalytical Association from 1925 to 1934. She continued her practice and teaching while continuing to live under her father's roof in Vienna. Among her analysands was Erik Erikson. In 1935 she became director of the Vienna Psychoanalytical Training Institute. While it was not published in London until 1945, Anna Freud's *The Psychoanalytical Treatment of Children* contained an extensive lecture series on the subject that she had delivered before the Vienna Institute of Psychoanalysis in 1926.[13] She followed in 1937 with *The Ego and the Mechanisms of Defence*,[14] a central text in the new era of psychoanalytic ego psychology. Her most important contribution was the idea of ego development in the child in both normal and abnormal conditions. Psychoanalytic theories of development across the life span and the application of psychoanalysis to normal development then flourished, as they seemed through this work to have had the sanction of the Master himself. Ostensibly in this way, she became Freud's long sought heir apparent.

Anna Freud fled Vienna with her father in 1938 and settled in London, opening a practice and becoming heavily involved with the local psychoanalytic community. However, she soon clashed with Melanie Klein over the methods and direction of child analysis, but the real underlying tension was over who would actually represent the psychoanalytic legacy. This led to the creation of two entirely different schools of thought, Anna's theories of child development and Melanie's new theory of object relations, based on the mother–infant bond; while further elaborations, neither of them deviated from the classical psychoanalytic framework previously established by Freud.[15]

Jones in Britain

Alfred Ernest Jones (1879–1958) was born in Wales, and in 1901 took a medical degree from the University of London.[16] In 1905, he came to hear of Freud's work through the surgeon Wilfred Trotter, later author of *Instincts of the Herd in Peace and War* (1916),[17] but, according to Andrew Paskauskas, Jones was not really converted to psychoanalysis until after the Clark Conference in 1909.[18] With James Jackson Putnam, Jones had participated in founding the American Psychoanalytical Association in 1912, and in 1913 founded the London Psycho-Analytic Society. He also began analysis with Sandor Ferenczi in 1913. In 1919 he founded the British Psycho-Analytical Society and served as president of the International Psychoanalytic Association from 1920 to 1924 and again from 1932 to 1949. Also in 1920 he founded the *International Journal of Psychoanalysis* and served as editor until 1939. In 1921 he launched the International Psychoanalytic Library, which published over 50 titles on psychoanalysis during his tenure as editor. He also obtained from Freud the exclusive rights to the English translation of Freud's work, and thereafter supervised James Strachey's translation, which became the *Standard Edition of the Collected Works of Sigmund Freud*. While still in print today, it has been said of this translation that Strachey substituted English folk tales for the Jewish ones Freud had originally recounted in German, and in this way anglicized psychoanalysis for English-speaking readers. At the end of his career, Jones undertook a biography of Freud in three volumes, which appeared between 1953 and 1957 to both acclaim and controversy.[19] Commenting on this work, Henry A. Murray later maintained that it was accurate in most cases where Jones was talking about others. In Jones's own case, however, he indulged in much over-elaboration, factual inaccuracy, and misplaced credit given to himself.[20]

Herbert Silberer

There were many minor disciples around Freud, in the sense of not well known outside psychoanalytic circles. Possibly the most short-lived was Herbert Silberer, a well-to-do, educated man from Vienna, who was a member of Freud's circle after the Clark University conference in 1909. He was interested in what his translator, Smith Ely Jelliffe, called a "paleo-psychology." This referred to the appearance of similar dynamics in dreams, fairy tales, myths, and legends of different cultures, to which Silberer gave a psychoanalytic interpretation. His approach differed somewhat from the more clinical analogies Freud made with cases of psychopathology, notwithstanding Freud's attraction to the idea that psychoanalysis digs deeper and deeper into strata of the unconscious, much as the archeologist would uncover layer after layer of a city from some ancient civilization in the past. Silberer's early research focused on problems of symbol formation, where he developed a technique for tapping into the hypnogogic state of mental imagery by positioning himself to hover for long periods at the interface between the waking consciousness and the sleep state.[21]

Also enamored with Jung before the split between Freud and Jung in 1913, Silberer took up the problems of mysticism and its symbolism and gravitated toward an analysis of the symbols of the European alchemical tradition long before Jung had this subject as his focus. Silberer's work, *Problems of Mysticism and Its Symbolism* (1917), is a case in point.[22] Opening with a long-hermetic parable, Silberer proceeded to equate Freud's method of dream interpretation to the non-pathological symbolism of alchemy and followed with an explanation of Freud's method of dream analysis, and then his own psychoanalytic interpretation of the material. How the alchemists would interpret it led to a discussion of the hermetic scholars and the Rosicrucians and Freemasons, and the problem of multiple interpretations.

In a bold departure from Freud's epistemology, Silberer devoted the second half of the book to a non-pathological, psychoanalytic interpretation of introversion as the proper orientation to understand the universal, interior spiritual quest for personal regeneration. Both Jung and Silberer mentioned the influence of each other's ideas on their own. When the work was first published in German, however, Freud took a dim view of it, and eventually Silberer was edged out of the psychoanalytic circle around the Master. The myth is that he fell into despair over Freud's rejection and hanged himself in 1923, but the story is disputed by recent evidence.[23]

Ludwig Binswanger

Ludwig Binswanger (1881–1966), at first a student of Jung's and then for a time ardent follower of Freud, was a grandson of Ludwig Binswanger, Sr., an enlightened Swiss physician who had founded the Bellevue Sanitarium at Kreuzlingen in 1857. Binswanger's father, Robert, was also a physician as well and Director at Bellevue until 1910, while Binswanger's uncle Otto was a professor of psychiatry at the University of Jena and director of the psychiatric clinic there. The young Binswanger first met Freud in 1896 at a conference on psychiatry and neurology. In addition, Binswanger Sr. had discussed Freud's work in a 1904 publication, *Die Hysteria*, so Freud was known to the Binswanger physicians from an early era.[24]

Later, in 1906, the young Ludwig Binswanger joined the staff at the Burghölzli under both Jung and Bleuler, where he completed his medical dissertation on the subject of association. Binswanger recalled that he joined the Burghölzli as a trainee physician when Eugen Bleuler was doing his preliminary work on *Dementia Praecox, or the Group of Schizophrenias* (1912)] which revolutionized the theory of *dementia praecox*. But it was C. G. Jung, then chief physician of the hospital, with whom he planned to write his doctoral thesis. Jung was already well known for his work on the Diagnostic Association Test and had completed his epoch-making work on the *Psychology of Dementia Praecox*.[25] Jung suggested the subject of Binswanger's thesis "The Psycho-Galvanic Reflex Phenomenon in the Association Test." This put Binswanger into close contact with Jung, who also agreed to be one of Binswanger's subjects.

When it was complete, Jung sent Freud a copy of the dissertation, lauding Binswanger's work. The document was all the more interesting because, though presented anonymously, much was revealed about Jung's own unconscious complexes, including his hopes and ambitions as well as his concerns in the period just before meeting with Freud for the first time. He had hopes for a son in his new marriage, his father had recently died, he fretted over money, and always there was this incessant complex over Goethe. His struggles for power and intimations of his exchange with his patient Sabina Spielrein were also evident.

In 1907 Binswanger accompanied Jung on his first meeting with Freud and noted with pleasure that Freud recognized Jung right away as his "son and heir." There can be little doubt that the luster of the Swiss medical tradition hung on both Jung and Binswanger in Freud's presence at that meeting, as Freud contemplated the future of psychoanalysis. If the Swiss Protestants were with him then psychoanalysis could not possibly be labeled strictly a Jewish science. In fact, as Jung's relation with Freud began to deteriorate in the years after the Clark conference, Freud was determined to keep up his Swiss connections, as evidenced by the so-called "Kreuzlingen gesture," where Freud came to visit Binswanger at one point and by-passed Jung near-by. Jung and Freud eventually parted ways in 1913, but the correspondence between Binswanger and Freud remained steady. Binswanger went overboard in his initial praise of psychoanalysis, though 10 years later declared that really only a few subjects were helped by it at the Bellevue Asylum, where Binswanger himself had become medical director in 1911 and remained for the next 46 years.

The relationship between Binswanger and Freud remained cordial up to the time of Freud's death in 1939, despite their theoretical divergence in the 1920s, when Binswanger became a figure in existential and phenomenological psychiatry, influenced heavily by Husserl, Heidegger, and Buber. His work is still largely unavailable in English, however, and the first inkling of the direction his ideas had taken did not come until 1958, when he analyzed the case of Ellen West in May, Angell, and Ellenberger's *Existence: A New Dimension in Existential Psychiatry*.[26]

James Jackson Putnam

James Jackson Putnam (1846–1917), distinguished Harvard professor of Neurology, co-founder of the American Neurological Association, scion of a long line of Boston Brahmins related to the Jacksons, the Cabots, and the Lowells, was Freud's big catch at the Clark University Conference in 1909. Putnam took the MD at Harvard Medical School along with his other close friends and medical school classmates, William James, Henry Pickering Bowditch, and Edward Emerson. He toured the German laboratories of Ludwig and Meynert, and on his return founded the laboratory of neuropathology at Harvard Medical School and immediately became identified with the Department of Diseases of the Nervous System at the Massachusetts General Hospital. He was the Hospital's first medical electrician in 1873, at which time he also founded the first Out-Patient Clinic for neurological patients. He specialized in aphasia, localization of brain function, and traumatic injuries to the nerves before taking up the study of the pathology of the emotions due to the scientific studies of William James, and he came to specialize in functional disorders of the nervous system with no known organic cause. He became an early follower of Charcot and advocate of psychotherapeutics before being introduced to the work of Breuer and Freud through William James. He had access to German translations of Freud's early shorter works on dreams and sexual psychopathology, which he applied in primitive clinical trials at the MGH between 1903 and 1905, culminating in his article "Recent Experiences in the Study and Treatment of Hysteria at the Massachusetts General Hospital" (1907),[27] published in the inaugural issue of Morton Prince's *Journal of Abnormal Psychology*. From 1906 to 1909, he became a primary mover in the Emmanuel Movement in Boston, the effort to combine the Christian teachings of character formation with the new methods in scientific psychotherapy.

Putnam did not actually read Freud's *Interpretation of Dreams* until the eve of the Clark Conference in 1909 (the English translation did not appear until 1913), where he suffered through the complete German edition. He was sufficiently impressed with Freud at the Conference that he converted to psychoanalysis, just as he was retiring from neurology at Harvard Medical School. From then on he became an avid supporter of Freud's methods on the international scene; he helped launch the American Psychoanalytical Association in 1912, and contributed numerous scientific papers at the various psychoanalytic congresses.[28]

Putnam's main difference from Freud was that he advocated a philosophy for psychoanalysis.[29] To cure his psychotherapeutic patients he believed one had to harness their will to live by appealing to their individual ideals and their highest aspirations. He found that his patients could not sublimate their primitive impulses just on the basis of an explanation of a Freudian concept. But he found they would engage in sublimating their instinctual impulses in service of actualizing their ideals. When he told this to Freud, the response was that it was all too Protestant for Freud, who referred to himself as "a godforsaken incredulous Jew." "But we need you for the movement," he told Putnam, "so by all means, keep writing."[30] There were other ardent Freudians in America at the time—Isador Coriat, William Healey, and Augusta Bronner in Boston, A. A. Brill in New York, Smith Ely Jelliffe and William Alonson White in Washington DC, but none with the stature of Putnam in American medicine in those early years.[31]

Abraham Arden Brill

A. A. Brill (1874–1948) became Freud's earliest American translator. As Paul Roazan has pointed out, he was Hungarian, so that neither English nor German was his native language and when rendering Freud's German into English often substituted his own examples when he could not understand Freud's or thought them too complex for English readers.[32] After he founded the New York Psychoanalytic Association in 1911, he became the recognized leader of psychoanalysis in America when his translation of Freud's *Interpretation of Dreams* appeared for the first time in English in 1913. Freud would have preferred Horace W. Frink, whom both he and Brill had analyzed, but his confidence proved overwhelming for the man. In addition, Frink had proposed marriage to one of his patients when both were married to someone else. When the other spouses unexpectedly died separately under different circumstances, but around the same time, the patient and therapist developed morbid guilt which, though they were then free to marry, prevented the event from occurring. Frink, suffering from acute depersonalization, later died in a mental institution in a state of manic excitement.

As for Brill, he had immigrated to America at 15, supporting himself by sweeping out bars, giving mandolin lessons, and teaching. He obtained the BA from New York University in 1901 and the MD from Columbia in 1903. He then went to Zurich to work under Bleuler and Jung and from there made his way to Vienna, where he met Freud and attended meetings of the Wednesday Society of analysts. He then returned to the United States and founded the New York Psychoanalytic Society where he remained for the rest of his life. He translated Freud's works and produced volumes on psychoanalysis himself. By the 1930s, however, he was viewed by the younger analysts as something of a has-been and was summarily pushed aside as the new training institutes were being formed in New York and elsewhere.

Karl Abraham

Freud called him the first German psychoanalyst.[33] He was Freud's close friend and there at the beginning of the Wednesday evening group when it first formed in 1902. Abraham was born into a well-to-do Jewish family, in Bremen, Germany in 1887. He obtained his medical training and afterward spent more than a half dozen years working in medical asylums, first in the State Hospital at Dalldorf and later at the Bürgholzli under Bleuler and Jung in Switzerland. His wife, also a physician, became a distinguished psychoanalyst in her own right. He moved with his family to Berlin, where he set up a private practice and in 1910 founded the Berlin Psychoanalytic Society. With the exception of his stint as a war psychiatrist, he presided over this group for 15 years. Eventually he analyzed Karen Horney, Sandor Rado, Ernest Himmel, and Felix Boehm. He was also a member of the Committee of the Seven Rings, which included Ferenczi, Jones, Sachs, Rank, and later Eidingon, formed to oust Jung and protect Freud's teachings from corruption.

Max Eitingon

Dubbed the first to come from a foreign country to study psychoanalysis, Max Eitingon, sent to Freud by Blüeler to find out what psychoanalysis had to contribute to psychiatry, came from Switzerland to attend two meetings of the Vienna Psychoanalytic Society in January, 1907.[34] He began the first of many long walks with Freud, commencing what Jones was later to call "the first training analysis."[35] Born in 1881 in Mogilev, Russia, and raised in wealthy circumstances by his Jewish parents, he was educated in Leipzig, and later pursued medicine and philosophy at Marburg. When he graduated from medical school in 1909, he moved to Berlin to join his friend Karl Abraham at the Psychoanalytic Institute. He remained there until the Nazis came to power, after which he immigrated to Palestine. He was the only psychoanalyst in the world who had independent means and proved to be a major force in financially underwriting the movement. As well, he was able to use his time initiating new programs, teaching psychoanalysis, and acting as an administrator as needed. He entered World War I as a colonel in the Austrian Medical Corps and made a name for himself studying war neuroses. He was to rise to prominence in the psychoanalytic movement for founding the polyclinic in Berlin, where budding psychoanalysts could be trained under proper supervision and have an empirical base in patient care. The idea that no one could do psychoanalysis that had not himself been analyzed was formalized in 1925, when Eitingon proposed the International

Training Commission. Here the Berlin model was adopted as a template for training analysts in the formation of other psychoanalytic institutes and served to focus and standardize the training and supervision of candidates throughout the movement. Eitingon presided over the Training Commission for almost a quarter of a century. As well, Eitingon was instrumental on more than one occasion in rescuing the Verlag, Freud's publishing house. For these efforts, Freud heaped upon him great praise, considering him like a son, who had helped both the movement and the Freud's family. Over the years, however, Eitingon's health began to deteriorate from a heart condition. He also became embroiled in the controversy over lay analysis. Freud came out in support of it, while Eitingon leaned toward requiring medical credentials. When the Nazis came to power in 1933, Eitingon determined to take his family and move to Palestine, with the vision that he could introduce psychoanalysis there. The University repelled him, but he was able to establish a private psychoanalytic institute, over which he presided for the remaining years of his life. He died January 30, 1943.

Oskar Pfister

Oskar Pfister (1873–1956) was a Swiss pastor from Zurich who became an analyst to his parishioners, writing about Christianity and psychoanalysis, children and the family, glossolalia, and automatic writing, and by so doing fueled the debates over lay analysis.[36] Only physicians were allowed to apply for training in the United States, while elsewhere numerous other individuals who were non-MDs gained recognition, Erik Erikson among them. European attitudes were much different than the Americans, which allowed such figures as Marie Bonaparte and Melanie Klein to rise to prominence within psychoanalytic circles. Freud composed an essay on the subject "The question of lay analysis,"[37] in which he favored the idea of training for non-MDs. Pfister, along with the socialite Lou Andreas Salomé, were friends with Freud in this category and he was glad to have them in his circle.

Pfister, with already a long-standing interest in psychology, apparently came to Freud through Jung around 1908. He was himself analyzed and turned afterward to his parishioners as a pastor-analyst, promulgating what Peter Gay called an undogmatic Protestant psychoanalysis. He charmed the entire Freud family on his visits to Vienna, and even went so far as to defend psychoanalysis when the Swiss pastors under whom he worked nearly succeeded in ousting him. He tended to his flock and had long discussions with Freud about religion, calling Jesus the first psychoanalyst and Freud more like a Christian than a Jew.[38]

Marie Bonaparte

In France, there was Marie Bonaparte (1881–1962) great-grand-niece of Napoleon I of France, also officially known as Princess Marie of Greece and Denmark. She first sought a consultation with Freud about her sexual frigidity, after which she went on the have affairs with several leading men other than her husband. She became a practicing analyst and introduced psychoanalysis into France when she founded the *Société Psychoanalytique de Paris* in 1926. That Freud's work was so long delayed can be attributed to the extenuating influence of the French Experimental Psychology of the Subconscious and the tradition of Charcot and Janet into the 1920s. She was an intimate in Freud's circle and socialized with Ernest Jones, Anna Freud, and other prominent psychoanalysts throughout England and Europe. She also contributed to the ransom money paid to the Nazis to free Freud from Vienna in 1938 and was responsible for preserving the Freud–Fliess letters for later publication.[39]

Psychoanalysis in France from then on became a particularly French institution with its own unique turn of influence. Jean Paul Sartre and Simone de Beauvoir both read Freud and absorbed psychoanalysis into their work. Sartre adapted it to his existential interpretation of experience by claiming that, while Freud was a genius in his own right, his emphasis on a reductive psychic determinism was incorrect. Sartre conceived instead a theory of psychoanalysis based on human freedom and the ability of the individual to define his or her own meaning in experience.[40] Freud expressed the idea that the neuroses reveal the sexual origin of the libido, while Sartre maintained that the interior life of the person, taken as a totality, is revealed in every gesture. Unlike Freud, he maintained that the ego is not in any privileged position to engage in self-knowledge, and he postulated transcendence of the ego through a radical critique of introspection. Moreover, he became the great author of the nihilism so characteristic of European existentialism and phenomenology, casting the individual's choices which define personality always in terms of the specter of nothingness that each one of us ultimately face.[41]

Lacan and Post-structuralism

Jacques Lacan (1901–1981) physician, psychoanalyst, and post-structuralist was born and raised in Paris, where he became heavily involved with Parisian writers, painters, and intellectuals in pre-World War II France. He associated with the surrealists and philosophically he was attracted to Jaspers, Heidegger, and Hegel. He was analyzed by Rudolph Lowenstein.

Lacan specialized in psychiatry, and in 1926, did his clinical training at St. Anne, the main psychiatric hospital in Paris, where he would later return and begin weekly seminars in 1951 that would continue for 30 years. As his theory began to develop, he encountered numerous forms of opposition from the International Psychoanalytical Association and particularly the French psychoanalysts. Eventually, he resigned from these groups to form his own organization, the *École Freudienne de Paris*. His major era of influence was the 1950s and 1960s. He joined the faculty at the *École Pratique des Hautes Etudes* and in 1964 began lecturing at the *École Normal Supérieure*, and then moved to the *Faculté de Droit*, where he continued to lecture for more than 20 years.

Trained in classical psychoanalysis, Lacan soon became disenchanted with the way analysts were misinterpreting Freud and he began a critique of the prevailing trends toward ego-psychology and object relations theory. He called for a return to Freud in the original texts as a way to show the subsequent deviations that had taken place. His main focus was on fusing the dynamics of the unconscious to language by way of a structural linguistics. One does not rescue the patient who has been traumatized or neurotically conflicted from control by a primitive unconscious through strengthening the executive functions of the ego. One learns to balance the functions of consciousness and the unconscious, both of which are equally complex. His concept of mirroring shows the "I" in contrast to itself with the development of language. The first stage in the development of the ego, and the initial step toward a colossal misunderstanding of who the person is, begins when the individual, in fact, first identifies with his own image in the mirror rather than who he is within. Who the child also becomes is contrasted with how the child is seen by others, particularly the all powerful mother, whose attention continues to be reinforced through language, which has both a conscious and an unconscious source. In this, the imaginary, the symbolic—meaning the linguistic, and the real are three different dimensions of experience that are central to the growth of the self.[42]

Melanie Klein

Melanie Klein (1882–1960) kept within the Freudian framework, but virtually founded her own school of thought under that umbrella. She was born and raised in Vienna, but had no graduate education. Rather, she was analyzed by Sandor Ferenczi during World War I, after which she became a practicing analyst working with children by 1919. She later sought an analysis with Karl Abraham in Berlin and began to generate her own interpretation of psychoanalysis with children, to the acclaim of other analysts. In 1926 she was invited by Ernest Jones to immigrate to London, where she remained for more than 30 years.[43]

Klein's major works included *The Psychoanalysis of Children* (1932), *Contributions to Psychoanalysis*, 1921–1945 (1948), *Narrative of a Child Analysis* (1961), and *Our Adult World and Other Essays* (1963).[44] She is considered to have deviated from Freud, in that she emphasized the child's more important bond with the mother, she believed fear and aggression were more influential in shaping early childhood development than the psychosexual stages of development, and she believed the superego began to make its appearance as early as 2 or 3 years of age. These ideas remain within a Freudian framework, however.

Klein's major emphasis was on the world of objects that the infant and child identified with and in this she is acclaimed as the mother of object relations theory. Freud had established that the important objects of the infant's earliest identifications are internalized as mental representations. Klein contended that these could be people, such as the mother and the father, but also parts of objects, such as the mother's breast, body odor, and voice, setting the stage for later neuroses to develop as personality was shaped first this way and then that depending on the objects of identification. The identification was both psychic and bodily. Fairbairn and others developed these ideas into formal object relations theory, which represented a major new arena of psychoanalytic discourse beyond a psychology of the ego and an era unique to the history of psychoanalysis in Britain. Anna Freud stood opposed to these ideas and became a countervailing force once she and her father immigrated to England in 1938. Eventually, Freudian and Kleinian therapy with children stood opposed to each other, although a reconciliation between the two schools emerged with the development of a third group somewhere in between, which defines the state of psychoanalysis in Britain today.

Donald W. Winnicott, for instance, was an English physician and psychoanalyst who worked with psychotic children and their mothers. He trained in medicine at Oxford and St. Bartholomew's Hospital Medical College and qualified in 1920. He then went to work at Paddington Green Children's Hospital in London, where he stayed for 40 years. Influenced by both Anna Freud and Melanie Klein, he supervised psychoanalysts of the day such as R. D. Liang. He was also associated with the translators of the Standard Edition of Freud's works, James and Alex Strachey, among others.[45]

Wilfred Bion (1897–1979) was a British psychoanalyst who became a pioneer in the application of Freudian theory to the dynamics of groups. He had undergone a training analysis from 1946 to 1952 with Melanie Klein.[46] Meanwhile, John Bowlby (1907–1990), physician and British psychoanalyst, had been influenced by Melanie Klein but whose ideas about mother–child attachment differed significantly from hers. Born into an upper middle class English household, Bowlby experienced his mother as loving, but restrained in the expression of her emotions, so she remained distant. He was raised by a nanny whom he considered a second mother, but who unfortunately left the family when he was 4. Boarding school at age 7 became yet another crisis of separation and anxiety, themes he would develop professionally in his later years. He attended Trinity College, Cambridge. He then trained in medicine at the University Hospital in London and specialized in adult psychiatry at the Maudsley Hospital. He qualified as a psychoanalyst in 1927 at the Institute for Psychoanalysis in London, where Melanie Klein was his supervisor, later associating himself with the Tavistock Clinic. In the ensuing years, his focus became normal and abnormal development in the child. Separation and loss were his main themes, which he eventually developed into a full-scale theory of attachment in the tradition of object relations.[47]

A seminal statement was his article "The Nature of the Child's Tie to his Mother," which appeared in the *International Journal of Psychoanalysis* in 1958.[48] There, drawing on literature from learning theory, Piaget, and psychoanalysis, he explicated four major theories describing the nature of mother–child bonding: the fulfillment of purely physiological needs, the theory of the mother's breast as the primary object, the theory of the need for human contact, and the theory revolving around the child's fury at being extracted from the womb. In any case, he pointed out that developmental psychologists do not agree on much beyond the fact that the mother is the primary object and that the foundation of personality is laid down in the mother–infant bond within the first 12 months of life.

Heinz Kohut

Meanwhile, there were other British analysts who had their own effect on the continued evolution of the field, widening the psychoanalytic interpretation of personality. Heinz Kohut was born in Vienna and received the MD from the University of Vienna. He fled Austria in 1939, the year after Freud left, and immigrated to Chicago, where he became a staunch advocate of the strict Freudian approach. Eventually, however, his thinking gave way to a more liberal conception of the ego and the self. Finally, he abandoned Freud's framework of a separate id, ego, and superego to develop a tripartite theory of the self. The study of the narcissistic personality was his point of departure and his conception of the self gave greater emphasis to relationships than Freudian psychology. His key text was *The Analysis of the Self* (1971), in which he coined the term narcissistic personality disorder.[49] He was certainly not the first to conceptualize the self in psychodynamic theories of personality, as Jung had preceded him by several decades. But he did write in an era when ego psychology and object relations had trumped Freud's previous focus on the primitive unconscious, and so could be credited with retrofitting psychoanalysis with the concept of the self to a greater extent than any other trained Freudian.

M. Masud R. Khan

One of the most interesting examples of psychoanalysis at mid-century is the case of Mohammed Masud Rasa Khan (1924–1989), whose flamboyant life and career as a training analyst, psychoanalytic insider, and Anglo-Pakistani aristocrat serves as a lens through which to view the development of the object relations school within the British Psychoanalytical Society and the International Psychoanalytic Association after World War II. His rise was meteoric, and his fall a major embarrassment to psychoanalysis. In retrospect, he was described by one commentator in terms of the harm done by an alcoholic married analyst who initiated sex with female patients, encouraged affairs between other patients, threatened patients who terminated treatment, and abandoned those who did not meet his own emotional needs. He also serves to highlight the larger enigma of how one translates the unconscious across cultures and the extent to which this translation succeeds or fails in the life of a single individual from a non-Western culture.

Khan was born in 1924, in an area of India known as the Punjab, which later became part of Pakistan. His father was a civil servant in the British Raj who then became a well-to-do landowner raising horses and his mother was described as a dreamy eyed dancer, one of several wives that created several households of children for the father. Both the father and the mother were absent for different portions of Khan's upbringing. At one point, between 4 and 6, he remained mute in his mother's enforced absence. Thus, he was later always in perpetual search for a father figure, and lack of maternal bonding probably contributed to his isolation and inwardness, which in turn expressed itself later as a tendency toward confabulation and fantasy. He was also born with a slight physical defect where one ear was larger than the other, a condition which further made him shy as well as an outcast among his peers. He was raised a Sunni Muslim but because of his father's accomplishments in the Indian government under the British, the household was thoroughly English. He was home schooled by a young female tutor who was herself a graduate of Oxford, before he attended nearby colleges associated first with the University of the Punjab and then the University of Lahore, where he earned Bachelors and Masters degrees in English literature, political science, and mystical Persian Sufism. In 1942 he experienced the death of his favorite sister, with whom he was deeply in love, after which he fell into a depression. Then his father died a year later.

Kahn's graduation coincided with Indian independence from the British, and he took advantage of the situation to immigrate to London at the age of 22, where, instead of proceeding to Oxford, he applied to become an analyst-in-training at the British Psychoanalytic Institute. The admissions committee looked favorably upon his materials and John Bowlby, the secretary, replied in the affirmative. Khan was supervised by both Melanie Klein and Anna Freud, associated with Wilfred Bion, Michael Balint, and W. R. D. Fairbairn, was analyzed by Ella Sharpe and John Rickman, and eventually wound up a protégé of Donald Winnicott. He became a credentialed analyst in 1950. The conversion to the psychoanalytic viewpoint had become complete and he was judged now able to inoculate others.

At the same time his star continued to rise within the psychoanalytic community. He went on to be appointed editor of the International Psychoanalytical Library, producing 26 volumes; he became editor of the *International Journal of Psycho-analysis*, and coeditor of the *Nouvelle revue de Psychanalyse*, for which he wrote 27 articles between 1970 and 1987. During this period he also produced a number of books of note, all of them have a bearing on his definition of personality, but cast into the particular epistemology of psychoanalysis. Two in particular were *The Privacy of the Self* (1974) and *Hidden Selves* (1983).[50]

In these works, largely through case studies, he developed the idea that all therapy is about self-experience. Most people act in a way that is not exactly consonant with their real inner self. Their entire situation colludes to hold them in place, extending this false self to the world, so that when they speak, they do not speak from the authentic center of themselves. What one needs is a holding environment where one's soul can be discovered in a private space, a space where no one can reach, where the self is beyond definition.

Such ideas are quite understandable to the educated reader, but they also reflect the approach of Sufism to the normal personality as an untamed horse, or a dog that has yet to be properly trained. With the absolute knowledge of God as the goal the individual enters into disciplined practice where self-management, the privacy of one's own thoughts through prayer and meditation, leads to self-knowledge and an absolute love of God.[51] In this regard, Christopher Bollas remarked that one of Khan's favorite Persian aphorisms was, "Where am I but in the place where no news comes to me, even about myself".[52]

He accepted all that Sigmund and Anna Freud had to say about the ego, its unconscious aspects, and its defenses; he followed closely the writings of Hartmann and Kris on psychoanalytic ego functioning; he internalized the object relations

hypotheses of Klein and Winnicott; but then fielded his own psychoanalytic interpretation of such concepts as the false self, by drawing on his own resources, such as
the Persian mystics. The fact that this remained only half conscious to himself was
the likely source of much of his neurotic behavior, except for the fact that his psychoanalytic interpreters still cleaved to a Judeo-Christian interpretation of human
sexuality, when Khan had the vast traditions of the Orient to draw from, though
unconsciously, as it was in his blood as well as his cultural milieu. What, after all,
could the White world comprehend of Kundalini Yoga?

But this was not always the case. As one of his biographers noted, within a colo-
nial system the original inhabitants establish a symbiotic relationship with their col-
onizers, such that the values of the colonizer are internalized as part of the self,
which creates a condition of unconscious identification.[53] Alliances and lieutenancy
are then the established norm, but for this harmony to proceed there must be a concomitant devaluing of the native self. Khan carried both this devaluing and this identification with him to London, where he transferred it into the more self-contained
epistemological framework of psychoanalysis and adopted a social role of associating himself with cricket, high tea, and the elite aristocracy of English and European
culture. He was a man of impeccable dress and decorum reflecting his confabu-
lated view of his own high station, as he strove to be more British than even the
British themselves. That this elitism slowly began to disintegrate over the years can
be inferred by his increased problems with alcohol, his tendency to give up expen-
sive suits for more native forms of dress, his all to frank published revelations of his
sexual exploits in therapy, and finally, at the end, his widely published anti-Semitic
tirade against the Jews which he had suppressed for so long.

In the end, suffering from lung cancer, his last book, *When Spring Comes*
(1988)[54] appeared, full of vitriol against the Jews, and containing descriptions of
what were judged as numerous countertransference violations, bi-sexual encounters, and his general mental instability. His credentials as a training analyst had been
revoked by the British Psychoanalytical Society in 1975 over similar complaints
and also personality conflicts with other members. Then, when the book came out
in 1988, the analysts had had enough, and his membership was cancelled altogether.
He died in London in 1989. The eventual cause of death was liver failure, caused
by his alcoholism but complicated by the effects of cancer. The origin was possibly
rage against himself. His body was flown back to Pakistan, where he was buried
next to his father. Tributes that followed were both scathing and laudatory, some
calling him insane, others a "prince of the psychoanalytic movement." Still others
took no note of his passing, or waited some years to render their opinion.

Islam is actually closer to Judaism and Christianity since the three constitute the
prophetic tradition in world religions. The Jews and the Arabs are both sons of Abraham, and Christianity represents the over-identification of the Christians with their
Judaic heritage. Islam, meanwhile, is the errant expression of the prophetic tradition because it also has roots in non-Western epistemologies, such as the indigenous
philosophies of India, and represents a potential bridge between these other ways
of knowing the ultimate and the Judeo-Christian outlook. Masud Khan struggled
with this paradox in his overidentification with the British but found a means of

expressing his lineage within psychoanalytic conceptions of personality and consciousness. Through psychoanalysis he had dialogued with the Jews as much as he was able in his lifetime, only to return to his native self at the end.

Ego Psychology

Ego psychology was a distinct outgrowth of Freud's earlier emphasis on the id, and the conflicts that arise between the instincts and the ego. At first it seems that the ego grew out of the id in Freud's theory, as in his essay on narcissism in 1914, until he began to elaborate more on ego functions and their relation to external material reality in "Group Psychology and the Analysis of the Ego" (1921); "The Ego and the Id" (1923), and "Inhibitions, Symptoms, and Anxiety" (1926). Anna Freud carried the theory of defenses forward (1937), as did Melanie Klein (1932b) and her variant of Freud in object relations theory.[55] But it was figures such as Rudolph Lowenstein, Heinz Hartmann, Ernst Kris, and David Rapaport who were most closely identified with ego psychology.

Heinz Hartmann (1894–1970) was born in Vienna and graduated with a degree in medicine from the University of Vienna in 1920. He began as a young man in pharmacology but soon switched to psychiatry, undertaking analytic training in Vienna, then Berlin. He returned to Vienna, where he worked at the Psychiatric Institute at the University of Vienna and then the Vienna Psychoanalytic Institute, before moving on to Paris and then New York. He edited the *International Journal for Psychoanalysis* and co-founded the *Psychoanalytic Study of the Child* with Anna Freud and Ernst Kris. He became medical director of the treatment clinic at the New York Psychoanalytic Institute and thereafter served as president of the various psychoanalytic associations both nationally and internationally.

His papers between 1922 and 1935 were on clinical topics related to personality and character development in twins. A second phase on psychoanalytic theory and methodology was followed by a phase on psychoanalysis and health, the attempt to adapt Freud's theory to the normal personality. A seminal work during this period was "Ego Psychology and the Problem of Adaptation" (1939).[56] Here, he made a clear distinction between instinctual conflicts between the ego and the id and non-pathological, autonomous adaptations of the ego, the so-called conflict free spheres of ego development, such as memory, thinking, and language.

Others, such as Ernst Kris and Rudolph Lowenstein joined him in elaborating on the functions of the ego that promote adaptation in the world of external material reality. This further fused biology with the forces of social adjustment, making psychoanalysis not only more of a cognitive but also a social psychology.

Ernest Kris (1900–1957) was born in Vienna and encouraged from an early age to study art.[57] He later earned the PhD in art history from the University of Vienna, after which he became assistant curator at the Vienna Kunsthistorisches Museum, which housed one of the great collections of art treasures in Europe. He soon developed an expertise in cameos and intaglios in the collection and was eventually recognized as a world expert. He met Freud through a mutual friend of the Freud family and began as a consultant to Freud's collection of artifacts. He then became a member of the Vienna Institute for Psychoanalysis and began an analysis with Helene Deutsch. He saw himself as an art historian, rather than a clinician, and published works on art and creativity from a psychoanalytic perspective. He did begin medical studies in 1933, but was diverted to other activities, when Freud put him in charge of editing the psychoanalytic journal, *Imago*. He became a training analyst at the Psychoanalytic Institute of Vienna but fled Austria, following Freud to London, in 1938. There, he trained analysts at the London Institute of Psychoanalysis.

He became involved in the analysis of enemy communications during World War II and was sent by the British Government to Canada to continue the work there. From Canada, he immigrated to New York in 1940, where he became a visiting professor at the New School for Social Research and a training analyst at the New York Psychoanalytic Institute. He also became an American citizen and joined the American Psychological Association. In his later years he began to focus on child psychoanalysis, leaving the world of museum artifacts behind. He established the Postgraduate Study Group of the New York Psychoanalytic Institute and two major projects, the Longitudinal Study at the Yale University Child Study Center in New Haven and The Gifted Adolescent Research Project at the New York Psychoanalytic Institute.

A work that defined his key contribution to psychoanalysis was *Psychoanalytic Explorations in Art* (1952).[58] Employing the basic principles of psychoanalytic ego psychology, he divided the process of artistic creation into inspiration and elaboration. Inspiration drives the artist to create in a rapturous state, while elaboration focuses on the solution of a deliberately defined specific problem. In both cases, regression into the unconscious plays a major part, as it acts in service of the ego as a kind of controlled madness. In addition to other works on ego-psychology, Kris also became well known for his editorship with Anna Freud of the Freud–Fleiss Letters[59] and for his theoretical papers published with Lowenstein and Hartmann.[60]

Rudolph Lowenstein (1898–1976) was born in Vienna and interrupted his study of medicine when he began an analysis with Hans Sachs in Berlin. He moved to Paris in 1925 and helped launch the *Société Psychanalytique de Paris* (SPP). He resumed his medical studies and was awarded the MD in 1935. He was mobilized into the French army in 1939, but eventually made his way to New York, where he continued his career as an analyst.

David Rapaport was born in Budapest, in 1900, raised in a middle class Jewish family, and at the University studied physics and mathematics.[61] He went to Palestine for 2 years to live on a Kibbutz and promote Zionism, where he married and began a family. He returned to Hungary in 1935, began to undertake psychoanalysis, and took the PhD in philosophy from the Royal University of Hungary in 1938. Immediately afterward he immigrated to the United States with his family, where he worked at Mt. Sinai Hospital and a state hospital in Kansas, before going to the Menninger Clinic in 1940. At the Menninger he began as head of the School of Clinical Psychology and director of research. *Emotions and Memory* appeared in 1942 and *Diagnostic Psychological Testing* in 1946–1948.[62] These are his best-known work in psychoanalytic ego psychology. *Organization and Pathology of Thought*, a collection of papers, appeared in 1951.[63] He left Menninger's to go to the Austen Riggs Center in Stockbridge, Massachusetts, where he worked until his death from a heart attack in 1960. Though he had been analyzed he never practiced psychoanalysis himself and was known instead as a theoretician, concerning himself with ego development and problems of metapsychology.[64]

The Menninger Clinic

The history of the Menninger Clinic began when Charles Frederick Menninger took his medical degree at the Hahnemann Medical College in Chicago, where he was trained in homeopathic medicine. In Topeka, Kansas, he began a medical practice and eventually broke with the homeopaths to join the ranks of the local physicians trained in allopathic medicine. After visiting the Mayo Clinic in 1908, he resolved to begin a group medical practice in Topeka serving psychiatric patients. With his son, Karl Menninger, a graduate of Harvard Medical School, Class of 1917, he launched the Menninger Diagnostic Clinic. They were soon joined by his other son William, who had trained at Cornell Medical College. At the time of their formal organization as a sanitarium in 1925, it was one of the only two mental health facilities in the United States to specialize in psychoanalysis,[65] to which the Menningers added the idea of group practice and the concepts of milieu therapy and moral management, a program of humane care pioneered by Quaker physicians who ran the English asylums at Gheel and elsewhere in the 19th century.[66]

Devoted to medical practice, research, and education, their facility became the Menninger Foundation in 1941 and a few years later, the Menninger School of Psychiatry. They specialized in treating a small group of patients diagnosed as neurotic or psychotic while expanding their facilities to focus on the training of psychiatrists and psychologists. After World War II, the facility was transformed from a small family operation housing 60 beds to one of the largest programs devoted to training in psychology, psychiatry, and psychoanalysis in the world. While the number of patients remained small the staff expanded. This was due largely to support from the federal government through the GI Bill, which provided funds to train needed mental health care workers who could deal with the problems of returning servicemen. To this end, they began to accept annually entering classes of 100 psychiatric residents who already held the MD and 10 psychologists who came to the Menninger to earn a degree in clinical psychology from the University of Kansas.

The treatment program was designed specifically for each patient rather than treatment regimes organized by diagnosis. The approach was holistic, in that it provided adequate time for work, education, play, rest, socialization, and time alone for reading and reflection. The central figure was the primary physician, who directed psychologists, nurses, social workers, interns, and all staff who had contact with the patient. Each patient had different needs and the entire staff was alerted to these in each case.

That psychoanalysis was at the core of their curriculum there could be no doubt. Their northwest office building housed offices of the Topeka Psychoanalytic

Institute and the Topeka Psychoanalytic Society. Nevertheless, the atmosphere was eclectic, optimistic, and pragmatic in the American tradition. David Rapaport mixed diagnostic testing with Freud's theories of psychology and metapsychology. George Kline and Phil Holzman ran a laboratory of experimental psychology. Gardner and Lois Murphy came for 12 years, during which he served as director of research. Rudolf Ekstein and Robert Wallerstein lectured on psychotherapy and produced *The Teaching and Learning of Psychotherapy* (1958).[67] Margaret Brenman and Merton Gill worked on hypnosis and related states. Henri Ellenberger was in residence for several years and lectured on what would become his *Discovery of the Unconscious*.[68] Helmuth Kaiser came and presented on his theories about communication between patient and therapist. The theories of Wilhelm Reich, Milton Erickson, and Carl Rogers were explored. Otto and Pauline Kernberg were there. And Erik Erikson gave lectures that became *Childhood and Society* (1950).[69] Frieda Fromm-Reichmann came from the Chestnut Lodge, while Margaret Mahler and Margaret Mead lectured, as did Ludwig von Bertalanffy and S. I. Hayakawa. Aldous Huxley and Isaac Bachevis Singer presented. Even Anna Freud visited several times. In addition, Elmer and Alyce Green launched the Voluntary Control of Internal States Project through the Menninger's Biofeedback Laboratory, which they founded. Such a spectrum of expertise defines the way psychoanalysis had been absorbed into its uniquely American variety.

Franz Alexander

With regard to the problem of personality in psychoanalysis, we can cite no better example than that of Franz Alexander (1891–1964). Franz Alexander was born in Budapest, immigrated to Berlin, where he was the first graduate of the Berlin Psychoanalytic Institute, which he then ran until immigrating to the United States. He was the first training analyst in Boston before being called to the University of Chicago in 1931 to become its first visiting professor of psychoanalysis. He founded the Chicago Psychoanalytic Institute, which became an international center for training and research into psychoanalytic concepts. Among his trainees were Karl and William Menninger, Leo Bartemeier, and Gregory Zilboorg.

The quintessential statement on Freud's dynamic theory of personality we would expect to find in Alexander's *Psychoanalysis of the Total Personality: The Application of Freud's Theory of the Ego to the Neuroses*, first translated into English as a Nervous and Mental Disease Monograph in 1930.[70] But the result was heavily qualified. The work recited the epochs of psychoanalytic history beginning with the era of Charcot, then Breuer, identifying trauma, repression, abreaction, and catharsis as the essential elements. Then followed Freud's period of isolation, where Freud abandoned hypnosis for free association, discovered the sexual component of the neuroses, and emerged with his new system, psychoanalysis. The first two eras were totally dominated by a focus on repression and the instincts, and to object libido. Only later did Freud turn his attention to the psychoses, which may contain manifestations of the neuroses, and to the narcissistic neuroses, which is the ego involved in self-preservation and also self-love. From this, Freud concluded that the ego is the true reservoir of the libido. His later formulation of the id, controlled by the ego, which is in turn overseen by the superego, led him to the formulation that the neuroses represent a conflict between the id and the ego (the instinctive needs), the psychoses represent a conflict between the ego and the outward world, and the narcissistic neuroses a struggle between the ego and the superego. These must be understood within the larger framework of the two kinds of instincts: *eros*, the life force, and *thanatos*, the death instinct.

Alexander's work claimed as original only his extension of the Master's theory to a further understanding of neurotic self-punishment. The id demands gratification, the superego punishment and retribution. The ego mediates between the organism and the environment through object cathexis, but participates, as well, as a central player in the drama being played out between instincts and ideals within. In this, the ego demonstrates an unconscious aspect in the form of preverbal instinctive needs at odds with the inculcated rules of the superego just below the surface of consciousness. The person becomes resigned to his or her illness. A neurotic illness can then become a permanent part of personality through the individual's adjustment to their infirmity, making it difficult to give it up once they have become comfortable with its chronicity.

But the real question for us is, what does Alexander mean by the "total personality"? Obviously it is id, ego, and superego across a spectrum from waking consciousness to the unconscious, itself made up of instincts as well as conscience. Reason was still the highest function Freud could conceive, even though it was the most fragile under stress and trauma. There is no spiritual dimension to personality, only the introjection of external rules and values from parents and culture. It is no wonder then that Freud viewed religion as just another neurosis, since his model is incapable of differentiating between the external teachings of organized religion and a generic spiritual dimension to personality inherent in each person that can be cultivated independently of external social institutions.

Finally, it is paradoxical that when you ask the educated man or women on the street, "What is psychology?" or "What is psychiatry?" they will most likely say Freud, when Freudian theory has lost most of its power to influence these disciplines in the academy. In fact, as we have said earlier, there is one line of interpretation, which suggests that Freud never had the impact on psychology and psychiatry that most people think that he had had. This is due to the fact that scientific laboratory psychology has been dominated first by physiological psychology and psychophysics, then behaviorism, and now cognitive science, while scientific psychiatry has always been grounded in medicine, its most pervasive advances occurring in psychopharmacology, both instances where psychoanalysis never had any influence. Yet history shows how pervasive psychoanalysis has been in culture at large. It is this paradox that shows how successful Freud was in his insistence that psychoanalysis was a science and in its persistence in American psychiatry, despite its dubious status as such. It is also a condition that has allowed for the radicalization of depth psychology in popular culture beyond anything Freud could ever have dreamed. All did not emanate from Freud, by any means, but his influence did significantly shape what was to come.

Notes

1. Gay, 1988, p. 173.
2. See Freud, S., Ferenczi, S., Brabant-Geroo, E., Falzeder, E., & Giampieri-Deutsch, P. (1993–2000). *The correspondence of Sigmund Freud and Sandor Ferenczi* (3 Vols.). Cambridge, MA: Belknap Press of Harvard University.
3. Ferenczi, S., & Rank, O. (1925/1986). *The development of psycho-analysis.* Madison, CT: International Universities Press.
4. Ferenczi, S. (1916). *Contributions to psycho-analysis* (E. Jones, Trans). Boston: R. G. Badger.
5. Ellenberger, 1970, p. 844.
6. Rank, O. (1907). *Der kuňstler: Ansaïze zu e. sexual-psychologie* [The artist: Approches to sexual psychology]. Leipzig: International Psychoanalytic, Verlag.
7. Rank, O. (1909). *Der mythus von der geburt des helden versuch einer psychologischen mythendeutun* [The myth of the birth of the hero]. Schriften zur Angewandten Seelenkunde, Heft 5. Leipzig: Deuticke.
8. Rank, O. (1912). *Das inzest-motiv in dichtung und sage: Grundzüge e. psychologie d. dichterischen schaffens* [The incest motif in poetry and saga]. Leipzig: Deuticke.
9. Rank, O. (1924). *Das trauma der geburt und seine bedeutung fuř die psychoanalyse* [The trauma of birth and its significance for psychoanalysis]. Internationale Psychoanalytische Bibliothek. Leipzig: Internationaler Psychoanalytischer Verlag.
10. Rank, O. (1996). In R. Kramer, & R. May, (Ed.), *A psychology of difference: The American lectures.* Princeton, NJ: Princeton University Press.
11. Becker, E. (1973). *The denial of death.* New York: Free Press. Becker was always puzzled why E. G. Boring never reviewed his work in *Contemporary Psychology.* (Personal Communication, Association for Humanistic Psychology Conference, 1976. Austin, TX)
12. A useful biography is Coles, R. (1992). *Anna Freud: The dream of psychoanalysis.* Reading, MA: Addison-Wesley.
13. I have used Freud, A. (1946). *The psychoanalytical treatment of children: Technical lectures and essays.* London: Imago Publishing Company.
14. See Freud, A. (1937). *The ego and the mechanisms of defence.* The International Psychoanalytical Library, No. 30. London: Hogarth press, and the Institute of Psycho-analysis.
15. Freud, A. (1967–1981). *The writings of Anna Freud* (8 Vols.). New York: International Universities Press, including Freud, A. (1922–1935). *The writings of Anna Freud: Vol. 1. Introduction to psychoanalysis: lectures for child analysts and teachers.* New York: International Universities Press; Freud, A. (1936). *The writings of Anna Freud:* Vol. 2. Ego and the mechanisms of defence. New York: International Universities Press; Freud, A. (1939–1945). *The writings of Anna Freud: Vol. 3. Infants without families reports on the Hampstead Nurseries by Anna Freud.* New York: International Universities Press; Freud, A. (1945–1956). *The writings of Anna Freud: Vol. 4. Indications for child analysis and other papers.* New York: International Universities Press; Freud, A. (1956–1965). *The writings of Anna Freud: Vol. 5. Research at the Hampstead Child-Therapy Clinic and other papers.* New York: International Universities Press; Freud, A. (1965). *The writings of Anna Freud: Vol. 6. Normality and pathology in childhood: Assessments of development.* New York: International Universities Press; Freud, A. (1966–1970). *The writings of Anna Freud: Vol. 7. Problems of psychoanalytic training, diagnosis, and the technique of therapy.* New York: International Universities Press; Freud, A. (1970–1980). *The writings of Anna Freud: Vol. 8. Psychoanalytic psychology of normal development.* New York: International Universities Press.
16. Jones, E. (1959). *Free associations: Memories of a psycho-analyst.* London: Hogarth Press.
17. Trotter, W. (1916). *Instincts of the herd in peace and war.* New York: The Macmillan Company.

18. Paskauskas, A. (Ed.). (1995). *The complete correspondence of Sigmund Freud and Ernest Jones, 1908–1939*. Cambridge, MA: Belknap Press of Harvard University Press. (1st edition 1993; Reprint edition 1995)

19. Jones, E. (1954–1958). *Sigmund Freud: Life and work* (3 Vols.). London: Hogarth Press.

20. H. A. Murray, personal communication, March 5, 1985. Cambridge, Massachusetts.

21. Silberer, H. (1951). A method of eliciting autosymbolic phenomena. In D. Rapaport, D. (Ed.), *Organization and pathology of thought* (pp. 195–207). New York: Columbia University Press.

22. Silberer, H. (1917). *Problems of mysticism and its symbolism* (S. E. Jelliffe, Trans.). New York: Moffat, Yard and Company.

23. Nitzschke, B. (1989). Sigmund Freud and Herbert Silberer: Conjectures on the addressee of a letter by Freud written in 1922. *Review of the International History of Psychoanalysis, 2,* 267–77.

24. From a summary prepared by Thomas J. Martinez, 3rd, by permission.

25. Jung, C. G. (1907a). *Über die psychologie der dementia praecox: Ein versuch* [The psychology of dementia praecox]. Halle a S.: Verlagsbuchhandlung Carl Marhold.

26. May, R., Angel, E., & Ellenberger, H. F. (1958). *Existence: A new dimension in psychiatry.* New York: Basic Books; Binswanger, L. (1963). *Being-in-the-world: Selected papers of Ludwig Binswanger* (J. Needleman, Trans.). New York: Basic Books; see also Binswanger, L. (1957). *Sigmund Freud: Reminiscences of a friendship* (N. Guterman, Trans.). New York: Grune & Stratton.

27. Putnam, J. J. (1907). Recent experiences in the study and treatment of hysteria at the Massachusetts General Hospital; with remarks on Freud's method of treatment by "psychoanalysis." *Journal of Abnormal Psychology, 1*(1), 26–41.

28. Vasile, R. G. (1977). *James Jackson Putnam, from neurology to psychoanalysis: A study of the reception and promulgation of Freudian psychoanalytic theory in America, 1895–1918.* Oceanside, NY: Dabor Science Publications.

29. See Taylor, E. I. (1985b). James Jackson Putnam's fateful meeting with Freud: The 1909 Clark University Conference. *Voices: The Art and Science of Psychotherapy, 21*(1), 78–89; also Taylor, E. I. (1988). On the first use of 'psychoanalysis' at the Massachusetts General Hospital, 1903–1905, *Journal of the History of Medicine and Allied Sciences, 43*(4), 447–471.

30. Hale, N. G. (1971b). *James Jackson Putnam and psychoanalysis; Letters between Putnam and Sigmund Freud, Ernest Jones, William James, Sandor Ferenczi, and Morton Prince, 1877–1917.* Cambridge, MA: Harvard University Press.

31. For an important review of the Boston scene, see Gifford, S. (2003). Émigré analysts in Boston, 1930–1940. *International Forum of Psychoanalysis, 12,* 1–9.

31. Roazan, P. (1975). *Freud and his followers.* New York: A. A. Knopf, pp. 380–381.

33. Summarized from Grotjahn, M. (1966). Karl Abraham: The first German psychoanalyst. In F. Alexander, S. Eisenstein, & M. Grotjahn (Eds.), *Psychoanalytic pioneers* (pp. 1–13). New York: Basic Books.

33. Summarized from Pomar, S. L. (1966). Max Eitingon: The organization of psychoanalytic training. In F. Alexander, S. Eisenstein, & M. Grotjahn (Eds.), *Psychoanalytic pioneers* (pp. 51–62). New York: Basic Books.

35. Pomar, 1966, p. 51.

36. His work, *The Psychoanalytic Method,* was translated into English in 1915. See Pfister, O. R. (1915). *The psychoanalytic method.* London: K. Paul, Trench, Trubner.

37. Freud, S. (1926). The question of lay analysis. In J. Strachey (Ed. & Trans.), *The standard edition of the complete psychological works of Sigmund Freud* (Vol. 20, pp. 177–250). London: Hogarth Press.

38. Gay, P. (1988). *Freud: A life for our time.* New York: W. W. Norton, pp. 190–193.

39. Bertin, C. (1982). *Marie Bonaparte: A life.* New Haven, CT: Yale University Press.

40. See Cannon, B. (1991). *Sartre and psychoanalysis: An existentialist challenge to clinical metatheory.* Lawrence, KS: University Press of Kansas.

41. See Sartre, J.-P. (1957). *The transcendence of the ego: An existentialist theory of conscious-ness.* New York: Noonday Press; Sartre, J.-P. (1956). *Being and nothingness: An essay on phenomenological ontology.* New York: Philosophical Library.

42. Lacan, J. (1977). *The seminar, Book 11, The four fundamental concepts of psychoanalysis* (J.-A. Miller Ed., A. Sheridan, Trans.). New York: W. W. Norton & Company; Lacan, J. (1988a). *The seminar of Jacques Lacan: Book 1, Freud's papers on technique, 1953–1954* (J.-A. Miller, Ed., J. Forrester, Trans.). New York: W. W. Norton & Company; Lacan, J. (1988b). *The seminar, book 2. The ego in Freud's theory and in the technique of psycho-analysis, 1954–1955* (J.-A. Miller, Ed., S. Tomaselli, Trans.). New York: W. W. Norton & Company; Lacan, J. (1993). *The seminar, book 3, The psychoses* (J.-A. Miller, Ed., R. Grigg, Trans.). New York: W. W. Norton & Company; Lacan, J. (1992). *The seminar, book 7, the ethics of psychoanalysis, 1959–1960* (J.-A. Miller, Ed., D. Porter, Trans.). New York: W. W. Norton & Company; Lacan, J. (1998). *The seminar, book 20, on feminine sexuality, the limits of love and knowledge* (J.-A. Miller, Ed., B. Fink, Trans.). New York: W. W. Norton & Com-pany; Lacan, J. (2006). *Ecrits: The first complete edition in English* (B. Fink, Trans.). New York: W.W. Norton & Company; Lacan, J. (2007). *The seminar, book 17, the other side of psychoanalysis* (J.-A. Miller, Ed., R. Grigg, Trans.). New York: W. W. Norton & Company.

43. Klein, M, (1975). *The writings of Melanie Klein* (4 Vols.). The International Psycho-Analytical Library. London: Hogarth Press including: Klein, M. (1975a). *The writings of Melanie Klein: Love, guilt and reparation and other works 1921–1945* (Vol. 1, No. 103). The International Psycho-Analytical Library. London: Hogarth Press; Klein, M. (1975b). *The writings of Melanie Klein: The psycho-analysis of children* (Vol. 2, No. 220). The International Psycho-Analytical Library. London: Hogarth Press; Klein, M. (1975c). *The writings of Melanie Klein: Envy and gratitude and other works 1946–1963* (Vol. 3, No. 104). The International Psycho-Analytical Library. London: Hogarth Press; Klein, M. (1975d). *The writings of Melanie Klein: Narrative of a child analysis* (Vol. 4, No. 55). The International Psycho-Analytical Library. London: Hogarth Press. All reprinted by Virago, 1988.

44. Klein, M. (1932). *The psycho-analysis of children* (A. Strachey, Trans.). London: L. & V. Woolf at the Hogarth Press and the Institute of Psycho-analysis; Klein, M. (1948). *Contribu-tions to psycho-analysis, 1921–1945.* London: Hogarth Press; Klein, M. (1961). *Narrative of a child analysis: The conduct of the psycho-analysis of children as seen in the treatment of a ten-year-old boy.* London: Hogarth Press and the Institute of Psycho-Analysis; Klein, M. (1963). *Our adult world and other essays.* New York: Basic Books.

45. Winnicott, D. W. (1958). *Collected papers: Through paediatrics to psycho-analysis.* London: Tavistock Publications; New York: Basic Books; Winnicott, D. W. (1975). *Collected papers: Through paediatrics to psycho-analysis.* London: Hogarth Press and the Institute of Psycho-analysis; Winnicott, D. W. (1992). *Collected papers: Through paediatrics to psycho-analysis.* London: Institute of Psychoanalysis and Karnac Books; Winnicott, D. W. (1992). *Collected papers: Through paediatrics to psycho-analysis.* New York: Brunner/Mazel.

46. See for instance, Bion, W. R. (1948). *Experiences in groups: Human relations, Vols. I–IV, 1948–1951.* Reprinted in *Experiences in groups.* (1961). London: Tavistock; and Bion, W. R. (1957). The differentiation of the psychotic from the non-psychotic personalities. *International Journal of Psycho-analysis, 38,* 266–275. Reprinted in *Second thoughts.* (1967). London: Heinemann. Nancy Julia Chodorow (1944–) was born in New York. She received her BA from Radcliffe College, where she focused on personality and culture in an environ-ment that was dominated by an enveloping feminist epistemology. She took her PhD from Brandeis University in 1975, where she came under influence of psychoanalytic sociologist Philip Slater, whose explanation for male dominance is that men fear women, which has become an institutionalized attitude. Chodorow was also influenced by Karen Horney and Melanie Klein. She teaches sociology at University of California, Berkeley. Some of her works include: *The reproduction of mothering* (1978). Berkeley, Los Angeles: University of California Press; *Feminism and psychoanalytic theory* (1989). London, New Haven, CT: Yale

University Press; *Femininities, masculinities, sexualities: Freud and beyond* (1994). Lexington, KY: The University Press of Kentucky; *The power of feelings: Personal meaning in psychoanalysis, gender, and culture* (1999). London, New Haven, CT: Yale University Press.

47. Bowlby, J. (1969–1982). *Attachment and loss: Vol. 1. Attachment*. London: Hogarth Press; Bowlby, J. (1973a). *Attachment and loss: Vol. 1. Attachment*. New York: Basic Books; Bowlby, J. (1971). *Attachment and loss: Vol. 1. Attachment*. Harmondsworth, UK: Penguin; Bowlby, J. (1973b). *Attachment and loss: Vol. 2. Separation: Anxiety and anger*. London: Hogarth Press; Bowlby, J. (1973c). *Attachment and loss: Vol. 2. Separation: Anxiety and anger*. New York: Basic Books; Bowlby, J. (1975). *Attachment and loss: Vol. 2. Separation: Anxiety and anger*. Harmondsworth: Penguin; Bowlby, J. (1980). *Attachment and loss: Vol. 3. Loss: Sadness and depression*. New York: Basic Books; Bowlby, J. (1981). *Attachment and loss: Loss: Sadness and depression*. Harmondsworth, UK: Penguin. See also Van Dijken, K. S., Van der Veer, R., Van IJzendoorn, M. H., & Kuipers, H. J. (1998). Bowlby before Bowlby: The sources of an intellectual departure in psychoanalysis and psychology. *Journal of the History of the Behavioral Sciences, 34*(3), 247–269.
48. Bowlby, J. (1958). The nature of the child's tie to his mother. *International Journal of Psycho-Analysis, 39*(5), 350–373.
49. Kohut, H. (1971). *The analysis of the self: A systematic analysis of the treatment of the narcissistic personality disorders*. New York: International Universities Press.
50. Khan, M. M. R. (1974). *The privacy of the self: Papers on psychoanalytic theory and technique*. New York: International Universities Press; Khan, M. M. R. (1983). *Hidden selves: Between theory and practice in psychoanalysis*. New York: International Universities Press.
51. Schimmel, A. (1975). *The mystical dimensions of Islam*. Chapel Hill, NC: University of North Carolina Press.
52. Bollas, C., Pontalis, J.-B., & Didier, A., et al. (1989). In memoriam: Masud Khan, 1924–1989. *Nouvelle Revue de Psychanalyse, 40*, 333–359.
53. Roger. W. (2005). *Masud Khan: The myth and the reality*. Foreword by Pearl King. London: Free Association Books.
54. Khan, M. M. R. (1988). *When spring comes: Awakenings in clinical psychoanalysis*. London: Chatto and Windus.
55. Klein, M. (1932b). *The psycho-analysis of children*. (A. Strachey, Trans.). London: L. & V. Woolf at the Hogarth Press and the Institute of Psychoanalysis; Freud, A. (1937). *The ego and mechanisms of defence*. London: Hogarth Press.
56. Hartmann, H. (1939). Ich-psychologie und anpassungsproblem. *Internationale Zeitschrift für Psychoanalyse, 24*, 62–135; First English edition (1958), "Ego psychology and the problem of adaptation." *Journal of the American Psychoanalytic Association, Monographs 1*. New York: International Universities Press.
57. Ritvo, S. & Ritvo, L. (1966). Ernest Kris, 1900–1957. In F. Alexander, S. Eisenstein, & M. Grotjahn (Eds.), *Psychoanalytic pioneers* (pp. 484–500). New York: Basic Books.
58. Kris, E. (1952). *Psychoanalytic explorations in art*. New York: International Universities Press.
59. Kris, E. (1954). Introduction. In M. Bonaparte, A. Freud, & E. Kris (Eds.), *The origins of psychoanalysis: Letters to Wilhelm Fliess, drafts and notes, 1887–1902, by Sigmund Freud*. New York: Basic Books.
60. For instance, Hartmann, H., & Kris, E. (1945). The genetic approach to psychoanalysis. *Psychoanalytic study of the child* (Vol. 1). New York: International Universities Press; Hartmann, H., Kris, E., & Lowenstein, R. (1946). Comments on the theory of psychic structure. *Psychoanalytic study of the child* (Vol. 2). New York: International Universities Press; Hartmann, H., Kris, E. & Lowenstein, R. (1949). Notes on the theory of aggression. *Psychoanalytic study of the child* (Vols. 3, 4). New York: International Universities Press; Hartmann, H., Kris, E., & Lowenstein, R. (1953). The function of theory in psychoanalysis. In R. M. Lowenstein (Ed.), *Drives, affects, and behavior*. New York: International Universities Press.
61. Gill, M. M. (1961). David Rapaport (1911–1960). *Bulletin of the American Psychoanalytic Association, 17*, 755–759.

62. Rapaport, D. (1942). *Emotions and memory*. Baltimore, MD: The Williams & Wilkins Company; Rapaport, D. (1945). *Diagnostic psychological testing: The theory, statistical evaluation, and diagnostic application of a battery of tests*. Chicago: The Year Book Publishers Inc.
63. Rapaport, D. (Ed., & Trans.). (1951). *Organization and pathology of thought: Selected sources*. New York: Columbia University Press. See also, Rapaport, D., Schaefer, R., & Gill, M. M. (1946). *Manual of diagnostic psychological testing. II. Diagnostic testing of personality and ideational content* (Vol. 3, No. 1). New York: Macy, Josiah Jr. Foundation.
64. Rapaport, D. (1958). A historical survey of psychoanalytic ego-psychology. *Bulletin of the Philadelphia Association for Psychoanalysis, 8*, 105–120; Rapaport, D., & Gill, M. M. (1959). The points of view and assumptions of metapsychology. *International Journal of Psycho-analysis, 40*, 1–10.
65. The other was the Chestnut Lodge, according to Schlesinger, H. J. (2007). The treatment program at Menninger. *American Imago, 64*(2), 229–240.
66. See Friedman, L. J. (1990). *Menninger: The family and the clinic*. New York: A. A. Knopf; Schlesinger (2007).
67. Ekstein, R., & Wallerstein, R. S. (1958). *The teaching and learning of psychotherapy*. New York: Basic Books; London: Imago Publication Company.
68. Ellenberger (1970).
69. Erikson, E. H. (1950). *Childhood and society*. New York: W. W. Norton.
70. Alexander, F., Glueck, B., Lewin, B. D., & Brill, A. A. (1930). *The psychoanalysis of the total personality: The application of Freud's theory of the ego to the neuroses*. Nervous and Mental Disease Monograph Series, No. 52. New York: Nervous and Mental Disease Publishing Company.

Chapter 5
The Neo-Freudians

From the 1920s onward, the battle over the unconscious was being fought and lost in the fields of academic laboratory psychology in the United States. In the opening decades of the 20th century, first, the specter of Pavlov and then Watson began to dominate the academic laboratories with theories of learning and their emphasis on classical conditioning. In the 19-teens and twenties, Thorndike's theory of selecting and connecting and Toleman's conceptions of latent learning had their adherents, while Kohler's studies of insight learning, which had suddenly burst upon the scene with the publication of *The Mentality of Apes* (1925)[1] never made any impact among the experimentalists. After Skinner's *Behavior of Organisms* (1938),[2] operant conditioning came into vogue, solidifying the pervasive infusion of behaviorism as the reigning ideology guiding how psychology as an entire field ought to be defined.[3]

Meanwhile, reductionistic operationism, epitomized by Boring's misinterpretation of Bridgman,[4] received significant reinforcement with the appearance of the psychophysicist S. S. Steven's *Handbook of Experimental Psychology* (1951),[5] which became the bible of laboratory research. Clark Hull at Yale captured the era with his formula for the hypotheticodeductive method, declaring it the central motif unifying scientific psychology. Moreover, that way of defining psychology now had its own historical foundations in the form of Boring's bible, *A History of Experimental Psychology*.[6] Sigmund Koch came to call it "The Age of Theory," because its framers sought to dominate all other theories.

Meanwhile, valiant but in the end not very successful attempts were carried on to prove that psychoanalysis was a science. Robert Sears and Saul Rosenzweig labored to produce a body of experimental proofs on the subject. Dollard and Miller sought to fuse psychoanalysis with learning theory with their studies on frustration and aggression. The Rockefeller philanthropy threw large amounts of money at Franz Alexander in Chicago to carry on such investigations. The battle, in fact, rages to this day but under the names of different investigators. The language of psychoanalysis has become more accepted, but also defined more in terms of a non-Freudian "cognitive unconscious."[7]

Depth psychology, meanwhile, was undergoing its own transformations. The farther it got away from the orthodox Freudians, the more deeply it penetrated as well as helped to shape the soft psychologies of personality, abnormal, social, and clinical psychology. In psychiatry, it came to control the clinical teaching of

E. Taylor, *The Mystery of Personality*, Library of the History of Psychology Theories, DOI 10.1007/978-0-387-98104-8_5, © Springer Science+Business Media, LLC 2009

medical residents whose attention was directed to the ambulatory psychoneuroses, once the office practice of psychotherapy became economically viable, and the psychotherapists stayed away from the psychotics under asylum care. At the same time, however, there were numerous examples that attempted to treat schizophrenia by psychogenic means in the mental hospitals.

By these means, depth psychology became radically disenfranchised from biological psychiatry, which controlled the laboratories. The biological psychiatrists fought back with the somatic therapies such as psychosurgery, shock therapy, and the soon to flourish industry of psychopharmacology. At the same time, the depth psychologies were being absorbed by a kind of osmosis into the other social sciences, such as sociology and anthropology. The effect there was to produce a socialized form of psychoanalysis, in which less emphasis was placed on the dynamics of the individual unconscious and more on ego adaptation, social forces that shaped the individual within society, and the application of dynamic theories to entire cultures.

Within the clinical domain, two competing models of the person then emerged. One focused on the definition of personality as a function of internal psychic forces, while the other came to define personality as a function of external social forces within the family, the clan, the state, one's culture, and even the race. Social psychologists became radicalized, as exemplified by the founding of the Society for the Psychological Study of Social Issues in 1936, which attracted liberal psychologists as well as socialists into populist movements and social reform.[8] Psychology suddenly became overtly politicized, as more socialist influences were brought to bear on its interpretation, particularly through radicals reading Freud and Marx in the counterculture and later through the Neo-Freudians, who became the real purveyors of psychoanalysis throughout modern popular culture. They were intermingled with the existentialist theologians, the Jungians, and the gestaltists, but particularly influenced by the fusion of dynamic theories of personality with new developments in anthropology in what was to be called the "Culture and Personality movement." Depth psychology became associated with more phenomenological approaches emphasizing interior experience, while the concept of the unconscious was also being adapted to explanations already extant linking the individual to external social forces.[9] The situation in New York was a case in point.

In the United States, once the so-called classical period of Freud, Jung, and Adler started to cool down in Europe by the end of the 1920s, the influence of their dynamic theories of personality were already heating up in places like Washington, Boston, and New York. According to historian Nathan G. Hale, Jr., Smith Ely Jelliffe from St. Elizabeth's Hospital, co-founder of the *Psychoanalytic Review* with William Alanson White, was in high demand in Washington, while Beatrice Hinkle, Jung's American translator, was most frequently consulted in New York.[10] Meanwhile, the New York Psychoanalytic Society and Institute remained the bastion of Freudian orthodoxy. They date the founding of the original society from 1911 by A. A. Brill, making it the oldest psychoanalytic organization in the United States. Though he originally came to Freud through Jung, Brill had been meeting with physicians interested in psychoanalysis since 1908 and himself lectured widely on Freud's ideas, especially to professional associations of New York physicians. He also launched a significant translation project that produced the first English language edition of the *Interpretation of Dreams* (1913).[11]

In addition to Brill, significant numbers of American physicians who had sought a direct analysis with Freud in Vienna after the World War I returned to New York, and were soon joined by others who had undergone analysis at the Berlin, Budapest, and Vienna Institutes. Bronislav Onuf, Clarence Oberndorf, Sándor Lorand, Fritz Wittels, Abram Kardiner were among them.[12]

The society launched a series of successful lectures in 1922 that led to the formation of their educational committee. The committee blossomed to establish the first psychoanalytic training institute in the United States in 1931. They were soon joined by fleeing psychoanalytic émigrés from Europe, which further expanded their numbers. Probably more than any other Institute subsequently founded in America, the New York group saw themselves as the most orthodox, and endeavoring to preserve the Master's teachings against all deviation and corruption, as Freud himself was endeavoring to do in Vienna.

The major issue during the 1920s was over the question of lay analysis. Freud had championed the idea and supported numerous analysands, such as Oskar Pfister, a Swiss minister, as the various Institutes were being founded. But in the United States, psychoanalysis became the exclusive province of the physicians and hence remained a branch of psychiatry. This, plus the attempt to keep the teachings pure, created a narrow focus for orthodox psychoanalysis, which had the effect of fostering an alteration and expansion of Freudian ideas just beyond the psychoanalysts' doorstep. These included, among others, The Karen Horney Institute, The William Alanson White Institute, The cultural anthropologists at Columbia, faculty at Union Theological Seminary and The New School for Social Research, Jungians who had founded the Analytical Psychology Club, theologians at the Union Theological Seminary, and individual personalities at such places as Brooklyn College, The City University of New York, and Sarah Lawrence.

The Expansion of Psychoanalysis

As the analytic émigrés began pouring into the United States by the mid-1930s, one informal but highly influential group responsible for the widespread reinterpretation and dissemination of psychoanalysis throughout American culture was already underway. This was the Zodiac Club, which hovered around the American psychiatrist Harry Stack Sullivan beginning in 1931. Through Sullivan and the Zodiac Club, psychoanalysis found its way into various avenues of the social sciences related to psychology and psychiatry, particularly sociology, anthropology, and linguistics. Beyond these boundaries several personalities constellating around Sullivan, including Erik Fromm and Karen Horney, applied their version of psychoanalytic ideas to contemporary problems such as gender issues, totalitarianism, the meaning of love and freedom, and the fate of modern civilization. Through their best-selling books, depth psychology in the Freudian mold found able interpreters who by their very deviations served to elevate psychoanalysis to the status of a cultural phenomenon in the West.

The Zodiac Club first convened in 1931, during Prohibition, when Harry Stack Sullivan, Clara Thompson, William Silverberg, and later a few others began meeting in a New York speakeasy on Monday evenings for dinner, drinks, and discussion of psychiatry, mainly Freud's ideas. The three had known each other from time they had spent in Baltimore, where Thompson had convened what they then called the Miracle Club, because patients seemed to miraculously get better after their case was discussed by the group.

According to one biographer, the newly reconvened New York circle was named the Zodiac Club on a whim by Sullivan.[13] Each member was required to represent themselves through the symbol of some appropriate animal, the exact reason for which has not yet been told. Sullivan became a horse. Thompson became a puma. Silverberg became a gazelle. Later, others were to join this group, including Karen Horney, Erik Fromm, Ruth Benedict, Margaret Mead, Ralph Linton, and Edward Sapir. In all, the Zodiac Club became a convergence of intellectual influences from Chicago, New York, New Haven, and Washington, linking some of the keenest minds from those environments in the social and behavioral sciences. For the dozen or so years that it lasted, its members produced some remarkable cultural benchmarks. Not the least of these was a few national best sellers, including Horney's *The Neurotic Personality of Our Time* (1937) and Fromm's *Escape from Freedom* (1941).[14]

As for the group's internal dynamics, while Sullivan's stature and ideas dominated, he himself was also changed the more theoretical the discussions became. Thompson was his devoted follower, but she also introduced him to orthodox psychoanalysis and feminine psychology. In a certain sense, she was just as much at the center of the group as the more conspicuous Sullivan. Horney, another important woman in the group, appreciated Sullivan's ideas, but her psychology was already well formed from her contact with Freud before she arrived. Fromm, on the other hand, continued to go through large changes from all quarters. But overall, everyone operated more or less as independent entities. Each one had their own positions and there seems to have been more interaction and cross-fertilization rather than competition. Ideas and insights were aired and discussed; then each person applied the result in their own domain. Occasionally, some mutual project would emerge. One of the big issues they discussed, for instance, was female sexuality, which led to collaboration between Thompson and Horney.

Just who were these people? And what was the trajectory of their lives that allowed them to intersect at just this moment in both the popular and the professional histories of psychoanalysis in America?

Sullivan

Harry Stack Sullivan, the man at the center of the Zodiac Club, has been variously characterized as a withdrawn and cantankerous drunk, a pretentious high stepper, opportunistic, power-driven, irresponsible about money, who, nevertheless, could also rise to great heights as a sophisticated compassionate human being.[15] He was born in 1892 in rural Chenango County, New York, part of the great "Burned Over District," of Joseph Smith and Ellen White. Sullivan grew up on a farm, the only child of a poor Irish Catholic family. He attended Columbia University for two semesters until he fell in with a gang of near-do-wells and got into trouble with the police, after which, he disappeared for 2 years. His biographer suggests that during this period he may have had the first of several schizophrenic-like episodes and was hospitalized for a time.[16]

In 1911, he entered the Chicago College of Medicine and Surgery, then an unaccredited facility, which was the medical branch of Valparaiso University in Indiana. He completed his class work in 1915, but was not awarded the MD until 1917. Between 1916 and 1921, he worked in the area of industrial surgery and then enlisted briefly in the army as a military surgeon. After the war he continued to find employment as an assistant district medical officer in Chicago assisting in the rehabilitation of soldiers and sailors. He seems to have gone through another schizophrenic-like episode during this period as well.

In 1921 Sullivan passed the Civil Service examination and was assigned as a neuropsychiatrist to St. Elizabeth's Hospital in Washington, DC as a liaison officer for the Veterans Bureau. There he came under the influence of William Alanson White, who was to have an important effect on his subsequent career. At St. Elizabeth's he also began working with schizophrenic patients.

This arrangement lasted until 1922, when Sullivan went to the Sheppard and Enoch Pratt Hospital in Maryland as an Assistant Psychiatrist, where he remained for 8 years. During this period, he became a renowned clinician and a pioneer in integrating psychiatry with the social sciences. He adapted psychoanalysis to the treatment of the psychoses; he began research into the nature of schizophrenic thought processes; and he became preoccupied with the important period of pre-adolescence. When he was given his own ward, he began successfully experimenting with the social relationships of schizophrenics.

In this milieu, the therapeutic interventions he designed and the innovations he instituted drew national attention. He also developed a strong stand against chemical restraints, lobotomy, and electroconvulsive shock therapy, believing that they interfered with patient's interpersonal learning, which he believed was the very source of their recovery. Schizophrenics were not lost souls, but more like normals than psychiatry suspected. All of us, Sullivan believed, had access to the schizophrenic process, particularly in the adolescent years, and in these experiences he found the link between the healthy and the insane personality.

It was also during this period that he first met Clara Thompson, life-long friend, professional colleague, disciple, and his training analyst, who introduced him to the work of Adolf Meyer and the psychobiosocial approach in psychiatry. Their relationship, intimate in every way but sexual, was probably the closest Sullivan had with any woman. They never married and he remained a bachelor his entire life.

In 1930, he moved to New York, where he opened a private practice and became involved in psychoanalytic politics. His fortunes declined somewhat as a result of the depression and he was forced to declare bankruptcy in 1932. Nevertheless, his professional activities on behalf of psychiatry continued. During this period he began attending seminars at Yale by Edward Sapir in personality and culture. Here Sullivan found that his writings were being used as collateral readings. He established ongoing contact with Harold Lasswell, the sociologist at the University of Chicago who collaborated with Sapir. Meanwhile, he continued to work with William Alanson White on the national scene promoting psychiatric education and research.

By the time the Zodiac Club got underway in New York, Sullivan's career was also gaining momentum. As a way to organize his professional activities, he launched the William Alanson White Foundation, incorporated in 1933. Under this rubric, he founded the Washington School of Psychiatry in 1936, which began as a way to bring psychiatry more into general medicine. It soon became an interdisciplinary school for training in a wide range of specialties. Then in 1938, Sullivan launched *Psychiatry*, an interdisciplinary journal. At the same time, in conjunction with William Alanson White, Sullivan became deeply involved in the politics of the American Psychiatric Association.

One of the only two books that Sullivan published in his lifetime also appeared during the period of the Zodiac Club, his *Conceptions of Modern Psychiatry* (1947).[17] These were the first William Alanson White Memorial Lectures, given by Sullivan before a public audience in October and November of 1939. They were printed in *Psychiatry* during 1940 and eventually reprinted in book form by the William Alanson White Foundation in 1947. Here Sullivan summarized his theories of adolescent and adult schizophrenia, outlined his methods for social re-education, and acknowledged his debt to his many intellectual mentors. Freud, whom he had never actually met, he said was one of them.

The big influences on his intellectual life, according to Sullivan, himself, were psychoanalysis, which he got through his own reading and through Clara Thompson's work with Sandor Ferenczi, and the psychobiosocial approach of Adolf Meyer, also a big influence on Thompson. There were also the writings of the Chicago sociologists, such as George Herbert Mead, cultural anthropologists like Bronislaw Malinowski, Edward Sapir, and Ruth Benedict, and the writings of the physicist, P. W. Bridgman, a man who had been significantly influenced by Jamesean pragmatism while an undergraduate at Harvard. Sullivan also showed that he was deeply immersed in the Chicago brand of American pragmatism, which was another of his connections to the earlier visionary tradition of Emerson and James.

Sullivan's conception of personality was like James's, in that he believed we had as many personalities as we had interpersonal relations. Since personality could only be known in interaction with others, Sullivan questioned whether or not the idea of a person was even really justified. What we are is not fixed, but malleable, on-going, and in a constant state of change.

In 1939, Sullivan left New York and moved to Baltimore, where he remained for the rest of his life. Beginning in 1940, he participated in the formation of national screening plans for the Selective Service, and in 1942 began teaching at the Chestnut Lodge, a hospital for psychotic patients.

He became seriously ill in 1945, but recovered enough to embark upon a new direction of inquiry, the contribution of the social sciences to world peace. As a final gesture, in collaboration with Gordon Allport and others, Sullivan helped produce the pioneering volume, *Tensions That Cause Wars*. He died in Paris, in 1949, just before the book was published.[18]

Karen Horney

Karen Danielson Horney, one of the few non-Jewish émigrés who fled to the United States from the Third Reich in the early 1930s, played a major role in Americanizing psychoanalysis. While the orthodox analysts prefer to see her as primarily a social theorist, her main contribution to American folk culture came through her differences with Freud over the nature of feminine psychology.[19]

Born in Hamburg, Germany in 1885, of Dutch and Norwegian parents, she married Oscar Horney, an attorney, in 1909 and produced three children before she was divorced. She received the MD at the University of Berlin in 1913, after which she became interested in psychoanalysis. She was analyzed by Karl Abraham and Hans Sachs, opened a private practice, and around 1919, joined the faculty at the Berlin Psychoanalytic Institute. Eventually, she would also ascend to membership and educational responsibilities in the International Psychoanalytical Association.

With regard to her primary professional accomplishments, however, during the next 13 years she produced a series of papers on the psychology of women which demonstrated that she was far in advance of her time in declaring the independent status of women's psychosexual development. Her ideas also showed that she differed significantly from Freud on concepts disciples such as Helena Deutsch and Karl Abraham thought so basic that Horney was eventually shunned from the society.[20]

Freud had very little to say about the psychology of women, except to solidify the images of dependence, motherhood, and male sex object, by maintaining that the feminine personality develops from penis envy. All young girls suffer neurotically from not having the visible male organ of power, according to Freud. Elaborating on Freud's thesis, Abraham further explained that the girl invents the theory of castration to explain why she has no male organ. Her childhood explanation is that she once had one, but it was cut off; the vagina is the remaining wound. Eventually resolving herself to the fact that she will never receive a penis, the young girl is able to substitute the wish for a penis with the desire to have a child by the father. The child develops an intense rivalry with the mother for the affections of the father, but these feelings go underground during the latency period. Eventually, these affections emerge again in adolescence as the search for an appropriate male object, in all likelihood one that reminds her of her father.

Helena Deutsch, being one of the key women in Freud's inner circle who defended this orthodox view, took Abraham's discussion one step further. She maintained that the woman must be masochistically subjected by the penis in order to discover her own vagina and that while sexual orgasm occurs for the male at copulation, it occurs for the female only at the moment she gives birth.[21]

Horney, always referring to her extensive clinical experience, tried to reconcile psychoanalysis with the reality of the feminine. Females, she maintained (still in Freudian terms), have their own independent experience of sexuality surrounding their genital organs. But these experiences empower rather than debilitate them. She also believed that Freud's formulation was offensive to women as well as contrary to biological science. Moreover, Freud seemed to be viewing the psychosexual development of males and females from the masculine point of view. Freud believed so much in the primacy of the phallus that the experience of the male sets the standard for what the female will do as the appropriate follower. Thus he had said, "We deal only with one libido, which behaves in a male way."[22]

Horney, on the other hand, following the philosopher and sociologist, Georg Simmel, and the psychoanalyst, Georg Groddeck, made a case for the explanation that we live in an atmosphere that is so thoroughly masculine that the radically different culture of the feminine is misinterpreted and ignored. "It seems to me," Horney concluded, "impossible to judge to how great a degree the unconscious motives for the flight from womanhood are reinforced by the actual social subordination of women."[23] Since much of psychoanalysis was based on clinical observations of the neurotic personality, the psychology that Horney went on to develop called, as well, for a more intensive study of healthy women.

By 1932, Horney's position among the orthodox had naturally become quite strained. Freud was also to have characterized her as "able," but "mean," a comment that was no doubt a virtual kiss of death for any further chances of advancement within the psychoanalytic community in Europe. As well, the political situation in Germany was becoming increasingly unstable, and while a non-Jew, and not in danger on that account, her biographer notes that to Horney it was obvious that the world around her, which she loved so dearly, was rapidly disintegrating. Just at that same time, as if a breeze from above, when Franz Alexander called from the United States to invite her to become associate director of the newly founded Chicago Psychoanalytic Institute, she accepted.

Horney, accompanied by her daughters, went to Chicago, where she spent 2 years at the Chicago Institute, working under Alexander, her former student from Berlin. She planned the analytic training program, taught courses to staff and candidates, for 5 hours each day carried on a patient practice, and managed to pass the state medical license exam with distinction. She also renewed her acquaintance with Erich Fromm, who came as a visiting lecturer in 1933. Horney, with Fromm and Frieda Fromm-Reichmann, had studied psychoanalysis together in Berlin. Now, according to her biographer, Horney became both intellectually and romantically involved with Fromm during his Chicago stay.[24] Horney also became the gracious hostess. She entertained Karl and William Menninger when they came through from Topeka. She also met Harry Stack Sullivan during this time, a man whom she would interact with again in New York.

Psychoanalysis in the United States during the early 1930s was an internecine war. The New York and Washington-Baltimore Societies were each vying for control of the American Psychoanalytic Association, which had recently declared its independence from the International Psychoanalytical Association over supervision and accreditation of candidates. The battle lines were drawn between the orthodox and the heterodox with regard to interpretation of Freud's ideas and between the European-trained analysts and their American-trained counterparts. The prize was, of course, who would become the Freud of the New World. In the midst of this commotion, for a variety of reasons, Horney moved to New York in 1934.

There she was also an outcast because of her non-conformist attitudes toward Freudian thought. The New York Society, meanwhile, was the oldest psychoanalytic group in the United States, and, as many of its older members had been with Freud in Vienna, the New York group saw itself as the last bastion against all infidels. Nevertheless, Horney was accepted for membership. Her accreditation was recognized and she began to supervise candidates.

Her real reference group seems to have been elsewhere, however. Erich Fromm moved to New York the same year she did and, taking up together again, they became close companions. Through him she met the Christian theologian, Paul Tillich and his wife Hannah, and leftist thinkers such as Max Horkheimer and Theodore Adorno. She also began a long and enduring relationship with the New School for Social Research, a veritable university in exile for European scholars fleeing Germany.

This was the era of the Zodiac Club and the years of Horney's greatest flowering. Her psychology became more informed by sociological and anthropological factors. In her lecturing she became charismatic, speaking to the inner life of her listeners as much as transmitting and analyzing information.

Her first book, *The Neurotic Personality of Our Time*, became a best seller. It went through 13 printings in 10 years and her paperback editions sold over a half million copies. Although based on lectures to a lay audience through the New School, she had written it, she said, for "psychiatrists, psychoanalysts, psychosociologists, [and] social workers."[25] She presented a new definition of neurosis based, not on repressed infantile sexuality, but on the driving need for love and appreciation. Lack of love, she said, led to behavior that was impelled by anxiety and expressed in the manner of an "indiscriminate hunger." Further, she believed that because emotional isolation was particularly widespread in modern America we suffer from a collective neurosis. The antidote was to develop warm and loving relationships, without overemphasizing the sexual component as the orthodox Freudians had done.

Her old student from Berlin and Chicago, Franz Alexander, gave the book grudging acceptance. John Dollard, the Yale sociologist, praised Horney for her "stubborn thinking through and literal realistic expression" of her patients' character. Margaret Mead thought the emphasis on cultural determinants a "creative hypothesis." In this new direction, Horney believed that the form of the neurosis was not universal across cultures but depends on its social circumstances. Even more horrifying to the orthodox analysts, she said that the Oedipus complex was not universal, but generated through cultural expectations and, moreover, a form of neurotic behavior in itself.

Such pronouncements caused much indignation in what remained of Freud's circle. In London, Ernest Jones proclaimed that, by deemphasizing sexuality, Horney had uttered a "dangerous half-truth." At the same time, American analysts castigated her for presenting Freud's work in too offhand a way. Their inevitable conclusion was that she was merely expressing repressed anger at her own father, confusing Freud for him.

But then, as if the theoretical deviations she had made from orthodox psychoanalysis in the past were not enough, Horney's work went through further refinements during the 1940s. She became convinced through her studies of social anthropology that the entire theory of psychoanalysis was not universal and value free but actually a culture-bound enterprise. She also called into question the necessity of deep interpretation. It was not always necessary, she thought, to enter into a protracted analysis of the patient's past if the present was not clearly understood. She thus came to believe that there is not an inviolable connection between events of early childhood and present symptoms. There only was a connection when current problems in fact led back to some precipitating cause.

More books from her pen on such subjects brought her additional popular acclaim and professional censure. Among the most popular were *Self-analysis* and *New Ways in Psychoanalysis*.[26] Finally, the political situation at the New York Institute became so tense over her further deviations that members such as Lawrence Kubie and Gregory Zilboorg, who controlled the education committee, conspired to revoke her status as a supervisor. When she was finally demoted to lecturer, she walked out, taking Clara Thompson and a band of students with her. As a result, the Karen Horney Institute for Psychoanalysis was founded, which continues to train analysts in the main themes of her life work: the psychology of women, social factors in the origin of the neurosis, and an experiential approach to clinical practice that is not rigidly confined by preconceived theories.

Then in 1951, Horney embarked upon the final excursion of her life, a 2-month, all expense paid trip to Japan, which had been underwritten by a grateful patient. She was accompanied by friends and family and led by 80-year-old D. T. Suzuki and his assistant Richard DeMartino. Horney lectured at the beginning of her stay, but the bulk of her time was spent traveling to Japan's religious shrines, marveling at the gardens, practicing some meditation, and being exposed to Zen philosophy. It was a profoundly important experience for her personally and she endeavored while there and on her return to compare the psychologies of East and West.

The trip was important for three reasons. First, when upon initial application a visa was denied to her, she discovered for the first time that instead of a mild mannered and very apolitical psychologist, the FBI and the House Committee on Un-American Activities had been tracking her as a communist sympathizer. Subsequently, when her dossier was released by the Freedom of Information Act, her biographer discovered that Horney was suspected of left wing sympathies because she had been actively helping refugees come into the United States during the 1930s, and she had been associated with the New School for Social Research, thought to be a subversive organization by paranoid zealots in the government. In addition, the post-mistress at her Maine retreat had kept the FBI constantly informed about supposed enemy agents with foreign accents coming and going to her home, as well as alleged Morse code communications sent and received to overhead planes.

Horney was originally denied entrance to postwar Japan on the grounds that she would spread the word of communism there. Eventually, however, she was permitted entry because of contacts she had in the Immigration Office.

Second, her connections to Suzuki and her interest in non-Western forms of depth psychology make her a significant transition figure from the psychoanalytic underground to the American counterculture movement.

Third, the trip had religious implications of great peace and joy for her that went far beyond her professional work. It was a final moment to savor. Although she did not yet know it, she was harboring cancer in its advanced stages. Several episodes during that previous year should have been taken as warning signs, but she ignored them at the time. She died in 1952, just 4 months after her return from Asia.

Erich Fromm

The man who was the most successful in getting the message of the new psychology across to the Western world was Erich Fromm, Hassidic mystic, Marxist, psychoanalyst, psychologist of religion, and interpreter of our contemporary *angst*. A recent analysis of Fromm divides his career into three parts: the period from 1929 to 1935, which was his Freudo-Marxist phase; 1936 to 1960, which marked his increasing preoccupation with religious and theological topics; and the final phase, 1960 to 1980, where he returned to Freud against the ever increasing tide of the human potential movement.[27] In this, with regard to psychoanalysis, he has been characterized as the loyal opposition, although the orthodox analysts would never have conceded even that.

Fromm was born March 23, 1900 in Frankfurt, Germany, the only child of a broken marriage. The father, a small wine merchant of modest means, was descended from a long line of rabbis and was very active in the Jewish community. He hoped his son would likewise become a rabbi, a fact which may have driven the young Erich toward an early interest in spirituality and away from aspirations of material gain.

As a child, Fromm received intense indoctrination into Talmudic studies. His most influential mentor was R. Nehemiah Nobel, a mystic, Goethe enthusiast, and neo-Kantian. According to one interpreter, Nobel-mixed conventional Talmudic instruction with mysticism, philosophy, socialism, and psychoanalysis, a curious combination of radicalism and orthodoxy, which Fromm seems to have adopted throughout the course of his own career. Through Nobel, Fromm became an ardent Zionist.

His most recent biographer recounts that, during this period, the two most traumatic experiences of Fromm's early life were the suicide of a young relative whom he admired, and the carnage of World War I. In the first instance, Fromm became preoccupied with questions of love and death; in the second, he developed a deep mistrust for authoritarian forms of control and for social institutions that fostered aggression and conflict. These were themes he would develop for the rest of his life.

From Frankfurt, Fromm went on to study sociology in Heidelberg. Here, he became acquainted with Chabad Hassidism through the socialist and mystic, R. Salman Baruch Rabinkow. Rabinkow's teachings spoke to the common people in terms of devotion and faith. He taught the inner Kabalistic symbolism of everyday activities, thus elevating simple acts to the level of religious observance. Meanwhile, Fromm continued with his academic studies and graduated from the University of Heidelberg with a doctorate in sociology.

He returned to Frankfurt in 1920 to edit a small Jewish newspaper, where he also became involved in establishing several secular Jewish study groups. Through these organizations he came into contact with such distinguished thinkers as Martin Buber and Gerschom Scholem. At the same time, he met Frieda Reichmann, a Jewish psychoanalyst, 10 years his senior and soon to be his wife, with whom he entered therapy. He went on to undergo supervisory training in Munich with Wilhelm Wittenberg and in Frankfurt with Karl Landauer. He followed these episodes with further psychoanalytic training under Hans Sachs and Theodore Reik in Berlin. Here, he also met Karen Horney, the woman with whom he would later become amorously involved in America.

Fromm married Frieda Reichmann in 1926. In 1927, with his new wife, Fromm returned to Southern Germany to begin clinical practice and to co-find the Frankfurt Psychoanalytic Institute. At this point in his life, he repudiated Zionism, gave up his religious observances, and declared himself a Trotskyite. Dividing his time between Frankfurt and Berlin, he became associated with the Frankfurt Institute for Social Research, where he steeped himself in Marxist social science. While he co-authored a landmark study of authoritarianism among German workers by combining standard polling methods with projective techniques, his major theoretical contribution at this time was the application of psychoanalysis to an understanding of matriarchal societies. Toward the end of this period, he also separated from his wife after 4 years of marriage.

In 1933 Fromm immigrated to the United States. He had been invited by Karen Horney to help launch the Chicago Psychoanalytic Institute, but differences between Horney and Alexander caused him to leave for New York after a year, where he opened a private practice and rejoined the faculty at the Frankfurt Institute, which had then recently re-located to Columbia University. This relationship lasted until 1938, when he had a falling out with leaders such as Herbert Marcuse and Theodore Adorno. Fromm was in his thirties during this period, a lay analyst, avowed socialist, and a Jewish émigré who considered himself a psychoanalyst, but who opposed Freud's sexual theories and Freud's excessive patriarchal orientation. It was an odd combination that made him an outsider, especially in psychoanalytic circles. But it was the right combination for reaching the American public at the time.

He was undoubtedly helped along in no small measure by his association with members of the Zodiac Club because of the broadening influence that their discussions would have on his thinking. They were also a conduit, through which he would come to understand the pragmatic, eclectic, and pluralistic character of American popular consciousness.

His first literary success was *Escape from Freedom*,[28] which came out in 1941 and subsequently went into 26 printings by 1965. He characterized this book as an attempt to show that totalitarian movements appealed to our deep-seated cravings to escape from the freedom we had originally won by overthrowing the feudal system of medieval times. Totalitarianism appealed because we were still not yet free enough to build a meaningful life based on reason and love. Hence in this incomplete state, we sought new security in submission to a leader, a race, or a state. Through this submission, we become automatons and enter willingly into acts of destructiveness. His great revelation was that the same seeds that led to the development of the Third Reich existed in the Free World, because the monopolistic character of industrialization always left the individual feeling insignificant and powerless. One solution, he believed, was to work for the collective mental health of our social relationships.

In an unprecedented editorial decision, Harry Stack Sullivan arranged in a special issue of *Psychiatry* for eight different reviews of Fromm's book. In keeping with the interdisciplinary nature of the journal, contributing were psychiatrists such as Thomas Gil and Ernest Hadley, anthropologists Ashley Montague and Ruth Benedict, the theologian Anton Boisen, the Baltimore analyst, Lewis Hill, and others. The orthodox analysts were, of course, annoyed with the work. Otto Fenichel, for instance, damned it with feint praise by saying that everything good in it was not new and everything new was not good. Nevertheless, coming on the eve of World War II, Fromm's interpretation helped to answer why Nazism arose. It was a question being asked worldwide and Fromm gave one of the first authoritative answers. The normal, socially adjusted person fears the burden of individual freedom and to alleviate the alienation gravitates instead toward submission to an organized authority.

In subsequent books, almost equally popular, Fromm continued to analyze the problem of alienation in modern society. His innovation was to rely extensively on the basic principles of depth psychology, but to substitute Freud's scheme of libido development for one related to the evolution of character in interpersonal terms. This new orientation he chose to call in 1955, "humanistic psychoanalysis," by which he meant that:

> The basic passions of man are not rooted in his instinctive needs, but in the specific conditions of human existence, in the need to find a new relatedness to man and nature after having lost the primary relatedness of the pre-human stage.[29]

Following Horney, Fromm's prescription for pervasive illness of our culture was love, the only satisfactory answer to modern existence. His *Art of Loving* (1956)[30] became another international best seller. The slim 112 page book went into 34 printings and was eventually translated into 17 languages, with over 1,500,000 copies sold in English alone. Practically no American female teenager alive between 1956 and 1970 was without a copy of this book. It was virtually emblematic of an era.

In it, Fromm examined love as art and theory, concluding that we experience different forms depending on the object. There is brotherly love, motherly love, erotic love, self-love, and love of God. This last was most revealing, because he cast his discussion into strictly secular terms, but spoke of spiritual love only in a theistic sense. God for him was generic, but his underlying assumptions after all rested with a neutered and secularized conception of God still embedded in the Judeo-Christian tradition. It was prime example of the American shadow culture, because it was not orthodox Christianity, Judaism, psychoanalysis, or science, but actually a blend of all these stripped of their linguistic trappings. It was highly relevant for a modern American audience, but it was certainly irrelevant for an orthodox Buddhist, Confucian, Taoist or other non-Western, non-theistic religious person. Nevertheless, it did address the spread of industrialism and its effects on the emotional life of the individual, since this was essentially a Western movement.

It was a book of many paradoxes. While Fromm espoused reason as the final standard, he maintained that love and a psychology of the unconscious was the key to fixing the problem. He also mixed his metaphors when referring to Asian ideas, juxtaposing East and West in the same sentence. Consequently, although he referred to Zen in his prescription for how to love when he enjoined the development of concentration, patience, and supreme concern for the object loved, his source was a Western interpreter of Zen, hence a text not from the orthodox Zen canon but from the literature of American folk psychology.

He took up the religious theme again in works such as *The Revolution of Hope* (1968),[31] not as popular as the rest of his works, but a clear statement again that we are trapped in meaningless work and compulsive consumption. The only answer is to reinstate the person and not materialism at the center of cultural existence. Under the steps to humanize a technological society, he called for psychospiritual renewal. He said, "Man's development requires his capacity to transcend the narrow prison of his ego, his selfishness, his separation from his fellow man, and, hence, his basic loneliness. This transcendence is the condition for being open and related to the world. . . ."[32] Mixing up the traditions again into the same soup, in a footnote he suggested that this is a common goal not only of Judeo-Christian religion as well as Buddhism but also of Marxist ideology.

Here, in such a work, we have completed the cycle, having transformed psychoanalysis from an orthodox Freudian system into a prescription for living that again injects the iconography of the transcendent back into the discussion. Nevertheless, when the counterculture movement came in the 1960s, Fromm became one of its harshest critics, returning to a singular defense of Freud's ideas. In 1959, he published *Sigmund Freud and his Mission*, in which he paradoxically reaffirmed Freud's view that:

> Belief in God is a fixation to the longing for an all protecting father figure, an expression of a wish to be helped and saved, when in reality man can, if not save himself, at least help himself, only by waking up from childish illusions and by using his own strength, his reason and skills.[33]

Reason and transcendence seem to clash in his thought, yet their juxtaposition was precisely the key to his success.

In addition to the fame afforded by his writings, Fromm continued to have both a professional career as a psychotherapist and a personal life. He had remarried in

1944, and in 1946 he became director of clinical training at the William Alanson White Institute until 1950, when he moved to Mexico. There he soon founded the Mexican Institute of Psychoanalysis. He traveled extensively in the Soviet Union during the 1960s preaching a popular form of Marxist Humanism. After his second wife died, he remarried again and moved to Switzerland in 1974. There, he died in 1980, by then somewhat forgotten by the American public.

Clara Thompson

Clara Mabel Thompson, American psychiatrist and psychoanalyst, was born in Providence, Rhode Island in 1893 from a long line of Calvinist seafaring men and dutiful New England housewives.[34] Her father was a self-made man who rose from the trade of tailor to become president of his own wholesale drug company. Her mother was a quiet but forceful housewife who created a loving family environment that made Clara's early life carefree and untroubled.

Thompson was graduated from Brown University in 1916 with honors and entered Johns Hopkins Medical School. She spent one summer at the St. Elizabeth's Hospital in Washington, DC, where she came under the influence of William Alanson White, which probably inclined her toward psychiatry as her medical specialty. After completing her clinical requirements she took a 3-year residency at the Phipps Clinic under Adolf Meyer, but she terminated this arrangement in 1925 when she entered psychoanalysis against Meyer's better judgment.

From Hopkins, Thompson went into private practice with the support of Harry Stack Sullivan, who had by then moved to Baltimore and was working at the Sheppard and Enoch Pratt Hospital. According to her biographer, Thompson and Sullivan had met in 1923. Thompson later described her relationship to Sullivan as the most important in her life. They continued to work closely together until Sullivan's death in 1949. It was Sullivan who had encouraged Clara Thompson to go to Budapest and be analyzed by Sandor Ferenczi, which she began in 1928 and continued until 1933. Thompson was to return and teach Sullivan what she had learned. But Ferenczi had deviated from Freud so markedly by then that he was quite outside the psychoanalytic circle. He believed that patients had to be loved and accepted by the therapist if they were to get well, while Freud enjoined against any emotional involvement with the patient whatsoever. As a result, Thompson's training later played against her in the eyes of the orthodox analysts when she went to New York City in 1933, where Sullivan had already moved. Here, she became an intimate in the Zodiac Club, fusing herself in many respects to Sullivan's own career.

Club interchange was marred in 1943, however, by a major schism. Horney walked out of the New York Psychoanalytic Society in 1941 after being demoted for her errant views, and with Clara Thompson and others set up the Association for the Advancement of Psychoanalysis. Two years later Horney drummed Fromm out of the organization for being a non-MD, as she, herself, had been shunned by the New York Psychoanalytic Society. The suspicion was, however, that Horney's personal relationship with Fromm had come to an end and the non-MD issue was the pretext for severing the ties that remained. Thompson and Sullivan resigned in protest and Thompson set up her own training institute with Sullivan, Erich Fromm, and his ex-wife Frieda Fromm-Reichmann. Thompson made it the New York branch of the Washington School of Psychiatry. This organization later became the William Alanson White Institute for Psychiatry, Psychoanalysis, and Psychology, which she headed from 1946 until her death in December, 1958.

In 1950, Thompson produced a masterful rendering of *Psychoanalysis: Evolution and Development*,[35] a review of theory and therapy from Freud's early formulations up to the work of Horney, Fromm, and Sullivan. She noted particularly the manner in which psychoanalysis had become more social and interpersonal in the hands of the American interpreters. She reserved the finale of the book for an examination of Sullivan's work and gave extensive comparisons between his theories and others in their little group. The work showed that psychoanalysis may have begun with Freud, but its finest reformulations had then recently emerged in the United States, especially around the work of Sullivan.

Her book was followed a year later by a symposium on Harry Stack Sullivan and his wide-ranging influence, held at the William Alanson White Institute. There, Thompson compared Sullivan to Freud and concluded that, while their approach to therapy was quite similar, their vision of personality was quite different. Sullivan believed that psychoanalysis was indeed appropriate with schizophrenics and that the bond that is established between therapist and patient, while interpersonal, is non-sexual. Freud believed that schizophrenics had decompensated so much that no direct patient–therapist relationship, and hence no free association, was possible. Sullivan maintained, however, that the patient's bizarre symptoms were a non-verbal way in which the schizophrenic was trying to communicate, and these could be read like any other symbol system. Not what was hidden inside the person, he said, but what went on between people was the arena where psychopathology developed. Thus, for Sullivan, the social milieu of the hospital ward became sine qua non, the testing ground for the reconstruction of health.

In the same symposium, Gardner Murphy and others compared Sullivan's work to the field theory of Kurt Lewin and the group work of J. L. Moreno, inventor of psychodrama. They outlined his extensive influence in social psychology, counting him as one of the seven greatest personalities to have shaped the field, and they showed his considerable influence on sociology in both theory and method. Indeed, Sullivan was responsible for hundreds of introductions between researchers in different disciplines and for providing a format through which psychoanalysis had become more extensively diffused throughout the social sciences.

Thus, the Zodiac Club played a major role in the history of psychoanalysis. One of the ways in which its members collectively did this was to shift the emphasis from sexuality to character development and from the patient's past to the problems of the present. Such deviations from analytic doctrine were precisely the reasons why psychoanalysis was able to permeate further into popular American culture, as the lives of the more influential members show. Beyond their era, others were to follow who performed the same task but in ways that stretched psychoanalysis beyond its very limits.

Rollo May

Also a member of the Sullivanian group and one who pushed such limits was Rollo May (1909–1994), former minister turned philosopher, existential psychotherapist, and co-founder of the humanistic movement in psychology. The first son and second child of a family with six children, May was born, April 21, 1909, in Ada, Ohio and raised in Michigan. He graduated in 1930 with a BA from Oberlin College, and from 1930 to 1933 taught at the American University in Salonika, Greece and also studied briefly with Alfred Adler. He received the Bachelors of Divinity degree in 1938 from Union Theological Seminary, where he had come under the influence of Paul Tillich and Reinhold Niebuhr. In 1938 he married Florence DeFrees and was ordained as a Congregational minister. But in the early 1940s, during a near-death struggle with tuberculosis, he lost his Christian faith and afterward resigned from the ministry. In 1949 he received the PhD summa cum laude from Teachers College, Columbia University, later receiving honorary doctorates from 10 or more institutions.

Turning to existentialism, under the profound influence of Paul Tillich, he absorbed the philosophies of Kierkegaard and Nietzsche, calling for recognition of both the creative and the demonic in our potential.[36] Emphasizing the optimistic, eclectic, and pragmatic nature of a uniquely American perspective in the tradition of William James, May soon became a major force in the flowering of existential and phenomenological psychotherapies within the burgeoning movement of humanistic psychology. As Carl Rogers proposed the client-centered approach in therapy and Abraham Maslow emphasized the self-actualizing aspect of personality, May defined the psychotherapeutic hour as a living laboratory—the existential crucible—of personality change.

While he had already published *The Springs of Creative Living* (1940) and *The Art of Counseling* (1939), in 1950 he produced his much acclaimed, *The Meaning of Anxiety* (1950, revised 1977), which was the first book to examine the stress on the organism at the dawn of the Atomic Age. He followed with *Psychology and the Human Dilemma* (1967, revised 1978), *Dreams and Symbols* (with Leopold Caliger, 1968), *Love and Will* (1969), *Power and Innocence: A Search for the Sources of Violence* (1972), *The Courage to Create* (1975), *Freedom and Destiny* (1981), *The Discovery of Being* (1983), *Politics and Innocence* (1986), *The Cry for Myth* (1992), and with Kirk Schneider, *The Psychology of Existence: An Integrative, Clinical Perspective* (1995).[37]

His most historic work, however, he published in 1958 with Henri Ellenberger and Ernest Angel, *Existence: A New Dimension in Psychiatry and Psychology*,[38] which later led to his being called the father of American existential psychology. Throughout most of his career he was associated with the William Alanson White Institute of Psychiatry, Psychology, and Psychoanalysis in New York City. There, he served as professor of psychiatry and as a supervisory and training analyst.

Variously, May was also lecturer in psychotherapy at the New School for Social Research (New York City, 1955–1976) and visiting professor at Harvard (1964), Princeton (1967), Yale (1972), Brooklyn College (1974–1975), Dean's Scholar at New York University (1971), and Regent's Professor at the University of

California, Santa Cruz (1973). After moving to California in 1975, he resumed his private practice and served in various ancillary capacities at the Saybrook Institute and the California School of Professional Psychology.

Like so many others, May fielded his own theory of personality. In one sense, his stages of personality were really dimensions of consciousness.

There is first of all, the condition of Innocence. This is the stage where the infant has no developed ego and has yet to go through the process of socialization. It is pre-egoic, pre-self-conscious, and premoral. The main drive is to fulfill one's basic needs. Then there is the stage of rebellion. This is the adolescent stage of developing one's ego through an exaggerated self-consciousness that defines the individual as different from the adults. It is the yearning for freedom, but without the acceptance of responsibility. Then there is the ordinary state of the normal adult ego. One aspires toward adjustment to the norms of society. Freedom is possible but too demanding, so one reverts back to social conformity and submission to the rules of authority. Finally, May recognizes the creative state. It is one of existential authenticity, beyond even self-actualization. While it is the acceptance of one's destiny, it is also the courage to be in the face of non-being.

May also proposed a theory of motivation based upon "the diamonic." In his book, *Love and Will*, he described the diamonic as:

> Any natural function which has the power to take over the whole person. Sex, eros, anger, rage, the craving for power are examples. The diamonic can be either creative or destructive and is normally both. . . . When this power goes awry and one element usurps control over the total personality we have 'diamonic possession,' the traditional name through history for psychosis.[39]

Eros—love, is a diamon, as is the will. Love in its creative aspect is seen as all good, but its destructive side produces infatuation, blind attachment, and a pathological sense of entitlement. Similarly, the will allows us to reach out and overcome inertia, to affect novel responses, and to assert ourselves against all odds. Its destructive side produces the will to power, overbearing control over others, the insistence of one's own way despite the weight of circumstances, and megalomaniacal behavior.

Frieda Fromm-Reichmann

Also a member of the Sullivanian group was Frieda Fromm-Reichmann. Born in 1890 in Königsberg, East Prussia, the eldest of five sisters, in the absence of any brothers, she was encouraged by her parents to attend medical school. She graduated from the University of Königsberg in 1914 with a specialization in psychiatry. During World War I she worked at the Institute of Kurt Goldstein, treating soldiers with injuries of the brain. Afterward, through Freud's works, she was led to analytic training at Heidelberg. There in 1926 she met Erich Fromm, whom she married. Together, they founded the Psychoanalytic Training Institute of Southwestern

Germany and opened an asylum for patient care. She separated from Fromm in 1933 when the Nazis came to power and made her way to the United States from France through Palestine, arriving in 1935. She became a part of Harry Stack Sullivan's circle and joined the staff at Chestnut Lodge in Maryland. There she developed a technique of modified psychoanalytic therapy of schizophrenia, which she called "psychoanalytically oriented psychotherapy." Rejecting Freud's sexual theories, she opted instead for a more motherly approach to the therapeutic relationship, working long term with schizophrenics, a population Freud thought immune to the effects of dynamic psychotherapy. Her most important work was *Principles of Intensive Psychotherapy* (1950). A former patient wrote of her treatment under Fromm-Reichmann in a fictionalized account, widely read as *I Never Promised You a Rose Garden.*[40]

Erik Erikson

Foremost among the American variants of psychoanalysis has been the work of Erik Erikson. Direct disciple of the Freud circle, he was analyzed by Anna Freud before he came to the United States and, after he arrived and left Harvard for Yale, became connected to Sullivan's circle. On his own he went on to establish an entire new field of endeavor subsequently referred to as psychohistory.

Erikson was born, June 15, 1902 near Frankfurt, Germany. His parents were Danish, having themselves been brought up in Copenhagen.[41] Little information exists on the father. The mother, widely read in Danish literature, was attracted to Kierkegaard and also read American writers such as Emerson. She was divorced before her son was born and when he was 3 years she moved from Denmark to Germany. In Karlsrhue, she met and fell in love with a Jewish physician. They married and afterward the boy was given the stepfather's name, Homberger, which he later changed to Erikson.

Erikson thus grew up in somewhat fortunate circumstances for the times. He attended primary school until he was 10 and then the Gymnasium, where he studied scientific and technical subjects and also the standard round of Greek, Latin, and German literature. He graduated when he was 18 and instead of going off to the university wandered around Europe for a year. When he returned to Karlsrhue he enrolled in the *Badische Landekunstschuke*, an art school where he remained a year before attending the more famous *Kunstakademie* in Munich. While he drew and etched, his primary medium was wood, enormous pieces which, along with other artists, he was able to show in Munich's fashionable Glaspalast.

Two years later, Erikson moved to Florence, still a wandering artist trying to find which road to take in the world. He had two important American friends in Italy, one, Peter Blos, a child psychoanalyst and writer, and the other, Oscar Stonorov, a Philadelphia architect turned sculptor. Later, after Erikson had returned to Karlsrhue and was preparing to teach art, Blos contacted him about a job teaching in a special school based on psychoanalytic principles.

Blos had been studying biology in Vienna and while there had met Dorothy Burlingame, a wealthy American woman with four children who was an analytic patient and close friends with Anna Freud. Burlingame had retained Blos to tutor her children in the sciences and drill them in German and during that time he, too, had come to know the Freud family. After 2 years had passed, although quite successful with the children, Blos began to have thoughts about leaving. Both Mrs. Burlingame and Anna Freud conspired, however, to keep him on by offering him the opportunity to establish a school of his own. He agreed, under the condition that he have an assistant. The man he had in mind was a brilliant young artist friend of his named Erik Erikson.

The women agreed and after preliminary negotiations, Erikson accepted the invitation. A building was purchased and the children, largely American and English boys and girls, were recruited mainly from the families of parents who were either patients themselves, or psychoanalysts-in-training.

Blos and Erikson were given complete freedom to establish the curriculum. Their choice was a progressive, open atmosphere based on the responsibilities of equal citizenship for all. There were no grades and children were taught as individuals. Intellectual subjects, such as science, language, and geography, were taught, as well as the arts and all forms of creative expression. It became a living laboratory for innovative education as well as a proving ground for the new area of psychoanalytic child psychiatry.

Erikson also underwent an analysis of his own during 1927 and 1928. Having been granted a scholarship, he traveled daily to Freud's home at Bergasse 19 to be seen by Anna Freud. At the same time, he studied clinical psychoanalysis with August Aichhorn, Edward Bibring, Helene Deutsch, Heinz Hartmann, and Ernst Kris, and he also received training in the educational methods of Maria Montessori. He was one of the few men to graduate from the *Lehrerinnenverein*, the Montessori Teacher's Association.

As well, in 1929 at a Mardi Gras Ball he met Joan Serson, a Canadian-American and teacher of modern dance who had been educated at Columbia and the University of Pennsylvania in sociology. They married a few months later and within a short time produced the first two of their three children. In all, Erikson remained 7 years in Vienna. The result was that, despite the fact that he had no advanced degree, the artist gradually became a husband, father, teacher, and a practicing psychoanalyst, himself.

Perhaps the most important theoretical development during this period became Erikson's interest in the spontaneous play of children. Between his own analysis and his work teaching, he became a pioneer in play therapy. Play, he found, was a means by which the symbolism of the unconscious could be expressed in children too small to engage in the traditional psychoanalytic method of free association employed with adults. Instead of merely getting the adults to recreate their past through analysis, it now became possible to study these developmental processes directly with children through the symbolism of play. These innovations were to have an important impact on the future development of child analysis.

In 1933, on the eve of Hitler's ascent to power, Erikson finished his analytic training and was advanced to full membership in the Vienna Psychoanalytic

Society. Afterward, he and his family left right away for Denmark. Through the help of Marie Bonaparte, herself an accomplished Freudian and member of the Danish Royal Family, Erikson tried to establish himself there. Circumstances were against him, however. Instead, through a chance meeting with Hans Sachs, close associate of Freud's and then a training analyst in Boston, Erikson's attention was drawn to America.

After some hurried arrangements, the Eriksons left for Boston and, having found suitable arrangements in an apartment on Memorial Drive in Cambridge, were settled in the New World by Christmas, 1933. Because of his status within the Vienna Psychoanalytic community, Erikson was afforded a superior welcome. He quickly found a half-time position at Harvard Medical School in psychiatry under Stanley Cobb and another half-time job with the personality theorist Henry Murray, working at the Harvard Psychological Clinic. He also began consultation work with the Judge Baker Guidance Center and he opened up a private practice in psychotherapy on Marlborough Street in Boston's fashionable Back Bay.

Erikson was now exposed to a new population of patients, and his horizons broadened considerably. In addition to his research with Harvard students, he came to treat American adolescents and the working class poor. Most of his research, however, began to focus not on neurotic children, but on moderately healthy college men. Meanwhile, his intellectual scope also expanded as he developed new relationships with such lights as Margaret Mead, Gregory Bateson, Scudder McKeel, Kurt Lewin, and Ruth Benedict, who all passed through Harvard during this time. Eventually a summary of his research appeared in the psychoanalytic literature and he became an important contributor to Henry A. Murray's *Explorations in Personality* (1938).[42]

Erikson's first stint in Cambridge lasted until 1936, after which he went to the Yale Institute of Human Relations. He soon became an instructor in psychiatry at Yale Medical School, and an assistant professor in the college. While at Yale, in addition to his family being enlarged by a third child, Erikson carried on research and became more deeply interested in anthropology. Here, he also came into contact with Harry Stack Sullivan and others already blending psychoanalysis with the social sciences.

Meanwhile, after his first year, through Scudder McKeel, Erikson arranged to spend time working with Sioux Indian children on the Pine Ridge Reservation in South Dakota. There he studied child-rearing practices, family relationships, and patterns of adolescent development. This work also allowed him to cast his psychoanalytic discussion of personality into a cross-cultural perspective.

"Observations on Sioux Education" appeared in print in 1939, just as the Eriksons left the East Coast for California.[43] In San Francisco Erikson set up an analytic practice with children and in Berkeley he became associated with Institute of Child Welfare at the University of California. His focus was again on normal children and predictions he might make about their future course of development, but his subject cohorts also gave him a good look at racial and class differences that became readily apparent in the lives of the children he encountered from the poorer sections of Oakland and Berkeley. He also had the opportunity to study the Yurok Indians of Northern California.

The war was also on and as a part of his contribution; Erikson worked with the Office of Strategic Services and the Committee on Morale. He wrote on submarine psychology, the possibility of doing psychological research in internment camps, and the interrogation of prisoners, and he contributed various analyses of mental imagery in Hitler's speeches. Some of his work on this last topic appeared in Harry Stack Sullivan's journal *Psychiatry* and Murray and Kluckhohn's pioneering volume *Personality in Nature, Society and Culture*, which is to say that more and more Erikson became an important contributor to the culture and personality movement in both psychology and psychiatry. At the same time, he was becoming a major re-interpreter of psychoanalysis in a social context.

The first of the epoch works of his career, *Childhood and Society*, appeared in 1950. In addition to the social and cultural aspects of personality, he presented his now famous longitudinal theory of personality development. It was a major revision of Freud's original scheme of infantile sexual stages, but now writ much larger across the entire human life span. Erikson defined the life cycle in eight stages, each with its own developmental tasks that the person either succeeded or failed to achieve.

At the oral and sensory stage, the issues are trust versus mistrust. At the muscular and anal stage, the issues are autonomy versus shame and doubt. At the genital and locomotor stage, the issues are initiative versus guilt. During the latency period, the issues are industry versus inferiority. During puberty and adolescence, the issues are the establishment of basic identity versus falling into role confusion. In young adulthood, the issues are intimacy versus isolation. In adulthood they are generativity versus stagnation. And in the final stage of maturity, the closing years of life, they are ego integrity versus despair.[44]

Erikson followed with other works, but the one for which he is also most well known was *Identity, Youth and Crisis* (1968).[45] His primary construct was the ego's resolution of its place in its social context. Personality, the self, and the construct of the person, commensurate with the developing ego psychology of his time, was identity. Without a stable sense of identity, the individual went into an unstable identity confusion, which became popularly known through Erikson's work as the identity conflict. Adolescents were particularly prone to it in the transition to young adulthood, but the era of the 1960s had more intense transformations going on with the young, largely having to do with shifting values in society, the rejection of white middle class goals, norms, and expectations and a movement toward experimentation with heretofore unheard of life styles on a wider scale than the dominant culture could fathom.

The concept first emerged in the clinical treatment of mental abnormalities experienced by war veterans. Erikson wrote:

> Most of our patients, so we concluded at that time, had neither been 'shellshocked' nor become malingerers, but had through the exigencies of war lost a sense of personal sameness and historical continuity. They were impaired in that central control over themselves for which, in the psychoanalytic scheme, only the 'inner agency' of the ego could be held responsible. Therefore, I spoke of a loss of 'ego identity.'[46]

Erikson developed this concept to apply not only to psychopathology but also to cases of exceptional abilities, such as the creative genius found in authors such as George Bernard Shaw and William James. It was also a phenomenon that could be identified with the striving of entire groups of people, such as Blacks involved in the American Civil Rights Movement. Erikson's ideas burst upon the wider cultural scene just when psychoanalysis began to dominate clinical teaching in psychology and psychiatry and an expansive postwar period had begun in American culture, though 20 years later psychoanalysis itself had begun to wane. At the time, his was a new psychology of the whole person, the individual now understood in a cultural context, yet his ideas still had all the elements of the older more strictly Freudian psychology embedded within them.

Just before *Childhood and Society* broke upon the scene, however, Erikson became embroiled in a controversy with the Regents at the University of California over a loyalty oath they required renouncing all forms of communism. Erikson, of course, was no communist but he was more appalled at the fascistic tendencies he saw in the McCarthyite movement to root out not only suspected communists, but anyone else with deviant new thoughts. He avoided being fired over not taking the loyalty oath by publicly declaring that he had no allegiance to communism. But just as soon as the air had cleared, he wasted no time in resigning.

Through contacts at the Menninger Clinic in Topeka, he was offered a position at the Austin Riggs Center in Stockbridge, Massachusetts. A rural village to be sure, but since the Riggs was a leading center of psychoanalytic training on the east coast, he accepted. He also began an exhausting schedule by commuting at the same time to Pittsburgh to teach at the Western Psychiatric Institute.

Over the next 20 years Erikson published numerous papers on psychoanalytic topics, received hundreds of letters, and lectured around the world, even spending an extended period at one point in India. Two of his several books that broke new ground during this period were *Young Man Luther* (1958) and *Gandhi's Truth* (1969), massive biographical studies that established the term psychohistory as synonymous with the Eriksonian and psychoanalytic mode of interpretation.[47]

In the early 1960s Erikson returned to Harvard to teach in the Social Relations Department, an interdisciplinary program in the social sciences that had been started by Gordon Allport, Clyde Kluckhohn, Talcott Parsons, and Henry Murray in 1946 to counter the trend toward reductionism in the laboratory sciences. There, Erikson taught enormously popular courses on the human life cycle and led a continuing seminar on the lives of great historic figures.

Eventually, he and his wife began to spend more and more time in California, but in the 1980s, they were drawn back to Harvard through the efforts of Dr. John Mack, a professor of psychiatry at Harvard Medical School, where the Erik and Joan Erikson Center was established through the Cambridge City Hospital. This particular wing of the Psychiatry Department at Harvard had become a hotbed of radicalism in the late 1970s. While psychoanalysis, behaviorism, and cognitive science continued to dominate the Psychology Department in the School of Arts and Sciences at Harvard, vast innovations in psychology were still taking place in the various departments of psychiatry at the medical school that were associated with the different teaching hospitals. At the Cambridge City Hospital, Charles Ducey, who had worked with Murray, and Daniel Brown, a clinical psychologist interested in hypnosis and Buddhist meditation, ran a seminar on cross-cultural approaches to psychoanalysis. Mitchell Weiss, who taught traditional outpatient psychiatry, was also a specialist in Indian Aryavedic medicine. John Mack, a tenured professor, was known for his psychological biography on Lawrence of Arabia and had started the Center for Psychological Studies in the Nuclear Age. He was interested in promoting a dialogue between Russians and Americans and in studying children's perceptions of "The Enemy." He was also an est graduate and a friend of Werner Erhard, who gave the keynote presentation at the opening of the Erikson Center. Mack then entered into perhaps the most controversial work of his career, phenomenological accounts of alien abduction.[48]

Largely as a result of the Erikson Center and along with close personal support given by other faculty in comparative religions and the psychology of religion at Harvard, the Eriksons moved back to Cambridge. While Erikson and his wife became beloved personalities, his psychology has become worldwide. His model of developmental stages, for instance, ranks with those of Kohlberg and Piaget as permanent fixtures in the field of child development.

The most important point, however, is that as a psychoanalytic theoretician, as one who had known Freud and been directly analyzed in the old Vienna tradition, from the post war period to the present, Erikson had no rivals equivalent in stature in America. In a very real sense, out of all the other voices, and quite without meaning to, it was he who became the American Freud.

Notes

1.   Köhler, W., & Winter, E. (1925). *The mentality of apes.* London: K. Paul, Trench, Trubner & Company; New York: Harcourt, Brace & Company.

2.   Skinner, B. F. (1938). *The behavior of organisms: An experimental analysis.* Upper Saddle River, NJ: Prentice-Hall; New York: Appleton-Century-Crofts.

3.   The entire field was later rechristened behavior science and Skinner recommended at that point that we discard the outmoded word psychology.

4.   Koch, S. (1992). Psychology's Bridgman vs. Bridgman's Bridgman. *Theory & Psychology, 2*(3), 261–290.

5.   Stevens, S. S. (1951). *Handbook of experimental psychology.* New York: Wiley & Sons.

6.   Boring (1929/1950).

7.   Eagle, M. N. (1987). The psychoanalytic and the cognitive unconscious. In R. Stern (Ed.), *Theories of the unconscious and theories of the self* (pp. 155–189). Hillsdale, NJ: Analytic Press; Kihlstrom, J. F. (1987). The cognitive unconscious. *Science, 237*(4821), 1445–1452; Shevrin, H., & Dickman, S. (1980). The cognitive unconscious: A necessary assumption for all psychological theory? *American Psychologist, 35*(5), 421–434; Piaget, J. (1973). The affective unconscious and the cognitive unconscious. *Journal of the American Psychoanalytic Association, 21*(2), 249–261.

8.   Cartwright, D. (1979). Contemporary social psychology in historical perspective. *Social Psychology Quarterly, 42*(1), 82–93; Cartwright, D. (1948). Social psychology in the United States during the Second World War. *Human Relations,*

1(3), 333–352; Nicholson, I. (1997a). The politics of scientific social reform, 1936–1960: Goodwin Watson and the Society for the Psychological Study of Social Issues. *Journal of the History of the Behavioral Sciences, 33*, 39–60.

9. The dating of this distinction is purely arbitrary. Sociology, not yet even a recognized discipline at Harvard in the late 1890s, had been implicitly defined by at least two streams: growing railroad interests and their influence on defining economics in the field of business, and the fledging Social Gospel Movement emanating from Francis Greenwood Peabody's course on the "Ethics of the Social Question," originally offered in the Divinity School. Inner experience versus the social contract was not a new issue when applied to the emergence of depth-psychology.

10. Hale (1995).

11. Freud, S. (1913). *The Interpretation of dreams* (A. A. Brill, Trans.). New York: The Macmillan Company; London: George Allen and Unwin.

12. Others included Arlow, Bornstein, Brenner, K. R. Eissler and R. Eissler, Greenacre, Hartmann, Isakower, Jacobson, E. Kris and M. Kris, Lewin, Loewenstein, Mahler, Nunberg, and A. Reich.

13. Hale, 1995, Vol. 1.

14. Horney (1937); Fromm, E. (1941). *Escape from freedom.* New York: Farrar & Rinehart.

15. I have relied heavily on Perry, H. S. (1982). *Psychiatrist of America: The life of Harry Stack Sullivan.* Cambridge, MA: Harvard University Press, but also referred to Mullahy, P. (1973). *The beginnings of modern American psychiatry: The ideas of Harry Stack Sullivan.* Boston: Houghton Mifflin.

16. Perry, H. S. (1982). *Psychiatrist of America: The life of Harry Stack Sullivan.* Cambridge, MA: Harvard University Press.

17. Sullivan, H. S., & Mullahy, P. (1947). *Conceptions of modern psychiatry.* William Alanson White Memorial Lectures. Washington, DC: W. A. White Psychiatric Foundation.

18. Cantril, H. (1950). *Tensions that cause wars, common statements and individual papers by a group of social scientists brought together by UNESCO.* Urbana: University of Illinois Press.

19. Natterson, J. M. (1966). Karen Horney, 1885–1952. In F. Alexander, S. Eisenstein, and M. Grotjahn *Psychoanalytic pioneers* (pp. 450–451). New York: Basic Books; Quinn, S. (1988). *A mind of her own: The life of Karen Horney.* New York: Addison Wesley.

20. The following discussion follows closely Quinn's significant chapter, "Freud, Horney, and the Psychoanalytic View of Women," pp. 205–241.

21. Quinn (1988).

22. Quinn, 1988, p. 233.

23. Quinn, 1988, p. 225.

24. Quinn (1988).

25. Quinn, 1988, p. 308.

26. Horney, K. (1942). *Self-analysis.* New York: W. W. Norton & Company; Horney, K. (1939). *New ways in psychoanalysis.* New York: W. W. Norton & Company.

27. In the following section, I have followed closely the biographical chapter from Burston, D. (1991). *The legacy of Erich Fromm* (pp.1–29). Cambridge, MA: Harvard University Press.

28. Fromm (1941).

29. Fromm, E. (1955). *The sane society.* New York: Holt, Reinhart & Winston, p. viii.

30. Fromm, E. (1956). *The art of loving.* New York: Harper.

31. Fromm, E. (1968). *The revolution of hope, toward a humanized technology.* New York: Harper & Row.

32. Fromm, 1968, p.135.

33. Fromm, E. (1959). *Sigmund Freud and his mission, an analysis of his personality and influence.* New York: Harper, p. 101.
34. Perry, H. S. (1980). Clara Thompson. In B. Sicherman, & C. H. Green (Eds.), *Notable American women: The modern period. A biographical dictionary* (pp. 680–683). Cambridge, MA: Belknap Press of Harvard University.
35. Thompson, C. (1950). *Psychoanalysis: Evolution and development.* New York: Hermitage House.
36. May used the word diamonic.
37. May, R. (1939) *The art of counseling.* New York: Abingdon Press; May, R. (1940). *The springs of creative living, a study of human nature and God.* New York, Nashville: Abingdon-Cokesbury Press; May, R. (1950). *The meaning of anxiety.* New York: The Ronald Press Company (revised 1977, New York: W. W. Norton); May, R. (1967). *Psychology and the human dilemma.* New York: W. W. Norton & Company; Princeton, NJ: Van Nostrand (revised 1979, New York: W. W. Norton & Company and Princeton, NJ: Van Nostrand); May, R., & Caliger, L. (1968). *Dreams and symbols.* New York: Basic Books; May, R. (1969a). *Love and will.* New York: W. W. Norton & Company; May, R. (1972). *Power and innocence: A search for the sources of violence.* New York: W. W. Norton & Company; May, R. (1975). *The courage to create.* New York: Bantam Books; May, R. (1981). *Freedom and destiny.* New York: W. W. Norton & Company; May, R. (1983). *The discovery of being: Writings in existential psychology.* New York: W. W. Norton & Company; May, R. (1986). *Politics and innocence.* Dallas, TX: Saybrook Publishers, New York: W. W. Norton & Company; May, R. (1991). *The cry for myth.* New York: W. W. Norton & Company; May, R., & Schneider, K. J. (1995). *The psychology of existence: An integrative, clinical perspective.* New York: McGraw-Hill.
38. May, Angel, & Ellenberger (1958).
39. May, 1969a, p. 123.
40. See Fromm-Reichmann, F. (1950). *Principles of intensive psychotherapy.* Chicago: University of Chicago Press, and Fromm-Reichmann, F. (1960). *Principles of intensive psychotherapy.* Chicago: Phoenix Books; Also Hornstein, G. A., & Fromm-Reichmann, F. (2000). *To redeem one person is to redeem the world: The life of Frieda Fromm-Reichmann.* New York: Free Press. Also, Greenberg, J. (1964). *I never promised you a rose garden.* New York: New American Library.
41. This section relies heavily on Coles, R. (1970). *Erik H. Erikson: The growth of his work.* Boston: Little, Brown.
42. Murray, H. A., and the Workers at the Harvard Psychological Clinic. (1938). *Explorations in personality: A clinical and experimental study of fifty men of college age.* New York: Oxford University Press.
43. Erikson, E. (1939). Observations on Sioux Education. *Journal of Psychology, 7,* 101–156.
44. Erikson, E. (1950). *Childhood and society.* New York: W. W. Norton.
45. Erikson, E. (1968). *Identity, youth, and crisis.* New York: W. W. Norton.
46. Quoted in Nisbet, R. A. (1968, March 31). *Review of Identity, youth, and crisis by Erik Erikson. New York Times.*
47. Erikson, E. (1958). *Young man Luther: A study in psychoanalysis and history.* New York: W. W. Norton; Erikson, E. (1969). *Gandhi's truth: On the origins of militant nonviolence.* New York: W. W. Norton.
48. Until his recent untimely death, the late John Mack had been investigating claims of alien abduction. Mack, J. E. (1995). *Abduction: Human encounters with aliens.* New York: Ballantine Books.

Chapter 6
Jung and Complex Psychology

> *My complex psychology was in place long before I met Freud.*
> C. G. Jung

Jung's early interest in a dynamic psychology of the subconscious is evident in Aniela Jaffé's biography, *Memories, Dreams, Reflections* (1963a), historically put forward as a book by Jung himself.[1] There, Jaffé has Jung recounting from a young age his preoccupation with dreams, visions, and inner psychic events related to an understanding of his own personality.[2] We see this interest again in 1898 when Jung read DuPrel, Swedenborg, Passavant and others, and decided, because of the absence of any such dynamic language in the prevailing mental science of the times, to go into psychiatry as a specialty. His dissertation on Hélène Preiswerk, his studies of the Word Association Test, and his psychotherapeutic work with hospitalized schizophrenics under Bleuler transformed a youthful interest into a full-fledged and life-long quest for a dynamic psychology of the interior life.

Early on, Jung followed James, Janet, Flournoy, and Myers on the reality of the buried idea. He was, after all, a 20th-century exponent of the symbolic hypothesis, but in the tradition of the late 19th-century psychologies of transcendence. His conception was that psychic elements had broken off from waking consciousness, where they floated around in the subconscious, acting according to laws of their own. Moreover, they carried with them a certain amount of energic valence. In their continued evolution, these subconscious elements attracted similar experiences to themselves and grew in psychic power by appropriating the energy of those other fragments, until they were strong enough to present themselves above the surface by bursting forth into the field of waking consciousness as a physical or psychological symptom, or possibly even in the appearance of a full-blown, distinct personality. One sees this in mediumship, as well as hysterical symptoms and cases of multiple personality. Such psychic elements Jung came to call complexes. More controversially, Jung also held that such complexes might also be influenced by motifs deeply within the person, from a universal substrate, creating images that had never before been conscious. Their origin, he would maintain, was the collective unconscious, a suprapersonal substrate common to all humanity. He would later come to call this dynamic picture of the total psyche by the name complex psychology, an

E. Taylor, *The Mystery of Personality*, Library of the History of Psychology Theories, DOI 10.1007/978-0-387-98104-8_6, © Springer Science+Business Media, LLC 2009

appellation he actually preferred to analytical psychology, as his theories have come
to be known in common parlance.

This psychology Jung seemed at first to set aside during the years he was with
Freud, during which he produced no new significant original work of his own. His
Psychology of Dementia Praecox (1906)[3] was translated into English by Frederick
Peterson and A. A. Brill in 1909, to which Peterson appended an introduction. This
earlier version is a rare edition of the work, which was re-issued in 1934 by Brill,
minus Peterson's introduction. The later issue, which is the version universally cited
by psychoanalysts-turned historians, was then made out to be primarily a Freudian
document, which it was not.

In that work, Jung's research with schizophrenics had convinced him that while
psychotics may have experienced a break with external material reality and apparently live in a world of their own fantasies that was heavily influenced by motifs
from the collective unconscious, there was internal consistency to their pathology.
One had to find ways to enter into this world and locate the central concepts, memories, and experiences that organize it. In that way, a rapport can be established
where before there was none, and a dialogue initiated in which the patient, cut off
from everyone else, plays a key part along with the therapist in order to return to
normal functioning. The attempt to understand the content of the schizophrenics'
interior worldview led Jung to compare their hallucinations to those of dreams
and primitive cultures, as well as to the more primitive developmental state of
children, a contribution that had profoundly affected Freud's ideas on the same
subject.

There were significant differences, however. When Freud talked about resistance,
he meant the attempt of the ego to keep unacceptable impulses below the surface of
consciousness. Jung's idea of a complex involved not only the notion that powerful ideas float around in the unconscious, drawing their energy from among other
sources, long-term stress, repressed memories of trauma, and the experience of unresolved intrapsychic conflict. They might also derive from deeper levels of the psyche, which Jung believed represented as much a universal reservoir of the highest
and best in our humanity, which is the source of our urge toward integration and
wholeness, as well as the vast primitive domain of the instincts, including the psychopathology that comes from a complete disintegration of personality.

The experience with Freud was intense, and the separation had large consequences for Jung because the break was like a divorce, or a death in the family,
as Jung had been embraced as Freud's heir apparent to the psychoanalytic movement and groomed as his successor to the literature, the apparatus, and the ideas to
which Freud had so closely identified.[4] They had differed over the nature of psychic energy, which eventually revealed entirely different conceptions of personality
and consciousness, but Jung was also struggling with the problem that as long as
he was ensconced within the psychoanalytic bubble Freud had created, he was not
himself. After his break with Freud, Jung resigned his appointment as lecturer at the
University of Zürich, cut back his therapeutic practice, resigned his editorship of the
psychoanalytic journal he had been editing since 1908, and turned within. As Freud
had done after 1896, Jung entered a period of deep inward reflection; Ellenberger

called it a "creative illness"; Jung, however, referred to it as his confrontation with the unconscious.[5]

Most of us live our entire lives oriented to the demands of the external environment without ever understanding that there are other worlds within. Some accident, a temporary illness, possibly a vision or a near-death experience, a certain poetic sensitivity, a religious quest, or simply an active urge to understand more about ourselves may push us beyond the immediate barriers that prevent us from even acknowledging the reality of the unconscious. Its exploration is fraught with psychic dangers and for these reasons most turn away. But in the lives of many others, a moment comes when we not only discover the existence of a vast domain within, but are faced with a choice that may end up having lifetime consequences, to either go forward with such an exploration or turn away from it, possibly forever. What hangs in the balance is what kind of person we shall elect to become and to what extent we shall come to know ourselves. Dangerous though it may be, Jung came to believe that one must take the risk if growth and transformation toward a fully embodied self-hood is to take place. This begins with some initial confrontation between consciousness and the unconscious, such as that which began for Jung after his break with Freud.[6]

Jung followed his dreams closely and also experienced intense images in the waking state. The work he produced, but never published during this time, was "Seven Sermons to the Dead," basically a mythological paean to the personality and life style he was leaving behind. But the real tome that gave an account of what he was going through inwardly has come to be known as "The Red Book," in which he kept his recopied drawings and visions and their psychological commentary, derived from a more tentative notebook he referred to as "The Black Book." According to the Jung scholar Sonu Shamdasani, however, "The Red Book" was not a diary, but a literary work about a new kind of psychology.[7]

Among other strategies on which he relied, such as dream interpretation and free association, Jung mastered the technique that he would later refer to as active imagination or "visionary meditation." It was a method of lowering the horizon of waking consciousness so that the level of dream imagery now came into the waking state, where consciousness could enter into a more direct dialogue with the unconscious. The dialogue began with meditation on an image, since the imaginal is the doorway into the unconscious, and thereafter the image would eventually begin to undergo its own process of internal transformation.

The difference between Freud and Jung on this matter is that Freud relied on free associations and the description of dreams to get at the patient's unconscious material. It was all primarily verbal. In this sense, Freud's method did not differ from any other practiced at the time, such as that developed by DuBois or Dejerine, where therapy was all talk. Among other things, Jung's approach was more imaginal. He drew and painted what he could not intellectually articulate and later encouraged his patients to enter into such artistic productions, not to exhibit in the art galleries, or simply to develop their artistic sensibilities, but as mere process activity. It was based on the idea that often the hands know how to solve a riddle with which the intellect struggles in vein. Eventually, such activity began to depict interior domains beyond the waking state which contained numinous material never before made conscious, yet nevertheless was an integral part of the person's psychic make up. Jung did, however, credit Freud's method of free association as the origin of his own newer approach.[8]

Jung employed the technique of active imagination in composing "The Red Book."[9] The Jung scholar, Wendy Swan, has studied this period most intensively, focusing on what Jung said about active imagination as an emerging technique, after which she demonstrated its application in the work of one of Jung's analysands at the time, Tina Keller.[10] Her investigations have shown that Jung himself published accounts of his patients' experiences with the technique; he used the visionary paintings of Christiana Morgan[11] as the basis for the *Visions Seminar* (1930–1934/1997) and the mandalas of Kristine Mann[12] for his essay "A Study in the Process of Individuation" (1950/1969a).

Regarding the creative nature of the interior quest, when Jung bolted from the psychoanalytic fold, Freud and his followers were worried that he had been so closely identified with the psychoanalytic vanguard that he would take the movement with him, as far as international recognition was concerned. The fact that dozens of US newspapers from small towns to big cities reviewed Jung's *Psychology of the Unconscious* (1916a)[13] was an indication of the widespread popularity of dynamic psychotherapy, which, although the historians tend to focus on its use in the treatment of psychopathology, was also seen as a vehicle for self-knowledge and higher consciousness in popular high culture.

Individuation, or the coming to self-hood by means of the transcendent function, became the new focus of Jung's research.[14] Essentially, as personality develops, the ego takes control of the executive functions required to adjust primitive impulses to the demands of the external world. At a certain point, however, a confrontation with the unconscious begins. This is the beginning of the dialog between the ego and the inner, larger and more all-encompassing self of the person in which control of personality shifts from the ego to the self as the person matures spiritually throughout the course of their life.

World War I began in 1914, just as Jung was still immersed in his creative illness in neutral Switzerland, and as he began to emerge from this deep inwardly directed period, the war was coming to an end. Still, even before the Clark Conference in 1909, as a result of his earlier connections to Adolf Meyer and the American circle around William James and James Jackson Putnam, Jung had continued to treat members of the McCormick and Rockefeller families, extraordinarily wealthy members of the American aristocracy. In 1916, Edith Rockefeller endowed the Analytical Psychology Club in Zurich.[15] The Club was organized around the analysands who had come in increasing numbers and was designed to provide a social outlet during their stay in Zurich, which sometimes lasted several years. Around the club other gatherings formed, made up of physicians whom Jung met with regularly to discuss his ideas, and those who were closest to Jung as both his analysands and assistants, to whom he referred patients which he would see simultaneously or take on later, or he would start with and whom these assistant analysts would continue to see alone. Collectively, this assemblage was his inner circle, mainly in Zurich, and which, along with the later Eranos conferences, started at Ascona by Olga Froebe-Kapetyn, and finally his courses at the Swiss Technical Institute, became the collective intellectual platform from which Jung would continue to develop and try out his ideas.[16]

Jung's lectures were always filled with patients as well as professionals interested in his work. Early on, there was also a contingent of wealthy upper-class women from the Zurich well-to-do who became known as the "fur-coat ladies." They sat in the back and at times they would overwhelm the lecture hall and dominate Jung's attention during the questions. They represented yet another contingency of what came to be referred to somewhat pejoratively as "Jung's women." This was a significant circle of students, analysands, and occasionally, it has always been rumored, paramours who stayed near him sometimes for decades, even a lifetime.[17] Some, such as Toni Wolff, significantly influenced Jung's work. Others were his assistants in his immediate circle, such as Maria Moltzer and Ruth Bailey, and later Marie Louise von Franz and Aniela Jaffé, while still others were analysands. In the early days this included such figures as Beatrice Hinkle, Eleanor Bertine, Esther Harding, Constance Long, and later Kristine Mann, Francis Wickes, and Christiana Morgan. Still later were Jane Cabot Reid and Carol Sawyer Baumann. The most immediate group was subsequently referred to as "The Valkyries." In one sense, out of the milieu they created, the outline for an archetypal psychology of the feminine would emerge and then disappear again, then reappear, often beyond the ken of Jung himself, a man struggling to come to terms with the repressed feminine within his own unconscious, even though he had been the one to launch these women on the process of individuation in the first place.[18]

His system was rapidly jelling at the time, as we have said, not just around the treatment of psychological pathology, but around the idea of a growth-oriented dimension to personality. According to the Jung scholar, Amy Colwell Bluhm, who has reconstructed the evolution of Jung's conception of individuation, the progression of Jung's thought in these early years is significant, as his major tenets move from nascent suggestions to amplified concepts.[19] The process of individuation, along with Jung's notions of the collective unconscious, the persona, the anima and animus, the transference, psychic compensation, the transcendent function, the archetypes, and the self, all go through marked development in this relatively short period of his thought.

Archetypes and the Collective Unconscious

The archetypes, Jung considered to be inborn patterns of apprehension based on the evolution of biological structures in the brain, though they were susceptible to modification by consciousness depending on the extent to which a person remained passive and therefore controlled by their indigenous forms or proactive, able to direct their form toward creative growth. They appear most clearly in dreams. According to Jung, dreams were not wish fulfillments, but "a spontaneous self-portrayal, in symbolic form, of the actual condition of the unconscious."[20] And in the same manner that dreams were a way in which the unconscious was able to communicate with waking consciousness, archetypes were the mediating links between the personal unconscious and the collective unconscious. According to Shamdasani, following the ideas of Jakob Burkhardt, Jung began to talk about primordial images in his writings in 1911, to which he had given the name archetypes by 1916. By this term he meant phylogenetic mythological images residing in a suprapersonal, collective reservoir he called the collective unconscious within each person. The process of self-realization was inherent to this domain; a journey Jung believed was quickened by analysis. For Jung, the existence of such a collective reservoir was proven in dreams, as their analysis showed an inherent relation between the hallucinations of the psychotic, myths of primitive cultures, and children's fantasies.

Honegger's dream of the solar phallus man became for Jung a paradigm case. Honegger was a psychotic patient who described a hallucination previously described in an old Mithraic religious text about which he could have had no previous knowledge.[21] Likewise, Kristine Mann's vision of the lotus and the star, which she painted as one of her crowning mandalas in a series depicting her journey toward individuation, had been described in a Chinese Taoist text centuries earlier which she had never seen and about which she, too, had no prior knowledge.[22] One only has to look beyond the borders of Western culture to discover the 1,600-year-old tradition of the *alaya-vijnana*, or storehouse consciousness in Chinese Mahayana Buddhism, to recognize that it is the complete absence of the iconography of the collective unconscious that is so shocking in the West, not that it is scientific blasphemy to propose it.

Jung's point was that just as dreams may depict the archaic past of the individual, archetypes reflected the collective past of the race, chiefly through the lines of one's ancestors. Just as ontogeny could recapitulate phylogeny in the biological realm, it could do so as well in the psychic domain. Totems that unite a person with their ancestors, the performance of rituals passed down through the generations, songs, dances, and instruments, even meditative visualizations allow one not only to engage in a *participation mystique* with the past, but they unite the past with the present, as if a portal had opened, and we had access to that distant domain but in the present.

Freud, after all, had returned to the time of Oedipus and claimed that we reenact that drama over and over in the weaning of our children. Even Wundt had turned to ethnopsychology and the language and symbolism of mythology to widen the purview of psychology beyond the laboratory. As Shamdasani points out, with regard to myths, Wundt was merely interested in their content; Jung took them as collective expressions of libido and posited different lineages of myths from different cultures as a way to understand the collective unconscious of any given culture.[23] The Greeks had Oedipus, the Germans their Faust, the Americans their George Washington and their Davy Crockett, and so on. Myths are not symbolic stories of things that have already happened; they live in the present moment and give depth and power to immediate personal experience.

The archetypes themselves were inherited inborn ways of expressing universal motifs common to all humanity that each individual holds within him or herself. The Mother and Father archetype, the archetype of the *puer aeternitatis*, or eternal youth, the archetype of the Self, the archetype of God[24] were all forms of representation within each person that control and shape our thinking that are biological and inborn, but the actualization of which in the process of individuation liberates their bound up energy for personal and creative growth at the psychic level.

We have various archetypes at the level of the personal unconscious shaping our perceptions of who we think we are. They provide specific functions that keep us entrenched in our same old habits, but also actually protect us from being inundated by contents from the collective reservoir. The masculine and feminine archetypes, which he called the *animus* and the *anima*, Jung believed, were the guardians to the inner door, which led from the personal unconscious into the larger, deeper, and more vast reservoir of the collective unconscious.[25]

Jung's first major work signaling a post-Freudian era had appeared in 1911, *Wandlungen und symbole der libido*.[26] Its content had been delivered at Fordham in 1912. The published version appeared in German in two parts, one in 1911 and the other in 1912, and the English language version followed in 1916 under the title *The Psychology of the Unconscious*, translated by Beatrice Hinkle.[27] Hinkle, a native Californian, had earned the MD and held a public health appointment as physician to the city of San Francisco in her early career before she met Jung, where she became a fierce defender of women's rights. She had originally intended to go to Vienna to see Freud, but, like so many other physicians, went through Jung and Zurich to get there. But Jung had recently broken with Freud. She ended up staying in Zurich and being analyzed by Jung. She translated *Wandlungen und symbole der libido*, which was published to wide acclaim in the United States under the English title *Psychology of the Unconscious*.

The work was an analysis of the fantasies of Miss Frank Miller, a conflicted young American woman who had been in and out of asylums her young adult life, being plagued by fantasies and depression. In both the United States and Europe she performed on stage these fully developed fantastic scenarios in which she was an Egyptian princess, or an American Indian maiden. Her performances were a kind of tableau, giving the impression that she was many persons in one body from completely different cultures and time periods, all accurately and convincingly reproduced. She had written up these scenarios, which came to be referred to as The Miller Fantasies, and Theodore Flournoy had published them in his journal, *Archives de Psychologie*, squeezed in next to an article by William James in 1904. It was Flournoy who drew Jung's attention to them, which Jung then turned around and used as the basis for *Wandlungen und symbole der Libido*, precipitating the break with Freud.

Jung first developed the thesis that the relation between the incest fantasy and the Oedipus myth in Freud's work pointed to living history—that myths are the means by which the past can be reawakened in the present in order to understand their effect on us today. They are symbolic representations of universal human experiences common to humanity at all times in history. In the same manner, dream meanings within the individual are psychological. They are symbolic, not literal. Myths are the mass dream of a people, whereas dreams are the myth of the individual. The individual dream is the vehicle for the exploration of the unconscious, at the same time it is an expression of the collective myth. Libido is the expression of psychic energy within the person; it appears to be purely sexual and biological until it is spiritualized through the use of symbols, as the person awakens to the universal within and invests symbols with personal meaning.

This investment is what Jung came to call the hero's journey—a turning within, a confrontation with the unconscious, and a rebirth—a dying in order to come to life, so that a higher state of consciousness and a new, more spiritually realized being can emerge. This is the meaning of the Greek tragedies, and the hero myths of nations—that spiritual life becomes possible through the sacrifice of one's worldly personality. The most powerful example of this motif in the Western world, Jung pointed out, is the myth of the resurrection of Jesus, upon which the entire Christian scheme of salvation is based.

The problem is that retreating within is most often interpreted as a pathological regression and therefore a disintegration of personality. Only in extraordinary individuals, or because of extraordinary events in the life of common individuals, since it is not usually the norm, is a detachment from external material reality voluntarily sought. The goal is to transcend the incessant union between the inner life world of the person and sense attachment to external material reality. A primitive and undeveloped relationship with the unconscious lies on one side and the ego lies on the other. The ego maintains a constant attachment to external material reality through the senses and overemphasizes reason as the only seemingly plausible compensation for what appears to consciousness as the primitive forces of the unconscious.

Jung gave the Freudians their due, particularly citing Freud's work and those of his disciples in this direction. But Jung was clear that they had not taken their case far enough, which his text intended to, do. He then expanded on the universal conception of the mother and the pre-Oedipal phase of the mother–child relationship as one of nutritive love. The Oedipal phase, as Freud described it, is the fear-based explanation—that the child desires the mother but fears the father. In the growth-oriented explanation, as Jung saw it, the hero's journey is one of liberation or individuation as he would later call it, from the mother and the father. In the Oedipal phase, the child succeeds in the first step toward individuation when he opts for the idealized version, where the mother, through the mother imago, becomes the divine mother, the nurturing Earth, and Mother Nature, among the pantheon of all divine mothers, which the male child will use to find a woman whom he will marry and who will beget and nurture his own children.

Similarly with the father imago, this will lead the person to God consciousness. No man ascends to the throne of the deity, Melville once said, except through the temple of the father. For the father imago, according to Jung, is not merely a psychic reaction to the immediate father, but to the universal and primitive form of the father established since the archaic past, referring to the mythological power of the sun; fire, which all cultures presume to be of spiritual origin; and the creative masculine deity.[28] Freud maintained that it was the fear of castration that set the male child on the right path, as far as same sex identification was concerned. Jung believed it is the numinous character of the image that allows the child to escape the course of the immediate family drama and establish the proper primordial relationships to the mother and father at that stage of development in which the child has now taken a first step toward the spiritualization of the libido. Spiritual self-actualization is also the means by which the transition from the narrow circle of the family and its complex dynamics to the wider human society may be made easier, if it is going to happen successfully at all.

The period of Jung's creative illness then intervened from about 1913 to 1918, during which time he wrote *Seven Sermons to the Dead*,[29] composed the Red and Black Books, published a number of short papers, and saw Beatrice Hinkle's translation of *Psychology of the Unconscious* appear in English. Finally, he emerged from his long hibernation with the appearance of *Psychological Types*, which was published in German in 1921 and in English in 1923. The English version sold 22,000 copies and, according to the editors of Jung's *Collected Works*, was translated into Dutch, French, Greek, Italian, Japanese, Portuguese, Russian, Spanish, and Swedish. It was Jung's attempt to differentiate himself from both Freud and Adler, to justify the inwardness of his own personal quest, and to show that the interior life had a transcendent as well as pathological dimension.

Psychological Types

When it first appeared in 1921, Jung's *Psychological Types* broke new ground as far as dynamic theories of personality were concerned. But it also gave tremendous stimulus to the budding typologists already into statistics who quickly appropriated his ideas as a major advance in trait theory among the experimentalists in psychology. Within a short time, introversion and extraversion became the most enduring constructs of his book and were eventually operationalized in personality inventories such as the Myers–Briggs Type Indicator as fixed traits called introversion and extroversion, including a change in the spelling of extraversion. They also became the focus of later research by experimentalists such as Hans Eysenck in constructing a statistically based theory of personality. By then, the categories had nothing to do with Jung, his theories, the epistemology underlying them, or even the original constructs themselves.

Statistical psychologists took introversion and extraversion as pigeon holes in which to insert their subjects, so that they could proceed with the measurement of additional traits, the sum total of which was presumed to equal the person. Others took them as measures of character development and proceeded to divide the world into just these two categories. Jung employed them, however, as guides in reconstructing the larger picture of the entire person. They were directions in which psychic energy tended to flow rather that fixed entities by which a specific structure could be identified. Shamdasani notes Jung's own comments to the effect that "My typology. . . is not a physiognomy and not an anthropological system, but a critical psychology dealing with the organization and delimitation of psychic processes that can be shown to be typical."[30] And elsewhere, "I have never occupied myself with the so-called character. My intentions and interests are also in no way directed to characterology, but in complete contrast, to typology. But not in the sense that I have established types in order to classify people with, but to have a schema with which I can order psychological material."[31]

Thus, the theory of the functions—that we are introverted or extraverted, further differentiated by functions he referred to as thinking, feeling, sensing, and intuiting—was concerned with types of psychological occurrences, not typification as characters. One would need 27 categories or more just to give a semi-accurate characterization of mentally differentiated persons, he said. In fact, it would not be such a great stretch of the imagination to interpret Jung's comments about physiognomy as a suggestion that what we have in modern trait theory is nothing less than a new phrenology—the measurement of hypothetical categories of personality that may justify psychology as an empirically oriented science, but one that fails to grasp the essential uniqueness of the person who is now objectified at a level of characterization that permits comparisons, but who is then represented as just another thing. In contrast, Jung was looking to get at the unique person who was before him in order to help that person learn how to live. By objectifying their subjects, trait theorists are more interested in their own scientific identity, believing that classification is the first step to eventual control of the phenomenon under study.

Jung's problem was he believed that individuals were unique souls connected to a universal psychic substrate in the unconscious and believed that, like William James before him, if there actually was a God, he came from within. But upon such theories no science could be based. As Shamdasani points out, Jung's characterization of the types was an attempt to put a rein somewhere on the essential unfathomable nature of the psyche and to delimit the problem of the personal equation, so that a provisional science of the person could commence.[32]

Jung had broadcast his ideas about types as early as 1913 at the Psychoanalytic Congress in Munich, the last time he and Freud had met in person. He first differentiated between the neurotic and the psychotic, emphasizing the emotionality in the one as opposed to the complete indifference in the other. Fantasies in the neurotic condition are clearly connected to the antecedent history of the individual patient, while the imagery of schizophrenics is related more to dreams than the content of the waking rational state. They exude a mythological, archaic character reminiscent of the primitive imagination. The movement of the neuroses is outward, that of schizophrenia inward, until a period of morbid compensation thrusts the schizophrenic into the limelight with his bizarre and extravagant behavior.

Jung proposed in 1912 to use the terms extraversion and introversion to refer to these two opposite movements of the libido. He equated regressive extraversion with Freud's idea of the transference, where the subject projects upon the object his own illusions. Regressive introversion, Jung considered the opposite phenomenon, where the schizophrenic's fantastic ideas refer back to himself. When the hysteric is extroverted, he protects himself from disagreeable memories by repression; when introverted, he resorts to devaluation of the objective world. Both can also be observed in the same individual. Indeed, the normal personality exhibits similar shifts, which may have become an integral part of personality development since childhood.

Jung then quoted William James's distinction between tender and tough-minded individuals, the spiritually oriented and the materially oriented types, suggesting that the libido is localized in different places in different people. Ostwald divided men into classicists and romantics; Worringer divided them into the empathetic types and the abstract types; Schiller the naive and the sentimental. In Nietzsche, it is the contrast between the Apollonian and the Dionysian; in linguistics, it is the difference between the transitive and intransitive verbs. In psychiatry, we have the distinction made by Otto Gross of the two types of inferiority, that of the diffuse and shallow consciousness and that of the contracted and deep consciousness. Jung then contrasted Freud and Adler's theories, saying that Freud's were reductive, pluralistic, sensationalistic, and causal, while Adler's were intellectualistic, monistic, and finalistic. What psychology was to do with these two contrasting types to give them equal stature, he left as a question for the future.

By 1921, in *Psychological Types*, the typological psychology Jung outlined was wholly different because more mature, except that he did retain the earlier distinction between introversion and extraversion. He considered the type problem as bequeathed to us from antiquity, touching on Gnosticism, and Christianity. He then turned to German philosophy and the classic distinction between idealist and realist, before reviewing the Apollonian versus Dionysian types. The type problem in poetry came in for examination, as well as in psychopathology and esthetics. When he came to philosophy, he devoted the entire section to William James's various distinctions on the subject.

In the final chapter, he presented his theory of introversion and extraversion as general attitudes of consciousness, with their principle subordinate functions of thinking, feeling, sensing, and intuiting. Because of the universal psychic law of compensation, every conscious orientation implies its undeveloped, unconscious opposite. Extraverts struggle with a repressed introversion, while introverts struggle with extraverted tendencies that usually remain undeveloped in the unconscious, until brought into consciousness through analysis or some other means.

Further, the types have their opposites as well—thinking is usually opposed to feeling, sensing opposed to intuiting, and so on, which must also be confronted in the process of individuation. Also, the male ego, dominated by the feminine principle within his own unconscious psyche, must encounter the unconscious *anima* and come to terms with it in order to transcend the opposites and by so doing gain access to the collective unconscious. Similarly with the woman, who must confront her own repressed *animus*, the male principle, within her own female psyche. Coming to terms with it means transcending the polarities and thus gaining access to deeper regions within, beyond the limits of the individual ego.[33]

We may say that, by 1921, most of Jung's major formulations defining his dynamic psychology of personality had emerged, even if only in rudimentary form, which he clarified later. This early period has been summarized in Jung's *Two Essays on Analytical Psychology* (1953)—"On the Psychology of the Unconscious" and "The Relations between the Ego and the Unconscious."[34] Curiously, however, typology as a subject never took up Jung's time again in his career to the extent that it did in 1921, except as a means to refer to the subject he was developing at hand. It was more of a justification for an inward psychology that was to take up virtually all his time for the rest of his life. Only the trait theorists ran with it, distorting it beyond all recognition of its original formulation. As well, the tendency to categorize individuals according to a fixed scheme has permeated successive generations of Jungian analysts to some extent, despite Jung's warnings.

The Architecture of the Psyche

The structure of the psyche as Jung eventually saw it began with the persona. This is the mask that we all wear and project out onto the world. It is the most superficial aspect of personality because it is the way we see ourselves as we believe the world sees us, or as we would like the world to see us. The persona protects the ego from full disclosure of oneself to others. The ego, meanwhile, holds a similar executive function to the ego in Freud's model and can be equated with normal everyday waking rational consciousness, to the extent to which most of us are able to achieve it. It is the reality principle, the I or the me about which the cognitive behaviorists make their primary observations.

At the same time, the ego and the personal unconscious remain separated by the shadow, which is represented by all the undeveloped characteristics of personality that the ego denies or is conscious of enough to want to hide from the external world. However, the shadow is also the guardian of the inner door. It prevents material from the personal unconscious from flooding the field of waking consciousness, except that the barrier is permeable, in the sense that memories, dreams, and other kinds of imagery do get through. It also admits the impressions of daily experience (Fig. 6.1).

Thus, the personal unconscious functions much like Freud's conception of the preconscious, to a large extent. It is also the medium through which the archetypes make their way into the field of waking rational consciousness in symbolic form. The anomaly is that they come from within, from the collective reservoir, and not from external sources.

During the 1920s, Jung traveled back to the United States to visit the Pueblo Indians and also embarked upon a safari to Africa and a visit to Egypt. The purpose of these excursions was not only to verify aspects of his theories about the collective unconscious, but more pointedly they were way stations on the journey toward his own goal of individuation to which he had committed himself so many years earlier. Jung commenced delivery of a series of papers at the now famous Eranos Conferences in Ascona, Switzerland; lectured at the Tavistock Clinic in London in 1935; journeyed to India at the invitation of the British Government to celebrate the 25th anniversary of the University of Calcutta in 1938, after receiving an honorary doctorate from Oxford and being elected to the Royal Society of Medicine. He returned to the United States again on further two occasions, once to receive an honorary LLD from Harvard in 1936 and again in 1938 to deliver the Terry Lectures on Psychology and Religion at Yale.

THE EXTERNAL WORLD

THE PERSONA

THE EGO

THE SHADOW

THE PERSONAL UNCONSCIOUS

THE ANIMUS AND ANIMA

THE COLLECTIVE UNCONSCIOUS

Fig. 6.1   Jung's architecture of the psyche

Several of his papers are particularly instructive for revealing details of his mature psychology. His friend, the sinologist Richard Wilhelm, had translated the *T'ai I Chin Hua Tsung Chih* or *Secret of the Golden Flower*, first published in 1929, and asked Jung to write a psychological commentary to accompany the text.[35] Jung had been struggling to understand the symbolism of the collective unconscious through Gnostic and early Christian documents, but had run into difficulties because of the obscurity of recessions he had to work with that had been written and rewritten many times over. In *The Secret of the Golden Flower*, a text on Chinese yoga and alchemy, he found what he had been searching for, clearly articulated links to the symbolism of the modern psyche. This revelation led him to turn back to the literature of the West and initiate an in-depth investigation of the European alchemical tradition.

He did this because he believed the collective unconscious is common to all mankind, and does not consist of contents merely capable of becoming conscious, but of latent predispositions causing identical reactions across cultures. Modern depth psychology provides us with a way to make visible these recurring patterns. But we are required to discover these patterns through our own means; otherwise, we take over a tradition that is not our own, which creates its own form of psychopathology.

He then considered the iconography particular to the Chinese Taoist texts, such as the meaning of the Tao, the nature of the opposites, the motif of the circle with the center as a protective mechanism to prevent consciousness from being overwhelmed by the unconscious. He also considered the goal of wholeness through an exploration of mystical states.

In his essay on "Yoga and the West" (1936/1969b),[36] Jung reviewed the history of Christianity, dating the introduction of Oriental syncretism from the Hellenistic period in the Pythagorean cults and Gnosticism, but really making its incursion with the development of Protestantism. Nineteenth-century expressions such as theosophy and anthroposophy, which supported the mass introduction of Hinduism and Buddhism into popular culture, he considered sects of Protestantism. The particular appeal of yoga was psychic and physical hygiene independent of religion, largely due to the claim that it was scientific, which drew the attention of educated intellectuals. He cautioned that the West needs to develop its own form of yoga out of Christianity rather than import a foreign system. We must do this if we are to heal the cultural split we ourselves have created between mind and body. We must find our own way to allow the unconscious, which now traps the majority of our personality, to come more into the field of waking awareness and contribute to the general expansion of world consciousness.

In his Foreword to the German edition of D.T Suzuki's *Introduction to Zen Buddhism* (1939/1969c),[37] Jung pointed out the unique nature of Zen—that it was entirely a presuppositionless philosophy. In this, one can immediately draw analogies to Western phenomenology, such as Amedeo Giorgi's phenomenological psychological method, where the observer is trained to be devoid of interpretation. In Zen this leads to a state of emptiness or *wu*, which necessarily sets the contents of the unconscious aside and creates the conditions for a break through experience such as that described in the literature on *satori*.

Jung's view was that the unconscious is an irrepresentable totality of all subliminal psychic factors, a "total vision" *in potentia*.[38] From this totality we pluck bits and pieces and integrate them into waking consciousness and as we do this, "a form of psychic existence results which corresponds better to the whole of the individual's personality, and so abolishes the fruitless conflicts between the conscious and unconscious self."[39] Most people in the West lack the mental discipline necessary to achieve true satori, however, so this more piecemeal approach better serves our purposes.

Jung also contributed psychological commentaries to Evans-Wentz's translation of the *Tibetan Book of the Dead* and also *The Tibetan Book of the Great Liberation*.[40] *The Tibetan Book of the Dead*, a profound document unto itself, remains obscure because it is essentially beyond the ken of most rationalists to read anything about life after death, let alone a document based on the principles of karma and reincarnation. Their response is always to rationalize away such phenomena. Those who have ingested entheogens, or themselves have had profound experiences that have taken them beyond waking consciousness and into the realms of the unconscious, understand this book immediately, however. For it posits a dynamic relation between inner exploration in this waking life, the moment of one's death, and its aftermath.

The text first describes the moment of death, in which the supreme white light of ultimate liberation is revealed to the dead person. But due to their impurities, they cannot bear it. While still remaining a possibility throughout a symbolic period of 49 days, the karma of the individual descends into the realms of the heavens and hells caused by the person's own illusions. Eventually spiraling down to the primitive, animal level, it fantasizes mating couples and is then caught in the womb of one of them, being reborn again into physical existence but with no conscious memory of the past.

Here, in the context of a wider and deeper context of the unconscious, Jung gave a significant recapitulation of the strengths and weaknesses of Freudian psychoanalysis, which is well worth the attention of readers interested in this subject. He kept this text with him closely, and from it, he said, derived "significant insights."[41]

In his psychological commentary on *The Tibetan Book of the Great Liberation* (1954), Jung went to great lengths to indicate that the meaning of Mind in Tibetan Buddhism is a metaphysical concept, while in Western psychology it remains anchored only to waking rational consciousness, with only a skeptical association to the reality of the unconscious. Having said that, the symbolism of the unconscious, and the general notion of a collective unconscious, is the closest we come in the West to the expression of Universal Mind, which is understood matter of factly throughout Asian philosophy. The concepts are not immediately transferable, however, such as when the Western non-dualists make a claim about the nature of ultimate reality, forgetting that their ability to assert such a claim as a superior way of knowing creates the very duality from which the rationalist seeks to escape. Liberation means freeing ourselves from the tyranny of waking consciousness, where the major portion of our personality remains trapped in the unconscious. Liberation is when the ego gives up control and the center of personality moves more into the domain of the unconscious to liberate the self. Its ultimate nature, according to Hindu psychology, is that the individual *jiva* is the Supreme Self, *Atman*. For the Buddhists, the ultimate nature of the self is empty (*sunya*) and nonexistent (*anatta*), ideas, as we have said, quite outside the ken of Western rational consciousness.

The Voidness of liberation in an Eastern sense, Jung says, means that we would have to spend all our time there permanently and teaching that doctrine to Westerners seems pointless. For liberation, to be a possibility for us, means the union of opposites, particularly through the difficult task of reconciling introversion with extraversion by means of the transcendent function. So again, Jung turns the teachings of a non-Western epistemology toward a more functional psychology of individuation.

The period of the 1930s represented another major turning point in Jung's career, as his work began in earnest on the European alchemical tradition and its relation to archetypal symbolism. Here, he was searching for the so-called yoga of the West, the path toward self-realization unique to our own lineage. This took him full circle, back to an analysis of the documents of Christianity.

In *Alchemical Studies*, Jung's editors presented the psychological commentary on *The Secret of the Golden Flower*, as well as alchemical essays on Paracelsus as a spiritual phenomenon, the Spirit Mercurius, and the history and interpretation of the symbolism of the tree in alchemy.[42] Jung's final and major work on alchemy was

Mysterium Conjunctionis: An Inquiry into the Separation and Synthesis of Psychic Opposites in Alchemy.[43] Here, he noted that the alchemists were dealing with the central problem of Western consciousness, namely, how to heal the break between the world of the rationalist and the larger domain of the rationalists' own spirit.

His Work on Christian Symbolism

I shall take only one example, Jung's *Answer to Job* (1952/1969f).[44] It is a difficult text to summarize in a short space. Briefly, in the Old Testament, Satan wagers God that a perfect man can be shown false by taking everything he loves away and punishing him unfairly. He will abandon his belief in God and become like Satan. God takes the challenge and selects Job, a perfect disciple. He casts him out, makes him lose his servants, his lands, and his entire fortune. His sons and daughters are killed and his friends abandon him. Job is reduced to nothing. Along the way what friends he has left counsel him this way and that, mainly pointing out that God has forsaken him, so, what kind of a God is that? Job even wavers a little, himself, but only for an instant. In the end he is permitted to talk to God directly, who first chastises him further as nothing but a mere worm, but then recants and returns to him his lands, his cattle, his fortunes, and his children in greater measure than before because of his steadfastness.

Jung's analysis is that God's behavior has to be understood in terms of the way Yahweh is defined in the Old Testament—a thoroughly jealous God who is all rules and no mercy. The historical significance of the story is that in his abject poverty, Job stands before God with the complete understanding that he has no recourse but to take whatever God metes out as his fate. Yahweh is God and Job is man. That is the nature of the relationship. But the God of the Old Testament has lapses. He pretends that He does not really care what happens to man, whether good or evil befalls him, but secretly He needs man, who worships and adores God nonetheless. In his downtroddenness and utter wretched state, Job sees that he is powerless against God's whims.

This elevates him to a new status, however, because that insight represents awakened intelligence, which God seems not to have immediately noticed or planned. This quickens the evolution of God in the Old Testament, from a God who is not a man, to the God of the New Testament, who sends his only begotten son in the form of a man to take on the sins of the world. In other words, the torment of Job, the man, in the Old Testament is answered in the New Testament through Christ's suffering as a man on the cross for the sins of all mankind. God is on a journey to become man. Jung then implies that the larger picture over the millennia since the crucifixion is the realization by the Christian world of the reality of God in man. This is hinted in the present day evolution of depth psychology, especially those systems that speak to the growth-oriented dimension of personality, where the goal of individuation for the *animus* is perfection, and for the *anima*, completeness. Organized religion may have its vicissitudes and may appear in some quarters to have waned with the rise of modernism, but what has grown stronger is the realization of a growth-oriented, spiritual dimension to each personality, regardless of religious affiliation that is accessible through depth psychology in a secular age.

Also during this period, Jung gave numerous seminars, the transcripts of which have floated around for years in mimeograph form in the libraries of the various Jungian Institutes. Recently, several of these have found their way into print. *The Visions Seminar* Jung taught from 1930 to 1934, based on the artwork of Christiana Morgan, was a seminar on the psychology of active imagination. In the Kundalini Yoga seminar Jung delivered in 1932, the first four chapters were a scholarly commentary delivered by J. W. Hauer, German expert in comparative religions, on the *Sat Chakra Nirupana*, a Sanskrit text from the Hindu Tantra on the *chakras*, or centers of vital energy in the body.[45] The second four chapters were lectures given by Jung on the same subject, except now translated for his audience of Jungians into a psychology of individuation.[46] Another was *The Children's Dream Seminars*, given from 1936 to 1940. These contained an invaluable template described by Jung himself of how the dreams are to be analyzed, followed by an extensive collection of dreams that Jung interpreted which had been remembered from childhood by adult subjects.[47]

Jung also carried on significant correspondence with a number of intellectuals in the context of friendships that sometimes lasted several decades. Aside from Freud, there were the letters between Jung and the Catholic Dominican priest, Victor White, on the problem of evil.[48] Jung's letters to and from the physicist Wolfgang Pauli, a member of Niels Bohr's Copenhagen Circle, which went on for 25 years (1932–1957), led Jung to the idea of synchronicity as an acausal connecting principle, while for Pauli, they led to the introduction of the language of depth psychology into quantum physics. Through his relation with the sinologist, Richard Wilhelm, Jung was led to the study of alchemy, and through the comparative religionist, Wilhelm Hauer, Jung was introduced to the symbolism of Kundalini Yoga. Further, Jung's encounters with the Sanskrit scholar Heinrich Zimmer led Jung to the translation of religious experience into psychotherapeutically useful insights about the process of self-knowledge.[49]

The 1930s was also the period of Jung's controversial relationship with the International Society for Medical Psychotherapy, an organization that eventually was influenced by the Nazis. While later admitting he had made a mistake in his early assessment of the situation in Germany, Jung's reputation in the West suffered, especially among Jewish psychoanalysts who cleaved to Freud's assessment of Jung as an anti-Semite, and because of continued opposition by niche groups has remained deeply distorted in some circles to this day.[50] One rumor circulating around the time of the Harvard Tercentenary in 1936 was that Jung was Hitler's private psychiatrist, who flew to Berchtesgaden every weekend to consult with the Fürher. But Jung was never a Nazi sympathizer and had never met Hitler. On the other hand, during the 1940s, Jung was involved with "Wild Bill" Donovan, consulting with the Office of Strategic Services.[51]

During the years of World War II, Jung retreated to his books, his psychotherapeutic practice, and to his tower on Lake Zurich at Bollingen, where he continued to write on spiritual themes, Eastern and Western religions, and the evolution of the psyche. A special chair was created for him in medical psychology at the University of Basel in 1944, but illness forced him to resign after only 1 year. He retired in 1947 and continued work on such subjects as synchronicity, alchemy, the *I Ching*, and the mystical union of opposites, and to articulate his conception of a cross-cultural phenomenological psychology of individuation. His wife died in 1955.

In 1958, Aniela Jaffé, with assistance from Jung, began work on what became *Memories, Dreams, Reflections*, an influential spiritual statement that remains in print to this day.[52] Sections of the English translation linking Jung to James, Flournoy, and others were excised by the editors and the publishers, however, so the two prevailing influences on his thinking that were left appeared to be only Freud and God. More recently, the so-called New Jung Scholarship has documented these and other omissions. Other works of the later period for which Jung has also become known include *The Undiscovered Self* (1958), *Flying Saucers: A Modern Myth of Things Seen in the Skies* (1959), and *Man and his Symbols* (1964).[53] He died after a brief illness at his home in Kusnacht, near Zurich, June 6, 1961.

The Diffusion of Jung's Ideas

We have said that in the early days of Jung's association with Freud, numerous physicians first passed through Zurich in order to get to Freud in Vienna. From that time, Jung also began to attract his own followers, many of them women. Beatrice Hinkle (1874–1953) was an early analysand of Jung. Born in San Francisco, the daughter of a physician, she married a lawyer. She herself graduated from Cooper Medical School in 1899, just after her husband died, leaving her with two children. Appointed physician to the city of San Francisco, she became interested in psychotherapy after working with patients suffering from an epidemic of bubonic plague and noting their different psychological reactions to the same disease. She moved to New York City in 1905 after the 1904 California earthquake, where she co-founded one of the first psychotherapeutic clinics in the United States at Cornell University Medical School.

While she was involved with hypnosis, yoga, and psychoanalysis, rather than Freud, she gravitated to Jung, studying with him from about 1911 to 1915, when she returned to New York.[54] As we have said earlier, she published a translation of Jung's original German edition of *Symbols of Transformation* (1912) under the title of *Psychology of the Unconscious* (1916b).[55] One of her analysands recommended the well-known anthologist Louis Untermeyer to her, whom she employed to translate some of the poetry in *Psychology of the Unconscious*. Untermeyer went on to write extensively on Jungian psychology, dedicate a book of his poetry to both Jung and Hinkle, and was a lay analyst. He was also a long-time friend and correspondent with Henry A. Murray

Hinkle became associated with other analysands returning from Zurich and a knot of them, mostly women physicians, developed into the New York group. These included figures such as Eleanor Bertine, M. Esther Harding, Constance Long, and Kristine Mann, while Frances Wickes later followed. Christiana Morgan came into Jung's orbit, from Boston, through Henry A. Murray.[56]

Jung's Immediate Circle[57]

Aniela Jaffé (1903–1991) was Jung's long-time private secretary, who co-wrote *Memories, Dreams, Reflections*, Jung's alleged autobiography. From a German Jewish family, she fled the Nazis in 1933 before she could complete her doctorate in psychology from the University of Hamburg. She immigrated to Switzerland, where she underwent an analysis with Liliane Frey and then Jung himself. She was first secretary of the Jung Institute when it opened in 1948, and she became Jung's private secretary in 1955 until his death in 1961. She carried on an active analytic practice, although not formally credentialed, edited several works of Jung's with others, wrote *The Myth of Meaning* (1970), and with C. G. Jung wrote *Word and Image* (1979).[58]

Jolande Jacobi (1890–1973) of Hungarian Jewish descent, met Jung in the early 1920s when he came to one of her salons, held in her apartment, which was a meeting place for writers and artists in the early 1920s. Beginning in 1934, she studied psychology under Charlotte and Karl Bühler at the University of Vienna, where she eventually received her degree, commuting to Zurich in order to be analyzed by Jung. She was instrumental in the founding of the Jung Institute in Zurich and endowing a foundation that collected paintings from many analysands from around the world. She was a prodigious writer of articles and books, among them *The Psychology of C. G. Jung* (1942), *Complex/Archetype/Symbol* (1959), and was one of the co-authors of *Man and His Symbols* (1964) with Jung.[59]

Barbara Hannah (1891–1986) was born in Brighton, England. Her father was a bishop in the Anglican Church. She was in different ways, according to Kirsch, sometimes as close to Jung as Jolande Jacobi. She was reserved and aloof, described as the archetypal English spinster, reminding one sometimes of the witch in Hansel and Gretel. Even she declared that Jung had softened her aggressive masculine impulses, says Kirsch. She went to Zurich to study with Jung after reading his essay "Women in Europe" (1927).[60] Jung put her to work, which eventually turned into an analysis, and afterward, she engaged in extensive writing and teaching. She wrote numerous books but is perhaps best known for her biography of Jung, a work lauded by some Jung scholars as still the best rendering of the maestro.[61]

Franz Riklin (1909–1969) was a Swiss physician whose father was also a psychiatrist, while his mother was Jung's cousin. Riklin co-authored *Studies in Word Association* in 1904 with Jung[62] was analyzed by Jung, did his psychiatric training at the Bürgholzli, and ran his own private analytic practice while he taught at the Jung Institute for 25 years. It was he who organized the *festschrift* on Jung's 80th birthday. He was also a leading figure in the founding of the International Association for Analytical Psychology.

Helton Goodwin "Peter" Baynes (1882–1943) was a British physician and an early analysand of Jung. He was Jung's assistant in Zurich and organized Jung's trip to Africa in 1925. He spent a year in Northern California in 1928, where he met Joseph Henderson and encouraged him into Jungian analysis. Before the *Collected Works*, Baynes translated various volumes of Jung's works into English, among them *Psychological Types* (1921a) and *Contributions to Analytical Psychology*

(1928a), and in collaboration with his third wife, Cary Baynes, *Two Essays on Analytical Psychology* (1928b). He also wrote two books of his own, *Mythology of the Soul* (1940) and *Germany Possessed* (1941).[63] Cary Baynes, herself, also later translated the *I Ching* (1968) from German to English and was co-translator of Jung's *Modern Man in Search of a Soul* (1959b).[64] In Kirsch's opinion, Peter Baynes was known as an effective and a dynamic interpreter of Jung's ideas.

Gerhard Adler (1904–1988), of German Jewish origin, was analyzed by James Kirsch, Thomas Kirsch's father in 1929 in Berlin, and from 1931 to 1934 by Jung. Adler earned the PhD in psychology and afterward immigrated to England with his wife in 1935. He was the author of *Studies in Analytical Psychology* (1948) and *The Living Symbol* (1961), a case study of a Jungian analysis.[65] Adler was close with Jung for almost 30 years; co-editor with Aniela Jaffé of a 2-volume set of Jung's published letters, and member of the editorial board of Jung's *Collected Works*.[66]

Michael Fordham (1905–1995) was dubbed by Kirsch as one of the most creative first-generation analysts after Jung and the undisputed leader of analytical psychology in England for over 50 years. He studied medicine and physiology at Cambridge University, was analyzed by H. G. Baynes, a family friend, and then went to Zurich, but was unable to arrange an analysis with Jung. He returned to England and resumed with Baynes, then, with Jung's permission, switched to Hilda Kirsch, Thomas Kirsch's mother, as her first analytic patient. When he developed an erotic transference toward her, she invited him to dinner to meet her husband, which immediately solved that problem. He was analyzed by her from 1936 to 1940, he said, to good effect, after which she abruptly had to terminate on immigrating to the United States in 1940.

Peter Baynes had used Fordham's analysis and artistic drawings in *Mythology of the Soul*, concluding erroneously there that he was a schizophrenic. As a child psychiatrist, Fordham was influenced by Melanie Kline. Jung, who did not see children in analysis himself, believed that one need only analyze the unconscious of the parent to cure the neuroses of the patient's child. Meanwhile, Fordham developed analytic theory around the nature of the child as a way to understand its psychic development in *The Life of Childhood* (1944).[67] He was responsible for the mixing of analytical psychology with object relations theory in England, although he considered himself a Jungian to the end.

Carl Alfred Meier (1905–1995) was originally Jung's "crown prince." Born in 1905 in the same town where Emma Jung was from, Meier met Jung as a young boy. He graduated from the University of Zurich, interned at the Burghölzli, and then underwent an analysis with Jung in the late 1920s. He was secretary of the International Medical Society for Psychotherapy the last 6 months of Jung's tenure as president, trying to rescue psychotherapy from the Nazis. Kirsch thinks he was the most important male figure around Jung, who was otherwise surrounded by women. He inherited Jung's patients, succeeded him as professor at the Swiss Technical Institute in Zürich, and generally acted as his right-hand man for almost 30 years. Interested in the relation between quantum physics and analytical psychology, he was a close friend to Wolfgang Pauli and edited the Jung–Pauli correspondence. Meier wrote numerous books interpreting Jung's theories. They fell out with each other in 1957, however, and thereafter he withdrew from analytical psychology. He died in 1995.

There were significant others. James and Hilde Kirsch founded the Analytical Psychology Club in Los Angeles. Sir Laurens van der Post was a friend and biographer of Jung's. Joseph Wheelright and his wife, Jane, founded the Jung Institute in San Francisco and shaped its early training program. Ann Ulanov teaches at the Union Theological Seminary and writes on Jung in the context of Christian spirituality. Edwin Eidinger, a Yale MD, who trained at the New York Institute, was known for his book, *Ego and Archetype: Individuation and the Religious Function of the Psyche* (1972).[68] Christopher Whitmont trained in New York, but was also a homeopathic physician.

Similarly, June Singer wrote on Jung and William Blake and was instrumental in the transpersonal interpretation of Jung. Jean Shinoda Bolen and Clarissa Pinkola Estés have both written best sellers from a Jungian perspective. Joseph Cambray, Linda Carter, Claire Douglas, John Beebe, Andrew Samuels, Murray Stein, A. Guggenbuhl-Craig, and Hester Solomon have been contemporary key figures in the International Association of Analytical Psychology, the official credentialing body of Jungian analysts.[69]

At the same time, local organizations have flourished even though in the beginning they had no official status. Among them, Ruth Thacker Frye launched the C. G. Jung Educational Center in Houston, Texas in 1958 with Jung's blessing and influenced Carolyn Fay and others to support it. It is now a fully fledged Society and an accredited training program in analytical psychology, most recently guided by James Hollis.

Eisendrath's Three Schools

The Cambridge Companion to Jung, edited by Polly Young-Eisendrath and Terrance Dawson (1997),[70] identifies three schools of contemporary Jungian thought: The lineage around the Jung Institute in Zurich, a breakaway line led by Marie Louise von Franz, and then those who are the followers of James Hillman.

The Jung Institute of Zürich was first founded in 1948 around those who were closest to Jung. After Jung died in 1961 and this generation themselves aged and began passing from the scene, new, younger personalities began to emerge. James Hillman was one, and Adolf Guggenbuhl-Craig another. Hillman, who had become Director of Training, had a falling out with the Institute over an affair he had carried on that involved the civil courts. Half wanted him to go and the other wanted him to stay. Guggenbuhl Craig, who held the key position on the Curatorium, which oversaw the Institute, put changes in place that were not popular, such as the inauguration of training courses in Jungian group therapy that many of the older analysts, such as Marie-Louise von Franz, believed deviated too much from the process of individuation in the person, which was Jung's primary focus. As a result, several of the older analysts left the institute to form their own separate training group.

Marie Louise von Franz (1915–1998) was German born and later became a Swiss citizen. She met Jung when she was 18 on a class trip. In exchange for analytic sessions, which she could not then afford, she translated Latin and Greek alchemical texts for Jung, which he needed at the time. She completed her PhD in classical philology in 1943 and wrote thereafter on fairy tales. She was active in founding the Jung Institute and attracted a large following to her lectures and seminars over the years. While remaining close to Jung, she moved in with Barbara Hannah and they lived together for decades, devoted to Jung's cause. She became Jung's primary interpreter internationally and opposed divergences such as those of Michael Fordham. She founded her own independent Jungian Institute in Zürich in the 1980s. At the time of her death, Thomas Kirsch mentions that she was working on the texts of a Shiite alchemical mystic.

James Hillman (1926–), an American from New Jersey, went to Zürich to study with Jung and ended up earning a PhD from the University of Zürich as well as becoming a credentialed analyst. According to Kirsch, he entered private practice in Zürich and became director of studies at the Jung Institute there. He resigned in 1969 over the affair previously mentioned, which had by then developed into an international incident. Hillman remained in Zürich until 1978 and then immigrated to Dallas, Texas, where he taught at the University of Dallas, which had a doctoral program at the time in phenomenological psychology under Robert Sardello and Robert Romanyshyn. Later, he settled in Thompson, Connecticut, as an internationally noted author and lecturer, affiliated at-a-distance with Pacifica, a doctoral program in Santa Barbara, California, which is devoted to training graduate students in depth psychology. He was the main motivating force behind Spring Publications and launched *Spring*, a journal devoted to analytical psychology, now published by Nancy Kater. His main focus after leaving analytic practice has been to elaborate on the diseases of cultural consciousness, by way of what he calls archetypal psychology, a "therapy of ideas."[71]

Current Status

The current status of Jungian thought remains paradoxical. On the one hand, credentialed Jungian analysts have been increasingly trying to associate themselves with the Freudians regarding the perception of their accepted professional status within private clinical practice. At the same time they are trying to distance themselves from the association of Jung with the psychotherapeutic counterculture. Most Freudians in the United States hold either the MD as physicians and psychiatrists or the PhD in psychology. Most Jungians may or may not have a PhD and it might just as frequently be in English as psychology. There are probably many more credentialed Freudians than credentialed Jungians, but the influence of Jung on the psychotherapeutic counterculture has been so large that today more people are probably familiar with his ideas than with Freud's. Within the academy, psychoanalysis is still taught, associated mostly now with psychoanalytically assisted psychotherapy in clinical licensure programs in psychology and psychiatry. It was also associated with the radical feminists, who tend to be almost exclusively Freudians if they acknowledge depth psychology at all. Freudian analysts are occasionally recognized in the standard histories of psychology and psychiatry, but Jungians, and especially Jung himself, are never mentioned. There never has been a set of Jung's collected works exhibited at an annual meeting of the American Psychological Association, for instance, and where Jung is mentioned in textbooks, it is always erroneously assumed he was just a student and a mere dissenter from Freud.

At the same time, within the Freudian and Jungian professional organizations, the clinical literature on Freudian and Jungian analysis remains hermetically sealed. Most scholarship on Jungian analysis remains unavailable to general readers or scholars outside Jung circles except through the popular press. Their respective books and journals are not indexed in the standard databases in psychology and psychiatry; PsychAbstracts and PubMed. Further, Jungian historians tend not to be in communication with historians of psychology or psychiatry and hence each does not refer to the others' work. Nevertheless, the popular Jung literature continues to generate huge amounts of money for its publishers, likely more so these days than for Freud's work. Jungian models of personality and consciousness tend to be flourishing internationally, likely because of their cross-cultural character, while Freudian models remain largely anchored in Judeo-Christian culture and their structure tends to be superimposed onto non-Western cultures, that are then read through a Freudian lens, instead of being heard for what they intrinsically have to say themselves about the human condition.

In this regard, there can be no doubt that Freud's ideas have influenced modernist culture. The formally organized Jungians appear to agree, as they have committed themselves to an interpretation of their own agenda, recognition, and survival as a professional institution under the rubric of "Family Matters." The gist of it has been that Jungians have decided to interpret their lineage as Freudians turned Jungian and have sought to identify with the established Freudian movement as legitimate professionals in modern society. In this vein, Jungian therapy emphasizes an analysis of the defense mechanisms and the transference and the study of a patient's dreams. It may introduce an examination of psychological types and symbolism of the archetypes. But in the end, Jungian analysis begins to look more normative with regard to the goal of therapy as adjustment to external social norms, rather than an emphasis on the idea that the self-actualizing goals of the individuating person are not always the same as the adjustment needs of society.

The interpretation of Jung within the American psychotherapeutic counterculture, however, may incorporate non-Western forms of healing, homeopathy, the identification of personal mythologies, alchemical symbolism, and other iconography that are distinctively not Freudian. But the credentialed Jungians remain split between identifying with the Freudian establishment and their own unique lineage, which reaches deep into the psychotherapeutic counterculture and fans out into the mythology of world cultures.

Notes

1. Who actually wrote the work, Jaffé or Jung, remains a matter of interpretation. [Jung, C. G. (1963a). *Memories, dreams, reflections*. A. Jaffé (Recorder & Ed.). (R. & C. Winston, Trans.). New York: Vintage Books.]

2. For the disputed authorship of this work, see Shamdasani, S. (1995). Memories, dreams, omissions. *Journal of Archetype and Culture, 57*, 115–137. Jung did not want to have the book included in his collected works, partly because it was composed largely of verbatim quotes that Jaffé had attributed directly to Jung, but which were the result of edited protocols that she herself had composed after her interviews with him.

3. Jung, C. G. (1909). *The psychology of dementia praecox* (F. Peterson, & A. A. Brill, Trans.). *Nervous and Mental Disease Monograph, 3*. New York: The Journal of Nervous and Mental Disease Publication Company (Original work published 1906). See also Jung (1907a).

4. McGuire, W. (Ed.). (1974). *The Freud-Jung letters: The correspondence between Sigmund Freud and C. G. Jung*. Bollingen Series, 94. Princeton, NJ: Princeton University Press.

5. According to Swan, during his 1925 seminar on analytical psychology, Jung explained that his personal examination of fantasy material began near the end of 1912 when he had a dream which revealed that "the unconscious did not consist of inert material only, but that there was something living down there." He went on to state, "I was greatly excited at the idea of there being something living in me that I did not know anything about." As a result of this awareness, Jung commenced a systematic attempt to examine his own unconscious. Jung, C. G. (1989). *Analytical psychology: Notes of the seminar given in 1925* (W. McGuire, Ed.). Princeton, NJ: Princeton University Press, p. 40. (Original lectures delivered October 15, 1930–March 21, 1934)

6. It also has to do with the personal equation, the direction in which our psychic energy flows, and what draws many people into the helping professions in the first place. Contrary to the popular stereotype, it is not because they are damaged themselves, and therefore driven by a lack or a need, but that they are impelled toward self-realization and drawn to the helping professions, since every encounter with another human being is seen as a chance to advance forward in the inward domain oneself.

7. S. Shamdasani (personal communication, New York City, October, 16 2007).

8. In his 1931 essay, "The Aims of Psychotherapy," Jung credited Freud's method of word association as the origin of his own method for working with the unconscious: "as to the problem of my technique, I ask myself how far I am indebted to Freud's authority for its achievement. Nevertheless I learned from Freud's method of free association, and I regard my technique as a direct continuation of the same" (pp. 46, 47, para. 100, trans. mod); Jung, C. G. (1966). The aims of psychotherapy. In H. Read, M. Fordham, G. Adler, & W. McGuire (Eds.). R. F. C. Hull (Trans.), *Collected works of C. G. Jung* (Vol. 16, pp. 35–52). Princeton, NJ: Princeton University Press. (Original work published 1931)]

9. "I wrote everything down very carefully" (Jung, 1925/1989, p. 47). "I wrote these fantasies down first in the Black Book; later I transferred them to the Red Book, which I also embellished with drawings. It contains most of my mandala drawings" (Jung, 1963, p. 188).

10. Swan, W. (2007). *C. G. Jung and active imagination: A case study of Tina Keller*, Saarbrucken, Germany: VDM Verlag.

11. Some secondary accounts of Jung's patients' experiences with the technique exist in the published literature, such as the biographical writings of Douglas (1997, 1993, 1990) and Robinson (1992) based on Christiana Morgan's analytic notebooks and visions. A recently published work by Reid (2001) describes Catharine Rush Cabot's analytic relationship to Jung using excerpts from Cabot's diaries, but it does not address the topic of Jung's practice of active imagination (Reid, 2001). See Douglas, C. (1997). (Ed.). *Visions: Notes of the seminar given in 1930–1934* by C. G. Jung (Vol. 1, 2). Princeton, NJ: Princeton University Press; Douglas, C. (1993). *Translate this darkness: The life of Christiana Morgan*. New York: Simon & Schuster; Douglas, C. (1990). *The woman in the mirror: Analytical psychology and the feminine*. Boston: Sigo Press; Robinson, F. (1992). *Love's story told: A life of Henry A. Murray*. Cambridge, MA: Harvard University Press; Reid, J. C. (2001). *Jung, my mother, and I: The analytic diaries of Catherine Rush Cabot*. Einsiedeln, Switzerland: Daimon Verlag.

12. Jung, C. G. (1969a). A study in the process of individuation. In H. Read, M. Fordham, G. Adler, & W. McGuire (Eds.). R. F. C. Hull (Trans.), *Collected works of C. G. Jung* (Vol. 9, part 1, pp. 290–354). Princeton, NJ: Princeton University Press. (Original work published 1950)

13. Jung, C. G. (1916a). *Psychology of the unconscious: A study of the transformations and symbolisms of the libido, a contribution to the history of the evolution of thought*. London: Kegan, Paul, Trench, Trubner.

14. Transcendence refers to the interaction and integration of the opposites as well as their transcendence without loss of individual identity.

15. Shamdasani, S. (1998). *Cult Fictions: C. G. Jung and the founding of analytical psychology*. London, New York: Routledge.

16. The caliber of professionals who presented at the Eranos Conferences over the years gives an indication of Jung's intellectual milieu. They included, among others, Mircea Eliade, Heinrich Zimmer, Paul Tillich, D. T. Suzuki, Paul Corbin, Roberto Assagioli, Ernst Benz, Frederik Jakobus Johannes Buytendijk, Joseph Campbell, Marie-Louise von Franz, Gerald Holton, Aniela Jaffé, Erich Neumann, Laurens van der Post, Ira Progoff, Gershem Sholem, James Hillman, and so on. See Campbell, J. (Ed.). (1964a). *Papers from the Eranos yearbooks* (Vol. 5). Bollingen Series XXX. New York: Pantheon.

17. Anthony, M. (1999). *Jung's circle of women: The valkyries*. York Beach, ME: Nicholas-Hays.

18. Douglas (1997).

19. Bluhm, A. C. (2005). *Turning toward individuation: Carol Sawyer Baumann's interpretation of Jung, 1927–1931*. Unpublished doctoral dissertation, Saybrook Graduate School and Research Center, San Francisco, CA.

20. Shamdasani, S. (2003). *Jung and the making of modern psychology: The dream of a science*. New York, London: Cambridge University Press, p. 149.

21. Honegger, a patient and later a student, had reported a hallucination where he saw in the sun a kind of upright tail, which Jung took to be an erect penis. When Honegger reported moving his head back and forth, the penis in the sun swung back and forth as well, creating the winds of the earth. Jung later found a description of this same motif in an obscure text on Mithraic liturgy (Shamdasani, 2003, p. 219).

22. Jung, C. G. (1971). *Archetypes and the collective unconscious*. In H. Read, M. Fordham, G. Adler, & W. McGuire (Eds.). R. F. C. Hull (Trans.). *Collected works of C. G. Jung* (Vol. 9.1) Princeton, NJ: Princeton University Press. (Original work published 1934)

23. Shamdasani (2003).

24. Jung even proposed an archetype of place. See Martinez, T. J., & Taylor, E. I. (1998, Fall/Winter). "Yes, in you the tempest rages": The archetypal significance of America in Jung's own process of individuation. *Spring: A Journal of Archetype and Culture*, *64*, 32–56.

25. Shamdasani notes that around the time of the release of *Psychological Types*, other schemes of personality integration based on the type problem also appeared. Beatrice Hinkle, who had been analyzed by Jung, listened to the development of his early formulations, even translated his works into English, proposed a scheme of her own quite different from Jung's, in which introversion and extraversion were further divided into objective, simple, and subjective subtypes. [Jung, C. G. (1976). *Psychological types*. In H. Read, M, Fordham, G. Adler, & W. McGuire (Eds.). R. F. C. Hull (Trans.), *Collected works of C. G. Jung* (Vol. 6). Princeton, NJ: Princeton University Press. (Original work published 1921)]

26. Jung, C. G. (1912). *Wandlungen und symbole der libido: Beiträge zur entwicklungsgeschichte des denkens* [Transformations and symbols of the libido: Contributions to the development history of thinking]. München, Deutscher Taschenbuch Verlag; reprinted 1991.

27. Taylor, E. I. (2001a). Foreword: The Americanization of Jungian ideas. In C. G. Jung (2001). *Psychology of the unconscious: A study of the transformations and symbolisms of the libido: A contribution to the history of the evolution of thought, Collected works of C. G. Jung, Supplementary Vol. B*. (W. McGuire, Ed., B. Hinkle, Trans.), (pp. xvii–xxvi). Princeton, NJ: Princeton University Press.

28. In religion, in this regard, Jung had said in *Psychology of the Unconscious*, we find the regressive reanimation of the mother-and-father imago made into an organized system. (Jung, 2001, p. 86)

29. See Jung, C. G. (1916/1963). Appendix V: Septem sermones ad mortuos [seven sermons to the dead]. Written by Basilides in Alexandria. (Jung, 1963a, pp. 378–390).

30. Shamdasani, 2003, p. 87.
31. Shamdasani, 2003, p. 86.
32. Shamdasani, 2003, pp. 88–90.
33. Juxtaposition of the opposites onto one another is not logical because in logic the whole can never be more than the sum of the parts. In the case of transcendence, however, the whole is always greater than the sum of the parts, because the process is non-logical and non-rational, which is not the same as irrational. The artist can tolerate the ambiguity of it, while the rationalist cannot.
34. Jung, C. G. (1953). *Two essays on analytical psychology.* In R. F. C Hull (Trans.), *Collected works of C. G. Jung* (Vol. 7). Bollingen Series XX. Princeton NJ: Princeton University Press. (Original works, On the psychology of the unconscious, published 1916; The relations between the ego and the unconscious, published 1928)
35. Jung, C. G. (1968). *Alchemical studies,* Commentary on *The Secret of the Golden Flower.*" In H. Read, M. Fordham, G. Adler, & W. McGuire (Eds.). R. F. C. (Trans.), *Collected works of C. G. Jung* (Vol. 13, pp. 1–57). Princeton NJ: Princeton University Press. (Original work published 1929)
36. Jung, C. G. (1969b), *Psychology and religion: West and east* was originally published in English in 1936 as "Yoga and the West" in *Prabuddha Bharata.* [Jung, C. G. (1969b). Yoga and the west. In H. Read, M. Fordham, G. Adler, & W. McGuire (Eds.). R. F. C. Hull (Trans.), *Collected works of C. G. Jung* (Vol. 11, 2nd ed., pp. 529–537). Princeton NJ: Princeton University Press. (Original work published 1936)
37. Jung, C. G. (1969c). Foreword to the German edition of D.T Suzuki's *Introduction to Zen Buddhism.* In H. Read, M. Fordham, G. Adler, & W. McGuire (Eds.) (R. F. C. Hull, Trans.), *Psychology and Religion: West and east, Collected Works of C. G. Jung* (Vol. 11, 2nd ed., pp. 538–557). Princeton NJ: Princeton University Press. (Original work published 1939)
38. Jung, 1969b, p. 551.
39. Jung, 1969b, p. 552.
40. Jung, C. G. (1969d). Psychological commentary on *The Tibetan book of the dead* was first published in German in 1935. See H. Read, M. Fordham, G. Adler, & W. McGuire (Eds.), *Psychology and religion: West and east.* R. F. C. Hull (Trans.), *Collected works of C. G. Jung* (Vol. 11, 2nd ed., pp. 509–528). Princeton NJ: Princeton University Press. Also, Jung, C. G. (1969e). Psychological commentary on *The Tibetan book of the great liberation,* first published in English in 1954. In H. Read, M. Fordham, G. Adler, & W. McGuire (Eds.), *Psychology and religion: West and east. Collected works of C. G. Jung* (Vol. 11, 2nd ed., pp. 475–508). Princeton NJ: Princeton University Press.
41. Jung, 1969c, p. 511.
42. Jung (1968).
43. Jung, C. G. (1963b). *Mysterium conjunctionis: An inquiry into the separation and synthesis of psychic opposites in alchemy.* In H. Read, M. Fordham, G. Adler, & W. McGuire (Eds.) (R. F. C. Hull, Trans.), *Collected works of C. G. Jung* (Vol. 14, 2nd ed., pp. 475–508). Princeton, NJ: Princeton University Press. (Original work published 1955–1956)
44. Jung, C. G. (1969f). Answer to Job. In H. Read, M. Fordham, G. Adler, & W. McGuire (Eds.), (R. F. C. Hull, Trans.), *Collected works of C. G. Jung* (Vol. 11, pp. 355–470). Princeton, NJ: Princeton University Press. (Original work published 1952)
45. Pietikainen, P. (2007). The Volk and its unconscious: Jung, Hauer and the 'German Revolution.' *Journal of Contemporary History, 35*(4), 523–539.
46. A translation does not always have to confine itself to working from one foreign language to another. It can also be undertaken from one epistemology to another, such as taking an account of a religious experience from a non-Western culture, and translating it into a form useful for a psychology of personal transformation in a Western cultural context. See Starcher, D. C. (1999). The chakra system of Tantric yoga: *The Sat-Cakra Nirupana, interpreted within the context of a growth-oriented depth psychology. Dissertation Abstracts International, B 64/10.* (UMI No. 3110201)
47. Jung, C. G. (2008). In L. Jung & M. Meyer-Grass (Eds.) (E. Falzeder & T. Woolfson, Trans.), *Children's dreams: Notes from the seminar given in 1936–1940.* Princeton, NJ: Princeton University Press. The Philemon Series.
48. Lammers, A. C., Cunningham, A., & Stein, M. (Eds.). (2007). *The Jung-White letters.* New York: Routledge. The Philemon Series.

49. Zimmer, H. (n.d.). Some remarks about Henry R. Zimmer. In *Two lectures*. Privately printed. Cambridge, MA: Harvard University. See also Case, M. H. (1994). *Heinrich Zimmer: Coming into his own*. Princeton, NJ: Princeton University Press.

50. Maidenbaum, A., & Martin, S. A. (Eds.). (1991). *Lingering shadows: Jungians, Freudians, and anti-Semitism*. Boston: Shambhala: Distributed by Random House.

51. Maidenbaum & Martin, 1991.

52. Jung (1963a).

53. Jung, C. G. (1958). *The undiscovered self*. Boston: Little, Brown; Jung, C. G. (1959a). *Flying saucers: A modern myth of things seen in the skies*. New York: Harcourt, Brace; Jung, C. G., & Franz, M.-L. v. (1964). *Man and his symbols*. Garden City, NY: Doubleday.

54. McGuire reports that she was denied membership in the New York Psychoanalytic Society in 1915 because she was a Jungian. Introduction. *Psychology of the Unconscious*. Princeton, NJ: Princeton University Press.

55. Jung, C. G. (1916b). *Psychology of the unconscious: A study of the transformations and symbolisms of the libido* (B. Hinkle, Trans.). New York: Moffat, Yard and Company.

56. Others included Helene Preiswerk, Sabina Spielrein, Miss Frank Miller, Fanny Bowditch Katz, Toni Wolff, Maria Moltzer, Ruth Bailey, Tina Keller, Jane Cabot Reid, Carol Sawyer Baumann. There was also, of course, Jung's wife, Emma.

57. I have drawn liberally here from Kirsch, T. B. (2000). *The Jungians: A comparative and historical perspective*. London: Routledge; Samuels, A. (1985). *Jung and the post-Jungians*. London: Routledge and K. Paul; Anthony, M. (1999). *Jung's circle of women: The valkyries*. York Beach, ME: Nicholas-Hays; Hall, N. (1988). *Those women*. Dallas, TX: Spring Publications.

58. Jaffé, A. (1970). *The myth of meaning in the work of C. G. Jung*. London: Hodder & Stoughton; Jaffé, A. (1979). *C. G. Jung, word and image*. Bollingen Series, 97, 2. Princeton, NJ: Princeton University Press.

59. Jacobi, J. S., & Bash, K. W. (1942). *The psychology of C. G. Jung: An introduction with illustrations*. London: Routledge & Kegan Paul; Jacobi, J. S. (1959). *Complex/archetype/symbol in the psychology of C. G. Jung*. Bollingen Series, 57, Princeton, NJ: Princeton University Press; Jung & Franz (1964).

60. Jung, C. G. (1927). Women in Europe. In *Collected works of C. G. Jung* (Vol. 10, pp. 113–133). London: Routledge & Kegan Paul.

61. Anthony, 1999, pp. 87–88.

62. Eder, M., Wehrlin, K., Riklin, F., & Jung, C. G. (1969). *Studies in word-association: Experiments in the diagnosis of psychopathological conditions carried out at the Psychiatric Clinic of the University of Zurich under the direction of C. G Jung*. New York: Russell & Russell. (Original work published 1904–1909)

63. Jung, C. G. (1921a). *Psychological types* (H. G. Baynes, Trans.). London: Kegan Paul Trench Trubner; Jung, C. G. (1928a). *Contributions to analytical psychology*. London: Routledge & Kegan Paul; Jung, C. G. (1928b). *Two essays on analytical psychology* (H. G. & C. F. Baynes, Trans.). New York: Dodd, Mead and Company; Baynes, H. G. (1940). *Mythology of the soul: A research into the unconscious from schizophrenic dreams and drawings*. London: RKP; Baynes, H. G. (1941). *Germany possessed*. With an introduction by Hermann Rauschning. London: RKP.

64. Wilhelm, R., & Baynes, C. F. (1968). *The I ching, or, book of changes*. London: Routledge & Kegan Paul; Jung, C. G. (1959b). (W. Dell & C. F. Baynes, Trans.), *Modern Man in search of a soul*. London: Routledge & Paul.

65. Adler, G. (1968). *Studies in analytical psychology*. New York: Greenwood Press; Adler, G. (1961). *The living symbol: A case study in the process of individuation*. London: Routledge & Kegan Paul; New York: Pantheon Books.

66. Jung, C. G. (1957–1990). *Collected works of C. G. Jung* (Vols. 1–20). (H. Read, M. Fordham, G. Adler, & W. McGuire, Eds., R. F. C. Hull, Trans.). Princeton, NJ: Princeton University Press.

67. Fordham, M. (1944). *The life of childhood: A contribution to analytical psychology*. London: Paul, Trench, Trubner.

68. Edinger, E. F. (1972). *Ego and archetype: Individuation and the religious function of the psyche*. New York: Putnam for the C.G. Jung Foundation for Analytical Psychology.

69. See, for instance, Cambray, J., & Carter, L. (Eds.). (2004). *Analytical psychology: Contemporary perspectives in Jungian analysis*. Hove, New York: Brunner-Routledge.

70. Young-Eisendrath, P., & Dawson, T. (Eds.). (1997). *The Cambridge companion to Jung*. Cambridge [Cambridgeshire]: Cambridge University Press.
71. Hillman, J. (2004). *Archetypal psychology* (3rd ed.). Putnam, CT: Spring Publications.

Chapter 7
Adler's *Menschenkenntnis*

I never was a student of Freud
Adler to Abraham Maslow, 1934

Alfred Adler (1870–1937), Viennese physician and founder of individual psychology, proclaimed loudly to Abraham Maslow in 1934 that he had never been a student of Freud's. Jung said the same thing, but the *Encyclopedia Britannica*, Ernest Jones, and most of the Freudians who followed Freud said otherwise. Are we to believe the protagonist when he talks about himself? After all, that is what Ernest Jones asked the world to do in his three-volume life of Freud whenever Jones referred to himself. Or should we rely on the allegedly more objective opinion of others? Either is, of course, dangerous if you do not ask about motive, point of view, and precisely when such statements were made. There is no doubt, however, that Adler's individual psychology is nothing like Freud's psychoanalysis or Jung's complex psychology. For himself, Adler focused on *Menschenkenntnis*, the intuitive, practical understanding of human beings in their natural and social context, and the ways in which the individual developed with regard to social feeling (*gemeinschaftsgefuhl*). As a result, his theories had a completely different life of their own than any of the other depth psychologies.

Adler was born outside Vienna in 1870, the second child in a family of six children.[1] He seems to have been closer to his father, a grain merchant, than to his mother. He also had an antagonistic relationship with his only older brother. Early schooling was unremarkable. His training in medical school taught him to pay attention to the patient as a whole and that the emotional disposition of the physician had also to be taken into account. He joined the student socialist movement and became an advocate for reforms. In this circle, he met his future wife. Here he also absorbed a certain amount of Marxist philosophy that influenced his later work on the influence of environmental and economic factors on personality. He became interested in the common man. He received the MD in 1895, was married in 1897, and his first child arrived in 1898. The same year, his first book appeared, *Health Manual for the Tailoring Trade*.[2] In 1902, he also began publishing in a newly launched medical journal, in which he was the main contributor.

He began his medical practice in a lower middle-class section of Vienna, next to a well-known amusement park. There, he served a mixed clientele of professional,

E. Taylor, *The Mystery of Personality*, Library of the History of Psychology Theories,
DOI 10.1007/978-0-387-98104-8_7, © Springer Science+Business Media, LLC 2009

waiters, acrobats, and artists, and there he first began to understand the weaknesses of apparently strong people—that their strengths often grew out of their compensation for their inferiorities. He became particularly adroit at both diagnosis and treatment. He also studied his own children and developed theories of education and child guidance.

Adler first encountered Freud in 1902 by reading his work, which had immediately engendered opposition from the established medical community. Without having actually met the author, Adler defended Freud's right to a fair hearing in print on two occasions, one of which was a response to *The Interpretation of Dreams*. Adler also adapted Freud's methods to his own independent ends, as he would do throughout the course of their relationship. He had already been reading Charcot and Janet when he heard Freud lecture for the first time in 1899. In 1901, Freud invited him to discuss his ideas before his Wednesday evening circle. Adler joined in 1902, but never saw himself as an acolyte or disciple. Freud nonetheless maneuvered things to make him stay, which he did for 9 years. Adler not only began to advocate for psychoanalysis, a term that meant something much more general at that time than today. He also published several works on the subject. But these works were a continuation of his own ideas. In a break with the ethnic identification of psychoanalysis with Judaism, for instance, he converted to Protestantism in 1904, demonstrating ideological commitments beyond the Freudian circle. By then, in his writings he had already established the idea of organ inferiority, the ideas of the pampered child, self-confidence and courage, and a complete theory of education.

In 1907, Adler published an influential monograph, *Studie über Minderwertigkeit von Organen*, translated into English as *Studies of Organ Inferiority* (1917).[3] In it, he put forth the idea that all mental inferiority stems from organ inferiority, which the individual deals with either through denial or through compensation. Freud thought it an important contribution to psychoanalysis and hence began the idea of the inferiority complex, attributed to Freud, but originated by Adler. Despite the fact that Adler was 14 years younger than Freud, each absorbed much from the other, which Adler's followers later meticulously tried to catalog. Adler proposed a separate aggressive drive, for instance, which Freud rejected at the time, but later embraced after Adler had left the fold. Adler first defined the inferiority complex, which later authors attributed to Freud, and so on. The list is long. He was one of the original four who first constituted Freud's circle and was a member of the inner group until 1911.

At the same time, working on his own ideas, Adler turned out to be mainly a listener, which annoyed the Jewish analysts following Freud, and he often took contentious positions toward what was being discussed, so he was not popular to begin with. Thus, he could not identify with their general feelings of persecution, either as Jews or as psychoanalysts. It was always Freud who was the bridge builder. Adler thought the drives to be very important, but he did not assign sexuality the valence that Freud did.

The open split between them began at the Nuremberg Conference in 1910, when Freud engineered Jung into the presidency of the International Psychoanalytic Association and turned his back on the older Viennese group made up of his Jewish followers. To appease them, he put Adler in charge and allowed them to start a new journal, edited by Stekel and Adler. Adler strongly emphasized physiology and heredity more than Freud and did not believe that early sexual development was decisive for the making of character. He rejected the theory of the sexual etiology of the neuroses, the Oedipus complex, the child's psychosexual stages of development, and the centrality of sexuality as a definition of libido. Instead, he believed every neurotic seeks to compensate for some organic imperfection. Biology was destiny. Neurosis was a failed compensation for inferiority feelings. Infantile traumas have significance only in relation to the inferiority of organs. The child loves others first, not his body as Freud maintained. Thus, the sexual component was never central to Adler's theory.[4] Adler used terms to fit his own meanings. Society finds its center in man's bisexuality, for instance, that is, in the interaction of man and woman and their division of labor. This is quite different from Freud's idea about the inherent bisexuality of all individuals, or Jung's idea that symbolically, males and females carry archetypes of their gender opposites in the unconscious.

As he did first with Jung and later with James Jackson Putnam, Freud tolerated these deviancies. Freud gave Adler free reign during the early years and even ignored his criticisms, instead considering Adler's ideas as valuable supplements to psychoanalysis. Later, however, Adler accused Freud of creating a philosophy without love. Freud's reaction was what Adler called the revenge of the insulted Goddess Libido. Adler aired his views on problems with psychoanalysis and also the topic of the masculine protest, a man's overreaction to the stereotype of his own masculine prowess, in February, 1911 and Freud finally openly attacked him. Within a short time, Adler was relieved of his presidency of the Vienna Psychoanalytic Society and asked to step down as editor of the local psychoanalytic journal. Freud then denounced him as paranoid and delusional. Adler, in turn, claimed that Freud was trying to castrate him in public. That was the end of it. By the end of the year, Adler and 10 followers left to form their own group.

After that, Freud literally wrote Adler out of the history of psychoanalysis. For his part, Adler reformed his own followers around a more liberal idea of depth psychology and as a result, they flourished. That was in 1911. By 1912 he was ready to release his newest book, *The Neurotic Constitution,* which elaborated on the theory of psychogenesis, the hyper-division of the opposites such as the masculine and feminine, and the masculine protest. In it, he fused depth psychology with Marxist social theory, believing that the individual owed much to the culture in which he was immersed. Organ inferiority and the aggressive drive within the individual he now adapted to understanding the neurotic character. The theme of the work was that all the activities of the neurotic conspire toward one goal, driven by impulses of the person toward social interest (*gemeinschaftsgefeuhl*), especially of a spiritual or cosmic nature. Publication of the work was delayed. In 1913, Adler's group became known as the Society for Individual Psychology and they launched a journal. Suddenly, however, World War I broke out and their efforts scattered, as many were drafted into the military. Adler himself was mobilized in the army as World War I broke out, where he served as a military doctor. After the War, *The Neurotic Constitution* was finally published in 1916 (English translation, 1917).

Adler's most important years were during the Weimar Republic between 1920 and 1932. In the new climate, he rejected politics and threw his energies into his own system for reform, individual psychology. Adler remained for most of his career in Vienna. He had become an Austrian citizen in 1911, but had difficulty launching a school of thought recognized as independent of Freudianism. He was rejected for the position of *privatdozent* at the University by Warner-Jauregg, for instance, because he was considered a Freudian.

At the same time, his journal, launched in 1914, which was suspended during the War, afterward was restarted as an international publication, and then renamed when it moved to the United States as the *Journal for Individual Psychology*. Adlerian groups by then had spread throughout Europe and the United States. Adler traveled, lectured, was awarded a professorship, and expanded his publications. He also began traveling extensively in the United States, attending, for instance, the Wittenberg Symposium in Springfield, Ohio in 1927.

In 1924, Adler had become a member of the Teachers College at the Pedagogical Institute of the City of Vienna. There, he influenced hundreds of teachers who came to his lectures voluntarily of their own accord. He taught an innovative method of case study research for teachers, in which individual psychology was applied directly to students in the classroom, the effect of which was often immediate on the child's behavior. As an extension of these lectures, child guidance clinics of a voluntary nature were developed along the lines of Adler's teachings. The child being studied had to be accompanied by a parent as well as his teacher, in which the child was a co-participant in diagnosing the problem and discovering its solution. The clinics were tremendously successful and were flooded with applicants. Adler himself worked at one of these clinics and through direct demonstration in front of small audiences of professionals further extended his influence. At one point, in Vienna alone, there were 28 child guidance clinics managed by the Vienna section of the International Association for Individual Psychology. Other clinics operated in Munich and Berlin.

In 1924, he published *The Practice and Theory of Individual Psychology*. In it he maintained that individual psychology covers the whole range of psychology in one survey, and as a result it is able to mirror the individual unity of personality. [5] The contents of the work were individual lectures, first on general topics of individual psychology, and then more specific ones followed on its application.

Individual psychology, he said, does not deny, as other theories do, experience, conscious intent, artistic and creative vision, and intuition itself. He espoused rather, a comparative individual psychology by starting with the assumption of unity within the individual. In this sense, he said, his method was similar to that of William Stern. The path the individual follows is important, because it tells us what the person's goal is. It tells us his "life line." We are always goal oriented, especially with regard to our living out of an "imagined terminal goal"—something that has not come about yet, but toward which we aspire and strive to achieve. All thoughts, words, and deeds are then preparations for achieving that goal: "All psychical powers are under the control of a directive idea, and all expressions of emotion, feeling, thinking, willing, acting, dreaming, as well as psychopathological phenomena are permeated by one unified life plan."[6] The general mood of the person is always one of compensation from inferiorities. He gave as an example the man with a bad memory. The man usually is not suffering from a hereditary problem or some intellectual defect. With regard to the overall scheme of things in his life plan, he is just under the sway of something he does not want to remember. Similarly, traits of character are always adjustments to the individual's life plan.

Community feeling (*gemeinschaftsgefeuhl*), the development of an appreciation for social relationships, became the primary avenue through which a person was able to strive for superiority and to exercise his power over others. It was physiologically rooted, and the person's attitude about it could always be traced back to an origin in early childhood. There, compensation for physical inferiorities began to express itself psychologically as the child developed, which then found expression in the social sphere of adolescence and of adulthood. These lines of development since childhood, he thought, could only be broken by "an exceedingly high degree of introspection" or though psychotherapy.

Adler also continued to develop his ideas on sexual hermaphroditism and the masculine protest. Each of us, regardless of our gender, has masculine and feminine traits that define our personality. Some traits are more enduring than others, but what prevails is largely guided by the individual's life plan. At the same time community feelings help shape identity. Men, in particular, are encouraged to express themselves as real men, which takes the form of an overexaggeration of the image of what the accepted male image would look like. The urge toward an ideal of perfection begins in childhood in terms of compensation for physical inferiorities. This might take the form of deficient height, weight, physical prowess, or size of one's sex organs. Psychologically it extends into the expression of masculine rather than feminine traits of personality. Overcompensation for inferiorities by exaggerating masculine traits Adler referred to as the masculine protest.

He then followed with chapters on hallucinations, dreams, the masculine attitude in female neurotics, homosexuality, compulsions, hunger strikes, the role of the unconscious in neuroses, the importance of early childhood education, and the case of demoralized children.

In 1927, *Menschenkenntnis* appeared, translated into English as *Understanding Human Nature*.[7] It was a major summary of his dynamic theory, in that it was not so much a preconceived theory as an intuitive characterization of personality, which could be reached by anyone putting any thought into the subject. The character of the individual in normal adult life, he said there, is already laid down within the first 4 years and changes very little from that time. The study of children is therefore recommended as the place to start in understanding human nature. If you want to change the behavior patterns in maturity, then start with those laid down in earliest childhood. From there we are led to pedagogy and the wider field of education if we want to understand the science of human nature.

Adler believed that empathy comes through having lived through psychic crises, not from reading books. What one should look for was the unique core of the person, the soul. From the very beginning, Adler made use of the soul as a referent to the individual. From this we see that the psychic organ is always goal oriented.

It demonstrates purposive teleology. Life is a preparation always for some future situation. In this way the soul is always associated with movement.

The soul that cannot withstand the pressures of survival on its own necessarily joins the herd for increased protection. This leads to the communal life because man, unlike other animals, cannot exist by himself in nature. Weak animals never live in solitude. Instead, one is surrounded by layers of protection, from help during childbirth, to protection in the first few days of life, to avoiding the vagaries that beset the survival of children in the early years. Inferiority and insecurity are thus built into the individual's constitution. Desire, will, understanding, and speech have all grown up to assist the person who is inferior in nature to adapt in the communal life. Legal codes, totems, taboos, education, and laws all then become necessary in regulating this relationship. Adaptation to the community is the most important function of the individual soul.

Every type has a meaning only when we understand its relationship to its environment. The soul is born in early childhood in those situations whose function is to make normal life possible. The different types of individuals begin in this early period. The goal is maximum satisfaction of the instincts with the least possible friction. Similarly, reflections of the environment are to be found in the behavior of every child.

Creative education can always come out of striving to accommodate one's inferiorities. It begins with organ inferiority and proceeds to psychological, then sociological weaknesses. The sense organs are the first to show these tendencies to adaptation. Usually a child overemphasizes one or the other of them and though compensation develops a repertoire of identifiable traits to his or her personality. Sense organs lead to perceptions and to the creation of memory and imagination. Fantasy is yet another creative activity of the soul, always concerned with the future. The striving for power often plays a dominant role. This also implies a goal, usually one involving social recognition and significance. It is well developed in the weak that use it to deprecate reality and elevate themselves to a fictional level in their own imagination. Thus the main outlines of his theory were laid out. The unique expression of the soul begins to flourish in the recognition of organ inferiority, which generalizes to psychological and sociological adjustments, and the paramount importance of social striving.

The Case of Fritz

Several volumes appeared during this time explicating Adler's method with examples.[8] A case in point was a demonstration Adler himself gave in *Guiding the Child* (1930a).[9] The case was a 12-year-old boy named Fritz, whose mother had brought him to the Clinic with the complaint of enuresis. Adler explained that the boy was militant and probably pampered when younger but since had been displaced by other siblings. He did not feel well and made excessive demands on his mother. He was slovenly, had difficulty eating, and wanted always to be the center of attention. He seemed to do well in school, however. It was important to get all the details of the study to get the origin of these behaviors. The fact that the boy wet himself during the day suggested there is no violent struggle at the root, only on the outside. Further, he never wet himself when his mother was with him or he was at school. He may have feel he was the cause of his mother's troubles. The boy lived with his grandparents, who pampered him. Before that, the child used to sleep with the parents. If he slept in his mother's bed, Adler noted, he would not wet himself.

Four years earlier the boy had come down with an osteomyelitic condition. His leg was in danger of being amputated. This was an important source for his feelings of inferiority. He stayed out of school for 3 years. He returned, only to be enrolled in special education classes. He always interrupted the other students, trying to get recognized. He had a brother 4 years older who was also his father's favorite. This made the younger boy the problem. As a result, the boy adopted this mantle and often played the role of the clown. For these things, Adler characterized him as an ambitious weakling. On the positive side, Fritz had no difficulty eating, so the parents were doing something right; similarly with washing and dressing.

Adler then made it known that both the parents and the grandparents were blood relations. This was discouraging and a source of social weakness. The possibility of organ inferiority was therefore very high. The child also had whooping cough and bladder trouble, which would promote pampering. He occasionally cried out at night. He walked at 16 months and talked at 3 years. This is late and indicates an over involvement by the mother. In features, Fritz appeared slightly mongoloid, which would exacerbate the situation because of a tendency to start out in a feeble-minded class to begin with.

Up to this point, Adler had been lecturing to the professional audience. He then asked that the mother be brought in. His intent was to win her over to a new program of re-education for her son. Adler began by praising the child, a behavior which the mother usually minimized. He asked the mother what the child would like to become. She replied, a cabinetmaker. He asked what the father did and she said he was a dental mechanic. So Adler concluded that it was a compatible wish, which the mother seemed to not see. Adler asked if the boy had any friends. Yes, but all younger ones, she replied. How was he in dealing with money? Ok, she said. Has he been to one of three clinics before? Yes, evidently, but got into a fight. Was he reliable? Yes. How was he with the older brother? She dissembled and made up how well they got along.

At that point, the child then entered the room. Adler addressed him directly. He asked him how he was getting along in school, but then stated he usually acts cowardly because he had no confidence in himself: "You are overwhelmed by arithmetic. We could help you do better if you are interested. You would then be able to go to a higher school. We should like you to come to our clinic. You will have a good time there. We shall work together and you shall improve. I was also poor in arithmetic but soon learned to excel above everyone else. What would your teacher think of that?" The boy made a positive, enthusiastic reply. Adler then told the boy to come again and in the same sentence admonished him to ignore what others say about him. "And don't wet yourself at home when criticized. You must help me," Adler tells him. "May I rely on you?" The child then left the room.

In addition to the accounts by Adler and his colleagues in Vienna, there were other publications. There was also *The Case of Miss R.* (1929), the interpretation of a life story, which followed a patient into neurosis across the life span and proposed an innovative method for reading and creating case histories.[10] "The Pattern of Life" were lectures he gave at the New School for Social Research in 1929, in which a number of cases were presented. These endeavors abruptly ended in 1934, however, when the fascists took over the Austrian Republic. Already aware of the pending problem that the Nazis' rise to power entailed, Adler had long before been expanding his operations internationally and replanting himself elsewhere. As we said, after World War I the *Journal of Individual Psychology* resumed publication in 1923 and it added editors such as the Americans G. Stanley Hall and William Ernest Hocking when it migrated to the United States.

When the lecture invitations began to increase, Adler took it as a personal challenge to learn English in order to accept more of them. In the first half of 1927, he gave talks at the New School for Social Research, the New York Academy of Medicine, various child guidance and mental hygiene associations, local churches, and Institutes, and he held clinics at two New York Hospitals. In Boston, he was the guest of William Healy and he lectured at Harvard, introduced by Morton Prince. One of his articles also appeared in Prince's *Journal of Abnormal and Social Psychology*. In Providence he lectured at Brown, as well as local schools. In Chicago he lectured at the University of Chicago and spoke to professional meetings sponsored by the Board of Education. Two thousand five hundred were turned away trying to get tickets to his lectures for teachers. He then proceeded on to lecture in Pennsylvania, Indiana, Ohio, Wisconsin, and California to wide acclaim. He returned in 1928 to receive the LLD from Wittenberg College and he returned again 1929–1930 as lecturer at Columbia. Back home, he became medical director of a clinic for neurotics and was named Citizen of Vienna in 1930. It should have been a day of celebration, but he was publicly greeted by the mayor as a deserving pupil of Freud, which angered him.

His message, by that time in his life, which impressed so many, was that leading children in the formative years to a useful life would change both our quality of life and our history, while the children at the same time would be protected from neuroses and delinquency.

By then, there were active groups devoted to Adlerian psychology in Belgium, Czechoslovakia, Denmark, England, France, Greece, Hungary, Italy, the Netherlands, Poland, Rumania, Spain, Switzerland, Turkey, and the United States.[11] Tirelessly traveling and lecturing, while also trying to find his daughter who was at that time lost somewhere in Russia, he died in Scotland in 1937.

Ellenberger summed Adler's teachings in a series of axioms[12]: Man was a unity, a whole, not conscious and unconscious, and not divided into id, ego, and superego. Adler's conception of personality was based on the idea of dynamism, that is, life cannot be conceived without movement. We think forward and have goals and intentionality. There is always in the life of the individual a sense of cosmic influence. We live always in a sense of community feeling and within an individual conception of the cosmos. Also, there is a spontaneous structuration of the parts in a whole. That is, all functions conspire toward the whole of individuality. There is always action and reaction between the individual and the environment; this underlay the dynamics of interpersonal relationships. There is a law of absolute truth, even if it is a fictitious norm set up for the conduct the individual and governing his or her relation to community feeling, deviation from which causes psychopathology, perversions, and criminality. These premises define the relation of humans to nature, social groups, and with each other; they form the basis for the interrelation of the individual to the community. Adler also believed that individuals are divided into visual, auditive, or motor types.[13]

Every individual also has a style of life, a phrase Adler employed instead of the construct of personality. An individual's style of life is discovered by investigation of present attitudes, earliest memories, childhood activities, adolescent wishes, and dreams. These sources reveal the individual's perception of the world and hence his or her style of living. Each person also has a secret goal they are attempting to attain. Dreams reveal this, as well as reveal a tentative solution to the dreamer's immediate problems. The key question to ask for Adler was "What is the patient's life goal?" "What is their life style?" To know these things, one had to work with children. So he worked with patients and their families and did extensive work in schools. Later he would found his own kindergarten classes for therapeutic education.[14]

Adler's Influence

Adler attracted numerous adherents during his own lifetime. Two of his children even followed in his footsteps, Kurt, his only son, and his daughter Alexandra. Contrary to his father's aversion for numbers, Kurt Adler was a numerical genius from an early age.[15] He took a PhD from the University of Vienna in physics and mathematics in 1935 and he then earned an MD in 1941 from the Long Island College of Medicine. Though an MD and a psychiatrist, he always referred to himself as a psychologist. He worked as a psychiatrist for the US Army during World War II, and afterward carried on a private practice in New York City for 45 years, until he died in 1997. He believed, as his father did, that mental health is achieved through integration into a community, when the person merges his or her own self-interest with the common interest of humanity.

Alfred Adler's daughter, Alexandra, also made a name for herself in individual psychology. Her father died in 1937 in the middle of a lecture series, which she endeavored to complete. Afterward, she helped to found The Alfred Adler Institute in New York. In 1952, Rudolph Dreikurs, MD, founded Alfred Adler Institute in Chicago, now the Adler Institute of Professional Psychology, and between the two of them Adlerian psychology flourished in Chicago and New York as separate centers of activity. Prior to that time, Alexandra Adler had undertaken a major study of the traumatic neuroses when in 1942, among many other physicians; she examined the victims of the Cocoanut Grove fire, a devastating incident in a crowded Boston nightclub that resulted in 442 deaths and 166 injured. Her report highlighted the fact that symptoms of depression and anxiety associated with traumatic exposure may be more permanent and persistent than originally thought due to persistent emotional factors long after the physical injuries had healed.[16] She was remembered as a brilliant researcher, neurologist, and psychiatrist. She was also noted as one of the first women neurologists at Harvard Medical School. She died on January 4, 2001 at age 99.

Another ardent Adlerian, Alexander Müller, a Jewish psychiatrist, was born in Hungary in 1895 and studied medicine in Vienna. He was drafted as a soldier, however, in World War I and spent 4 years as a prisoner of war in Russia. After the war he helped Adler found numerous child guidance clinics and also was active in therapy, teaching, lecturing, and the training of therapists. When the Nazis came to power, he and his family emigrated, trying to settle in several different countries before landing in Holland. When the Nazis invaded Holland, they fled back to Hungary, where he was interred in a concentration camp. After liberation, he returned to Holland until 1952, when he was invited to become a lecturer in Zürich at the Institute for Applied Psychology. He became the director of the Swiss Society for Individual Psychology and secretary of the International Association for Individual psychology before retirement. He died in 1968.

Lydia Sicher, MD, psychiatrist and PhD, was born in Vienna in 1890 and took her MD at the University of Vienna in 1916. During World War I, she was a physician and First Lieutenant in the Austrian army. Afterward, skilled in surgery, pathological anatomy, and radiology, she worked in Vienna under Wagner-Jauregg in neurology and psychiatry for 6 years.

Sicher met Adler in 1919 and was drawn to his work over that of Freud's. She became director of Adler's clinic when he left for the United States in 1929 and she ran it until it was closed by the Nazis in 1938. By then, she and her colleagues had treated over 3,000 patients using Adler's methods. She traveled widely throughout Europe while also running the clinic, until she immigrated to the United States in 1939. She spent 2 years in Utah, lecturing and seeing patients, until 1941, when she moved to Los Angeles and founded the first Adlerian Society there. She was also president of the American Society of Adlerian Psychology and was a member of the editorial board of the *Journal of Individual Psychology*.

Sophia deVries was born in Holland in 1901, took a BA in education and earned a teaching credential by 1919. Thereafter she started working with children. Soon, she went to Italy and studied with Maria Montessori. She first heard Adler lecture in Amsterdam, but it was not until 1935 that she went to Vienna, where she took courses given by Alfred Adler, Lydia Sicher, Alexander Müller, Rudolf Dreikurs, August Eichorn, and Karl Bühler. Her "study analysis," a process of supervised analysis by a qualified Adlerian, was with Sicher, who was Adler's first assistant, and her case supervision was provided by Müller, who was a close co-worker of Adler.

During the War, the Nazis forbid the practice of Adlerian psychology, but she continued anyway, largely in isolation. After the war, in 1945, the Adlerian training group was re-established in Holland. She was chosen for the Scientific Committee on Adlerian Psychology and taught courses with Alexander Müller in Amsterdam. She immigrated to the United States in 1948, settled in Southern California, and worked closely with Lydia Sicher. She moved to Northern California in 1952, worked as a case worker for Lincoln Child Center in Oakland, and continued to teach and develop a private practice.

For nearly 20 years, deVries served as a mentor and consultant to the Alfred Adler Institute of San Francisco, offering study groups, case studies of individuals, supervision, and study-analyses to students. Toward the end of her career, she became a major figure in the Adler translation project.

Anthony Bruck was a tireless lay advocate of individual psychology. He was multilingual from an early age and earned an MBA in Vienna. He moved to the United States in 1922. He had been introduced to Adler's essays before emigrating and in 1926, when he heard Adler was coming to the United States, wrote, introduced himself, and was able to arrange lectures for Adler in New York. That began a period when he became involved in all aspects of Adlerian psychology. He was the secretary of the Adler study group that met at the New School for Social Research, he attended all of Adler's lectures and became close to Adler himself. He returned to Vienna in 1931 and visited all 32 of the Adlerian Child Guidance Clinics and joined the Adlerians at the Café Shiller for extensive discussions. Thereafter, at Adler's encouragement, he traveled and lectured widely at universities and clinics throughout Central America, parts of Europe, and also the Middle East, returning to the United States in 1947. He lectured and traveled widely there, particularly in California, before returning to New York in 1977. Having been a confidant to Adler, he was close with his immediate disciples as well, who remembered him as a significant influence on their community.

Henry Stein,[17] a PhD in psychology, first encountered Adlerian psychology in the 1970s in the Bay Area of San Francisco, California. There, he was directed to Sophia deVries, who was well connected to the other Adlerians and depth psychologists of the day and she eventually became his teacher. As we noted before, she had studied with Alfred Adler, Carl Jung, August Eichorn, Ludwig Klages, and Maria Montessori. She did her study analysis with Lydia Sicher and received her case supervision from Alexander Müller.

She first suggested a study analysis where Stein would read a series of Adler's books to study the theory, and then in a weekly meeting, discuss with her each idea and its application to his personal and professional life. Eventually, he studied with her for more than 20 years. She in turn introduced Stein to Anthony Bruck and others and to a cache of unpublished documents that constitute the Adler archives.

Under deVries's guidance, Stein read all of Adler's writings that he could find, discovering that many of them were still not translated into English. She suggested that he learn German, so that he could then read the untranslated material. The result, with a group of German-speaking Adlerian translators more skilled than he, was the recently published clinical writings of Alfred Adler in 12 volumes.[18]

The Ansbachers

We may say that Adler's influence was far reaching, but remains widely unknown, especially today. While he did study psychopathology, his real focus was on education, which was not considered a hot topic in any case, but it was the field where the person could be studied as a whole and their hopes and strivings identified so as to bring about the development of their highest potential, beginning at an early age.

Even before he had met Adler through Maslow, Heinz Ansbacher came into psychology through popular lectures Adler had delivered at Columbia University in 1930. Meanwhile, Rowena Ansbacher had studied with Adler in Vienna in 1928. Thereafter, both came to know him intimately until the time of his death in 1937. Heinz Ansbacher and his wife went on to become Adler's tireless advocates, making his writings more widely known in the English language literature.

In *The Individual Psychology of Alfred Adler: A Systematic Presentation in Selections from his Writings* (1956), the Ansbachers' thesis was that Adler was the original field theorist of a dynamic psychology as a social science.[19] In his subjectivist orientation, Adler was the complete antithesis of Freud's objectivist epistemology. The essential problem, they noted, over and over, was how few really knew Adler's work. This was exacerbated by the unsystematic nature of his writings. Their volume hoped to correct that by collecting his papers in approximate chronological order and then thematically in the middle around the exposition of his theories. They were particularly aided in this regard, they said, by encouragement from Abraham Maslow and also the guiding hand of Gordon Willard Allport, and Gardner Murphy, among others.

In the introductory chapters, the editors went to great lengths to differentiate Adler from Freud and at the same time to explain Adler's system. Individual psychology was, first of all, a subjective depth psychology. By this they meant that it goes beyond surface phenomena to take unconscious motivation into account, but it does not hypostatize or reify the unconscious as a separate theoretical construct. It was dynamic, in that it incorporated strivings held by the person that they did not themselves fully understand, but which had definite effects as goals and ideals.

They went to great lengths to review William James's differentiation of personality types as tender and tough minded, classing Adler in the tender and Freud in the tough-minded columns. Freud was a biologically oriented reductionist bent on proving psychoanalysis a science. Adler was interested in the subjective interpretation of life from the person's point of view and gave more emphasis to experiential meaning rather than an externalist description of biology in shaping character. The Ansbachers then compared Adler to other psychological systems, finding him compatible with the personalistic psychology of William Stern, whose psychology represented a science of immediate experience which was experienced by the goal-directed person. The individual was a self-consistent unity always striving toward an ideal. Adler himself even remarked on their similarities.

Adler's was an idiographic science, the Ansbachers also pointed out. It was made up of laws that pertain to the individual case only, at the same time it was nomothetic, governed by general laws such as compensation for inferiority, but the focus was always on the individual, one's style of life, and opinion of the self, geared toward specific individual goals. The next step, the Ansbachers maintained, was to compare Adler to Allport and also to the psychology of Gardner Murphy.

They cited Adler's holism as a link to gestalt psychology. Solomon Asch, they pointed out, employed the same term as Adler—social interest—in differentiating himself from the socialization advocated by Freud. They reserved a special section comparing Adler to Kurt Lewin. Indeed, Lewin himself believed that the gestaltists had provided experimental evidence for the correctness of Adler's views.[20] First, they were similar in that they both rejected classification systems. Second, for both, dynamic forces were not fixed quantities of energy, but relational and changing. Adler's concept of movement was Lewin's concept of vector—the expression of a force directed from one point to another. For these reasons the Ansbachers classed Adler as the original field theorist in psychology.

His psychology, the Ansbachers continued, was also descriptive and not explanatory. This linked him to Dilthey, Spranger, and Jaspers. Even the early psychoanalysts commented on this similarity between Adler and Jaspers regarding the neuroses. The Ansbachers compared Adler favorably to the phenomenological psychology of Donald Snygg and Arthur Combs, and the existentialists, and finally to the client-centered theory of personality put forth by Carl Rogers.[21] Indeed, many of the later variations of Freud's theories among the neo-Freudians, they further pointed out, could be called instead, neo-Adlerian.

For his part, Adler came to depth psychology as a physician in general medicine and true to his training stayed there by emphasizing biology and physiology over unconscious mental mechanisms. He strove instead for a psychology that would lead to a more holistic biology.

In this regard, the true meaning of holism, according to Jan Smuts, makes room for a new science of personality, which "as the synthetic science of human nature, will form the crown of all the sciences, and, in turn, become the basis of a new Ethic, a new Metaphysic." As a method of approach to this new science Smuts proposed a comparative study of carefully documented biographies that will enable man to formulate the laws of personal evolution. It should come as no surprise that Smuts and Adler corresponded.[22]

Adler always maintained the originality of his own work. Nevertheless, he felt he had advocated for psychoanalysis in the Viennese medical community for many years and played some role in its acceptance as a science. But he also did not understand why he had to do his own work under Freud's shadow. One interpretation, of course, was that he could not see the bubble he was working in, in which, one could say, he was unconsciously dreaming, not his own dream, but Freud's dream, which centered in Freud's mind always around Freud and no one else.

May and Adler

Meanwhile, in 1932, Rollo May, a 20-year-old graduate from Oberlin College, had just arrived for a 3-year stint teaching English at Anatolia College in Saloniki,

Greece. Idealistic and starry-eyed, all he knew about Greece he had learned in *Bulfinch's Mythology*. He was in love with the place, in love with his students, in love with learning, and decidedly stuck in the classical Greek mindset. He was on a search, he later wrote, for beauty.[23]

But after 2 years the blush had worn off and May found himself in a lonely depression. Athens and Delphi no longer amazed him. He became neurasthenic; he lost energy, and took to his bed. He understood that he had to change, to adopt new values, and a new way of seeing, if he was to pull out of this slump. That summer, he took off for the mountains. He walked through a cold and snowy night beyond the inhabitants on the slopes and by morning had reached one of the remote villages high up beyond modern civilization, where no one spoke any English. He arranged a room and spent a number of days by the fire at an inn; writing on odd slips of paper all the thoughts that were streaming into his mind. He was engaging in a primitive form of self-analysis. Both a budding poet and an amateur artist, he had brought the tools of those trades, so began chronicling both the inward and the outward journey he was taking in pencil and in paint.

Eight weeks later, in May of 1932, May found himself enrolled in Alfred Adler's seminar at Semerling, a resort in the mountains above Vienna. We have little data on the content of these seminars, but May later proclaimed them seminal in the development of his thought about human nature. This was also as close to psychoanalysis as he would come, until later when he developed friendships with various American analysts and became a pupil of Paul Tillich, who had his own interpretations of Freud. The point was, it was this early direct contact with Adler, not Freud, that most influenced May with regard to dynamic theories of personality.

There was a strong personal reward that came out of the seminars as well. While there, he met an older American woman who had been watching him draw and she invited him to join a group of 18 students traveling through central Europe that summer visiting the peasant villages, and he accepted. They began in Vienna, proceeded to Hungary, then to Czechoslovakia, where May was exposed to art, music, dancing, and beauty. He returned to his teaching in the fall, a new man.

Adler and Maslow

From 1932 on, Adler himself became a visiting professor at Long Island College of Medicine. Finally, in 1934, he immigrated to the United States with his wife and lived at the Gramercy Hotel. There, he met Abraham Maslow. Maslow had been first introduced to the writings of Freud and Adler in 1932 and was fascinated by their differences, but also their relevance to his own work on dominance, power, and sexual hierarchies in primates. He came to believe at that time that Adler's work seemed more realistic—that hierarchy determined sexual behavior, not the other way around.

Maslow had graduated from the University of Wisconsin under Harry Harlow with a PhD in comparative animal psychology, and at that time he was a committed experimentalist. By 1935 he had a secure postdoctoral fellowship under E. L. Thorndike at Columbia, was married, and comfortably settled in New York. New York at the time was a hot bed of displaced émigré social thinkers and Adler was one of them. Maslow immediately sought out his company. Adler used to run Friday evening seminars in his hotel suite, where Maslow soon became a frequent guest. According to Maslow's biographer, 40 years his senior, Adler soon became Maslow's mentor.[24] To Maslow's complete surprise, the Friday groups were quite small, which gave him more time for intensive interaction. He brought numerous friends and colleagues to hear Adler lecture and to meet with him personally. One of them, he said, was Heinze Ansbacher.

Adler's influence on Maslow was allegedly enormous. He had convinced Maslow of the importance of social interest and reinforced the biological bases of the neuroses. But more importantly, Maslow got the meaning of *Menschenkenntnis*—it was an intuitive picture of the total person in the context of his or her environment. They saw each other intensively for an 18-month period and then had a falling out, after which Maslow ceased coming around. Adler died a short time later.

Adler's Influence on Victor Frankl

Possibly one of Adler's most significant admirers was Victor Frankl, founder of Logotherapy and a major pioneer in the development of existential psychiatry. Frankl had been particularly attracted to Adler's conception of cosmic feeling in the individual.

Of Jewish ancestry, Frankl was born March 26, 1905, son of Gabriel and Elsa Frankl.[25] His father was a government employee and his mother a housewife. Already drawn toward psychology, in his last years in high school he wrote a psychoanalytic study of Schopenhauer, published in the *International Journal of Psychoanalysis*, and opened a correspondence with Sigmund Freud. A medical student at age 20, he finally met Freud in 1925. By then, however, he had fallen under the influence of Alfred Adler's theories, soon publishing "Psychotherapy and Weltanschauung" in Adler's *International Journal of Individual Psychology*.[26] He was graduated from the University of Vienna with the MD in 1930. By 1940 he had become director of neurology at the Rothschild Hospital in Vienna and a year later married Mathilde Grosser. In 1942, however, they were both arrested by the Nazis and sent to the concentration camps. His father, mother, and brother died there, along with Mathilde, who managed to stay alive until 1945.

Frankl, himself, survived both Auschwitz and Dachau. Despite 3 years of the most abject horror, under constant threat of death, he lived to write about his experiences. There were, he came to believe, dimensions of consciousness so much deeper and more profound than that addressed by psychoanalysis that some completely new and revolutionary theory was in order. Out of this realization he evolved a new kind of therapy addressing the existential dimension of human experience, which he came to call Logotherapy, the discovery of meaning as a way to reach the deepest aspects of the soul.

While he eventually wrote some 20 volumes in German on the technical aspects of Logotherapy, American audiences heard of it for the first time through the English translation of *The Doctor and the Soul* (1955), renamed *From Death Camp to Existentialism* (1959), and later renamed again *Man's Search for Meaning* (1963).[27] The book appeared with a preface by the distinguished personality-social psychologist at Harvard, Gordon Willard Allport, the man who was primarily responsible for seeing its publication through the Beacon Press edition and who sponsored Frankl's introduction to the American psychological community. As a result, Frankl came to the United States as a visiting professor at Harvard in 1961, before he went on to Southern Methodist University in 1966, Stanford in 1971, and Duquesne in 1972. As a lecturer he was in international demand. His books have been translated into 14 languages and the US edition of *Man's Search for Meaning* by itself sold more than 4 million copies.

In this work, Frankl gave an account of his own experiences in the camps, followed by an essay on the basic principles of Logotherapy.[28] His intention, however, was not to write a systematic autobiography, but to sketch firsthand the psychology of the concentration camp prisoner in order for the reader to understand the genesis of Logotherapy. He was quite clear that it was impossible for us who were never there to ever understand what happened to those interned. We who had never gone through it could never really know the true extent of the suffering, crucifixion, and death of so many. He did not wish to tell about the worst kind of person that emerged under these extraordinary circumstances; he wished only to show that something really hopeful and important came to him about the human condition. He discovered heroic people who found a way to live, even if only briefly, by actualizing their highest values in the midst constant torture and death. He was self-consciously aware at the outset, he said, that those who were not there could never know, and of those who were, "the best of us did not come back."

The experiences in the camps, he said, proceeded through three distinct phases: the shock upon being arrested, the abject apathy that emerged in the face of the constant terrors, and the anesthesia that followed liberation.

In the first phase, shock set in somewhere between the time of arrest and the first hours after arrival in the camps. Thousands were rounded up and herded onto cattle cars, then compressed so tightly that few could even crouch down. With no food, ventilation, or sanitary facilities, the trains carried them for days, finally disgorging them at their destination. During this time, most maintained an attitude of utter disbelief that all this could be happening. Bewildered, cold, and hungry, they arrived only to stand a long time for inspection as an officer beckoned them to the right or the left. They did not yet know that one way meant immediate death in the gas chambers, the other way meant assignment to a work detail. Ninety percent of the 2,500 who arrived with him, Frankl said, were sent to death at the first selection.

Those who were left were then herded into buildings where their bags and parcels were taken from them. At first, unwilling to give up everything they had brought, many clung to the past, to a piece of jewelry, a wedding ring, a watch. Frankl kept a manuscript hidden under his coat until at one point they all realized, one by one, that everything would be taken away. They were stripped naked and every single hair was shaved off their bodies. Then they were given old clothes that had belonged to dead prisoners. Kickings, beatings, and brutal killings occurred all around them, carried out by the most sadistic and horrible means. Finally, by being successively subjected to the lowest of degradations, with the punishment of death hanging over them for showing even the slightest disgust, all delusion of reprieve finally vanished.

Then the second stage began, that of apathy. This was emotional death, a necessary survival mechanism. Nothing became too terrible to witness. One did not avert one's eyes any more, whatever the episode. While a reaction could mean one's own death, because of attracting the guards' attention, the real effect was nothing so rationally mediated. Rather, each one in turn experienced a complete numbing of all emotional sensibilities. Soon, it became impossible to react; but this, too, had survival value, because it helped each prisoner become insensitive to the daily and hourly beatings. Prevailing on such a large scale, apathy made a prisoner frightened to take any initiative whatsoever. Fate became one's master and was not to be tempted.

The prisoners were forced by these outward circumstances to turn within. But when they did so, they opened themselves up, one degree or another to the reality of interior vision. Sleep and, hence, dreaming became a kind of drug, a temporary respite. The most ghastly moment of each day, Frankl said, was awakening, because it brought one back to face the horror. Sleep, when it could be had, took place eventually under the most extraordinary of conditions. As for dreaming, once Frankl thought to wake up his neighbor from a terrible nightmare, but he suddenly left off, realizing that nothing could be worse then to subject the man once again to their present waking reality.

He reported that under these outward circumstances there was an extreme intensification of inner life. There were numerous instances of time distortion, for instance. Each hour would pass by with excruciating slowness. A minute might seem like an eternity. A day seemed longer than a week. Also, an inward curiosity about one's personal circumstances would develop. With each new insult more horrible than the one before, living on the edge, not knowing if that was to be the final moment on earth, each situation brought a curious detachment, a removed pondering as to which way the outcome might go. A certain dark humor also became another of the soul's weapons in the fight for self-preservation. A certain mass forgetfulness of norms and values might occur, as in one reported instance of cannibalism. Anything that led to survival was the key. All else was forgotten.

He also gave many instances of dissociated states of consciousness. In tears from pain, walking many miles to a distant work site in cold bitter winds, wearing only rags and torn shoes, Frankl had been thinking of endless little problems—Would he get enough food that day? Could he fix his broken shoelace? Could he trade a cigarette he had for extra bread? Suddenly, he became disgusted with these trivial thoughts and, desiring to turn away from them, he saw himself standing on a platform in a well-lit and warm lecture hall, lecturing to an interested audience on the psychology of the concentration camp! Everything pressing on him, all the little problems he thought about while he marched through the cold and the wind, he then saw remotely, from an objective viewpoint. In this way he was able to rise above his emotional suffering at that moment.

He also noted the psychic influence of the mind on health and disease. On the one hand, the will to live produced remarkable instances of self-healing. Despite severe vitamin deficiency and inability to brush their teeth, everyone's gums remained generally healthy. Sores and abrasions did not suppurate, despite the constant infestation of lice and the dirt and grime from wearing the same clothes for 6 months at a time without washing. Many common minor physical and mental complaints simply disappeared in the face of the larger daily task of survival at all costs.

On the other hand, the mind could play a role for ill. One patient, for instance, had a dream in which he was granted the opportunity to ask one question. He asked when the war would be over for him and the dream gave a precise date. Accordingly, he announced to his friends that the Armistice would come and the war would be ending on that specific date. But as the months past and the date neared it appeared that the fighting would continue. Suddenly, he came down with a mysterious fever and died. It was, of course, the exact date foretold to him in his dream.

As well, thoughts of suicide were common. While generally each man clung to life, the real danger to everyone was the prisoner who lost faith in the future. It usually started when the person refused to get up. He would not get dressed and wash or go out onto the parade ground. Under other circumstances, a prisoner might refuse to go to sick bay when mortally ill. Such a person would just lay there in his own excrement, just waiting for the end.

The highest achievement of all, however, was the rising of a spiritual consciousness. "We who lived in the concentration camps can remember the men who walked through the huts comforting others, giving away their last piece of bread."[29] Most importantly, Frankl noted that how a person reacted was an inward decision, not mediated by any outward circumstances. Each person chose the stance they would take toward what happened to them. In this inward attitude they were completely free. For some, each situation brought out their worst or appealed to their weakest aspect, and this aspect they became. For others, each situation was a test of inward spiritual strength. They would ask of themselves, not "Why is this happening to me?" but "Am I worthy of my sufferings?"

Some of these people who knew they were about to die and who had made peace within themselves appeared angelic and could commune with the simplest levels of living nature—a twig, a blade of grass, as if all was one. For them, self-realization for just one moment became a reality.

At one point, Frankl recounted marching to a work detail amidst fierce kicks and the crushing blows of gun butts. Stumbling on for miles, through ice and wind, the prisoners supported each other. The man next to him furtively wondered what their wives would think if they could see what pitiful condition their men were in. After this, as they continued along, they both knew they were thinking of their wives. Frankl wrote:

> Occasionally I looked at the sky, where the stars were fading and the pink light of the
> morning was beginning to spread behind a dark bank of clouds. But my mind clung to my
> wife's image, imagining it with an uncanny acuteness. I heard her answering me, saw her

smile, her frank and encouraging look. Real or not, her look was then more luminous than the sun which was beginning to rise. A thought transfixed me: for the first time in my life I saw the truth as it is set into song by so many poets, proclaimed as the final wisdom by so many thinkers. The truth–that love is the ultimate and highest goal to which man can aspire. Then I grasped the meaning of the greatest secret that human poetry and human thought and belief have to impart: *The salvation of man is through love and in love.* I understood how a man who has nothing left in this world still may know bliss, be it only for a brief moment, in the contemplation of his beloved. In a position of utter desolation, when man cannot express himself in positive action, when his only achievement may consist in enduring his sufferings in the right way–an honorable way–in such a position man can, through loving contemplation of the image he carries of his beloved, achieve fulfillment.[30]

Meaning could emerge in the midst of suffering. To illustrate this Frankl recounted the episode of a prisoner who stole some potatoes from the storehouse. When he was discovered the camp commandant threatened to deprive everyone of food until the culprit was given up. Instead of betraying him, all 2,500 inmates chose to fast. That night in Frankl's hut the men were depressed. As tempers flared up, the lights went out, making things even worse. The hut leader got up to quiet their fears and once he had their attention, he asked a surprised Frankl to address them on ways to prevent despair and suicide. Extemporizing, Frankl rose from his own cold, exhausted, and hungry state to speak to the collective group in such great despair about hope and meaning. He appealed to their dreams and their memories, to people whom they had lost, or to those who might still be alive whom they had loved. Live for them, he said.

In order not to sound biblical, he quoted from poets and essayists, "What does not kill me makes me stronger." They all had small things to be glad for, an extra bowl of soup, the hope of a light work detail, escaping once again the daily dreaded selection. Meaning could be found even in the most profound suffering, because we always have the choice of what attitude we will take toward what happens to us. Suffering gives us hidden opportunities for new achievement. Because everyone in the room was still alive, life still expected something from them. Life questions us and it is upon us to take responsibility to find the right answers to fulfill the tasks it sets for each individual. Once we have discovered for ourselves a reason to live, we can endure anything. "He who has a why can bear with almost any how." When the lights came on again and he stopped talking, many came before him thankful and weeping.

Then there was the final phase, the psychology of the prisoner after liberation. Frankl recounts that after so many years, after so many false hopes, the human soul had been torn open, its depths had become overexposed. Consequently, when liberation came, its reality could not be immediately grasped.

In many instances, Frankl noted that the pressure bearing down on people for years to be silent suddenly was released and made them talk, irresistibly. Sometimes, after many days or months of this kind of chatter, the first glimmer of feeling might emerge, although this was not universally the case. After what they had seen and experienced, others never opened again.

Frankl recounted the story of one of his first walks outside the camps with a compatriot, who in his glee on being released insisted on trampling down a field of young crops. Frankl objected, but the man replied angrily that he had lost his wife and children in the gas chambers; hadn't he a right to trample down a few stalks of oats? For many like him, Frankl noted, there was only the moral deformity, the bitterness, and the disillusionment that followed. Former prisoners would return to their home towns only to find everyone in their family gone. Strangers lived in their houses. Those who had not been through the camps merely shrugged their shoulders. They did not know what had gone on. And if they did, what could they have done about it? The former prisoners soon came to realize that no earthly happiness could compensate them for all they had suffered. After so many years of withstanding the absolute limit of suffering, they were introduced to a new kind of suffering that had no limits. In the end, liberation, the day, which for so long had been a dream, was followed by an eerie transition, after which, the horrors of the camps were remembered as if a nightmare.

Logotherapy

Even before the war Frankl had been working on the problems of existential anxiety in psychotherapy. But afterward this kind of anxiety evolved into the central focus of his worldview. Logotherapy, a therapy of the soul in the search for meaning, became the third school of Viennese psychiatry, after Freudian and Adlerian psychology. Frankl's position was that the basis of all human striving was not to overcome the conflicts between biological urges and the extent of their fulfillment, but to discover reasons to live. We are impelled not by our repressions but by our values and ideals. Neurosis, he came to believe, was the necessary result of putting sense gratification before meaning.

Frankl made many comparisons between his approach and that of Freud. Freud stayed focused on the psychological expression of biological needs, while Logotherapy "dared to enter the human dimension." Its focus on meaning went beyond mere adjustment to the norms of a society and entered into the existential nature of personal experience. Frankl saw in this that the therapist's job was to pilot patients through the existential crisis until they discovered where they were heading in their life. For some, this was not the real issue; in these cases, he practiced classical psychoanalysis. For others, this was the central problem, and so logotherapeutic interventions were necessary, which carried the patient and the therapist beyond the more limited frame of reference conceived by Freud. Adler had first showed him the way.

Frankl tried to get the patient to ask the deeper questions about personal existence, to see that even the simplest of daily tasks carried large spiritual consequences, in that all things are transitory, that life is finite, and that the end is final. He said, "The logotherapist's role consists of widening and broadening the visual field of the patient so that the whole spectrum of potential meaning becomes conscious and visible to him."[31] This widening to a world beyond the self he further called "the self-transcendence of human existence."

He encouraged his patients to take up a cause, to love something or someone, and to stand for some principle. Only in this way is character refined and perfected. Meaning should be the goal, not happiness or self-actualization, as these are mere side effects of transcendence; they are byproducts, not the goals, of a well-lived life.

Meaning, in this regard, can be created in several ways. The most difficult is through the actualization of values. Normally, we wait until the last minute and then make do with each situation we are presented with in life. Sometimes, however, we are able to see that by starting with the small things and putting them in order, by slowing accruing the success that comes from mastery of events over which we do have control, that the highest of what we cherish can come into being.

The other way, which is the path most readily open to most of us, is to find meaning in the attitude we take toward our suffering. No person is free from this dimension of human experience. Yet, as Frankl found in the concentration camps, we are likewise free to determine the attitude we will take toward what happens to us. Each struggle presents us with a new opportunity for transcendence and inward growth. In this his theories sound much like Buddhist thought, which, like Logotherapy, emphasizes the transitoriness of all existence, existential emptiness, and the transcendence of suffering. Yet his occasional references to belief in God, his emphasis on depth psychology as a secularized religious language, and his references to transcendent consciousness made Frankl's work tremendously popular with English-speaking audiences, especially in the field of pastoral theology. This may explain why his work has been closely embraced by the popular Christian world. Meanwhile, it has been rejected by the orthodox psychoanalysts, received somewhat coolly within Orthodox Judaism, and hardly mentioned by technical scholars of the Holocaust. Despite the fact that Frankl spent most of his life in Vienna and had always been an Austrian citizen, he remained, after all, for the very reasons he is considered suspect by these other sources, a folk hero, particularly among the existential-humanistic psychologists.

Finally, there are numerous ways in which we can see Adler in Frankl's work. The intuitive nature of Adler's vision of the person leads to a deepening of the existential point of view with regard to human experience. It is not the happiness psychology of Prof. Seligman, or a denial of the dark side of human nature, but a full bodied and direct encounter with pain, conflict, suffering, and death as a means toward self-transcendence. Frankl's was a case study of Adler's theories, particularly the need for social feeling (*gemeinschaftsgefeuhl*) to understand the existential context of personal autonomy (*Menschenkenntnis*). The biological roots of one's psychological sense of inferiority lead to compensation and the striving for superiority in the context of social feeling. Whatever we are in the secular domain, within the inner life of the person, there is the capacity to experience cosmic feeling, to live "as if" there will be a better day, and to understand love as the ultimate experience of self-transcendence. Freud did not take up these topics. Instead, the way for Frankl was through Adler.

These influences cause us to look a little more deeply into Adler's life and work. One always presumes that when we talk about depth psychology we must be talking about the lineage from Freud. We have shown thus far, however, that there was a flourishing dynamic psychology of the subconscious many years before Freud that had emerged upon the international scene. Adler's work, moreover, came out of his interest in psychology, but within the context of Adler's own medical background. Adler's ideas, such as the inferiority complex, were taken over by the psychoanalysts and wrongly since then attributed to Freud, and while Adler's theories were clearly psychodynamic, they rejected most of the major presuppositions Freud had put forth about the unconscious and the nature of psychic energy. Adler championed psychoanalysis without being Freud's disciple.

This can be seen in the many ways in which Adler's individual psychology is totally unlike psychoanalysis. In fact, a further elaboration of Adler's thinking shows him to have had a greater impact on a normative psychology of the individual, which Freud did not write much about, and, further, it was direct contact with the Adlerian, not the Freudian system, that so inspired later pioneers such as Maslow, May, and Frankl in the rise of existential-humanistic and transpersonal psychology.[32]

Notes

1. I have relied heavily on Ellenberger, 1970, pp. 571–656; and Ansbacher, H. L., & Ansbacher, R. R. (Eds.). (1964). *Alfred Adler: Superiority and social interest: A collection of later writings*, with a biographical essay by Carl Fürtmuller. Evanston, IL: Northwestern University Press.
2. Adler, A. (2002a). Health manual for the tailoring trade. In H. T. Stein (Ed). (G. L. Liebenau, Trans), *The collected clinical works of Alfred Adler (1898–1909)* (Vol. 2.1, pp. 1–14). Bellingham, WA: Classical Adlerian Translation Project. (Original work published 1898); Adler, A. (1898). *Gesundheitsbuch für das Schneidergewerbe*, No. 5 of the series: *Weigweiser der Gewerbehygiene*, G. Golebiewski (Ed.). Berlin: Carl Heymanns.
3. Adler, A. (1917). Study of organ inferiority and its psychical compensation: A contribution to clinical medicine. *Nervous and Mental Disease Monograph Series, 24*. (S. E. Jelliffe, Trans.). New York: The Nervous and Mental Disease Publishing Company; Adler, A. (2002b). A study of organ inferiority and its philosophical and psychological meaning. H. T. Stein (Ed.) (G. L. Liebenau, Trans.), *The Collected clinical works of Alfred Alder (1898–1909)* (Vol. 2.2, pp. 78–85). Bellingham, WA: Classical Adlerian Translation Project. (Original work published 1907); Adler, A. (1907). *Studie über Minderwertigkeit von Organen* [Study of organ inferiority].Vienna: Urban und Schwartenberg.
4. Adler, A. (1916). *The neurotic constitution: Outlines of a comparative individualistic psychology and psychotherapy* (B. Glueck & J. E. Lind, Trans.). New York: Moffat, Yard.
5. Adler, A. (1935). Introduction. *International Journal of Individual Psychology, 1*(1), p. 5; Adler, A. (1924). *The practice and theory of individual psychology*. London: K. Paul, Trench, Trubner & Company, Ltd; New York, Harcourt, Brace & company.
6. Adler, 1935, p. 6.
7. Adler, A. (1927). *Understanding human nature*. New York: Greenberg; Adler, A. (1927). *Menschenkenntnis*. [Understanding human nature]. Leipzig: Hirzel.
8. Adler, A. (1930a). *Guiding the child on the principles of individual psychology* (B. Ginzburg, Trans.). London: George Allen and Unwin; New York: Greenberg.
9. Adler, 1930a, pp. 127–147.
10. Adler, A. (1929). *The case of Miss R.: The interpretation of a life story* (E & F. Jensen, Trans.). New York: Greenberg.

11. Fürtmuller, C., & Adler, A. (1964). A bibliographical essay. In H. L. Ansbacher, & R. R. Ansbacher (Eds.). *Alfred Adler: Superiority and social interest: A collection of later writings.* Evanston, IL: Northwestern University Press, p. 383.

12. Ellenberger, 1970, pp. 609–613.

13. Adler, 1930a, p. 62.

14. See, Adler (1930a); Adler, A. (1930b). *The pattern of life* (B. Wolfe, Ed.). New York: Cosmopolitan Book Corporation; Murchison, C. (Ed.). (1930). *Psychologies of 1930,* by Alfred Adler, Madison Bentley, Edwin G. Boring [and others]. Worcester, MA: Clark University Press; London, H. Milford, Oxford University Press.

15. Kaiser, C. (1995). An interview with Kurt Adler (1905–1997) on his 90th birthday. Adler Institute of Zurich, Adler Institute Homepage. http://ourworld.compuserve.com/homepages/hstein/kurt-90.htm

16. Adler, A. (1945). Two different types of post-traumatic neuroses. *American Journal of Psychiatry, 102,* 237–240.

17. Stein, H. T. (2002–2006). *The collected clinical works of Alfred Adler* (Vols.1–12). Bellingham, WA: Classical Adlerian Translation Project.

18. Stein, H. T. (2007). Adler's legacy: Past, present, and future. Ansbacher Lecture. Annual Conference, North American Society for Adlerian Psychology, May 24, 2007. Vancouver, BC. Adler Home Page. http://ourworld.compuserve.com/homepages/hstein/adlers-legacy.htm

19. Ansbacher, H., & Ansbacher, R. (Eds.). (1956). *The individual psychology of Alfred Adler: A systematic presentation in selections from his writings.* New York: Harper & Row.

20. Ansbacher & Ansbacher, 1956, p. 12.

21. Ansbacher & Ansbacher, 1956, p. 15. These are clearly the Ansbachers' interpretations as a form of comparison, not the articulation of a lineage.

22. Smuts, J. C. (1926). *Holism and evolution.* New York, London: Macmillan. See also, Ellenberger, 1970, p. 631.

23. May, R. (1985). *My quest for beauty.* San Francisco: Saybrook.

24. Hoffman E. (1988). *The right to be human: A biography of Abraham Maslow.* Los Angeles: J. P. Tarcher, pp. 102–106.

25. Biographical material in this section comes from *Contemporary Authors.* http://gale.cengage.com/pdf/facts/ca.pdf

26. Frankl, V. (1925). Psychotherapie und Weltanshauung [Psychotherapy and weltanschauung]. *International Zeitschrift fur Individualpsychologie, 3,* 250–252.

27. Frankl, V. E. (1955). *The doctor and the soul: An introduction to logotherapy.* New York: Knopf; Frankl, V. E. (1959). *From death-camp to existentialism: A psychiatrist's path to a new therapy.* Boston: Beacon Press; Frankl, V. E. (1963). *Man's search for meaning: An introduction to logotherapy* (I. Lasch, Trans.). Boston: Beacon Press.

28. I have used Frankl, V. E. (1992). *Man's search for meaning: An introduction to logotherapy* (4th ed.). Boston: Beacon Press.

29. Frankl, 1992, p. 75.

30. Frankl, 1992, p. 49.

31. Frankl, 1992, p. 115.

32. Ansbacher, H. L. (1990, Fall). Alfred Adler's influence on the three leading cofounders of humanistic psychology. *Journal of Humanistic Psychology, 30*(4), 45–53.

Chapter 8
Psychodynamics, Gestalt Psychology, and Personality Theory at Harvard

Harvard likes to be either first or last in everything.
E. G. Boring

For almost half a century, from the day Edwin G. Boring first walked into the halls at Harvard to assume his teaching duties in 1921, to the day that he died in 1967 in Stillman Infirmary, the status and relevance of dynamic theories of personality as a legitimate science played a central role in defining what was even allowed to be called psychology at the University. Boring was against the molar, the psychodynamic, and a science that was person centered because he judged them to be unscientific and he spent his entire career defending that principle. What hung in the balance, insofar as Harvard contributes to the gold standard of what happens in institutions of higher learning in the West, was the more ethereal fate of such theories in the academy and in the wider discipline of psychology at large, both nationally and internationally, influencing their status, then as today.

On the one side, representing psychology as a laboratory science, was E. G. Boring, student of Titchener in the direct lineage of Wundt. Then there was Boring's protégé, Stanley Smith Stevens, experimental psychologist and psychophysicist *par excellence*, and others, such as Edwin Newman, J. G. Beebe-Center, and Karl Lashley, and later B. F. Skinner. Eventually, on the other side stood Gordon Willard Allport, pioneer personality-social psychologist; Henry A. Murray, physician, biochemist, and specialist in abnormal psychology who ran the Harvard Psychological Clinic; and others, such as Clyde Kluckhohn, Robert White, and the aging Morton Prince in psychology; Talcot Parsons and George Homans in sociology; Stanley Cobb in psychiatry, who was Harvard's Bullard Professor of Neuropathology at the Medical School and chief of psychiatry at the Massachusetts General Hospital; and L. J. Henderson, physical chemist and Harvard powerbroker, who paradoxically sponsored both Henry Murray and B. F. Skinner at the same time in psychology. Looming in the background were students such as Saul Rosenzweig, Donald McKinnon, Hadley Cantril, Jerome Bruner, James Grier Miller, and others.

There were also other faculty, such as Pitirim Sorokin, the fiery and rhetorical sociologist into revolutions, and Samuel Stouffer, the statistician. Beyond Harvard, but close in its shadow, was Gardner Murphy, who took an MA in psychology at Harvard and his doctorate at Columbia under William James's old student Robert

E. Taylor, *The Mystery of Personality*, Library of the History of Psychology Theories, DOI 10.1007/978-0-387-98104-8_8, © Springer Science+Business Media, LLC 2009

Woodworth. Afterward, Murphy returned briefly to teach parapsychology at Harvard in the 1920s; and others, such as Erik Erikson, who first came to Harvard in 1933, and without a college degree of any kind, joined the faculty in both psychology and psychiatry through the influence of Cobb and Murray.

But the man who was probably most influential behind the scenes in shaping the scientific study of personality in the 1930s at Harvard as a Galilean rather than a mere Newtonian science was a German émigré and gestalt psychologist, who only taught from 1938 to 1940 as a visiting professor. That was Kurt Lewin. In the minds of Allport and Murray, Lewin confirmed their emphasis on the possibility of constructing a science of the whole person over against the reductionists who had taken over almost the entire field of psychology. At the same time, their appropriation of Lewin's topological field theory made a place in their definition of scientific psychology for dynamic theories of personality, admittedly more of the gestaltist rather than the Freudian variety alone. Complex as the history of it is, we can only give a bare sketch here.

Edwin G. Boring was a central figure. He was raised in a Quaker-Moravian household in Philadelphia, in a communal arrangement run on strict spiritual values of a fundamentalist sort.[1] The 22 people living communally under two conjoined roofs, which included Boring and his mother and father, were led by two aging spinster sisters, whose purity, as well as absolute authority, were unquestioned. Boring's father, a druggist, appears to have held a relatively minor status in the hierarchy of things, leaving a gap that was soon to be filled by a towering and charismatic figure in the history of psychology, Edward Bradford Titchener. Boring attended Cornell and majored in engineering, but his senior year decided on a course in psychology. Psychology at Cornell was defined by the dictates of E. B. Titchener, originally an Oxford trained Englishman who had taken his PhD under Wilhelm Wundt in Leipzig in experimental psychology, and who had then immigrated to the United States. There, he set up an experimental laboratory at Cornell University as a young professor and launched a formidable research enterprise in which he intended to establish German structuralism in the experimental laboratory tradition as the only psychology worthy of the name. His method was the introspective analysis of consciousness, which he trained his students to do in the laboratory, along with the mastery of all the other accoutrements of Teutonic psychology, which included physiological recordings, psychophysical measurements, and reaction time experiments. Aspiring to become the American Wundt, Titchener even rejected as still too eclectic the overly scientific emphasis of the newly established American Psychological Association once he had come to Cornell. In a huff over some issue at some point, Titchener founded his own group, The Society of Experimental Psychologists, which ran as an independent society until 1938.[2] Within his own domain, he remained in control of how psychology was to be defined, having his own standards. He even lectured in his academic gown, which he later said, allowed him to be dictatorial.

Boring took Titchener's introductory psychology course, which he himself would later adapt to the Harvard curriculum. At the end, as he walked out the door for the last time, he had to pass Titchener, who stood there in his academic robes returning each student's final exam. As he passed across the threshold, Titchener looked down at him and, handing him his exam, declared in a stentorian voice, "*You* have the psychological attitude," a compliment that he extended to no other student. It was a prescient moment for Boring, who went off to do engineering for a steel company in Bethlehem, Pennsylvania. After a year, Boring decided that engineering was not for him and returned to Cornell to take the PhD under Titchener's guidance. To underscore the fatherly nature of Titchener's influence over him, when Boring met his wife-to-be in the laboratory, and then married her, and they went on their honeymoon, after a certain number of days had passed, Titchener sent a telegram that the honeymoon was over; it was time to return to the laboratory as there was work to be done. They, of course, complied.

Titchener's fortunes appeared to be changing as well. Upon Hugo Münsterberg's death at the podium while lecturing to students at Radcliffe, Harvard made an offer to Titchener to replace Münsterberg as the senior professor in experimental psychology. Titchener played President Lowell to the maximum with one demand after another, to the point where the offer was withdrawn. So Titchener was out, but Boring was soon in.[3] Boring arrived in 1921, with the intent of living out Titchener's will at Harvard. This meant that he intended to establish experimental psychology in the Wundtian tradition, at Harvard and elsewhere from that vantage point if he could.[4] The project was temporarily put on hold when he became involved in a serious auto accident and completely lost his memory for a time. His was but a trial run teaching at Harvard as an instructor for a semester. He went to Clark University, after G. Stanley Hall offered him a professorship in experimental psychology. There he taught briefly until he was summarily dismissed related to a misunderstanding over which he had no control. He was able to return to Harvard, where he remained until his death almost 50 years later. Upon his return, however, through a series of political intricacies, while Boring was able to come, Floyd Allport, who was Gordon Allport's older brother, and Herbert Sydney Langfeld, Gordon Allport's dissertation chair, were forced to leave.

Floyd Allport and his younger brother Gordon had come from a conservative Midwestern background of four children. They were born in Indiana and grew up in Ohio. Their father was a naturopathic physician, while their mother was a school teacher. She had come from a line of Free Methodists, who practiced stricter prohibitions than even the mainstream Methodist Church. She had rebelled against Free Methodism as an adult, converting first to New Thought and then Christian Science. Gordon Allport himself later returned to mainstream Christianity to become a high Episcopalian.

Gordon matriculated at Harvard in 1915, because his brother Floyd was already there, teaching as Münsterberg's assistant. As an undergraduate, he majored in psychology and did volunteer work through the Phillips Brooks House, the social service organization for undergraduates at Harvard. Also a member at Phillips Brooks House was Richard Clarke Cabot, ethicist, cardiologist, former student of William James, member with others such as L. J. Henderson and Walter Cannon in the so-called Royce circle, and founder of the Department of Social Services and later chief of the West medical service at the Massachusetts General Hospital. But Allport said in his own autobiography that he did not really get to know Cabot until he began teaching in the Department of Social Ethics in 1924.[5] Cabot had been instrumental in developing The Boston School of Social Work at Simmons College in 1904, the first professional school of social work in the United States, and involved with founding the Department of Social Ethics at Harvard under Rev. Francis Greenwood Peabody in 1905. Cabot's emphasis was on development of the spiritual dimension of personality in a secular age, and his connections to religion, philosophy, and psychology at Harvard satisfied Allport's alternate urge to lean toward the ministry. As a beginning student, Allport did volunteer social work through The Phillips Brooks House. In this regard, Cabot, among others, was also Allport's link to the Jamesean ethos at Harvard.

Allport graduated in 1919. During W.W.I, he had been an inductee in the Student's Army Training Corps, where social service continued to play a most important role in his life. After graduation, he then spent a year teaching at Robert College in Turkey, and afterward returned to Harvard, where he received his PhD in psychology in 1922 under Herbert S. Langfeld, James Ford, and William McDougall with a dissertation on trait theory.

Allport retold an amusing story in his autobiography while he was preparing his dissertation that serves as a clue to his mettle. Titchener was visiting Clark University with some of his graduate students as Boring's guest and they invited Langfeld and Allport from Harvard to join their seminar. When they got there, Titchener dominated the conversation for most of the time, and then at the very end permitted each graduate student to state the topic of his research project, which he had assigned them. When they got around to Allport, Allport announced he was studying the traits of personality, and got a reception of glowering silence. Afterward, Titchener pulled Langfeld aside and demanded to know why he had permitted Allport to choose that topic. On the return trip to Cambridge, Allport was devastated that he had been rebuked by the great Titchener and he was tremendously embarrassed. He confessed to Langfeld that he was really unprepared in biology, mathematics, and the more experimental laboratory aspects of science, until Langfeld interrupted him and said. "Don't worry, there are many humanistic pastures in psychology." And besides, he declared, "you don't really care what Titchener thinks." Suddenly, it was a revelation for Allport to be able to admit that actually he really didn't care what Titchener thought. He could be committed to psychology, but still go his own way.

The dissertation was entitled "An Experimental Study of the Traits of Personality, with Application to the Problem of Social Diagnosis" (1922).[6] It had absolutely nothing to do with dynamic theories of personality except that Allport reviewed briefly the work of Janet, Freud, and Prince but in a historical section that showed he was no historian. He also adapted Jung's traits of introversion and extraversion to an elaborate statistical study, but he misspelled the word as "extroversion" and admitted that he had significantly modified what Jung had originally been getting at. It was mostly a classic experimentally oriented document in the lineage of Floyd Allport, J. B. Watson, and Walter Dearborn that attempted to establish not only trait theory, but psychology and its methods as an experimental laboratory science. The applied part went one step farther in its advance of social psychology as the experimental analysis of behavior.

After completing his dissertation, Allport then spent 2 years studying abroad in Germany and England, where he was influenced by German holism, the study of character and temperament, graphology, the theories of Eduard Spranger, the personalism of William Stern, and gestalt psychology.[7]

There is also the matter of Sigmund Freud, whom Allport met on his trip. Traveling through Vienna with some extra time on his hands, the young and self-assured Allport, the recent Harvard graduate, decided that while he was in Vienna he might drop by and meet Freud to see what he was like. Quite otherwise unannounced, he called to say he was coming and Freud acquiesced. On the way over in a tram, he observed a prim and fussy hausfrau reprimanding a little boy in her charge. The seat was apparently dirty and the boy did not want to sit down and there was some unpleasant exchange between them. When Allport arrived at Bergasse 19, he was ushered in and sat down. There was then a moment of awkward silence, as Freud sat expectantly waiting to hear why Allport had wanted to see him. Allport, for his part, became extremely uncomfortable and thought to himself that he would just describe what happened on the tram, so he blurted out the story. Freud leaned forward and asked simply, "And was that little boy you?" Allport was then tremendously annoyed. Of course the little boy wasn't him. Why was Freud reading something into Allport's account? This he thought quite presumptuous, and left immediately. He remained indignant about Freud for the rest of his life, which, at the moment further confirmed his original behavioristic leanings. As it turned out, he may have held a grudge personally against Freud for what Allport perceived was a misplaced embarrassment, but he would later turn approvingly to psychoanalysis and incorporate an Americanized version of the unconscious into his own model of personality.

One of the influences that worked to liberalize Allport's thinking about a dynamic theory of personality was gestalt psychology, a psychology which, paradoxically, had no theory about the unconscious, but rather was derived from the German experimental laboratory tradition, but not the Wundtian.

German psychology had become somewhat transformed during the Weimar Republic. Wundt had died in 1920 and the influence of his school was waning, but by no means dead. The effect of World War I on Germany was to stimulate an era of holism in German science unprecedented in its previous history. Gestalt psychology, which had developed around Wertheimer, Koffka, and Köhler in Stumpf's laboratory after 1905, also came to include Kurt Lewin who would have a central influence on Allport's theories.

Allport was also significantly influenced by Edward Spranger. Spranger was a philosopher of education and follower of Wilhelm Dilthey who radically opposed the methods of natural science and preferred those of a more humanistically oriented psychology, which he called *Geisteswissenschaften*. Spranger even demanded a return of the word psychology from the experimentalists so it could be more properly employed for the science of a meaningful and fulfilled life. He developed a typological theory of personality based on six ideal categories, although individuals could be characterized as mixtures of each one. They were the theoretical, economic, aesthetic, social, religious, and a power type, with one type predominating over the others.[8] He believed sufficiently in the principle of individuality that he openly stood against the mass testing of students in the gymnasium in the early 1920s.

Allport was also attracted to the Graphology movement in Germany of Ludwig Klages. This was a popular movement that believed handwriting analysis was a key to understanding an individual's soul, and was a more accurate predictor of job performance than standardized tests.[9] Mitchell Ash reports that Klages's work was based on the ideas of the Romantic philosopher Carl Gustav Carus, who believed that expressive movements of a person's body were the key to understanding their character. Allport would exploit this idea later in his own theories to counter the influence of the nomothetic reductionists who wanted American psychology to focus only on mass statistics.

The psychologist who seemed to have the biggest looming influence on Gordon Allport's theorizing was William Stern, the man in the Clark University photo of 1909 standing next to William James. It was he who advocated a personalistic psychology, meaning a science that was centered on the person. Stern had studied at Berlin with Ebbinghaus and Stumpf, and was noted for his differential psychology and contributions to education, and remembered for his psychophysical work and the invention of the tone variator.[10] His great criticism of the gestaltists was "No Gestalt without a Gestalter," in that he sought to shift the focus of psychology from the interaction of the organism and the environment to personality as the central motif of perception.

Stern, known as a pioneer in differential psychology, was born and raised in Berlin in 1871 and was weaned away from Ebbinghaus by the works of Lazarus and of Paulsen, leading him to the synthesis of cultural and experimental science in 1893 in his doctoral dissertation.[11] He went to Breslau thereafter and developed the tone variator for which he is remembered by the experimentalists,[12] but he also discussed the conscious present, presaging the phenomenology of gestalt psychology. His works on differential psychology followed in which he declared that individuality would be the psychological problem of the 20th century. He also founded a journal and an Institute. His philosophy he called critical personalism, which he characterized in the context of the second law of thermodynamics and its relevance for mental science. He also formulated the intelligence quotient, or IQ, in 1912, and pioneered in the use of the diary to chronicle adolescent development. He fled Hitler in 1933, first through Holland, and went on to the United States, where he later became a professor at Duke from 1934 to 1938, teaching at Harvard summer school in 1936. In 1938 the English translation of his pioneering text *General Psychology from the Personalistic Standpoint*[13] appeared, but he suddenly died that year.[14] For Stern, all difficulties were resolved in the person. "This concept and this concept alone...could provide the substantiality, the causality, and the individuality required in every mature psychological analysis."[15]

The other figure who came to profoundly influence Allport was Kurt Lewin. Lewin began publishing during the World War I. One of his important papers was on camouflage and the war landscape. The other was a critique of G. E. Müller and Herman Ebbinghaus. He gained an international reputation, however, through a series of papers published between 1926 and 1930 in the *Psychologische Forschung*, the gestaltist's journal, entitled *Untersuchungen zur Handlungs-und Affekt-Psychologie*. He electrified psychologists at the 1929 International Congress of Psychology in New Haven with a film about an 18-month-old child learning to sit down on a stone, upsetting a number of prevailing behavioristic notions about intelligent learning in children at a young age. Allport was exposed to Wertheimer, Koffka, and Kohler's work on his first trip to Germany, but he said in his autobiography that he only came to know about Lewin at that period second hand.

Lewin had originally been a student of Carl Stumpf, like Koffka and Köhler, and he employed gestalt concepts in his experimental research. He also worked closely with Köhler and Wertheimer in the 1920s, but Mitchell Ash presents him as something of an outsider. He was more interested in practical application than pure laboratory work, and he also had a radically different idea about how science should be conducted, and his political and philosophical opinions were well formed before he appropriated from the gestaltists.

Lewin was born in Prussia in 1890 into a Jewish family that celebrated the Protestant religious calendar. His bent was to combine philosophy with natural science, while politically he considered himself a socialist. Like James, he considered science to be pluralistic, developing a comparative theory in which science was empirical, practical, and pluralistic. It was not possible, in other words, to reduce the concepts of biology to physics. Nor was it possible to unify science under just one banner.

Instead, Lewin proposed to marry theory with action. He developed a topological psychology that employed the concept of field forces to understand the total situation. Behavior was always a function of the totality of the organism and the environment. His *métier* was always constructing a geometrical life space in his mind with which he could conceptualize a problem, and the product of his thinking was always a concrete experiment to test the question at hand. Later, this penchant for deriving the solution out of the problem itself instead of superimposing preconceived categories onto it became formalized into a method called action research. For Lewin, research was social practice, even to the point of recreating real life situations in the laboratory.

In the years he taught at the Psychological Institute at the University of Berlin, Lewin attracted a devoted following of students. He was always available, affable, and outgoing and a keen listener of what others had to say. But he was deep and inward in his contemplation of the problems he was working on, which he always tended to fit into his own scheme of things. He sought a geometry for psychology that would define space–time relations in terms of psychological fields of force that more accurately represented organism–environment interactions than performance oriented concepts of measurement. This idea in particular appealed to Allport, as he, too, sought to integrate the principles of gestalt psychology into his evolving conception of the person.

In 1924 Allport returned to Harvard as an instructor in the Department of Social Ethics, where he taught the first course in the United States on the psychology of personality entitled "Personality and its Social Amelioration" that year.[16] In 1926 he became an assistant professor at Dartmouth College, returning to Harvard in 1930, the same year that Henry A. Murray's apprenticeship ended as Morton Prince's assistant at the Harvard Psychological Clinic, and Murray ascended to the directorship of the clinic, intent on establishing psychoanalysis at Harvard with the help of his compatriot at the Medical School, Stanley Cobb.

Henry A. Murray

Henry Alexander Murray, MD, PhD, clinical psychologist, personality theorist, and ardent Melvillian, was born in 1893 into privileged circumstances. His father's relatives are listed in *Burke's Peerage* and his mother's father was a wealthy New York financier. He saw his first person hypnotized when he was age 9, on a luxury liner returning from England with his parents. An animated conversation was going on at the table next to them which involved some guests and a distinguished looking educated gentleman who held himself with some force of character. The discussion was about hypnosis, and to prove a point, the gentleman interrupted the waiter who was in the middle of clearing the table before them. In front of everyone in the room, he asked the waiter to participate in a brief experiment, placed him into a hypnotic trance, and demonstrated some of the standard effects.[17]

Murray prepared at Groton Academy and entered Harvard University in 1911, four years ahead of Gordon Allport, to major in the three Rs, as he told it,— "rowing, rum, and romanticism." He lived in palatial surroundings in an apartment on Harvard's "Gold Coast" along Mount Auburn Street and soon married Josephine Rantoul, sister of his class treasurer (Class of 1915). Thereafter, he earned the MA in Biology and MD from Columbia College of Physician and Surgeons in 1921 before returning to Cambridge, Massachusetts, where he worked for the physical chemist, L. J. Henderson, empirically verifying the Henderson–Hasselbach equation.[18] This equation attempted to measure simultaneously 17 different variables in a sample of blood, which, according to Murray, later led to the development of blood plasma. The work by Murray and his co-worker Franklin Chambers McLean was to become the model that Murray would later use to develop an entirely new and original theory of personality, called personology—the multivariate study of the individual at many different levels of complexity by a team of trained investigators.[19] Once the empirical work verifying the theory behind Henderson's equation had been completed from the laboratory of physical chemistry in Boylston Hall, Murray went on to study aging in chick embryos at the Rockefeller University.

While he was gone, the aging Morton Prince, neurologist of William James's era and specialist in dissociation theory and multiple personality, approached the Harvard Corporation with an unusual offer. He wished to endow what would be called The Harvard Psychological Clinic, which would be devoted to the scientific study of personality. Seeing the new trends in experimental behaviorism and psychoanalysis, he hoped to preserve the tradition in experimental psychopathology that, with William James and James Jackson Putnam, he had helped launch so long ago. The only clause was that the clinic had to be situated in the psychology department in the School of Arts and Sciences as a research enterprise, not in the medical school as a therapeutic clinic. In this way, Prince believed that he was striking a blow for the larger view of the person by going right into the Lions' Den of the reductionists.

Harvard accepted the terms and gave Prince a courtesy appointment as Assistant Professor of Abnormal Psychology. But, due to the machinations of L. J. Henderson, Prince was not permitted to appoint his own assistant. In 1926, the same year that Gordon Allport left Harvard for Dartmouth, Henderson offered the position to Henry A. Murray, who accepted, despite having no formal background in psychology but with plenty of experimental laboratory training in science as a physician and biochemist. The first thing Murray did was to take a sabbatical and return to England to finish up a PhD in biochemistry in Haldane's laboratory at the University of Cambridge, awarded 1927.

It was a strange and wonderful year. Murray and Christiana Morgan, a young married socialite who had been having an affair with Murray's older brother, became enamored of each other and began a relationship of their own. Murray was conflicted as to what to do about this situation, since he himself was married, until he decided while he was in England to visit Carl Jung in Zurich and talk over the matter. The details of how he knew to call on Jung are sketchy, but he knew all about Jung through Louis Untermeyer.[20] Also, Murray had been able to rent F. W. H. Myers's old house while in Cambridge, William James's close compatriot in the field of psychical research, and James had been one of Jung's early heroes.[21] At any rate, Murray did meet Jung that year, they sailed up and down Lake Zurich discussing many issues, among them Murray's plight, and launched a lifetime friendship that they had a chance to rekindle on several occasions that lasted up to the time of Jung's death in 1961. Not the least of these connections, Murray introduced Jung to Christiana Morgan. Both she and her husband went into analysis with Jung. In therapy, her paintings using the technique of active imagination depicted her inward struggle toward individuation. Afterward, Jung used them as the basis for his Visions Seminar in Zurich from 1930 to 1934.[22]

The other important event to note about Murray's crossing the Atlantic in 1926 was his introduction to the works of Herman Melville. On announcing his intention to go abroad, one of Murray's Harvard school mates had given him a copy of *Moby Dick*[23] to tuck into his jacket pocket for the long hours on deck when there was nothing to do. Murray accepted it without much thought and proceeded to embark on his trip.

Halfway across the ocean, he received an urgent call to rush to the Captain's Cabin, where he found the famous surgeon Sir John Bland Sutton, of the Royal Academy, standing over the prostrate captain. The captain was an extremely large, fat man who was desperately in need of an emergency appendectomy. Sir John would perform the surgery, would Murray care to assist him by administering the anesthetic, since he was the only other physician on board? During the operation, which Murray afterward reported was a success, but extremely bloody due to the Captain's obesity, Sutton went on and on about Herman Melville and why he, Sir John, happened to be on board just this ship at that time. It seems he had been involved with the Royal Society in giving a giant whale skeleton as a gift to a museum and as an enthusiast of Melville he had vowed afterward to visit the little church in New Bedford, Massachusetts that for its minister's pulpit had a whaling ship's fo'c'sle where the captain usually stands on board his ship. It was the last place where Melville stood on dry land before setting sail at age 25 in 1838, not to return again for 2 years. Glad the captain lived, Murray was even more agog with the Melville story, since he still had the copy of *Moby Dick* in his jacket pocket, which immediately afterward, he read from cover to cover.

On his return to the United States in 1927, Murray immediately went to see Raymond Weaver, a professor of English at New York University who had been the first to write a biography of Melville, just then recently published more than 30 years after the mariner had died in obscurity in 1891. Murray wanted to know if Weaver would mind if an upstart from the domain of the sciences who was interested psychology tried to write a study of Melville. Weaver was not only enthusiastic, but also introduced him to Melville's heirs in Pittsfield, Massachusetts. The sisters were deathly afraid of outsiders, and especially those wanting to write about their relation to Herman Melville. They thought the death of Allan Melville, Herman's father, from maniacal insanity had put a hereditary taint on the family and that succeeding generations would be judged in that light once Melville's own life became unearthed.

But they readily accepted Murray for several reasons. First, he bore a striking resemblance to their absent younger brother. Second, because Allan Melville, Herman's father, had died of lobar pneumonia. Murray had treated such patients as a young medical resident and was able to assure them that lobar pneumonia had a maniacal phase at the end, just before death. They embraced him, invited him to stay as their guest, and allowed him to sleep in Melville's bed, which was still intact. Murray later reported that the experience gave him fantastic dreams, which afterward he could not remember. Before he left, they loaded him up with original manuscripts they still had of some of Melville's most important works, which he subsequently returned. Murray later reported that he worked for several years collecting more documentation before writing up a draft of a biography he called "Young Melville." It was the story based on Melville's own quote, "From my 25th year, I date my life," referring to the day he had left dry land for the sea.[24]

By then, Murray was well into his new position as director of the Harvard Psychological Clinic, which had developed a reputation as a haven for Freudian and Jungian analysis in Boston. The unpublished draft of the Melville biography was written from a psychodynamic perspective, which everyone who read it presumed was Freudian. It was psychological, in that Murray tried to fathom Melville's state of mind; it was interpersonal, since he examined in detail the relation of the boy to his parents and grandparents, and siblings; and it was developmental, since he was trying to understand the evolution of Melville's personality from birth to age 25.

The central psychodynamic issue that Murray believed was his most original contribution to Melville scholarship was the *amfortas* wound, the blow that struck Melville so deep that he never recovered, a blow that sent him to sea in the first place, and though a profoundly spiritual man, made him an atheist and turned him forever from the Christian scheme of salvation. This wound was sustained by Melville, Murray inferred, from knowledge communicated to him from his uncle, that Allan

Melville, devout father, primary font of his son's early religious and moral upbring-ing, God-fearing man and pious Calvinist in the Dutch Reformed Church, had sired an illegitimate daughter. Herman Melville went to great lengths to discover who she was, and to locate her whereabouts, according to Murray. But then Melville argued with his mother over revealing the great secret, so his half-sister could be brought into the family. But the rift between mother and son was not mendable and he stormed out, leaving that day for the sea, the day he first dated as the beginning of his life of true spiritual seeing, which before had all been but an illusion.

Distraught that his best friend, Lewis Mumford, had deadpanned the draft as too psychoanalytic, and frustrated because he kept writing and re-writing every sentence because he wanted to write like Melville, Murray tore the draft apart and started again. He would try to revise it twice more over the next 30 years, but to no avail. And for the rest of his life there was a whale on everything Murray owned, as if he, too, was searching for the great white beast. Meanwhile, Mumford went out and quickly published his own biography of Melville. Murray appeared nonplussed because he actually had another agenda than being the second person to publish a biography of Herman Melville. Melville, in fact, in the tradition of James's Leonora Piper and Theodore Flournoy's Helene Smith, was Murray's paradigm case—the single case study for the recapitulation of his budding personological system.[25]

At the same time, however, though it remained unpublished, the work had a tremendous impact on stimulating Melville scholarship in the field of compara-tive literature. This was partly due to Ray Weaver, partly to Murray's upper-class stature in the intellectual world at Harvard, and elsewhere, which was fast becom-ing international, and partly due to a number of long papers and book introduc-tions to Melville's collected works, where Murray's ideas found wide circulation. A younger generation of scholars working on Melville soon found their way to Mur-ray's door at Harvard to fathom what he had been getting at and to see or hear about the phantom document. In this way, Murray also participated in the dissemination of psychoanalytic ideas in their application to literary criticism in the 1930s.

In any event, Christiana Morgan, Carl Jung, and Herman Melville all happened at once to Murray in 1926, and they would form a trinity of affinity, as Robert Rieber calls such concatenations, influencing the course of Murray's development of a dynamic theory of personality to come.

Murray returned in 1927 to teach classes and assist Prince in running the clinic. Prince would lecture to large audiences of undergraduates, but at his advanced age, his energy was spent and the classes were considered dull and boring by most students, except by a few, such as David Shakow and Saul Rosenzweig, who, as acquaintances with the James family heirs and in with Murray, understood the his-tory of what was going on in front of them. At the same time, Murray began to broadcast widely his new interest in Melville and word was out that he was working on a biography.

The young B. F. Skinner turned up in one of his classes, the first course in psy-chology Skinner had ever taken, as he had been an English major at Scranton Col-lege, but he had already determined that behavioristic learning theory was to be his chosen epistemology by the time he had come to Harvard. In his three-volume autobiography, Skinner recounts that after the very first class he went up to Murray and somewhat smugly said, "Why Professor Murray, I see that you are a *literary* psychologist," but we have no record of Murray's immediate response, only the record of their almost-never-on and nearly-always-off-again relationship over the next 60 years.

Prince died suddenly in 1930 and overnight Murray became the director of the clinic, which allowed him to set the course of his own agenda. Prince had wanted the legacy of hypnosis and dissociation to be continued at the clinic, but only the young graduate student Robert White was pursuing those topics. White would go on to pioneer in the single case study in the investigation of whole lives, following Murray's lead, but at the beginning, he was the one Murray could point to who was reviving Prince's tradition. Murray, meanwhile, in 1930 was more interested in psychodynamic psychology and the theories of Freud and Jung.

Stanley Cobb

Stanley Cobb was born in 1887, in Brookline, Massachusetts, into the Victorian era, just 22 years after the cessation of the American Civil War.[26] His father, also born in Brookline, was a business man who made his money filling in the South Bay of Boston after the Back Bay had already been over colonized by other investors; meanwhile, Cobb's mother was a native New Yorker. The family lived in Milton, just south of the city, and Cobb attended Milton Academy, once his mother finally decided to let him go to school at all. By then he was 8, having spent the early period being home schooled and set loose in nature to investigate for himself. Cobb became an avid birder, keen naturalist, and a fine artist of wildlife and landscapes. He later said he came to medicine through biology, referring to this early period when he spent most of his time in the woods. He did better in the sciences than the humanities, roomed with Emerson's grandson, was a member of all the most coveted clubs, and so had an active social life associated with the Boston and Concord scene. He graduated from Harvard College in 1911.

Cobb had petitioned Hugo Münsterberg to undergo hypnosis, as Cobb suffered from congenital stuttering. Münsterberg referred him elsewhere, but it was only a temporary success. In the beginning of his training for the MD, Cobb was still able to ride a horse everyday to get to the Medical School. He also was enlisted in the Massachusetts National Guard. The only point to note here is that his very bad stutter always disappeared when he sang bawdy songs with his Army reserve classmates.

At Harvard Medical School Cobb came under the influence of David Cheever, Walter Cannon, Otto Folin, and L. J. Henderson, among others. His advisor was William T. Councilman, professor of neuropathology, who was father to Christiana Councilman Morgan, who would later become involved with Henry A. Murray. His cadaver mate was Carl Binger, who would be analyzed by Jung in 1929, and go on to become a leading figure in psychoanalysis. Cobb also interned under Harvey Cushing at the Peter Bent Brigham Hospital. He missed Freud, Jung, and Ferenczi at the Putnam Camp when they came in 1909, but he was an attendee there socially in 1913, where he met his future wife, Elizabeth Mason Almy. His stuttering seemed to improve after he got married.

After their honeymoon the couple moved to Baltimore, where Cobb did a post-doctoral fellowship in neurophysiology and psychiatry, under Adolf Meyer. For 3 years, Cobb worked in the new area called psychobiology, an integrative approach to psychiatry that was at once psychological, biological, and social. One of his innovations in teaching medical students was that Meyer had them write out their psychiatric life histories. Meyer later developed this into the Life Chart method, which Cobb also later employed in patient care and student teaching at Harvard. Meyer remained a significant and immediate influence in Cobb's career for over 15 years.

Cobb entered military service in 1918, but was released early in May, 1919, due to the Armistice. David Lynn Edsall summoned him at one point and made him an offer to return to Harvard, which Cobb subsequently accepted. His base of operations in neurology and psychiatry was to be the Massachusetts General Hospital and he worked with Walter Cannon at the Medical School, while he also opened a private practice. His first teaching duties were with Richard Cabot, professor of clinical medicine, and Allport's old mentor, who was also Cobb's wife's second cousin. The most influential person on Cobb's career at that time became William Herman, a young medical intern. Cobb's biographers describe Herman as a junior Moses. He went from the MGH to work with Meyer at Hopkins and afterward underwent a Freudian and Jungian analysis. On his return, Herman led Cobb through the maze of analytic psychiatry in detail, and then married Cobb's secretary.

Meanwhile, Cobb's old cadaver mate, Carl Binger, had introduced Cobb to his then current roommate in New York, Alan Gregg. As an undergraduate, Gregg had accompanied the group that escorted Freud, Jung, and Ferenczi to the Putnam Camp after the 1909 Clark Conference. After attending Harvard Medical School, Gregg began work for the Rockefeller Foundation. The Flexner Report of 1910, sponsored by the Foundation, had been a major call to arms for Western medicine to upgrade its scientific and medical research and to require the MD of all licensed physicians. Gregg soon became involved in distributing large sums of money and traveling around the world founding medical schools. At one point he was responsible for eradicating certain kinds of diseases from microorganisms in countries that benefited from advanced scientific medical education he had funded.

Through Gregg, Cobb met the senior members of the Rockefeller Foundation and they agreed to fund the development of a new center for neurology at Harvard. Neurology had been centered at the Massachusetts General Hospital under James Jackson Putnam since the 1870s, but Putnam had retired in 1912, after converting from neurology to psychoanalysis, and then he died in 1917. The new center would be based at the Boston City Hospital. The result was the Channing and Thorndike research laboratories, which attracted such greats as Derrick Denny-Brown, the neurosurgeon, and later Houston Merrit, discoverer of the anti-epileptic drug Dilantin. The Rockefeller Foundation earnestly desired Cobb to lead the new enterprise, and proposed sending him to Europe for 2 years, with his wife, two children, and their nanny, to investigate neuropsychiatry there and recommend what would make Harvard the premier research facility in that subject in the world.

Meanwhile, Alan Gregg and David Lynn Edsall, Dean of Harvard Medical School, who was also on the Rockefeller Board, wrote up a position paper and presented to the Foundation a proposal to fund the scientific study of personality. The Foundation agreed and this money eventually went to founding liaison psychiatry in a general hospital setting when Cobb opened the Department of Psychiatry at the MGH in 1934. The department at the MGH soon became the centerpiece of the Rockefeller's program to train psychiatrists who passed through there and then went on to found similar departments in other teaching hospitals throughout the United States. The money also went to the Yale Institute of Human Relations, the scientific study of psychoanalytic concepts at the Chicago Psychoanalytic Institute under Franz Alexander, and it went to support Henry Murray's endeavors at the Harvard Psychological Clinic.

Cobb returned from Europe and took over neurological research at the Boston City Hospital and also became involved in planning the founding of the Department of Psychiatry at the MGH, which did not actually open for several more years. When it did happen, they just switched staff. Major figures in neurology at the MGH went to the City Hospital and Cobb and his staff moved into the MGH.

Cobb's service was staffed mainly by psychiatrists and social workers trained under Adolf Meyer. Their focus was mainly adult psychiatry, but Cobb also quickly established a children's unit, although it was housed over next to pediatrics. At that point, a major transition began to occur with the coming of Erik Erikson, Erich Lindemann, Gibby Dawes, and Felix and Helena Deutsch, who were all psychoanalysts with direct connections to Freud in Vienna. Suddenly, all the Myerians on the staff were in analysis, desiring to become Freudians. The Rockefeller grant that founded the Department was pioneering, in that it was the first time that Rockefeller had agreed to subsidize not only patient care as part of the package, but it also subsidized a select group of Harvard medical students to undergo Freudian analysis.

Meanwhile, still back in the early 1930s, activities were afoot to found an Institute devoted to psychoanalysis in Boston. Franz Alexander arrived as the senior training analyst and Murray allowed him to meet on Fridays at the Harvard Psychological Clinic, which made the place a hot bed of mainly Freudian but also Jungian activity. The reputation of the clinic could hardly have been further sullied in the eyes of the experimentalists in the Department of Psychology, then still in Emerson Hall. Meanwhile, the clinic was located separately over on Plympton Street in an elegant wooden house. The joke was, "Wysteria on the outside; hysteria on the inside."

Indeed, animosity had developed between Boring and Murray over many issues. Murray believed that Boring was particularly piqued because everywhere he turned he was being trumped by Murray. Murray himself later said that he believed Boring thought Murray himself was the source of Boring's ulcer. More to the point, Boring was no doubt galled that while he invited everyone to bring their lunch to the laboratory on Fridays and he provided the burnt coffee, Murray was over at the Harvard Psychological Clinic entertaining visiting dignitaries with catered meals in elegant surroundings.

This later developed into a significant issue, as Boring launched a program to test psychoanalytic concepts by calling on a number of experimental psychologists who had undertaken therapy to submit evaluations of their treatment. These were subsequently published in one of the APA's psychological journals. Boring himself did not fare well, as his analyst suddenly left town and Boring had a panic attack. His only recourse was to call on Murray for assistance, which assuredly heightened the approach-avoidance conflict that had developed between them.

At any rate, after a year Alexander was called to the Chicago Psychoanalytic Institute, and Hans Sachs, one of Freud's original circle, arrived in Boston as the designated training analyst. Sachs was a lawyer, but, because of his advanced status in the newly forming psychoanalytic community, was permitted to attend grand rounds with Cobb and the other physicians. Both Murray and Cobb were actively involved in the budding psychoanalytic community, which solidified into a formal institute in 1933. Both, however, were asked to resign from the local psychoanalytic society and were not permitted to join the new Institute, as neither was recognized as having undergone a formal training analysis, a new pre-requisite for membership.[27] Neither hardly needed the psychoanalysts for verification of their professional status in the world and both allowed the purists to retreat into the world of their own meetings. Meanwhile, both Cobb and Murray colluded to continue to introduce psychoanalysis into the Harvard curriculum and to wrest control away from Vienna as to who would be the right and most qualified candidates to do so.

Murray was surrounded by both Freudians and Jungians, as the clinic became known as a center for psychotherapeutic research and at the cutting edge of dynamic theories of personality. It also quickly became a haven for brilliant, well-qualified women whose intelligence went unnoticed in the more male-dominated power circles involving dynamic psychology and psychiatry. Christiana Morgan, Cecelia Robertson (later Mrs. Walter Bogner), who first proposed the idea for the Thematic Apperception Test, Josephine Murray, MD, who was Murray's daughter, Cobb's wife, Elizabeth, Eleanor Jones, Esther Whitman, Ruth Peterson, and Maria Rickers-Ovsiankina, Kurt Lewin's former student from Berlin, were among them. Cobb similarly fostered the careers of numerous women in psychiatry and social work at a time when this was not the vogue, including Lucy Jessner, Jenny Velderhaus, Elizabeth Zetzel, and Eleanor Pavenstedt. Cobb had also contemplated a central role for Bill Herman in his new Department, but Herman died prematurely in 1935, much to Cobb's personal dismay.

Boring and Psychoanalysis

Boring himself underwent a psychoanalysis from September 1934 to June, 1935. He reported that he had had 168 analytic sessions—five every week, which he later described in an article "Was This Analysis a Success?"[28] He made almost every one of them. He wept. He threw things. He expressed a great deal of emotion. Four years later, however, he was still unable to assess the significance of his experience in therapy. He entered therapy a psychologist committed to scientific productivity. Believing more in his persistence than any tendency toward genius, he worked an 80 hour week, 50 weeks of the year. He had already published his *A History of Experimental Psychology* (1929)[29] and with that behind him, started on *The Physical Dimension of Consciousness* (1933).[30] He then promptly fell into a deep emotional crisis. By his own account, he suffered from inattention. His thinking became autistic, and he felt an emotional disturbance that led him to believe he was depressed. He felt as if all his accomplishments lay behind him. His friends urged him to get help. So he turned to psychoanalysis. He rationalized that the analysis of an experimental psychologist might reveal some insightful cross-fertilizations.

After an aborted beginning with someone whom he disliked, he met Han Sachs, one of Freud's closest disciples, who had emigrated from Berlin to become the senior training analyst in Boston upon the departure of Franz Alexander for Chicago. He liked the man and thought they would get along well. Throughout the analysis, however, Boring felt an inadequacy of the basic theory itself. It seemed too loose and mixed volunteerism with determinism. He also felt he was unable to adequately establish a transference relationship with Sachs, the foundation on which all successful psychoanalysis is based. For this reason, he judged his analysis to be a failure. He also said they discovered no significant forgotten memories or any significant dreams.[31]

Many issues therefore went unresolved. These included Boring's relation to his mother and father; Titchener as the great father figure in Boring's life; and Boring's reputation as a historian rather than an experimentalist when he wanted to be seen as an experimentalist. And was it that Boring was driving himself too hard and just overworked? Or was Murray himself the cause of Boring's ulcer?

We know, however, that the analysis definitely had an effect on Boring. When Sachs went on vacation and returned to Europe for the summer, Boring had a panic attack. He desperately sought help and had nowhere to turn. So, he tried to contact Harry Murray. At the time, Murray was up at his cabin, vacationing on the St. Lawrence Seaway. He was being visited there by a number of colleagues, Erik Erikson among them, and also Murray's young teenage nephew, who later grew up to became a Unitarian minister in Williamsburg, Virginia. Discovering they were there, Boring drove up in his car. He was welcomed when he finally arrived. They were in the middle of a softball game. Invited to join them, although not an athletic person and not in that good a physical condition, Boring took off his shirt and played throughout the afternoon, sustaining a serious sunburn by nightfall. That night, after dinner, sitting around the living room, someone made the proposal to engage in a trivial pursuit-like game, where questions international in scope on a variety of subjects were posed to each participant. The one answering the most questions correctly was declared the winner. Murray reported that this was exactly the kind of game that Boring loved and in which he excelled, but Boring was so out of sorts that night that the teenage nephew soundly trounced him. The entire episode suggested that Boring had, after all, established a certain dependence on his therapist, whose unexpected absence drove him to desperate behavior and uncertain surges in emotion.

The Macropersonality Theorists

Besides Murray taking over the clinic, the other interesting event of 1930 was that Gordon Allport had returned to Harvard from Dartmouth, bringing graduate students such as Hadley Cantril with him. He reappeared ostensibly with Boring's blessing to assist in dismantling the old Department of Social Ethics and to assist in the establishment of a new Department of Sociology. Psychology was not yet a full-fledged Department in the University, but more a semi-independent concentration still operating under the Department of Philosophy, as it had been since William James's time. Boring knew that big changes were coming and Allport, he believed at the time, would make a good chair of psychology when it achieved its full independence.

Allport launched a pioneering research program in personality-social psychology. He studied traits, developed the Allport–Vernon–Lindsay Study of Values, and pioneered in the psychological study of newspapers and radio. He was also editor of the *Journal of Abnormal and Social Psychology* from 1937 to 1949, a co-founder of the Society for the Psychological Study of Social Issues, and in 1939, president of the American Psychological Association.

We should conjecture at this point on the historical relationship between depth psychology and social psychology in the history of personality theory. The question is an important one, because Allport showed signs of being able to amenably combine normative trait theory with depth psychology and also sociological theories of personality which posited cultural factors as the essential origin of personal identity. The formation of personal identity clearly originated in deep structures within the dynamic unconscious, according to the psychoanalysts, an interpretation that was soundly rejected by both the measurement-oriented trait theorists known as experimental social psychologists, and a new breed of radical socialist theorists in psychology at the other end of the political spectrum—we shall refer to them as socialist psychologists,—because many of them were involved with the populist causes of the 1930s.[32]

Allport, for his part, known as a personality-social psychologist, produced one of the primary texts in personality theory during this period, further launching the field in the 1930s and marking it as an era of the macropersonality theorists—those who rejected a reductionistic science based in the laboratory behavior of the white rat and who argued instead for a science of the whole person. This text was Allport's *Personality: A Psychological Interpretation* (1937).[33]

To begin with, Allport's move away from a strict trait theory was palpable. He gave, for instance, a hefty 15-page summary of Adler and Freud, relying mainly on Freud's then recently published *New Introductory Lectures on Psychoanalysis* (1932–1933),[34] and interpretations of Freud by Franz Alexander and Ives Hendrick.[35] He did learn well from his brother Floyd's tack of reinterpreting dynamic concepts, except now, instead of the behaviorist manifesto we got in Allport's dissertation of 1922, brother Gordon wanted to establish a dynamic psychology beyond Freud that retained instincts, traits, and motives but reorganized them into a gestalt that remained a science but focused on the unique totality of the person.

Drawing on the distinction by Wilhelm Windelband, Allport said personality must always be idiographic, so the focus of the work would be on the single case, not the nomothetic—generalizations of large-scale sample sizes. He knew this was a bold statement to make in a discipline already gone berserk with large-scale statistical measurements. But he intended with his text to expand the horizons of psychology.

He began with historical definitions, and then turned to psychophysiology, learning, and the evolution of the self. He introduced his concept of the functional autonomy of motives—that is, the persistence of behaviors and traits beyond their original reinforcers—as a way to understand the mature personality as different from the same self that had been in the child's body.[36] In terms of the structure of personality, he introduced his own definition of traits and developed them into a theory leading to the unity of personality, relying on gestalt principles to identify the total person, which was greater than the sum of the parts. Four chapters on methods of assessment were followed by two chapters on our ability to judge people and the place of intuition in any kind of personality theory, which, such theory he said in the end, must be both empirical and intuitive.

The type of psychology that treats motives, which explains why people do what they do, he said, is called a dynamic psychology. It is not merely a descriptive psychology; it strikes for a cause and is therefore bolder than a psychology that endeavors merely to establish a mathematical function between a stimulus and a response. A dynamic psychology seeks to be more than a matter of coefficients of correlation; it seeks first and foremost a sound and adequate theory of the nature of human dispositions. Current dynamic theories cannot bear the weight of a single full bodied personality because they are too general, too abstract, and too rigid. William McDougall, Allport says, states that only instincts can be the prime movers, few in number, common in all men, and established at birth. The psychoanalysts hold the same over-simplified theory—all human motives are canalized into one basic sexual instinct. He then gave examples from Freud, Rank, Adler, Murray, and others. They all had in common the reduction of every elaborate and individual motive to a limited number of basic interests shared by all men and presumably innate. The fact that such dynamic theories are all so different attests to their failure to successfully describe the person and his or her unique individuality.

But how can you have a science of the unique? His answer was the theory of the functional autonomy of motives. The new dynamic psychology he proposed accounted for the infinitely varying living systems that define the person contemporaneously, even though they may have grown out of previous systems, which had served different purposes. Now, they are functionally independent of them.

Allport positioned James as a foundational source for Allport's own idea of functional autonomy. James spoke about the transitoriness of instincts, by which he meant one may appear, but once in a lifetime, whereupon it promptly disappears through its transformation into habits. The psychology of personality therefore must be a psychology of post-instinctive behavior. He also cited Robert Woodworth's idea of the transformation of "mechanisms" into "drives": "The fundamental drive toward a certain end may be hunger, sex, pugnacity or what not, but once the activity is started, the means to the end becomes an object of interest on its own account." [37]

Allport also said that the same conception can be found in the writings of William Stern and E. C. Tolman. It was a principle of dynamic development, allowing room to describe and understand the person's growth toward mature selfhood and unity. He would later refer to this kind of psychology as a science of the person.

Two primary sources for understanding the whole person that he put forward in his text of 1937 were depth psychology and gestalt psychology. In his discussion of cardinal traits, for instance, Allport discussed congruence—that between the subjects' own perception of himself and the actual condition of the self, and also the observer's perception of the same thing. Concerning the concept of a root quality, called a radix by the gestalt theorist Max Wertheimer, Allport said:

> The cardinal trait, or *radix*, has been represented in a slightly different way by Henry A. Murray under the title of unity-thema. According to this conception, too, the dominant tendencies of a life are said to derive from a single central dynamic principle, which if properly understood would explain the collaborating and the conflicting actions of the person. But according to Murray, the unity-thema often springs from fixations formed early in life, and can be accurately discovered only through psychoanalytic exploration. Here, then, is the principle of congruence from a Freudian rendering.[38]

Surveying the methods for studying the whole person, Allport had liberalized his position tremendously since his dissertation in 1922. In addition to describing methods directly taken from dynamic theories of the unconscious, he associated all these with Morgan and Murray's "thematic apperception test," which he listed all under the same rubric of "Depth-analysis."[39]

Specifically, the psychiatric interview, through questioning and listening, discovers "hidden motives and obscure sequences of behavior." It is often supplemented with auxiliary techniques, such as free association, dream analysis, hypnotism, and automatic writing. And to these more familiar methods, he said, may be added a "whole groups of ingenious techniques" for the analysis of fantasies, "which are considered by all depth psychologists to be of primary importance in the investigation of personality." These involve analyzing the content of day dreams, getting the subject to discuss favorite themes in plays, novels, and literature, the administration of word association tests, the method of free association, the induction of trance states, what he called similes tests, where the subject must give in three minutes all the similes he can think of to the phrase "as unhappy as. . ."; musical reverie tests, picture completion tests, word projection tests, and then Allport described the Thematic Apperception Test, being then still under construction by Christiana Morgan and Henry A. Murray. According to Allport, the ambiguous picture contains people in vague or suggestive situations the same age as the subject, who makes up a brief story based on the ambiguous stimuli in which he or she usually puts themselves in the role of the main character.

Allport's discussion of unity in personality also focused on gestalt psychology, not the unity of substructures as expressed in the writings of Wertheimer, Koffka, and Köhler. Instead, when considering whether or not personality as a whole is a gestalt, he chose the work of Lewin, particularly his *Principles of Topological Psychology* (1936), because Lewin said yes to the question "is a science of the whole person possible?" and he supported it with his own experimental evidence. Allport said:

> Personality, Lewin says in effect, is indeed a Gestalt, but it is a Gestalt that has greater or less unity, depending upon its own individual nature, upon the condition of the organism and the field in which it is behaving. Perhaps no other psychologist has succeeded quite so well at depicting at one in the same time so many of the intricate issues involved, and the unity of personality is always a matter of degree.[40]

The key here for Allport was that the single case study is elevated to a position of highest respectability in psychological research. He questioned the use of the word dynamic in the title of Lewin's book, however. The relation of the individual to the environment is ever changing and therefore dynamic but, according to Allport, Lewin's topology cannot seem to explain stability over time especially in regard to unity of various levels of traits. Nevertheless "the topological treatment of unity is one of the most fruitful to be found in the entire literature of personality."[41] Lewin most certainly would have listened attentively, and then asked permission to draw one of his J-curves, after which he would probably give a topological explanation of the subject.

For his part, in 1938, Murray, with the help of others at the clinic, produced his first major work on psychology, *Explorations in Personality: A Clinical and Experimental Study of Fifty Men of College Age* (1938).[42] The official authors were "The Workers of the Harvard Psychological Clinic," whose names were then listed. There were 27 of them, including Murray's own. But history always records the book as his, which annoyed him. Among the more well known were Donald McKinnon, Nevitt Sanford, Erik Erikson, Saul Rosenzweig, William G. Barrett, Walter Langer, Christiana Morgan, Jerome Frank, Elizabeth Cobb, Merrill Moore, and Maria Rickers-Ovsiankina, to name only a few. Murray, himself, was listed as assistant professor of psychology.

No publisher would take the book until a subvention was offered with it and Murray's friend Felix Frankfurter made a few phone calls. Oxford Press finally published it. The work was dedicated to five individuals: to Morton Prince, who had the vision, raised the endowment, and was the clinic's first director; to Sigmund Freud, whose genius contributed the most fruitful working hypotheses; to Lawrence J. Henderson, whose exposition of scientific procedure established a methodological standard; to Alfred North Whitehead, whose philosophy of the organism supplied the necessary underlying generalities; and finally, to Carl G. Jung, "whose writings were a hive of great suggestiveness." This wording was quintessential Murray.

So it was not just a collection of articles. Murray defined the procedure for achieving unity among individual investigators: all experimenters studied the same 50 subjects with the same concepts actively in mind and then in assembly, a meeting being devoted in each case, to report findings toward a common purpose—the formulation of the personality of every subject. He called this kind of research a Jeffersonian democracy, because of the freedom each investigator coveted and so was given. The conditions under which the subjects were studied were as much as possible those of everyday life. They employed the Lewinian model, Murray said:

responses of subjects were compared under two different conditions and the results compared for normative responses as well as deviations, and of what kind, thus capturing the whole of the groups' responses as well as those of the individual subjects, rather than just a statistical take on one or two variables. This was a book, in other words, based on Galilean and not Newtonian science.

The 50 subjects became the most studied subjects in the history of psychology. Everything that could possibly be known about them was collected. They were measured with tests, their unconscious was probed with free associations, and they were repeatedly interviewed over a 3-year period. As the data rolled in, it became obvious that the investigators needed to construct out of all this an adequate framework for defining personality. Each investigator was asked to give up some of their independence for the sake of the larger agenda. Murray admitted that in the end they never did really succeed in merging their respective ideologies:

> How could such a thing come to pass in a group composed of poets, physicists, sociologists, anthropologists, criminologists, physicians: of democrats, fascists, communists, anarchists; of Jews, Agnostics, Atheists; of pluralists, monists, solipsists; of behaviourists, configurationists, dynamicists, psychoanalysts; of Freudians, Jungians, Rankians, Adlerians, Lewinians, and Allportians?[43]

All these vagaries, he said, were expressed somewhere through the book. He then indicated in so many words that the orientation of the book was primarily psychodynamic:

> In our explorations we attempted to get below the social derm of personalities. Indeed, we became so bent upon the search for covert springs of fantasy and action that we slighted necessarily some of the more obvious and common phases of behaviour. This has resulted in a certain distortion which may seem great to those whose vivid experiences are limited to what is outwardly perceived and public, to what is rational and consciously intended.[44]

In the very beginning he was absolutely clear about the point of view adopted in the book—"that personalities constitute the subject matter of psychology, the live history of a single man being a unit with which this discipline has to deal."[45] He realized that he was deviating from the custom in academic psychology to concentrate almost completely on the perceptive and cognitive functions of the organism or more recently the behavior of animals. He was intent here on not only defining the field of personality, but on setting nothing less than a new course for psychology.

Regarding psychoanalysis, Murray cited examples from Freud, claimed that the interpretations of the personologists were liberal but not as liberal as that of the psychoanalysts, and he quoted Jung directly on matters of differing interpretation among scientists. Attempting to bring order to the budding field of personology, the clinic team drew on McDougall's classification of propensities, or driving instinctual forces, rather than the Freudian list of basic instincts. When looking at dimensions, functions, vectors, modes, or traits, they followed "heavily" Jung, Stern, and Allport. When they were concerned with genesis, history, and development they followed both the work of Pavlov and the gestalt psychologists, "and by such psychoanalytic concepts as fixation, substitution, compensation, sublimation, and regression."[46] In defining their theory of the total personality they desired to proceed according to certain principles. Murray then gave a footnote of acknowledgment to L. J. Henderson, who was then teaching the sociology of Vilfredo Pareto in the Sociology Department.

He also had an entire section in the introduction in which he compared the method of the clinic to the psychoanalysts and the academic personologists, by which he said that he meant Allport. Most psychoanalyses take 200 hours; the clinic's subjects were studied for a total of about thirty-five 1-hour sessions, of which about 5 hours were devoted to the recovery of past experiences; their viewpoint was also not one sided, so the subject did not get tangled up in the personality of the therapist; plus the relation between consciousness and the unconscious can be seen in a greater relief because of the addition of the social emphasis; the clinic also focused on relatively normal subjects, while the psychoanalysts usually dealt with more neurotic types; also, small as the subject sample was, the clinic staff was able to study individual differences; they were also not averse to employing experimental methods, which psychoanalysts usually did not do. Nevertheless, he stated, critical though we may be, "we are not unmindful of the fact that from the start it [psychoanalysis] has been our most constant guide and source of illumination. Without it these studies would never have been planned or finished." From Allport, on the other hand, they derived much in respect to "orderly method of procedure and proper statistical treatment of our findings."

Thus, Murray concluded:

> Our work is the natural child of the deep, significant, metaphorical, provocative, and questionable speculations of psychoanalysis and the precise, systematic, statistical, trivial, and artificial methods of academic personology. Our hope is that we have inherited more of the virtues than the vices of our parents.[47]

Murray then set out to outline the proposal for a theory of personality, drawing on the works of William McDougall, E. C. Tolman, a heavy emphasis on Kurt Lewin, a smattering of Köhler, Erikson, Skinner, and James, then a good deal of Sigmund Freud, Carl Jung (Murray spelt introversion and extraversion correctly), and Alfred Adler, but mainly Freud. After a description of the variables of personality, the ability to judge persons, a discussion of child development, and the methods of testing the subjects, he and his co-authors finished with the detailed analysis of a single subject, the Case of Ernest, which was actually contributed by Robert White. It was a *tour de force* that launched a new generation of personality theorists, the lineage of which continues, altho somewhat dissipated today.

Meanwhile, Cobb had been busy launching psychoanalysis at the Harvard Medical School. The Department of Psychiatry at the Massachusetts General Hospital had been launched in 1934, effectively elevating liaison psychiatry in a general hospital setting to a new status within psychiatry. The Rockefeller money supported the project, paid salaries, administrative costs, and the alteration of infrastructure to get the Department started. Entirely new, he said, was that for the first time, Rockefeller money included underwriting a certain number of beds for patient care at the MGH and also the cost of psychoanalysis for young medical residents. Two of these included Jock Murray and Walter Kauffman, men who would rise to the top of the profession during the war years and help in determining the course of psychiatry in subsequent decades. This included marrying psychoanalysis to the programs of the Veterans Administration, which led to an unprecedented era of psychoanalytic influence in the clinical teaching and practice of psychology and psychiatry. That influence lasted into the late 1960s.[48]

The political payoff for Murray was also soon realized when Murray's academic appointment came up for review in 1938. The examining committee consisted of Boring, Lashley, two Deans, Allport, and Cobb.[49] President Conant assembled the group together in his office for the first time just to get acquainted and conversation went back and forth somewhat informally about Murray. At one point Allport said that he thought he was the most important psychologist at Harvard since William James. Lashley was aghast at such a statement and immediately rose to proclaim that, to the contrary, William James was the biggest mistake to have happened to Harvard and to psychology. Voices rose in both contradiction and agreement at once and an uproar was eminent. Conant seized the moment to rise himself and suggest that the meeting be adjourned, but that they all shake hands before leaving, so the meeting would end on a positive note.

The evaluation took much longer than expected—2 years. In the final decision, there were three votes against—Boring, Lashley and one of the Deans, and three votes in favor, Cobb, Allport, and the other Dean. Conant broke the tie in favor of Murray, because Cobb had presciently gone back to the Rockefeller Foundation and gotten them to commit more money to the Harvard Psychological Clinic, if Murray was permitted to stay.

The only caveat was that Murray was not granted tenure and not awarded a full professorship, thus ameliorating somewhat the reaction of the naysayers. At the same time, Lashley, who had in the beginning been recruited as one of the world's great physiological psychologists, was able to retain his faculty position at Harvard, but as a research professor who drifted away toward the Yerkes Primate Research Center and ceased to be a force in the Department. Such was the fate of the man who vilified James. True, James was only a sometime laboratory psychologist, but a beloved figure nonetheless in the pantheon of Harvard professors whose reputation had reached mythic proportions in the history of the University.

Ross Stagner and The Murphys

Meanwhile, during this time, the field of personality was blooming. Three other early pioneers in this work were Ross Stagner, and Gardner and Lois Murphy. The same year that Allport produced his text, Stagner, Assistant Professor of Psychology at the University of Akron, produced his *Psychology of Personality* (1937), a study of normal personality development rather than abnormal psychology.[50] The work also included a chapter on personality and culture by Abraham Maslow.

Stagner decided that traits should not be confused with types because traits could be precisely measured while types were general orientations that broke down under minute analysis. In this he broke with the gestaltists, such as Lewin, who advocated studying the ideal type as more instructive for seeing variations in real-life situations. He did advocate studying the total personality, however, which could be done by analysis of the single case at a point in time, or more dynamically, along three dimensions: the individual in relation to disease, the study of normal development, and the study of personality as an expression of its cultural milieu. This approach stands in contrast to trait theory, which asks the person to answer a list of questions, the results of which are factored into fixed tendencies, the sum total of which is never really calculated.

He also devoted an entire section to the dynamics of personality, in which he considered appetites and aversions, the theories of Freud, Adler, and Lewin, and the cultural interpretation of motivation. Appetites and aversions had been avoided by philosophers interested in psychology since the time of Aristotle and Aurelius, focusing instead on the rational aspects of humans, which made them neglect the irrational side. This side reveals motivation in the form of conscious and unconscious drives. Tabooed appetites can then also be studied, as well as what motivates learning, all of which constitutes the dynamics of personality.

Stagner then presented three such dynamic theories. Freud has been misunderstood for many reasons, not the least of these is the mistranslation of certain words such as lust, instinct, and libido. He then reviewed the basic ideas of Freudian theory, commenting on the pleasure principle, the reality principle, repetition compulsions, and the like. It took him five full pages to mention the word sex, which he then skipped over in favor of a further discussion of behavior shaped by the Id, Ego, and Superego. After ten pages of rhetoric, he finally got into psychosexual stages of development and the Oedipus phase, concluding that sexual factors remain Freud's most important contribution to a dynamic study of personality.

Stagner's treatment of Adler is much shorter. He mistakenly called Adler a student of Freud and then proceeded to explicate his theory. The life plan of the person is formulated in response to perceived organ inferiority and its compensation. The environment is mastered by the will to power in order to overcome inferiority. Social norms require the perfect masculine form, prowess, strength, and mastery, which in the inferior individual are experienced as "the masculine protest." While apparently built on a negative epistemology, Adler's theory had great success in helping school children overcome feelings of inferiority while learning successively how to assert themselves at a young age.

Kurt Lewin's dynamic of theory of personality then came in for treatment in a section even shorter than Adler's. Lewin's theory, Stagner said, is based on two fundamental concepts: external valence, the demand characteristics of objects in the environment, and internal tension, which builds with unfulfilled needs. The child in infancy who pushes things out of the crib will later learn to push things under the rug, which may later develop into the predilection to hide things, then to lying behavior. A common need or tension persists in each example which requires expression and determines behavior. Tensions can also be task specific. Zeigarnik noted that when subjects were given tasks to perform, where some were allowed to finish and others not, then asked to remember the whole set of tasks, most often they reported thinking about the unfinished ones. Rickers-Ovsiankina employed the same tasks but allowed the subjects to go back and play with them during a free time at the end. Subjects almost always returned to the unfinished tasks. Goals may also be substituted for one another, providing they are similar and the replacement is not more difficult. Stagner noted in conclusion that, in typical gestalt fashion, these studies emphasized the here-and-now, while Freud and Adler required delving into the subjects' past. All were designed to get at dynamic sources of motivation. The final third of the book emphasized social and cultural determinates shaping personality.

Stagner did not actually have the stature in psychology or the reputation already garnered by personality theorists such as Murray and Allport, but his legacy has demanded attention by prominent psychologists such as the late Ernest Hilgard nonetheless. The suggestion is that Stagner was actually less controversial among later experimentalists and for that reason probably more accepted.

Gardner and Lois Murphy

Despite the fact that they were an integral part of the Murray-Allport circle, two early personality-social psychologists similarly shunted to the wayside by historians or cut up piecemeal by those who took only parts of their psychology were Gardner and Lois Murphy. Lois was best known for her work in child psychology and psychoanalysis, while Gardner was not only a major player as a personality theorist but also a distinguished parapsychologist, a fact conveniently often dropped from his biography because both mainstream interpreters and younger human science scholars cannot bear to associate themselves with what they assuredly label the occult and the unscientific, when they know absolutely nothing about these subjects or the history of their scientific study.

Gardner Murphy was born in 1895 and died in 1979.[51] During his early life he spent several years in Concord, Massachusetts, and for that episode now lies buried next to his wife Lois in Sleepy Hollow Cemetery, next to Authors' Ridge, where Emerson, Thoreau, Hawthorne, and the Alcotts rest. He took his undergraduate degree at Yale and from 1916 to 1917 went to Harvard to earn the MA in psychology. Robert Mearns Yerkes, who was teaching there, became his lifelong friend. Murphy later recounted that he took uninspired courses from Herbert S. Langfeld, Hugo Münsterberg, and Edwin B. Holt. But he remained eclectic. Murphy was simultaneously enrolled in physiological psychology, history of religions, and philosophy. One result, he renounced the Episcopalianism of his family. He became an ethical humanist, more at home with the Quaker meeting than a High Mass. But it was psychical research that captivated his imagination. As a boy, he had been introduced to the subject in his Grandpa King's library when he found a copy of Sir William Barrett's *Psychical Research*[52] and devoured it in its entirety, and he was familiar with William James's famous case of the medium, Mrs. Leonora Piper, as Grandpa King was her lawyer. But the scientific study of the paranormal did not suggest itself to him directly until he began to work with Leonard Troland at Harvard. Troland drew him into the experimental method and the two entered into laboratory investigations that launched Murphy for the rest of his career into the field of what J. B. Rhine later called parapsychology, despite the fact that Murphy became best known as a personality-social psychologist. Along with Murphy, Troland also involved George Estabrooks, and the young graduate student, Harry Helson.

While at Harvard, Murphy also was drawn into subjects such as esthetics and beauty, and he learned Freudian psychoanalysis as well as Jamesean pragmatism and the philosophy of Henri Bergson.[53] These were his entry into psychodynamic psychology, which became foundational to his later theory of personality. And although they lived in completely different worlds, Murphy, the struggling graduate student, and Murray, the flamboyant coxswain on the rowing team, Murray had just left Harvard a year before Murphy was there. Allport, however, Murphy must have actually known from those early days, as Allport was a sophomore from 1916 to 1917, and in the same environment in which everyone pretty much knew everyone else.

On Meeting Gordon Allport

According to Lois, however, she and Gardner first met Allport at the Hanover Conference on Personality and Culture in 1930, just as Allport was returning to Harvard from 4 years at Dartmouth. Their subsequent meetings, according to Lois, always emphasized Allport's work on gestalt psychology. At the same time, Allport's *Studies in Expressive Movement* (1933)[54] reinforced Murphy's appreciation for the contribution the experimental approach could make to personality. Allport, for his part, visited them in their home in Brooklyn, traveled to see them on several occasions to their summer home, Birchlea, in New Hampshire, and endlessly discussed personality and social psychology and how to help the fleeing Jewish refugees, such as Werner Wolff. As well, Allport could not speak highly enough of Murphy's writing style.

Lois maintained that she and Gardner first met Henry A. Murray at Harvard in 1936, at a meeting of Kurt Lewin's topological psychology group. They developed a lasting friendship with Murray, visiting with him at meetings of the American Psychological Association, and they corresponded and read each others' writings throughout the years that followed. Murray himself visited them in New Hampshire, as Allport and others had done, and Murray came to see Murphy in Washington, DC, during his final illness.[55]

Murphy, with the help of Friedrich Jensen, an MD from Freiberg-im-Breisgau, and John Levy, a New York psychoanalyst who also taught at Columbia, also produced one of the earliest texts in personality psychology, *Approaches to Personality: Some Contemporary Conceptions Used in Psychology and Psychiatry*, first published in 1932.[56] The work was based on what Murphy described as a "polydimensional eclecticism" and was likely a more accurate reflection of the American temper, which is at once pragmatic, eclectic, and more optimistically oriented than the texts that followed. The later texts tried to paint the picture of psychology as science unified around reductionistic empiricism and trait theory, where personality psychology largely remains today. Under "Experimental Psychology," gestalt theory, the French and American schools of dissociation, and Russian and American theories of conditioned learning were considered. The second section considers the psychodynamic theories of Freud, Jung, and Adler, while the final section presents the study of personality from the standpoint of child guidance. The focus throughout is on the individual case study and the genetic method, by which the authors meant to refer to developmental stages across the life span, but with a particular emphasis on the early years of development. Levy, in particular, equated the study of personality with understanding the "total behavior" of the child.

Murphy and Lewin

This was also the time that the Murphys first met Kurt Lewin. Lewin arrived from Germany just after their book *Experimental Social Psychology*[57] was published in 1931. Murphy wrote that Lewin "cut a meteoric flight through our experience of personality-social research...from 1932 until his death in 1947."[58] He first met Lewin at the Columbia University Faculty Club in 1932 and he was immediately struck, not only by Lewin's new methods but also the kind of new leadership that he represented that would soon be guiding the development of experimental-social psychology. Both Gardner and Lois recognized that Lewin had not yet quite worked out his field theory, but it was obviously so close to what they were doing that they were immediately attracted to it. They joined the topological psychology group on two occasions, when Margaret Mead, Edward C. Tolman, Kurt Koffka, and Erikson were there as well. At one point, Murphy copied Lewin's style to develop his own version of field theory for an APA address delivered in 1946. Murphy, along with Horace Kallen, also tried to get Lewin a position at the New School for Social Research, but was effectively blocked by Wolfgang Kohler, who had always considered Lewin an outsider from the true circle of gestaltists.

But Murphy also differed with Lewin on many points. He complained that Lewin would only work with a cross-section of behavior, not with a history of how the behavior came into being. He also felt that Lewin had not shown the non-utility of breaking the whole into clarifiable parts and that he neglected a psychology of individual differences. Nor had he shown how his ellipses were related to mathematics or statistics. Nevertheless, Gardner Murphy proclaimed, "Lewinian theory was rapidly elevated to a position of great importance."

The Princeton Conference on Personality and Gestalt Psychology

Gestalt psychology was a growing dynamic force behind the scenes as the new field of personality psychology begin to blossom in full force in the 1930s. One example was the Conference on Personality Development and Gestalt Psychology, held on January 18, 19, and 20, 1935, at Princeton University. Originally called by

Lawrence Frank,[59] head of the General Education Board of the Laura Spellman Rockefeller Fund, the conference was designed to identify significant concepts in gestalt psychology for understanding the problem of development in personality. It was Frank's conviction that no orderly system of development had yet been worked out for personality, in spite of widespread interest in the problem. Psychoanalysts were a possible exception, probably because they operated within a closed theoretical system, but psychologists were seldom satisfied that Freud's theories held the entire story. Gestalt psychology appeared to have numerous contacts with the subject of personality and the conference was convened, Frank said, to get these connections in better perspective. He specifically pointed out that the experts that had been invited included "all leading gestalt visitors" and some Americans, but no psychoanalysts.

Those in attendance included Gordon Allport from Harvard University; W. E. Blatz from the University of Toronto; Barbara Burks from the Child Development Institute, Teachers College, Columbia University; Mrs. Mary Fisher from Sarah Lawrence College; Kurt Koffka, then at Smith College in Northampton, Massachusetts; Wolfgang Köhler, who was then visiting faculty at Harvard University; Kurt Lewin, then at Cornell; Norman Maier from the University of Michigan; Mark May from Yale; Gardner and Lois Murphy from Columbia University; Willard Olson from the University of Michigan; George Stoddard from the State University of Iowa; and Max Wertheimer, who was at that time at the New School for Social Research in New York City.

Gordon Allport's typewritten notes from the event indicted that, like many such conferences, this one was slow in getting started. Frank opened the conference with an eloquent quotation from L. L. Thurstone,[60] advocating a longitudinal, genetic, and psychiatric approach to personality, which was not based on cross-sectional research. The point Frank appeared to be making to Allport was that Americans allow nature to slip out of their hands by their one-sided and narrow-minded use of cross-sectional, quantitative methodology.

Allport described the initial interactions as "some preliminary skirmishing to find out what the cardinal problem for discussion should be." In a separate insertion with an ink pen, Allport noted the general conclusion to be "what is the genetic problem in the psychology of personality." Here he has crossed out "psychological," opting for "genetic," indicating that the issue to be discussed was the overall problem of the psychological development of the person over the life span.

As the Chairman, Frank proposed that the answer was a problem of "Becoming," a key concept in his developmental theory of how children learn and what social scientists ought to be studying. To the idea of becoming, Allport wryly noted in his notes, "Becoming organized (including, of course, disorganized)." The various combatants then weighed in. W. E. Blatz from the University of Toronto objected to Frank's characterization as seeming to overemphasize formal education over experience. Blatz's position was that learning that is important for personality has no relation to academic learning, particularly when expressed in terms such as frequency and recency. Growth that takes place from traumatic experiences would be closer to the actual case of experiential learning. Wertheimer jumped in and emphasized the point that, from the perspective of gestalt psychology, learning depends on personality, rather than determining it. Maier from Michigan thought of organization of personality in terms of individuation and equivalence of stimuli, which sounded to Allport like "a kind of situational identical element theory." Throughout the conversation, Allport noted, "this dispute persisted," referring to whether personality depended on the organization within the person, or organization of the environment. Allport also noted that at the beginning, a certain amount of skepticism that things would ever gel hung in the air, although this markedly diminished later on in the conference.

Kohler, whom Allport characterized as "the bad boy of the conference," then asserted that psychology was not ripe for the study of personality. We are not sure what this means, but it almost certainly refers to the maturity of psychology as an experimental science, being at that moment too atomistic and reductionist, and narrow in methodology to grasp the bigger picture of human functioning. He also expressed the view, "reminding one of Watson," Allport notes, that nothing is innate in personality except biological qualities. Allport later went back and decided in a penned addition that this was a "decidedly contrary consideration."

Lawrence Frank commented that he too also despaired of the strictly scientific approach, because no single variable can be interpreted in one unequivocal way. There is all manner of construction surrounding the same facts. A variable secured still names all manner of things. One of the Murphys chimed in that we cannot even adequately measure the environment, let alone personality, which depends on the environment and other things as well. Allport characterized them all as situationists, especially Frank, the Murphys, and Stoddard, most of whom were pessimistic, simply because they had not distinguished the environment from the person. He noted that "one does get dizzy when the two are combined." Also, he noted that everyone at least agreed to the point that some behavior may be due to different causes. "Hence, the problem of cause and effect becomes immensely confused." But, in spite of the original skepticism, the conference finally got down to work.

Allport noted that "abstract discussion got nowhere." In spite of the chairman's rhetoric, there continued to be a lot of general demand to hear concrete reports of investigations. A discussion then ensued after Olson from Michigan presented data from a study that attempted to predict delinquency among 3,000 children in which teacher's ratings were compared to judges' disposition of cases. Allport noted that the results showed teachers and judges seemed to have similar prejudices. Olson thought the study to be a gestalt investigation because of the global scoring used. Koffka, Wertheimer, and Lewin each pointed out faults with that point of view. Generally, it was considered macroscopic, when gestalt studies tended to be much more microscopic with regard to prediction. Kohler then interjected a comment that Allport noted was "shocking as usual." He said we definitely need the large scale as well as the atomistic point of view. "Facts are always acceptable to Gestalt." In any case, he advised them all to leave Olson alone. Olson was describing a "nice, typical, American problem," Kohler said. It was "Good common sense American psychology." Lewin added that one must know what aggressiveness is to the child.

Persistence may vary but it was always persistence. He gave the example of a child always giving a tool away is just as persistent a mode of conduct as always keeping it. In general, however, it was clear to Allport that "Gestalt does not recognize a nomographic method (or pooling variables) as a Gestalt method."

As the conference progressed, Professor Stoddard of Iowa observed four special points that were emerging for him: the importance of case histories, interest in ascendance and submission, types of change in personality, and the gestalt approach to a good interview.

Concerning case histories, he particularly noted the case history of one child, connected with the work of A. R. Lauria, which seemed to indicate that numerous problems in the child could be traced to a single root—the fact that the mother was a prostitute. In this particular case, all problems, affective organization, and mental content "derived therefrom." Stoddard appeared to be speaking generally on this point, as Allport noted "this though Stoddard did not recognize it, a decidedly agreeable conception to Gestalt."

Stoddard also thought there was "much interest in ascendance submission. He had found in several studies that it was possible to change submission but not ascendance. Why?" Allport's notes ask in answer: "difficult to find situations that encourage a submissiveness in training?" He felt there was a wrong emphasis here on the situation. He referred to Köhler's idea that we strive to "maximize the ego at all times?" That submission is a form of life most easily admitted in our culture? Or was this trend a function of biological drives?

Regarding types of change in personality, Stoddard contrasted the sudden with the gradual. Re-education should be gradual, especially when we are confronted with the person's statement that it does not feel right to do things in a new way. Allport then noted Stoddard's point that "even sudden re-orientation may require long preparation." Finally, Stoddard noted a defining idea for interviewing, namely, "Never put in a question on blind hope. Always have a hypothesis for every question, or leave it out."

There was much more, but suffice it to say that the gestaltists and the personality theorists were melding behind the scenes, even as the founders of the gestalt lineage were being welcomed by the laboratory experimentalists in American universities, but not really permitted to get a foothold. The core of experimental psychology at Harvard was, after all, Wundtian. Psychology as a whole embraced the gestaltists to the extent that it absorbed most of their major constructs, such as the relation between figure and ground, insight learning, isomorphism, and the concept of *Gestalten* itself, into the flow of what was taught as introductory, general psychology. But the gestaltists themselves were never able to successfully challenge the American experimentalists directly, and their potential as a significant movement soon dissipated. Gestalt psychology did continue to have a significant impact within the community of the macropersonality theorists, and then flourished in the American psychotherapeutic counterculture in the 1960s around Fritz and Laura Perls and Fritz's controversial decision to call his approach gestalt therapy. A more direct example of the influence of gestalt psychology on personality theory, however, was Lewin at Harvard.

Lewin at Harvard

In 1931, Lewin had proposed his famous distinction between Aristotelian and Galilean modes of thought in psychological science.[61] He asked, "Is it possible to find general laws that apply to the individual? Can we determine general laws and at the same time do precise experiments on individual emotional life? Is it possible to study and explain inner emotional processes as quantitatively and objectively as physics has done in its own realm?"

Lewin's position was that large-scale samples are not needed to find general laws. Such laws can be found in the concrete example of the single case. To this idea, Lewin added that, yes, general laws can be known from the single case, but only if the case is known in its totality. This point marked Galileo's historic break with Aristotle.

Aristotelian ways of thinking were static. They broke phenomena up into their opposites—light dark, good–bad, black–white. Galilean thinking on the other hand considered the opposites to lie along an unbroken continuum. Psychology, too, must adopt the dynamic conception of sequence instead of the static concept of paired opposites. The Aristotelian standard for establishing laws required many repetitions that were predictable and orderly so that validity can be established. The Galilean required only that the phenomenon actually be observed; how many times were not important. This would mean that psychology would have to become more like astronomy or oceanography, where single events were not only legitimate, but the key to understanding the nature of real life. It was not the frequency of occurrence that was decisive, but the exact description of all the forces acting in the present, both inner needs and from the outward environment. Behavior can be known and predicted, but only if the total psychological field has been defined. Large-scale samples miss these dimensions of the total person and the total field because they only deliver information about one or two aspects of the whole, not the totality of the person and the situation itself.

The Galilean was essentially Murray's approach to the multivariate study of the concrete individual simultaneously at many different levels of complexity. It was also Allport's emphasis on individual personality as a total gestalt. The piece was widely read and contributed to Lewin's growing international reputation.

The Topology Club met annually at different Universities. In 1936 it met at Harvard, where both Murray and Allport gave papers. The meeting was also attended by among others, David Shakow, Donald McKinnon, David Kretch, Ruth Benedict, Tamara Dembo, Harold Lasswell, and Gardner Murphy.[62] At one point, Morrow reports that Lewin and Murray were both at the blackboard comparing both their systems, chalk dust everywhere. Murray suddenly exclaimed, but how with this maze of lines and cross hatchings can you represent qualitatively different motives, vectors, and goals? Lewin's humorous reply was that he would simply employ different colors of chalk.

Gardner Murphy remembered being captivated by the charm and the convenience of Lewin's broad conceptualizations and graphic displays. Murphy went on to attempt to describe his own version of field theory at the 1936 meeting of the

American Psychological Association. He felt that the conception of psychological space needed to be worked out further and that Lewin might sometimes be obscuring the person's idiosyncratic life space with what was actually the sociological space around him.[63]

Donald McKinnon, one of Murray's students, wrote that when he was at Harvard in the 1920s, psychologists had good experimental methods, but they were applying them to insignificant problems, while the psychoanalysts were dealing with real-life situations but their methods were inadequate. McKinnon wanted to build a bridge between the two, and when he discovered Lewin, he thought he had found someone already doing just that. Lewin was not interested in psychoanalysis, however, but he was vitally involved with dynamic problems of motivation. McKinnon traveled to Berlin to work with him. Karl Zener and Donald Adams had preceded him. Jerome Frank also came from Harvard and joined Lewin's inner circle.

Morrow, Lewin's biographer, reports that Lewin spent two spring terms at Harvard, one in 1938 and the other in 1939. He spent most of his time with Murray over at the Harvard Psychological Clinic, where he held his seminars. He rejected the Department's main focus on the elegant experiment, because an artificial emphasis on operationism was always superimposed in between the experimenter and the subject. Lewin preferred instead the realities of everyday life and the freedom from constraint he found at the clinic. But Marrow also reports that Lewin was on good terms with everyone, including Boring, Stevens, and Lashley. He described Allport as a good friend. Allport was interested in Lewin giving greater consideration to attitudes, and, if we are to believe Morrow's claim, he wanted Lewin to incorporate more psychoanalytic concepts into his system. Allport recalled later that Lewin would always listen thoughtfully, and then draw one of his j curves. He might then incorporate the thought into his own system by way of expanding his own theories rather than taking on the theories of others. During the Harvard seminars Lewin met several investigators who later began to work closely with him, including Mason Haire, Jack French, Dorwin Cartwright, John Harding, and Eliot Jacques. Lewin wanted to be invited to Harvard, but Morrow described him as so different from Allport and so similar to Murray that difficulties continually abounded between them, though they were always quite friendly.

Lewin returned to Iowa, where he headed his own research team and encountered the Harvard researchers again through the Office of Special Services and the Office for Navel Research. Murray, for his part, employed Lewin's research approach again in *The Assessment of Men*,[64] which was the training program Murray and his colleagues designed to select and prepare secret operatives to be dropped behind enemy lines in Europe. Lewin made close contact again with Murray and Allport later after the War, when he founded the MIT Center for Group Dynamics in 1946, employing numerous colleagues from his Iowa days, such as Leon Festinger. The program at the Center was to be completely new, focused on the dynamics of groups as a whole. Action theory was to underpin its methods. The Center was situated in the Department of Economics and Social Sciences and had little regard for disciplinary boundaries. They quickly established close relations with Allport and Murray at Harvard and shared graduate students under a long-standing arrangement between the two

Universities allowing students to cross-reference courses. The Center worked on group productivity, group communications, social perception, intergroup relations, group membership and individual adjustment, and finally the improvement of group functioning.

Boring Performs a Commissurotomy on Psychology

Meanwhile, the same year Lewin developed his Center at MIT, one of the single most important events in the history of academic psychology in the 20th century took place when the split occurred in Psychology at Harvard. The measurement-oriented laboratory men became the Department of Psychology, strictly so-called, while personality, abnormal, social, and clinical joined with similar dissidents in cultural anthropology and sociology to form the new Department of Social Relations.

The reason for its importance was its effect on higher learning in psychology in the United States. President Conant was certainly aware of the tensions in the various departments of the social sciences and assembled a blue ribbon commission to examine the status of psychology and make recommendations. The Chair was Alan Greg, then director for the Medical Sciences at the Rockefeller Foundation. Other members included Chester I. Bernard, President of the New Jersey Bell Telephone Company; Detlev Bronk, Johnson Professor of Biophysics at the University of Pennsylvania; Leonard Carmichael, president of Tufts University; John Dollard, professor of social anthropology at Yale; Thomas French, associate director of the Institute for Psychoanalysis, Chicago; Ernest Hilgard, professor of psychology at Stanford; Walter S. Hunter, professor of psychology at Brown University; Edward L. Thorndike, professor of psychology, *emeritus*, Teachers College, Columbia; Louis L. Thurstone, Charles F. Grey Distinguished Service Professor of Psychology, University of Chicago; John C. Whitehorn, Henry Phipps Professor of Psychiatry and Psychiatrist in Chief, Johns Hopkins University; and Robert M. Yerkes, professor of psychobiology, *emeritus*, Yale University.

The Commission was appointed May 1945 but the formal report was not issued until 1947. The project had definitely evolved from one of assessing the status of psychology at Harvard, through to the ideal status of psychology in a university, to finally the main consideration of the Commission's Report as stated in its title, *The Place of Psychology in an Ideal University* (1947).[65] The reason for this was that psychology cannot be considered in a vacuum, and to describe its place as a separate discipline also infused throughout various other disciplines in the University required the Commission to step back and look at the structure of the University as a whole.

Their definition of psychology was brilliant. Psychology is what psychologists actually do and teach. But they then limited their definition to "the science of human and animal behavior, both individual and social."[66] But then they expanded on even that definition: "psychology is the systematic study, by any and all applicable and fruitful methods, of organisms in relation to their behavior, environmental relations, and experience." Even so, such a psychology made up of purely intuitive and imaginative perceptions was not amenable to experimental verification or validation by way of prediction. The discipline is instead hierarchical, studying the most elementary phenomena first, and then working up to the more complex. The majority of the committee wanted to place psychology as one of the biological sciences, but several dissenters were permitted to make their views known in initialized footnotes. In this case, several maintained that exploratory tendencies and novel hypotheses and an open-ended attitude toward radically new methods, procedures, and problems were essential to the acquisition of new knowledge, especially since many advances are made at the borderlines of conventionally defined disciplines.

Personality they considered a subset of clinical psychology. Social psychology they agonized over as to whether it should be taught in psychology or sociology. Experimentation and controlled observation are the touchstones of scientific psychology, but not all of science relies on the experimental method—astronomy, for instance. They recognized that science does not start with experimentation. "Too great concentration on experimentation may involve costly oversights, for experiment is not the beginning of science nor yet its only cachet of respectability."[67] There are effective clinical methods to consider. The anamnesis—the story of the illness as told by the patient, or the life history, are methods that supply important information.

Their conclusion had several parts. First, they believed that "arrangements that encourage the exclusive domination of psychology by the laboratory would sacrifice the unity of the subject, belie its freedom, and limit its opportunity."[68] Second, their solution was to allow the central department, no matter how small, to decide on its own focus of specialization, but to have every other psychologist in the university of whatever kind have a courtesy appointment on the faculty of that Department.

However, as the committee deliberated, the Armed Forces were beginning demobilization, and the rush to solve the problem at Harvard became acute before the arrival of waves of returning students. So, while the blue ribbon panel eventually recommended fusion of the various parts of psychology as a discipline throughout the ideal University, Harvard moved under Boring's leadership to effect a fission—a splitting apart of the experimental and "social" theorists, which actually was perceived as the separation of the experimental and clinical traditions— the hard from the soft sciences in psychology. And while few universities rushed out and formed their own Department of Social Relations, the effect of the severance was that the experimentalists in the laboratories consolidated their control over psychology departments throughout the United States, while the clinicians were simply forced to go elsewhere. In Harvard's case it was into the Department of Social Relations. By the 1970s clinical psychology had gone to the School of Education, and after that, out of the University's School of Arts and Sciences altogether.[69]

Along with Allport and Murray, there was Murray's friend, Clyde Kluckhohn, cultural theorist, specialist in Navaho witchcraft, eminent teacher to successive generations of Harvard students, famed American long rider, and according to Talcott Parsons, certainly one of the most notable anthropologists of the 20th century. Kluckhohn first encountered the Navaho while at a ranch in the Southwest while he was recuperating from a severe illness that had caused him to drop out of Princeton after his first year. He was 21 at the time. He became fluent in their language and society, lived with them for extended periods of time, and traveled to remote sites of their culture. He was known to them affectionately by his Navaho name, "Hasteen Clyde."

He published his first book in 1927, *To the Foot of the Rainbow*,[70] an account of his pack trip across the American Southwest. He completed his AB at the University of Wisconsin in 1928, studied in Vienna and was a Rhodes Scholar at Oxford, after which he taught at the University of Arizona. He completed his doctorate at Harvard in 1936. He kept in constant touch with the Navaho people during this period and made numerous trips back to the Southwest. He kept up these close contacts for the rest of his life. In particular, he began a longitudinal study of a single Navaho community, which produced heretofore unknown discoveries about their customs and culture. Over the years, he became a major contributor to the refinement of ethnographic methods. He studied their chants and song ceremonials, their childrearing practices, and combined psychoanalysis, analysis of social structure, and learning theory in his pioneering study *Navaho Witchcraft* (1944).[71] He made major contributions to the field of anthropology and was elected president of the American Anthropological Association in 1947.

He was at once the consummate scientist and humanist, writing on topics from population genetics to psychoanalysis. *Mirror for Man*[72] and *Culture: A Critical Review of Concepts and Definitions*[73] allowed him to make generalizations across cultures about structures and values. These culminated in his Cooperative Study of Values in Five Cultures project. Talcott Parsons noted that Kluckhohn was one of the principle founders and mainstays of the Laboratory and Department of Social Relations and a prominent citizen of the university as a whole. Kluckhohn also had numerous friends, among them, he was an old friend of John Dollard from their days as students at Wisconsin, and he was close friends of Alexander and Dorothea Leighton. Abram Kardiner and Ralph Linton, and Robert Merton were also his friends and colleagues. He was also influenced to varying degrees by Boas, Sapir, and to a lesser extent Ruth Benedict. He died of a heart attack in 1960, while typing in an isolated cabin near Santa Fe.

There was also Pitirim Aleksandrovich Sorokin (1889–1968).[74] Sorokin was born in Russia into an alcoholic and violent family life where his mother died when he was young. He was raised by an uncle into mysticism and Russian Orthodox symbolism. His early life was one of a constantly starving young revolutionary against the Tzar, for which he was jailed several times. In jail, he did have access to food, a bed, and especially books, of which he took full advantages to continue his studies. He taught for the Soviets between 1919 and 1922, until they, too, jailed him. Nevertheless, he established the first Department of Sociology at the University of Petrograd in 1919.

As a sociologist, Sorokin was influenced by Durkheim, Spencer, and Comte, and in psychology by Pavlov. His books carried such titles as *The Sociology of Revolution* (1925/1967),[75] *The Crisis of our Age* (1941),[76] *Power and Morality* (1959),[77] and *Hunger as a Factor in Human Affairs* (1975).[78] His basic thesis as a criminal anthropologist was that in societies where extreme poverty existed side by side with plenty, criminality would go up due to class struggle and the breakdown of the protection of possessions. Individuals followed either the laws of the spirit or the laws of sensate pleasure, which then defined the direction of culture. In this way, a culture either deteriorated or flourished. In a successful society, God, Sorokin believed, ruled through the State. C. Wright Mills was heavily influenced by his writings and Robert Merton was one of his students.

When Sorokin first came to Harvard in 1930, there was no Department of Sociology, so he began teaching in the Department of Economics. There he met a young instructor named Talcott Parsons. Sorokin was the only professor in Sociology when it finally was established and Parsons also came over from Economics, but with a lower rank. Nevertheless, Parsons was eventually able to make his influence known through his theory of action and became a powerbroker within his own domain. He was more in the tradition of American functionalism than Sorokin and made a stronger alliance with others such as Murray and Allport. Sorokin entered into bitter struggle with Parsons along the way. Parsons followed the Chicago School, which Sorokin thought too philosophical and indecisive, while Sorokin himself was more sensate. Between 1937 and 1941, Sorokin published a four-volume work with the help of numerous scholars and students, *Social and Cultural Dynamics*.[79] After he gave up the chairmanship of Sociology in 1942, the department was reorganized under Parsons, and Sorokin went on to found the Center for Creative Altruism, but was no longer a force on the Harvard scene as he had been before.

Parsons (1902–1979), born in Colorado Springs, majored in biology and anthropology at Amherst, attended the London School of Economics, and received his PhD from the University of Heidelberg in sociology and economics. After a stint teaching at Amherst, he began teaching at Harvard as an instructor in 1927 and, after joining Sorokin in the newly founded Department of Sociology, rose rapidly with the success of such major works as *The Structure of Social Action* (1937),[80] which was a review of Weber, Durkheim, and Pareto in an attempt to derive general principles governing social systems. At one point he became much enamored with psychoanalysis, undergoing training himself as a lay analyst and incorporating psychoanalytic ideas into his theories. This he followed with such works as *Essays in Sociological Theory: Pure and Applied* (1949)[81] and *The Social System* (1951),[82] in which he argued for homeostasis as well as a holistic approach to the study of social systems, and the multi-authored volume *Toward A General Theory of Action* (1951).[83]

There is discussion among historians of the social sciences regarding the so-called Parsons School of Sociology, some contending that Parsons founded the Department of Social Relations himself to further his own ends (he was merely the Chairman, a low man's job at Harvard). In reality, there were bigger egos than his own that he had to deal with and the situation was more one of unruly optimism in which criticism, debate, and freewheeling discussion prevailed rather than a strong leader in charge of a hierarchy. An example was The 1949 Carnegie Seminar, sponsored by the Carnegie endowment, which became the basis for *Toward a General Theory of Action*. According to Lawrence Nichols, West Virginia University, who has been mining the transcripts of this seminar, Parsons had advocates in Shils, E. C. Tolman, there on a visiting professorship, and Freed Bales, mainly an observer. Clyde Kluckhohn, Samuel Stouffer, and Richard Sheldon remained friendly critics, while the dissenters were Allport, Murray, and Robert Sears.[84]

Yet another figure at the time was George C. Homans, founder of behavioral sociology and expert in the social group. Homans was born in Boston in 1910 and died in Cambridge, Massachusetts in 1989. He was one of the original Harvard Society of Fellows, along with B. F. Skinner and Willard van Orman Quine, and best known for a work he published on Pareto and another on 13th-century English villagers.[85] He found his way onto the University faculty through L. J. Henderson, champion of Pareto's philosophy, and Elton Mayo over in the Business School, who was working on the famous Hawthorne experiments.[86] There, much more enamored with Pierre Janet than with Freud, Mayo introduced Homans to the literature of psychodynamics.

There can be little doubt where Homans stood in relation to psychology. At one point he contributed to a volume on *Explanation in the Behavioral Sciences* and there wrote on "The relevance of psychology to the explanation of social phenomena." Others, such as Charles Taylor, Stephen Tolman, Karl Pribram, Noam Chomsky, and Hans Eysenck also contributed. Homans focused on the necessary and sufficient conditions for a theory to be considered scientific and relied heavily on the epistemology of behaviorism to prove his point. Psychology, he thought, was one of the many disciplines which he subsumed under sociology, since interactions between people constitutes the majority of that discipline. Personality he defined as "that precariously integrated group of interrelated responses that makes a man an individual." No other theory in psychology was considered, except in one section where he compared conditioned learning in the growth of the child and Freud's conceptions of the Id, Ego, and Superego, did not find the theories incompatible, and concluded that Freud could be considered "the first great behavioral psychologist."[87]

When Homans was discharged from the Armed Services and returned to Harvard in the spring term of 1945–1946, he was given one of two tenured positions newly created for the Department of Social Relations by Dean Paul Buck. The other went to Samuel Stouffer, a statistician. At the first faculty meeting of the School of Arts and Sciences that he attended the Department was voted into existence. Homans mentioned in his autobiography how different he was from the rest of the Social Relations Faculty; "If the founding fathers had fully understood how different, in some ways, though not in all, my ideas from theirs, I doubt if they would have shown themselves so ready to welcome this viper into their bosoms."[88] He got along well with most of the senior people. Murray, for instance, had been an old friend of the Homans family and they both shared an interest in Melville, but for very different reasons. But Homans was closest to the junior faculty and the graduate students. Among them, he named Jerry Bruner, Oscar Handlin, Florence Kluckhohn, Barrington Moore, Jr., Robert White, Richard Sheldon, David Aberle, David Schneider, Hank Riecken, Joe Kahl, Chuck Tilly, Kim Romney, Dan Rosenblatt, and others.

His differences with the department were all intellectual, he reported. He thought all the social sciences should be integrated under the same principles. The only problem was he thought these were the principles of behavior. The lineage of culture and personality theorists he called the "culture–vultures," especially Kluckhohn. Of Freud, he remained "totally skeptical." Durkheim he believed wrong in his idea that society was an entity, "something more than the resultant of individual human beings." He was also in favor of the new effort in the Social Relations Department to move away from pure theory methodologically and to bring in more statistics, although he could not do any such calculations himself. Stouffer did get up before 700 undergraduates in the intro course, however, and announce that statistical polling was now so accurate that they knew ahead of time that Dewey would win over Truman in the national election the next day, but that gaffe was not serious enough for statistical methodology to be abandoned even in Social Relations. Homans also noted that experimental social psychologists tended to not engage themselves in much fieldwork. While it was true that the thrust of the Department of Social Relations remained more in the direction of the human sciences, using the ethnographic approach and the case study method, it continued to fight the encroachment of reductionistic empiricism into its domain. Homans reported in this regard the attempt to have an on-going seminar in methods in social relations. After a year it was discontinued, because everyone seemed to have different methods and no one was really interested in changing.

Similarly, the lines of communication in the faculty remained akimbo. The plan was that there would be two committees, a senior one and a junior one. The senior faculty met once a week and occasionally sent memoranda down to the junior faculty for comment and feedback. But they never seemed to take the feedback seriously. Thus, when *Toward a General Theory of Social Action* came out in 1951, it seemed mainly about the theories of Parsons and Shils, not much about the work of the other senior people. It was then handed down to the junior faculty for approval, who were enjoined to take it up as the official doctrine of the Department and a guide to all future research and teaching. Homans stood up and, quite to everyone's surprise because he was normally so mild-mannered, declared that quite impossible; there were no absolute doctrines in science, and Stouffer stood up and agreed with him. To Homan's surprise, Parsons, the chairman of the Department, retreated on the matter, although his theories continued to dominate students in sociology in the Department for some years.

The majority of students came originally as returning servicemen and saw in the new fusion a possible answer to what they had seen of human nature's destructiveness during the War. Some sense that society could be changed for the better seemed afoot. Eventually, as these numbers declined, the main thrust of the students entering the concentration became personality psychology and self-development, while the zeal to change society as a whole waned. Eventually, the largest numbers of students were undergraduates who did not continue on in any one of the specific disciplines that initiated the Department in the first place. The Department never offered a single doctorate, for instance, but gave degrees in clinical psychology (really personality), social psychology, social anthropology, and sociology, so its influence in the wider world remained diffuse.

Nevertheless, in 1946, when it was first founded, the announcements of the new experiment were all glorious, great advances in learning were forecast, and a new interdisciplinary era for psychology was supposedly ushered in. At its very outset, Social Relations even drew the largest classes in the University. The darker side of it, however, was that tensions had mounted unbearably between the experimentalists, who advocated reductionistic operationism and subsumed psychology under the allegedly more important rubric of empirical laboratory science, and the humanists who, most of them, embraced dynamic theories of the unconscious, performed experiments of a more qualitative nature in science, but held the person as central to the discipline, not the identity of the psychologist as a scientist.

Boring, himself, unable to hold the reins of strong and unruly egos, must have secretly harbored a certain sense of glee at the loss of unity he had attempted to demonstrate on the surface. Meanwhile, down below, the split allowed for the inward fulfillment of a deeper agenda that had brought Boring to Harvard in the first place—to achieve Titchener's goal to establish a general Wundtian laboratory science as the only basis for a legitimate experimental psychology. In 1946, the soft sciences were out and the hard sciences were in as far as the definition of psychology was concerned at the University.

A milestone back in 1934 had been when psychology, which had always been harbored in the Philosophy Department since William James's time, was established, but still within the Department of Philosophy as its own semi-independent committee. Boring introduced the measure in the general faculty meeting and it passed. Then, in 1938, with regard to a wider discussion of semi-independent committees that existed within several Departments, Boring rose in the faculty meeting and proposed the abolition of all committees and the elevation of each to its own Departmental status. Where most other universities had long ago separated psychology from philosophy, Harvard was the last to do so, and at that late date. Eight years later, in 1946, the separation of psychology as a laboratory science from psychologically oriented studies under the rubric of Social Relations brought a quarter of a century of engineering on Boring's part to a point of glorious fulfillment. He just could not tell anyone, as he was only half-aware of it himself. But it did represent the completion of a lifework and the fulfillment of a great spiritual task. Psychology, without its excess baggage, was now truly scientific.

As he headed into retirement, Boring produced a second edition to his *A History of Experimental Psychology* (1950).[89] There, contrary to the 1929 edition, where James had founded the first experimental laboratory at Harvard in 1875, the origin myth was born, that, no! Wundt had now founded the first laboratory of experimental psychology, at Leipzig, but 4 years later in 1879. Here at last was a true scientific, laboratory-oriented Father of the field, but, of course, Grandfather to Boring, as Titchener had fulfilled the role of Wundt's spiritual son in America, and Boring had engineered the legacy at Harvard as Titchener's faithful intellectual offspring. Boring had at last secured the record of his lineage for posterity, and the Freuds, the Jungs, the Murrays, and the Allports were not in it.

Endnotes

1. Boring, E. G. (1961). *Psychologist at large: An autobiography and selected essays*. New York: Basic Books, pp. 3–84.
2. Boring, E. G. (1938). The society of experimental psychologists: 1904–1938. *American Journal of Psychology, 51*(2), 410–423.
3. "Titchener mistrusted the Harvard situation. If he went, he needed to dominate it, and to help with that he wished to bring me along as his adjutant to implement his biddings" (Boring, 1961, p. 29).
4. Boring remarked in his autobiography that Harvard likes to be either first or last in everything, and in the case of separating psychology from philosophy, they were last. Most other American universities, especially with the establishment of their graduate schools, had established psychology as a laboratory science independent of philosophy decades earlier. Johns Hopkins, Clark, University of Chicago, and most others had done so by the end of the 19th century. Harvard did not officially separate psychology from the Philosophy Department until 1938. In 1936, it was Boring who stood up and proposed making psychology a separate committee within philosophy, which was approved, and in 1938, he proudly arose again and proposed to abolish all committees throughout the School of Arts and Sciences, elevating them to the official status of independent Departments in their own right, which was also approved.
5. Allport, G. W. (1967). Autobiography. In E. G. Boring, & G. Lindzey (Eds.), *A history of psychology in autobiography* (Vol. 5, pp. 3–25). New York: Appleton-Century-Crofts.
6. Allport, G. W. (1923). *An Experimental study of the traits of personality, with application to the problem of Social diagnosis*. Unpublished doctoral dissertation, Harvard University, Cambridge, MA.
7. The otherwise excellent biography of Allport does not develop Allport's connections to gestalt psychology, despite Allport's own statements to the contrary as to its importance. See Nicholson, I. (2003). *Inventing personality: Gordon Allport and the science of selfhood*. Washington, DC: American Psychological Association. Insight into the Murray–Allport relationship, and hence what was really going on in the department in the 1930s, was also under-represented.
8. Ash, M. G. (1995). *Gestalt psychology in German culture, 1890–1967*. Cambridge, New York: Cambridge University Press, p. 290.
9. Ash, 1995, pp. 290–291.
10. Boring, 1950, p. 430.
11. Allport, G. W. (1938). William Stern: 1871–1938. *American Journal of Psychology, 51*(4), 770–773.
12. This instrument measured a continuous tone changing dynamically into another tone, rather than the traditional method of comparing two tones for a just noticeable difference.
13. Stern, W., & Spoerl, H. D. (1938). *General psychology from the personalistic standpoint*. New York: The Macmillan Company.
14. Material adapted from Ash (1995).
15. Adapted from Allport, 1938, pp. 770–774.
16. Nicholson, I. (1997b). To "Correlate Psychology and Social Ethics": Gordon Allport and the first course in American personality psychology. *Journal of Personality, 65*(3), 773–742. I disagree with Prof. Nicholson in his interpretation of Allport on personality and character, due to the lack of any discussion of Francis Peabody's "Ethics of the Social Question," upon which the Department of Social Ethics was originally founded and Allport's sense of what he later defined as the psychology of religion also found there.
17. H. A. Murray (personal communication, March, 27, 1982).
18. H. A. Murray (personal communication, May, 24, 1984).
19. H. A. Murray (personal communication, July, 16, 1984).

20. H. A. Murray (personal communication, April 17, 1987).

21. Murray later reported that the real estate broker had told him that the grandfather clock had stopped the moment of Myers's death in 1901 and had not worked since, but when Murray first stormed into the study and banged the door on entering the clock started working again. (H. A. Murray, personal communication, April 28, 1985).

22. Douglas, C. (Ed). (1997). *Visions: Notes of the seminar given in 1930–1934 by C. G. Jung.* Princeton, NJ: Princeton University Press.

23. Melville, H. (1851). *Moby-Dick: Or, the whale.* New York: Harper.

24. H.A.Murray (personal communication, November 5, 1985).

25. H. A. Murray (personal communication, January, 6, 1987). Historically, of course, the two periods are linked. Both psychologists and physicians were working on the lives of individuals and the psychology they generated was person centered. Gordon Allport, following Wilhelm Windelband, wrote extensively on ideographic versus nomothetic approaches to generate knowledge in psychology. The ideographic studies the person in-depth, while the nomothetic studies a single variable in large population samples. He lamented that by the late 1930s, most of psychology had turned to the study of the white rat and to nomothetic methods, though he and other personality theorists were the big holdouts. See, Allport, G. W. (1968). *The person in psychology: Selected essays.* Boston: Beacon Press. Reviewing the history of personality theory, Winter and Barenbaum imply that psychologists in general cannot handle the single case study, since they were originally trained exclusively in nomothetic methods. See Winter, D. G., & Barenbaum, N. B. (1999). History of modern personality theory and research. In L. A. Pervin and O. P. John (Eds.), *Handbook of personality: Theory and research* (2nd ed., pp. 3–27). New York: Guilford. Humanistic psychologists have continued the clinical tradition of the single case study in their pursuit of a person-centered science. See again, Kreuter (2006). *Victim vulnerability: An existential-humanistic interpretation of a single case study.* New York: Nova Science Publishers.

26. White, B., Wolf, R., & Taylor, E. I. (1984). *Stanley Cobb: A builder of the modern neurosciences.* Boston: Francis A. Countway Library of Medicine.

27. Anderson, J. W. (1988). Henry A. Murray's early career: A psychobiographical exploration. *Journal of Personality, 56*(1), 139–171.

28. Boring, E. G. (1940). Was this analysis a success? *Journal of Abnormal and Social Psychology, 55*(1), 2–3, 3–10.

29. Boring (1929).

30. Boring, E. G. (1933). *The physical dimensions of consciousness.* New York, London: The Century Company.

31. This was very much like L. J. Henderson, the physical chemist who sponsored Skinner at the Harvard Society of Fellows, as well as originally hiring Murray. Henderson, a skeptic toward psychoanalysis from the beginning, once reported that he had talked into a dictaphone machine for 3 hours, had it transcribed, and on reading it found not one allusion to sexual matters. (The late John Adams Abbott, first assistant resident in the Department of Psychiatry at the MGH in 1934; J. A. Abbott, personal Communication, June, 5, 1984).

32. The distinction between depth psychology and social psychology became quite pronounced later, when radical political psychologists into race, class, and gender in the 1960s, who had no depth psychology beyond an ambivalent relationship to Freud, insisted that personality was defined by impersonal social forces acting on the individual but controlled by a ruling elite that had to be overthrown if the oppressed classed were to be emancipated. On the origin of SPSSI, see Nicholson (1997a).

33. Allport, G. W. (1937). *Personality: A psychological interpretation.* New York: Henry Holt and Company.

34. Freud, S. (1932–1933). New introductory lectures on psycho-analysis. In J. Strachey (Ed. & Trans.), *The standard edition of the complete psychological works of Sigmund Freud* (Vol. 22, pp. 1–182). London: Hogarth Press.

35. Hendrick, I. (1934). *Facts and theories in psychoanalysis.* New York: A. A. Knopf.

36. Allport is probably best known for his concept of functional autonomy—to give a learning theorists' definition: the persistence of habits long after the original precipitating reinforcer has ceased to be a cause. His conception was more all embracing because it engaged psychologists in looking at the organism in the here and now as a dynamic entity whose interrelated systems were always changing, despite certain enduring characteristics.

37. Woodworth, R. S. (1918). *Dynamic psychology.* New York: Columbia University Press. p. 201

38. Allport, 1937, p. 358.

39. Allport, 1937, p. 386.

40. He was referring to Lewin, K. (1936). *Principles of topological psychology.* New York: McGraw-Hill. The quote comes from Allport, 1937, p. 363.

41. Allport, 1937 p. 365.

42. Murray & the Workers at the Harvard Psychological Clinic (1938).

43. Murray et al., 1938, p. xi.

44. Murray et al., 1938, p. xii.

45. Murray et al., 1938, p. 3.

46. Murray et al., 1938, p. 25.

47. Murray et al., 1938, pp. 33–34.

48. Hale (1995).

49. A protégé of John B. Watson, Lashley's interest was in teaching the neural mechanisms of the conditioned response. Experiments that destroyed parts of the frontal lobe to discover their effect on learning in the white rat became the subject of his major work, *Brain Mechanisms and Intelligence: A Quantitative Study of Injuries to the Brain*, which came out in 1929. His work focused on conditioned learning theory in psychology and localization of function in neurology. This led him to the search for the engram, which he believed to be a neurological trace created in the brain though learning, though he never found it. See Lashley, K. S. (1929). *Brain mechanisms and intelligence: A quantitative study of injuries to the brain.* Chicago: University of Chicago Press; Lashley, K. S. (1935). The mechanism of vision, Part 12: Nervous structures concerned in the acquisition and retention of habits based on reactions to light. *Comparative Psychology Monographs 11*, 43–79; Lashley, K. S. (1950). In search of the engram. *Society of Experimental Biology, Symposium 4*, 454–482.

50. Stagner, R. (1937). *Psychology of personality.* New York: McGraw-Hill Book Company.

51. Murphy, L. (1990). *Gardner Murphy: Integrating, expanding, and humanizing psychology.* Jefferson, NC: McFarland. See also Murphy, L. (Ed.). (1989). *There is more beyond: Selected papers of Gardner Murphy.* Jefferson, NC: McFarland and Company.

52. Barrett, W. (1911). *Psychical research.* New York: Henry Holt.

53. Murphy, L, 1990, pp. 90–91.

54. Allport, G. W., Vernon, P. E., & Powers, E. (1933). *Studies in expressive movement.* New York: The Macmillan Company.

55. Murphy, L., 1990, pp. 175–176.

56. Murphy, G., Jensen, F., & Levy, J. (1935). *Approaches to personality: Some contemporary conceptions used in psychology and psychiatry* (2nd printing). New York: Coward-McCann, Inc.

57. Murphy, G., & Murphy, L. (1931). *Experimental social psychology.* New York: Harper.

58. Murphy, L. 1990, p. 164.

59. Lawrence K. Frank (1890–1968) was born in Cincinnati, OH, and died in Boston. He received his bachelor's degree in economics from Columbia University in 1912. He first worked as a systems analyst for the New York Telephone Company, but in 1923 began to work at the Laura Spellman Rockefeller Memorial. He later worked for the Josiah Macy, Jr. Foundation and the Caroline Zachary Institute of Human Development. He retired in 1955 to Boston. Influential in the Child Development movement he also helped define what came to be called the "behavioral sciences." As associate director of the Spellman Fund, one of the leading financiers of child development research during the 1930s and 1940s, he championed the new

holistic interdisciplinary paradigm of human development that recognized individual differences among particular children, and which incorporated knowledge not only from evolutionary natural science, but from the social sciences as well. Applying this holistic paradigm to developmental theory, Frank argued that the central problem of child development research was to understand the development of the whole child. He advocated that researchers be child centered by understanding that children are emerging, becoming, and dynamically learning. Portions excerpted from "What is 'Normal' Adolescent Growth?" A Paper Presented at the History of Childhood in America Conference, August 5, 6, 2000, Washington, DC by Heather Munro Prescott, Central Connecticut State University (Information, courtesy of Pamela Matz, Widener Library, reference desk).

60. Thurstone began his studies as an electrical engineer, developing several motion picture innovations that attracted the attention of, and led to an offer of employment with Thomas Edison in 1912. However, Thurstone was more interested in studying the "learning function," and continued his academic studies at the University of Chicago. He later stated that G. H. Mead's lectures on social psychology were the greatest influence on his development in psychology. In his early work in psychology, Thurstone rejected the popular stimulus-oriented psychology in favor of a person-centered approach.

61. Lewin, K. (1931). The conflict between Aristotelian and Galilean modes of thought in contemporary psychology. *Journal of genetic psychology, 5,* 141–177.

62. Morrow, A. J. (1969). *The practical theorist: The life and work of Kurt Lewin.* New York and London: Basic Books, pp. 112–113.

63. Morrow, 1969, p. 138.

64. Murray, H. A. (1948). *Assessment of men: Selection of personnel for the Office of Strategic Services.* New York: Rinehart.

65. Gregg, A. (1947). *The place of psychology in an ideal university: The report of the university commission to advise on the future of psychology at Harvard.* Cambridge: Harvard University Press.

66. Gregg, 1947, p. 2.

67. Gregg, 1947, p. 6.

68. Gregg, 1947, p. 42.

69. Eventually, clinical psychology art Harvard landed in the postgraduate APA approved clinical programs associated with the different departments of psychiatry at the various teaching hospitals at the Harvard Medical School.

70. Kluckhohn, C. (1927). *To the foot of the rainbow: A tale of twenty-five hundred miles of wandering on horseback through southwest enchanted land.* New York, London: Century Company.

71. Kluckhohn, C. (1944). *Navaho witchcraft.* Cambridge, MA: The Peabody Museum.

72. Kluckhohn, C. (1949). *Mirror for man: Relation of anthropology to modern life.* New York: Whittlesey/McGraw-Hill Book Company.

73. Kroeber, A. L., & Kluckhohn, C. (1952). *Culture: A critical review of concepts and definitions.* Cambridge, MA: The Museum.

74. Sorokin, P. A. (1963). *A long journey: The autobiography of Pitirim A. Sorokin.* New Haven, CT: College and University Press.

75. Sorokin, P. A. (1925). *The sociology of revolution.* Philadelphia: J. B. Lippincott Company.

76. Sorokin, P. A. (1941). *The crisis of our age: The social and cultural outlook.* New York: E. P. Dutton; Sorokin, P. A. (1992) (2nd revised ed.). London: Oneworld.

77. Sorokin, P. A., & Lunden, W. A. (1959). *Power and morality: Who shall guard the guardians?* Boston: P. Sargent.

78. Sorokin, P. A. (1975). *Hunger as a factor in human affairs* (E. P. Sorokin, Trans.). Gainesville, FL: University Presses of Florida.; See also Sorokin, P. A. (1950). *Altruistic love: A study of American "good neighbors" and Christian saints.* Boston: Beacon Press; Sorokin, P. A. (1947). *Society, culture, and personality: Their structure and dynamics, a system of general sociology.* New York: Harper.

79. Sorokin, P. A. (1937–1941). *Social and cultural dynamics.* New York: American Book Company.
80. Parsons, T. (1937). *The structure of social action.* New York: McGraw-Hill Book Company.
81. Parsons, T. (1949). *Essays in sociological theory, pure and applied.* Glencoe, IL: Free Press. See also Parsons, T. (1942). Age and sex in the social structure. *American Sociological Review, 7*(5), 604–616.
82. Parsons, T. (1951). *The social system.* Glencoe, IL: Free Press.
83. Parsons, T., & Shils, E. (1951). *Toward a general theory of action.* Cambridge, MA: Harvard University Press.
84. Nichols, L. (2006, June). *The genesis of the Parsons school in sociology: Dialogue versus charisma in the 1949 Carnegie Seminar.* Paper presented at the 38th Annual Meeting of Cheiron, International Society for History in the Behavioral and Social Sciences, Sarah Lawrence College, Bronxville, NY.
85. Homans, G. C., & Curtis, C. P. (1934). *An introduction to Pareto: His sociology.* New York: A. A. Knopf; and Homans, G. C. (1941). *English villagers of the thirteenth century.* Cambridge, MA: Harvard University Press.
86. Mayo, E. (1933). *The human problems of an industrial civilization.* Boston: Graduate School of Business Administration, Harvard University; and Mayo, E. (1945). *The social problems of an industrial civilization.* Boston: Graduate School of Business Administration, Harvard University.
87. Homans, G. (1970). The relevance of psychology to the explanation of social phenomena. In R. T. Borger & F. Cioffi (Eds.), *Explanation in the behavioral sciences* (pp. 313–329). Cambridge, MA: Cambridge University Press. Eysenck, in the same volume, wrote on "Explanation and the Concept of Personality." While he identified the *Geisteswissenschaften,* or ideographic psychologists like Allport, from the *Naturwissenschaften,* or nomothetic psychologists such as himself, he was careful to point out that the Allport types operated outside the bounds of the exact sciences. The rest of the chapter was an analysis of the hypotheticodeductive model of research, demonstrating how measurable personality variables are at the heart of other measured variables in an experiment and need to be accounted for. See Eysenck, H. J. (1970). Explanation and the concept of personality. In R. T. Borger & F. Cioffi (Eds.), *Explanation in the behavioral sciences* (pp. 387–424). Cambridge, MA: Cambridge University Press.
88. Homans, G. S. (1984). *Coming to my senses: The autobiography of a sociologist.* New Brunswick, NJ: Transaction Books, p. 296.
89. Boring (1950).

Chapter 9
Anthropologists, Gestaltists, Jungians, and the Pastoral Theologians of New York

One of the more important circles in New York that had embraced dynamic psychology and used it to promote a theory of culture and personality flourished around the anthropologists at Columbia, emanating from the intellectual lineage of Franz Boas, Ruth Benedict, and Margaret Mead. Boas, who had first taught at Clark and the University of Chicago, was a German émigré who has variously been called the father of modern anthropology. He specialized in native cultures and languages, and launched the new but controversial idea that there were no genetic differences between the races in terms of abilities. All races that had survived were equal in endowment. Their radical differences were primarily cultural and historical. Others in this arc included Edward Sapir, Ruth Benedict, Margaret Mead, and, by association with Mead, figures such as Gregory Bateson.[1]

The circle was a tight one. Boas had Sapir, whose specialty was linguistics and culture, and Benedict and Mead for students. Boas and Sapir clashed in their own ways but believed each other to be a worthy adversary. Benedict, while primarily a student of Boas, drew heavily from Sapir; Mead saw herself as a student of both Boas and Benedict, but was clearly Benedict's disciple. They were all drawn together by anthropology, but more importantly Sapir, Benedict, and Mead were all aspiring poets who maintained an even tighter circle in that domain. Benedict and Mead remained in New York, while Sapir went to work first in Canada, then Chicago, migrating to Yale in 1931, where he founded the Department of Anthropology, remaining there until his death.

In addition, others, such as Abram Kardiner, had studied with Boas. Kardiner had also been analyzed by Freud, and so developed a cultural approach to analyzing personality. He did a seminar on psychoanalytic anthropology attended by Erich Fromm, Abraham Maslow, Harry Stack Sullivan, and John Dollard from Yale, each of whom would show up occasionally. He criticized Benedict, whom he did not like very well, because of what he called her exaggerations and omissions.

Benedict, nevertheless, was preeminent in her own field. Ruth Fulton was born in 1887 in New York City, her father was a surgeon and her mother a teacher and librarian. Her father died when she was almost 2 years old. She was raised in upstate New York with her sisters, attended Vassar (Class of '09) and married Stanley Benedict in 1914. From 1919 to 1921 she attended The New School for Social Research and completed her PhD at Columbia under Franz Boas in 1923 with a dissertation on

E. Taylor, *The Mystery of Personality*, Library of the History of Psychology Theories, DOI 10.1007/978-0-387-98104-8_9, © Springer Science+Business Media, LLC 2009

"The Concept of the Guardian Spirit in North America." Even before she graduated she had contributed to the literature with "The Vision in Plains Culture" (1922),[2] a psychological study of visionary experience as a rite of passage determining a young man's place in the tribe. She began teaching at Barnard College and then joined the faculty in anthropology at Columbia, where she finally attained the rank of full professor just 11 weeks before she died in 1948. Her major works were *Patterns of Culture* (1934),[3] in which she compared three different pre-industrial societies; *Race: Science, and Politics* (1940),[4] a study of racial prejudice in the United States; and *The Chrysanthemum and the Sword* (1946),[5] an analysis of patterns in Japanese culture. She was a major figure in the personality and culture movement, which she developed beginning with field studies on Native American Indian tribes of the Southwest.

Benedict's husband died in 1936; meanwhile, throughout her adult life she carried on what one writer referred to as an androgynous relationship with Margaret Mead, herself married four times. A small, frail, shy person of strikingly beautiful appearance who nevertheless wielded tremendous influence over most of the men with whom she worked, Benedict broke the gender barrier in the professoriate and dominated developments in cultural anthropology to the late 1940s by applying dynamic theories of personality to the study of primitive societies. A case in point were articles such as "Psychological Types in the Cultures of the Southwest" (1930),[6] where she first developed her conception of the Apollonian type, which stays within the norm of others, even in the state of exaltation, and the Dionysian, which reaches for excess to transcend the bounds of everyday experience in order to stand outside it, often to receive power to take back in return. This explains the use of datura, peyote, and even alcohol in different Indian rituals of the Dionysian type, and their complete absence among the Pueblo. They are the defining types ruling out shamanic experience or counting it in as integral to the particular tribe. Another was "Anthropology and the Abnormal" (1933), [7] which established that what we consider abnormal in our culture can be considered quite normal and not maladjusted in a variety of different non-white cultures. Trance and epilepsy are notorious examples. Homosexuality is another. In yet another culture, the man considered rich has nothing, for he has given everything away. The poor man is one with many possessions. The implications of this are staggering, because they mean our cultural values are relative and not absolute, and not sacrosanct or ordained by God, to be superimposed on others. Maslow called her "the Benedictine enigma." "She was messianic, like the rest of us," he said, referring to the reform spirit of the 1930s.[8]

Benedict was also close friends with Karen Horney. In that sense, like Mead, she could be characterized as a Neo-Freudian. She drew from Adler and Jung but dipped into Freud selectively. Her work had the effect of drawing Horney away from a strictly Freudian view to a Neo-Freudian one in which culture played a more central role in personality development. She reviewed Horney's *Neurotic Personality of Our Time* in 1938.[9] She also reviewed Erich Fromm's *Escape from Freedom*.[10] The only psychologist she cited in *Patterns of Culture* was her friend, Gardner Murphy. In addition, both Mead and Benedict were friends with Harry Murray.[11] Maslow also referred to her in *The Farther Reaches of Human Nature* (1971),[12] Words came to her intuitively, he said. Maslow traced part of his theory of self-actualization back to Benedict's Apollonian and Dionysian drives, describing the self-actualized individual as an "Apollonian mystic."[13] Benedict was Maslow's case study of a self-actualizing personality. At her funeral, a stunned Erik Erikson, who with his wife Joan had been a close friend, announced to all in his eulogy that she was not the question, she was the answer.

In many ways, however, Benedict was eclipsed by her even more famous student, Margaret Mead.[14] Mead had taken an MA in psychology with a thesis on intelligence in Italian-American immigrants before taking the doctorate in anthropology under Benedict. Her great work became *Coming of Age in Samoa* (1928),[15] a study of adolescent puberty rites, especially among young women. In the beginning, Mead absorbed Kurt Koffka's *Principles of Gestalt Psychology*[16] in 1935, at the same time she was struggling to free herself from measurement-oriented psychology. She started with the galvanic skin response and ended up with Jung's psychological types. On Freud's influence, which was considerable, she asked the question, if primitive adults resembled our children, as Freud maintained, what must the primitive children be like? She found none of the prelogical thinking in young Samoans that Freud's theory predicted. She did seem to find evidence for fixation at the oral, anal, and phallic stages that Freud predicted, but as individual characteristics, each one defining an entire tribe. In the end, however, she considered Freud's views on primitive man to be armchair philosophy. Instead, she was influenced by Benedict's great arc of personality potential,[17] the idea that each culture selected only certain traits to emphasize.[18] Like Benedict, Mead was way ahead of the Western dynamic theorists. She married Gregory Bateson in 1936 and the two of them went off to Indonesia for 2 years to study dissociative trance states as a culturally sanctioned institution among the Balinese.

Mead, Benedict, and Sapir were considered the initiators of the school of personality and culture, although there were others before them. W. H. R. Rivers, Cambridge Don, who died in 1922, had been interested in evolution, the unconscious, and its early origins in primitive cultures. In 1924, the British Association for the Advancement of Science, meeting in Toronto, held a section on anthropology where everyone was talking about Jung's psychological types. But the Boas school, and that of others, such as Clyde Kluckhohn at Harvard, led the field of psychological anthropology, which flourished until the 1950s, blending depth psychology and projective measures with models of psychological types.[19] In 1927, Sapir had delivered a paper on "The Unconscious Patterning of Behavior in Society," which was thought to launch the movement, but Benedict and Mead were considered the leading figures in the school. The Hanover Conference, held in 1934 by Lawrence Frank of the Commonwealth Fund, led to a joint publication between Mead and Benedict, *Cooperation and Competition among Primitive Peoples* (1937),[20] which influenced the course of the discipline, in addition to their other best-selling works individually written.

At a conference held at Dartmouth at in 1967,[21] Anthony Wallace, anthropologist at the University of Pennsylvania, outlined the direction of culture and personality studies. He believed anthropologists were ahead of cognitive psychologists on their understanding of what was in people's minds. But he did hark back, quoting appreciatively from an article in 1913 by A. A. Brill on the Eskimos, suggesting that from the standpoint of a dynamic theory of the unconscious, anthropology as a field, even as late as the 1960s, was in many ways still mired in classical Freudian thinking.

The New School for Social Research

Meanwhile, there was the New School for Social Research. Founded in 1919 by historian, George Beard, economists Thorstein Veblen and James Harvey Robinson, and progressive philosopher John Dewey, its first president was Alvin Johnson, who served from 1921 to 1945. On Johnson's watch, the Graduate Faculty, then the intellectual heart of the New School, became the University in Exile from 1933 until the end of World War II and served as a base for scholars who had been driven from their academic posts by the fascists and the Nazis. Among these émigrés were political philosophers Hannah Arendt and Leo Strauss, the phenomenologist Aron Gurwitsch, and the acknowledged founder of gestalt psychology, Max Wertheimer. In 1935, Karen Horney lectured at the New School for Social Research and was invited by W. W. Norton to write a book that became *The Neurotic Personality of Our Time* (1937),[22] based on those lectures. Thereafter, she continued to lecture at the New School on a regular basis.[23] The New School remained a hotbed of radicalism, socially, politically, and scientifically, and loomed large as a haven for errant theorists and their theories about consciousness and personality.

The Gestaltists

Gestalt psychology—originally a laboratory-based theory of perception, which later became a scientific study of the totality of one's experience, came to define personality as always greater than the sum of its parts. The movement originated in Germany before World War I. It was a science built from the top down, based on a phenomenological perspective, rather than the atomism of the logical reductionists. It was also a distinctive rebuttal to the rational associationism of experimental psychology in Germany at the time. Its official founding is dated from 1912, when Max Wertheimer (1880–1943) published the results of experimental studies undertaken in Frankfurt with his colleagues Kurt Koffka (1886–1941) and Wolfgang Köhler (1887–1967) on the so-called Phi phenomenon—the effect of apparent movement when two stationary flashing lights are put side by side, which is the basic principle behind motion seen in the successive frames of a movie camera. The brain perceives movement in terms of the totality of its experience—the best gestalt it can muster from the conditions of the moment— not by means of perceiving its individual parts, as the psychophysicists believed. Wertheimer, Köhler, Koffka, and their students were successful in extending the gestalt movement beyond perception to problems in learning, cognition, motivation, and personality, and into other areas extending outside psychology, including esthetics and economics. All three migrated to the United States beginning in the 1920s, where they were welcomed with open arms, except that the powerbrokers in American experimental psychology were careful not to let their ideas become too influential in the academy, since the experimental laboratory tradition in the United States owed so much to its association with Boring and Titchener's Wundtian experimentalism, which the perceptual laboratory studies of gestalt had been so successful in criticizing.

Koffka received the PhD under Carl Stumpf at the University of Berlin in 1909 and taught at the University of Giessen from 1911 to 1924. In 1924, his work, *The Growth of the Mind*,[24] for which he became best known, applied gestalt principles to child psychology. In 1924 he also began trips to the United States and in 1927 was appointed to the faculty at Smith College in Northampton, Massachusetts, where he remained the rest of his career.

Köhler took his PhD under Stumpf at the University of Berlin in 1909 on the subject of hearing and taught at Frankfurt briefly before taking charge of the anthropoid research station of the Prussian Academy of Sciences at Tenerife, Canary Islands, from 1913 to 1920. There he studied learning in apes and published his groundbreaking results in 1917, *The Mentality of Apes*,[25] in which he demonstrated the centrality of insight in learning, quite upsetting the theories of blind conditioning put forward by Ivan Pavlov in Russia and James B. Watson in the United States. In 1921, Köhler became head of the Psychological Institute and professor of philosophy at the University of Berlin. He published *Gestalt Psychology* in 1929,[26] but was soon chased out of Germany by the Nazis. In 1935, he became a professor of psychology at Swarthmore College in Pennsylvania until 1955.

Max Wertheimer, originally born in Prague, in 1880, went from music and then law into psychology, where he studied with Stumpf at Friedrich-Wilhelm University before Stumpf went to Berlin. Wertheimer took his doctorate at the University of Würzburg in 1904, on the forensic problem of human testimony. Wertheimer was first on the faculty of the University of Frankfurt, before becoming a lecturer at Friedrich-Wilhelm University in Berlin from 1916 to 1929. During this time he co-founded *Psychologische Forschung*, the journal of the new gestalt movement. He returned to Frankfurt as professor of psychology in 1929, where he became a vocal critic of educational programs that emphasized logic and association, arguing instead for perceptual wholes and a focus on the overall structure of experience. He fled from Germany in 1933 and became a professor at the New School for Social Research in New York City, where he remained until his death. His only notable book was *Productive Thinking*,[27] published posthumously in 1945.

Wertheimer was one of the original 12 refugees who arrived at the New School in 1933.[28] Helping to co-found the Graduate Faculty for Political and Social Science, he was the only psychologist. But he was soon joined by his friend Horace Kallen, William James's former student, who helped him organize the graduate program in psychology and philosophy. Wertheimer taught a seminar on research methods that was quite popular from 1933 to 1944. During this time he became a mentor to Abraham Maslow, then teaching at Brooklyn College. Maslow cherished

Wertheimer as his most inspired teacher and Wertheimer responded accordingly. Wertheimer believed that learning happens not through trial and error, but through insight, totally contradicting the thrust of learning theorists in the United States at the time. He himself was a spontaneous person, who appreciated the function of play and of humor. He was generally good natured and could readily laugh at himself. He also had a vast knowledge of history, philosophy, and the arts, as well as science, and he taught psychology at all levels, including the psychology of art, music, teaching and education, logic and the scientific method, as well as specialized courses in gestalt psychology. He was a man who could ask the big questions. Ethics, values, and personal perceptions were crucial to understanding human experience, and psychology had a duty to find ways to study them. Maslow's biographer also indicated that Maslow was introduced to Oriental philosophy through Wertheimer's work. Western psychologists were too goal oriented and needed to study non-goal-oriented experience, such as play, wonder, awe, esthetics, and mysticism. As a result, Maslow was particularly attracted to Chinese Taoism, which played a later part in defining the self-actualizing personality. Wertheimer pointed Maslow toward the study of peak experiences. He also consulted with Maslow on his own research, expanding Maslow's focus considerably.

So while Koffka and Köhler were around and people were reading their works, it was Wertheimer who played such a significant role in the New York scene, especially through his connections to other German émigrés as diverse as the brain neuropathologist Kurt Goldstein and the Lutheran theologian Paul Tillich, neither of whom were gestaltists but who were sympathetic to its teachings, closely related to the other German émigrés in the neighborhood, and also closely allied to the new developments in scientific studies of the unconscious and dynamic theories of personality.

Kurt Goldstein

Goldstein was born November 6, 1878, in Upper Silesia, seventh of nine children. His father was an owner of a lumber yard, who brought up his children in a very large, agnostic Jewish family. Goldstein's cousin was Ernst Cassirer, who influenced him intellectually. As a young man, Goldstein moved from Breslau to Heidelberg, studying philosophy and literature, then back to Breslau to study medicine and nervous and mental diseases. He studied under Karl Wernicke in the pathological laboratory, was drawn to neuro-embryology, the correlation between psychiatric symptoms and postmortem findings, and problems of aphasia. He received the MD in 1903.

His specialty was the brain and spinal cord, working with Ludwig Eidinger in Frankfurt am Main and others. In 1906 Goldstein joined the psychiatric clinic at the University of Königsberg. There he worked with psychotic patients who had basically been abandoned by the system.

In 1914 Goldstein joined Eidinger at the Neurological Institute at Frankfurt. From there, in cooperation with the military establishment, he founded his own institute for the study of brain injured soldiers during World War I. He hired the gestalt psychologist Adhemer Gelb, who had taken his doctorate with Carl Stumpf. The institute quickly developed into a large and highly successful treatment center for neuropsychiatric disorders. Soon, advanced students and junior colleagues flocked to the place, including Frieda Fromm-Reichmann and Aron Gurwitsch. Major publications in neuropathology followed.

Goldstein took up an interest in psychotherapy in the 1920s. He studied Freud's writings and rejected most of them on the basis of his own extensive knowledge of neuropsychiatric patients, but gave serious consideration to depth psychology and the way in which it was conceptualized. In 1927, he published on the relationship between psychoanalysis and biology. He became a professor of neurology at Frankfurt. He co-founded the *Psychologische Forschung* and was one of the founders of the International Society for Psychotherapy. A major professorship opened to him at the University of Berlin in 1930, which he took. But when Hitler came to power, he was briefly jailed and then thrown out of Germany. Rockefeller Foundation money supported him for a year in Amsterdam, during which time he wrote his definitive text, *The Organism* (1934). An English translation, *The Organism: A Holistic Approach to Biology Derived from Pathological Data in Man* appeared in 1939[29] with a forward by Karl Lashley.

Lashley, no mean intellect himself, seemed to grasp the larger agenda of the whole organism that Goldstein wanted to put forward, yet Lashley explained it in atomistic terms of the correlation and integration of the vital functions, which Goldstein explicitly stated was in error. In the text, Goldstein proceeded to define his subject as the total response of the organism to his experience. His subjects were severely brain-injured soldiers whose attempt at recovery showed remarkable plasticity of not only the nervous system but the organism as a whole. He reviewed the reflex theory of nervous action and theories of conditioning and found them inadequate to understanding the phenomena he had observed in his subjects. What he found was that atomistic theories that tried to build a definition of the organism from the ground up failed, because their models were too static and missed the dynamic interrelation of the parts. Consideration first of the milieu of the total organism succeeded much better in explaining the patient's attempt at recovery.

This theory Goldstein explained in terms of coordinated centers in which the distribution of excitation depends on the condition of the organism as a whole. Different patterns are required than those employed in the more atomistic and therefore static models, so he proposed the alternating figure-ground of the gestaltists as a more viable explanatory device to understand abnormal symptoms and their relation to each other and the whole. Dedifferentiation was another principle that applied—the tendency for growth to move in the direction of greater differentiation and in traumatic pathology to revert back to less differentiated forms. Similarly, the atomist wanted to break down the subject into various drives and instincts. Goldstein contended, however, that there is really only one drive and that is self-actualization—that the organism from birth to death always strives to actualize its highest potentials to extract the maximum out of its existence. Brain-injured soldiers show this consistently in compensating for severe damage. Weak striving as well as overwhelming catastrophic events, however, show how both organic and habitual preferences in the individual go awry. Nevertheless, recovery always proceeds in the direction of compensation to resurrect the total whole. He included chapters analyzing the theory of consciousness and the unconscious and introduced instead the "good gestalt" as a way to see the larger picture that was not fractionated by a theoretically ordained interpretation of experience.

Goldstein's investigation of the new dynamic psychiatry in the late 1920s, led to his first formal statements on the wholistic approach in biology. His emigration in 1935 to the United States, when he was already in his mid-fifties, with a spectacular career already behind in the German medical literature, led him to a second although itinerate and less stable era in which he exerted a profound influence on neurology, psychiatry, and psychology. He began in New York City with a private practice and a clinical professorship at Columbia, and a position at the Laboratory of Neurophysiology at Montefiore Hospital. With Martin Scheerer, he published *Abstract and Concrete Behavior: An Experimental Study with Special Tests* (1941).[30] In 1938–1939 he was invited to give the William James Lectures at Harvard, which became *Human Nature in the Light of Psychopathology* (1940),[31] published with a foreword by Gordon Allport.

For purposes of our discussion the most interesting chapter in this work is "The Structure of Personality." In it, Goldstein notes the fantastic intercorrelation between very subtle neurological styles or preferences and minute variations of mental functioning, the totality of which defines the unique individual. He examined the presuppositions of trait theory and declared them useful for establishing trends within the person, but maintained that they are useless as representations of large-scale samples, because one not only looses the dynamic nature of the interaction of traits within the person but also is incapable of presenting the details of the individual except in terms of averages to which there is a probability the individual might or might not conform.

He became clinical professor of psychology at Tufts University in Medford, Massachusetts in 1940, where he remained for 5 years, funded by Rockefeller money. *Aftereffects of Brain Injuries in War* (1942)[32] appeared during that time and *Language and Language Disturbances* (1948)[33] thereafter. He visited Worcester State Hospital frequently at the invitation of David Shakow, and in 1944 also published with Eugenia Hanfmann and Maria Rickers-Ovsiankina, *Case Lunati: Extreme Concretization of Behavior due to Damage of the Brain Cortex*.[34] He visited with Allport in Cambridge and Lashley whenever Lashley came to town. He also became associated with a small group of German émigrés in Boston, which came to include over the years Mary Ann and Hans Lucas Teuber and Paul Tillich. Goldstein went back to New York City and taught at the New School for Social Research and City College, but then returned shortly thereafter to teach at Brandeis, commuting each week from New York. He was 80 in 1958 and special issues of the *Journal of Individual Psychology* and the *American Journal of Psychotherapy* were issued in his honor. He died September 19, 1965. A memorial volume appeared in 1968, *The Reach of the Mind*,[35] edited by Marianne Simmel, with contributions from, among others,

Erich Fromm, Aron Gurwitsch, Eugenia Hanfmann, Rollo May, Gardner Murphy, David Shakow, and Silvan Tomkins.

He was a man of his era, encountering gestalt psychology, psychoanalysis, phenomenology, and existentialism and deriving from them a wholistic biology of his own making that linked biology and psychology to a science of the whole person.[36]

The Jungians

There was also the Analytical Psychology Club of New York, founded around a group of devoted Jungians who were all physicians and close friends who had all been analyzed by Jung and comprised the earliest group of Jung's followers in the United States. As we said earlier, they included Beatrice Hinkle, the first to translate Jung's works into English, Kristine Mann, ardent Swedenborgian and co-founder of the Analytical Psychology Club, whose personal library became basis for the present Kristine Mann Library; Eleanor Bertine and Esther Harding, Constance Long, and later, Frances Wickes.

Kristine Mann (1873–1945) was said to be the subject of C. G. Jung's "A Study in the Process of Individuation," in which Jung interpreted a series of 24 paintings of a Miss X.[37] Mann was born on August 29, 1873, in Orange, NJ, where her father, Charles Holbrook Mann, was a New Church minister. He had discovered the writings of Swedenborg during his Civil War experiences and had become a convert. Her mother, Clausine Borschenius, who had come to America from Denmark at the age of 14, had become interested in Swedenborg while working her way through Northwestern University. Thus it was a distinctly New Church environment in which Kristine Mann grew up, a home in which the two realities, spiritual and physical, were accepted as the basis of life. But Charles Mann was no orthodox Swedenborgian; he was a follower of that brilliant though eccentric thinker, Henry James, Sr., from whom he derived the anti-ecclesiastical tendencies that brought him into conflict with his church.

Kristine Mann began summers on Bailey Island in Maine when she was 11. She graduated from Smith College and afterward studied German in Berlin. She took the MA in English at the University of Michigan, and she taught at Vassar for 4 years before moving to New York City to teach English and take graduate courses in psychology, among other subjects at Columbia. Interested in the health and education of women, age 36, she entered Columbia Medical School and received the MD in 1913. She worked in various capacities in women's health and did wartime service in the same area, working with women in ordinance.

Mann was identified as one of a group of women from Vassar who gravitated toward Jungian psychology around the same time.[38] While teaching there, she developed lasting friendships with three of her students who themselves went on to become physicians in an era when women were still pioneers in the study and practice of medicine: They included Cary Fink (later de Angulo and then Baynes) '06 (MD, Johns Hopkins, 1911), Elizabeth Goodrich (later Whitney) '07 (MD,

Stanford, 1914), and Eleanor Bertine '08 (summa cum laude and Phi Beta Kappa; MD, Cornell, 1913). Like Mann, all three women played major roles in the early history of analytical psychology in New York.

Eleanor Bertine, meanwhile, set up a medical practice and numbered many business and professional women among her patients. She also served as consulting physician to the New York Reformatory for Women, but resigned in protest when her objections to the inmates' appalling living conditions met with no response. At the war's end, the War Work Council of the YWCA appointed Bertine to direct a radical educational program supported by its leftover war-work funds. It sponsored lectures on sex education (decorously referred to as mental hygiene) by women physicians for women in colleges and universities in 40 states; Bertine herself, Mann, and Dr. Margaret Doolittle Nordfeldt, Vassar 1893 (MD, Boston University, 1898), were among the speakers. All three had read Jung and were eager to follow Hinkle's footsteps and study with him.

Bertine traveled first to London, in 1920, to begin analysis with Dr. Constance Long, the first English woman to follow Jung's methods. In 1921–1922, Mann and Bertine were both analyzed by Jung in Zurich, after which they established their own practices in New York as the second and third Jungians to treat analytic patients in the United States. Becoming friends and staunch allies of Jung, both regularly crossed the Atlantic to continue analysis and attend Jung's seminars.

In New York, the fledgling Jungian band gathered around Bertine and Mann, and when Esther Harding, a British medical doctor and early and distinguished disciple of Jung, emigrated from England in 1924 to join them, the three doctors composed a powerful trio. In 1936 they created the Analytical Psychology Club of New York and were active leaders in its educational programs.

At her death in 1945, Kristine Mann left her personal library to the Analytical Psychology Club. Today, after years of building its collections, the Kristine Mann Library boasts the most extensive holdings in analytical psychology of any library in the world. Bertine and Harding went on to spearhead the establishment of New York's Jung Foundation and Training Institute in 1962.

Esther Harding (1888–1971), along with Kristine Mann and Eleanor Bertine, spent many summers in their compound in Bailey Island, Maine, where in 1936, C. G. Jung presented what is known as the Bailey Island Seminar, the first of his two-part American seminar on Dream Symbols. The second part of the seminar was held in New York a year later and is known as the New York Seminar. A version of these seminars was published in volume 12 of Jung's *Collected Works*, as "Individual Dream Symbolism in Relation to Alchemy." Many years after Jung's death, the dreamer was identified as physicist Wolfgang Pauli.[39]

Edward Christopher Whitmont

Jungian analyst, homeopath, dowser, poet, teacher to many generations of devoted students, and a co-founder of the C. G. Jung Training Center in New York, Edward Whitmont, according to one of his students, embodied "the journey to the Great

Man within."[40] He was born in Vienna in 1912 of Polish parents and raised in an orthodox Jewish family. Deeply introspective as an only child, he lived in the interior world of dreams, myths, fairy tales, and Wagnerian music. He became an ardent socialist and trained in medicine at the University of Vienna, after which he passed into the anthroposophy of Rudolf Steiner, homeopathy, psychosomatics, alchemy, and Jungian psychology. He escaped from the Nazis, but his parents perished in the concentration camps. In the United States, he taught homeopathy before he sought out Esther Harding and encountered Jung's ideas. He went back to Vienna after the War and did further analytic training with Gustav Richard Heyer, despite Heyer's former association with the Nazis. But Whitmont was best known for his own synthesis of depth psychology and its unique application to himself, his students, and his patients.[41]

Joseph Campbell

Joseph Campbell was probably most well known of the New York Jungians, but as a scholar, since he was not a therapist.[42] Campbell was born in 1904 in New York City and raised in upstate New York in an upper-class family. He was the eldest of two children. He attended Canterbury Preparatory School in New Milford and continued to develop an interest in Native American culture, which he had discovered as a young boy. He briefly attended Dartmouth College, but transferred to Columbia University where he was a member of the track team and played the saxophone in jazz bands. On one of the trips to California he took with these bands, he met Jiddu Krishnamurti, the charismatic Hindu philosopher in 1924, which led to a lifelong friendship and to the study of Hinduism and Buddhism.

Instead of continuing on to graduate school, upon graduation in 1925, he bought an old car and spent the year driving to the West Coast, where he fell in with John Steinbeck and his wife and lived with them outside Monterey until their divorce. He earned the MA from Columbia in 1927 and traveled to Europe to study for 2 years. While he later studied Sanskrit and Indo-European philology at the University of Munich, he never earned the PhD. Nevertheless, he went on to a distinguished teaching career at Sarah Lawrence College, beginning in 1934, where he developed an international reputation as a philologist, editor, translator, and interpreter of world mythology.

His interpretation, however, was decidedly Jungian and psychological, which alienated him from the formal scholars in the Universities. He became editor of the Bollingen Series for Princeton University Press and translated the Eranos Yearbooks into English. He also completed the translations of the indologist Heinrich Zimmer, a close friend and confidant of C. G. Jung, and brought such works to English-speaking audiences as Zimmer's *Philosophies of India*.[43]

In 1938, he married Jean Erdman, and in 1944 published *A Skeleton Key to Finnegan's Wake*,[44] which brought him some notice. He followed this work in 1949 with *The Hero with a Thousand Faces*,[45] an account of the distillation of motifs from his study of world cultures. He suggested, as Mircea Eliade was also delineating, that the hero of so many of the worlds myths makes a characteristic journey into the depths of the unconscious, struggles with immense forces there, overcomes adversity, and is spiritually transformed as a result. He then emerges back into the world to affect the lives of others who are also on that inward journey. Again, borrowing heavily from Jung's psychology, Campbell understood that myths are the collective roadmaps of different cultures, pointing the way toward individuation and wholeness for the individual and hence the culture at large. The work was reviewed as interesting, but a little fantastic. He did receive an award for the book from the American Academy of Arts and Letters. The work also drew the attention of the New York intellectuals into culture and personality, further linking depth psychology (but of the Jungian not the Freudian variety) to the various conceptions of personality emerging on the scene. His influence was farther out in what is already visible as a psychotherapeutic counterculture operating beyond the clinics and the laboratories.

After *Hero with a Thousand Faces*, Campbell continued to teach at Sarah Lawrence and elsewhere. In 1956, he began lecturing at the Foreign Service Institute at the State Department in Washington, DC. His next major project was a four part series on *The Masks of God*,[46] the different conceptions of spiritual experience across cultures. *Primitive Mythology*[47] was published in 1959; *Oriental Mythology*[48] was published in 1962. *Occidental Mythology*[49] was published in 1964; and in 1968 the final volume, *Creative Mythology*[50] appeared. Along with numerous other works, such as *Flight of the Wild Gander*[51] in 1969, in 1970 he edited *Myths, Dreams, and Religion* [52]; in 1972 *Myths to Live By*,[53] and in 1974 published *The Mythic Image*.[54] Toward the end of his life he planned out an *Atlas of World Mythology*,[55] but had some trouble-finding publishers, as it was a multivolume endeavor.

The true significance of Campbell's work remains obscure even to his own community of followers, who are largely therapists, as the implications of an atlas of world mythology has yet to be fathomed from a scholarly standpoint. The transpersonal psychologist Dale Starcher has identified an important lineage linking the work of scholars in comparative religions to a spiritually oriented depth psychology operating within the psychotherapeutic counterculture in which Campbell played a prominent part. The link is between the ideas of Mircea Eliade and their influence on Heinrich Zimmer, whose interpretation of Asian philosophies was taken up by Carl Jung, upon which Joseph Campbell elaborated. Essentially, Eliade posited a cross-cultural comparative science of religions that presumed universal forms of expression within the experience of the individual. Zimmer demonstrated this in his indological studies published in German from the Sanskrit literature, which Campbell translated into English and employed in his mapping out of world mythologies, and Jung expressed in the psychological language of individuation. This lineage essentially defines the way in which a religious experience from a non-Western culture can be translated into a psychotherapeutically useful tool relevant to a spiritual psychology of self-realization in a Western context.[56]

Then, in the mid-1980s, Campbell was interviewed by Bill Moyers for National Public Television. The response of the national audience was tremendous, as the series was a powerful affirmation of the interior quest for self-realization and there was obviously a need for some understanding of this phenomena not being provided by the modern definition of psychology as an empirical and reductionistic science. Princeton University Press, which had ended the Bollingen Series and receded from their former pace of republishing Jung's works, all the sudden had to resurrect their Jungian list, which included works by Campbell. The demand for what Campbell was discussing overwhelmed the publishers. As one point of reference, just at the height of his new found popularity, in 1987, Campbell died in Honolulu, Hawaii. Then in 1989, 2 years after his death, his book *Hero with a Thousand Faces*, which had first appeared in 1949, finally made the *New York Times Best Seller List.*

There was also a small but significant backlash against Campbell's televised series. Some commentators were so outraged that they tried to associate him with anti-Semitism, and the Nazis. Scholars of folklore tried to say his work was not credible. He was also attacked for enunciating the phrase "Follow your bliss," as the encomium against the ravages of modernity, being accused as a narcissistic hedonist. The overwhelmingly positive response, however, muted his detractors.

Tillich at Union and Columbia

Dynamic theories of personality turned out to be the bridge between psychology and religion in the 20th century, beginning with the Emmanuel Movement in Boston.[57] The Movement, which married the Christian teachings of character formation with major advances in scientific psychotherapy, turned out to be Chapter One of the clinical pastoral education movement in the United States. The center of this movement shifted from Massachusetts in the late 1920s to Chicago, following the influence of the Rev. Anton Boisen, and to New York with the involvement of Helen Flanders Dunbar, a physician and pioneer in psychosomatic medicine. Depth psychology then became an integral part of a revival of Protestant Christianity in the 1930s and 1940s, particularly through the work of Paul Tillich, professor at Union Theological Seminary who also had a joint appointment at Columbia. Christian existentialist and eminent figure in pastoral psychology, Tillich's position was that in the modern age, we need something more than traditional religion to guide us; we need a theology of culture. By this he meant that Christianity was fast ceasing to be an influential force on industrial society and must invigorate itself by encountering the significant movements of the day. These included such forces as socialism, existentialism, and science, as well as psychoanalysis, believing that such dialogues would lead to an altogether new theology of culture.

Tillich came to the United States at the invitation of his good friend Reinhold Niebuhr to join the faculty at Union. Probably one of the most influential Protestant theologians of the 20th century,[58] from the moment he arrived from Germany as an émigré fleeing Hitler in 1934 to his death in 1966, Tillich surrounded himself with not only religious scholars but also philosophers, psychologists, and psychiatrists who shared his vision. He was close friends with Kurt Goldstein. He reviewed Erich

Fromm. He spoke lovingly at the funeral of Karen Horney. He had a significant influence on Carl Rogers. He was friend and mentor to Rollo May, and more.

May recounted his impressions in notes he made for a biography, eventually published as *Paulus*, which turned out to be more of a personal tribute.[59] May had first met Tillich in 1934, the day he arrived in New York. Tillich went looking for his room at the Union Theological Seminary, where he was to teach, there, as well as at Columbia across the street, until 1955. May became an auditor of Tillich's lectures, then a student and then a close friend. Their meeting occurred just after May had returned from his travels in Greece and his then recent summer seminar with Alfred Adler. It was during the holidays so no one was there. May encountered only a man who appeared to be lost, wandering down the hall. Without any introductions, May showed him to his room and thought no more of it, but remembered the chiseled features of a strong face.

Later, when he went to hear the new professor whose name he did not recognize, on "The Spiritual Implications of Psychoanalysis," it turned out to be Tillich. The seminar was small with a handful of students and several faculties. The students would laugh at Tillich's mistakes in English, as he talked at each meeting. Later, May sent him an anonymous letter, letting Tillich know that the laughter was not personal and that the students really valued his ideas. Tillich later found out that May had sent it and thanked him, saying it had meant a great deal personally at an anxiety ridden and uncertain time.

May immediately identified Tillich with the spirit of ancient Greece. In Tillich's presence one's spiritual self could emerge from underground. Whatever he discussed mattered. When he spoke about being, you felt he was speaking about your being. One felt as he lectured that you were standing on the top of a mountain surveying a vast landscape—the spirit of the ancient Greeks in one direction, the Middle Ages in another, the Renaissance in another, and the modern period in yet another.

With his father, early on, Tillich had engaged in long conversations about philosophy that had led to a breakthrough in his own independent thinking. This then spread to all areas of his thought. Forever after that, he remained immune to any attempt to surrender this autonomy. Tillich began his career as a philosophical idealist, deciding to become a philosopher on the death of his mother when he was 18. He took his university degree and was ordained in the Lutheran church.

But he converted to existentialism in a single day. This occurred when Tillich was a chaplain at the Battle of the Marne. On the day in particular, they brought in a group of soldiers, many of whom were his friends. As they lay there in varying stages of carnage and death, Tillich went into shock. He tried reading Nietzsche to recover, finding some solace of momentary ecstasy amidst the forests of ruin around him. The big question for Tillich became "How is there something rather than nothing?" His answer was that when your destiny is made immediately available to your experience and your understanding, truth must be wedded to action.

As for May, 3 years after he had graduated from Union he was back working at Columbia on a PhD in clinical psychology. He had become an ordained minister, written *The Art of Counseling*[60] and *The Springs of Creative Living*,[61] but then contracted tuberculosis. Two years in a hospital at Lake Saranac in New York, at one point in a state of near-death, convinced him that that he no longer believed in the Christian scheme of salvation and that he had to leave his vocation as a minister. He even cancelled the second edition of his book, then doing quite well. Back at Columbia, again under Tillich, he moved from Christianity to existentialism, which he fused with his earlier emersion in classical Greek culture. Tillich had him study theories of anxiety. Tillich was unmerciful in this quest. "Study everything on the subject," he said. No exceptions. It took 8 years for May to write the book *The Meaning of Anxiety,*[62] which became a best seller. He and Tillich struggled with the question of anxiety, not just normal forms, but the *angst* that characterized the individual's response to death and to non-being. His response to May's *Meaning of Anxiety* became Tillich's Terry Lectures of 1950, later published as *The Courage to Be.*[63]

In that work, Tillich introduced the concept of ecstatic or transcendent reason. This is not just logic, but reason that embraces values, ethics, and justice. It connects logic and intellectual life to the cosmos and admits what is of ultimate concern to the individual, which was Tillich's definition of what is truly the spiritual core within the individual in a secular age. For mere reason is always shaken and overpowered by that which is of ultimate concern. It is the courage to leap into the realm of mythology when the truth one wishes to express requires it. At the same time, the abyss is a realm of creative chaos that transcends values. It is transmoral. It is mystic illumination—the holy void, the tolerance of ambiguity, the attraction to the gray areas of life because of their hidden possibilities.

"Living on the boundary" for Tillich meant finding oneself at the interface between opposing forces, between consciousness and the unconscious, philosophy and theology, the intellectuals and common men and women, and heteronomy, or rules, and autonomy, which is freedom, but which must be guided by Theonomy, the Divine law, which envisions a situation in which norms and values express the convictions and commitments of free individuals in a free society.

But the price of loving the abyss is *angst*, anxiety, and the subjective side of the tension between being and non-being. "New knowledge can be won only through breaking a taboo." "All autonomous thinking is accomplished by a consciousness of guilt."[64]

According to May, Tillich penetrated the women he met psychologically and spiritually. There was much libido in his presence, which delighted women who came near him.[65] For Tillich, himself, every one of these encounters with a new person was anxiety creating. Anxiety is the dread of freedom. When human beings are in conflict, the unconscious becomes visible.[66] But can we ask the big questions of life too strongly, so that we are brought to the edge of the abyss of madness? According to May, Tillich lived perpetually at that boundary.

Truth is dynamic; it occurs in the middle of struggle and destiny. Live Dionysian and think Apollonian; one is then always living in an open and a dynamic condition. Peace is their dynamic equilibrium. Risk is one of those existential qualities. The experience of the abyss was also the "holy void"—chaos, crying to be made into form.

Tillich's method was one of correlation. Our existential questions stand on one side; their theological answers on the other. Courage, for example, is the fundamental virtue upon which all other virtues depend. Self-affirmation wards off non-being, illness, death, and our intellectual limitations. It is the source of meaning. But it is always self-formation "in spite of . . ." something. "The self is the stronger the more non-being it can take into itself." In the face of non-being, we answer instead with a courageous, yes!

Tillich also talked about the God beyond God. God does not exist. He is rather being itself. So to argue that God exists is to deny his existence. There was a cosmic basis to his reason and his reason was always open ended.

Meanwhile, Tillich's engagement with depth psychology was profound. He recognized that we are living in an age of psychology in which man himself has become his own problem. As May pointed out, "the culture in which Tillich lived in Europe was self-consciously Freudian."[67] Tillich's mysticism, however, remained rooted in Boehme, Schelling, and Nietzsche. As far as his relation to Freud, Tillich had a quasi analysis with an unknown associate. Once he came out of a therapeutic session and tried to strangle his wife. On another occasion he fled from the room believing he had seen his father as a snake.

Following Jung, Tillich says, personality is the generally acknowledged term associated with unity. A neurosis is a disturbance in its development. Personality is the development of the whole person, the unique indivisible unit. It means wholeness—a vocation performed. This demands that physicians pay attention to positive health as well as illness, on which they now focus too much.

For Tillich, there is a psychic reality in both body and mind, one unconscious, the other conscious. The unconscious becomes actually what it potentially is, and for which it strives, by reaching the state of waking rational consciousness. Consciousness, for Tillich, included the potentialities driving within the unconscious as its vital reservoir. Potentiality is not actuality, but neither is it nothing; it is *potentia*, power: the most destructive power, if it conquers the mental unity of consciousness after having been repressed; the most creative power, if it enters and widens consciousness through union with the objective structures of reality. The success of this union determines the integration (or disintegration) of the personality; it decides between disease and health; and between destruction and salvation. But the use of words such as ego, self, and personality, Tillich believed, remains ambiguous. The indefinite character of modern terminology reveals the immature stage of the self-interpretation of man in our age.[68]

May had also participated with Tillich and others in the New York Psychology Group. This was a series of meetings that began with Seward Hiltner, professor of theology and personality at Princeton Theological Seminary and a central figure in the pastoral counseling movement. The meetings also prominently featured Erich Fromm. The meetings, in the form of a conference, were sponsored by the National Council on Higher Education in 1941 at Keuka College in New York. The Group met 29 times on Friday evenings from 1942 to 1945. A professional stenographer was hired to come to each session and detailed notes were taken. Participants included, among others, Rollo May, Carl Rogers, Erich Fromm, Ruth Benedict, Frances Wickes, as well as Hiltner and Tillich.[69]

The first year the theme was the psychology of faith, especially the dynamics of faith and the relationship between the faith and the healthy personality. Tillich soon emerged as a champion of the transcendent, the unconditioned, and what was infinite and ultimate in life. Fromm stood out as an advocate for the actualization of human potential with a more humanist and this worldly concern. For Fromm we are estranged from ourselves and others. For Tillich we are separated from the very ground and source of our being.

The second year it was the psychology of love; that is, love as an expression of the entire personality, not just a feeling, instinct, or idea. Hiltner articulated the outlines of self-love, love of others, and love of God. Fromm retorted with a psychoanalytic interpretation. He articulated certain key attitudes that one has a right to expect love from others, that if one wants love, one has to take it, or else one remains withdrawn. He associated these attitudes with Freud's oral stage of development. Love was based on feeding. In the passive aggressive kind of love, one's mouth is always open and receptive to being fed. In the aggressive mode one goes out looking for attachment, snatching it by one's jaws as it were. The passive mode is withdrawn, cut off, and tight lipped. Wickes invoked the Jungian ideas of the shadow within ourselves and coming to terms with our own dark side. We are then able to engage in the *participation mystique*, the merging with others and the collective. Love then emerges out of the unconscious and comes into consciousness in its more mature form. Sexual love and love in primitive cultures were also considered.

The third year it was the psychology of conscience. Fromm again dominated. Conscience was the Freudian superego, comprised of the internalized laws and prohibitions of the Father, if the Oedipus conflict is successfully resolved. Guilt then becomes not disobedience to a higher law, but a form of self-mutilation, since the original fear of punishment from the Father remains castration. Conscience for Tillich, on the other hand, was not the internalization of rules and regulations, but the shift from external standards to internal ones, in which the depth and profundity of one's internal realizations become the standard because what is eternally true is inscribed in the heart of every person. This he called transmoral conscience, that which goes beyond mere laws and penetrates into the ground of our being. God is in us and can be seen as the inner light. Conscience does not make laws; it enforces them, but at the same time it is also a call back to ourselves. The fourth year was dedicated to the psychology of helping.

According to Allison Stokes in *Ministry after Freud* (1985),[70] these meetings were central to the post-World War II movement called Religion and Health and its participants contributed many of the major texts used in theology schools in pastoral counseling by the 1970s.[71] The seminars also provoked a deep disquiet in Tillich's thinking as he sought to reconcile the Christian scheme of salvation with existentialism and psychoanalysis. Freud's complete rejection of religion served as a counterforce for Tillich's own conclusions—that psychoanalysis pointed to a larger and more all-encompassing form of depth psychology that involved the process of spiritual self-actualization beyond a psychology of the neurosis. This more all-encompassing form of depth psychology he found in existentialism, which acknowledged the generic dimension of spiritual experience within the person independent of any particular theological or psychological system.

At Tillich's memorial service in 1966, May remarked that psychologists and psychiatrists came to hear him in droves. Why? Anxiety, despair, and guilt are not only part of the human condition but also become sources for the courage to be. Their work with patients can then be infused with deeper understanding and mercy, even the quality of grace. "It seems to me," May concluded, "that Tillich is the therapist for the therapists."[72]

Abraham Maslow

Yet another key figure in the New York scene was Abraham Maslow, who taught at Brooklyn College. Maslow, born of Russian Jewish parents who had settled in New York, was the eldest of four children. Throughout his life he made no secret that he hated his mother, while he remained friendly but emotionally distant from his father. He attended Cornell for 1 year and took psychology with E. B. Titchener. Thus, he began his career as an experimentalist in the laboratory. He fell in with Harry Harlow, Clark Hull, William H. Sheldon and others at the University of Wisconsin, where he did his doctorate on dominance and sexuality in primates. Thoroughly imbued with the experimentists' methods at the time, he saw himself as an avid follower of the doctrines of behaviorism.

Freshly minted with the new doctorate, he entered medical school, an experiment that lasted just 1 year. But then, through the strong support of Gardner Murphy, a postdoctoral fellowship suddenly came through as a research assistant to E. L. Thorndike at Columbia, where Thorndike gave him a completely free hand to pursue whatever kind of research he wanted. Ostensibly, he was to work on Thorndike's project, "Human Nature and the Social Order." Meanwhile, Maslow also launched a project of his own that lasted into the 1940s—the study of power and sexual dominance in females of the human species.

At the same time, after graduation, through Gardner Murphy and Ashley Montague, Maslow took a teaching job at Brooklyn College. Maslow spent some time studying with Alfred Adler in New York as well. He became friends with Max Wertheimer, Kurt Goldstein, and others at the New School for Social Research, and also established a friendship with Ruth Benedict and Margaret Mead, as well as Karen Horney and Erick Fromm.[73] Wertheimer and Benedict, as we have already said, were two of the most self-actualized persons he had ever met.

Benedict arranged for him to live with the Blackfoot Indians in Alberta, Canada to get field experience and test his theories on dominance and sexuality, which he found all wrong when working with a non-European population secure in their own identity and less stressed than whites, whom he found as a culture to be much more affluent but more insecure.

As a result of this experience, Maslow abandoned the concept of cultural relativity—the idea that another culture can be successfully understood by comparing it to the norms and values of one's own culture. Instead, he began to focus on the unique individual and one's inner most values, goals, and aspirations. His early New York years taught him three things: Learn to look within, strive to develop your potential, and think for yourself. His biographer, Edward Hoffman, credits Max Wertheimer, the co-founder of gestalt psychology, with influencing Maslow in the direction of the normal and ideal types of personality, when Maslow first taught a course in "The Normal Personality" in 1940. Solomon Asch and Herman Witkin were among his other colleagues. Solomon Asch became his close friend.[74]

Maslow's Blackfoot Indian experience had convinced him that a man's personality was by far more important than his class membership. The birth of his first child also caused him to abandon the cherished beliefs he had previously held about Watsonian behaviorism. At that point, he preferred Goldstein's conception that we come into the world as a total psychophysical human being. Also, Maslow was a close colleague and friend to Gardner Murphy. For Maslow, psychoanalysis, gestalt, behaviorist, and now organismic psychology fused into a new conception of personality.

Maslow himself eventually underwent a partial psychoanalysis with Emil Oberholzer, a Swiss psychoanalyst. Abram Kardiner, whom we have already mentioned, was another influential psychoanalyst on his thinking. His emphasis was on anthropology. Maslow also later underwent an analysis with Felix Deutsch and Harry Rand, a local analyst who was his best friend.[75]

From these experiences, Maslow's own outlook was gradually changing. Shortly after the United States entered World War II, Maslow had a peak experience, the effects of which never left him. It was while watching a rag tag parade of veterans full of boy scouts and old fat people that had blocked his way home one evening. He found himself weeping, and afterward committed the rest of his life to "a psychology for the peace table." This would take the form of a comprehensive theory of motivation.

Since 1935, Wertheimer and Benedict, we have said, had been his two prototypes. In 1941, he co-authored *Principles of Abnormal Psychology*, where he included a chapter on the normal personality, identified by 12 broad categories and several dozen specific ones, and he also added a section on the ideal personality.[76] Thereafter, he queried his Brooklyn College students on the subject between 1943 and 1944 to identify good human beings, almost healthy, even saintly people, who were basically satisfied and self-fulfilled. He was interested in people who were at peace, who had experienced contentment, calmness, the full utilization of capacities, full creativity, and who had demonstrated success in interpersonal relationships.

During this period he articulated his theory of the hierarchy of needs. He called them five sets of goals or purposes or needs which are set in the following order of prepotency: First, satisfaction or gratification of body needs; second, the safety needs; third, love, affection, warmth, acceptance, a place in the group; fourth, desire for self-esteem, self-respect, self-confidence, for the feeling of strength or adequacy; fifth, self-actualization, self-fulfillment, self-expression, working out of one's own fundamental personality, the fulfillment of its potentialities, the use of its capacities, the tendency to be the most that one is capable of being. Later, he would add a sixth level, self-transcendence.[77]

At this time, he also outlined but never completed a magnum opus of 21 chapters overhauling psychology that would, he hoped, have the same effect on transforming the field as James's *Principles of Psychology*[78] had in 1890. It was based on the idea that the obsession psychologists had with methods had created a poverty of ideas.[79] For his new psychology of the normal personality, he drew heavily on Karen Horney and others. The issue became for him who was self-actualized and who was not. But asked this way, the concept appeared to be just another personality type. The non-self-actualizers, that is, most of us—were over here, and the self-actualizers—a few genius types, were over there. But in early January, 1946 Maslow slowly realized that there is a self-actualizing dimension to every personality. There was a higher dimension to ourselves to which each person could appeal. Such types are intensely private and also prone to mystical experiences (Jung's introverts?) and tend to see the world more accurately than the more anxiety ridden. Yet at the same time, they had their persona in the world. They fit in wherever they went. Ninety-nine percent of the time they obeyed the folkways and mores of their immediate social situation, yet as each person penetrated into the higher reality of who they were, they became more like other such personalities across cultures than they resembled the members of their own culture.

Maslow lived in California for a year from 1946 to 1947 and there became friends with Elsa Frankel-Brunswick at UC Berkeley. In her European period, before the Nazis invaded Austria, she had done a biographical study of 400 persons, living and dead. While psychoanalytically inclined, she was also a strong phenomenologist and enamored with gestalt psychology. She organized an informal seminar for Maslow that included David Kretch, Donald McKinnon, David Mandelbaum, an anthropologist, Nevitt Sanford, and E. C. Tolman, who met weekly. Maslow filtered his new ideas about motivation and personality through them.

Then, in 1949, the Stanford psychologist Ernest Hilgard first introduced him to the California psychotherapist Anthony Sutich. As a teenager in the early 1920s, Sutich had sustained a major injury in which he was almost totally paralyzed. For the rest of his life—he died in 1977—he remained confined to a gurney, able to move only his hand and to partially turn his head. But he could still think and talk. He harnessed all his resources to keep going, received tutoring with the help of supporters such as Mrs. Frederick Terman. Originally a student of Lewis Terman in psychology at Stanford she had married Lewis Terman's son, Frederick, engineer, later provost at Stanford, and founder of Silicon Valley. Sutich even became a labor activist. His friends used to carry him on the gurney everywhere around Palo Alto. He met Ernest Hilgard, who permitted him to attend his courses in psychology at Stanford. Graduate students carried Sutich up five flights of stairs to the lecture hall. Constantly in rehabilitation therapy, Sutich nevertheless never lost his zest for life. He was a constant inspiration to other handicapped people.[80]

Eventually, his caregivers, who had no physical infirmities themselves, would come to him with their personal problems. How could he be making it in his condition, while they struggled with no clue as to how to achieve his peaceful state of mind, despite all odds? He always spoke to the total person in their immediate life situation. He appealed to the growth-oriented dimension of their personality.

He encouraged them to look deeply into the spiritual meaning of events for that person. Soon, he was able to conduct a limited practice seeing clients and his counseling efforts flourished. He did this, almost totally paralyzed from his gurney.

Eventually, Hilgard introduced Sutich to Gordon Allport, who was then still editor of the *Journal of Abnormal and Social Psychology*. Sutich submitted an article on the ethics of psychotherapy.[81] One-to-one therapy is really group work, Sutich maintained, because each person is connected at any given time to about 35 other people who benefit from the individual's growth toward health. He also maintained that psychologists should be ethically bound to communicate the results of their tests to their clients, which they did not do at the time. When licensure requirements became required in California, Sutich's colleagues who were already members of the American Psychological Association arranged for him to become a member himself and to be grandfathered into the licensure program at the state level. Sutich had an extensive mailing list, and Hilgard thought Maslow would be another good contact. Maslow and Sutich eventually combined mailing lists, which became the initial roster of invitees to join the American Association for Humanistic Psychology. Hilgard paid for their telephone bills, as Sutich stuck to his gurney and Maslow began to travel all around the United States. Sutich later became the founding editor of the *Journal of Humanistic Psychology* in 1961 with Maslow as principal contributor. The two of them then went on to found the *Journal of Transpersonal Psychology* in 1969. But we are getting ahead of the narrative.

Maslow returned to Brooklyn with his family in 1949 after 2 years in California. On his return to the East Coast, Maslow continued to teach courses in personality and abnormal psychology at Brooklyn College and to search for a health-centered psychology. He was friend and colleague with Werner Wolff of Bard College. Maslow first published "Self Actualizing People: A Study of Psychological Health" in Wolff's ill-fated journal *Personality Symposia #1 on Values* (1950),[82] in which Maslow drew his examples from historical and public figures such as Thomas Jefferson, Albert Einstein, and Eleanor Roosevelt. There, he identified 13 features of the self-actualizing personality. Rogers at Chicago considered it a conceptual breakthrough and dispersed it among students and colleagues. Maslow further circulated it in mimeographed form.

Maslow also had close ties to Henry A. Murray and his students. Murray's papers contained many unpublished final drafts of papers Maslow had sent to Murray before they were eventually published, and they met frequently over the years after Maslow immigrated to Brandeis. Maslow also published with Donald Mckinnon, former student of the gestalt psychologists in Berlin who had worked closely with Murray afterward at Harvard.[83] Maslow's biographer, Edward Hoffman, recounts that, in addition to Max Wertheimer and Ruth Benedict, Erick Fromm, Karen Horney, Kurt Goldstein, Carl Rogers, David Levy, Abram Kardiner, Andras Angyal,[84] S. I. Hayakawa, and David Reisman constituted Maslow's most important intellectual influences at this time.

Approached by Brandeis in 1951, Maslow accepted their offer to move to Boston and found their new psychology department.[85] He published *Motivation and Personality*[86] in 1954, which had chapters on what Maslow called "positive psychology." He identified boredom, anhedonia, authoritarianism, prejudice, and loss of life purpose and meaning as true pathologies unrecognized by the rest of psychology. Our question should be "adjusted to what?" Mainstream psychology concerns itself with the irrelevant, however. To this, Maslow proclaimed, "What is not worth doing is not worth doing well." Instead, we should study self-actualization, "a development of personality which frees the person from the deficiency problems of growth, and from the... neurotic problems of life, so that he is able to face, endure, and grapple with the real problems of the human condition."[87] With this new psychology, Maslow would go on to influence personality theory, as well as the field of motivation, and beyond those, business management, marketing, education, counseling, and psychotherapy.

Werner Wolff

Another prominent person involved with dynamic theories of personality during this period who was operating from the New York area was Werner Wolff (1904–1957). Wolff had completed his doctorate under Max Wertheimer at the University of Berlin in 1930. Throughout the 1930s he was associated with various clinics and hospitals in Germany and Spain. He immigrated to the United States in the early 1940s, where he developed a circle of professional relationships at Columbia, Harvard, Brooklyn College, and Vassar. Wertheimer had been his teacher, Gertrude Schmeidler his classmate, and they were now in New York. He had also been influenced by William Stern, and as a result was led to Gordon Allport and Robert K. Frank, among others.

Wolff, a professor of psychology at Bard College in upstate New York, was also listed on the faculty at Columbia. His first book in English was *The Expression of Personality: An Experimental Depth Psychology* (1943).[88] It was a hybrid combining the epistemologies of gestalt psychology and the depth psychologies of Freud, Jung, and Adler, made all the more unique because the discussion was grounded in a mix of theory and empirical experiments. Wolff had dedicated the book to Max Wertheimer.

Gardner Murphy was the General Editor and lent a preface. In it, he credited Allport and Lindsey's *Studies in Expressive movement* (1933) as the key document that first introduced psychologists to Wolff's work, generating much excitement. It should be taken in the end, Murphy maintained, as a text in experimental psychology.

The book was divided into three parts. The first section made the case for the unity of personality. By this, Wolff meant not only the psychological configuration of the person but also the relation of the mental to the physical dimensions of personality. Specifically, he was interested in the ways that outward expressive behavior could reveal the interior life of the unique individual. Expressive movement became his specific focus. He also recognized that, despite the fact that personality was a total gestalt, the methods of science would be inherently limited to only parts of the phenomena involved. Nevertheless, the problem of personality could still be approached by looking at individual differences, general dynamics that linked the person to their cultural environment, and structural features that define the basic personality.

The second section dealt with self-confrontation. By this Wolff referred to the ability of the individual to make accurate judgments about one's self as well as others, including the overall process of self-assessment. This gave him an opportunity to examine in detail the errors of judges used in psychological experiments and also what came to later be called the experimenter bias effect—that the personality of the experimenter might have as much to do with the outcome of the study as the more objective rendering of the hypothesis, method, procedure, and so forth.

Wolff devised numerous experiments employing unconscious self-judgments. This construct refers to a method whereby the person is asked to judge personality from data that contain their own anonymous self-judgments. This could be the sound of a sequence of voices, while unbeknownst to the subject; their own voice had been inserted.[89] Another would be having the subject assess their own performance on some motor task, which was being surreptitiously filmed, then showing the film back to the subject for discussion of the discrepancies between the overt self-judgment and what was on the film. Another might be, can the subject recognize their own shadow profile out of a lineup of other similar shadow profiles, and so on.

The third section of Wolff's book looked at personality diagnosis. In this, he devised ingenious experiments to study facial expressions using a method that corrected for facial asymmetry; he studied the person's unique gait, employed handwriting analysis, and also gestures and placement of the hands, the uniqueness of the person's voice, rhythmical patterns in tapping, breathing, and writing, and tachistoscopic studies of self-recognition.

Wolff's conclusions were important for understanding a person-centered science. One was that we have two vocabularies; the subjective vocabulary versus the objective vocabulary. The subjective vocabulary is the one the individual employs to describe who he or she is in their interior life. The objective vocabulary is the language of consensus out in culture that tries to describe who we are, usually based only on overt cues. To be called an introvert usually carries the designation of a withdrawn isolate that lacks adequate social skills. For that person, however, to call oneself an introvert might mean one who interacts out in the world but from the frame of reference of a rich and fantastic interior life to which the extrovert does not have access.

Another important conclusion was that the value of a trait depends on its embeddedness in the context of other traits and on the frame of reference of the interpreter. First, traits cannot be mathematically summed, so the total picture will always remain piecemeal. Second, we may be able to identify the form of the trait, but that does not specify its function. To be feminine for a woman usually refers to biological attributes, while to be feminine for a man connotes a totally different function. To be intelligent may mean one is a good memorizer or one is able to grasp and solve a complex problem. There is an absence of dynamism inherent in trait theory when taken by itself. Third, how a trait shall be defined also involves the experimenter's own philosophical frame of reference, which is almost never taken into account.

Finally, possibly more than any other gestalt psychologist at the time, Wolff came closest to articulating a bridge between depth psychology and empirical measurement with regard to dynamic theories of personality, while going straight to the heart of the relation between overt behavior and internal experience. His work has remained totally obscure, and been long forgotten, however.[90]

Allport, along with Otto Klineberg, Lyle Lanier, Lois Murphy, Joseph Stone, and Barbara Burks all read over the manuscript. Emilio Mira at Barcelona, Phillip Vernon in Glasgow, Hadley Cantril at Princeton, and Gordon Allport and William Huntley at Harvard replicated his experiments and helped him to establish what he called "experimental depth psychology."

Gardner and Lois Murphy in New York

As we have said in the last chapter, Murphy's first major book was his *Historical Introduction to Modern Psychology*[91] in 1929, which he followed with a string of works, among them, with Lois, *Experimental Social Psychology* (1931),[92] *Approaches to Personality* (1932)[93] with F. Jensen, and *A Briefer General Psychology*[94] in 1935. He also became general editor for the *Harper Psychology Series* in 1931, until 1964, and, with Otto Klineberg, handled all the dissertations in social psychology at Columbia after 1929.

By Murphy's own account he was caught up in the excitement of applying experimental methods to any and all subjects, as the horizon seemed unlimited in the 1920s. He was most profoundly influenced in this regard by Floyd Allport, as Floyd's brother, Gordon would also come to be. Gardner and Floyd had been graduate students together at Harvard and they both had a mutual interest in social psychology. For his part, rejecting the rigidity of the behaviorists' viewpoint, Murphy delved into the personal world of the social initiator and the social responder. He tested out many of these ideas teaching Woodworth's course in Social Psychology from 1924 to 1929 and a course in Personality in 1935. He and Lois also attended the personality and culture seminar organized by Edward Sapir and the Social Science Research Council at Hanover, in 1930. At the same time, Murphy was developing into one of the premier parapsychologists in the United States, a move he largely kept separate from his contributions to mainstream personality and social psychology for obvious political reasons.

The 1930s, Murphy wrote, were exciting years in New York intellectual circles. The highpoint of his professional career, he recounted, was a conversation he had at the King's Crown Hotel in 1933 with Max Wertheimer and William Stern.[95] Through Lois he met Erik Erikson, Peter Blos, and Fritz Reidl. He came to know Ruth Benedict and Margaret Mead and was profoundly influenced by their work. He and Lois took Benedict's course at Columbia in anthropology. He was quite close to Maslow's friend the psychoanalyst David Levy, and he collaborated with

Rensis Likert on the measurement of social attitudes, which led to Likert and Murphy's *Public Opinion and the Individual* (1938).[96] Also, he was very active in the newly formed Society for the Psychological Study of Social Issues. He later said that in his professional life, he was two-thirds social psychologist and one-third parapsychologist at the time. By the end of the decade he was drawing on seven major approaches: the organic and biological, the behavioristic, the approach of the gestaltists, self-psychology, psychoanalysis, largely of Freud, but with some Jung and Adler, and a combination of these from the standpoint of traditional social science, which culminated for him in field theory.

The growth of personality within the field of social psychology became his focus, and forever after, he strove to develop his own conception of field theory in psychology—by which he meant the merging of the two subdisciplines of personality and social psychology. Abraham Kardiner, Henry A. Murray, Kurt Lewin, and J. L. Moreno were his major guiding lights. The result he summarized in his 1947 text *Personality: A Bio-social Approach*,[97] and *Human Potentialities* (1958),[98] which he wrote after 6 months in India with Lois studying the Hindu/Muslim conflict for UNESCO.

Gardner Murphy's Biosocial Approach

Personality: A Biosocial Approach to Origins and Structures appeared in 1947. Murphy opened the work by calling forth a theme similar to one articulated by James, who had said, "our knowledge a drop, our ignorance a sea." Rather than begin with absolute certainty in the gains of materialistic science as the reductionists tended always to do, implying that their interpretation was always the only real truth, Murphy preferred simply to clarify the little we really did know. The principles already established with certainty and their application he intended to forego, in place of a greater emphasis on research hypotheses suggested by what we know and speculations suggesting the unlimited possibilities that might at some future date be brought into the purview of measurable science. The book was not a vault of trade secrets, but an explorer's kit with the standard tools and maps supplied, still provisional though they were. He recommended David Rapaport's two volume *Diagnostic Psychological Testing*[99] and Sylvan Tomkins's *Contemporary Psychopathology*[100] for all the data that had been collected on quantitative problems. That was not his aim. And he said he intended to consider the overwhelming literature on psychoanalysis only at those points where it interfaced with his own conceptions. It was not a textbook on psychotherapy or the scientific method. It was simply an attempt to summarize what we know about how personality grows. He particularly acknowledged Gordon Allport, Ernest Hilgard, Margaret Mead, Bela Mittleman, Ruth Monroe, David Rapaport, Saul Rosenzweig and L. Joseph Stone. He also dedicated the work to his wife, Lois, whom he said as a professional companion was practically a co-author of the book.

This gives us an important clue to the psychodynamic cast of the work, as Rapaport was a pioneer ego psychologist, Rosenzweig a personologist and protégé of Murray, while Murphy's wife, Lois, a psychoanalytically oriented child psychologist with a systematic knowledge of Eastern thought. The foundation of the work encompassed all these epistemologies. Personality in general as opposed to the personality of the individual person would be his focus. Thus, he would have little to say about traits. Rather, he believed that the use of the principles of psychology to understand the whole of the individual personality constituted what he called a general psychology of personality. Individuality was still to be the focus, in the sense of a general psychology that studies the totality of the person and the organic systematic relations that obtain within it.

Personality must be considered as an object or an event; it must be identified by its internal structure and by the field of its external relations. His approach would be through field theory, where the barrier between organism and environment was in perpetual redefinition. That way, the totality could be always kept in view, even as he had to perpetually resort to different theories and different points of view to explain himself. His references made clear he was drawing on Lewin's conception of field theory here and amplifying it in his own way. In fact, while the idea of gestalt is mentioned in numerous places throughout the book, it is always to Lewin's work, especially *A Dynamic Theory of Personality* (1934),[101] and almost never, except in one or two cases, to any of the other gestaltists.

The structure of the book began with the biological and physiological conditions affecting the growth of personality, before turning to the impact of learning and habit once the biological direction of the individual's development had been established. Biology and physiological psychology underlay the first phase of development, while behaviorism and experimental learning theory underlay the second. The psychodynamic then follows, in which Murphy devoted an entire major section of the work. This included Freudian psychoanalysis and the attendant contributions of Jung and Adler, which were invoked where applicable to understanding the relation of the instincts to the development of emotions, the dynamics of the unconscious, types of personality, the establishment of the ego as the executor of personality, and the superego as its guiding principle of adaptation to external social reality. Murphy, like Allport, also discussed traits in the context of a gestalt of the whole person. He followed this with a section that placed the individual in a social context, fulfilling the organism–environment gestalt required of the field theory approach.

But before he even began the first chapter on organic foundations, he wanted to summarize the wholistic approach with an example that also demonstrated some of the difficulties between theory and real life. To do this, he chose to give a detailed summary of one of his great heroes, the life of William James.

The section specifically devoted to psychodynamics focused on Freud's further remarks on the neuro-psychoses of defense (1896);[102] *The Interpretation of Dreams* (1900);[103] *Three Essays on the Theory of Sexuality* (1905b);[104] *Totem and Taboo* (1912/1913);[105] *On The History of the Psycho-analytic Movement* (1914);[106] *A General Introduction to Psychoanalysis* (1920b);[107] *The Ego and the Id* (1923);[108] *Group Psychology and the Analysis of the Ego* (1921);[109] *Beyond the Pleasure Principle* (1920a);[110] *Some Character-Types met with in Psycho-analytic Work* (1916);[111] and *New Introductory Lectures on Psycho-analysis* (1932–1933).[112]

The only work of Anna Freud cited was *The Ego and Mechanisms of Defence* (1946).[113] Works by Ernest Jones, Wilhelm Stekel, Franz Alexander, A. A. Brill, Abraham Kardiner, Alfred Adler, Erik Erikson, John Dollard and Neal Miller, Erich Fromm, and Karen Horney were also integrated into the text.

In the same section on Freud, Murphy cited Jung's *Studies in Word Association* (1904–1907)[114] and *The Psychology of Dementia Praecox* (1907b),[115] except that he really used the 1936 reissue; he also referred to Jung's "The Theory of Psychoanalysis" (1913);[116] Hinkle's translation of *Psychology of the Unconscious* (1916b);[117] and *Psychological Types* (1921b).[118]

It should also be mentioned that Murphy referenced Janet and made several of his concepts, such as canalization, central to the discussion. He had an intriguing section on dissociation and multiple personality, and he cited F. W. H. Myers and made reference to the psychical research literature of Myers's era unobtrusively in a few places, despite the fact that he was then, among other things, director of research at the American Society for Psychical Research and could have overwhelmed the book with contemporary experimental studies from that field.

At the end of the book, he also took up some of the larger questions of the psychologists' perspective, referring to Hindu and Buddhist conceptions of the self and personality. In deference to his audience, however, he said that he kept these out of the main part of the text, as he wished to address the core epistemology that then prevailed in Western psychology. But he remained keenly aware that Western psychologists remained totally unconscious to the possibility that their view of ultimate truth could be culture bound and therefore only relative when compared to the highly sophisticated but radically different epistemological assumptions about personality and consciousness held by non-Western cultures, but articulated from a more experiential and symbolic viewpoint.

Human Potentialities (1958), which further developed the outlines of his field theory, began as an address Murphy gave to the American Psychological Association in 1953 when he received the Kurt Lewin Memorial Award. The nominating committee had been made up of Abraham Maslow, Jerome Bruner, and Gordon Allport. In the end, the paper turned out to be a full length book. He began by asking, "What are the potentialities latent within individual personality and within human society?" He listed such subjects as the life space—the inner world of the individual and the external environment, which taken together comprise the entire field. Second, was man's endless becoming. There is no Platonic "basic human nature", such that man is basically good or basically evil. The inner and outer are two phases of the same reality. Understanding this leads to the discovery of a new conception of human nature. There was also the idea of an evolution of new forms. In the world of music, to go along with his own vocal chords man has invented vibrating strings. The beautiful music of a virtuoso violinist makes us feel deep and satisfying experiences as human beings that are entirely new. Where are these in our psychologists' list of textbook drives?

If it is true that we penetrate into an altogether newer and higher dimension of experience, then what is the range of human potentialities? What are the modes of reciprocal interdependence between the violin and the musician that create something beyond the mere sum of the two? This is something more than just striving for a science of persons. We need a field science of human possibilities that is at once quantitative and qualitative, but also admits new elements, and is configurational, meaning amenable to reorganization. The conception of personality represented by field theory envisages the appearance of attitudes, outlooks, and feeling tones which were never released before, and which go on proliferating, or exploding into amazing new forms.

The years he spent at City College produced students such as Jerome Levine, Leo Postman, Roy Schafer, Harold Prochansky, and others. At CUNY, they worked on experimental studies of drive, feeling, affect, and motive inspired by Henry Murray's theories, which Leo Postman and Jerome Bruner continued at Harvard after World War II.

Gardner Murphy addressed the then current impact of Freudian psychology at the annual meeting of the American Psychological Association in 1956.[119] Freud, he said there, "always had the artistic feeling for the integrity of the dynamic whole."[120] As a consequence, a dynamic view of personality could not have emerged without Freud's contribution. He admitted he was a Freudian. But having said that, he also had to admit that at the same time he was a Darwinian, a Pavlovian, an Adlerian, a Sullivanian, a Thurstonian, a Tolmanian, and more.

The central plan for the Freudian epoch was the reality of the unconscious, a demonstration that the psychopathology of everyday life was a deterministic process, which included Freud's understanding of the role of the parents in the development of conscience. Freud was the first to emphasize drives in the preservation of the life process and that these tendencies were more primordial than the phenomena of consciousness. This meant that the ego was derivative rather than a primary expression and that all psychological activity is driven by life tensions seeking resolution. In this, Freud had his greatest impact on personality theory as well as clinical, abnormal, and social psychology, less on the fields of perception and learning, and at that time virtually no influence on the intelligence testing movement or on reductionistic biology.

The larger point, however, was that psychology leads us not so much toward the impossible fusion of specific, incompatible constructs but rather to a larger picture of the organism as a whole. In this, the central theme, delivered by Freud as well as others, was that the individual responds simultaneously to the environment and to himself or herself trying to make an integral response while both are still continually changing. It is at this more general level of analysis that we not only find verification for some of Freud's major ideas but also the possibility for a more flexible system of an integrated psychology.

From New York, Gardner and Lois Murphy went to the Menninger Foundation for 14 years, where Gardner became director of research and assisted in the birth of humanistic and transpersonal psychology. Maslow went from Brooklyn College to Brandeis. Tillich gravitated to Harvard. The denouement of the era related to the history of dynamic theories of personality occurred when Gordon Allport, originally the poster boy for reductionistic trait theory in the 1920s, went down to New Haven and delivered the Terry Lectures on psychology and religion in 1954, which was later published as *Becoming: Basic Considerations for a Psychology of Personality* (1955).[121] He had come a long way in his thinking about a science of the whole person, and he was by then not the trait theorist in the way he is still most recently depicted.

With Allport's Terry Lectures at Yale, his theory of a dynamic psychology of personality had become full fledged. Personality and consciousness were in a constant state of evolution. The early stages of becoming could be understood with reference to psychodynamic theory. Freud and Adler were a bit too rigid in claiming that all is fixed by age 3 or 4, but their work, especially Freud's, Allport claimed, had been verified by a significant body of literature and considerably clarified by researchers such as Anna Freud, Renee Spitz, John Levy, and John Bowlby. In the second stage of life, traces of social neuroses can be identified, but the person mellows as the lower order needs are fulfilled in a way that permits greater levels of self-actualization and socialization. His own work, that of Abraham Maslow and Pitirim Sorokin, would be representative examples. Creative becoming, however, transcends the superego. Tribal customs make a person into a mirror, while the springs of creative becoming light the lamp of individuality within. To understand this antinomy, he referred the reader to Henri Bergson's, *The Two Sources of Morality and Religion.*[122]

Freud should be given credit for rescuing the ego through three decades of reductionistic positivism. Freud's early ego defined the assertive aggressive side that held the instincts in check; Freud's later ego became a rational though passive agency reflecting the conscience of the superego, while building compromises between the two. It took the Neo-Freudians to enlarge the sphere of the ego and make it more active beyond what Freud was able to conceptualize. Indeed the era of ego psychology had to come about, due to the failure of the positivists to achieve anything significant from merely their measurement of traits, claiming they now knew the total personality. In this Allport was in agreement with Bergson's *Introduction to Metaphysics* (1912).[123]

An answer to this dilemma, Allport said, can be found in Adler's admonition that psychologists would not need to posit an ego if they would just spend more time defining the individual's life style, most of which would then account for what was then defined as ego function. Following Whitehead, what is important is radically different from mere matters of fact to the person, such as keeping to the right in traffic or using good manners.

Behaviors must be propriate to be important. Here then is the key concept in Allport's mature psychology—the proprium and its difference from the self. He attributed the meaning of this concept to James's conception of the self in *The Principles of Psychology* (1890a). There James differentiated between the empirical self, the "Me," and the knowing self, the "I." The empirical "Me" is made up of the material, social and spiritual selves. Allport noted Henry David Spoerl's references to Swedenborg, where the term actually originated. Allport's intention was to expand James's scheme.

The bodily me is composed of the streams that emanate from within the individual—viscera, muscles, tendons, semicircular canals, etc., that is, totally unconscious until they rise to the surface during moments of excitement and energy expenditure. The first mark of the proprium is the feeling of effort, the felt bodily sensations. He located the ego at a point midway between the eyes, that is, slightly behind them within the head, as the center where we reconnoiter what is left and what is right. He proposed a dramatic and immediate test—swallowing one's own saliva. No problem. But to drink a glass full of the same stuff is repugnant. What is in us is warm and ours; what is outside is not us and alien.

The second quality of the proprium is self-identity. This probably does not develop until age 5, Allport said, when we can finally begin to make a clear distinction between self and not self. Another characteristic is ego enhancement, which refers more to selfishness and pride. It is unabashed self-seeking. Self-love, however, may be prominent, but it does not have to be sovereign.

Yet another is characteristic of the proprium is ego extension. This is the identification of what we own with who we are. It is the extension of our identity to include all that we own, all that we call mine. Yet another is rational agency. Here, Allport credited Freud for advances unrecognized "sixty years earlier": "It is thanks to Freud that we understand the strategies of denial, repression, displacement, reaction formation, rationalization and the like better than did our ancestors."[124] But the ego, of course, is much more. He then cited the Thomists, who understood the higher order functions of the ego, and mused how odd it is to combine Freud, "the supreme irrationalist of our age," with the Catholics, but both prepared then modern cognitive psychology to deal with the central functions of the proprium.

The proprium also functions with regard to our self-image, or what Allport equated with our phenomenal self. This involves the way we presently see ourselves, as well as our aspiration for ourselves in the future. Allport compared it to Karen Horney's idealized self-image.[125] It is the focus of present day psychotherapy.

Allport then considered propriate striving, the nature of motivation itself. The familiar formulas of drives and their conditioning suffice at low levels of behavior, but once the personality enters the stage of ego extension and developed a self-image with visions of self-perfection, then, he believed, psychologists need to think about motivation of a different order that involves propriate striving. He then invoked Kurt Goldstein's conception of self-actualization developed by Maslow, McDougall's self-regarding sentiment, or the fortified ego of the Neo-Freudians. However, beset by conflicts, the goal of propriate striving is the unity of the personality, which harnesses interest, tendency, disposition, expectation, planning, problem solving, and intentionality.

But what about the Me? The knowing self that knows all these others' aspects of the proprium? James says, however, that there is no synthesizer, no self of selves. The direct experience of the self in the form of an I cannot be just another aspect of the me. Allport resorts to Kant here by saying that Kant says the I knows itself through the me and can never be directly known by itself. James makes the distinction between knowledge about versus direct acquaintance with, meaning that our awareness always flips back and forth between the direct experience of a thing, versus our understanding of it through our intellectual categories. Allport was more familiar with James's *Principles* than his radical empiricism, but he had thought through the problem of the observer far enough to see the same implications that

James was getting at. In any event, that we do know and know as much is the clear eight functions of the proprium.

Allport then returned to the question as to whether or not a concept of the self was necessary in the psychology of personality. One cannot answer categorically since it all depends on how the construct of the self is used. For those who felt the need to postulate a permanent enduring self, he referred to Peter Bertocci's "The Psychological Self, the Ego, and Personality."[126] His own term, the Proprium, he admitted was only "our temporarily neutral term for the central interlocking operations of personality."[127] What is unnecessary and inadmissible, he said, was "a self (or soul) that is said to perform acts, to solve problems, to steer conduct, in a transpsychological manner, inaccessible to psychological analysis."[128]

To buttress his position he turned to the existentialists, focusing particularly on the work of Paul Tillich. True, he said, that Freud had brought forward the importance of anxiety, especially that aroused by guilt and fear of punishment, but he had little to say about the dread of non-being, death, and still less about the apparent meaninglessness of existence. Because psychology in general remains deficiency motivated, it also has little to say about striving and courage. Existentialism, on the other hand:

> Admits all the evidence that depth psychology can deliver, including every fragment of prose, passion, guilt, and anguish in a man's nature, and it accepts the facts of opportunism and tribalism that characterize primitive behavior in an advanced society, but it also gives "due weight to the dynamic possibilities that lie in self-knowledge . . . ." [129]

Stated theologically, it deals with all the factors which a modern doctrine of regeneration would have to deal.

He then acknowledged the pessimism of the European variety of existential thought and its essential transformation as an American variety. This included Neo-Freudian conceptions of a "productive personality," developments in pastoral counseling, and also humanistic psychology, including the works of Goldstein, Maslow, Rogers, and May. He also added the tradition of personalism in philosophy, a lineage from Bordon Parker Bowne to Peter Bertocci, which had helped spawn a monistic, theistically oriented psychology of religion.

Tillich, Allport pointed out, was particularly impressed with American resiliency in these expressions. Such resiliency Tillich attributed to the American emphasis on pragmatism, process philosophy, progressive education, and crusading democracy. However, problems of freedom, values, and the will, which underlay Tillich's own metaphysics, were avoided in modern deterministic psychology.

Elsewhere in his text, Allport could not help invoking the construct of the unconscious, although he appeared to do so reluctantly. In one place he was discussing how every psychologist knows that most acts are performed in accordance with superordinate systems of motivation. We can sometimes counter these forces in a reflective moment, showing we have the freedom to do so. He then appended a footnote in which he interpreted Freud's discussion of anxiety. According to psychoanalysis, a defeated impulse is thought to be repressed and therefore continues to plague the individual from the unconscious. Allport added a new interpretation—that when propriate striving is involved, the impulse that would normally exist in the limbo of the unconscious just fades away. He pointed out where Freud himself said that sometimes it is difficult to discriminate "between a mere repression and the true disappearance of an old desire or impulse."[130]

When Allport turned to the religious sentiment, he blatantly made it clear that depth psychology had made us aware of the crucial role of unconscious processes in defining our orientation toward religion. He chastised the psychoanalysts, however, for locating religious belief exclusively in the defensive functions of the ego rather than placing the religious sentiment at the core of personality itself, where Allport believed it belongs. He avoided Freud's thesis that religion is merely the sublimation of repressed sexual impulses and instead referred merely to religious beliefs fortifying one against anxiety and uncertainty. What he really wanted to emphasize was that it also provides forward intention at each stage of becoming and the pursuit of what is meaningful to what he called the "totality of Being."

He ended with reference to his own ground breaking work, *The Individual and his Religion* (1950).[131] This was important because it marked him as a pioneer in yet another subfield—the psychology of religion.[132] In *Becoming*, depth psychology, especially forms both built upon, but also beyond psychoanalysis, shows where spirituality and personality theory began to coalesce.

At the same time, the Harvard and New York scenes began to merge. Allport, along with Murray and the Murphys, and those around them were to become the God fathers and God mothers of a non-reductionistic movement to construct a science of the whole person. Their emphasis on the whole person set the stage for the incorporation and expansion of dynamic theories of personality in what came to be known as humanistic psychology.

Notes

1. Gregory Bateson was born in Grantchester, England, on May 9, 1904, son of the zoologist and geneticist, William Bateson. Gregory Bateson studied at the University of Geneva, then at Cambridge where he received an AB in 1925. He involved himself with anthropology, psychiatry, biological evolution, and genetics and the new epistemology stemming from systems theory and ecology. His initial period in anthropology led him to New Guinea, which he summarized in "Social Structure of the Iatmul People of the Sepik River" (1932). He received the MA from Cambridge and was elected to the Council of Fellows of St. John's College, Cambridge, in 1931 and again in 1934. He returned to Indonesia during the period 1936–1938 to do research in Bali, and in 1938 to the Iatmul of New Guinea. In 1938 he was William Wyse scholar at Cambridge. He went to the United States in 1940 as a specialist in Balinese material at the American Museum of Natural History, New York City, and later (1942–1943) was anthropological film analyst at the Museum of Modern Arts New York City. He appears to have been a successful grant gypsy, receiving funds from such sources as the Macy Foundation, the Rockefellers, and the National Institutes of Health. Bateson was overseas with the OSS in 1943 through 1945 and returned to New York as a Guggenheim Fellow and became visiting professor in the graduate faculty at the New School, New York City, and at Harvard in 1947–1948 before moving to California and then Hawaii. A polymath, his double-bind theory of schizophrenia had many adherents in the social sciences and he was widely known throughout the psychotherapeutic counterculture among educated psychologists.
2. Benedict, R. (1922). The vision in plains culture. *American Anthropologist, 24*, 1–23.
3. Benedict, R. (1934). *Patterns of culture*. Boston: Houghton Mifflin.

4. Benedict, R. (1940). *Race, science, and politics*. New York: Modern Age Books.
5. Benedict, R. (1946). *The chrysanthemum and the sword: Patterns of Japanese culture*. Boston: Houghton Mifflin.
6. Benedict R. (1930). Psychological types in the cultures of the Southwest. *Proceedings of the 23rd International Congress of Americanists*, September, 1928, 572–581.
7. Benedict, R. (1933). Anthropology and the abnormal. *Journal of General Psychology, 10*, 59–82.
8. Bannar, L. (2003). *Intertwined lives: Margaret Mead, Ruth Benedict, and their circle*. New York: Alfred A. Knopf, p. 203. For definitive accounts of Mead, see, Bateson, M. K. (1984). *.With a daughter's eye: A memoir of Margaret Mead and Gregory Bateson*. NY: William Morrow and Co.; Howard, J. (1984). *Margaret Mead: A life*. New York: Simon & Schuster.
9. Benedict, R. (1938). Review of *The neurotic personality of our time*. *Journal of Abnormal Psychology, 33*, 133–135.
10. Benedict, R. (1942). Review of *Escape from freedom. Psychiatry, 5*(1), 111–113.
11. Bannar, 2003, p. 415.
12. Maslow, A. H. (1971). *The farther reaches of human nature* (p. 200). New York: Viking Press.
13. Bannar, 2003, p. 295.
14. Margaret Mead was born December 16, 1901, Philadelphia, PA, and died on November 15, 1978, in New York City. She entered DePauw University in 1919 but transferred to Barnard College a year later, from which she graduated in 1923. From there, she entered the graduate school of Columbia University. Mead received an MA in 1924 and a PhD in 1929. In 1925, she began to write the first of her 23 books, *Coming of age in Samoa* (1928; new ed., 1968). She spent her career at the American Museum of Natural History in New York, working in anthropology and psychology.
15. Mead, M. (1928). *Coming of age in Samoa: A psychological study of primitive youth for Western civilization*. New York: Blue Ribbon Books.
16. Koffka, K. (1935). *Principles of gestalt psychology*. New York: Harcourt, Brace and Company.
17. Mead, M. (1972). *Blackberry winter, my earlier years*. New York: Simon & Schuster.
18. Mead, 1972, p. 217.
19. John Dollard (1900–1980) was another figure in this field who in 1935 wrote *Criteria for the life history: With analysis of six notable documents*. New Haven: Yale University Press. The work originated at the suggestion of Gordon Allport, Mark May, and Gardner Murphy, a subcommittee on culture and personality of the Social Science Research Council. It establishes the criteria necessary for constructing a life history and then presents six cases in which the criteria is applied. The first, 31 contacts with a 7-year-old boy, came from the *Dynamics of Therapy* by Otto Ranks's student Jessie Taft. The second came from one of Freud's cases, "Analysis of a Phobia of a Seven Year Old Boy." The third came from a case by W. I. Thomas and Florian Znaniecki, "Life Record of an Immigrant," taken from *The Polish Peasant in Europe and America*. The fourth was "The Jack-Roller" by Clifford Shaw; the fifth came from *Experiment in Autobiography*, by H. G. Wells, and the sixth "Crashing Thunder," which came from *The Autobiography of an American Indian*, by Paul Radin, and also drew on Jung's typology. Dollard's conclusions had to do with how culture bound our psychology really is.
20. Mead, M. (Ed.). (1937). *Cooperation and competition among primitive peoples*. New York: McGraw-Hill.
21. Fernandez, J. W. (1968). *Report of the 1967 seminar on culture and personality* (pp. 188–214). Hanover, NH: Dartmouth Comparative Studies Center.
22. Horney (1937).
23. Continuing in the tradition of intellectual radicalism, the New School today offers students systematic training in Continental philosophy; Aristotle is emphasized from the classical period. Locke and Hume of the British Empiricists, Kant and Hegel, Kierkegaard and Nietzsche, as founders of existentialism, Husserl and Heidegger of the phenomenologists; Freud, but not Jung, Marx on economic theory, Wittgenstein of the positivists, and Foucault and Derrida of the post-modernists. Critical Theory of the Frankfurt School is particularly emphasized, especially the work of Max Horkheimer, Walter Benjamin, Theodor Adorno, Hannah Arendt, Herbert Marcuse, and Jürgen Habermas.
24. Koffka, K. (1924). *The growth of the mind: An introduction to child psychology* (R. Morris, Trans.). New York: Harcourt, Brace & Company.

25. Köhler, W. (1925). *The mentality of apes*. New York: Harcourt, Brace & Company. (Original work published in 1917 as *Intelligenzenprüfungen an Anthropoiden; Intelligenzenprüfungen an Menschenaffen*, 1921).
26. Köhler, W. (1929). *Gestalt psychology*. New York: H. Liveright.
27. Wertheimer, M. (1945). *Productive thinking*. New York: Harper & Row.
28. Adapted from Hoffmann, E. (1988). *The right to be human: A biography of Abraham Maslow*. Los Angeles: Jeremy P. Tarcher, pp. 93–94.
29. Goldstein, K. (1939). *The organism: A holistic approach to biology derived from pathological data in man*. New York: American Book Company.
30. Goldstein, K. (1941). *Abstract and concrete behavior: An experimental study with special tests*. Evanston, IL: The American Psychological Association.
31. Goldstein, K. (1940). *Human nature in the light of psychopathology*. Cambridge, MA: Harvard University Press.
32. Goldstein, K. (1942). *Aftereffects of brain injuries in war, their evaluation and treatment: The application of psychologic methods in the clinic*. New York: Grune & Stratton.
33. Goldstein, K. (1948). *Language and language disturbances: Aphasic symptom complexes and their significance for medicine and theory of language*. New York: Grune & Stratton.
34. Hanfman, E., Rickers-Ovsiankina, M., & Goldstein, K. (1944). *Case Lunati: Extreme concretization of behavior due to damage of the brain cortex*. Evanston, IL: The American Psychological Association.
35. Simmel, M. L. (Ed.). (1968). *The Reach of the mind: Essays in memory of Kurt Goldstein*. New York: Springer.
36. Goldstein, K. L. (1959). Notes on the development of my concepts. *Journal of Individual Psychology, 15*, 5–14; See also, Purdy, D. M. (1937). The biological psychology of Kurt Goldstein. *Journal of Personality, 5*(4), 321–330.
37. Jung, C. G. (1934). A study in the process of individuation. In H. Read, M. Fordham, & G. Adler (Eds.), *The archetypes and the collective unconscious: Vol. 9.1, Collected works* (pp. 290–354). London: Routledge and Kegan Paul.
38. Darlington, B. (1998, Winter). Vassar's Jung Folks. *Vassar Quarterly, 95*(1), 18–23.
39. Meier, C. A. (Ed) (2001). *Atom and archetype: The Pauli/Jung letters, 1932–1958*. Princeton, NJ: Princeton University Press.
40. Szalay, S. (1998). Tributes to Whitmont. *The American Homeopath, 4*, 63–67.
41. Whitmont, E. C., & Perera, S. B. (1989). *Dreams: A portal to the source*. London, New York: Routledge; Whitmont, E. C. (1982). *Psyche and substance: Essays on homeopathy in the light of Jungian psychology*. Berkeley, CA: North Atlantic Books; Whitmont, E. C. (1982). *Return of the goddess*. New York: Crossroad; Whitmont, E. C. (1969). *The symbolic quest: Basic concepts of analytical psychology*. New York: Putnam.
42. Larsen, S., & Larsen, R. (1991). *A fire in the mind: The life of Joseph Campbell*. New York: Doubleday.
43. Zimmer, H. R. (1952). *Philosophies of India* (J. Campbell, Ed.). London: Routledge & Kegan Paul.
44. Campbell, J. (1944). *A skeleton key to Finnegan's wake*. New York: Harcourt, Brace and Company.
45. Campbell, J. (1949). *Hero with a thousand faces*. New York: Pantheon.
46. Campbell, J. (1959–1968). *The masks of God*. New York: Viking Press.
47. Campbell, J. (1959). *Primitive mythology*. New York: Viking Press.
48. Campbell, J. (1962). *Oriental mythology*. New York: Viking Press.
49. Campbell, J. (1964b). *Occidental mythology*. New York: Viking Press.
50. Campbell, J. (1968). *Creative mythology*. New York: Viking Press.
51. Campbell, J. (1969). *The flight of the wild gander: Explorations in the mythological dimension*. New York: Viking Press.
52. Campbell, J. (1970). *Myths, dreams, and religion*. New York: E. P. Dutton.
53. Campbell, J. (1972). *Myths to live by*. New York: Viking Press.
54. Campbell, J. (1974). *The mythic image*. Princeton, NJ: Princeton University Press.
55. Campbell, J. (1988). *Historical atlas of world mythology*. New York: Perennial Library.
56. Starcher (1999).

57. Gifford, S. (1997). *The Emmanuel Movement (Boston, 1904–1929): Origins of group treatment and the assault on lay psychotherapy.* Boston: Countway Library of Medicine. Dist by Harvard University Press.
58. Others, in my opinion, include Dietrich Bonhoeffer, Karl Barth, Bishop Desmond Tutu, Martin Luther King, Jr., and Cornell West.
59. May, R. (1973). *Paulus: Reminiscences of a friendship.* New York: Harper & Row.
60. May (1939).
61. May (1940).
62. May (1950).
63. Tillich, P. (1952). *The courage to be.* New Haven, CT: Yale University Press.
64. May, 1973, p. 75.
65. May, 1973, p. 29.
66. May, 1973, p. 44.
67. May, 1973, p. 52.
68. May, 1973, pp. 51–55.
69. Others included clinical psychologist Harry Bone; Thomas Bigham, a professor at General Theological Seminary (Episcopal); psychiatrist Gotthard Booth; Davis Roberts and Harrison Elliott, who were professors at Union Seminary; hospital chaplain Otis Rice; psychoanalysts Ernest Schachtel and Greta Frankley; Jungian analysts, Elined Prys Kotschnig, Violet de Lazlo, Frances Wickes, Martha Glickman, Elizabeth Rohrbach, and E. McClung Fleming; Walter Gotschnig, educator; anthropologist Ruth Benedict; and Kent Fellow Helen Nichol. Others came and went but these were the most frequent attendees; Cooper, T. D. (2006). *Paul Tillich and psychology: Historic and contemporary explorations in theology, psychotherapy and ethics.* Macon, GA: Mercer University Press, p. 100. A slightly different list is presented by Allison Stokes, (1985). *Ministry after Freud.* New York: Pilgrim Press, pp. 11–12, which was Cooper's original source.
70. Stokes, A. (1985). *Ministry after Freud.* New York: Pilgrim Press.
71. Stokes, 1985, pp. 113–114.
72. Stokes, 1985, p. 111.
73. Hoffman, E. (1988). *The right to be human: A biography of Abraham Maslow.* Los Angeles: J. P. Tarcher, p. 87.
74. Solomon Asch (September 14, 1907–February 20, 1996) was a world-renowned American gestalt psychologist and pioneer in social psychology. He was born in Warsaw, Poland, and immigrated to the United States in 1920. He received his Bachelor's degree from the College of the City of New York in 1928. At Columbia University, he received his Master's degree in 1930 and PhD in 1932. He had been a professor of psychology at Swarthmore College for 19 years, working with psychologists including Wolfgang Köhler. He became famous in the 1950s, following experiments which showed how the effect of social pressure can make a person believe an obviously wrong opinion is correct. He inspired the work of the controversial psychologist Stanley Milgram and supervised his PhD at Harvard University. See Asch, S. (1946). Forming impressions of personality. *Journal of Abnormal and Social Psychology, 41,* 258–290.
75. Summarized from Hoffman, 1988, pp 203–210.
76. Maslow, A. H., & Mittelmann, B. (1941). *Principles of abnormal psychology: The dynamics of psychic illness.* New York: Harper and Brothers. Also, Maslow, A. H. (1943). The dynamics of personality organization I & II. *Psychological Review, 50,* 514–39, 541–58.
77. Koltko-Rivera, Mark E. (2006). Rediscovering the later version of Maslow's hierarchy of needs: Self-transcendence and opportunities for theory, research, and unification. *Review of General Psychology, 10*(4), December 2006. pp. 302–317.
78. James, W. (1890a). *The principles of psychology* (2 Vols.). New York: Henry Holt and Company.
79. See Maslow, A. H. (1946). Problem centering versus means centering in science. *Philosophy of Science, 13,* 326–331. Also, Taylor, E. I. (2009). The Zen doctrine of no-method. *The Humanistic Psychologist.* Also Watson, R. L. (1975). *Scientists are human.* New York: Arno Press.
80. Sutich, A. (Personal Communication, January 5, 1970).
81. Sutich, A. (1944). Toward a professional code for psychological consultants. *The Journal of Abnormal and Social Psychology, 39*(3), July 1944. pp. 329–350.
82. Maslow, A. H. (1950). Self-actualizing people: A study of psychological health, *Personality Symposia: Symposium 1 on Values* (pp. 11–34). New York: Grune & Stratton, pp. 11–34.

83. Maslow, A, H., & McKinnon, D. (1951). Personality. In H. Helson (Ed.), *Theoretical foundations of modern psychology*. New York: Van Nostrand.

84. Andras Angyal immigrated to the United States and worked at Johns Hopkins with Adolf Meyer before becoming resident director of research at the Worcester State Hospital in Massachusetts. Angyal's book, *Foundations for a Science of Personality*, New York: The Commonwealth Fund appeared in 1941. It was a classic text in the new holistic psychology of the person. Drawing heavily on the earlier work of Stern, the theoretical biologist von Uexküll, and the vitalist Hans Driesh, Angyal presented a theoretical framework for a science of the person that was clearly an extension of the Jamesean, Lewinian, and personological point of view of Murray as far as then contemporary trends in personality were concerned in English-speaking countries. The work is remarkable for the phenomenological cast of the argument, which Angyal put forward with hardly any references to other authors. He introduced the concept of the biosphere, by which he meant the total organism–environment life space, but he intended to advance Lewin's formulae by depicting geometrically the dynamic, evolving character of the individual unit. The term dynamic, meant for him the movement toward self-expansion and psychic growth. He also considered the extension of the person into superordinate units, by which he meant kinship, social relationships, identification with objects including one's own phylogeny as well as one's physiology. This process came about by what he called homonomy and he tried to work out these relationships in the language of biological systems, but from a theoretical standpoint. He granted autonomy to the psychological domain, however, and therefore referred to Freudian concepts of the unconscious, discussed instincts and the functions of the will, and gave an extensive discussion of symbolism, but generally fielded his own understanding of a science of the whole person. It was a strange and wonderful mix of Old World holistic science, such as what was found in Germany between the two World Wars, and the newer developments of the personologists pointing to a holistic psychology of the future.

85. Feigenbaum, Kenneth (2008). Maslow's founding of the Brandeis Psychology Department. Society for the History of Psychology, Annual Meeting of the American Psychological Association, Boston, Massachusetts, 2008.

86. Maslow, A. H. (1954). *Motivation and personality*. New York: Harper & Row.

87. Hoffman, 1988, p. 257—Maslow soon became involved in the Nebraska Symposium on Motivation and developed a list of 40 growth-oriented scholars such as Allport, Angyal, Charlotte Bühler, Fromm, Goldstein, Paul Goodman, Rollo May, Ashley Montague, Charles Morris, Lewis Mumford, David Reisman, Carl Rogers, Pitirim Sorokin, and Paul Tillich. Maslow's circle at Brandeis also included Herbert Marcuse, the radical leftist from the Frankfurt School who fused Freud and Marx.

88. Wolff, W. (1943). *The expression of personality: Experimental depth psychology*. New York, London: Harper & Brothers.

89. The recognition level in one series of trials was less than 30%. When tested again weeks later and this time told their voice was among the others, the recognition level dropped to zero. When asked to self-consciously pick out their own voice from a sequence of other voices, they got worse the more effort they put into it. Meanwhile, the subjects in general were able to make assessments of their own personalities from the stimuli presented; they just did not know they were assessing themselves. Subjects generally agreed with others in their perceptions of themselves, but with more intensity of exaggeration; they also judged themselves more severely while generally the assessment of others was usually more positive. Subjects were also more uniformly positive about their assessment of personality when they did not know they were judging themselves (Wolff, 1943, pp. 64–65).

90. See also, Wolff, W. (1948). *Diagrams of the unconscious: Handwriting and personality in measurement, experiment and analysis*. New York: Grune & Stratton.

91. Murphy, G. (1929). *An historical introduction to modern psychology*. London: K. Paul, Trench, Trubner & Company; New York: Harcourt, Brace & Company.

92. Murphy, G., & Murphy, L. B. (1931). *Experimental social psychology*. New York: Harper & Row.

93. Murphy, G., & Jensen, F. (1932). *Approaches to personality: Some contemporary conceptions used in psychology with psychiatry*. New York: Coward-McCann.

94. Murphy, G. (1935). *A briefer general psychology*. New York, London: Harper & Row.

95. Murphy, L. B. (Ed.). (1989). *There is more beyond: Selected papers of Gardner Murphy.* Jefferson, NC: McFarland & Company.

96. Murphy, G., & Likert, R. (1938). *Public opinion and the individual: A psychological study of student attitudes on public questions, with a retest five years later.* New York, London: Harper & Brothers.

97. Murphy, G. (1947). *Personality: A biosocial approach to origins and structures.* New York: Harper & Brothers.

98. Murphy, G. (1958). *Human potentialities.* New York: Basic Books.

99. Rapaport, D. (1945–46). *Diagnostic psychological testing* (2 Vols.). Chicago: The Year Book Publishers, Inc.

100. Tomkins, S. S. (1943). *Contemporary psychopathology.* Cambridge, MA: Harvard University Press.

101. Lewin (1934).

102. Freud, S. (1896). Further remarks on the neuro-psychoses of defense. In J. Strachey (Ed. & Trans.), *The standard edition of the complete psychological works of Sigmund Freud* (Vol. 2, pp. 41–61). London: Hogarth Press.

103. Freud (1900).

104. Freud (1905b).

105. Freud (1912–1913).

106. Freud, S. (1914). On the history of the psychoanalytic movement. In J. Strachey (Ed. & Trans.), *The standard edition of the complete psychological works of Sigmund Freud* (Vol. 14, pp. 1–66). London: Hogarth Press.

107. Freud, S. (1920b). *A general introduction to psychoanalysis.* (G. Stanley Hall, Trans.). New York: Horace Liveright.

108. Freud (1923).

109. Freud (1921).

110. Freud (1920a).

111. Freud, S. (1916). Some character-types met with in psycho-analytic work. In J. Strachey (Ed. & Trans.), *The standard edition of the complete psychological works of Sigmund Freud* (Vol. 14, pp. 309–336). London: Hogarth Press.

112. Freud (1932–1933).

113. Freud, A. (1946). *The ego and mechanisms of defence.* New York: International Universities Press.

114. Jung, C. G. (1904–1907). Studies in word association. In H. Read, M. Fordham, & G. Adler (Eds.), *Experimental researches: Vol. 2, Collected works.* London: Routledge and Kegan Paul.

115. Jung, C. G. (1907b). The psychology of dementia praecox. In H. Read, M. Fordham, & G. Adler (Eds.), *The psychogenesis of mental disease: Vol. 3, Collected works.* London: Routledge and Kegan Paul.

116. Jung, C. G. (1913). The theory of psychoanalysis. In H. Read, M. Fordham, & G. Adler (Eds.), *Freud and psychoanalysis: Vol. 3, Collected works.* London: Routledge and Kegan Paul.

117. Jung (1916b).

118. Jung, C. G. (1921b). Psychological types. In H. Read, M. Fordham, & G. Adler (Eds.), *Collected works, Vol. 6.* London: Routledge and Kegan Paul.

119. Murphy, G. (1956). The current impact of Freud on psychology. In L. B. Murphy (Ed.), (1989), *There is more beyond: Selected papers of Gardner Murphy* (pp. 58–74). Jefferson, NC: McFarland & Company.

120. Murphy, 1956, p. 59.

121. Allport, G. W. (1955). *Becoming: Basic considerations for a psychology of personality.* New Haven, CT: Yale University Press.

122. Bergson, H. (1935). *The two sources of morality and religion.* New York: Henry Holt.

123. Bergson, H. (1912). *Introduction to metaphysics.* New York: G Putnam's Sons. See Allport, 1955, p. 38.

124. Allport, 1955, p. 46.

125. Horney, K. (1950). *Neurosis and human growth: The struggle toward self-realization.* New York: W. W. Norton.

126. Bertocci, P. (1945). The psychological self, the ego, and personality. *Psychological Review, 52,* 91–99.

127. Allport, 1955, p. 54.
128. Allport, 1955, p. 55.
129. Allport, 1955, p. 80.
130. Allport, 1955, p. 86.
131. Allport, G. (1950). *The individual and his religion.* New York: The MacMillan Company.
132. There are actually two lineages called the psychology of religion, one in religious studies and the other in academic psychology. The one in religious studies is where pastoral psychology views the care of souls as the job of the minister, but primarily in a Judeo-Christian, monotheistic, and largely Protestant context. Psychology of religion within psychology as a discipline is almost always generally constrained by empirical reductionism, which translates as the measurement of religious behavior. Religious scholars are permitted to study mysticism as a topic in the psychology of religion, for instance, while psychologists of religion in psychology generally confine themselves to the assessment of beliefs and the measurement of institutional affiliation. Again, the focus has been primarily on monotheistic Judeo-Christian religion, or the measurement of other organized religions according to a test designed by Christian adherents who are trained in reductionistic empiricism. There are distinguished exceptions in psychology, however, from William James to James Bissett Pratt, to Walter Houston Clark and Arlo Strunk. These last two had been students of Allport.

Chapter 10
An Existential-Humanistic and Transpersonally Oriented Depth Psychology

All of us are called to make something of life that respects yet
reaches beyond our mere materiality and vitality
Adrian van Kaam

Beyond a mere ego-centered concept, dynamic theories of personality merged between the 1940s and the 1960s to produce existential-humanistic and transpersonal psychology. The creative and diamonic forces at work that allowed this to come about were many.[1] First, was the Americanization of European forms of existentialism and phenomenology and their absorption into the new movement called humanistic psychology. This led to the valorization of the psychotherapeutic hour over artificial modeling in the laboratory, as well as a major epistemological critique of positivistic reductionism in experimental science. Second, was the radicalization of psychoanalysis, leading to forms of depth psychology that mixed the iconography of the transcendent and new experiential forms of learning with radical forms of social activism directed against traditional psychology and psychiatry. Third, was the psychedelic revolution, which displaced psychoanalysis as the primary vehicle for inner exploration in modern popular culture and at the same time led to experiences both wider and deeper than traditional forms of Western psychology and psychiatry could fathom and to concepts of personality and methods of transforming consciousness from such sources as classical Asian psychology, which could speak more directly to the breadth and depth of people's internal phenomenological experiences. This, in turn, led to major developments in the counterculture incorporating meditation and psychotherapy, psychotherapy and shamanic states of consciousness, and now alternative and complementary therapies into Western concepts of psychology. Depth psychology and existential phenomenology, within an existential-humanistic and transpersonal context, remain major portals into this contemporary frame of reference, having a major impact at the interface between the delivery of clinical services and consumer demand that continues unabated to this day.

Meanwhile, the new rubric in cognitive psychology for spirituality became resilience, directly traceable to the incursion of the psychotherapeutic counterculture into mainstream psychology.[2] There is also Seligman's cognitive rendition, which he calls positive psychology, both of which have unexamined implications

E. Taylor, *The Mystery of Personality*, Library of the History of Psychology Theories, DOI 10.1007/978-0-387-98104-8_10, © Springer Science+Business Media, LLC 2009

for an altogether new definition of personality. But the cognitivists themselves are not allowed to broach them. Their epistemology forbids self-reflection and considers it unscientific. So they steal the limelight from the counterculture theorists while remaining in the reductionists' fold. This means that traditional histories of mainstream academic psychology can conveniently ignore developments in the psychotherapeutic counterculture and act as if they either never happened or they are acknowledged at all, they are not considered worthy of being called psychology.[3] In this way, academic psychology has remained safe within the confines of its outmoded 19th-century definition of itself as aligned with the physical sciences but is considered in American culture at large, beyond the walls of the academy and the publicly regulated clinics, as largely irrelevant to post-modern experience.

The reason for this is that humanistic psychology was willing to embrace a wider view of personality than mainstream trait theorists because it acknowledged a growth-oriented dimension to personality. The humanistic movement also fused constructs of personality with an expanded theory of consciousness before the neurosciences even broached the subject. This new outlook, in turn, had implications for the way then present day science was being conducted and so raised epistemological questions about fundamentalist influences keeping science in a state of preadolescence while the most important problems of personality and consciousness went unaddressed. Such questions were then taken up at the perimeter of science, which, within the academy, were those points where psychology touched biology, anthropology, sociology, and the arts and humanities, as well as religious studies. A major incursion was human science and the development of qualitative methods.[4]

A case in point is the evolution of dynamic theories of personality after the passing of the macropersonality theorists, such as Murray, Allport, and the Murphys, whose era was the 1930s and 1940s, and who began to pass from the scene in the early 1960s. Almost all their students eventually became assimilated into variations of in reductionistic academic science or psychoanalysis, although many tried valiantly to maintain their identity. Sylvan Tomkins, Salvatore Maddi, Brewster Smith, and now Dan McAdams would be distinguished examples. William McKinley Runyan and James William Anderson would be others. Meanwhile, their teachers went in another direction completely and became the grandfathers and grandmothers at the birth of the existential-humanistic movement, which originated out of the older lineage of personality, abnormal, social, and clinical psychology, and has since flourished in the psychotherapeutic counterculture, where it has helped to spawn a cultural revolution from the bottom up.[5]

This is to say that humanistic psychology is generally remembered along with encounter groups, sex therapy workshops, psychedelic drugs, and the American counterculture movement because it was believed by its proponents to promote a new experiential psychology based on the development of intuitions and the free expression of emotions, rather than relying primarily on reason or science. It has also been variously associated with the larger Western philosophical tradition of humanism, as in the type of discourse that focuses on the person, explicated from the time of the Greeks to the Renaissance. But humanism and humanistic psychology are not identical. Humanistic psychology has more recently become associated with the term transpersonal, referring to higher states of consciousness accessible through deliberate forms of spiritual practice; and it is sometimes used interchangeably with the term human science, a more recent quasi-intellectual movement of social criticism, mostly European in origin, that had its roots in the ideas of Wilhelm Dilthey and arose from continental interpretations of Husserlian and Heideggerian phenomenology contrasting the natural from the human sciences. More recently human science, in the form of a branch but not the trunk, derives its inspiration from the Marxism of the Frankfurt School as well as teachings attributed to writers such as Derrida, Lacan, Habermas, and Foucault.

A more focused historical analysis, however, suggests that humanistic psychology flourished as a viable form of discourse in academic psychology, roughly from about the early 1940s to the early 1970s. During this period, humanistic psychologists introduced a number of lucid ideas that not only suggested integrating psychology around a common theme of the person but also held the promise of initiating a new and unprecedented dialogue between the science and the humanities within the structure of the Western university system. In 1941, Carl Rogers, self-described as an educational psychologist with religious leanings, introduced the technique of client-centered or non-directive therapy, the first successful and uniquely American challenge to Viennese psychoanalysis, which had dominated clinical psychology and psychiatry up to that time. In 1954, Abraham Maslow, by then a repentant comparative animal psychologist who had become interested in human motivation, introduced the idea of the self-actualizing personality—that our definition of normality should be based on the best examples of humanity, not on a comparison with psychopathology or as defined by a statistical average.

As a herald of what was to come in the interdisciplinary understanding of personality, consciousness, and psychotherapy, in 1956, Clark Moustakas, existential psychologist at the Merrill Palmer School in Detroit who specialized in play therapy with children, published a remarkable collection of papers under the title of *The Self* (1956).[6] Frances Wilson, professor of child development at Cornell contributed on esthetic growth through art; psychoanalyst Karen Horney posited a growth-oriented dimension to personality despite the vicissitudes of a neurotic culture; anthropologist Dorothy Lee wrote on being and values in primitive cultures; and Marie Ramsey, professor of education, wrote on self-actualization in exceptional children. There were also papers on personality derived from the indigenous psychologies of India; but most importantly, the majority of essays were a Who's Who of the emerging humanistic movement in psychology. These included Abraham Maslow, Carl Rogers, Kurt Goldstein, Andras Angyal, Carl Jung, Erich Fromm, Jean Paul Sartre, and others. The focus on the self was not its measurement but its direct experience, on the actualization of its potential, on a striving toward health as intrinsic to human motivation, on the existential difficulties inherent in interior exploration, but on a vision of personality that went far beyond the mere measurement of outward behavior.

Carrying the existential impulse forward, in 1958, Rollo May, along with Henri Ellenberger and others, became a central figure uniting the separate European traditions of existentialism and phenomenology under the umbrella of humanistic psychology in the form of existential-phenomenological psychotherapy. Thereafter, others such as Charlotte Bühler, James Bugental, Adrian van Kaam, and Sydney Jourard wrote tirelessly on humanistic themes in existential psychology. It was Rogers, Maslow, and May, however, who, in the face of formidable opposition from behaviorists and psychoanalysts alike, collectively established a new norm for psychology as a whole, declaring that humanistic psychology, at the center of their vision of a transformed discipline, was person-centered, growth oriented, and existential in orientation, and that its agenda was to put reductionistic experimentalism on notice that the era of its almost complete hegemony had come to an end.

Against this backdrop, figures out in the wider culture, such as Alan Watts, a student of Zen teachings and Episcopal minister by training; his teacher the aging D. T. Suzuki; the former theosophist, Jiddhu Krishnamurti; Indian yogis such as Swami Rama; psychophysiologists such as Elmer and Alyce Green; indologists and religious philosophers like Frederick Spiegelberg and Huston Smith; and Vedantic practitioners such as Aldous Huxley and Gerald Heard, were increasingly able to inoculate Westerners with concepts of consciousness and techniques of meditation drawn from classical Asian psychology and other world religions. This was also the era when psychedelic drugs were first introduced into the general population by the Central Intelligence Agency and began to have an increasingly widespread social effect on the resurgence of a popular spiritual psychology.[7]

Humanistic psychology, then, which began originally as a legitimate form of academic discourse, did not appear on the scene de novo. One major line of influence had grown out of the older personality and social psychologies developed by previous figures such as Gordon Allport, Henry A. Murray, and Gardner and Lois Murphy during the 1930s and 1940s. These older psychologists had been the first generation after William James to successfully resist the takeover of academic psychology by reductionistic empiricism, which in James's time meant the structuralism of Titchener and Münsterberg and the atomism of Cattell and Witmer. After James, the opposition became the conditioning theories of Pavlov and Watson and the tyranny of testing. After 1930, control over the definition of scientific psychology meant the laboratory experimentalism of Boring, Stevens, Lashley, Hull, and Spence. After the era of the personality-social psychologists, humanistic psychologists continued to carry on this debate and to field an alternative psychology, which raged at the national level in the academy into the early 1960s.

The most notable of these exchanges was carried on in public between Carl Rogers and B. F. Skinner on at least four separate occasions between 1956 and 1964. While the experimentalists continued to believe that their man Skinner was repeatedly able to keep the world safe for reductionism, a far more ominous sign signaling the decline of their epistemology was massing with publication during the same period of Sigmund Koch's monumental six volume work *Psychology: A Study of a Science* (1958–1963), a reassessment of experimental psychology at mid-century commissioned by the American Psychological Association.[8] In it, 87 of the world's premier scientific psychologists assessed the rules linking quantification to theory construction against what they had actually accomplished over a lifetime of their own individual work. The result was a correlation so low that it became a massive indictment of psychologists' agenda to establish psychology as a reductionistic and positivist enterprise. The work also became a landmark symbolizing the era of de-regulation in academic psychology that followed, thus opening the door to the further development of humanistic psychology as a potential new leading movement that would reshape the discipline.

One of the more important comprehensive summaries solicited by Sigmund Koch for his massive re-evaluation of the presuppositions of scientific psychology at mid-century was that presented by Carl Rogers.[9] Rogers's piece was entitled, "A Theory of Therapy, Personality, and Interpersonal Relationships, as Developed in the Client-centered Framework." Rogers found the original assignment quite forced, as he had never expressed his project in terms of dependent, independent, and intervening variables, so he presented instead the organic evolution of his work. He did, however, have a healthy respect for quantifiable studies, but the difference was that these were not primary; they were secondary to understanding the mystery of the person. They were ways to check one's self, to corroborate, to confirm or deny certain hypotheses, but these were not the purpose of the work. The purpose of the work was the person. It was the person who was at the center of his scientific theory, not justification for psychology as a science.

First of all, he considered the development of client-centered therapy to be a group effort, not his singly and alone, and he went to great lengths to identify who his colleagues were at different stages of the theory. He began with a little autobiography.[10] He had come from a Midwestern Christian conservative background and was raised on a farm, where he became deeply involved in the statistics of large-scale agricultural production and husbandry. He went through the physical and biological sciences in college but also studied history for a time. He questioned the fundamentalist religion of his upbringing, especially after a year in China, and on his return and graduation entered Union Theological Seminary. From there he moved across the street to Teachers College Columbia, where he encountered the ideas of E. L. Thorndike and John Dewey and was introduced to clinical psychology by Leta Hollingworth. He did a year of internship at a newly founded Institute of Child Guidance where he was introduced to the ideas of Freud by David Levy and Lawson Lawry. Here, he first began to do therapy. He spent the next 12 years at a community child guidance clinic in Rochester, New York, completely divorced from the psychology going on at the University of Rochester nearby. The faculty in psychology rejected his work as real psychology, although he did some teaching in the other departments. Instead of the laboratory, he focused on his patients. The result of both the therapy and his research was *The Clinical Treatment of the Problem Child* (1939a).[11] During the second half of this period, he was influenced by the works of Otto Rank, and his students, including Jessie Taft and Frederick Allen. From these encounters he reoriented his research toward the actual experience of the client, not with the testing of some intellectual theory in a laboratory.

Rogers then took a full-time faculty position at the University of Ohio, where more rigorous standards of research met his clinical formulations. He rose to the occasion with a program of rigorous testing and the result was *Counseling and Psychotherapy: Newer Concepts in Practice* (1942a).[12] He then moved to the

University of Chicago and encountered there a broad and deep interdisciplinary eclecticism more than anything he had encountered before. By the time he wrote for Koch's project, he was at the University of Wisconsin. What he presented, therefore, represented 30 years of work with patients, whose experience had become the sole focus of his research. Out of this population he generated a theory of therapy, personality, and interpersonal relationships.

His primary distinction was to show that the basic data of a scientific psychology could be generated out of the psychotherapeutic hour, not the laboratory. Its focus was the inward ordering of experience, not the measurement of behavior; his approach was scientific even if the first steps were crude and only suggestive. His science was dynamic and not static. Establishing the methods of the laboratory as the only legitimate standard for psychology produced a sterile pseudoscience "of no particular importance." Nor was advanced theoretical physics a correct model for psychology. He was certain psychology was nowhere near this same status. Every theory contains error and mistaken inference. The book is never finished and therefore never closed. Too many small caliber minds in psychology jump to accept a theory as the dogma of truth. While he was thinking of the behaviorists in this regard, he was also referring to the Freudians. Freud may have had some good ideas from an intuitive level, but they kept changing. His disciples, meanwhile, had already cast his theory in stone.

Only a complete theory will show us what God and man are, Rogers said, but this is probably unattainable, even if a lofty goal to strive for. At the same time, every theory cannot cover everything. More realistically, "every theory deserves the greatest respect in the area from which it was drawn from the facts and a decreasing degree of respect as it makes its predictions in areas more and more remote from its origins."[13] Finally, he believed that subjective experience was primary in every endeavor, including that of objective science. Operational definitions, experimental method, and mathematical proof are the best way of avoiding self-deception, but they are not the purpose of the research. They do not provide us with the final truth, only the individual perceptions of what appears to each person to be such knowledge.

He then presented his theoretical model. In the center, beginning with the experience of the person, was his theory of therapy. Branching off from it in all four directions were its important developments. The first was a theory of personality. The second was a theory of interpersonal relationships. The third was a theory of the fully functioning person, while the fourth involved the theoretical implications for various human activities, including family life, education and learning, group leadership, and the resolution of group conflict.

With regard to the theory of therapy and personality change, the basic conditions for therapy to take place are several. Two people first must be in contact. The client will normally be in a state of incongruence, feeling vulnerable and anxious. The therapist should feel congruent in the relationship and also feel unconditional positive regard toward the client; the therapist should feel an empathetic understanding of the client's internal frame of reference, and finally, that the client should perceive this regard and this empathy from the therapist (Fig. 10.1).

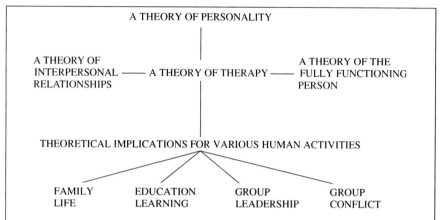

Fig. 10.1 Rogers's theory of personality emanating from psychotherapy
Rogers, C. R. (1959). A theory of therapy, personality, and interpersonal relationships, as developed in the client centered framework. In S. Koch (Ed.), *Psychology: A study of a science* (Vol. 3, pp. 184-257). New York: McGraw-Hill.

Concerning the theory of personality, Rogers assembled from the therapeutic hour experiences that led to a model of personality development and dynamics of behavior. He first articulated the attributes of the human infant, who perceives his experience as reality, that is, his own internal frame of reference, as more central than any other experience. His tendency is to actualize himself as an organism and he interacts with reality according to this tendency. In this behavior, he acts as an organized whole, as a total gestalt. He is attracted to positive experiences and repelled by negative ones. This motivational system is inherent.

He then turned to the development of the self. Since self-experience is primary, development proceeds in the direction of self-awareness and the development of the infant's concept of the self. In this, positive regard develops as a permanent need. It soon becomes directed toward others and supercedes the previous organismic valuing process. Self-regard emerges because not all experiences are unconditionally positive, in which case the organism's own self-perceptions carry him or her through.

Incongruence develops when expectations regarding positive regard are not forthcoming. The results tend to be distorted and perceived selectively, in some cases being denied to awareness, but nevertheless preserved as past experiences. An incongruence develops between self and experience, which can lead to discrepancies in behavior.

The expectation of threats and the development of defenses then occur, influencing perceptions of self-worth. Here, Rogers, without attribution, acknowledges Freud's conceptualization of the defense mechanisms—rationalization, compensation, fantasy, projection, compulsions, phobias, etc. Neurotic and psychotic diagnoses are avoided in favor of a greater or lesser degree of congruence experienced by the person. Subception is a term Rogers frequently used. Non-specific anxiety, for instance, is experienced as incongruence, the degree to which it is dependent on the extent of the self-structure which is threatened. Anxiety is subceived. When anxiety breaks through into awareness, the gestalt of the self-structure is broken and an open state of disorganization results. Conversely, the process of reintegration occurs when the threatening experience must be accurately symbolized in awareness and assimilated into the self-structure.

Rogers then engaged in an extensive list of operational definitions that could be used empirically to test these hypotheses regarding the development of different types of personalities and their reintegration as fully functioning persons. He enumerated the characteristics of the fully functioning person, and from this vantage point fielded a theory of interpersonal relationships. The final section was on the application of the theory to family life, education, group leadership, and the resolution of group conflict. All these areas Rogers eventually went on to develop. Indeed, his work on the resolution of international conflict led to his nomination for the Nobel Peace Prize before he died.

Another landmark event in the early history of humanistic psychology was the appearance of *Existence: A New Dimension in Psychology and Psychiatry* in 1958, edited by Rollo May, Ernest Angell, and Henri Ellenberger.[14] May began the volume with an essay on the origins and significance of the existential movement in psychology.[15] The goal was to know the patient as he or she really is. We must ask, "Are we seeing him or her in their real world?"

Ludwig Binswanger and Martin Heidegger were the early voices of the modern period who developed *daseinsanalysis*—the existential-analytic movement in psychology and psychiatry. It was the study of not just an ill man, but the total person in his life context. Eugene Minkowski, Erwin Straus, and V. E. von Gebsattel represented the first, phenomenological stage of this movement. Binswanger, along with A. Storch, Medard Boss, G. Bally, Roland Kuhn, J. H. van den Berg, and F. J. Buytendijk represented the second, more existential stage. Gebsattel, Medard Boss, and G. Bally were Freudian analysts, along with Binswanger himself, who was also significantly influenced by Jung.[16]

As Straus maintained, the unconscious ideas of the patient were more often than not the conscious theories of the therapist. Existential analysis, on the other hand, was focused on the patient's existence, not the therapist's theory. In this way, according to Binswanger, existential analysis was able to widen and deepen psychoanalysis. The person was not studied according to some external standard, but according to the interior disruption of the person's own *condition humaine*. Life histories, narratives, and the single case study were the bulwark of the existentialist's research methods. Such qualitative methods lent themselves naturally to the psychotherapeutic hour and into the depths of the therapist–patient relationship. Binswanger's presentation of the case of Ellen West in the latter half of the book was a case in point.

The gist of the humanistic movement, however, was not therapy, but the place of the individual embedded in the whole of the human condition, and the eventual achievement of a union between science and humanism. The part about humanism was obvious, but the founders also had about them the air of pure science as well, in that they searched, not for techniques for their own sake, but for the foundation upon which all techniques rest. Existentialism was "an expression of the profound dimensions of the modern emotional and spiritual temper and is shown in almost all aspects of our culture."[17]

Meanwhile, the cleavage between the subject and the object Binswanger had called the cancer of all psychology up to now.

The existential lineage comes through Socrates, Augustine, to Pascal, Kierkegaard, Schelling, then Nietzsche, Dilthey, and even James, Whitehead, Bergson, and Sartre, Berdyaev, Jaspers, Gabriel Marcel, Ortega y Gassett, Unamno, and Tillich in our own time. It is everywhere throughout culture, in the writings of Camus and Kafka, and in the art of van Gogh, Cezanne, and Picasso. It is primarily ontological, in that its focus is on our current state of being. The great edifice of science has very little to do with our current state of being. Quoting Tillich, May says: "Reality or Being is not the object of cognitive experience, but is rather existence, ... reality as immediately experienced, with the accent on the inner, personal, character of man's immediate experience."[18] The focus of existential psychology is not on objective man, but on the living man and living woman who are doing the experiencing. It is psychology as ontology.

Existentialists themselves begin with Martin Heidegger and his *Being and Time* (1962/1927), because he reflected the scientific temper, at least in the European sense.[19] But May chose to embark on an earlier historical comparison of Kierkegaard and Nietzsche and the relation of their ideas to psychoanalysis.[20] First, May maintained that existentialism and psychoanalysis arose out of the same cultural situation. Both were a reaction to industrialism and its impact on the psyche, where anxiety, despair, and alienation from oneself and society were mutual themes. Freud wrote about fragmentation of the person and repression of instinctual drives, while Kierkegaard wrote about anxiety, self-estrangement, depression, and despair. Nietzsche wrote about "the bad smell of a soul gone stale" and its effect on resentment, hostility, and aggression. Victorian man saw himself divided by science into reason, the will, and the emotions and trusted that this was the way to examine oneself—piecemeal. What followed, however, was a compartmentalization of culture along the same lines as the radical fragmentation and repression within the personality. Most importantly, what Kierkegaard, Nietzsche, and Freud also had in common was that they theorized upon themselves as a single case study.

Kierkegaard had asked "What does it mean to be an authentic person?" He found truth as defined in relationship, which set him to the question of whether or not man can be divorced from nature, subject from object. His answer, contradicting the entire Copernican revolution upon which then modern science was based, was that the separation of subject and object was entirely false, and in this he predates the quantum physicists who later launched the same answer. Truth is not defined solely in terms of external objects. There is also an internal phenomenological truth based on what an idea means to a person, whether or not it is true or false according to external circumstances. In this, he also predates Rank and Sullivan. We react to what we are committed to. The antidote we seek is recovery of self-consciousness—the will to power. By this Nietzsche meant the ability to overcome disease and suffering, and the potential to actualize one's destiny—that is, May says, self-realization of the individual in the fullest sense.

May compared Nietzsche to Freud on concepts such as repression, reaction formation, and the relation between artistic energy and one's sexuality. They also shared a common understanding about ecstatic reason, that is, reason that spills over into intuition as well as wonder. But Freud lost this sense when he later developed his arguments too rigidly for psychoanalysis as a rigorous science. Reason then became logical and static in his epistemology—a mere method. May finally concluded that "almost all the specific ideas which later appeared in psychoanalysis could be found in Nietzsche in greater breadth and in Kierkegaard in greater depth."[21] The three of them, at least, directed our attention back to the person having the experience as central to our understanding of man.

Papers then followed by May and Ellenberger on the clinical aspects of psychiatric phenomenology and existential analysis. A section followed of essays by Eugene Minkowski, Erwin Straus, and V. E. von Gebsattel representing phenomenology. A final section on existential analysis presented three papers by Ludwig Binswanger, one of which was the case of Ellen West, concluding with an additional case by Roland Kuhn.

Binswanger presents "The Case of Ellen West" as an example of an attempt to understand schizophrenia from an existential, an anthropological, and a psychotherapeutic orientation. The time period for the case is the end of the World War I, when Ellen voluntarily sought treatment and entered the Bellevue psychiatric facility at Kreuzlingen, where Binswanger was in charge. The anamnesis revealed that Ellen arrived at Binswanger's facility after attempts at treatment with two other un-named psychiatrists (Eugen Bleuler, who gave a psychoanalytic interpretation, and Emil Kraepelin, who gave a more biological one). With respect to their understanding of the case, Bleuler's psychoanalytic interpretation pointed to the unconscious repression of vital drives and instincts, whereas Kraepelin described her condition as the development and gradual manifestation of a pathological personality. Binswanger and Bleuler were in agreement that Ellen's difficulties were an expression of her schizophrenia, but also acknowledged the relevant psychodynamic, developmental considerations, and morbid propensities in her character. After 4 months of treatment and observation, Binswanger revealed that they could no longer keep her at Bellevue and this meant that she would probably take her own life. Binswanger released her and, in effect, acceded with her wish to do so.

The death of Ellen West occurred in early April of 1918, after a 4-month stay at Kreuzlingen, despite Binswanger's best efforts at convincing her to embrace life. Existential analysis exposes the failure of psychiatric theories and psychoanalytic determinations to understand her illness and predicament, without a supporting anthropologically oriented clinical orientation. The existential analytic understanding of the life and death of Ellen West reveals the pathological manifestation of several dominating ideas (related to her weight, in her words, "either thin, or dead," or "nothing") and a subsequent self-imposed "imprisonment in a world design ... restricted ... [and] ruled by very few themes."[22] We apprehend this imprisonment in the rejection of her body, of life, and the world, and understand it as part of the gradual disappearing of vital aspects of her existence. The existential anthropological contribution to the analysis rests in its illumination of this restriction

and imprisonment, as a disappearing of existence not simply biologically appre-
hended through drive theories or as disease, but also as an expression of transcendence. This insight can be expressed by the fact that, "the human being is in the
world, has a world, and at the same time *longs to get beyond it.*" Hence, the desire
for transcendence by first disappearing through anorexia and then in the incessant desire for death appears in the final analysis as a tragic and truncated expression of "an ambivalent and ultimately negative obsession" with "being beyond the
world."[23]

Existence was the first popular work to expose the general reader to existential
psychology. It was followed a year later, in 1959, by a landmark conference at the
annual meeting of the American Psychological Association in Cincinnati. Abraham
Maslow, Rollo May, and Herman Feifel were presenters at this symposium, and Carl
Rogers and Gordon Allport were discussants. The symposium at the APA Convention represented the first meeting of American psychologists in a public forum to
discuss this topic. Two years after the symposium Rollo May (1961) edited *Existential Psychology*, a compendium of the talks given at that meeting.[24]

The symposium began with a discussion of the emergence on the American
scene of existential psychology by Rollo May, a paper by Abraham H. Maslow
on the value of existential psychology to American psychotherapists, a discussion
on the relevance of death in psychology by Herman Feifel, a chapter on the existential bases of psychotherapy by Rollo May, a delineation of the objective versus the
existential view of psychology by Carl R. Rogers, and a commentary on the above
papers by Carl Rogers and Gordon W. Allport.

Carl Rogers (1959), the first discussant (APA Editor, 1959), had recognized the
phenomenological and existential influences in his own thinking when he published
Client-centered Therapy in 1951.[25] He had also been deeply influenced by Paul
Tillich. Even so, he never completely identified himself with these philosophies, a
fact which was probably due to his sincere and continued concern with the objective
verification of his subjective findings. According to Spiegelberg, Rogers's objective
leaning was at least as strong as the subjective influence in his work.[26] This predis-
position led him to focus his presentation on two divergent trends in therapy: the
"objective" trend, which he identified with learning theory and operant conditioning, described as reductionistic, operational, and experimental; and the "existential"
trend, which he described as being concerned with the whole spectrum of human
behavior, a behavior which is more complex than that of laboratory animals in many
significant ways.

Rogers elaborated by describing the objective trend as one which moved away
from the philosophical and vague, toward the concrete, the operationally defined,
and the specific. In this view, the road to progress in therapy was to reinforce the
behaviors in clients that exemplified the direction for improvement that the therapist
conceived of as appropriate. He pointed out that this trend had behind it the weight
of then current mainstream attitudes in American psychology.

Rogers identified the existential trend in psychology with the psychotherapists,
and with Abraham Maslow, Rollo May, Gordon Allport, himself, and others. This
trend, he emphasized, recognized the need for the therapist to be real, empathic,

accepting, and openly and freely him or herself. In Rogers's own experience, such a therapeutic relationship allowed the client to be open to many possibilities including considering what in him or herself was real; becoming confirmed in both what he or she was, and in his or her own potentialities; becoming affirmed, although fearfully, in a separate and unique identity; becoming the architect of the future while perceiving future possibilities; and facing what it would mean to be or not to be.

Rogers suggested that these two trends, the objective and the existential, which seemed to represent two divergent and disparate modes of science, might find rapprochement in empiricism itself. According to Rogers, what a positivistic scientist might view as Rollo May's vague philosophical principles, could easily be deduced as testable hypothesis. In the balance of his presentation he offered examples of this possibility. For example, if one looks at May's first principle that neurosis was a method that a person used to preserve his or her own center or existence, a testable hypothesis might be: "The more the self of the person is threatened, the more he will exhibit defensive neurotic behavior."[27] Rogers elucidated several other plausible and convincing examples in his talk.

Notwithstanding Rogers's insistence on the need for objective proofs, in his final argument he confirmed that, in his own experience "the warm, subjective, human encounter of two persons is more effective in facilitating change than is the most precise set of techniques growing out of learning theory or operant conditioning"[28]

The second discussant, Gordon Allport (1959), commented on what he called four crucial issues from the presented papers. These four issues included Maslow's question concerning what European existentialism had to offer American psychologists. Allport began his discussion on this question by suggesting that all rational attendees at the symposium had to admit to being repelled by the European style of philosophizing and writing. He declared that American psychology had recast, "imported ideas bringing order, clarity, and empirical testing to bear on them."[29] With these qualifications in mind, he admitted that *"existentialism deepens the concepts that define the human condition ...* [and] *prepares the way (for the first time) for a psychology of mankind"* [his italics].[30]

Death was the second crucial topic which Allport reviewed. He supported Feifel's assertion that death is a large part of a person's philosophy of life and lamented the lack of death's inclusion in psychology's study of personality, and in the practice of psychotherapy. He also suggested that persons whose religious values were more comprehensive and integrated into their lives would have less fear of death, while those who had defensive, escapist, and ethnocentric religious values would be more fearful of death.

Allport's third crucial issue was the European preoccupation with dread, anguish, and despair. He suggested that trends in American existentialism were more optimistic in their orientation. These trends included client-centered therapies, growth and self-actualization-oriented therapies, and ego therapies.

Finally, Allport took issue with a point made by Rollo May in his talk on the existential bases of psychotherapy. He understood May as presenting phenomenology— or the client's own view of himself as a unique being-in-the-world—as the first stage of therapy, and possibly, the only stage needed. Allport recognized May's description of the true existential-phenomenologist as one who would realize the "full reality and richness,"[31] and ultimately the why of a situation. Even so, Allport argued that the unconscious of Mrs. Hutchens, a case presented by May in support of his six ontological characteristics, was "filled with Freudian, not existential, furniture."[32] Allport also argued that May relied heavily on psychoanalytic techniques in his existential analysis of this case.

Allport, himself, suggested that the phenomenological view may be the preliminary as well as the ultimate stage of therapy. Having reflected this understanding, Allport still concluded his presentation by suggesting that psychology needed to distinguish between client presentations in which the existential layer was the whole of the personality, and presentations in which the existential layer was a mask for deeper rumblings of the unconscious.

Even though it had been a prominent influence in European psychology for 2 decades, existential psychology was practically unknown in America until 2 years prior to this symposium (May, 1969). In the preface to the second edition of *Existential Psychology*,[33] May stated that a nearly exhaustive listing of psychologically oriented, existential writings in English included only 185 citations in 1961, while 8 years later there were close to 1000. During those 8 years, the vocabulary of existentialism had become an integral part of the language in American psychology. It was no longer a foreign school of thought, but had become an attitude that permeated many types of therapy and had also exercised an influence on the therapies that acted as correctives to orthodox psychoanalysis. Without being a separate school in its own right, it had become allied with the third force in psychology and the term existential-humanistic psychology had become commonplace.

Rollo May lent the final thought. His fervent wish was that existential-phenomenological philosophy might become a base for a science of individuals that would not fragmentize and destroy our humanity as it went about studying who we are as persons.[34]

Meanwhile, humanistic psychology was also flourishing abroad. Within a few years of its founding as The American Association for Humanistic Psychology, there were so many international organizations sprouting that they dropped the "American" part of the title. The history of the movement in England has been sketched by John Rowan.[35] Rowan, originally an English socialist radical, turned to psychotherapy and took his PhD from Middlesex University. He became extremely well connected in the various psychological and psychotherapeutic organizations in professional psychology representing the humanistic point of view, while keeping a private practice going in London. He has had a number of popular books published, among them *Ordinary Ecstasy* (1976).[36] More recently he has become associated with transpersonal psychology (Fig. 10.2).

Rowan has developed a theory of the normal personality by relying on the research of others and drawing on his own intuitive norms as a longtime psychotherapist in private practice. His theory focuses on the normal development of subpersonalities.[37] Rowan proposes that the infant's initial state of a "primordial paradise" is shattered through the experience of trauma and abuse. Faced with what

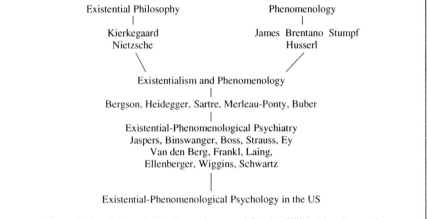

Fig. 10.2 The evolution of the continental philosophies of existentialism and phenomenology into existential-phenomenology psychotherapy operating under the umbrella of humanistic psychology in the United States.

Existentialism begins with Kierkegaard and Nietzsche. The Husserlians presume they own the term phenomenology but they were preceded by Hegel. James, Brentano, and Stumpf. Existentialism and phenomenology became associated with each other through the writings of Bergson, Sartre, Heidegger, and Merleau-Ponty. Buber and Tillich, both theologians, stand out as independent interpreters. Existential-Phenomenological psychiatry is associated with Jaspers, Binswanger, Boss, Straus, Ey, Van den berg, Frankl, Laing, and Ellenberger. Existential-Phenomenological Psychology we associate with figures such as Allport, McLeod, Angyal, van Kaam, Snygg and Combs, Tillich, May, Bugental, Moustakas, Jourard, Gendlin, Yalom, Giorgi, Schneider, Greening, Wertz, and to a certain extent, Polkinghorne. The list is not exhaustive.

feels like a very real threat of extinction, Rowan argues that the young infant defends itself by splitting—turning away its original paradisiacal self and putting in its place a "not-OK-me"—a tactic which it then adopts again and again as a means of surviving potentially annihilating experiences. These produce various subpersonalities which the growing person uses for adaptation throughout life.

One of humanistic psychology's most well-known British proponents was Ronald Laing, who expressed his views on existentialism, psychotherapy, psychoanalysis, and personality in, among other works, *The Divided Self* (1960).[38] Liang claimed there to have bounced his ideas off the works of Kierkegaard, Jaspers, Heidegger, Sartre, Binswanger, and Tillich, and he honored Minkowski, but assured the reader that what was presented were chiefly his own thoughts on existential psychology and psychiatry, based on clinical work at the Tavistock Clinic that he had completed by 1956.

He opened with a statement on the existential-phenomenological foundations for a science of persons. The divided self of the schizophrenic refers to the connection with the world that had been rent asunder, and also the rift with the self. The schizoid experiences this as two selves, or a mind split from the body, or an alienation from

others. Laing's purpose was to describe the existential and phenomenological context of the schizophrenic's words and deeds—a picture of his or her whole being-
in-the-world. His text was directed at psychiatrists who had many cases, but never
experienced one as a person, or two people with some familiarity with this type of
madness, but not from a clinical standpoint.

At the outset, he rejected classification. Words normally do what the
schizophrenic breakdown does; they divide the person into mind and body, psyche and soma, psychological and physical personality, the self, and the organism.
One must rather start from an organic unity. The term he used to refer to that is *existence*, one's being-in-the-world. Only existential and phenomenological psychology
looks to the whole, where other nomenclatures fail in psychology and psychiatry. A
person's being, which is the totality of who they are, is the beginning, just seen from
different points of view. Each of us sees people from our own point of view, which
may lead to entirely different kinds of action directed toward the same object. He
referred to these as different experimental gestalts, since there is only one person
actually there.

The individual looks at another individual the same way, either as a person or
as an organism, depending on whether he experiences the other person subjectively
or objectively. Laing was quite clear that a science of persons begins and ends with
one's relationship to the other as a person. One maintains this point of view through
intention. In this way, "the other" remains a self-acting agent. Yet such a science
eludes psychology and psychiatry, because " an authentic science of persons has
hardly got started by reason of the inveterate tendency to depersonalize or reify
persons."[39] Schizophrenics do this and we call them crazy, yet it seems perfectly
plausible for scientists to do it trying to understand persons. Odd, no?

> The experience of one's self and others as persons is understanding generally—how to
> understand the divided self of the schizophrenic as an authentic person. This is the dilemma
> of all psychology and psychiatry, except they begin with a dualism to start with and pretend
> that the unification of personality they speak of is actually true. For how can one remain
> scientific and objective without depersonalizing the schizophrenic as a means to model his
> ailment? A science of persons is primary and self validating.[40]

But, while no science yet exists to understand how this is so. Laing saw his task
as a difficult one in the absence of such attempts to avoid this, but unfortunately is
labeled subjective, unscientific, and mystical for doing so. He cited the efforts of
Freud as an example, a great hero to him, who had descended into the underworld
and encountered stark terrors, but lived to tell about it as a sane man.

Meanwhile, in Italy, Assagioli had launched psychosynthesis. Psychosynthesis
was one of the more important examples of a dynamic theory of personality to
appear on the American scene in the early 1960s. It was a theory of personality which, in its most mature form, was developed by the same Roberto Assagioli, whom we originally associated with the late 19th-century French-Swiss-
English-and-American psychotherapeutic axis as a young medical student in Italy
in 1911.

Assagioli spent his entire professional career in Florence, founding there the
Institute for Psychosynthesis. Because of the nature of his system which paralleled Jung's to a remarkable degree and his ready access to Eranos, the retreat and

conference center on Lake Maggiore on the Swiss-Italian border, where Jung delivered some of his most important papers, Assagioli himself was a frequent guest and presenter. By the 1960s, when Assagioli was in his late seventies, psychosynthesis emerged as a significant counterculture psychotherapy in the Western hemisphere, because of interest in Assagioli's work by Michael Murphy, co-founder of Esalen Institute in Big Sur, California. Murphy, himself, was versed in the models of personality and consciousness of the 19th century, being one of the few authors who had thoroughly read and absorbed the subliminal psychology of F. W. H. Myers and brought those historical insights forward under the framework of humanistic and transpersonal psychology.[41] Assagioli published a number of books on his system, but the one to highlight here is *Psychosynthesis: A Manual of Principles and Techniques* (1964), second in the Esalen series brought out by Viking Press.[42]

Assagioli opened his text by noting the similarities and dissimilarities between psychosynthesis and existential psychotherapy, referencing Adrian van Kaam and echoing Maslow's 1959 paper on "Remarks on existentialism and psychology." The method of starting from within, with the self and its presence, is the same. We find the same emphasis in Allport, Goldstein, Fromm, Moustakas, and Erikson and in such personalists as Tournier and Baudoin, Assagioli maintained. This self is in a constant state of becoming, where meaning is central to life. Ethical, noetic, and religious values are central, as in the work of Frankl. Choice and responsibility follow. Anxiety and suffering are taken fully into account. The role of the future in creating a dynamic present makes them similar, as does the centrality of the person, which he compared to Allport's theory of the idiographic personality. Each one requiring a new method.

They are different in many ways, however. Psychosynthesis emphasizes the will much more than most existential therapies. Psychosynthesis also emphasizes more the experience of the pure self in the immediate moment independent of the content of consciousness. Psychosynthesis emphasizes the positive joyous and peak experiences, some of which Maslow had written about. As such, self-realization is actively induced in psychosynthesis. Loneliness is neither ultimate nor essential. It is a temporary condition. The goal is the harmony of the sexes and one's connection to humanity. Following Sorokin and Fromm and others, Assagioli said, its emphasis is ultimately on love and its many forms. Psychosynthesis uses active techniques to direct psychological energies to actualize one's potential and to achieve higher states of consciousness. He believed the personality could be recreated along entirely new lines. The necessary techniques are defined by the uniqueness of each person. At the same time, however, psychosynthesis is neither a religion nor a philosophical system. It is a psychological framework for the actualization of the person, which may incorporate religious and philosophical concerns, but is not meant as a replacement for them. Rather, it is a "scientific psychodynamic."[43] It is appropriate in the treatment of the neurosis, but its real purpose is the spiritual transformation of the person into their highest and best form. It does this by reclaiming the will for the ego in a way that no other psychology has yet proposed.

He then rehearsed the history of dynamic psychology, from Janet and Breuer and Freud, to the Neo-Freudians and to Jung, and beyond his theories to that of the existentialists such as Binswanger and Frankl. He linked psychosynthesis to developments in psychosomatic medicine, the psychology of religion, investigation of mystical states, the work of the parapsychologists, non-Western epistemologies, especially Hindu psychology. He reviewed the links to Allport, Angyal, Goldstein, Maslow, Murphy, Perls, Progoff, and Stern. Social psychology and anthropology were noted, citing Sullivan, Lewin, Murray, Allport, and Sorokin at Harvard, and the work of Margaret Mead. He also included the techniques of the waking dream of Robert Desoille and Jacob Moreno's psychodrama, as well as the work of Ruth Munroe and Gardner Murphy.

Assagioli then made the attempt to depict his model of consciousness. He acknowledged the spectrum from the lower order domain of psychopathology and the primitive and instinctual; the centrality of the waking consciousness the domain in which the ego functions, but then posited a superconscious state in the individual, all of which was surrounded by the collective unconscious of humanity. The superconscious condition, like the lowest domain, remains unconscious but is nevertheless the source of artistic, scientific, and esthetic creativity and the spring of heroic, humanitarian, and altruistic action.

The ego, in contrast, exists in a state of conditioning, being attached to external objects through the senses and beset by habits, attitudes, and compulsions from within. It remains at the mercy of circumstances as long as the individual does not recognize that there is an internal life beyond external control, that there is a higher as well as the lower domain within, and that the higher domain is actualized by training of the will. This, however, takes knowledge of one's own personality, control of its various elements, discovery of one's true self as a unifying center, and a means to accomplish that goal, which is psychosynthesis.

While the majority of psychologists who refer to the term self-actualization usually have only had exposure to the writings of Abraham Maslow on the subject, Assagioli, relying partly on Maslow, developed it in more elaborate and refined detail, including its vicissitudes. Writing on the relationship of self-actualization to psychopathology, he presented the idea that much of what we consider psychopathic may be the result of thwarted spiritual growth. He enumerated four critical stages: crises preceding spiritual awakening, crises caused by spiritual awakening, reactions to spiritual awakening, and phases in the process of transmutation.[44]

Finally, Assagioli suggested that the therapist who has all the credentials is not always the most qualified to treat the patient, if the therapist himself has not engaged in this process of deep, inward reflection. He recommended a two-fold competence for practitioners, one that they be trained professionals, but also two, that they be experienced travelers along the path of self-realization. Though rarely found in formal programs leading to clinical licensure, the need for such types may be even greater than before.

Meanwhile, since 1949, Abraham Maslow had been in constant contact with the California psychotherapist, Anthony Sutich, and the two had combined mailing lists of professionals across several disciplines who were interested in seeing the evolution of a new kind of psychology. Such interest reached a critical mass in 1961 when the *Journal of Humanistic Psychology* was officially launched, with Sutich as editor and Maslow as contributor, after Allport, behind the scenes, had arranged an anonymous grant for $1,000 from the Psychological Foundation. The informal mailing list of Maslow and Sutich, once merged, became the first official list of subscribers, a group who formally banded together to found the American Association for Humanistic Psychology (AAHP) in order to financially support the journal.

Over the next 2 years, Esalen Institute, in Big Sur, California, was officially founded by Michael Murphy and Richard Price and launched its first programs in human potential with workshops by Willis Harman, Alan Watts, and others, spawning a national but disconnected network of similar growth centers fostering the new psychology.[45] Meanwhile, the first official meeting of AAHP convened in Philadelphia in 1963, attended by 75 people. At that meeting James F. T. Bugental, an existential psychotherapist, author of a then recently published and widely read article, "Humanistic Psychology: A New Breakthrough" in the *American Psychologist*, was elected president.[46] Also at that same meeting, a committee on theory for humanistic psychology was founded, chaired by Robert Knapp of Wesleyan University.

The following year, in November, 1964, Knapp was able to convene the first Old Saybrook Conference in Saybrook, Connecticut, supported by $5,000 from the Hazen Foundation, in order to bring scholars together to examine humanistic theory.[47] Formal invitations were extended by Victor Butterfield, then president of Wesleyan, and the meeting was held in the Wesleyan campus and nearby, in Old Saybrook, Connecticut, at the Old Saybrook Inn. At that conference, Allport, Murray, the Murphys, and others of the older generation of established personality theorists, such as George Kelley and Robert White, met together with Maslow, Rogers, May, Bugental, Moustakas, Bühler, and others such as Floyd Matson and Anthony Sutich to discuss where they had come from and where they were going and to pass the torch from the older to the new generation of theorists. Most, but not all, of the papers were published the following year in the *Journal of Humanistic Psychology*.

Henry A. Murray gave the opening keynote address.[48] He divided himself up into three alters so he could conveniently express the multiple points of view that constituted the new movement. The three parts of him all stood upon Mt. Pisgah, surveying the wasteland that psychology had become in one direction with regard to personality and consciousness, while they could also look toward the Promised Land that psychology was about to evolve into by turning toward the other direction. Between the three of them, they described the dehumanizing effect that experimental psychology in general and particularly at Harvard had wrought on the rest of psychology, and the scientific ideology of precision and irrelevance that had descended on both psychology and culture as a result. Alternately, one of them gave a glimpse of what a humanistically infused psychology of the future might also look like.

First, the coming psychology would focus on human beings rather than animals as objects of devoted study. Second, it would study the whole person, by which Murray meant all the salient and essential parts, properties, or aspects of a personality, as well as personality as an organ or a system in the sense that the whole is always greater than the sum of the parts. Third, it would study the historic personality—the whole person from birth to death, or from birth till the present moment of its existence, or from one to another point in the life span. Fourth, it would investigate the much neglected interior, experiential, phenomenological, or existential aspect of personality, which Murray took to be a basic and essential component to the external, behavioral component. Fifth, is the on-going study of personality in nature, society, and culture, rather than the study of thoughts, feelings, and acts in an artificial laboratory situation. Sixth, a humanistically oriented psychology of the future would encompass the largely neglected positive, joyful, and fruitful experiences of a person's life, as well as its most admirable dispositions and endeavors. Seventh, it would pay attention to a miscellany of concepts, such as that of choice or decision, and that of voluntary action or will, which were eliminated by both behaviorism and Freudianism, but are indispensable, as Rank insisted and May pointed out, to an adequate humanistic psychology. Finally, the eighth element is what Murray referred to as a philosophy of life or a system of desirable values to be experienced in conduct as time goes on. It is at this point that the humanistic psychologist steps out of his or her traditional scientific role, that of describing and conceptualizing the values entertained by others, and becomes a selector or creator of values in his own right.

The three alters then began all talking at once about Freud, Jung, Adler, McClelland, Goldstein, Maslow, Rogers, and Allport, as well as Robert White and Erik Erikson, so Murray decided that right there was a good place to end the keynote talk.

The problem was, however, that the new lights emerging on the scene had their own agenda, so that there was not exactly continuity of content between the old and the new theories. At the same time, researchers such as Maslow, Rogers, and May were in the process of leaving their positions as psychotherapists and professors within the mainstream culture of the East Coast establishment for more innovative opportunities in California. As well, most of the humanistic psychologists were only a few years younger than their counterparts in the older personality theory, and within a few years after that would themselves be either dead or have retired from the scene.

Also in 1964, the *Transparent Self* appeared, by Sidney Jourard, a statement about the process of self-actualization, in which the projected self and the real self within are in congruence.[49] Self-disclosure, its central theme, was defined by Jourard as the accurate portrayal of the self to others. Jourard (1926–1974) was an important figure in the development of humanistic psychology as a legitimate academic field of inquiry that pioneered in self-disclosure and body awareness. Born a Canadian, he took an MA at the University of Toronto in 1948 and the PhD in clinical psychology from the University of Buffalo in 1953. His dissertation was on the ego strength as measured by the Rorschach. He then produced a series of papers on body-cathexis and the self, focusing on the ideal self versus the real person.[50] He also developed an instrument to assess the extent of the discrepancy, the Jourard Self-Disclosure Questionnaire.

During this time jourard taught at Emory University and the University of Alabama Medical College. He joined the faculty at University of Florida in 1958. That year he also published papers on self-disclosure, and his first book, *Personal*

Adjustment (1958).[51] His emphasis then turned to the dynamics of psychotherapy, particularly the I–Thou relationship that developed between patient and therapist instead of an attitude of manipulation.[52] These insights came from his private practice which he pursued for 20 years.

When the *Transparent Self* came out in 1964, it created a sensation. Later he would be elected president of the newly formed American Association for Humanistic Psychology. After *The Transparent Self*, Jourard's writing took a distinctly existentialist turn. He began publishing in the existentialist journals, dialoging in public with known figures of the movement, meanwhile criticizing experimental reductionism in psychological science and writing on intersubjectivity and the experimenter bias effect.[53] He followed with three more books, *Disclosing Man to Himself* (1968), *Self-disclosure* (1971), and *The Healthy Personality: An Approach from the Viewpoint of Humanistic Psychology* (1974).[54] This last work went through four editions by 1980.

The last 10 years of his life he gave up private practice and did workshops and seminars on encounter at Esalen and elsewhere. He died unexpectedly at the age of 48 when an old antique sports car he was working under suddenly collapsed, and humanistic psychology lost one of its leading lights.

Also in 1964, Adrian van Kaam's *Religion and Personality* appeared.[55] The paperback edition followed in 1968. The work was significant for several reasons. It advocated for a growth-oriented dimension to personality. It acknowledged an individualized psychology of self-realization, but at the same time, it equated spirituality with the organized religious teachings of Catholicism, which empowered others in the pastoral counseling movement and the field of the psychology of religion who were ordained in specific denominations to speak to the process of spiritual self-realization through their respective denominational teachings. It also brought pastoral counselors more deeply into the humanistic movement in psychology and allied humanistic psychology with the psychology of religion.

Author of at least 30 books and hundreds of articles, van Kaam was a Dutch phenomenologist and an ordained Spiritan Catholic priest who earned his doctorate in psychology at Case Western Reserve, but whose major ideas, which he variously referred to as Formative Spirituality or Formation Anthropology, originated from his earlier work in Holland in the 1940s.[56] Van Kaam entered a Catholic community, the Spiritans, when he was 12. He had received a classical humanistic education from the gymnasium as a young man and continued to study philosophy and theology in seminary when the Germans invaded Holland. Due to logistical problems he was kept out of the seminary during the infamous Hunger Winter of 1944–1945, being forced to alternately hide and live on forged papers in the south, and working with the Dutch resistance to gather food for the starving populace. His ordination to the priesthood had to be delayed until after the war, in July of 1946 to be exact.

During his training, he had befriended another seminarian, Marinus Scholtes, whose life was profoundly mystical, but who died at age 21. Years later, van Kaam and a group of spiritual travelers he had gathered around him, including his colleague, Doctor Susan Muto, edited and published the young man's manuscript,

Become Jesus: The Diary of a Soul Touched by God.[57] The project brought laity together with clergy and strengthened the already established (in 1979) Epiphany Association. "Epiphany" means appearance or manifestation of the mystery to human beings in their distinctive humanness, which became van Kaam's guiding theme. The pioneering group in the Netherlands prior to and during the war was led by a former Benedictine who was the head of the choir in van Kaam's parish. Anton Toneman used the music of the church to spread the humanistic spirit of the Benedictines. Through others in the group, van Kaam was touched by a distinctively Dutch spirituality with its own ecclesial-experiential expression that had developed in Holland over the centuries.

In this line of thought, discursive meditation was not the same as contemplation. Contemplation transcends the discursive analytical mind. It grants one the grace of quiet presence. So an understanding of the approach to the unfolding of the spiritual life for each person was necessary before the experience of the actual revelations of the spirit could take place. These early pioneers wished to renew, to some degree, the classic experiential humanistic spirituality of their faith groupings.

The focus of attention was on the disclosure of one's own unique-communal life call:

> Was I being faithful to Christ, the Church, the Gospel, or not? The masters have much to say on this point, both humanistically and spiritually. What we were doing then, I am still doing now. It is the work I call formation theology to distinguish it from the first and most necessary study of informational theology. It is the art and discipline of giving form to one's faith experience as served by an ecclesial humane formation tradition. It is an approach to theological reflection that develops in respectful dialogue with our personal and shared humanity and its treasures of true humanism.[58]

After the war was over and van Kaam was reunited with his other seminarians, he completed his studies, graduated first in his class, and was inducted into the priesthood in 1946. Thereafter, he was assigned to teach courses in both philosophical anthropology and the philosophy of science at the Seminary.

When the then Vatican Secretary of State, Giovanni Baptista Montini, later Pope Paul VI, learned of his project he arranged through the proper channels of authority for van Kaam to be freed to pursue this unique way of thinking about the person as distinctively human under the then Dutch Life Schools of Formation for Young Adults. Then, in the early 1950s the then president of Duquesne University in Pittsburgh came to van Kaam's Seminary, spoke with him at length, and invited him to come to teach at Duquesne, where he wanted van Kaam to establish in the Psychology Department a new track called "psychology as a human science." Van Kaam had no degree in psychology, but the President foresaw no problem, provided the young priest was willing to get a PhD in psychology while pioneering this new approach. Receiving permission to do so and following his arrival in the United States in 1954, van Kaam taught his first courses in the department. Then he was set free to study at three universities. At Case Western University in Cleveland he worked with Calvin Hall, a historian of personality theory. At the end of his work there, he went on to study at the University of Chicago under Carl Rogers. He also went to the Alfred Adler Institute where he met, among others, Professor Heinz Ansbacher. After that he studied under Abraham Maslow of Brandeis University. His doctoral dissertation for Case Western was on the "Experience of Really Feeling Understood by a Person." At Duquesne, van Kaam continued to develop psychology as a human science and presented his version to other faculty, such as Amedeo Giorgi.

To build psychology as a distinctively human science, he turned to all the previous writing and research he had done in formation anthropology, which he had already developed in Holland. He translated this work into psychological language. In due course he published seven volumes about the field called *formative spirituality*, volumes in which he laid out the basics of formation science and anthropology. As it was, in the years between 1954 and 1963, he translated this work into humanistic psychological terminology with some implicit references to formation theology.

In those early years, he was also a new voice in the field of existential psychology, which he based uniquely on the Thomistic structure of "essence-existence." The same year he published *Religion and Personality*, he published a breakthrough book titled, *Existential Foundations of Psychology*,[59] his statement on a humanistic anthropological psychology. It contains certain insights pertaining to an anthropological phenomenology, is still considered a basic text in this field, and once issued it was reprinted many times over.

To van Kaam's surprise, the book evoked tremendous interest. He was invited to speak in many places. Maslow invited him to teach his courses at Brandeis University for a whole year when he went on sabbatical. He was invited to Harvard to speak to the faculty and students of psychiatry. Soon, he would become internationally known, as he became even further immersed in humanistic psychology and its adherents. These included theorists like Andras Angyal, under whom he studied at Brandeis, Roberto Assagioli, Charlotte Bühler, who came to Duquesne and who published an article in his journal, and of course, there was Viktor Frankl. Frankl visited Duquesne on several occasions, and van Kaam stayed at his home in Austria. He remembered Kurt Goldstein, whom he had met at Brandeis as well and later visited with him at his home in New York. There was also Sidney Jourard who came several times to van Kaam's sessions at Duquesne, as did Gordon Allport.

The positive response was gratifying. Van Kaam said he simply presented the main lines of the humanistic formation anthropology he had developed in Holland, but he put it into a kind of psychological terminology enabling him to stress the humanness of this psychology. These travels kept him in contact with all kinds of people. He attracted a following and got a certain name among colleagues in the field of existential psychology like Rollo May and Henry Elkin and the man who had trained him in client-centered therapy, Carl Rogers.

At Duquesne, van Kaam formed a group of people who would try to integrate into psychology, humanistic, phenomenological, existential, and anthropological thinking. Duquesne was a unique school in the 1960s and 1970s, its so-called creative golden age. Van Kaam himself edited *Review of Existential Psychology and Psychiatry* and published three classics together with numerous articles.[60]

Meanwhile, new developments in humanistic psychology were accelerating within both mainstream psychology and the burgeoning psychotherapeutic counterculture. In 1965, Fritz Perls, Charlotte Selver, and Will Schutz established themselves at Esalen. Thereafter, gestalt therapy, experiential encounter, and sensitivity training groups experienced phenomenal growth after 1969. In 1966, an innovative program in humanistic psychology at Sonoma State College was launched as part of the school's extension program, and within this context, Eleanor Criswell, a professor of psychology there, first proposed the formation of a Humanistic Psychology Institute, envisioned as the PhD granting wing of the new movement. In 1971, along with co-sponsorship with AAHP, this program was officially launched, and, in 1981 became fully accredited as an MA and PhD program in psychology, organizational systems, and human science under the present name of the Saybrook Graduate School and Research Center.

Also, by the late 1960s, the new humanistic orientation was reaching into sociology, anthropology, nursing, dentistry, and elsewhere. In 1968, Harvard Business School Professor Anthony Athos published *Behavior in Organizations*,[61] a text, inspired by the theories of Maslow and Rogers, which helped to launch the new field of organizational behavior in business schools throughout the United States. In 1969, West Georgia College in Carrolton, Georgia, founded an official graduate program in humanistic psychology, now in its 38th year. These events heralded the establishment of other academic programs elsewhere, such as PhD program in the history of consciousness at the University of California at Santa Cruz, as well as undergraduate programs at Johnson College at the University of the Redlands, Antioch College in Ohio, and Goddard in Vermont. Humanistic psychology also found one of its largest venues within the field of pastoral counseling, especially with the development of the Graduate Theological Union in Berkeley.

Humanistic psychology, meanwhile, was also drawing the occult and the theosophical into its circle, movements previously associated historically with spiritualism, which now were seen as more properly psychological. A case in point was the Doubleday edition of Dane Rudhyar's, *The Astrology of Personality*, which appeared in 1970.[62] The work was first published by an occult press in 1936 and reprinted in the Netherlands in 1963. By 1970, it had become a different text altogether, now drawing on the work of Jung and Maslow for an understanding of the process of self-realization and the use of astrology to achieve it. Mainstream psychologists cringed at the very sound of the title, as any association of personality with parapsychology, the occult, or anything having to do with astrology was considered the height of charlatanry and unworthy of a scientist to take seriously. Meanwhile, millions of people were using the various astrological systems as a language of inner experience with which to pursue the expansion of consciousness. The major transformation in public attitude was that traditionally astrology had been associated with magic, or, as applied to personality, it was thought to be in the esoteric schools something to be transcended. The rise of humanistic psychology focused it as an interior language related to personal growth.

Also, in 1971, against the better judgment of the officers of AAHP, which saw itself as a countercultural organization, and as a measure of how widespread the humanistic impulse had become even in American academic and clinical psychology, a group of influential psychologists within the American Psychological Association gathered enough signatures to found Division 32, the Division of Humanistic Psychology. The division is now in its 34th year of existence, and it maintains both a newsletter and an APA approved journal, *The Humanistic Psychologist*.[63]

At the same time Division 32 was being launched, similar developments were occurring out in the American psychotherapeutic counterculture at large. Chief among these was a major statement on life span development from a humanistic perspective by Charlotte Bühler and Fred Massarik. Massarik was on the faculty at UCLA and played a major role in launching organizational systems theory within business management. Bühler was another case altogether.

If Maslow was considered the Father of humanistic psychology, then Charlotte Malachowski Bühler might be considered its Mother.[64] Charlotte Bühler, German émigré psychologist who specialized in life span development and humanistic psychology, also made significant contributions in education, family studies, child psychology, psychological testing, clinical psychology, projective tests, and psychotherapy.[65] The existential humanistic psychologist, James Bugental, a colleague and close friend, characterized her as a formidable person who knew her own mind and set about doing things the way she believed they should be done. She could be imperious, humble, tough, gentle, petty, generous, formal, companionable, creative, and curiously blind. Before she immigrated to the United States, one writer characterized her as a cross between a typical Viennese social butterfly and an intellectual Prussian barracuda.[66] Tom Greening remembered that she and her husband Karl never achieved the recognition in the United States that they had in Europe, probably because of her attitude, but also because the Bühlers were neither psychoanalysts nor members of the Jewish refugee community (Charlotte herself was half Jewish, reared as a Protestant).

She was born in 1893 in Berlin, the eldest of two children. Her father was an architect and her mother an accomplished musician. She developed an interest in psychology and cognition at a young age, but wanted an answer to the big questions, such as "what is the essence of human nature?" When she read Ebbinghaus, she found him too atomistic. The penchant for the larger, more all-encompassing view never left her. She went on to study psychology at universities in Freiburg and Kiel, came briefly under the influence of Karl Stumpf in Berlin and was influenced by the early gestaltists. There she became interested in the "Aha! Experience," the experience of sudden insight. Stumpf sent her to Munich to study with Karl Bühler, who had named the phenomenon. At Munich she came under the influence of Oswald Külpe, whose student, Karl Bühler, became her advisor, upon Külpe's death.

Both began with a mutual interest in cognitive thought processes, but soon embarked on a whirlwind relationship. They were married in 1916. She was 23, he was 37. A year later she had her first child, received her PhD in 1918, and a year after that gave birth to their second child. Her dissertation, *Das Märchen und die Phantasie des Kindes*, was on children's fairy tales. In 1920, she took a job working for the school board as an employee of the Prussian government at the *Techniche Hochschule* in Dresden. There she began to collect diaries as a way to study the interior experiences of adolescent girls. Eventually she collected some 130 case studies from seven different countries, including the United States, and used them to write her book on the psychology of adolescence, *Das Seelenleben des Jugundlichen* (1922),[67] a work widely read in Germany and Austria.

In 1923, she and her family moved to Vienna, where Karl Bühler became a professor at the University and began to conduct research at the Vienna Psychological Institute, which he founded.[68] Charlotte began as an unpaid *privatdozent* and rose up in the ranks and became an associate professor (also unpaid). She was characterized as exploitative, dictatorial, and heavy handed as a teacher, meanwhile running the Vienna Institute with her husband as a major center of mainstream scientific research into the 1930s.

Psychoanalysis, for instance, was not permitted to be discussed. Yet her efforts led to major advances in child development and a cohesive group of free-thinking scientists. She also studied and traveled widely during this period. She went to Teachers College, Columbia University to study child and adolescent psychology with Edward Thorndike from 1924 to 1925, deciding the behaviorists were too molecular and too narrow in their thinking. Later in her experimental career, she would try to blend methods of describing behavior with phenomenological accounts presented by parents, teachers, and the children themselves. Her emphasis was, rather, more toward gestalt psychology, and the experimental science that characterized the reputation of the Institute Clinic. She became a visiting professor at Barnard College as a Rockefeller Fellow in 1929 and developed consultation work at child guidance centers in England, Holland, and Norway. When she returned from Columbia in 1925, she received a 10-year grant from the Rockefeller Foundation to fund her on-going work at the Vienna Institute's Child Guidance Center. Her research was also supported by the Ministry of Vienna in service of a school reform movement occurring at the time. However, her research was supposed to be confined to the goals of the school board, from which she often strayed. After one episode of criticism, she was remembered as writing:

> It is becoming clearer that we in youth psychology, as in psychology in general, cannot proceed from single investigations, but must ask ourselves: how does the growing person gradually gain his relationships to the world, its laws, tasks and possibilities? ... One sphere after the other opens itself to them, some of them through the school; that is its psychological significance.[69]

During the years that Karl Bühler headed the Institute and Charlotte served as chief administrator, there were many important students. There was Paul Lazarsfield, an educational statistician, who later became a famous sociologist in the United States. He was the son of Sophie Munk Lazarsfield, a well-known radical Adlerian analyst who practiced in both Vienna and New York. Marie Jahoda had been his first wife. She did research in the causes of anti-Semitism, became famous for her work on the F-scale in Adorno et al.'s study *The Authoritarian Personality* (1950) and later wrote a scientific critique of psychoanalysis, *Freud and the Dilemmas of Psychology* (1977).[70] Egon and Else Frenkel-Brunswick were two others under the Bühlers who immigrated to the United States. The list is long and distinguished, including Rowena Ansbacher, Lotte Danziger, Rudolf Ekstein, Fritz Redl, Rene Spitz, Edith Weisskopf, and others.[71]

After the Fascists took control of Vienna in 1933 and the Rockefeller grant dried up, the Bühlers got up their own private subscription fund to keep the Vienna Institute going. But when Karl was arrested by the Nazis in 1938, they made plans to immigrate to the United States. The Emergency Committee in Aid of Displaced Foreign Psychologists of the APA found a position for Karl in Minnesota and Charlotte followed in 1940.

She held a faculty position at the College of Saint Catherine in St. Paul, Minnesota. Later in 1941, she established a child guidance center in Worcester, Massachusetts, after which, back to the Midwest, she worked as a clinical psychologist at the Minneapolis General Hospital. Overall, Samantha Ragsdale notes that the Bühlers did not immediately adjust to American culture and were not well received by academic departments. The situation was so difficult that she did no writing between 1940 and 1950.[72]

The Bühlers moved to California in 1945, where Charlotte worked as a clinical psychologist at the Los Angeles County Hospital from 1945 to 1953. There, according to one source, she became a premier diagnostician and, despite her earlier opposition, a practicing psychoanalyst. She also served as assistant clinical professor of psychiatry at the University of Southern California Medical School for a portion of those years. Around this time, she also obtained US citizenship. In 1953, she began a private practice in Los Angeles, in Beverly Hills, identifying strongly with the new movement soon to be called humanistic psychology. She knew Carl Rogers, Gordon Allport, and Abraham Maslow, whose humanistic psychology was very much in accordance with her own, but her closest colleagues were Fred Massarik, at UCLA, and James Bugental, a theorist and psychotherapist in the tradition of existential-humanistic psychology. She became actively involved in the founding of the *Journal of Humanistic Psychology*, serving on its editorial board, and a founding member of the American Association for Humanistic Psychology. She later became a president of the Association. At the same time, she began to publish on humanistic psychology and its meaning, blending the ideals of the movement with her own theories.[73] However, she never produced a definitive work on her theories of personality and development across the life span.

We get a glimpse of this fusion in an introductory chapter on "The General Structure of the Human Life-cycle," which she published in *The Course of Human Life: A Study of Goals in the Humanistic Perspective*, co-edited with Fred Massarik.[74] There, she maintained that the life cycle has ten basic properties:

1) Each life cycle belongs to one individual. There is a maturational order, a sequence whose speed and quality can be influenced by learning and the impact of emotional experiences, as well as the intentional exploitations of one's gifts and opportunities. The life history contains the whole of the individual as he or she emerges in a given time and place. In the end the life terminates and what remains are evidences of the life in the stream of history.

2) The life cycle is of limited duration. We may live on in the memory of others, or in monuments we have created, there may even be an afterlife, but the physical life ends upon death.

3) Individual development proceeds according to a predictable ground plan. Periods of rapid growth are followed by plateaus of slower development and proliferation at that level, called stationary growth. These are followed by other distinct periods leading to the peak in midlife. Decline to varying degrees follows. Sexual activity, for instance, starts at the end of the first major growth period and stops before or during the final period of decline.

4) The phasic character of the ground plan constitutes the fourth element.

5) The succession of normally irreversible phases with definite direction is called development and represents the fifth property of the life cycle. In one's creative mentality, however, we find the exception to this rule, as either regression or self-actualization can occur at any time throughout the life cycle.

6) The individual remains continually active throughout the various phases. Circumstances change and the person continually attempts to adapt and consciously change conditions. Motives and goals play a major role.

7) Needs, which never let up, determine direction, except to the extent that goals of lifetime fulfillment and personal self-realization override them. Conscience rooted in the self instead of social rules can predominate. Thus, Bühler rejects Freud's assessment of thwarted life expectations as brilliant but normative and not in any way providing for the creative impulses of the self. Transcendence and the subconscious can be entirely new factors. Horney's conception of the whole person is inborn, while for Jung it is achieved. These are at least expressive of the true possibilities for the actualization of personal potential. She then discussed Gardner Murphy's conception of the self, as a reflection of three separate aspects of human nature. One is satisfaction of the biological organism; the other is maintained of the tastes and preference we have developed over a lifetime; and the third is our insatiable quest to understand our basic nature and to make this quest available to everyone.

8) The activities of the person are always goal directed. In this, she relied heavily on the studies of David McClelland on need for achievement.[75] At the same time, however, Bühler believed that inwardly directed goals reach toward existential authenticity (Bugental), while outwardly directed goals reach toward conformity with social norms. Authenticity comes from the core of the organism's basic system (she cites Horney's "real self"). This process goes beyond ego boundaries, which lack self-direction if they become too externally oriented. Beyond the ego, the inwardly directed self then becomes, as Allport calls it, "this awesome enigma," at the core of our being. It appears there to be all encompassing in one moment, then appears to be a chimera, completely gone in the next. She cited Tillich's writing on ultimate concern – that in which we are prepared to place our highest belief, the most far-reaching goal.

9) The dualism of human purpose—to seek to achieve self-realization, yet to remain petty and ego centered, the conflict between our needs and our goals, the general struggle with the opposites in our psychic life.

10) The fact that we live in the present but also have a spontaneous orientation to the past and the future. This is one source for the conflict between the opposites.

Inwardly determined fulfillment she decided was at the core of a meaningful life. In this she described the theories of Victor Frankl and Rollo May, reminding readers of the profound implication of Tillich's position reflected in *The Courage to Be* (1952)[76]—that we must have the courage to be oneself despite the doubts one may suffer about the meaning of existence. She noted the correspondence of these ideas with those of her husband, citing Karl Bühler in 1929, when he characterized "anything as meaningful that functions as a contributory constituent to a teleological whole..."[77]

In 1969, Carl Rogers founded his own independent facility, The Center for the Study of the Person, in La Jolla, while Sutich and Maslow bolted from the AAHP and its journal that same year to found the *Journal of Transpersonal Psychology* and, soon, its supporting organization. Their primary intent was to shift their attention from the study of human emotional development to the development of a psychology of spirituality. Meanwhile, in 1968 the AAHP had held its annual conference at the Fairmount Hotel in San Francisco, and, rather than the usual staid presentation of intellectual papers, was criticized by the management for staging a snake dance through the lobby. That year, the AAHP newsletter also began listing growth centers around the United States for the first time, all of which were unrelated to university-based psychology programs. These events were strong indications that humanistic psychology had effectively been taken over by the human potential movement by that time.

At the meeting of AAHP in Silver Springs, Maryland, in 1969, the "A" in the organization's title, referring to "American," was officially dropped because it had become such an international movement. By 1972, conferences were being held in London, Stockholm, Moscow, Hong Kong, Canton, Peking, Tokyo, and Hawaii. The most distinguishing memory of the 1969 conference in Maryland, however, was the group of nude sun bathers in the hotel fountain. That year the new AHP also co-sponsored, with the Menninger Foundation, the first of several conferences on the Voluntary Control of Internal States, held at Council Grove, Kansas. These proved to be the important transitional meetings leading up to the formation of the Association for Transpersonal Psychology in 1973 and established technologies such as biofeedback and meditation as important methods in the new psychology. To cap these events, also in 1969, Charles Tart, psychologist at the University of California at Davis, released his pioneering text, *Altered States of Consciousness*,[78] which quickly became the bible of the new psychological movement.

Maslow was elected president of the American Psychological Association for the academic year 1968 and 1969, but suffered a heart attack and continued only in a diminished capacity. He died in 1970. Afterward, humanistic psychology as an academic discourse arising out of personality theory and motivational psychology became almost completely absorbed by the American psychotherapeutic counter-culture. There, it is generally thought to have remained largely to this day, having fragmented into three general streams: (1) transpersonal interest in meditation and altered states of consciousness; (2) experiential encounter groups and somatic body work therapy; and (3) radical political psychology. Human science now meant deconstructionism, constructivism, radical feminism, peace psychology, and critical thinking, particularly in the liberal enclaves of intellectual learning in California. This line was dominated by what we might loosely call the University of California at Berkeley interpretation of the Frankfurt School.

Despite valiant efforts to stem the rising tide of cognitive behaviorism, such as Amedeo Giorgi's trenchant phenomenological critique *Psychology as a Human Science* (1970), and publication of Irvin Child's *Humanistic Psychology and the Research Tradition: Their Several Virtues* (1973),[79] humanistic psychology as a force for shaping academic psychology has remained in eclipse. Currently, AHP has become more and more marginalized from mainstream academic psychology, both intellectually and financially. It still reflects a significant portion of the counter-culture psychotherapic movement, however, which probably accounts for a major-ity of the psychotherapeutic practice now going on in the United States. The *JHP* and Saybrook have spun off from AHP as independent organizations with a life and structure of their own. Division 32 has remained a small division within the APA, alternately having harbored and jockeyed for position with the now disbanded Transpersonal Psychology Interest Group, which has never been able to achieve an independent status of its own from its humanistic parent. Human science scholars at one point found a venue at Saybrook and to a limited extent in Division 32 and in other of the innovative independent programs in psychology, such as the Institute for Transpersonal Psychology and the California Institute for Integral Studies. In these groups the split between the political radicals and the mystics of the 1960s contin-ues unabated. Qualitative methods reign, but the even newer trend to emerge is the ideal of race, class, and gender, compled with a turn back toward reductionistic main stream psychology.

Laura Perls and Natalie Rogers

Behind the first-generation founders of existential-humanistic and transpersonal psychology stand many interpretations of just what constitutes personality, its trans-formation, and how to achieve it. One of these is the experiential psychodynamics of Laura Posner Perls, wife of Fritz Perls, co-founder of gestalt therapy. Perls's writings made gestalt therapy a primary mainstay of the psychotherapeutic counterculture in the 1960s, influencing movements such as est (Erhard Seminar Training, always represented in lower case) and neurolinguistic programming, particularly dur-ing the 7 years Perls took over Esalen Institute for his own purposes between 1964 and 1971.[80] By then, he had separated from his wife and was espous-ing his mature (or immature) system focused on an experiential psychology of self-realization, an awakening of the senses, and consciousness in the here and now.

Gestalt therapy was the title Fritz coined to describe what was an amalgamation of psychoanalysis, existentialism, and holism, as described by Jan Smuts, whose work Perls had known from his years in South Africa, where Smuts had been the Prime Minister.[81] Laura Perls had never liked the choice, but Fritz Perls had worked briefly with Kurt Goldstein for a few months at Frankfurt and also dedicated one of his books to Max Wertheimer. So the name stuck. But the historians of experimental laboratory-oriented gestalt psychology, such as Mary Henle, later vehemently protested any association between Fritz Perls's gestalt therapy and gestalt psychology, defined as the tradition of Wertheimer, Koffka, and Köhler.[82]

However, Paul Shane, an existential-humanistic and transpersonal scholar and gestalt therapist, discovered a copy of Laura Perls's dissertation in the early 1980s in a shoe box, which he had found in a closet in Chicago. In German, the dissertation was an experimental laboratory study on the gestalt theory of color contrasts, which, under her maiden name of Laura Posner, Laura Perls had submitted successfully for the PhD under Adamar Gelb, at Frankfurt in 1933.[83] The smoking gun, in other words, was held by Laura Perls, not Fritz. He turned out to be the brilliant intuitive clinician, while she was the great intellect with the scientific background in their relationship. By the time he arrived at Esalen, however, all that was behind Fritz, who had freely appropriated from his ex-wife, his colleagues, and his friends, largely without attribution, which he had rolled over into his experience as a skilled clinician to construct his own system. Laura is only sometimes acknowledged as a co-founder of gestalt therapy, when, in fact, she was a prime mover in its development.[84]

The two of them shared, however, the vision of personality as a total psychophysical system, and they employed techniques designed to develop the intuitive, sensory, and emotional dimensions of the person. The intellectual, they left to the academy and to science, which in the history of Western thought had always treated everything as an appendage of the head. Their therapeutic regime they took as a necessary corrective. Laura, in particular, began to develop a dimension of experiential bodywork based on movement therapy.[85]

The essential but unanswered question for historians of psychology is how Laura Perls transmuted an experimental laboratory oriented but holistic psychology of perception into an experiential psychology of self-realization. It was a particularly feminine thing to do, as it was the direction her own personality took in its development, but it was based on her conception of science, first in terms of how we perceive the world in terms of wholes and then by considering personality as a total gestalt and defining the methods by which one transmutes those things from a psychology of the person in the mind of the teacher to the experiential life of the student or patient without losing sight of the whole human being. The calumny of the situation was that she was not acknowledged for her scientific background, probably because it was too great a leap to explain at the time within the intensity of the experiential milieu, except with reference to depth psychology, while at the same time her contribution was appropriated without proper attribution by Fritz, in all likelihood because she was a woman. The process by which she herself negotiated this transition has yet to be investigated, however.[86]

A second example of a wholistic psychology of personality anchored in a dynamic psychology of the unconscious is the program of Creative Connections developed by Natalie Rogers. Her father, Carl Rogers, had gone through several major phases of his therapeutic system, from empirical measurement of client-centered therapy to a science of the whole person, to a person-centered science, ending up in the more experiential domain of self-actualization in the context of group work, especially on an international level. Natalie Rogers worked intensively with her father during this last phase of his career, at the same time endeavoring to establish her autonomy from him through her association with radical feminism.[87] While her approach to a psychology of the whole person is intuitive, experiential, and somatic, its main focus building on art and movement therapy, it is a psychology of personality change nonetheless in the genre of an existential-humanistic and transpersonally oriented depth psychology.[88] The question for a post-modern psychology is what form the study of personality will take if the epistemology underlying how personality shall be studied scientifically is transformed to accommodate the experiential and the intuitive, in order that dynamic psychology shall still constitute a science of the whole person?

Transpersonal Psychology

A relatively new branch of American psychology that developed after 1969 out of humanistic psychology that focuses on meditation and altered states of consciousness became known as transpersonal psychology. While attempts have been made to suggest that transpersonal psychology is really very old, reaching back even to the spiritual concerns of the classical civilizations from antiquity, historically, it is an American phenomenon of the mid-20th century. One could stretch the point and say that it had an early era of godfathers in figures such as William James, Carl Jung, and Paul Tillich. William James's *Varieties of Religious Experience*[89] established the primacy of mystical experience for a cross-cultural comparative psychology of the subconscious. Then in 1905, James used the term transpersonal in a course prospectus at Harvard to describe the concept of "outside of" or "beyond" in relation to how humans experience the world. In 1914, C. G. Jung described *ueberpersonlich*, translated as "superpersonal" at the time, which, in 1942, he retranslated as "transpersonal."[90] Also, in 1954 Paul Tillich employed the term in *Love, Power, and Justice*[91] to refer to the ground and abyss within us.

Transpersonal themes certainly appeared between the 1940s and the 1960s in the works of such seminal writers as Aldous Huxley, who wrote *The Perennial Philosophy* (1945), having studied a variety of the world's religious systems, and *The Doors of Perception* (1954), after his own psychedelic experiences; Alan Watts followed with such early works as *The Way of Zen* (1957), *Psychotherapy East and West* (1961), and *The Joyous Cosmology* (1962).[92]

Insofar as transpersonal psychology was an outgrowth of humanistic psychology, it had a distinctly humanistic phase throughout the 1960s when humanistic psychologists were still a viable part of academic discourse in psychology. During this time, Maslow's self-actualizing personality and his hierarchy of needs continued to be discussed. Rogers's client-centered therapy emphasized empathy and unconditional positive regard for the client who was a growing, evolving organism, not merely a statistical average or a damaged individual. And Rollo May continued to write on the existential nature of the psychotherapeutic hour into the 1960s.

As we have indicated previously, the *Journal of Humanistic Psychology* was founded in 1961, while the American Association for Humanistic Psychology was launched in 1962. The main purpose of the Association was to support the journal. The First Old Saybrook Conference was held in Connecticut, co-sponsored by AAHP and Wesleyan University in November of 1964, which attempted to legitimize humanistic psychology within the academy. It was destined to be a failed agenda, however, as humanistic psychology was about to become fractionated and then almost completely absorbed into the psychotherapeutic counterculture, where it began to look more transpersonal, experiential, and radically political than humanistic.

The Old Saybrook Conference was followed in 1966 by such benchmark events as the Humanistic Theology Conference at Esalen.[93] This was a seminal event for many reasons. Maslow and Sutich were attending a conference at Esalen on the dialogue between humanistic psychologists and organized religion. They were sitting in an open seminar room with easy chairs exchanging ideas, when suddenly Fritz Perls and his entourage burst into the room. Fritz listened for a few moments and quickly determined in his own mind that nothing was really happening, so he dropped down on his stomach and slithered across the seminar room, finally attaching himself to the speaker's leg. Chaos ensued as some like Maslow and Sutich objected to the interruption, while Fritz's entourage were advocating the radical overthrow of speeches of any kind in favor of direct experience.

Both Maslow and Sutich left the conference immediately and therefore prematurely, convinced that humanistic psychology had become captivated by experiential extremists. They had already believed that what the new psychology needed was more of a focus on spirituality and higher states of consciousness. Events culminated in their overnight departure from humanistic psychology in 1969, when they turned over the reins of both the *Journal of Humanistic Psychology* and their involvement in the AHP to others and founded instead the *Journal of Transpersonal Psychology*, and its subsequent Association. They poured all their attention into this newest movement, which came to emphasize meditation and altered states of consciousness. As a result, many of the major popular voices in humanistic psychology–Elana Rubenfeld, George Leonard, Karl Pribram, Stanley Krippner, and others, followed them and suddenly became the keynote speakers at the new transpersonal conferences.

Maslow on Transcendence

Actually, Maslow was something of a paradox. He never sought out the counterculture psychotherapeutic movement. It found him. One day in the early 1960s he and his wife Bertha were driving down Highway 1 in Big Sur, California and were a little uncertain where they were. They pulled into a driveway to ask for directions and, by accident, it turned out to be Esalen Institute. He quickly discovered that everyone was sitting around reading and talking about his books, so he stayed. Thereafter, he became somewhat of a reluctant prophet. He wanted mainstream psychology to hear his ideas about the growth-oriented dimension to personality and about his theory of motivation, but the group that warmed most to him was the irregulars who were taking drugs and who were dropping out of academia in ever increasing numbers. He was embraced as a guru of the counterculture movement, yet he was for the Vietnam War and had proclaimed himself an avowed atheist. He was also a member of the American Humanist Association, which had been founded by Madeline Murray O'Hare. B. F. Skinner was also a member. Maslow also swore like a trooper. When his heirs decided, to publish his journals, they contemplated eliminating all the four letter words, but then the entire thing no longer was coherent, so they left them. Popular guru he may have been, but he never put himself forward as a holy man.

If psychologists remember him, it is usually for his conception of the self-actualizing personality and for his hierarchy of needs. This was the product of his early work up to the 1950s, however. Twenty years later, he had looked into Chinese Taoism, written about peak and plateau experiences, and generally had different thoughts about the spiritual life. He never directly professed a belief in God, but it was enough that he understood that each person had deep spiritual instincts, regardless of the way they expressed them.

In this regard, a year before he died, within his characterization of the self-actualizing dimension of human personality, Maslow posited the recurring experience of transcendence.[94] This concept is crucial to understanding the nature of personality posed by the new psychology, its radically different model of consciousness, as well as the critique of reductionistic science that accompanied its formulations. In general, transcendence means the ability to go beyond the mere rational ordering of sense data alone and to admit the emotional and intuitive parts of the human equation into the mix. This favors some combination of qualitative and quantitative methods in psychology as a science, in some way more than just the sum of the parts. Psychologically, it means going from a restricted state of waking consciousness, in which all is concrete and firmly attached to external waking material reality, with the attendant belief that that is the only reality possible, to a wider, higher, and deeper state of awareness, which is accessed not through logic but through insight.

Transcendence, for Maslow, referred to the very highest and most inclusive or holistic levels of human consciousness, behaving, and relating, as ends rather than means, to oneself, to significant others, to human beings in general, to other species, to nature, and to the cosmos. Here, holism should be taken in the sense of hierarchical integration, which also includes cognitive and value isomorphism.[95] He gave 35 operational definitions of the term.

It meant loss of ego-centered awareness; it mean identifying with being motivation rather than deficiency-oriented motivation; it meant passing from a state of boredom into one in which we see each moment under the eye of eternity; it meant resign above culture to the universal sense of our humanity; it meant rising above one's past; it means rising above the lower needs of the self; it means to experience the mystical; it means to struggle and overcome death, sickness, and pain, and to lay aside bitterness and anger; sometimes it means just letting things be; it means going beyond the we–they polarity; it implies becoming metamotivated in the sense of identifying with a higher purpose; it means to go beyond one's conditioning, such as ignoring advertising, or as Frankl maintained, even rising about the conditions of the concentration camps; it means to value and honor one's own opinions, even when unpopular; it means to go beyond the introjected values of the Freudian superego and rely on the depth of one's own insights for which path to follow; it means relating to the possible as well as the actual; it means to rise above dichotomies to superordinate wholes; it means to go beyond the dictates even of one's own will; it means to surpass one's own performance; it means actualizing potential divinity within ourselves; it means to rise above ethnocentrism and mere patriotic fervor; but without relinquishing being anchored in one's indigenous roots; it means to live casually in heaven; it means to speak and witness with equanimity and calm abiding; it means that facts and values become one; it means relinquishing attachment always to the negative; it means non-attachment to space, which then allows miracles to happen anywhere; it means to be able to enjoy fulfillment; it means the transformation of fear into courage; it means the forgiveness of human imperfections; it means to be more inclusive with regard to differences in beliefs. So one can see that these definitions go much beyond the conceptions of personality posed by the trait theorists. The important difference is the epistemological frame of reference between the two models, where one posits a growth-oriented dimension to personality and the other does not.

The late 1960s ushered in an era marked by the first generation of people who actually started to call themselves transpersonal psychologists. The seminal event of 1969 was publication of Charles Tart's *Altered States of Consciousness*, a pioneering text in transpersonal psychology that covered everything from meditation and dream psychology to paranormal events and the transcendent experience.[96] At the same time, the Voluntary Controls Project at the Menninger Foundation under Elmer and Alyce Green, in cooperation with the Association for Humanistic Psychology convened the First Council Grove Conference on the Voluntary Control of Internal States,[97] held in the outback of the Kansas prairie. Psychedelic drugs, North American Indian Shamanism, meditation, Asian psychologies, and mystical states of consciousness were all discussed openly. Eventually, there would be four such conferences at Council Grove between 1969 and 1972, their significance being that they were the transition conferences between what was officially called the humanistic and transpersonal movements in American psychology. Afterward, the Council Grove conferences continued on, but in a more diffuse form, in different places and under different venues, having served their primary function, namely, helping the major players transition to the first conference of the American Association for Transpersonal Psychology, which was held at Vallombrosa Conference Center, in Palo Alto, California in 1973.[98]

In the interim, much had happened. In 1970, Montague Ullman and Stanley Krippner, co-researchers at the Maimonides Dream Laboratory in Brooklyn, published *Dream Studies and Telepathy*, a pioneering work describing 10 years of research in parapsychology from the standpoint of experimental laboratory science. The work first appeared as a monograph of the Parapsychology Foundation, a non-profit organization originally founded by the British psychic, Eileen Garrett. This was followed by *Dream Telepathy*, which appeared through Macmillan in 1973, with an introduction by Gardner Murphy. Here again, psychical research was a taboo subject in academic laboratory studies of personality. Ullman and Krippner, however, endeavored to show that in a cohort of 100 subjects, it was possible to demonstrate empirically that telepathic communication between a dreaming subject while asleep and a waking percipient was possible. Papers were also included by Louisa Rhine on the commonality of such phenomena, and Charles Honorton, suggesting that dreams could foretell the future.

Ullman was a physician and psychiatrist with psychoanalytic training, while Krippner was a PhD psychologist who had previously been director of the Kent State University Child Study Center in Ohio. Krippner went on to publish extensively on dreams, parapsychology, hypnosis, dissociated personality, creativity, psychedelics, and psychic healing, among other subjects. In 1978 he drew important parallels between parapsychology and humanistic psychology and was also known for his investigation of parapsychology going on in the Soviet Union.[99]

Also during that same period, Maslow had died in June, 1970 and Sutich geared up to carry on by himself. The next year the Association for Transpersonal Psychology was officially formed in Palo Alto. John Cunningham Lilly also published his *Center of the Cyclone* (1972), a book that linked positive healthy states of meditation, psychedelic drug use among professionals, and communication with dolphins.[100]

Then in 1972, Charles Tart published his pioneering statement on state-specific sciences in *Science*, main organ of the American Association for the Advancement of Science.[101] His opening argument made the case that young people who have had experiences deeper and wider and more profound than those typically accepted in normative science usually do not go into science as a vocation, largely because the way science is currently constituted; extreme prejudices often surround established scientists with regard to novelty, or ideas that do not fit their accepted paradigm. Such prejudices are actually not very scientific, because they represent belief statements of the scientist about the nature of ultimate reality, not established facts about it.

Altered States of Consciousness Tart presented as a case in point. Scientists who live only in the normal everyday waking state tend not to acknowledge altered states of consciousness, except perhaps sleep, coma, and death. Any reports of those experiences are going to be labeled dysfunctional or psychotic. Having experienced such states, however, puts the scientist in a position to be a more objective observer and to draw more valid conclusions. The problem is that we have well-developed norms for the everyday waking state, but none for altered states of consciousness. Tart's suggestion was the establishment of the validity of state-specific sciences, where particular states are understood to have their own separate reality, their own presuppositions, their own laws of operation, and their own special content. He used the example of psychedelic intoxication with marijuana as an example, where phenomenological investigation of the state is quite possible, but not acknowledged by externalists who simply dismiss any value to it out of hand. What is at stake, however, is that only certain types of personalities therefore enter science, further skewing our perception of what is real to that which is defined by only those who are attached by way of the senses to objects in the external material world alone. Recognizing alternate realities would also show how varied different states of waking consciousness are as well. For example, some people think in images, others in words. Some can voluntarily anesthetize parts of their body, most cannot. Some recall past events by imaging the scene and looking at the relevant details; others use complex verbal processes with no images. All of the different modes of being when attached to objects in the external material world through the senses constitute the different types of personalities. Psychological science, however, should be more than merely the elaboration of just the one possible state of consciousness.

Echoing these same sentiments, in 1973, Jay Haley published *Uncommon Therapy*, which for the first time brought Milton Erickson and his approach to the attention of a wide reading audience.[102] Erickson (1901–1980) was probably the most influential hypnotherapist in the United States in the second half of the 20th century, particularly in the psychotherapeutic counterculture. He was born Aurum, Nevada, in 1901 and raised on a farm in Wisconsin. He was known to be dyslexic and learned things very slowly. From an early age, he was also guided by blinding visions, which always had a profound influence on shaping his sense of normal consciousness by always suggesting there was something more beyond. At age 17, he contracted polio, and nearly died. Determined to survive, he developed innovative techniques of physiological self-control. At the same time, he became a keen observer of people and their motives. He attended the University of Wisconsin and earned both the PhD and the MD.

His professor for the course in Medical Psychology was the youthful Clark Hull, who had been assigned the course which had been previously taught by Joseph Jastrow, despite the fact that he knew nothing about the subject. When Erickson heard him speak on the first day, he knew right away that he knew more than the professor about the subject. From then on, Erickson, himself a first year medical student, was merciless in his questions, challenging Hull at every turn and exposing his ignorance on topics such as hypnosis and the voluntary control of internal states, about which Erickson knew a great deal. Hull took up the challenge and embarked on an extensive experimental research program testing various aspects of hypnosis and its effects.

This culminated in the first major work of Hull's career, *Hypnosis and Suggestibility: An Experimental Approach* (1933).[103] When he later got to Yale, where he spent the rest of his career, his colleagues told him that studying such a topic for an experimentalist was unseemly, so Hull immediately embarked on a completely different course of investigation, using the basics of animal rat learning to launch his massive project to reform scientific psychology around the hypotheticodeductive method.

The other key event of 1973, beyond the first ATP conference at the Vallombrosa Conference Center,[104] was that Stanislav Grof launched the International

Transpersonal Association, which held its first conference in Iceland. Grof's view of the transpersonal was quite different from that of others, principally because he was an MD psychiatrist, not a psychologist. He therefore put himself forward as embracing a much wider notion of spirituality, consciousness, and healing than the merely psychological. This means that the transpersonal movement continued to expand, but now along the lines of the respectively different visions of Sutich and Grof.

Meanwhile, in yet another series of milestones, in 1975 Robert Frager launched the California Institute of Transpersonal Psychology, the PhD granting wing of the formal California Transpersonal movement; Robert Ornstein published *The Nature of Human Consciousness* (1973); and Stan Grof published his now pioneering work, *Realms of the Human Unconscious* (1975).[105]

Physician, psychiatrist, founder of the International Transpersonal Association in 1977, the man who coined the term transpersonal for the movement in the first place, and formulator of the technique of Holotropic Breathwork, Grof was born in 1931 in Prague, Czechoslovakia. He received his MD from Charles University in Prague in 1957, and the PhD in Medicine at the Czechoslovakian Academy of Sciences in 1965. He was then trained as a Freudian psychoanalyst. Grof immigrated to the United States in 1967. He was invited as an assistant professor of psychiatry at Johns Hopkins and went on to become chief of psychiatric research at the Maryland Psychiatric Research Center where he worked with extensively with alcoholics using LSD therapy when it was still legal in 1973. He moved to California in 1967 and lived at Esalen in Big Sur as a scholar in residence for 12 years, developing his method of Holotropic Breathwork, a technique he found could produce the same alterations in consciousness formally associated with LSD therapy. He now teaches at the California Institute of Integral Studies.

Realms of the Human Unconscious: Observations from LSD Research (1975) was Grof's first book. It was a report of nearly two decades of research with LSD in a psychotherapeutic milieu, in which a cartography of internal states of consciousness was presented representing people who had gone into deep states of spiritual experience. Grof based his observations on thousands of LSD sessions he had conducted as an aid to psychoanalysis in Prague. LSD, he believed was a powerful adjunct in therapy when used under properly controlled conditions. After these encounters, even skeptics, scientists, and radical Marxists were suddenly interested in states of consciousness that transcended their normal everyday waking condition. His major contribution was an exposition of the mythic and religious dimensions of personality that were revealed and the fact that LSD, like sensory deprivation, meditation, the final hours of life, heightens one's own naturally occurring psychological experiences rather than creating something artificial based on the pharmacology of the inducing stimulus.

He identified four levels of consciousness. The first level is sensory distortion, which gives way to the second level, that of the psychodynamic—repressed memories and the symbolic expression of conflicts, which tend to appear sequentially in LSD therapy until the original precipitating cause is revealed, in which case its hidden symptomatology ceases and does not appear again. There is then the level of perinatal experiences, states which invoke images of one's own birth and death, as well as rebirth while still in the body. There is then the transpersonal level, a breakthrough into the highest kinds of mystical and ecstatic experiences. What the person then chooses to become after such experiences lies at the root of the transformed personality, for which we as yet have no adequate psychology.

Also in 1975, Ken Wilber, age 26, a student in psychology at the Bachelor's level who had taken a few graduate courses in chemistry, published his first article in the *Journal of Transpersonal Psychology*, "Psychologia Perennis: The spectrum of consciousness."[106] In it, Wilber tried to link the then current transpersonal movement with a larger monistic and esoteric movement that periodically made itself known in the history of Western thought. Most notable, the Theosophical Society fielded such a monistic interpretation in the late 19th century, while the Vedantic Swamis revivified it again in the mid-1940s in the United States. The success of the piece was largely due to the extensive rewriting and editing done on the manuscript by Sutich's assistant, Miles Vich.[107] The effect that it had was to inculcate the monistic ideology into the interpretation of transpersonal experiences and to launch an interpretive frame of reference that precluded pluralistic ways of knowing the ultimate. Since then, Wilber has consolidated his thinking under the rubric of non-dualism, essentially the position of Sri Auribindo and Haridas Chaudhuri before him.

A year later, in 1976, events continued to heat up that would soon usher in a second, younger generation of transpersonal psychologists. For some years, Anthony Sutich had been collecting his memoirs while he also helped to launch these new movements, among them, the Humanistic Psychology Institute, which became the original PhD granting wing of the American Association of Humanistic Psychology. He had even received funding from Werner Erhard, founder of est, to bring the appropriate archival material together in book form. Sutich, although totally paralyzed from the neck down since 1921, had no formal degrees of any kind, but was a published author, founding editor of two journals and two associations, had been grandfathered into the American Psychological Association, and was a fully licensed psychotherapist in the state of California. By 1976, he was in his seventies and had begun to have increasing health problems. He died that year, but not before formally finishing his manuscript on the founding of humanistic and transpersonal psychology. For this accomplishment, through the Humanistic Psychology Institute's doctoral program which he helped to found, he was awarded his Doctorate of Philosophy in psychology on his death bed by Eleanor Criswell, James Fadiman, and Stanley Krippner. He passed away the next morning.

The editorship of the *Journal of Transpersonal Psychology* passed immediately to Sutich's assistant, Miles Vich. Meanwhile, James Fadiman and Robert Frager published their pioneering textbook in personality theory that same year, *Personality and Personal Growth*, which has since gone into five editions.[108] It was the first English language textbook in psychology and in personality theory to incorporate chapters on non-Western psychology. These and similar events marked the beginning of a new phase of the transpersonal movement, when a younger generation of transpersonalists who have associated their careers with the term took over the helm and retrenched in the spirit of Maslow and Sutich, but according to their own respective agendas. These included, among others, Miles Vich, Francis Vaughan, Roger Walsh, and John Welwood, most of whom were enamored with the writings of Ken Wilber, and soon became his chief spokespersons.

The following year, Wilber published *The Spectrum of Consciousness* (1977) through the Kern Foundation, which was taken up by the younger transpersonalists who had been around Sutich and who now elevated Wilber to the status of both a Freud and a Darwin of the consciousness movement. Because of their support and due to the positive popular reception of his ideas, Wilber emerged as the spokesperson for the "consciousness paradigm" around the *Journal of Transpersonal Psychology*. Other competing views were subtly excluded.

Aside from individual events, such as publication of a long awaited first book, *Beyond Biofeedback* (1977),[109] by Elmer and Alyce Green, the end of the 1970s posed a major challenge to the younger transpersonalists, as the key founding pioneers had passed from the scene and the legacy was passed on to a new generation of voices. Quite by accidental fiat, Stan Grof and his circle, including his wife Christina and devoted students such as Terrence McKenna, emerged as voices for the international transpersonal movement. Grof founded the International Transpersonal Association in 1976. Ken Wilber's writings continued to proliferate in the trade press, making it appear that at least in reputation, the names of Grof and Wilber became the more visible, and were associated with transpersonal psychology.

Throughout the decade other figures continued to emerge in the public eye as well, some of whom already had a long history of involvement with the movement. Only a few can be mentioned, including Willis Harman, president of the Institute of Noetic Sciences, Stanford professor and university trustee who had helped launch the programs at Esalen the early 1960s; Beverly Rubik, former director of the Center for Frontier Sciences at Temple University, a biophysicist interested in healing and consciousness; Ralph Metzner, another humanistic and transpersonal pioneer from the early days of the movement who wrote about entheogens and consciousness, Theodore Roszak, trenchant social critic and co-founder of eco psychology; Robert McDermott, Goethe scholar and exponent of Rudolf Steiner; the parapsychologist and social anthropologist Marilyn Schlitz; and the continued writings of Saybrook faculty, such as Ruth-Inge Heinze, David Lukoff, Stanley Krippner, Donald Rothberg, and Jeanne Achterberg.

Highlighting the difference between the fledgling institutionalized structures of transpersonal psychology and transpersonal psychology as a general force within the psychotherapeutic counterculture, the Dalai Lama received the Nobel Peace prize in 1989, which elevated his status among psychotherapeutically oriented practitioners of meditation and other forms of Asian disciplines and reaffirmed the merger between psychotherapy and spirituality. This is particularly important because psychotherapists who were adherents of Asian forms of spiritual practice soon became the new generation of younger voices calling for the introduction of Asian ideas into Western psychology. The problem was they were mostly adherents of the new religions, which did not appear to have anything to do with the way scientific psychology was defined in the West. Their zeal hurt their reception, largely because they were Bhaktins, followers of the path of *bhakti*, or devotion to the guru, which was anathema to behavioral scientists who largely identify themselves as atheists and now Christians. Eventually, these Occidental devotees began to master scientific methods and the mechanics of blind peer review. Meditation as a therapeutic regime, for instance, soon won grudging acceptance because there was now a body of empirical data substantiating the devotee's former passionate claims regarding the effects of meditation on stress reduction and various psychosomatic illnesses.[110]

Meanwhile, abroad, in 1990 the European Transpersonal Association was formed, which currently consists of 15 member countries, operating independently of the International Transpersonal Association. Recently, many of these different streams met in cyberspace for the first international transpersonal psychology conference on the Internet, an event that lasted 3 weeks.

The present status of transpersonal psychology remains a shifting congeries. On the one hand, as it was recently characterized by one Hari Krishna devotee, it still looks like the Northern California cult of consciousness that claims to have a monopoly on ultimate truth—a mere offshoot of an outdated humanistic psychology, which, as a parent movement, has already faded from the scene. On the other hand, there is a psychospiritual revolution now going on out in modern culture that is thoroughly transpersonal in direction and outlook, making it appear that modern transpersonalists are at the cutting edge of one of the newest and most influential social movements of the 21st century. While the movement has flagged in the United States, it is continuing to experience a meteoric expansion in central European countries.

Defining the parameters of the transpersonal movement remains an educated guess. A series of oral history interviews with both humanistic psychologists and major transpersonal figures suggests that throughout the 1980s and 1990s three distinct wings of the transpersonal movement emerged:

(1) Those transpersonalists exemplified by Grof, who believe that transpersonal experiences only occur in an altered state of consciousness, and Charles Tart, who has argued for state-specific sciences. This group also includes those who are engaged in generating maps of consciousness, generating scientific studies for the effectiveness of mind/body medicine and alternative therapies, and theorists correlating brain states with states of mind; (2) those transpersonalists exemplified by Wilber, who are popular writers generating books in the trade press outside academia, some of whom see themselves as enlightened beings who derive their source of knowledge from loving devotion to the gurus who have advanced them in meditation. These figures tend to consider all the different paths as leading to the same highest state of non-dual consciousness; and (3) probably the largest group, with no identifiable spokesperson, no guru, no school, no sacred text, and no special method, made up of those who feel that the transpersonal is a dimension of their own personality that is revealed in ordinary experiences, which they take 1 day at a time.

Another approach to estimating the size of the population involved in transpersonal ideas is to look at the characteristics of a subset of that population and then look for estimates of those subpopulations for which there is data in the population at large. Thus, factoring in such statistics as those gleaned from the health food movement, the alternative medicine and holistic health movement, the approximate number of meditators in the United States, the number of unlicensed psychotherapists, and approximations on the size of the women's spirituality movement, and the total number of people born between 1946 and 1956—the so-called Baby Boom generation, the total number of people interested in personal growth and planetary transformation has been estimated at about 40,000,000.[111]

Their Methods of Research

If we consider psychological science to proceed from the more reductionistic and empirical forms of measurement, and the psychoanalytic to emphasize the clinical method, defined as a dyadic or group dynamic, we may say generally that the existential-humanistic and transpersonal traditions rely more on phenomenology and direct experience. Experimental designs, paper-and-pencil tests, and psychophysiological measures characterize scientific empiricism. Free association, dream analysis, and the method of symbolism characterize the psychodynamic approach. Within the spectrum of quantitative and qualitative methods, the existential-humanistic and transpersonal point of view employs, for instance, Giorgi's phenomenological psychological method, the more heuristic approaches of Bugental and Kvale, the in-depth interview and the case study method, the non-directive methods of Rogers, historical and archival methods borrowed from the arts and humanities, the techniques of textual scholarship from the field of religious studies, and also practices from specific spiritual traditions (see Fig. 10.3).

Note that the list constitutes a spectrum from quantitative to qualitative within the discussion of methodology in the natural, social, and human sciences, to clinical methods commensurate with using the psychotherapeutic hour as the living laboratory of personal growth and transformation. Beyond these are the more experiential approaches to self-knowledge, which constitute their own special form of research, leading off into the methods of philosophy, religion, the arts, and the humanities.

Experimental	Psychodynamic	Existential-Humanistic
The laboratory	The clinic	The life world
Objective	Subjective	Phenomenological
Experimental variables	The unconscious	Transcendence
Quantification	Interpretation	Direct experience
Statistics	Case studies	Personality as a Gestalt
Nomothetic	Ideographic	Interpersonal
Traits	Defense mechanisms	Altered States of Consciousness

Fig. 10.3 Three ways of knowing in psychology
Adapted from Rogers, C. R. (1964). Toward a science of the person. In T. W. Wann (Ed.), *Behaviorism and phenomenology: Contrasting bases for modern psychology* (pp. 109–140). Chicago: The University of Chicago Press.

At the quantitative end of the spectrum, the subject is an object in nature to be studied by the experimenter. Here, manipulation, prediction, and control rest solely with the experimenter, whether the object studied is the group or the individual. The degree of control depends on whether the method is more quantitative or more qualitative. In general, the more precise the measurement, the more focused the results. This is extremely important, because the more you focus, the less you can say about the big picture.

Within the existential-humanistic tradition, on the other hand, following the orientation of Wertheimer, Koffka, Köhler, and Lewin, personality is approached as a total gestalt. With an emphasis on qualitative methods, the experimenter's presence in the outcome of the research is taken more self-consciously into account. Quantitative researchers say this is bad science because it is so imprecise. From the point of view of human science, however, qualitative measures more closely approximate the vagaries of the real human condition. Precision is necessary to build a science. Relevance gets at the meaning of the situation for the person with regard to the process of self-realization. Between exact scientific measurement and personal meaning there is almost always an inverse relationship. When one goes up, the other usually goes down, until a science reaches a more advanced state of maturity, which psychology has yet to do.

Note also that the clinical method still encompasses the dyadic relationship, except now, instead of the experimenter–subject bond; it is the therapist–client relationship. Traditionally, most clinical methods, except for the introduction of the Rogerian, non-directive approach, retain the authoritative position of the therapist. In either case, the psychotherapeutic hour becomes a living laboratory for research. This violates the quantitative scientist's sensibilities, however, which accounts for the extreme differences between the clinical and the experimental methods. The experimental method presumes that only exact science can inform what goes on in the clinic. The clinical method presumes that the experimentalists are dealing with abstract theories, while the clinical situation generates its own kind of science. Or at least this was Freud's contention when he declared psychoanalysis a science that was independent of psychology, psychiatry, and neurology.

Historical methods, which purport to be the method of the human sciences, constitute a discipline that comes out of the humanities. This is what gives it a somewhat questionable status in the history of medicine, the history of science, and the history of psychology. Historians are not scientists, except where they qualified in the sciences and slipped into the field of history as converts. But there should be no mistake. People of the number are not the same as people of the book. An excellent experimentalist is not *ipso facto* and excellent scholar. This misunderstanding goes to the core of the existential-humanistic position, namely, that psychology is both an art and a science, while it continues to be taught as if it were purely a science. The humanistic rationale is that history as a discipline in the humanities is ideally suited to critique a pathological focus on scientism in psychology as well as creating a bridge between the sciences and the humanities.

Experiential methods include transformational forms of individualized research directly experienced by the individual, methods of group experience, or also the methods in the humanities and in religious studies, since, while these can be more purely scholarly kinds of pursuits, they elucidate a personal, more humanistic, and spiritual component of personality. At the same time, the experiential also encompasses the performing and the fine arts, since these more directly reveal meaning and experience.

As for their relevance to methods in mainstream psychology, the primary question raised by the existential-humanistic psychologists concerns the phenomenology of the science-making process itself. In all objectivist science, with the exception of a few theorists in physics such as Niels Bohr, John Wheeler, and in psychologists such as William James, Amedeo Giorgi, Max Velmans, or Francisco Varela, there is no recognition of the subjective presence of the experimenter and his motives on the design, construction, execution, outcome, and interpretation of research. The existential-humanistic tradition re-injects this important element back into the discussion of methodology, particularly with regard to the new emphasis on the philosophical implications of the problem of consciousness in the neurosciences.

Their Model of Consciousness

The conception of consciousness fielded by the existential-humanistic and transpersonal tradition can be understood as a radicalization of depth psychology. Freud conceptualized psychoanalysis as a science, but hypostatized the unconscious, confusing his own for a more general dynamic psychology of the unconscious common to all human beings. The existential-humanistic psychologists, led by Rollo May, took up Victor Frankl, Ludwig Binswanger, Medard Boss, Karl Jaspers, Jean-Paul Sartre, and Martin Heidegger, and pioneered in the radicalization of depth psychology by stretching its boundaries to include phenomenological psychology, existential psychoanalysis, Reichean sexual therapy, and the archetypal psychology of Jung, among others, which eventually led some of them to the various Eastern meditative traditions.

Reductionistic empiricists in psychological science will acknowledge only the logical ordering of sense data. There is a positivistic consciousness, linking behavior and cognitive thought to brain neurophysiology. Consciousness, at best, ranges from coma to hyper-excitability. Psychoanalysts, at least, acknowledge the reality of the unconscious. The unconscious is that vast domain of submerged and more primitive possibilities, stretching back to previous levels of psychic and physical evolution, within us. It stands in relation to waking rational consciousness as unavailable, except through memories, dreams, fantasies, and all sorts of buried mental imagery. It is the more underdeveloped aspect of personality, while waking rational consciousness is the newer of the stages in the evolutionary scale, but more fragile and under assault in its constant battle to gain control over the environment.

Existential-humanistic and transpersonal psychology, on the other hand, acknowledges the importance of the waking state for the biological preservation of the physical body and cognizes the disintegration of personality in states of acute psychopathology. But its most important contribution is the assumption of a growth-oriented dimension to personality; a spectrum of human functioning in which we are called upon to actualize our highest potential and our best qualities as human beings. It posits a spectrum of higher states of consciousness—waking, dreaming, deep sleep, and the hypometabolic state of meditation, as well as visionary and mythic states that reflect self-realization, self-actualization, or individuation, as expressed in different cultures.

Their Approach to Indigenous Psychologies

Existential-humanistic and transpersonal perspectives also open us to considering the value of non-Western epistemologies, or what might also be called psychological anthropologies of world cultures. In order to get to these alternative ways of viewing personality and consciousness, one might usefully employ the analytic psychology of Carl Jung, for the reason that Jung's approach incorporates all that we know of the rational and analytic, while embracing not only the reality of the unconscious but also more radical expressions of depth psychology that include iconography of the transcendent.

Such epistemologies borrow heavily from the scholarly literature of religion and the humanities rather than confine themselves solely to the assumptions of the natural sciences. These may include literature from the prophetic traditions of the West, the cosmic civilizations of antiquity, the intuitive systems of Asia, the divinatory systems of Africa, and the shamanic cultures of Siberia, the Pacific, and the Americas (see Fig. 10.4).

The important difference is that the experimental and psychodynamic traditions superimpose their epistemology onto other cultures, whereas the existential-humanistic asks those other cultures to speak for themselves. The implications of this distinction are potentially far-reaching because the experimentalists' model judges non-Western systems to be insufficient a priori, without allowing them to speak for their own inner iconography because it is presumed that they do not measure up to the Western model in the first place. The existential-humanistic and transpersonal approach goes right to the heart of the discussion on such issues as

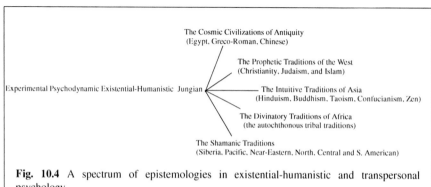

Fig. 10.4 A spectrum of epistemologies in existential-humanistic and transpersonal psychology

multiculturalism by recognizing the Western standard, but also by asking about alternate epistemologies upon which quite different approaches might be based.

The Western scientific approach investigates acupuncture and takes only that for which empirical evidence can be generated. The existential-humanistic approach reads *The Five Confucian Classics*[112] when it tries to understand acupuncture, because it knows that the treatment is bound up in a philosophy of self-realization, which requires the cultivation of character, along with the mere acquisition of technical, objective knowledge. This philosophy applies not only to the patient but also to the healer as well.

Thus, an existential-humanistic and transpersonally oriented depth psychology presents the larger discipline of psychology with an expanded definition of personality, a wider definition of consciousness, a more complete spectrum of methods for scientific inquiry, and an epistemology allowing psychology to dialogue with non-Western models of personality and consciousness.

A case in point is the Vedantic conception of personality in Hindu psychology. Reminding the reader of the religious, philosophical, and psychological roots commonly shared in these traditions, the person is expressed in terms of the individual human being, or *jiva* and its relation to *Atman*, the Supreme Self. The consciousness of the individual is identical to the ultimate spiritual consciousness of Brahma. "That art thou, O Svetaketu," it is declared in the *Upanishads*. But the normal individual does not realize this because of the veil of illusion, or *maya*, which keeps them in a state of *avidya*, or ignorance, Meditation (*dhyana*) causes one to break through this veil of illusion by detachment of the senses to their objects in the external material world and a turning within for purposes of self-realization. Achievement of this realization through intuitive insight produces the *jivanmukti*, one who is liberated while still in the body. Personality is transformed through the experience of transcendence. The one who acts and the one who watches from within are then recognized as the same.

In Yoga psychology, transcendence is achieved by practice of *sadhana*, spiritual discipline, the purpose of which is to generate heat (*tapas*), equated with the fire of transformation. Under the instruction of a spiritual teacher, one follows the blueprint laid down in the *ashtanga-marga*, or eight limbs. These involve (1) *yama* and (2) *niyama*, bodily and mental cleansing as preparation for entering the higher states; (3) *asana*, the practice of physical postures; (4) *pranayama*, the science of breath control; (5) *pratyahara*, withdrawal of the senses from attachment through the senses in either a pleasurable or a painful way to objects in the external material world; and then the three-fold tool of *samyama*; (6) *dharana*, attention; (7) *dhyana*, meditation; and (8) *samadhi*, absorption. Successful application of the eight limbs causes a quieting of consciousness (*cittavrittinirodha*) and an elimination of states of mind that are scattered and unfocused, (*kspita*), torpid (*mudha*), or obsessively attached to fixed ideas (*viksipta*). Application of the three-fold tool of *samyama* leads to insight into whatever the particular object of meditation may be (Figs. 10.5 and 10.6).

A series of more refined states of consciousness then follow focusing on absorption at the level of sense impressions, the ego, and the intellect, and the internal

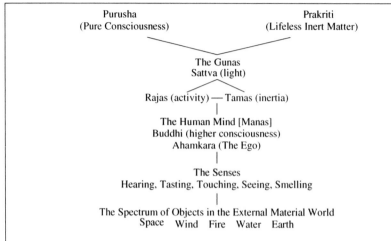

Fig. 10.5 The T*attvas* of the Samkhya-yoga school enumerating the categories of existence
Adapted from Larson, G. J., & Bhattacharya, R. S. (1987). *Samkhya: A Dualist tradition in
Indian philosophy*. Princeton, NJ: Princeton University Press, p. 53.

The Normal States of Consciousness
        Ksipta, the restless state
        Mudha, the torpid state
        Viksipta, the distracted state

Yogic States of Consciousness [Samyama]
        Ekagra, the focused state
        Niruddha, a complete cessation of
          all mental activity on the surface
          of consciousness
Samyama Consists of:
  Dharana –concentration on the object
  Dhyana –meditation [sustained concentration] on the object
  Samadhi –absorption into the object
   Samprajnata Samadhi –a continuously flowing stream of insights into the world of
      objects
     Savitarka Samadhi –gross objects as meditation
     Nirvitarka Samadhi –objectless concentration beyond gross objects
     Savichara Samadhi –subtle objects as meditation
     Nirvichara Samadhi –objectless concentration beyond subtle objects
     Sananda –Bliss as an object of meditation
     Nirananda –objectless concentration beyond bliss consciousness
     Asmita –the ego as an object of meditation
     Nirasmita –objectless concentration beyond the ego
   Asamprajnata Samadhi –isolation of pure consciousness from the objects of the
      continuously flowing stream of insights.

Fig. 10.6 Stages of consciousness leading to Samadhi in Samkhya-Yoga
Adapted from Mishra, R. S., Patanjali, B. S. M., & Patanjali, B. K. S. I. (1971). *The textbook of Yoga psychology, a new translation and interpretation of Patanjali's yoga sutras for
meaningful application in all modern psychologic disciplines*. New York: Julian Press.

spiritual sense, until the person is experiencing a continuously flowing stream of insights into the world of all objects (*samprajnatasamadhi*). This occurs at each level through generating more and more of the light of pure consciousness (*purusha*) through insight (*sattva*). The principles of energy (*rajas*), inertia (*tamas*), and light (sattva) go into equilibrium as one shifts one's attention from the objects of insight themselves to their illumined quality. By so doing, pure consciousness (*purusha*) is separated from lifeless inert matter (*prakriti*), and the person goes into a state of complete isolation, immersed in pure consciousness. This is the highest state, or *asamprajnatasamadhi*. As a result of attaining such a state, the adept is called a *kaivalyn*, one who is now liberated while still in the body, similar to the idea of the *jivanmukta* in Vedanta psychology.[113]

While the methods of yoga are generally appropriated by all schools of thought in Hindu psychology (*darshana*), they have also been absorbed into Buddhist psychology, which aims to achieve release from suffering (*dukkha*). Buddhist psychology is based on the idea that all things are impermanent (*anicca*), have no underlying substantial self to support them (*anatta*), and that clinging to the notion of substantiality is the cause of suffering (*dukkha*).

Within Buddhist psychology, normal personality is considered illusory, since there is no underlying permanent self to define it.[114] The normal identity is constructed out of a mere heap or conglomeration of conditions (*skandha*). They are *nama-rupa*, name and form; *vedana*, feelings; *samjna*, perception; *samskaras*, the unconscious seeds of waking conscious impression; and *vijnana*, personal consciousness. The first is the physical body, while the last four, the aggregates, are considered the ego or personality—that which detaches itself from the body at death and transmigrates to another body in the process of rebirth according to ones' *karma* (meaning thoughts, words, and deeds), until the final state of liberation (*moksha*) is achieved through good deeds, when rebirth ends.

The ideal of the liberated personality differs from school to school in Buddhist psychology. In Hinayana Buddhism, it is the *arahat*, one who has "reached the farther shore," by having achieved *nibanna* (Skt.: *nirvana*), "a burning out of the flame of desire." In the Mahayana philosophy, the ideal is to achieve *sunyata*, the state of complete emptiness. The ideal personality is the *bodhisattva*, one who is liberated while still in the body, who can step over into enlightenment at any time, but who has vowed to return to the world of suffering and assist all sentient beings down to the last blade of grass to pass over first.

Particularly relevant to the Tibetan Vajrayana Buddhist schools is the Tantric concept of the 84 *mahasiddhas* (Tib.: *Grub thob chen*), shared also with the Shaivite tradition of Hinduism. These are a collection of profiles of enlightened beings with exceptional powers representing no particular tradition but who are skilled adepts and complete Masters of the technologies of enlightenment. They are also called *hamsa*, or wild geese, suggesting that what we are actually dealing with is the generic experience of spirituality within each person regardless of lineage, independent of association with any one particular spiritual tradition.

Other Asian traditions also have conceptions of the liberated personality. In Chinese Confucianism, we might point to the ideal of the *chuntze*, "gentlemanliness based on strength of character rather than on hereditary feudal acquisition," or the Master of *wu-wei*, (non-doing) in popular Taoism. The point is that each culture has its conception of the ideal and expresses personality according to its own definition of human nature. As we have said, the existential-humanistic and transpersonal traditions at least listen to these other cultures, instead of superimposing a preconceived set of categories or measurable traits of Western origin onto them and then claiming that we somehow understand the people of that culture.[115]

This is but a limited attempt to summarize the definition of personality within the humanistic tradition in terms of what I would call an existential-humanistic and transpersonally oriented depth psychology.

Notes

1. Diamonic—that force which seeks to overcome the obstacles to development, whatever the cost, both guide and guardian.
2. Ellen Langer's mindfulness would be an example. See Alexander, C. N., & Langer, E. J. (Eds.). (1990). *Higher stages of human development: Perspectives on adult growth.* New York: Oxford University Press.
3. Professor Seligman's "positive psychology," would be a case in point. See Taylor, E. I. (2001b, Winter). Positive psychology versus Humanistic psychology: A reply to Prof. Seligman. *Journal of Humanistic Psychology: Special Issue, 41*(1), 13–29.
4. Messer, S. B., Sass, L. A., & Woolfolk, R. L. (1988). (Eds.), *Hermeneutics and psychological theory: Interpretive perspectives on personality, psychotherapy, and psychopathology.* New Brunswick, NJ: Rutgers University Press.
5. This is a difficult point to flesh out, as there is no question that the students of the macropersonality theorists defy classification and many took unique paths into the profession and influenced it accordingly. However, cognitive and not humanistic psychology became the reigning paradigm on the heels of behaviorism in university laboratories. See Baars, B. J. (1986). *The cognitive revolution in psychology.* New York: Guilford Press.
6. See Moustakas, C. E. (Ed.). (1956). *The self: Explorations in personal growth.* New York: Harper & Brothers; Moustakas, C. E., & Jayaswal, S. R. (1974). *The self: Explorations in personal growth.* New York, London: Harper & Row.
7. See Lee, M. A., & Shlain, B. (1992). *Acid dreams: The complete social history of LSD: The CIA, the sixties, and beyond.* New York: Grove Weidenfield.
8. Koch, S. (Ed.). (1959–1963). *Psychology: A study of a science* (6 Vols.). New York: McGraw-Hill.
9. Rogers, C. R. (1959). A theory of therapy, personality, and interpersonal relationships, as developed in the client centered framework. In S. Koch (Ed.), *Psychology: A study of a science* (Vol. 3, pp. 184–257). New York: McGraw-Hill.
10. See also, Kirschenbaum, H. (1979). *On becoming Carl Rogers.* New York: Delacorte Press.
11. Rogers, C. R. (1939a). *The clinical treatment of the problem child.* London: Allen & Unwin; Rogers, C. R. (1939b). In L. Carmichael (Ed.), *The clinical treatment of the problem child.* Boston, New York: Houghton Mifflin Company.
12. Rogers, C. R. (1942a). *Counseling and psychotherapy: Newer concepts in practice.* Cambridge, MA: Harvard University Press; Rogers, C. R., & Carmichael, L. (Ed.). (1942b). *Counseling and psychotherapy: Newer concepts in practice.* Boston, New York: Houghton Mifflin Company.
13. Rogers, 1959, p. 191.
14. May, Angel, & Ellenberger (1958).
15. Henri Ellenberger, Leslie Farber, Carl Rogers, Erwin Straus, and Paul Tillich, among others, had helped him develop the final draft.
16. For details on these figures, see Spiegelberg, H. (1972). *Phenomenology in psychology and psychiatry: A historical introduction.* Evanston, IL: Northwestern University Press.
17. May, Angel, & Ellenberger, 1958, p. 11.

18. May, Angel, & Ellenberger, 1958, p. 14.
19. See Heidegger, M. (1962). *Being and time* (J. Macquarrie, Trans.). London: S. C. M. Press.
20. He also directs the reader to Kaufmann, W. (1956). *Existentialism from Dostoevsky to Sartre*. New York: World Publishing Co., especially Karl Jaspers's essay "Kierkegaard and Nietzsche," pp. 131–157.
21. May, Angel, & Ellenberger, 1958, p. 33.
22. Binswanger, L. (1957). *Sigmund Freud: Reminiscences of a friendship*. New York: Grune & Stratton, p. 401.
23. May, Angel, & Ellenberger, 1958, p. 314.
24. May, R. (Ed.). (1961). *Existential psychology*. New York: Random House.
25. Rogers, C. R. (1951). *Client-centered therapy, its current practice, implications, and theory*. Boston: Houghton Mifflin.
26. See Spiegelberg on Rogers; Spiegelberg, H. (1972). *Phenomenology in psychology and psychiatry: A historical introduction*. Evanston, IL: Northwestern University Press.
27. Spiegelberg, 1972, p. 89.
28. Spiegelberg, 1972, p. 92.
29. Spiegelberg, 1972, p. 94.
30. May, 1961, p. 94.
31. May, 1961, p. 96.
32. May, 1961, p. 97.
33. May, R. (1969b). *Existential psychology* (2nd ed.). New York: Random House.
34. May, 1961, p. 83.
35. Frick, W. B. (1997). Interview with John Rowan. *Journal of Humanistic Psychology, 37*(1), 131–156.
36. Rowan, J. (1976). *Ordinary ecstasy. Humanistic psychology in action*. London, Boston: Routledge & Kegan Paul.
37. Rowan, J., & Cooper, M. (Eds.). (1999). *The plural self: Multiplicity in everyday life*. Thousand Oaks, CA: Sage Publications, pp. 11–27.
38. Laing, R. D. (1960). *The divided self*. London: Tavistock Publications. See also, Laing, R. D. (1961). *Self and others*. London: Tavistock Publications.
39. Laing, 1960, p. 21.
40. Laing, 1960, p. 22.
41. See in particular, Murphy, M. (1992). *The future of the body: Explorations into the further evolution of human nature*. Los Angeles: J. P. Tarcher. Assagioli also published in the first volume of the *Journal of Transpersonal Psychology*. Assagioli, R. (1969). Symbols of transpersonal experiences. *Journal of Transpersonal Psychology, 1*(1), 33–45.
42. Assagioli, R. (1976). *Psychosynthesis: A manual of principles and techniques*. Harmondsworth, England; New York: Penguin Book; Assagioli, R. (1964). *Psychosynthesis: A manual of principles and techniques*. New York: Holt, Rinehart & Winston; London: G. Allen & Unwin; New York: Viking Press, 1971.
43. Assagioli, 1976, p. 8.
44. Assagioli, 1976, p. 40.
45. See, for instance, Anderson, W. T. (1983). *The upstart spring: Esalen and the American awakening*. Reading, MA: Addison-Wesley, and Kripal, J. J (2007). *Esalen: America and the religion of no-religion*. Chicago: University of Chicago Press.
46. Bugental, J. F. T. (1963). Humanistic psychology: A new breakthrough. *American Psychologist, 18*, 563–567.
47. Knapp, R. (1949–1974). *Collected papers*. Archives of the History of American Psychology, Akron, OH: University of Akron. Also, Taylor, E. I., Martinez, S., & Martin, F. (Eds.). (2000). *Old Saybrook one: Landmark in the history of humanistic psychology: Commemorative edition*. Cambridge, MA: The Essene Press.
48. Taylor, E. I. (2000). "What is man, psychologist, that thou art so unmindful of him?": Henry A. Murray on the historical relation between classical personality theory and humanistic psychology. *Journal of Humanistic Psychology, 40*(3), 29–42.

49. Jourard, S. M. (1964). *The transparent self: Self-disclosure and well-being.* Princeton, NJ: Van Nostrand (revised edition, 1971, New York: Van Nostrand Reinhold).
50. Jourard, S. M., & Secord, P. F. (1953). Body-cathexis and personality. *British Journal of Psychology, 46*(2), 130–138.
51. Jourard, S. M. (1958a). *Personal adjustment: An approach through the study of healthy personality.* New York: Macmillan; Jourard, S. M. (1958b). A study of self-disclosure. *Scientific American, 198*(5), 77–82.
52. Jourard, S. M. (1959). I-Thou relationship versus manipulation in counseling and psychotherapy. *Journal of Individual Psychology, 15*(2), 174–179.
53. Jourard, S. M. (Ed.). (1967a). *To be or not to be... Existential-psychological perspectives on the self.* University of Florida Monographs, Social Sciences, #34. Gainesville: University of Florida Press; Jourard, S. M. (1967b). To be or not to be transparent. In S. M. Jourard (Ed.). *To be or not to be... Existential-psychological perspectives on the self:* University of Florida Monographs, Social Sciences, #34 (pp. 27–36). Gainesville, FL: University of Florida Press; Jourard, S. M. (1967c). Experimenter-subject dialogue: A paradigm for a humanistic science of psychology. In J. F. T. Bugental (Ed.), *Challenges of humanistic psychology* (pp. 109–116). New York: McGraw-Hill; Reprinted 1972 in A. G. Miller (Ed.), *The social psychology of psychological research* (pp. 14–24). London: The Free Press; Jourard, S. M., & Kormann, L. A. (1968). Getting to know the experimenter and its effect on psychological test performance. *Journal of Humanistic Psychology, 8*(2), 155–159; McLaughlin, F., Jourard, S. M., & Combs, A. W. (Eds.) (1971). Conversation: Two humanists. *Media & Methods, 8*(4), 24–29; Jourard, S. M. (1972). The transcending therapist. *Voices, 8*(3), 66–69; Jourard, S. M. (1971). Some ways of unembodiment and re-embodiment. *Somatics, 1*(1), 3–7.
54. Jourard, S. M. (1974). *Healthy personality: An approach from the viewpoint of humanistic psychology.* New York: The Macmillan Company.
55. Van Kaam, A. L. (1964). *Religion and personality.* Englewood Cliffs, NJ: Prentice-Hall.
56. Martin, F. A. (2001). Interview with Adrian van Kaam and Susan Muto, Pittsburgh, Pennsylvania, May 23, 1999. Appendix to *The meaning of humanistic psychology: Interviews with seventy-five living exponents.* Unpublished Doctoral Dissertation, Saybrook Graduate School and Research Center, San Francisco.
57. Scholtes, M. (1998). *Become Jesus: The diary of a soul touched by God.* Pittsburgh, PA: Dorrance Publications Company.
58. Martin, 1999, Interview with van Kaam.
59. Van Kaam, A. L. (1966a). *Existential foundations of psychology.* Pittsburgh, PA: Duquesne University Press.
60. Van Kaam, A. L. (1966b). *The art of existential counseling.* Wilkes-Barre, PA: Dimension Books.
61. Athos, A. G., & Coffey, R. E. (1968). *Behavior in organizations: A multidimensional view.* Englewood Cliffs, NJ: Prentice-Hall.
62. Rudhyar, D. (1970). *The astrology of personality: A re-formulation of astrological concepts and ideals in terms of contemporary psychology and philosophy.* New York: Doubleday.
63. See Aanstoos, C. M., Serlin, I., & Greening, T. (2004). A history of Division 32 (Humanistic Psychology). In D. A. Dewsbury (Ed.), *Unification through division: Histories of the divisions of the American Psychological Association* (Vol. 5, pp. xii, 197). Washington, DC: American Psychological Association. See also Popplestone, J. A. (1998). Virginia Staudt Sexton (1916–1997). *History of Psychology, 1*(1), 88–90.
64. Gavin, E. A. (1990). Charlotte M. Bühler (1893–1974). In A. N. O'Connell & F. F. Russo (Eds.), *Women in psychology: A bio-bibliographic sourcebook.* New York: Greenwood Press.
65. Schenk-Danziger, L. (1963). Fundamental ideas and theories in Charlotte Bühler's lifework. *Journal of Humanistic Psychology, 3*(2), 3–9. See also, Ragsdale, S. (n.d.). Charlotte Malachowski Buhler, Ph.D. (1893–1974). *Women's Intellectual Contributions to the Study of Mind and Society.* www.webster.edu/~woolflm/charlottebuhler.html; See also, Buhler, C. (1954). The reality principle: Discussion of theories and observational data. *American Journal of Psychotherapy, 8*(4), 626–647.
66. Gardner, S., & Stevens, G. (1992). *Red Vienna and the golden age of psychology: 1918-1938.* New York: Praeger, p. 151.
67. Bühler, C. (1922). *Das seelenleben des jugendlichen* [Psychology of adolescence]. Jena: Gustav Fischer.

68. Ash, M. G. (1987). Psychology and politics in Interwar Vienna: The Vienna Psychological Institute, 1922–1942. In M. G. Ash & W. R. Woodward (Eds.), *Psychology in twentieth-century thought and society* (pp 143–164). Cambridge, New York: Cambridge University Press.

69. Bühler, C. (1929). Jungendpsychologie und Schule. *Suddeutscher Monatshefte, 27,* 186, quoted in Ragsdale.

70. Adorno, T. W. (1950). *The authoritarian personality.* New York: Wiley, Science Editions; Jahoda, M. (1977). *Freud and the dilemmas of psychology.* London: Hogarth Press; New York: Basic Books.

71. Gardner & Stevens, 1992.

72. Ragsdale (n.d.).

73. Bühler, C. (1959). Theoretical aspects of life's basic tendencies. *American Journal of Psychotherapy, 13*(3), 501–581; Bühler, C. (1964). The human course of life in its goal aspects. *Journal of Humanistic Psychology, 4,* 1–17.

74. Bühler, C. (1968). The general structure of the human life cycle. In C. Bühler & F. Massarik (Eds.), *The course of human life: A study of goals in the humanistic perspective* (pp. 12–26). New York: Springer.

75. McClelland, D. (Ed.). (1953). *The achievement motive.* New York: Appleton-Century-Crofts.

76. Tillich, P. (1952). *The courage to be.* New Haven, CT: Yale University Press.

77. Gavin, E. A. (2000). Charlotte M. Buhler. In A. W. Kazdin (Ed.), *Encyclopedia of Psychology* (Vol. 1., pp. 482–483). Washington, DC: American Psychological Association; Also, Ragsdale (n.d.); Schenk-Danziger, L. (1963). Fundamental ideas and theories in Charlotte Bühler's lifework. *Journal of Humanistic Psychology, 3*(2), 3–9.

78. Tart, C. T. (1969). *Altered states of consciousness.* New York: Wiley.

79. Giorgi, A. (1970). *Psychology as a human science: A phenomenologically based approach.* New York: Harper & Row; Child, I. L. (1973). *Humanistic psychology and the research tradition: Their several virtues.* New York: Wiley.

80. See my summary of this episode in Taylor (1999).

81. Smuts, J. C. (1926). *Holism and evolution.* New York: The Macmillan Company.

82. Henle, M. (1978). Gestalt psychology and gestalt therapy. *Journal of the History of the Behavioral Sciences, 14,* 23–32.

83. Shane, P. (2002). *Return of the prodigal daughter: Historiography and the relationship between Gestalt psychology and Gestalt therapy.* Unpublished Doctoral Dissertation, Saybrook Graduate School and Research Center, San Francisco.

84. Hefferline and Goodman had appeared on some of Fritz's work as co-authors.

85. See, for instance, Bernstein, P. L. (1979). The use of symbolism within a gestalt movement therapy approach. In P. L. Bernstein (Ed.), *Eight theoretical approaches in dance movement therapy.* Dubuque, Iowa: Kendall/Hunt Publishing Company; Also, Wysong, J., & Rosenfeld, E. (1982). An oral history of Gestalt therapy: Interviews with Laura Perls, Isadore From, Erving Polster, Miriam Polster, Joe Wysong, Edward Rosenfeld. *Gestalt Journal, 1–3.*

86. Shane, P. (1999). *The contribution of Laura Perls to the development of Gestalt therapy.* Unpublished Master's thesis, Saybrook Graduate School and Research Center, San Francisco.

87. Rogers, N. (1980). *Emerging woman: A decade of midlife transitions.* Point Reyes, CA: Personal Press.

88. Rogers, N. (1993). *The creative connection: Expressive arts as healing.* Palo Alto, CA: Science & Behavior Books.

89. James (1902a).

90. Vich, M. (1988). Some historical sources of the term "transpersonal." *Journal of Transpersonal Psychology, 20*(2), 107–110.

91. Tillich, P. (1954). *Love, power, and justice.* New York, London: Oxford University Press.

92. Huxley, A. (1945). *The perennial philosophy.* New York, London: Harper & Brothers; Huxley, A. (1954). *The doors of perception.* New York: Harper & Brothers; Watts, A. (1957). *The way of Zen.* New York: Pantheon; Watts, A. (1961). *Psychotherapy east and west.* New York: Pantheon; Watts, A. (1962). *The joyous cosmology: Adventures in the chemistry of consciousness.* New York: Pantheon.

93. Sutich, A. (1976). *The founding of humanistic and transpersonal psychology: A personal account.* Unpublished Doctoral Dissertation, Humanistic Psychology Institute, San Francisco.

94. Maslow, A. H. (1969). Various meanings of transcendence. *Journal of Transpersonal Psychology*. *1*(1), 56–66.
95. Maslow, 1969, p. 66.
96. Tart, C. (Ed.). (1969). *Altered states of consciousness*. New York: Wiley.
97. Fadiman, J. (1969). The Council Grove conference on altered states of consciousness. *Journal of Humanistic Psychology*. *9*, 135–137.
98. Weide, T. N. (1973). Vallombrosa: A major transpersonal event. *Journal of Transpersonal Psychology*, *5*(2), 205–208.
99. Honorton, C., & Krippner, S. (1969). Hypnosis and ESP performance: A review of the experimental literature. *Journal of the American Society for Psychical Research, 63*, 214–252. Ullman, M. & Krippner, S. (1970). *Dream studies and telepathy: An experimental approach*. New York: Parapsychology Foundation; Ullman, M., & Krippner, S. (1973). *Dream telepathy*. New York: The Macmillan Company; Krippner, S. (1969). The psychedelic state, the hypnotic trance, and the creative act. In C. T. Tart (Ed.), *Altered states of consciousness: A book of readings* (pp. 271–290). New York: Wiley; Krippner, S. (1978). The interface between parapsychology and humanistic psychology. In M. Ebon (Ed.), *The Signet handbook of parapsychology* (pp. 79–87). New York: New American Library; Krippner, S. (1999). The varieties of dissociative experience: A transpersonal, postmodern model. *International Journal of Transpersonal Studies, 18*, 81–101; Krippner, S. (2000). *Varieties of anomalous experience: Examining the scientific evidence* (with E. Cardena & S. J. Lynn). Washington, DC: American Psychological Association; Krippner, S. (Ed.) (2003). *The psychological effects of war on civilians: An international perspective,* [co-edited with T. McIntyre; Foreword by S. Hobfall; Afterword by J. Achterberg.] Westport, CT: Praeger.
100. Lilly, J. C. (1972). *Center of the cyclone: An autobiography of inner space*. New York: Julian Press.
101. Tart, C. T. (1972). States of consciousness and state-specific sciences. *Science, 176*(4040), 1203–1210.
102. Haley, J. (1973). *Uncommon therapy: The psychiatric techniques of Milton H. Erickson, M.D.* New York: W. W. Norton.
103. Hull, C. L. (1933). *Hypnosis and suggestibility: An experimental approach*. New York, London: D. Appleton-Century Company.
104. Weide, T. N. (1973). Vallombrosa: A major transpersonal event. *Journal of Transpersonal Psychology*, *5*(2), 205–208; Wilber, K. (1977). *The spectrum of consciousness*. Wheaton, IL: Theosophical Publication House.
105. Ornstein, R. E (Ed.). (1973). *The nature of human consciousness: A book of readings.*New York: Viking; Ornstein, R. E. (1972). *The psychology of consciousness*. New York: Pengiun Books; Grof, S. (1975). *Realms of the human unconscious: Observations from LSD research*. New York: Viking Press.
106. Wilber, K. (1975). Psychologia perennis: The spectrum of consciousness. *Journal of Transpersonal Psychology, 7*(2), 105–132. See also, Vaughan, F. E. (1979). *Awakening intuition*. New York: Anchor Press; and Vaughan, F. E., & Walsh, R. N. (Eds.). (1980). *Beyond ego: Transpersonal dimensions in psychology*. Los Angeles: J. P. Tarcher, New York: Distributed by Martin's Press.
107. M. Vich (personal communication, March 10, 1988)
108. Fadiman, J., & Frager, R. (1976). *Personality and personal growth*. New York: Harper & Row
109. Green, E., & Green, A. (1977). *Beyond biofeedback*. New York: Delacorte Press/S. Lawrence.
110. Murphy, M., & Donovan, S. (1997). *The physical and psychological effects of meditation: A review of contemporary research with a comprehensive bibliography, (1931-1996)* (2nd ed.). Sausalito, CA: Institute of Noetic Sciences. See also Achterberg, J. (1985). *Imagery in healing: Shamanism and modern medicine*. Boston: New Science Library, Shambhala; New York: Distributed by Random House.
111. Ray, P. H., & Anderson, S. R. (2000). *The cultural creatives: How 50 million people are changing the world*. New York: Harmony Books.
112. Nylan, M. (2001). *The five Confucian classics*. New Haven, CT: Yale University Press.
113. See in particular, Das, K. C. (1975). *The concept of personality in Samkhya-yoga and the Gita.* Assam, India: Department of Publication, Gauhati University, in which the author built upon

the work of Gordon Allport, Robert Woodworth, and others. Also, Swami Akhilananda's *Hindu psychology.* (1946). New York: Harper & Brothers, with an introduction by Gordon Allport and a preface by Martin Luther King, Jr.'s teacher, Edgar Sheffield Brightman. Allport, along with George Hunston Williams, Peter Bertocci, and others at Harvard and Boston University were close friends with Akhilananda during the 1940s when he was head of the Vedanta Center in Boston at that time. Allport also served on the editorial board of *Psychologia,* the international journal of psychology the Orient. Watts, Huxley, Suzuki, and others were introducing Asian psychologies into the West during this same period.

114. Kalupahana, D. J. (1987). *The principles of Buddhist psychology.* Albany, NY: State University of New York Press; Guenther, H. V. (1952). *Yuganaddha: The Tantric view of life.* Banaras, India: Chowkhamba; Govinda, A. B. (1937). *The psychological attitude of early Buddhist philosophy and its systematic representation according to Abhidhamma tradition.* Patna, India: The University.

115. This is not to say, however, that the transpersonalists do not superimpose their own mainly white, Western, Judeo-Christian categories onto an interpretation of the Asian systems. Their purpose is to discover ostensibly what is ultimately true as they see it, while their effect is mainly to counter the great machine created by the reductionistic empiricists.

Chapter 11
Neuroscience and the Future of the Self

> *Some day we may have a general psychology which is also a*
> *psychology of personality as a whole.*
> Gordon Allport

Toward the end of the first decade of the 21st century, dynamic theories of personality have been relegated largely to clinical practice in psychology and psychiatry. Experimental research in personality theory has become largely dominated by trait theory, with some call for more narrative, psychobiographical methods from the periphery. Psychoanalysis has become colonized by PhD psychologists and left by the wayside by psychiatrists, who in the medical school curriculum have integrated it into more general "psychodynamically assisted" approaches to psychotherapy. The new focus on neuroscience has barely any reference to personality and has substituted this construct for a more cognitive and behavioral definition of the self. Borrowing a phrase from Fernando Vidal, Sonu Shamdasani has referred to this new focus as the ascendancy of "brainhood." The person is equal to the brain.[1]

Meanwhile, states of consciousness have continued to proliferate in the psychotherapeutic counterculture, where meditation and psychotherapy have evolved into more sophisticated discussions of shamanism and techniques of ecstasy from the iconography of non-Western, and largely non-technological cultures. The widespread, pervasive focus on spirituality in popular culture at large has forced the cognitivists to take up the study of the spiritual sources of resilience, the role of spirituality in therapy, and how to train therapists and researchers to integrate religious beliefs into their understanding of cognition. Neuroscience itself remains hostile to these discussions because of the unscientific nature of anything having to do with religion, and discussions about the nature of consciousness are almost totally confined to reductionistic conceptions of mind. Between parallel distributive processing theories, neural plasticity, and string theory, the person has nearly disappeared off the computer screen in the current milieu, though historically this may only be a temporary state of affairs. Meanwhile, the new rubric among the cognitivists has become "the Cognitive Neuroscience of Religion."[2]

E. Taylor, *The Mystery of Personality*, Library of the History of Psychology Theories, 315
DOI 10.1007/978-0-387-98104-8_11, © Springer Science+Business Media, LLC 2009

The Fate of Classical Personality Theories

Gordon Allport characterized European and American theories of personality in 1957, right about the time that physicists and biologists first started to talk to one another, but before seeds of the neurosciences had begun to sprout. This was also the period just before the humanistic revolution in psychology of the 1960s.[3] The problem was, at that moment in time, in both academic and clinical psychology things remained somewhat backward. Two World Wars and an intervening depression had marked a dramatic change in posture between the Old and the New World, although the Wundtian brand of experimental psychology still persisted in the United States in the idea that hard science meant the only real science worth pursuing in the academy. Only now, the child had become father of the man. Prior to 1914, Americans sent their finest minds to European universities. After 1945, the Americans assumed there was nothing to learn from Europe, while Europeans began to flock to the United States and Americans forgot their French and their German.

Allport maintained that, with regard to the specific field of personality psychology, marked differences remained, however. Americans tended to believe that personality was almost infinitely malleable, shaped by life history and social forces. In places like Switzerland, there was more emphasis on the relative constancy of basic character structure; sociology was less emphasized, while genetics, characterology, and constitutional psychiatry were foremost. The Americans stressed personality, while the Europeans continued to emphasize character, a pre-World War I construct. Americans viewed personality in terms of the more superficial, outward signs of behavior and motor activity, while the Europeans sought entry into the deeper structures of the individual. But the bifurcation was not really so clear. Britain and the United States shared numerous theories in common, such as the psychoanalytic, the factorial, the positivistic, the projective, and the interpersonal, so it is also appropriate to speak of an Anglo-American trend over against the European. The Germans had remained more phenomenological than behavioral and statistical, while the British, especially Hans Eysenck, considered Anglo-Saxon psychology to be more scientific, while Continental psychology remained more philosophical.

Allport then launched into some of the more substantive similarities and differences: Anglo-Saxon psychology adhered to the Lockean tradition in its definition of mental life—that the mind is a blank slate to begin with and does what the environment tells it to do, which it processes with simple ideas linked through association. The Continental tradition in contrast was more Leibnitzian and Kantian, emphasizing the rational categories of the monad. The intellect is proactive not merely reactive; the individual person strives toward a unique destiny; and persons fall into strata depending on their level of self-actualization, which ranges from bestial and animalistic to autonomous, compassionate, and altruistic. Personality is taken as a total gestalt. The Americans have remained compulsively focused on the nature–nurture controversy, while the Europeans ascribed a larger role to inborn ability and disposition.

Further, Continental theories concentrated on the whole person, while American theories were more atomistic, focusing on parts of the whole, such as traits, attitudes, syndromes, factors, and behaviors. Stern's personalism, Wertheimer's gestalt approach, and Lewin's topological psychology were all examples of "having your whole and analyzing it too." As was Spranger's *Verstehen*—an empathic, intuitive feeling of knowing a phenomenon from the inside. Existentialism also demanded allegiance to the entire subjective world of the individual. Anglo-Americans treat all this with suspicion, being dominated by associationism in its varied forms. Americans also tend to deny any internal unity to personality.

Likewise, American theories tended to be more melioristic and optimistic, while Continental theories of personality were more fatalistic and prone to pessimism. Here, Allport contrasted Freud's Germanic emphasis on a tyrannical Id and overbearing superego with newer developments in ego psychology and neo-Freudianism more characteristic of the Americans. Certainly the pessimism of European existentialism was to be contrasted with its more optimistic counterpart in American theories coming from Humanistic psychology, such as that of Carl Rogers. Allport selected out the writings of Paul Tillich for particular emphasis on American's "resilient courage."

European and American theories also differed on their emphasis on social interaction. Continental theories emphasized the self-contained person: American ones tended toward one's openness to the world. The pragmatic philosophies of James, Mead, and Dewey went on to inspire the sociology of Talcott Parsons and the social psychology of Floyd Allport. In such examples the emphasis was on external as opposed to internal structure.

They also differed on their emphasis on brain models. David Kretch, E. C. Tolman, and D. O. Hebb reflected the typical neurological urge among the Anglo-Americans to reduce personality to physiology; Walter Cannon, Karl Lashley, Wilder Penfield were all invoked in defining neurological substrates, as were Sir Charles Sherrington and Clark Hull. Even Wolfgang Köhler had contributed to this view with his work on isomorphism.

Finally, the ideal of rigorous positivism continued to prevail in the Anglo-American arc to a greater degree than anywhere else. Hans Eysenck, on the one hand, leveled three charges against European characterology. He found it obscure, philosophical, and unscientific and addicted to knocking down straw men. European opponents of this view characterize the American psychologists as "soulless mechanists, addicted to twitching muscles, mathematics, and raw meat."[4] On the other hand, Allport pointed out, "The central bulky problems of personality will remain untouched by 'science' if we are too niggardly concerning our conceptions of admissible procedures."[5] This made Freud's theories at the time, however unscientific, the more fruitful single source of insight into human personality than all of Eysenck's scales.

In the end, Allport posed Carl Rogers's self-revelation as a possible standard. Rogers knew that all the really important data about the person comes from actual human interaction, yet the need for irreproachable, repeatable, objective methods was also called for.

Science is a way to prevent me from deceiving myself in regard to my relatively formed subjective hunches which have developed out of the relationship between me and my material.
It is in this context, and perhaps only in this context, that the vast structure of operationism,
logical positivism, research design, tests of significance, etc., have had their place. They
exist, not for themselves, but as servants in the attempt to check the subjective feeling or
hunch or hypothesis of a person with objective fact.[6]

This view, Allport maintained, avoids the bigotry and sterility of the methodological purists and promotes the admission of fresh insights, phenomenological
deliverances, and hunches, which are now more freely allowed. In sum, it is difficult to separate theories of personality from the more general theories of psychology.
In this sense, Allport concluded, revealing his own prejudices, "some day we may
have a general psychology which is also a psychology of personality as a whole."

Twenty years later, a half a century of personality psychology was celebrated
in 1987 with publication of a commemorative volume recognizing the Allport and
Stegner texts of 1937, entitled *Fifty Years of Personality Psychology*.[7] But the problem here, too, was that academic psychologists could still not bring themselves to
acknowledge either the neurosciences, or the humanistic revolution that was blaz-
ing all around them. There were several venues, beginning with the Institute for
Personality Assessment and Research at the University of California, culminating
in a session at the annual convention of the American Psychological Association, in
August of that year, sponsored by the Division of Personality and Social Psychology. The published volume highlighted the opinions of 21 authors, many of whom
were direct students of Henry Murray and Gordon Allport. While representing possibly the extreme liberal wing of the scientific study of personality in the academy,
the picture they painted was one of almost zero progress in the field as far as altering
the stance of manipulation, prediction, and control was concerned.

Additionally, there were no women authors in the book, and issues of the historic
differences between personality theorists grounded in depth psychology and social
personality theorists who define the person in terms of impersonal social forces
were not mentioned. Neither was there mention of post-modernism, a movement
already by the 1980s in full swing—in fact, a movement by that time, which had
become a wave that had already crested. Freud and also Jung got exactly two references apiece in the entire text by the many authors who contributed papers. Gardner
Murphy was mentioned exactly once. The humanistic psychologists were mentioned
here and there but no conception of a growth-oriented dimension to personality was
anywhere broached, except to mention self-actualization as one genre of personality theory, but nothing philosophical was made of it as far as the transformation
of psychology's conception of the scope of personality was concerned. Existential-
humanistic concepts of the person were not broached at all.

The emphasis began on personal documents and the case study method, but
quickly turned to trait theory, culminating in the five factor theory, today now dominating the experimental literature. Psychodynamics were nearly absent throughout,
while the overall status of personality theory at large in psychology was depicted by
the late 1980s as extraordinarily low, ever since the gradual takeover of personality

theory by the epistemology of the social learning theorists in the early 1970s. Personality measurement was at least on the rise in industry by the late 1980s, and this was presented as the concluding, allegedly most positive note of the book.

Personality theory clearly had not moved any closer to fulfilling Allport's hope for a science of the whole person and its status today remains uncertain. According to Salvatore Maddi (1989), one of Murray's students, personality continues to be seen as a stable set of tendencies and characteristics that determine commonalities and differences in people's psychological behavior. These include thoughts, feelings, and actions that have continuity in time and that may not be easily understood as the sole result of the social and biological pressures of the moment.[8] However, such a definition continues to propel psychology forward as the enduring cognitive and behavioral study of personality traits.

Daniel McAdams, another protégé in the lineage of Henry Murray, challenged this view (1995, 1996) and contended that personality is best understood on three levels. First is the level of traits and dispositions. This is the five factor theory: (1) openness to experience, (2) conscientiousness, (3) introversion and extraversion, (4) agreeableness, and (5) neuroticism or negative affectivity.[9] The second is strivings and goals (Emmons, 1999). These are regulatory mechanisms that guide behaviors toward certain outcomes.[10] In other words, traits describe what a person has and strivings express what a person is trying to achieve. The third is identity, which involves life narrative, case materials, interviews, and intensive content analysis.[11] Barenbaum and White, however, have shown in their history of personality theory the inability of mainstream reductionists in psychology to deal with the case study method, which is at the heart of an identity-oriented psychology of personality. Instead, psychologists revert back to the measurements of traits, meanwhile practicing a form of tokenism by gesturing toward those who do case study research, implying that some do that too, whatever it is.

To McAdams's list I would add two additional levels of analysis: Fourth, a psychodynamic interpretation which takes account of unconscious determinates in the formation of personality, reported by a second person in dynamic interaction with the individual, such as a therapist trained in the language of the unconscious or the neuroscientist with experience in meditation and some knowledge of the world's contemplative traditions. A didactic training analysis would also be an example, which an initiate in meditation would also usually undergo.

And fifth, I would add level of or capacity for self-knowledge, which can only be communicated by the person, himself or herself. It may be a function of rational analysis of one's thoughts, words, or actions but also gained by intuitive insight. Intuitive insight is the individual's own idiosyncratic, phenomenological, and existential language of inner experience, expressed in terms of the poetic and visionary symbols they have discovered of their own personal destiny, gleaned from their various intentional excursions into the unconscious. This is exploration of the unconscious for purposes of character development instead of recovery from neurosis. Karen Horney described it within the context of psychoanalysis in *Self Analysis* (1942). Jung defined it as a journey over a lifetime of making the unconscious conscious in the process of normal spiritual growth. Swami Akhilananda described it as the essential process at work in Hindu psychology, which involves an awakening to a higher, deeper, and more profound state of consciousness.[12]

Attempting to accommodate the reductionists, McAdams has, meanwhile, argued for a New Big Five.[13] While trait theory has made great strides, it has yet to fulfill the historical mandate of the field envisioned by its founders, such as Allport and Murray, namely, the development of an integrative framework for understanding the whole person. McAdams proposes to marry trait theory to narrative life histories to achieve this end.[14] Five factor theorists, meanwhile, continue to ignore what they see as more qualitative methods, and are arguing instead for a marriage between the categories of the DSM-IV and the five factor theory, since the DSM has no standard of normality established by is a significant body of empirical data.[15]

But that is just the historical point. Personality psychology, particularly those models based on dynamic theories of the unconscious, was fading fast from psychology proper and replaced by a more normative concept of the self equal to traditional psychoanalytic definitions of the ego, now sanitized for the cognitivists.

The Self in Psychiatry

Thus, when we turn to the self in psychiatry, we see largely the same narrow focus as in academic psychology. Driving more nails into the coffin of the dynamic theorists, in 2002 the journal *Philosophy, Psychiatry, and Psychology* published a series of papers entitled "Dispensing with the Dynamic Unconscious."[16] O'Brian & Jureidini (2002), one a child psychiatrist with a new PhD in cognitive science and the other a lecturer on analytic philosophy, maintained that finally it was time to abandon altogether the concept of a dynamic unconscious. Their frame of reference, however, was confined to psychoanalysis, which they appeared to know only in a limited way. They cited Grunebaum (1984), who to this day still knows nothing about the history of the psychogenic hypothesis as it was anchored in 19th-century French neurophysiology, and Frederick Crews (1996), an English professor whose own Freudian analysis was apparently not successful, as primary sources for the strongest arguments exposing the methodological shortcomings besetting the psychoanalytic unconscious. O'Brian and Jureidini pointed out that psychoanalytic proponents counter with the new links between psychoanalysis and neural Darwinism that associate Freud's dynamic unconscious with the stronger empirical evidence for a cognitive unconscious. The counter strategy of the authors was to show the uselessness of a cognitive unconscious as a construct, thereby logically eliminating psychoanalytic conceptions about the unconscious once and for all.

In the next article, Woody (2002), a professor of philosophy at a small New England college, agreed with O'Brian and Jureidini that the dynamic unconscious must be dispensed with, arguing, in addition, that the problem was also the way psychoanalysts' understand consciousness. Consciousness, Woody quoted Freud as saying, is dependent on language, which differentiates us from the brutes. He then invoked William James's explanation of the psychologists' fallacy to understand the psychoanalysts' point of view, namely, "The great snare of the psychologist is the confusion of his own standpoint with that of the mental fact about which he is making his support."[17] In other words, Freud had merely superimposed his own state of mind onto the patients and confused their consciousness for his own. Woody did not consider that he too was doing the same thing.

Jerome Kroll, a psychiatrist at the University of Minnesota, countered with "The nine lives of the dynamic unconscious." He began by discounting the other authors' idea that repression is incompatible with subpersonal mental states understood in computational terms. And until cognitive psychologists learn how to cure a broken heart with a paper-and-pencil test, dynamic conceptions of the unconscious will stand as more useful and more relevant to human experience than the cognitivists' mechanical models.

O'Brian and Jureidini then returned with a rejoinder they called "The last rites of the dynamic unconscious." So, the journal editors somewhat unfairly pitted three articles against psychoanalysis to Kroll's single positive one, which was not a position paper to begin with but a response to O'Brian and Jureidini, who were advocates of reductionistic science, but not distinguished philosophers of it themselves, only academics who have identified themselves with science. In any event, the entire discussion highlights the continuing pejorative opinion of the run-of-the-mill, normative scientists for dynamic theories of consciousness and, by implication, the underlying models of personality that support them.[18]

A slightly more enlightened view can be found in Kircher and David's *The Self in Neuroscience and Psychiatry*(2003).[19] The authors limit their definition to begin with, however, by saying that the self refers to commonly shared experience and the fact that we know we are the same person across time.[20] They contrast phenomenology, the essence, content, or feel of a mental state, with analytic philosophy, the systematic and logical connections of knowledge. They then state that they represent the analytic point of view. Their history of the use of the term "the self" is one-sided, equating the self with everyday identity, while their attempt to draw on the literature of philosophy, cognitive science, neuroscience, and psychiatry comes off as quite vast for the little they derive from that literature. Perspectives from phenomenology, psychiatry/psychotherapy, and neuroscience they distinguish in terms of "first person science," what the person has to say out of their own lifeworld, and "third person science," objective knowledge about the individual, each with their own contributions. But in the end the authors attempt an unsophisticated Hegelian integration. They compare only the normal to the schizophrenic. Consciousness is limited to self-awareness. They believe there is a hierarchy—prereflexive, raw feelings, and qualia, after which is self-agency, self-coherence, self-affectivity, and finally self-history. To admit to the reality of the self, however, then usually leads most authors to a futile search for its neurological correlates. In addition, they grant the reality of the phenomenal self, but never apply it to themselves, which highlights the issue of control, but only control of others, as a central limitation of their scientific epistemology.[21]

In order to bridge the gap between mind and body, they think if they just set the philosophical discussion next to the neuroscientific one, then they will come up with causal connections. To do this, they artificially separate phenomenology from philosophy of mind. They claim phenomenology has to do with essences, while the philosophy of mind "based on concepts of analytical philosophy, is for our purposes, mainly concerned with the logical connection and systematization of our knowledge of the mind."[22] In other words, they distort the phenomenon under study to fit the limits of their already preconceived model.

Turkle on the Second Self

Even so, everywhere in the era of computational science, there appears to be a slide into mediocrity. Personality has become a moribund category in the wider domain of behavior science, as any need for a concept of the autonomous person has morphed into the self, equated strictly with atomistic traits that psychology tries to shape and reshape according to external norms. As personality has become the self, the self has become almost exclusively a focus on the ego, and then even here the definitions are not consistent. The favorite metaphor is to define it in terms of man–machine interaction, supported by the idea that we are not only creatures who think and feel, but we are also conditioned by our surroundings. The self then turns out, according to this view, to be our perceptions of how we see ourselves when shaped by things, events, and other persons around us.

Those who consider themselves experts on the subject, such as Professor Sherry Turkle, founder of the Initiative of Technology and Self at the Massachusetts Institute of Technology, have extended this discussion to include an investigation of interactions between humans and computers. Turkle believes that a definition of the self becomes crucial, if we are to fathom the ethical and moral relation of humans to machines, especially where machines are coming to take over more of the life space, but her conception fails to go beyond a secondary reading of Freud and her interpretation of Lacan from a feminist viewpoint.[23]

Ms. Turkle, who works in the context of the neurosciences, is to some degree emblematic of a larger movement in the vein of Human Science. Human Science traditionally has been understood as originally a form of biblical interpretation from the 19th century which evolved through writers such as William Dilthey and then the existential-phenomenologists, but which has in our own time also become associated with European and Marxist social movements, particularly from the Frankfurt School. Politically, the voices of the Frankfurt School were generally critical of the Western rational tradition and the control of institutions of culture by the bourgeois mentality and its ruling elites, mainly men. Lately, it has come to be a vehicle for the proliferation of an ideology that fuses race, class, and gender, limited to a radical feminist interpretation of Freud. Personality is most often defined in this line of thinking, not by internal psychodynamics, but by external social forces.[24]

Ulrich Neiser and the Cognitive Self

Ulrich Neiser, a central figure in the rise of cognitive science, has detailed what he means as the self. He admits at the outset that the self is a bundle of contradictions. The concept is advanced only by its different parts in psychology, as it is just a theory. It is what is reflected to us by others; the self is established by autobiographical memory, it refers to phenomenal experience. There is no centrally agreed upon theory of the self. Whatever it is, it is not generally considered a single entity in psychology

Neiser defines his own perspective as an ecologically oriented cognitive psychology. That is, a psychology where the self is defined by what information the person is using to search for self. Neiser's own work begins with publically available information; only then does it proceed to hypothetical structures. He posits five sources of self knowledge, each with different histories and pathologies: (1) the ecological self; (2) the interpersonal self; (3) the temporal or remembered self; (4) the private self, only available to the person; and finally, (5) the conceptual self, the largest, the theory provided for us by our culture concerning what human beings are.

The ecological self is based on perceptual information. This is James Gibson's term,[25] derived from optical information and bodily feelings, available from infancy, usually free from such pathology as hemineglect, and phantom limb. It begins with perception; move your finger and the optics change the object as it moves. Gibson's opinion was that visual systems evolve to take advantage of this information. Perceptions are usually veridical in place and time. All perception, however, is co-perception of self and world. It flows at an optical nodal point. Like a car next to you moving in traffic that is wall to wall, which makes it seem like you are moving when you are not. Fast looming, coming toward you, and object will create vertigo or throw children off balance. Not adults. This is all the ecological self. Another example would be when the child covers its eyes and says "You can't see me."

There is also the interpersonal self, meaning our relations with the social environment. Smiling and eye contact means we are in some relation with that person. You may not know me or my motives but we know we are looking at each other. This exists from birth. Baby gets disturbed when a video of mother is substituted for the real mother. So the interpersonal and the ecological self are both present; usually in fact, they cohere (annoying in darkness, however, because one is absent). Focusing exclusively on the interaction, such as between lovers, or in the case of mother/baby bonding, will sometimes do the same thing.

There is the remembered self; the self extended in time. I am not just who I am in the here and now. I have a history, memories, etc., which define who I am, as well. Not all memory involves the self. Memory for procedures, skills, and places seems independent of our memories of our self. Autobiographical memory is a good example of the extended self. Memories are not usually very narrative. They are more snapshots. Three-year-olds do not reminisce. Old people do. Your experiences define you, but children have not used them to define the self yet. This begins after age 4. We have childhood amnesia before that. Importantly, the remembered self is held together seamlessly with the ecological and the interpersonal self.

Then there is the private self. Here we have private experiences. Dreams, thoughts, pains—the realm of secrets for children. It starts after age 4.

There is then the conceptual self. Usually we define ourselves in terms of what other people have told us we are. These pieces of information include beliefs about who we are and who others are. I am American, a professor, a father, etc. I believe I have a liver. I've never seen it, but this is what I have been told. All concepts depend on theory. I simply call it myself. Beliefs about ourselves are not always true. They are moderately responsive to data but largely untrue, as when the skinny girl says, "I'm fat." Or the ugly man says "I'm handsome."

Neiser's conclusion was that private experience has to be accounted for, but too much should not be made of it, since the self is already largely defined elsewhere. We have to start with what is veridically there, what we perceive and who we are and who we are within the present. This is the cognitivists' point of view.

Seligman's Positive Psychology

More enigmatic than other expressions of reductionistic empiricism in cognitive psychology that are hostile toward dynamic conceptions of personality has been Martin Seligman's program called Positive Psychology. Seligman used his presidential address before the American Psychological Association in 1999 to launch Positive Psychology. It was a psychology of hope and optimism that he believed countered psychology's historical emphasis on suffering and the negative attributes of personality that thwarted adjustment.

There were two problems to this approach, however. The problem was that there was a distinguished lineage in psychology already laid down since the time of William James that had advocated the same kind of emphasis, so Seligman and his colleagues can claim no originality for the idea. James, Flournoy, and Myers, all advocated the growth-oriented dimension to personality. Even Théodule Ribot called his endeavors "positive psychology." Jung, Rank, Adler, and others promulgated a similar idea in the classical era of depth psychology, while Horney, Fromm, and Frankl did so among the Neo-Freudians. Goldstein and Wertheimer were similar advocates among the gestalt psychologists. Maslow, Rogers, May, Charlotte Bühler, and others did likewise among the humanistic psychologists. Maslow, in particular, focused on the concept of a positive psychology, long before Seligman.

Seligman, however, while appropriating their language, but with much less sophistication regarding the implications for a value-free science, has self-consciously divorced himself from any association with his forebears and claimed total originality for the idea of a positive psychology and himself its sole inventor.[26] His background is in cognitive psychology and attribution theory, and his major contribution has been to the literature on learned helplessness, shocking animals into complete submission until they learned to react always as victims of every stressor. Generalizing from animals to people, Professor Seligman is a classic trait theorist whose main thrust now has turned to a classification of virtues. Positive psychology for him is happiness psychology. If we would only look at the bright side of things, they would come about. But as a cognitive strategy, one can only deal with each single behavior one at a time. Each negative thought has to be conditioned to a positive one.

Prof. Seligman's second problem comes from his own colleagues, who argue that science is conceived of as value free and he is superimposing a value-laden judgment on its results. Who, then, determines what is positive and what is negative? By what criteria? The question of meaning cannot be approached by the objectivist epistemology of experimentalism and still remain within that definition of science.

Prof. Seligman has loudly claimed that the humanistic psychologists, while they may have dealt with these issues, are unscientific and do no research, so there is no body of evidence from their claims, which is actually not the case. Nor has he sufficiently addressed the questions about his own philosophy of science that have come from his more reductionistic colleagues. His project has been well endowed financially, and he has now moved into the lucrative field of executive coaching, an area previously mined successfully by predecessors in the psychotherapeutic counterculture such as Anthony Robbins and before him, Werner Erhard, the founder of est. The philosophical implications for science of what he has proposed have not been discussed within his own circle, however. Instead, with the imprimatur of the APA, he has moved into the popular domain, claiming to be more scientific than his predecessors.

To add to the paradox, Prof. Seligman's co-partner in Positive Psychology is the Hungarian cognitivist Mihaly Csikszentmihalyi from the University of Chicago. Csikszentmihalyi started his career studying creativity in art students and in the late 1980s developed a theory around the experience of flow, a state of optimum functioning, which he has interpreted within the context of evolutionary theory.[27] We are a function of our genes, our biology, and our social environment, but at the same time live in a cognitive world of ideas and emotions that flow onward throughout the life span. Sounding very Jamesean, he has described the self who simultaneously experiences and tries to cognitively understand that experience through memes, the basic building blocks of the consciousness that flows onward, comparable to the DNA of the physical body. Although this position of psychophysical parallelism hardly addresses the mind/body problem under which the cognitivists suffer, he acknowledges the reality of transcendence and the possibility of more evolved states of consciousness. The tone is hopeful, positive, and optimistic about what kind of a future we could create as individuals. Positive motivation in children, the optimal functioning of adolescents, flow in sports, and definitions of the good life have been his subjects. His new effort is positive aging.[28] His main audience remains the educated public and the followers of Seligman in cognitive psychology, not his more reductionistic and atomistic colleagues in science. He does not consider the philosophical implications of his view of the person for science, but follows Seligman's lead, and the historic lead of the Humanistic psychologists, in skirting the reductionists by presenting a charismatic, growth-oriented psychology right to the general public.

Genomics

The ultimate and final step in the technological redefinition of personality comes when scientists and engineers are able to gain total control over one's individuality. The mapping of the human genome provides just such a possibility, as the entire genotype and phenotype of the unique individual can be worked out, including their ancestry. The accepted methodological approach, however, remains the collection of DNA samples on human populations classed according to diagnostic criteria from the Diagnostic and Statistical Manual (DSM) widely used in psychology and psychiatry. Genetic markers are then sought for specific diseases or syndromes of symptoms, which would seem to invalidate the results because empirical evidence varies on the reliability and validity of the original psychiatric classification given to any one patient in the first place.

In other words, despite the fact that a science of the whole person has been flourishing within the history of psychology and psychiatry and also out in the psychotherapeutic counterculture, scientists safe within the academy can still assure themselves that the homunculus had at last been banned from the halls of higher learning. Personality, in the form of depth psychology, had gone the way of folk psychology, which, Fodor claimed, had now been replaced by the superior models of cognitive science.[29]

Neurophenomenology, Embodiment, and Experience

The nature of the Hard Problem in the neurosciences is understanding the relation of the brain to the mind. How is it that we can have an objective understanding of a thing and an experience of it and not be able to tie these two domains together? How is it that we can have a robust third person science which objectifies the person, and phenomenology—which could be construed as a first person science in which we systematically study the structure of experience, with no correlation between the two? One answer proposed by a new generation of cognitively oriented thinkers is to reexamine the relationship between the subject and the object within the context of the mind/body problem and to challenge, in the context of neuroscience, traditional definitions of scientific objectivity. This has taken several forms, one of which is the problem of embodiment.

The idea that personality is ensconced in a body is not new. William James investigated the difference between physical sensations and our emotional feelings and later said that the stream of consciousness is probably our breathing. His theory of emotion postulated that what emotion we will experience was dependent on our perception of the situation.

Similarly, Maurice Merleau-Ponty argued for the body as an innate structure, driving cognitive skills in a cultural environment:

> The body is our general medium for having a world. Sometimes it is restricted to the actions necessary for the conservation of life, and accordingly it posits around us a biological world;

at other times, elaborating upon these primary actions and moving from their literal to a figurative meaning, it manifests through them a core of new significance: this is true of motor habits [sic] such as dancing. Sometimes, finally, the meaning aimed at cannot be achieved by the body's natural means; it must then build itself an instrument, and it projects thereby around itself a cultural world.[30]

We have mentioned in a footnote the attempt to systematically understand personality through the form and shape of the body beginning with Kretchmer and extending to William H. Sheldon. But dynamic theories of the unconscious were not employed in those conceptualizations. Other reductionistic empiricists have attempted to look at personality and the body as well.[31] But it was Freud and Otto Weininger behind the scenes, and then, of course, Reich, and those after him such as Janov, who were steeped in the psychodynamic point of view, which they applied to consciousness of the body. This lineage, it has been recently claimed, has found its pinnacle at Esalen Institute, where psychotherapy has been fused with bodywork, and in the developing fields of health psychology called psychoneuroimmunology, the mind/body effect, and complementary and alternative therapies. Within the academy, the Women's Movement has developed its own literature on the subject.[32]

Descartes, however, had made the situation murky from the start by separating mind and body and then proceeding to develop a science of the physical without the mental, making their reconciliation impossible according to the accumulation of scientific evidence only on one side of the equation. Consequently, most experimental empiricists hold that consciousness, if it exists at all, is a mere epiphenomenon of our physiology and that there is no mental event that cannot be reduced to some biochemical process somewhere in the body. We have seen a different position, however, in the history of existential-humanistic and transpersonal psychology by investigators such as Kurt Goldstein and René DuBois and their arguments for a holistic biology.

Contemporary cardiologists, psychophysiologists, transpersonal psychologists, and neuroendocrinologists have also been trying to rectify Descartes error by establishing empirically the connection between states of consciousness, physiological control over normally unconscious bodily processes, and the growth-oriented dimension to personality. Only a few of these efforts can be recited here.

The first, established during the era of psychosomatic medicine, was that reaction to stress was a problem of personality. Selye had determined that all organisms functioned according to the General Adaptation Syndrome, that is, the body was capable of adapting to ever increasing levels of stress to the point of exhaustion and death. Trait theory prevailed in the 1950s within the psychosomatic movement with the identification of the Type A personality, the highly driven individual who succeeded in everything attempted except where power over events was thwarted. Thwarted Type A personalities were then thought to be at the highest risk for psychosomatic illness such as low back pain and irritable bowel syndrome as well as hypertension, heart attack, and stroke.

Herbert Benson, Harvard cardiologist, took the psychophysiology of the mind/body effect one step further by linking techniques in stress reduction with contemplative methods in the world's religions, the spiritual sense of well-being, and bodily health. His psychophysiological experiments led to the articulation of the relaxation response.[33] In 1973, Benson and his student, Robert Keith Wallace, took 26 subjects who were experienced transcendental meditators who all had the same training. The subjects meditated for two 20-minute periods per day and Benson studied their physiology while maintaining the meditative state. Subjects went through a premeditation phase, a meditation phase, and a post-meditation phase of 30 minutes each to give measures before, during, and after. Wallace and Benson measured heart rate, blood pressure, blood lactate, internal core body temperature, and respiration in terms of ratio and volume of gas exchange. They found a drop in oxygen consumption and CO_2 elimination, but the ratio did not change. They found a slowing in heart rate while blood pressure remained stable. And they found a dramatic decline in blood lactate, a measure of anaerobic metabolism that persisted even into the recovery phase. This was significant because it indicated an actual alteration in basic metabolism as the subject became more and more relaxed. They were also able to differentiate the physiology of meditation from that of sleep and hypnosis, indicating that meditation precipitates its own special state of consciousness.

Benson was later able to replicate these findings in normal subjects who were not transcendental meditators, eventually identifying the underlying physiological mechanism, which he called the relaxation response.[34] He was able to show that two 20-minute periods a day practicing the relaxation response could have significant clinical effects promoting health. Blood pressure medication could be cut in half, PMS symptoms could be relieved, and visits to the HMOs could be significantly decreased. He also demonstrated that the relaxation response was elicited after 20 minutes of exercise, causing a drop in metabolism as further exercise continued.

He linked the relaxation response to both the contemplative practice of prayer and meditation as a source of healing. It seemed to be a basic physiological mechanism, comparable to, but opposite in effect from the fight–flight response, as an evolutionary reflex. The fight–flight response geared us up for battle or escape by producing the high octane fuel of blood glucose, adrenalin, and other catecholamines, while the relaxation response relaxes us and makes us peaceful and renews our sense of well-being through deep concentrated relaxation. He and his colleagues eventually called the relaxation response an antibioscenescent, an evolutionary mechanism that serves to protect life once it is established. Benson and colleagues posited that its willful elicitation was the same as the more automatic, reflexive, and nonvoluntary reaction already called the placebo effect, which is the body's first line of defense against trauma and infection and also serves as preparation for coping with long-term illness or disability.[35]

Benson's work has many implications for personality. It means that Type A personalities could be trained to change their behavior, and hence their type. In addition, one could also say that intentional relaxation represents an appeal to the growth-oriented dimension of personality, regardless of a person's type.

Benson has encountered extreme resistance to his work by the scientific reductionists at Harvard, despite the fact that he has received major sources of private and governmental grant funding and published his experimental studies in some of the world's premier peer-reviewed journals in science. So far, there have been no book-length works in the peer-reviewed scientific literature, but he has produced some best sellers in the trade market. As a result he is more well known in the psychotherapeutic counterculture, while his body of data, meanwhile, has been appropriated by new adherents of complementary and alternative therapies, trying to show there is empirical evidence for non-traditional forms of healing that contain elements of the relaxation response. We might say in this regard that Benson's work, first and foremost, is a contribution to psychology as a science of the whole person, although his primary milieu has always been scientific medicine and cardiology. It is a contribution to the concept of embodiment, as it presents scientific evidence for a mind/body complex linking physiology with consciousness non-reductively, an assumption rejected out of hand by reductionistic science.

Another contributor to a wholistic definition of mind and body has been Elmer Green, psychophysiologist, pioneer in biofeedback research and energy medicine, and co-founder of the Biofeedback Research Society. Over his career, Green has presented empirical evidence for the voluntary control of internal states in yoga, meditation, cases of spiritual healing, and the patient's overall sense of spiritual well-being. He took a BA in physics in 1946, attended UCLA as a graduate student before joining the Naval Weapons Center in China Lake, California, working as a physicist in optics, electronics, and computing. He took a PhD in biopsychology at the University of Chicago in 1964 and with his wife and colleague Alyce established the Psychophysiology Laboratory at the Menninger Foundation in 1967. There they launched the Voluntary Controls Program in biofeedback and self-regulation and co-sponsored the Voluntary Control of Internal States conferences at Council Grove, Kansas. In addition to the intensive laboratory investigation of yoga adepts such as Swami Rama, the Green's established a successful nationwide program in biofeedback and self-control that combined Wolfgang Luthe's techniques of Autogenic Training with biofeedback techniques that could be taught to any normal, average individual.[36]

The gist of this training was to employ an electroencephalogram and a computer to give the subject feedback on alpha/theta activity from the occipital lobe. Using the Luthe's relaxation techniques, and by training the subjects to differentiate between the alpha state of waking alertness and theta states where mental imagery such as in REM sleep is generated, the Greens were able to teach subjects how to lower the threshold of consciousness and produce dream images in the state of full-waking consciousness. Their findings suggested that mental imagery might not only be the means by which consciousness communicated with normally unconscious physiological states, but also be the vehicle by which ultimately transforming states of consciousness, induced states of transcendence, and personality change occur.[37]

Another contributor to the idea of a non-reductive embodiment has been Candace Pert, a psychopharmacologist who is a former research professor at Georgetown University School of Medicine and past section chief at the National Institute of Mental Health. Pert received her undergraduate degree in biology from Bryn Mawr College and her PhD in pharmacology from Johns Hopkins School of Medicine. As a graduate student under Solomon Snyder, she discovered the receptor site for the body's natural opiates and opened an entirely new field of research into the endorphins, for which Snyder received the credit, since it was his laboratory and she was his graduate student. At the NIH she and her colleagues undertook extensive mapping of the neuropeptide receptor sites and found that they massed in the limbic system, on the dorsal horn of the spine, and throughout the gut. They also found communication between brain cells and floating cells in the immune system through the extra ambient cellular fluid. Additionally, she went on the develop Peptide T as a treatment for AIDS.

The psychosomatic network that she and her colleagues defined seemed to be diffused throughout the body linking the newly discovered parasynaptic information network with the hard wiring of the brain and nervous system. As cognitive mental processes were mediated by the brain, emotional cascades seemed to predominate in the alternate chemical network. This led Pert to hypothesize that the neuropeptide map she had drawn was the basis for understanding the biochemistry of the emotions. Moods, for instance, appeared to be defined by the alternate chemical network, so that intentional alteration of one's mood state could have a reciprocal effect on chemical mediation of receptors and their binding cites. Moreover, it was soon discovered that chemicals that controlled the transmission of the nervous impulse at the synapse also had dual functions as messengers between brain cells and neuropeptide receptor sites in the alternate chemical network. Since both neural and chemical systems appeared to work in tandem, the old distinction between mind and body was no longer relevant, calling for a new philosophy of mind–body interaction and hence, new conceptions of the biological underpinnings of the self that would be less focused on brain activity alone and more on the total physiochemistry of the person.

One such development was an area of investigation that came to be called psychoneuroimmunology, a designation embraced by the psychotherapeutic counterculture, but soundly rejected by reductionistic empiricists at the forefront of advances in neuroendocrinology. The philosophy of biochemistry Pert was looking for was trumped by the fact that neuroendocrinology already had a philosophy – that of reductionistic empiricism.

Pert found a ready audience, however, through such organizations as the New York Academy of Medicine, the National Institute for Clinical and Behavioral Medicine, and the Institute of Noetic Sciences. Her work soon reached a wide public audience, which she followed with a best-selling popular book, *Molecules of Emotion* (1997).[38]

Intersubjectivity

Enter upon the scene a new breed of post-modern thinkers.[39] Harry Hunt (2005), who combines neuroscience with Buddhist epistemology and transpersonal psychology, has attempted to argue for a new definition of psychology, which takes into account the personality of the scientist. But he backs into it from a hermeneutic analysis of psychology's current methods and theories a la Giambatista Vico and Wilhelm Dilthey.[40] His first concern is that to other sciences psychology looks like it is in complete disarray, with competing theories, methods, and faddish research topics. In actuality, according to him, taken as a human science, this is precisely what psychology ought to look like it if spans both the sciences and the humanities. Single, dominant theories based on cumulative evidence over generations are replaced with a pluralism of interpretations based on attitude and worldview of the researcher. Dilthey maintained that it is precisely this tension that keeps psychology together as a field. Each theory must also be judged in terms of its ecological validity, by which Hunt means its pragmatic effect in the world of application. So, what kind of a science is that?

Hunt's answer is a very forward looking one, if we accept the hypothesis that the materialistic side of the discipline has been fed inordinately while the phenomenological side starved almost to extinction. The difficulty, as Vico first pointed out, is that the phenomenological side studies itself, which seems to contradict the accepted theories of reductionism, objectification, operationism, and representation, upon which contemporary scientific psychology is based. Hunt's view, which accounts for both kinds of science, at least explains the current fragmentation.

But how does it allow us to address the so-called "Hard Problem" in the neurosciences, namely, the relation of the mind to the brain? The answer is important, because on the materialist side, personality is safely just a conglomeration of traits, but on the phenomenological side it is the individual self embedded in the experience of language, meaning, and culture. We may be able to stop the internecine war of competing epistemologies within the discipline, which is the least we should have accomplished in the past 100 years. This brings the person into the center of the equation and the problem of first, second, and third person science reappears as a central problem for psychology, which the reductionists still presently control and confine to the third person. The rest they do not have the slightest clue about how to handle. At best, they are facing what William James predicted in 1890, when he asked, "we might want psychology to become a science, but then again can we handle the psychology that it will become?" Hunt's conclusion is that rational–empirical theories about the nature of personality and consciousness are going to have to interact with the very kinds of folk psychology, that is, a psychology of immediate experience they have rejected as unscientific, in order to define themselves.

The late Francisco Varela, Chilean neuroscientist and evolutionary biologist, has carried the argument several steps further; first as the co-originator with Jose Maturana of the theory of autopoiesis, and second thorough reconstruction of our overly linear conception of evolution. Autopoiesis, the creation of consciousness out of self-referential systems,[41] abandons the black box theory of inputs and outputs and encourages us to think in terms of feedback loops, in which at all levels the organism is self-creating, always seeking to define and express itself.[42] Drawing on the non-reductive principle that personality is a total gestalt, which transcends the mere addition of its parts by always representing something greater, Varela explains emergent systems that are self-created, meaning systems at all levels—molecular, cellular, organ, and species levels.

At the time of his death he was particularly interested in embodiment, the diffusion of consciousness through every cell of the body, particularly the immune system, with its ability to differentiate self from not-self across changing developmental stages of the organism. This also includes the problem of how we continually renew ourselves at the microphysiogical level, yet manage to remain relatively the same person across the life span. More importantly, however, is the implication that embodiment encompasses a vision of the body as something more than mechanical systems. Varela's theory is that consciousness is a product of the interaction between the organism and the environment, but in more of a Buddhist than Christian sense. This is not a Cartesian split where the two must be somehow integrated, so much as a radically different conception of the interdependence of opposites and their ongoing evolution, as in the Buddhist sense of co-dependent origination, or, I would add, as in James's understanding of radical empiricism.

Similarly, the late Eugene d'Aquili and Andrew Newberg, two cognitive neuroscientists from the clinical faculty at the University of Pennsylvania, have studied the neurophysiological correlates of religious experience. Their claim is that we have circuits in the brain that account for different experiences: one being the experience of rational causality and another being holistic experiences of transcendence. Both have had profound evolutionary significance in shaping personality. Further, they believe they have isolated a neurophysiological circuit that identifies a continuum from esthetic to transcendent experiences.[43]

The discussion, which focuses on the theme of what they call "neurotheology," is somewhat philosophically naïve about unitive experience, since they cannot account for what James called "the ever not quite" in noetic pluralism, and they conflate the experience of God with Buddhist experiences of the ultimate, which are nontheistic. Additionally, they have used as subjects in their experiments both Christian nuns and those whom they refer to as Tibetan Buddhist meditators, who actually are not Tibetans, but Caucasians who have studied Tibetan Buddhist teachings. Their primary funding source is the Templeton Foundation, which has a prior implicit commitment to applying the methods of physics to illuminating the truths of Christianity. The Foundation's definition of psychology is chiefly cognitive and behavioral, while dynamic theories of the unconscious across cultures, especially non-Western and non-theistic ones, or non-Western conceptions of personality, they shy away from.

However, we live in an unprecedented era where, in our time, we have been witness to the end of the production phase of science and the beginning of its permanent maintenance phase.[44] For the past 400 years the scientific method has marched through first, the inorganic world, and then the organic. Employing the language of mathematics and objective classification, physics, chemistry, geology, astronomy and other disciplines associated with the physical sciences set the stage for mastery of the biological domain, as science simultaneously expanded into the world of plants and animals. Botany and physiology, particularly advances in the medical sciences, brought science to the threshold of sensory and rational psychology, now more complicated because of the simultaneous relation of psychology to theology and philosophy posed by the neurosciences.

Nevertheless, wresting psychology from a mechanical and Newtonian context has allowed a scientific psychology to develop over the past 150 years, but one that has marked the final production phase of science as a metadiscipline. After sensory and cognitive science, there is nowhere for the psychological sciences to go except, in their new maintenance phase, to encounter all that has been pushed aside to make progress as a science. Through interdisciplinary communication between physics and biology, science has now begun to confront the biology of consciousness, which, beyond the physical structures of the brain, involve the problem of the mind, the very organ that created science in the first place. Science is now confronting itself, but by so doing, its very identity is being called into question, admittedly now only by the gadflies of the culture wars. The implications are clear, however. Either science has to reconcile itself to the fact that it is now only one of many other forms of useful knowledge in culture, or else transform itself to be able to accommodate domains of human experience now excluded by its present epistemology.

This is because the old philosophical and religious questions that had been put aside and strictly banned from discussion throughout much of the 20th century are back with a vengeance. They are now eagerly pursued by the cognitive psychologists mainly in the tradition of learning theory, such as Daniel Dennett, and the analytic philosophers in the lineage of Aristotle, Kant, Hegel, and Quine, such as the Churchlands, who remain the most powerful controllers of the discussion in scientific circles. They have even coined a term for themselves—Neurophilosophers.

But now we have neurophenomenologists and neurotheology, which are natural outgrowths of this discussion by younger scientists who have newer philosophical sensibilities and a richer commitment to understanding spiritual experience. Their very ability to speak is based on the humanistic implications of the neuroscience revolution, which, in addition to accounting for the underlying biology, demand a philosophical and spiritual explanation for the problem of consciousness. The only problem is that the analytic philosophers with the microphone have had all such sensibilities winnowed out of them years ago, while most of the humanistically oriented psychologists and psychiatrists are largely unprepared to interpret these implications, because most remain oblivious to the fact that the long-awaited revolution in scientific thinking that they have been calling for is actually here.

The Phenomenology of the Science-Making Process Itself

William James had tried to understand the relation of the mind to the brain through his tripartite metaphysics of pragmatism, pluralism, and radical empiricism. Jung approached the problem through the personal equation in science, believing that the answer lay in the awakening of a dialogue between consciousness and the unconscious, allowing the unconscious access to expand the domain of the waking state. The macropersonality theorists of the 1930s and 1940s, the Jamesean lineage in psychology, argued for a science of the whole person. They became the grandfathers and grandmothers of the Humanistic movement of the 1960s, proponents of which argued for psychology as a person-centered science—person centered meaning the intersubjective relation between subject and object, client and therapist, subject and experimenter. At this point the study of personality as a total gestalt had faded with the passing of the classical Humanistic psychology of Maslow, Rogers, and May and the subsequent overcolonization of personality theory by the trait theorists. The revolution in the neuroscience obviated the need for elaborate theories of the unconscious as old arguments even about the reality of the unseen faded in the face of artificial intelligence and information-processing models positing a cognitive unconscious, which were taken as given in the new science. Functionally, the person appears to have disappeared as an object of study. In its place, an artificial matrix has been developed at the interface between human–computer interaction. There is the individual, but now made over into Prof. Turkle's second self. This is not the unconscious of the person, but the artificial, preprogrammed world of the computer manipulating the cognitive and behavioral life of the individual, whose real and independent identity has become of little scientific consequence to the cognitive researcher.

The intersubjective emphasis in the next historical phase attempting to solve the Hard Problem could possibly be a focus on the personality of the scientist himself or herself.[45] Here, the identity and outlook of the scientist is an important factor for understanding what the phenomenology of the science-making process means. We may define it as the scientist becoming more self-conscious of his or her presence on the design, selection of subjects, procedures, and interpretation of the results of the study, all of which should be a part of the normal disclosures communicated in the peer-reviewed literature once the study is published. It may involve the relative level of self-knowledge possessed by the investigator (Tart's state-specific sciences). It may incorporate a phenomenologically oriented psychological analysis of the process involved in hypothesis formulation. It may involve the deconstruction of the scientific experiment as essentially a study in social psychology. In medicine it may involve the articulation of a peri-operative psychology, that is, a psychology surrounding every phase of the psychotherapeutic hour or every step of a surgical operation. It may involve an estimate of the degree to which the study operates solely within the parameters of the ego and waking rational consciousness, or attempts to reach beyond that boundary into non-ordinary states. It may involve the assessment of the patient's state of consciousness as well as the therapists' or the experimenter's state of consciousness in relation to the subject's.

Revelation of the Epistemological Worldview of the Scientist

If we take a more phenomenological approach to understanding the experimental situation, it becomes essential to know the *eigenwelt*, or unique interior worldview of the experimenter. This contradicts the assumptions of reductionistic positivism, however, where the experimenter allegedly remains objective and his or her footprint is not supposed to influence the outcome of what is studied. From a phenomenological point of view, this is not only an unproven assumption, but impossible, regardless of what the objective experimentalist claims.

Rosenthal[46] has identified effects unintended by the scientist on the outcome of what he or she studies, though he has long claimed that the effect is less than 1%. Orne[47] has convincingly demonstrated that the subject is in a state of hypnotic rapport with the experimenter in the midst of the experiment, which is actually an exercise in social psychology. Kilhstrom,[48] who has conceptually separated psychoanalysis from a definition of the cognitive unconscious, acknowledges how the experimenter's viewpoint saturates every aspect of the experimental situation. Velmans[49] maintains that contemporary theories of consciousness in the neurosciences are incomplete unless they contain a reflexive element, that is, unless the scientist accounts for his or her own presence in the study. Giorgi[50] maintains that the unifying theme across experimental and clinical psychology is the phenomenological relationship between the subject and the experimenter and the therapist and the client. The centrality of the phenomenon of identity across the life span has been pointed out by Erikson, suggesting that the individual's choice of science as a vocation implicates their sense of personal identity in their judgments about what is science and what is not, while other authors have linked the personality of the scientist directly to the psychology of science.[51]

With regard to the phenomenology of the science-making process itself, one must then evaluate the experiment or the interpretation of other's work in terms of what level of experimental rhetoric is employed. What is the experimenter's preconceived attitude toward the unconscious? Is psychology pursued for its own sake as a science? Or are we focused on studying the mystery of the person, experimental science being one useful tool in that endeavor? These are questions that will help to define the intersubjective relation between the observer and the observed, which I hypothesize, brings us one step close to answering the Hard Problem in the neurosciences. That route is through not only the personality and state of consciousness of the scientist himself or herself but alsothrough a phenomenological analysis of how the experiment is conducted, and a more phenomenological approach to the subject's personality as a total gestalt. These considerations would be foundational to any depth psychology of the future.

Notes

1. Vidal, F. (2005). "Le sujet cérébral: une esquisse historique et conceptuelle," *PSN: Revue de Psychiatrie, Sciences humaines et Neurosciences, 3*(11), 37–48.
2. Taylor, E.I. (2008). "Come Hither and Be Measured": On the problematic relation between cognitive psychology and spiritual experience from a Jamesean point of view. Presented as the keynote address to The Conference on Religion and Cognitive Science. Co-sponsored by the Cognitive Science Program at the University of California at Berkeley and the Graduate Theological Union Berkeley, California, January 16, 2008.

3. Allport, G. (1957). European and American theories of personality. In H. P. David & H. von Bracken (Eds.), *Perspectives in personality theory* (pp. 3–26). New York: Basic Books. The work was the first volume of the new series by the International Union of Scientific Psychology so its breadth was truly international in character; at least as far as Western psychology was concerned.
4. Allport, 1957, p. 16.
5. Allport, 1957, p. 18.
6. Allport, 1957, p. 20.
7. Craik, K. H., Hogan, R., & Wolfe, R. N. (Eds.). (1993). *Fifty years of personality psychology*. New York: Plenum.
8. Craik, Hogan, & Wolfe, 1993, p. 8.
9. Norman, W. T. (1963). Toward an adequate taxonomy of personality attributes: Replicated factor structure in peer nomination personality ratings. *Journal of Abnormal and Social Psychology, 66,* 574–583; John, O. P. (1990). The "Big Five" factor taxonomy: Dimensions of personality in the natural language and in questionnaires. In L. A. Pervin (Ed.), *Handbook of personality: Theory and research* (pp. 66–100). New York: Guilford.
10. Emmons, R. A. (1999). *The psychology of ultimate concerns: Motivation and spirituality in personality*. New York: Guilford.
11. McAdams, D. P. (1995). What do we know when we know a person? *Journal of Personality, 63*(3), 365–396; McAdams, D. P. (1996). Personality, modernity, and the storied self: A contemporary framework for studying persons. *Psychological Inquiry, 7*(4), 295–321; McAdams, D. P., Diamond, A., de Saint, A. E., & Mansfield, E. (1997). Stories of commitment: The psychological construction of generative lives. *Journal of Personality and Social Psychology, 72*(3), 678–694. McAdams, D. P., Josselson, R., & Lieblich, A. (2006). *Identity and story: Creating self in narrative*. Washington, DC, US: American Psychological Association.
12. Horney (1942); Jung (1969a); Akhilananda (1946).
13. McAdams, D. P., & Pals, J. L. (2006). A new big five: Fundamental principles for an integrative science of personality. *American Psychologist, 61*(3), 204–217.
14. He is a clear example of the humanistic tradition of his mentor Murray, but now persisting in the established cognitive-behavioral environment. See, for instance, McAdams, D. P. (2006a). *The redemptive self: Stories Americans live by*. New York: Oxford University Press; McAdams, D. P. (2006b). *The person: A new introduction to personality psychology* (4th ed.). New York: Wiley; Bauer, J. J., McAdams, D. P., & Sakaeda, A. (2005). Interpreting the good life: Growth memories in the lives of mature, happy people. *Journal of Personality and Social Psychology, 88*(1), 203–217.
15. Widiger, T. A., & Trull, T. J. (2007). Plate tectonics in the classification of personality disorder: Shifting to a dimensional model. *American Psychologist, 62*(2), 71–83.
16. O'Brien, J., & Jureidini, G. (2002a). Dispensing with the dynamic unconscious. *Philosophy, Psychiatry and Psychology, 9*(2), 141–154; Woody, J. M. (2002). Dispensing with the dynamic unconscious. *Philosophy, Psychiatry and Psychology, 9*(2), 155–157; Kroll, J. (2002). The nine lives of the dynamic unconscious. *Philosophy, Psychiatry and Psychology, 9*(2), 168–169; O'Brien, J., & Jureidini, G. (2002b). The last rites of the dynamic unconscious. *Philosophy, Psychiatry and Psychology, 9*(2), 161–194.
17. James, 1890a, Vol. 1., p. 196.
18. See also, Kircher, T., & David, A. S. (2005). The self in neuroscience and psychiatry. *Educational Psychology in Practice, 21*(2), 156–157.
19. Kircher, T., & David, A. S. (2003). *The self in neuroscience and psychiatry*. London, New York: Cambridge University Press.
20. Kircher & David, 2003, p. 2.
21. Kircher & David, 2003, p. 450.
22. Kircher & David, 2003, p. 2.
23. Lasch, C. (1982). *The Freudian left and the theory of Cultural Revolution*. London: University College London; Robinson, P. A. (1969). *The Freudian left: Wilhelm Reich, Geza Roheim, Herbert Marcuse*. New York: Harper & Row; Marcuse, H. (1955). *Eros and civilization: A philosophical inquiry into Freud*. New York: Vintage.
24. See, for instance, Cantor, N., Zirkel, S., & Norem, J. K. (1993). Human personality: Asocial and reflexive? *Psychological Inquiry, 4*(4), 273–277.

25. Gibson, J. (1979). *The ecological approach to visual perception.* Hillsdale, NJ: Lawrence Erlbaum.
26. Taylor (2001b).
27. Csikszentmihalyi, M. (1991). *Flow: The psychology of optimal experience.* New York: Harper Perennial; Csikszentmihalyi, M. (1993). *The evolving self: A psychology for the third millennium.* New York: HarperCollins.
28. Csikszentmihalyi, M., & Csikszentmihalyi, I. S. (Eds.). (2006). *A life worth living: Contributions to positive psychology.* New York: Oxford University Press.
29. Fodor, J. (2000). *The mind doesn't work that way: The scope and limits of computational psychology.* Cambridge, MA: MIT Press.
30. Merleau-Ponty, M. (1962). *Phenomenology of perception* (C. Smith, Trans.). London: Routledge & Kegan Paul, p. 146.
31. Fischer, S., & Cleveland, S. (1968). *Body image and personality* (2nd ed.). New York: Dover.
32. Gilligan, C., Brown, L. M., & Rogers, A. G. (1988). *Psyche embedded: A place for body, relationships, and culture in personality theory.* Cambridge, MA: Harvard University, Graduate School of Education, Center for the Study of Gender, Education, and Human Development.
33. Wallace, R. K., & Benson, H. (1973). The physiology of meditation. In D. Shapiro, T. X. Barber, L. Dicara, J. Kamiya, N. Miller, & J. Stovya (Eds.), *Biofeedback and self control* (pp. 353–364). Chicago: Aldine.
34. Benson, H. (1975). *The relaxation response.* New York: Morrow.
35. Stefano, G. B., Fricchione, G. L., Slingsby, B. T., & Benson, H. (2001). The placebo effect and relaxation response: Neural processes and their coupling with constitutive nitric oxide. *Brain Research Reviews, 35,* 1–19.
36. Green, E., & Green, A. (1977). *Beyond biofeedback.* New York: Delacorte.
37. Working at the interface of psychology, physiology, and medicine he became a co-founder of the International Association for the Study of Subtle Energies and Energy Medicine.
38. Pert, C. (1997). *Molecules of emotion.* New York: Scribner.
39. Mostly all males. See, for instance, Beal, A. E., & Sternberg, R. J. (1993). *The psychology of gender.* New York: Guilford Press.
40. Hunt, H. T. (2005). Why psychology is/is not traditional science: The self referential basis of psychological research and theory. *Review of General Psychology, 9*(4), 358–374.
41. Varela, F. J. (1995). The emergent self. In J. Brockman (Ed.), *The third culture: Beyond the scientific revolution*(pp. 210–222). New York: Touchtone.
42. Varela, F. J., & Bruce, T. (2002). Consciousness in the neurosciences. *Journal of European Psychoanalysis, 14,* 109–122.
43. Newberg, A. B., & d'Aquili, E. (2000). The neuropsychology of religious and spiritual experience. In J. Andresen, & R. K. C. Forman (Eds.), *Cognitive models and spiritual maps: Interdisciplinary explorations of religious experience* (pp. 251–266). Charlottesville, VA: Imprint Academic.
44. MacMurray, J. (1939). *The boundaries of science: A study in the philosophy of psychology.* London: Faber and Faber, Ltd.
45. Stagner, R. (1988). *A history of psychological theories.* New York: Macmillan, London; Collier Macmillan; Silverman, H. (1977). *The human subject in the psychological laboratory.* New York: Pergamon Press; Bunge, M. A. (1962). *Intuition and science.* Englewood Cliffs, NJ: Prentice-Hall; Lowry, R. (1971). *The evolution of psychological theory: 1650 to the present.* Chicago: Aldine-Atherton.
46. Rosenthal, R. (1966). *Experimenter effects in behavioral research.* New York: Appleton-Century-Crofts.
47. Orne, M. T. (2002). On the social psychology of the psychological experiment: With particular reference to demand characteristics and their implications. *Prevention & Treatment, 5*(35); originally published 1962, *The American Psychologist, 17*(11), 776–783.
48. Kihlstrom, J. F. (2003). Expecting that a treatment will be given when it won't, and knowing that a treatment is being given when it is. *Prevention & Treatment, 6*(1), 4c. Also, Kihlstrom, J. F. (2002). Demand characteristics in the laboratory and the clinic: Conversations and collaborations with subjects and patients. *Prevention & Treatment, 5*(36c) [Special issue honoring Martin T. Orne]. Retrieved 5/20/08 from http://journals.apa.org/prevention/volume5/pre0050036c.html
49. Velmans, M. (1993). A reflexive science of consciousness. In *Experimental and theoretical studies of consciousness* (pp. 81–99). Ciba Foundation Symposium 174. Chichester, England: John Wiley & Sons.

50. Giorgi, A. (2006). The psychological phenomenological method. *Journal of Phenomenological Psychology, 37*(2), 284–285. And for a refutation of the idea that one could not access subjectivity without transforming it into an object, see Zahavi, D. (2005). *Subjectivity and selfhood: Investigating the first person perspective*. Cambridge, MA: MIT Press.

51. Feist, G. J. (1998). The psychology of science: Review and integration of a nascent discipline. *Review of General Psychology, 2*(1), 3–47; Roe, A. (1961). The psychology of the scientist. *Science, 134*, 456–459. Also, Erikson, E. (2008). The problem of ego identity. In D. L. Browning (Ed.), *Adolescent identities: A collection of readings* (pp. 223–240). New York: The Analytic Press/Taylor & Francis Group. See also, Maslow, A. H. (1966). *The psychology of science: A reconnaissance.* NY: Harper & Row.

Chapter 12
Epilogue

The ultimate in rigor is rigor mortis
E. Taylor

When we look back over the history of dynamic theories of personality, brief and incomplete as this sketch has been, and view it from the standpoint of the theorists themselves, not their detractors' version of it, we see several decisive trends. First, as we pointed out at the beginning, concepts of the ego, personality, and the self are often used interchangeably when they are historically different and completely unintegrated constructs with their own separate meaning, literature, and theorists. Second, as we also pointed out, attitudes about dynamic theories of personality imply models of consciousness, theories of personality, and techniques of psychotherapy that are always interrelated with each other. Third, the history of psychotherapeutics is still dominated by writers who know only the history of psychoanalysis, giving a distinct Freudo-centric spin on any subject that falls within the purview of depth psychology.

Fourth, traditional histories of personality theory omit the late 19th-century developments in multiple personality, skip the period of the so-called French-Swiss-English-and-American psychotherapeutic axis, except to mention Charcot without understanding his real milieu; then they ignore the interim era of character and temperament, go right to psychoanalysis, and then speak as if there were no other systems except Freud's or that Freud somehow "discovered the unconscious." Adler and Jung continue to be cast as errant disciples of Freud instead of depth psychologists in their own right. Janet is almost always pushed completely out of the picture.

Meanwhile, interest inventories, trait theory, the calculation of the IQ, and more sophisticated techniques of statistical inference became the main focus of the measurement-oriented reductionists after World War I, particularly from the 1920s onward, creating a psychology compatible with nomothetic reductionism. But these developments also obscured the macropersonality theorists of the 1930s and 1940s, who focused on the single case study, believed that personality was a total gestalt, and understood psychology as a study of the person and not the white rat. This caused a major rift between academic and clinical psychology, pitting tests and measurements and generalizations from animal studies against psychotherapeutics,

E. Taylor, *The Mystery of Personality*, Library of the History of Psychology Theories, 339
DOI 10.1007/978-0-387-98104-8_12, © Springer Science+Business Media, LLC 2009

developmental models, and dynamic theories of both personality and social psychology. To the experimentalists whose epistemology was dominated by behaviorism, any consideration of altered states of consciousness was fed into their contempt for Freud's theories, specifically the experimentalists' rejection of the Freudian conception of the unconscious. No other argument then needed to be mounted about possible competing theories, although in the early days of classical depth psychology, Adler and Jung were at least considered.

Meanwhile, an epistemological war began to develop between the dynamic theorists who saw the unconscious as the locus of change within the person and the social theorists who believed that impersonal forces within the group determined individual identity. Psychoanalytic ego psychology, a more social orientation to psychoanalysis, and the culture and personality movement were reactions to this split, while social psychology itself became more radical as organizations were founded such as the Society for the Psychological Study of Social Issues, arguing for a more socialist interpretation of psychology harnessed in service of political change out in culture at large. Traditional histories of personality theory only lightly touch upon the rift between the dynamic and the social theorists, and then instead hurry on to a discussion of the five factor model today, ignoring the rise of existential-humanistic and transpersonal psychology as a major development in the history of psychology, except to possibly mention Maslow, May, and Rogers, but out of context. Humanistic psychology flourished within the academy only into the 1960s. By then it had absorbed existential and phenomenological psychology into its purview and was driving new advances in pastoral counseling and social work as it temporarily took more of a position of influence in mainstream professional psychology. Here, the humanistic impulse passed more visibly out of the academy. Its proliferation out into the psychotherapeutic counterculture was reflected in women's consciousness raising groups, gestalt therapy workshops, encounter group methods, body work, radical sexual therapy, and interest in altered states of consciousness.

The so-called cognitive-behavioral viewpoint has dominated the modern era and defined experimental psychology in the context of the cognitive neurosciences, where any focus on the person has become obscured in discussions of parallel distributive processing models, artificial intelligence, and the mechanisms of synaptic transmission. These concerns have now evolved into discussions by reductionists about the putative relation between the mind and the brain and a new genre of literature referred to as 'the soft problem,' since the Hard Problem, the relation between the brain and the mind, cannot be solved by their present epistemology. In the domain of application, the new cognitive psychology has not been able to evolve past a focus such as Prof. Seligman's cultivation of positive, happy thoughts, one thought at a time, or Daniel Dennett's behavioristic interpretation of the evolution of consciousness.

Nevertheless, the uniqueness of the individual goes beyond the bounds of the present 19th-century definition of the scientific method in psychology by advocating that the person is much more than the sum of his or her traits. Objectivist methods ruled by a reductionistic and positivist epistemology have classically defined the person in scientific psychology in purely atomistic terms. Alternative ways of understanding personality have historically grown up to fill this gap between measurement and experience, including the traditions of depth psychology. Personality, abnormal, social, and clinical psychology were at first considered soft sciences; that is, they were thought of as the fleshy underbelly of putative real science, such as psychophysics, sensation and perception, learning theory, and mathematical psychology. The soft sciences gathered around themselves other related disciplines such as child psychology and developmental psychology across the life span, and overlapped with sociology, anthropology, and the arts and humanities. Only later were the soft sciences invaded by the empirical reductionists, mainly through tests and measurements, learning, and trait theory.

This has led to a situation where scientific psychology presently suffers from identification with an outmoded, reductionistic, and 19th-century Newtonian definition of the physical sciences, set in a complex labyrinth of myths around the founding of Wundt's laboratory in Leipzig in 1879, first articulated by E. G. Boring in the 1950 edition of his work, *A History of Experimental Psychology*. Experimental psychology has continued to identify with the physical sciences in its insistence that the field is a science. However, experimental psychology has failed to keep pace with developments in physics, such as the role of the observer in altering what is observed or the idea that there could be conflicting sets of data, both true, for the same phenomenon, both examples of which are elements of the so-called quantum philosophy.

Such an accommodation to the New Physics would have significantly altered the attitude of experimental psychologists toward the study of the person. Instead, the date psychology stopped maturing as a science patterned after physics can be precisely fixed as September 1927, when the quantum physicist Niels Bohr proposed the idea of complementarity at the international conference in Como, Italy, commemorating the 100th anniversary of the death of Volta. There Bohr outlined the evidence for the conclusion that all atomic structures can be successfully verified as both a wave of light and a particle of matter, but these two incompatible positions, while both can be demonstrated empirically, cannot be reconciled. The result in physics was an accommodation that both could be true simultaneously, which also had the unintended effect of relativizing the objectivist position in science. Experimental psychology did not absorb this lesson, but turned instead to the model of the double blind, randomized, placebo-controlled experiment, the measurement of a single variable in a large-scale sample, and the relativizing of the subject in the experiment, so that a rat, a pigeon, or a person could be equally substituted for each other.

Attempts at the experimental analysis of psychoanalytic concepts, beginning in the 1920s, became a veritable cottage industry among one segment of personality, social, and developmental theorists and have continued unabated up to today. But such efforts have usually been carried on by investigators already predisposed toward acknowledging the reality of the unconscious.

The inability of experimental psychology, based on the rational ordering of sense data alone, to acknowledge the reality of the unconscious remains as the most cogent historical example of scientific psychologists' inability to move past a Newtonian model of the physical sciences, similarly with the problem of acknowledging a growth-oriented dimension to personality. As a result of this outmoded identification with reductionistic measurement, the study of personality has drifted toward trait theory, a kind of lazy-man's science, which now has been elevated to the superior standard of what is considered real science in psychology.

Present day science, however, can only proceed up to the threshold of the known, as defined by the empirical measurement of what can be verified. Beyond that point is the entire domain of human experience in its breadth, depth, and history. This history has chronicled the use of images, symbols, and mythologies, both personal and collective, by human beings to articulate a vision of their personal destiny and their place in the structure and meaning of existence, long before the development of the rationalist tradition in Western science. Let us call it, an idiosyncratic, existential-phenomenological psychology based on mental imagery and intuitive insight, which allows the person to proceed into and out of the subconscious, sometimes daily, on a journey toward self-knowledge and the actualization of one's unique potential over a lifetime.

Institutions of high culture, such as the apparatus defining scientific research and its mechanism of funding, or clinical practice defined by third party insurance payments based on the measurement of traits, are at present themselves based on objectivist science and are therefore, by definition, more narrow than the breadth and depth of an individuals' contemporary lived experience.

The neuroscience revolution, however, demands an account of the dynamic relation between experience and understanding, between the brain and the mind. The phenomenology of the science-making process provides an avenue, namely, that with regard to the problem of consciousness, subject and object are intersubjectively intertwined, regardless of the reductionistic and objectivist epistemology that prevails in rhetoric of the experimentalists.

This poses a direct challenge to psychology as exclusively a science. Instead, it implies that psychology is not just a science. It is both an art and a science. The arts and humanities speak to psychology as a reductionistic science through narrative ways of knowing in a way that not only corrects for reductionistic objectivism but also uniquely situates psychology among the sciences. Understood as a phenomenological science, psychology not only reaches into the humanities but also sits at the foundation of science itself. This is because the interpretation of all measurements is always dependent on someone's individual consciousness somewhere. Such a view widens the purview of psychology as a science while it sets limits on the generalizability of reductionistic positivism by providing an adequate explanation for experiential self-knowledge and a language of interior experience based on intuitive insight. This would open predominantly White, Western, and Protestant views of the person to non-Western ways of defining personality. It would then become evident that depth psychology, as well as existentialism and phenomenology, are our ways in to these alternative epistemologies.

Indigenous Non-Western Conceptions of Personality

Let us return for a moment to the idea that historically in the United States, with the exception of the First Nations people who were here before us, we have largely evolved as a product of a Judeo-Christian, Greco-Roman, Western European, and Anglo-American definition of reality. This is a trajectory that has defined the major religious traditions in the West, produced science as we know it today, declared that our clocks shall be calculated from Greenwich Mean Time, and that our calendar shall be Gregorian. This trajectory has molded the course of our language and shaped our thinking as educated individuals into habitual ways of looking at things. Scientists like to believe that they are dealing only with the truth and that they remain skeptical until they have seen the evidence. Others, they say, deal in mere metaphysics, as scientists believe that only they are in possession of what is real. Thus, it is easy to confuse the scientific method, which helps us to better understand our reality, with the scientific worldview, which is a commitment to a specific belief about the universe, allegedly based on the facts of science. Could it be that, as we have fundamentalism in religion, so we have it as well in science?

We give Copernicus credit for the shift from a heliocentric view that the universe rotates around the person to a geocentric one, where the earth rotates around the sun. Yet, in a very real sense, there must be someone's consciousness somewhere to witness and chronicle this phenomenon. Phenomenologically, the universe still rotates around the individual, but this is a fact about consciousness, not a statement intelligible to materialistic scientists elaborating on the scientific worldview. Traditional Chinese medicine says that the brain is in the heart. Modern anatomy has quite discounted this claim, but there is also a concept in Buddhism describing a characteristic of the Buddha, called the *bodhi–citta*, the intelligent mind–heart of the Buddha. This is an attempt to address the problem using the method of symbolism in the transformation of personality—that wisdom is not an intellectual or cognitive activity by itself. It always involves an awakening of the heart and both must be cultivated together, although language makes them appear separate.

We have now reached the pinnacle of our confusion about the relation of the scientific method with the scientific worldview when we ask a Nobel Prize-winning physicist to talk on cosmology, previously the domain of the theologians and philosophers. Stephen Hawking's statements about the superiority of science seem more to be religious statements about his own personal beliefs, not the truth of all truths for us all. In believing with him, we have essentially reconstructed science as a religion, claiming at the same time that we are unbiased and as true scientists we remain uncontaminated by religion. It would be a rare experimental psychologist who could admit our methods and viewpoint are culture bound, which prevents us from listening to the indigenous psychologies of other cultures. Instead, we believe at the outset that these alternate epistemologies are inferior to the scientific worldview and if there is any merit to them, they must first yield to being assessed by our models and sanitized through our own cultural filters, both scientific and religious.

Other than a realization that psychological science presents only one of many other competing views of reality just as functional for healthy individuals, the only other way a true change in attitude by culture-bound psychologists to grasp the enormity of the problem might be a cross-cultural exchange of ideas between East and West unprecedented in the history of Western thought. We may say that the alternative reality tradition in Western cultural consciousness has been titrating non-Western ideas to us for 2 millennia. What I am referring to, however, is the opening of a new dialogue between Western scientists and non-Western views of personality and consciousness. This would occur along the lines of an epistemological shift so the context in which individual ideas are understood undergoes a massive realignment. Mundane ideas taken for granted would then have to be all reassessed, in the same manner as practical experience was subjected to numerical quantification in psychology in the opening decades of the 20th century. Everything had to be reassessed anew, as it would again under these new circumstances.

In this regard, we may conjecture about the outlines of a depth psychology to come. Throughout the 20th century, given a solely Western context, collective consciousness has focused on Freudian psychoanalysis. All else was thought to be a mere footnote. Should we experience a cross-cultural exchange of epistemologies of the magnitude I am describing, Freud would have to be reassessed. In my opinion, such a depth psychology of the future would be non-reductionistic, would change our understanding of waking rational consciousness in the evolutionary process, would be able to accommodate a wider range and depth of human experience than we do now, would be seen as foundational to the generation of all scientific knowledge, and at least would look more Jungian than Freudian, although both their names would likely not even be remembered.

No one can assess the current situation, however, and not see plainly that the traditional ways of defining the person in psychology are under assault. It has been one thing through the history of psychology to contest the reality of the self, as the experimentalists have persistently done. It is quite another that a tradition of the person has sprung up, endured, developed into maturity, and, with the humanistic implications of the neuroscience revolution now pressing in on us, been vindicated. There is no question, however, that these promulgators of a person-centered science in the past suffered the widespread, public and professional calumny of their detractors.

The Growth-Oriented Dimension of Personality

At the same time, let me say that the culture wars that have invaded the history and philosophy of science in the past quarter of a century have not swerved to address the fundamental basis of the mind/body problem. Instead, in psychology what has evolved is a radical feminist critique of positivism filtered through the lens of race, class, and gender, sometimes, as in the California variety of the movement, tempered with a Western reading of more exotic influences, such as a hint of Buddhist mindfulness. Dominated largely by a deconstructionist epistemology derived from European social criticism, what depth psychology there is in this movement is drawn largely from a feminist interpretation of Freud.

In contrast, the actual history of existential-humanistic and transpersonal psychology has evolved largely in the United States defining psychology as a person-centered science, where personality is considered a total gestalt, and experiential methods of self-realization are recognized as equally legitimate to statistics in generating the basic data of the discipline.

In this vein, as our analysis has suggested, dynamic theories of personality are hardly an anachronism. James showed clearly that a dynamic psychology of the subliminal was a sufficient challenge to reductionistic positivism to warrant a new epistemology for the way experimental psychology and science generally should be conducted. That was his radical empiricism. Though left undeveloped at the time of his death in 1910, with regard to not only science but also human thought in general, Whitehead was profoundly moved enough to declare that radical empiricism was the inauguration of an altogether new stage in philosophy, beyond symbolic logic and analytic methods.

During that same era, on the basis of his own intuition, Freud demanded that psychoanalysis be accepted as a science separate from neurology, psychology, and psychiatry, despite abandonment of his efforts to establish that fact with his Project for a Scientific Psychology. Jung, who historically was allied as much with James as Freud, conceived of analytical psychology as the bridge between science and religion, which permitted a cross-cultural, comparative psychology of mystical states of consciousness and linked psychology as much with the humanities as with the sciences. As we have said, the macropersonality theorists of the 1930s and 1940s understood this link, and, though fighting to maintain their own theoretical survival against the greater weight of the nomothetic psychologists of their own era, partly by drawing on the lineage of the gestalt laboratory psychologists and the cultural anthropologists, they became the god fathers and god mothers of the humanistic movement in psychology. Emanating out of counseling, motivation, and personality theory, humanistic psychology began to flourish with the failure of the unity of science movement driving reductionistic positivism. Humanistic psychology eventually came to also embrace existential-phenomenological psychology, more radical forms of depth psychology, and non-Western epistemologies, and it took on a distinct political tinge, as it simultaneously focused on the person in the body, emotional development, group dynamics, and altered states of consciousness. Intellectually, it was also poised to engage in epistemological critique of reductionistic positivism and the statistical definition of the person in mainstream psychology.

Unable to bear the weight of these forces all at once, humanistic psychology first bifurcated into the humanists and those interested in spiritual states of consciousness. It then further fractionated into those studying meditation and altered states of consciousness, those practicing experiential bodywork and group dynamics, and those pursuing a radical political psychology of social transformation that has come to be dominated by the ideology of race, class, and gender. Becoming absorbed into the psychotherapeutic counterculture, the humanistic movement in psychology moved out of academia over into the clinic, before being appropriated out in the wider culture by the folk-psychologists.

Meanwhile, the last place that interdisciplinary communication was thought possible began in the 1950s between physics and biology around the problem of consciousness. This eventually spawned the neuroscience revolution, which has cut across the boundaries of the traditional reductionistic disciplines, and is now drawing the greatest amount of research funding to the interface between molecular genetics, immunology, neurology, endocrinology, and experimental psychiatry. In this process, it has invaded psychology and appropriated the cognitivists' domain of sensation and perception, brain neuropsychology, psychophysiology, and learning theory, leaving the rest as kind of cannibalized shell.

The major research question of the neuroscience revolution circles around the biology of consciousness in search of a solution to the Hard Problem—that is, the relationship between the brain and the mind, between our objective understanding of reality and our direct experience of it.[1] This search has generated certain humanistic implications beyond the reductionistic epistemology that started the neuroscience revolution in the first place.

What are some of the humanistic implications of the neuroscience movement? These might include the role of the experimenter in the outcome of the study; the epistemological frame of reference under which the experiment is carried out; the theoretical persuasion of the experimenter; the focus on an individual's unique experience and momentary state of consciousness; and the ability to conceive of the person in terms other than the Western analytic model.

The Uniqueness of Each Person

Despite all that is said in empirical science and organized religion, the individual stands alone under the eye of eternity, or whatever higher power serves that function for different individuals. We come into the world as unique and irreplaceable. And while we always come in the context of the union of a male and a female, and therefore have a familial and social context, regardless of different definitions of the genders, no one else can take our place and be born for us, have just the reactions and make just the choices that each of us uniquely make, have the same experiences, love whom we have loved, hate whom we hate, pass on exactly the same genes, and in the end die instead for us. We do all these things singularly, in our uniqueness. We may trace our biological evolution with our DNA in the genes of our parents with some precision, but we still do not know the extent of how much of who we are is passed from generation to generation through the overlap of cognitive learning, or how much comes to us from the vast universe within from some collective pool of our psychic humanity.

In this regard, our uniqueness posses two problems for psychological science. Namely, we do not presently have a scientific psychology that accounts for the uniqueness of the individual. Our predilection is toward the average, toward the generalization, and toward the norms of the group. Likewise, we pit the individual against the collective, when all the new evidence points toward an intersubjective reality. We as much as create our reality as participate in it, but we have no science sophisticated enough to broach this possibility in anything except the most vague terms.

Further, intersubjectivity requires that we identify the primary presuppositions of the investigator and his or her particular philosophical outlook before we take the results and conclusion of the experiment at face value. The epistemology of the experimenter defines the epistemology of the experiment and its outcome. Psychology more accurately then becomes as much an art as a science, and its purview becomes clear, that it is first and foremost a science that is person centered (see Fig. 12.1)

Here, a person-centered science acknowledges the powerful effect of genetics and temperament on defining the person. But that is not all there is to the story. One must also consider the changing psychophysiology of the person over the life span; the role of learned behaviors in shaping particular personality styles; the individual's unique cognitive style; the individual's unconscious habits, attitudes, and memories, including the impact of the physical, psychological, and social environment; their dynamic repressions and sublimations; and their entire interior life world—including their existential and phenomenological states of consciousness in the immediate moment, ranging from the psychopathic to the transcendent, with waking consciousness somewhere in between. Finally, there is the state of consciousness of the observer of the person, so inextricably intertwined in any attempt to define someone else's personality.[2]

In such a person-centered science, the locus of control would not pass from the experimenter to the subject, because in reality the nature of the interaction is intersubjective. What such a psychology would look like would then mean a

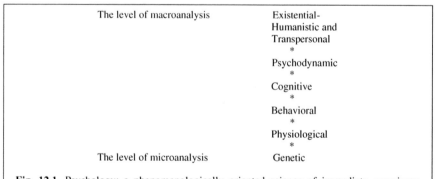

The level of macroanalysis	Existential-Humanistic and Transpersonal
	*
	Psychodynamic
	*
	Cognitive
	*
	Behavioral
	*
	Physiological
	*
The level of microanalysis	Genetic

Fig. 12.1 Psychology: a phenomenologically oriented science of immediate experience whose central focus as a person-centered science is the study of the individual and his or her life-space at many different levels of complexity through a variety of different methods Adapted from Strange, J. R., & Taylor, E. I. (1972). A theory of integrative levels useful in teaching psychology. Position paper. Department of Psychology, Southern Methodist University, Dallas Texas.

transformation of how psychology is defined today. The psychologist might still conduct research leading to the manipulation, prediction, and control of someone else's thoughts and behavior through models verified by statistical analysis, but the scientist would also have to concede to a more artistic approach to the understanding of interior experience, and in this sense, psychology as a science would become more observational. As an art, the individual and not the experimenter has at hand the method of symbolism in order to correct one's thinking, navigate the realms of the unconscious, and effect healing through psychogenesis as well as the voluntary control of internal states. Moreover, in the method of symbolism, we also have the harnessing of values, and the ability to make moral choices between right and wrong, a decision that always resides within the person alone. Through such encounters, the individual is empowered at the core. Reductionistic science cannot go there and moreover does not even belong in that domain, except perhaps to send a phenomenological observer. It may have to begin by approaching subjective experience from the periphery, but as it does, science begins to evolve into something else other than its traditional form.

Psychology as Epistemology

Finally, a history of dynamic theories of personality points to the need for a more sophisticated definition of psychology in the academy. Beyond the mere rational ordering of sense data alone, the scientist must be required to take the more subjective dimensions of human experience into account, particularly those drawing from his or her own emotional as well as intuitive nature. The logician and philosopher of science, Charles Sanders Pierce, has already laid the foundation for this work in his discussion of abduction, the use of intuition in the formulation, testing, and interpretation of hypotheses. Similarly, human science scholars have analyzed the extra-scientific factors in the science-making process and determined through their hermeneutic methods that normative science is gender biased, culture bound, and controlled, not by the neutral standards of objective, value-free research, but by a hidden and entrenched power elite with an agenda focused on perpetuating itself.

Expanding the sources of knowledge available to the scientific psychologist necessarily will broaden the definition and purview of personality in psychology. Such a new psychology, if we listen more closely to psychologists from William James and the macropersonality theorists to Amedeo Giorgi and neuroscientists such as Francisco Varela, would be much more phenomenological in character, and, consequently, in scope more like astronomy, geography, or oceanography, which are largely observational and permit one time unrepeatable events.

Meanwhile, the implications for psychology as a discipline go far beyond its present identity as a social science in the hierarchy of the sciences. Rather than being thought of as a derivative of the natural sciences, a more phenomenologically oriented psychology could be seen as foundational to all the sciences, since there can be no science anywhere without some consciousness somewhere to articulate it.

For such a transformed psychology, the person remains at once both focused and vast. The individual, at the center, remains incomparable in his or her uniqueness, like no other who has ever existed, yet at his or her farther reaches, within the capacity of each one's experience, the person is infinite. We may say of the person as Pascal has reminded us:

"Persona est circulus cuius centrum est ubique, cuis circumferentia vero nusquam."[3]

What we require is not a psychology perpetuated mainly for the sake of science, but a science equal to the mystery of the person.

Notes

1. Flanagan, O. (2008). *The really hard problem: Meaning in a material world*. Cambridge: MIT Press.
2. To say that such an inordinate focus on the individual misses the social dynamic is to completely misunderstand the existential state of consciousness within the person, in which all perceptions of the external world are based. To the social theorists, existentialism is a mere idea. To the existentialist, it is a central, interior experience. From this vantage point, there is no social group without there first being individuals. Phenomenal consciousness is inextricably intertwined with the external material world of objects and with other living beings. The social is comprehended through the individual.
3. Borges, H. L. (1999). Pascal's sphere. In E. Weinberger (Ed.) (E. Allen, S. J. Levine, & E. Weinberger, Trans.), *Selected non-fictions*. New York: Viking, p. 352.

Bibliography

Aanstoos, C. M., Serlin, I., & Greening, T. (2004). A history of Division 32 (Humanistic Psychology). In D. A. Dewsbury (Ed.), *Unification through division: Histories of the divisions of the American Psychological Association* (Vol. 5, pp. xii, 197). Washington, DC: American Psychological Association.

Achterberg, J. (1985). *Imagery in healing: Shamanism and modern medicine.* Boston: New Science Library, Shambhala; New York: Random House.

Adler, A. (1898). *Gesundheitsbuch für das Schneidergewerbe*, No. 5 of the series: *Weigweiser der Gewerbehygiene* (G. Golebiewski, Ed.). Berlin: Carl Heymanns.

Adler, A. (1907). *Studie über Minderwertigkeit von Organen* [Study of organ inferiority]. Vienna: Urban und Schwartenberg.

Adler, A. (1916). *The neurotic constitution: Outlines of a comparative individualistic psychology and psychotherapy* (B. Glueck & J. E. Lind, Trans.). New York: Moffat, Yard.

Adler, A. (1917). Study of organ inferiority and its psychical compensation: A contribution to clinical medicine. *Nervous and Mental Disease Monograph Series, 24* (S. E. Jelliffe, Trans.). New York: The Nervous and Mental Disease Publishing Company.

Adler, A. (1924). *The practice and theory of individual psychology.* London: K. Paul, Trench, Trubner & Company, Ltd; New York: Harcourt, Brace & company.

Adler, A. (1927). *Menschenkenntnis.* [Understanding human nature]. Leipzig: Hirzel; New York: Greenberg.

Adler, A. (1929). *The case of Miss R.: The interpretation of a life story* (E & F. Jensen, Trans.). New York: Greenberg.

Adler, A. (1930a). *Guiding the child on the principles of individual psychology* (B. Ginzburg, Trans.). London: George Allen and Unwin; New York: Greenberg.

Adler, A. (1930b). *The pattern of life* (B. Wolfe, Ed.). New York: Cosmopolitan Book Corporation.

Adler, A. (1935). Introduction. *International Journal of Individual Psychology, 1*(1), 5–8.

Adler, A. (1945). Two different types of post-traumatic neuroses. *American Journal of Psychiatry, 102*, 237–240.

Adler, G. (1961). *The living symbol: A case study in the process of individuation.* London: Routledge & Kegan Paul; New York: Pantheon Books.

Adler, G. (1968). *Studies in analytical psychology.* New York: Greenwood Press.

Adler, A. (2002a). Health manual for the tailoring trade. In H. T. Stein (Ed.) (G. L. Liebenau, Trans.), *The collected clinical works of Alfred Adler* (1898–1909) (Vol. 2.1, pp. 1–14). Bellingham, WA: Classical Adlerian Translation Project. (Original work published 1898).

Adler, A. (2002b). A study of organ inferiority and its philosophical and psychological meaning. In H. T. Stein (Ed.) (G. L. Liebenau, Trans.), *The Collected clinical works of Alfred Alder* (1898–1909) (Vol. 2.2, pp. 78–85). Bellingham, WA: Classical Adlerian Translation Project. (Original work published 1907).

Adorno, T. W. (1950). *The authoritarian personality.* New York: Wiley, Science Editions.

Akhilananda, S. (1946). *Hindu psychology: Its meaning for the West.* New York: Harper & Brothers.

Alexander, C. N., & Langer, E. J. (Eds.). (1990). *Higher stages of human development: Perspectives on adult growth.* New York: Oxford University Press.

Alexander, F., Glueck, B., Lewin, B. D., & Brill, A. A. (1930). *The psychoanalysis of the total personality: The application of Freud's theory of the ego to the neuroses.* Monograph series, No. 52. New York: Nervous and Mental Disease Publishing Company.

Alexander, F., & Ross, H. (Eds.). (1952). *Dynamic psychiatry.* Chicago: University of Chicago Press.

Alexander, F., & Selesnick, S. T. (1966). *The history of psychiatry: An evaluation of psychiatric thought and practice from prehistoric times to the present.* New York: Harper & Row.

Allen, G. W. (1967). *William James: A biography.* New York: Viking.

Allport, G. W. (1922). *An Experimental study of the traits of personality, with application to the problem of social diagnosis.* Unpublished doctoral dissertation, Harvard University, Cambridge, MA.

Allport, G. W. (1937). *Personality: A psychological interpretation.* New York: Henry Holt and Company.

Allport, G. W. (1938). William Stern: 1871–1938. *American Journal of Psychology, 51*(4), 770–773.

Allport, G. (1950). *The individual and his religion.* New York: The MacMillan Company.

Allport, G. W. (1955). *Becoming: Basic considerations for a psychology of personality.* New Haven, CT: Yale University Press.

Allport, G. W. (1957). European and American theories of personality. In H. P. David & H. von Bracken (Eds.), *Perspectives in personality theory* (pp. 3–26). New York: Basic Books.

Allport, G. W. (1967). Autobiography. In E. G. Boring & G. Lindzey (Eds.), *A history of psychology in autobiography* (Vol. 5, pp. 3–25). New York: Appleton-Century-Crofts.

Allport, G. W. (1968). *The person in psychology: Selected essays.* Boston: Beacon Press.

Allport, G. W., Vernon, P. E., & Powers, E. (1933). *Studies in expressive movement.* New York: The Macmillan Company.

Anderson, W. T. (1983). *The upstart spring: Esalen and the American awakening.* Reading, MA: Addison-Wesley.

Anderson, J. W. (1988). Henry A. Murray's early career: A psychobiographical exploration. *Journal of Personality, 56*(1), 139–171.

Angell, J. R. (1961). James Rowland Angell. In C. Murchison (Ed.), *A history of psychology in autobiography* (Vol. 3, pp. 1–38). New York: Russell and Russell.

Angyal, A. (1941). *Foundations for a science of personality.* New York: The Commonwealth Fund.

Ansbacher, H. L. (1990, Fall). Alfred Adler's influence on the three leading cofounders of humanistic psychology. *Journal of Humanistic Psychology, 30*(4), 45–53.

Ansbacher, H. L., & Ansbacher, R. R. (Eds.). (1956). *The individual psychology of Alfred Adler: A systematic presentation in selections from his writings.* New York: Harper & Row.

Ansbacher, H. L., & Ansbacher, R. R. (Eds.). (1964). *Alfred Adler: Superiority and social interest: A collection of later writings,* with a biographical essay by Carl Fürtmuller. Evanston, IL: Northwestern University Press.

Anthony, M. (1999). *Jung's circle of women: The valkyries.* York Beach, ME: Nicholas-Hays.

Aronson, J., & Rieff, P. (1966). *The triumph of the therapeutic: Uses of faith after Freud.* New York: Harper & Row.

Asch, S. (1946). Forming impressions of personality. *Journal of Abnormal and Social Psychology, 41,* 258–290.

Ash, M. G. (1987). Psychology and politics in Interwar Vienna: The Vienna Psychological Institute, 1922–1942. In M. G. Ash & W. R. Woodward (Eds.), *Psychology in twentieth-century thought and society* (pp. 143–164). Cambridge, New York: Cambridge University Press.

Ash, M. G. (1995). *Gestalt psychology in German culture, 1890–1967.* Cambridge, New York: Cambridge University Press.

Assagioli, R. (1909). La psichologia della ideé-forze e la psicagogia. *Revista di Psicologia Applicata, 5*(1), 371–393.

Assagioli, R. (1964). *Psychosynthesis: A manual of principles and techniques.* New York: Holt, Rinehart & Winston; London: G. Allen & Unwin.

Assagioli, R. (1969). Symbols of transpersonal experiences. *Journal of Transpersonal Psychology, 1*(1), 33–45.

Assagioli, R. (1976). *Psychosynthesis: A manual of principles and techniques.* Harmondsworth, England; New York: Penguin Book.

Athos, A. G., & Coffey, R. E. (1968). *Behavior in organizations: A multidimensional view.* Englewood Cliffs, NJ: Prentice-Hall.

Azam, E. (1887). *Hypnotisme, double conscience, et altérations de la personnalité.* Paris: J. B. Baillière et Fils.

Baars, B. J. (1986). *The cognitive revolution in psychology.* New York: Guilford Press.

Bair, D. (2003). *Jung: A biography.* Boston: Little, Brown and Company.

Bakan, D. (1958). *Sigmund Freud and the Jewish mystical tradition.* Princeton, NJ: Princeton University Press.

Baldwin, J. M. (Ed.). (1901/1960). *Dictionary of philosophy and psychology* (3 Vols.). Gloucester, MA: Peter Smith.

Bannar, L. (2003). *Intertwined lives: Margaret Mead, Ruth Benedict, and their circle.* New York: Alfred A. Knopf.

Barrett, W. (1911). *Psychical research.* New York: Henry Holt.

Bateson, M. K. (1984). *With a daughter's eye: A memoir of Margaret Mead and Gregory Bateson.* New York: William Morrow and Co.

Bauer, J. J., McAdams, D. P., & Sakaeda, A. R. (2005). Interpreting the good life: Growth memories in the lives of mature, happy people. *Journal of Personality and Social Psychology, 88*(1), 203–217.

Baynes, H. G. (1940). *Mythology of the soul: A research into the unconscious from schizophrenic dreams and drawings.* London: RKP.

Baynes, H. G. (1941). *Germany possessed (Introduction by Hermann Rauschning).* London: RKP.

Beal, A. E., & Sternberg, R. J. (1993). *The psychology of gender.* New York: Guilford Press.

Beard, G. M. (1873). The influence of the mind in the causation and cure of disease and the potency of expectation. *Journal of Nervous and Mental Diseases, 3,* 430–431.

Becker, E. (1973). *The denial of death.* New York: Free Press.

Benedict, R. (1922). The vision in plains culture. *American Anthropologist, 24,* 1–23.

Benedict R. (1930). Psychological types in the cultures of the Southwest. *Proceedings of the 23rd International Congress of Americanists,* September, 1928, 572–581.

Benedict, R. (1933). Anthropology and the abnormal. *Journal of General Psychology, 10,* 59–82.

Benedict, R. (1934). *Patterns of culture.* Boston: Houghton Mifflin.

Benedict, R. (1938, January). Review of the neurotic personality of our time. *Journal of Abnormal Psychology, 33,* 133–135.

Benedict, R. (1940). *Race, science, and politics.* New York: Modern Age Books.

Benedict, R. (1942). Review of escape from freedom. *Psychiatry, 5*(1), 111–113.

Benedict, R. (1946). *The chrysanthemum and the sword: Patterns of Japanese culture.* Boston: Houghton Mifflin.

Benson, H. (1975). *The relaxation response.* New York: Morrow.

Bergson, H. (1912). *Introduction to metaphysics.* New York: G Putnam's Sons.

Bergson, H. (1935). *The two sources of morality and religion.* New York: Henry Holt.

Bernheim, H. (1889). *Suggestive therapeutics: A treatise on the nature and uses of hypnotism* (C. A. Herter, Trans.). New York, London: G. P. Putnam's Sons.

Bernstein, P. L. (1979). The use of symbolism within a gestalt movement therapy approach. In P. L. Bernstein (Ed.), *Eight theoretical approaches in dance movement therapy.* Dubuque, IA: Kendall/Hunt Publishing Company.

Berrios, G. E., & Porter, R. (Eds.). (1995). *A history of clinical psychiatry: The origin and history of psychiatric disorders*. London, New Brunswick, NJ: Athlone Press; Somerset, NJ: Transaction Publishers.

Bertin, C. (1982). *Marie Bonaparte: A life*. New Haven, CT: Yale University Press.

Bertocci, P. (1945). The psychological self, the ego, and personality. *Psychological Review, 52*, 91–99.

Binet, A. (1890). *On double consciousness*. Chicago: Open Court.

Binet, A. (1892). *Les altérations de la personnalité*. Ancienne library. Germer Baillière et Cie. Paris: Félix Alcan.

Binswanger, L. (1957). *Sigmund Freud: Reminiscences of a friendship* (N. Guterman, Trans.). New York: Grune & Stratton.

Binswanger, L. (1963). *Being-in-the-world; selected papers of Ludwig Binswanger* (J. Needleman, Trans.). New York: Basic Books.

Bion, W. R. (1948). *Experiences in groups: Human relations, Vols. I–IV, 1948–1951*. Reprinted in *Experiences in groups*. (1961). London: Tavistock.

Bion, W. R. (1957). The differentiation of the psychotic from the non-psychotic personalities. *International Journal of Psycho-analysis, 38*, 266–275. Reprinted in *Second thoughts*. (1967). London: Heinemann.

Bluhm, A. C. (2005). *Turning toward individuation: Carol Sawyer Baumann's interpretation of Jung, 1927–1931*. Unpublished doctoral dissertation, Saybrook Graduate School and Research Center, San Francisco, CA.

Bluhm, A. C. (2006). Verification of C. G. Jung's analysis of Rowland Hazard and the history of Alcoholics Anonymous. *History of Psychology, 9*(4), 313–324.

Bollas, C., Pontalis, J-B., & Didier, A., et al. (1989). In memoriam: Masud Khan, 1924–1989. *Nouvelle Revue de Psychanalyse, 40*, 333–359.

Borges, H. L. (1999). Pascal's sphere. In E. Weinberger (Ed.) (E. Allen, S. J. Levine, & E. Weinberger, Trans.), *Selected non-fictions*. New York: Viking.

Boring, E. G. (1929). *A history of experimental psychology*. New York, London: The Century Company.

Boring, E. G. (1933). *The physical dimensions of consciousness*. New York, London: The Century Company.

Boring, E. G. (1938). The society of experimental psychologists: 1904–1938. *The American Journal of Psychology, 51*(2), 410–423.

Boring, E. G. (1940). Was this analysis a success? *Journal of Abnormal and Social Psychology, 55*(1), 2–3, 3–10.

Boring, E. G. (1950). *A history of experimental psychology* (2nd ed.). New York: Appleton-Century-Crofts.

Boring, E. G. (1961). *Psychologist at large: An autobiography and selected essays*. New York: Basic Books.

Bowlby, J. (1958). The nature of the child's tie to his mother. *International Journal of Psycho-analysis, 39*(5), 350–373.

Bowlby, J. (1969–1982). *Attachment and loss: Vol. 1. Attachment*. London: Hogarth Press.

Bowlby, J. (1971). *Attachment and loss: Vol. 1. Attachment*. Harmondsworth, UK: Penguin.

Bowlby, J. (1973a). *Attachment and loss: Vol. 1. Attachment*. New York: Basic Books.

Bowlby, J. (1973b). *Attachment and loss: Vol. 2. Separation: Anxiety and anger*. London: Hogarth Press.

Bowlby, J. (1973c). *Attachment and loss: Vol. 2. Separation: Anxiety and anger*. New York: Basic Books.

Bowlby, J. (1975). *Attachment and loss: Vol. 2. Separation: Anxiety and anger*. Harmondsworth: Penguin.

Bowlby, J. (1980). *Attachment and loss: Vol. 3. Loss: Sadness and depression*. New York: Basic Books.

Bowlby, J. (1981). *Attachment and loss: Loss: Sadness and depression*. Harmondsworth, UK: Penguin.

Braude, A. (1989). *Radical spirits: Spiritualism and women's rights in nineteenth-century America*. Boston: Beacon Press.

Breuer, J., & Freud, S. (1893). Studies on hysteria. On the psychical mechanism of hysterical phenomena: Preliminary communication. *The standard edition of the complete psychological works of Sigmund Freud* (Vol. 2, pp. 1–18). London: Hogarth Press.

Bugental, J. F. T. (1963). Humanistic psychology: A new breakthrough. *American Psychologist, 18*, 563–567.

Bühler, C. (1922). *Das seelenleben des jugendlichen* [Psychology of adolescence]. Jena: Gustav Fischer.

Bühler, C. (1929). Jungendpsychologie und Schule. *Suddeutscher Monatshefte, 27,* 186.

Bühler, C. (1954). The reality principle: Discussion of theories and observational data. *American Journal of Psychotherapy, 8*(4), 626–647.

Bühler, C. (1959). Theoretical aspects of life's basic tendencies. *American Journal of Psychotherapy, 13*(3), 501–581.

Bühler, C. (1964). The human course of life in its goal aspects. *Journal of Humanistic Psychology, 4,* 1–17.

Bühler, C. (1968). The general structure of the human life cycle. In C. Bühler & F. Massarik (Eds.), *The course of human life: A study of goals in the humanistic perspective* (pp. 12–26). New York: Springer.

Bunge, M. A. (1962). *Intuition and science*. Englewood Cliffs, NJ: Prentice-Hall.

Burnham, J. C. (1967). *Psychoanalysis and American medicine: 1894–1918: Medicine, science, and culture*. New York: International Universities Press.

Burston, D. (1991). *The legacy of Erich Fromm*. Cambridge, MA: Harvard University Press.

Calkins, M. W. (1915). The self in scientific psychology. *American Journal of Psychology, 26*, 495–524. Article retrieved October 1, 2007, from http://psychclassics. yorku.ca/Calkins/self.htm

Cambray, J., & Carter, L. (Eds.). (2004). *Analytical psychology: Contemporary perspectives in Jungian analysis*. Hove, New York: Brunner-Routledge.

Campbell, J. (1944). *A skeleton key to Finnegan's wake*. New York: Harcourt, Brace & Company.

Campbell, J. (1949). *Hero with a thousand faces*. New York: Pantheon.

Campbell, J. (1959). *Primitive mythology*. New York: Viking Press.

Campbell, J. (1959–1968). *The masks of God*. New York: Viking Press.

Campbell, J. (1962). *Oriental mythology*. New York: Viking Press.

Campbell, J. (Ed.). (1964a). *Papers from the Eranos yearbooks* (Vol. 5). Bollingen Series XXX. New York: Pantheon.

Campbell, J. (1964b). *Occidental mythology*. New York: Viking Press.

Campbell, J. (1968). *Creative mythology*. New York: Viking Press.

Campbell, J. (1969). *The flight of the wild gander: Explorations in the mythological dimension*. New York: Viking Press.

Campbell, J. (1970). *Myths, dreams, and religion*. New York: E. P. Dutton.

Campbell, J. (1972). *Myths to live by*. New York: Viking Press.

Campbell, J. (1974). *The mythic image*. Princeton, NJ: Princeton University Press.

Campbell, J. (1988). *Historical atlas of world mythology*. New York: Perennial Library.

Camus, J., & Pagniez, P. (1908–1909a). The history of psychotherapy. I. The psychotherapy of drugs (W. B. Parker, Ed., F. Peterson & E. Garrigue, Trans.). *Psychotherapy: A course of reading in sound psychology, sound medicine and sound religion, 1*(3), 64–71.

Camus, J., & Pagniez, P. (1908–1909b). The history of psychotherapy. II. Psychotherapy by means of miraculous (W. B. Parker, Ed., F. Peterson & E. Garrigue, Trans.). *Psychotherapy: A course of reading in sound psychology, sound medicine and sound religion, 1*(4), 54–64.

Camus, J., & Pagniez, P. (1908–1909c). The history of psychotherapy. III. The history of psychotherapy IV (W. B. Parker, Ed., F. Peterson & E. Garrigue, Trans.). *Psychotherapy: A course of reading in sound psychology, sound medicine and sound religion, 3*(1), 50–59.

Cannon, B. (1991). *Sartre and psychoanalysis: An existentialist challenge to clinical metatheory.* Lawrence, KS: University Press of Kansas.

Cantor, N., Zirkel, S., & Norem, J. K. (1993). Human personality: Asocial and reflexive? *Psychological Inquiry, 4*(4), 273–277.

Cantril, H. (1950). *Tensions that cause wars, common statements and individual papers by a group of social scientists brought together by UNESCO.* Urbana, IL: University of Illinois Press.

Cartwright, D. (1948). Social psychology in the United States during the Second World War. *Human Relations, 1*(3), 333–352.

Cartwright, D. (1979). Contemporary social psychology in historical perspective. *Social Psychology Quarterly, 42*(1), 82–93.

Case, M. H. (1994). *Heinrich Zimmer: Coming into his own.* Princeton, NJ: Princeton University Press.

Child, I. L. (1973). *Humanistic psychology and the research tradition: Their several virtues.* New York: Wiley.

Chodorow, N. J. (1978). *The reproduction of mothering.* Berkeley, LA: University of California Press.

Chodorow, N. J. (1989). *Feminism and psychoanalytic theory.* London, New Haven, CT: Yale University Press.

Chodorow, N. J. (1994). *Femininities, masculinities, sexualities: Freud and beyond.* Lexington, KY: The University Press of Kentucky.

Chodorow, N. J. (1999). *The power of feelings: Personal meaning in psychoanalysis, gender, and culture.* London, New Haven, CT: Yale University Press.

Claparède, E. (Ed.). (1910). *VIe Congrès International de Psychologie, 1909 Rapports et Comptes-Rendus.* Geneva: Kündig.

Clarke, J. F. (1882) *Self-culture: Physical, intellectual, moral, and spiritual.* Boston: James R. Osgood.

Coles, R. (1970). *Erik H. Erikson: The growth of his work.* Boston: Little, Brown.

Coles, R. (1992). *Anna Freud: The dream of psychoanalysis.* Reading, MA: Addison-Wesley.

Coon, D. (2000). Salvaging the self in a world without soul: William James's The Principles of Psychology. *History of Psychology, 3*(2), 83–103.

Cooper, T. D. (2006). *Paul Tillich and psychology: Historic and contemporary explorations in theology, psychotherapy and ethics.* Macon, GA: Mercer University Press.

Craik, K. H., Hogan, R., & Wolfe, R. N. (Eds.). (1993). *Fifty years of personality psychology.* New York: Plenum.

Crews, F. (1996). The verdict on Freud. *Psychological Science, 7*(2), 63–67.

Csikszentmihalyi, M. (1991). *Flow: The psychology of optimal experience.* New York: Harper Perennial.

Csikszentmihalyi, M. (1993). *The evolving self: A psychology for the third millennium.* New York: HarperCollins.

Csikszentmihalyi, M., & Csikszentmihalyi, I. S. (Eds.). (2006). *A life worth living: Contributions to positive psychology.* New York: Oxford University Press.

Darlington, B. (1998, winter). Vassar's jung folks. *Vassar Quarterly, 95*(1), 18–23.

Das, K. C. (1975). *The concept of personality in Samkhya-yoga and the Gita.* Assam, India: Department of Publication, Gawahati University.

De Bussy, J. H. (1908). Théories modernes sur la genèse de l'hystérie. *Compte rendu des Travaux du Premier Congrès International de Psychiatrie, de Neurologie, de Psychologie et de l'Assistance aux aliénés.* Amsterdam, September 2–7, 1907, pp. 264–270.

Dollard, J. (1935). *Criteria for the life history, with analysis of six notable documents.* New Haven: Yale University Press.

Dollard, J. (1939). *Frustration and aggression.* New Haven: Yale University Press.

Douglas, C. (1990). *The woman in the mirror: Analytical psychology and the feminine.* Boston: Sigo Press.

Douglas, C. (1993). *Translate this darkness: The life of Christiana Morgan*. New York: Simon & Schuster.

Douglas, C. (Ed.). (1997). *Visions: Notes of the seminar given in 1930–1934* by C. G. Jung (Vol. 1–2). Princeton, NJ: Princeton University Press.

Eagle, M. N. (1987). The psychoanalytic and the cognitive unconscious. In R. Stern (Ed.), *Theories of the unconscious and theories of the self* (pp. 155–189). Hillsdale, NJ: Analytic Press.

Eder, M., Wehrlin, K., Riklin, F., & Jung, C. G. (1969). *Studies in word-association: Experiments in the diagnosis of psychopathological conditions carried out at the Psychiatric Clinic of the University of Zurich under the direction of C. G Jung*. New York: Russell & Russell. (Original work published 1904–1909)

Edinger, E. F. (1972). *Ego and archetype: Individuation and the religious function of the psyche*. New York: Putnam.

Ehrenwald, J. (Ed.). (1976). *The History of psychotherapy: From healing magic to encounter*. New York: Jason Aronson Inc.

Ekstein, R., & Wallerstein, R. S. (1958). *The teaching and learning of psychotherapy*. New York: Basic Books; London: Imago Publication Company.

Ellenberger, H. (1970). *The discovery of the unconscious: The history and evolution of dynamic psychiatry*. New York: Basic Books.

Ellenberger, H. F. (1978). Pierre Janet and his American friends. In G. E. Gifford, Jr. (Ed.), *Psychoanalysis, psychotherapy, and the New England medical scene, 1894–1944* (pp. 63–72). New York: Science History Publications.

Ellenberger, H. (1993). The story of Anna O. A critical review with new data. In M. Micale (Ed.), *Beyond the unconscious: Essays of Henri F. Ellenberger in the history of psychiatry* (pp. 254–272). Princeton, NJ: Princeton University Press.

Emerson, R. W. (1850). *Representative men*. London: John Chapman.

Emmons, R. A. (1999). *The psychology of ultimate concerns: Motivation and spirituality in personality*. New York: Guilford.

Erikson, E. (1939). Observations on Sioux Education. *Journal of Psychology, 7*, 101–156.

Erikson, E. (1950). *Childhood and society*. New York: W. W. Norton.

Erikson, E. (1958). *Young man Luther: A study in psychoanalysis and history*. New York: W. W. Norton.

Erikson, E. (1968). *Identity, youth, and crisis*. New York: W. W. Norton.

Erikson, E. (1969). *Gandhi's truth; on the origins of militant nonviolence*. New York: W. W. Norton.

Erikson, E. (2008). The problem of ego identity. In D. L. Browning (Ed.), *Adolescent identities: A collection of readings* (pp. 223–240). New York: The Analytic Press/Taylor & Francis Group.

Eysenck, H. J. (1970). Explanation and the concept of personality. In R. T. Borger & F. Cioffi (Eds.), *Explanation in the behavioral sciences* (pp. 387–424). Cambridge, MA: Cambridge University Press.

Fadiman, J. (1969). The Council Grove conference on altered states of consciousness. *Journal of Humanistic Psychology, 9*, 135–137.

Fadiman, J., & Frager, R. (1976). *Personality and personal growth*. New York: Harper & Row.

Fancher, R. (1973). *Psychoanalytic psychology: The development of Freud's thought*. New York: W. W. Norton.

Feigenbaum, K. (2008). *Maslow's founding of the Brandeis Psychology Department*. Society for the History of Psychology, Annual Meeting of the American Psychological Association, Boston, MA, 2008.

Feist, G. J. (1998). The psychology of science: Review and integration of a nascent discipline. *Review of General Psychology, 2*(1), 3–47.

Féré, C. (1892). *La pathologie des émotions; études physiologiques et cliniques*. Paris, F. Alcan.

Féré, C. (1899a). *L'instinct sexuel; évolution et dissolution*. Paris: Félix Alcan.

Féré, C. (1899b). *The pathology of emotions: Physiological and clinical studies* (R. Park, Trans.). London: University Press.

Ferenczi, S. (1916). *Contributions to psycho-analysis* (E. Jones, Trans). Boston: R. G. Badger.

Ferenczi, S., & Rank, O. (1924). *Entwicklungsziele der Psychoanalyse zur Wechselbeziehung von Theorie und Praxis* [The development of psychoanalysis]. Neue Arbeiten zur ärztlichen Psychoanalyse, Heft 1. Wien: Internationaler Psychoanalytischer Verlag.

Ferenczi, S., & Rank, O. (1925/1986). *The development of psycho-analysis.* Madison, CT: International Universities Press.

Fernandez, J. W. (1968). *Report of the 1967 seminar on culture and personality* (pp. 188–214). Hanover, NH: Dartmouth Comparative Studies Center.

Fischer, S., & Cleveland, S. (1968). *Body image and personality* (2nd ed.). New York: Dover.

Fodor, J. (2000). *The mind doesn't work that way: The scope and limits of computational psychology.* Cambridge, MA: MIT Press.

Fordham, M. (1944). *The life of childhood: A contribution to analytical psychology.* London: Paul, Trench, Trubner.

Frankl, V. (1925). *Psychotherapie und weltanshauung* [Psychotherapy and weltanschauung]. *International Zeitschrift fur Individualpsychologie, 3,* 250–252.

Frankl, V. E. (1955). *The doctor and the soul: An introduction to logotherapy.* New York: Knopf.

Frankl, V. E. (1959). *From death-camp to existentialism: A psychiatrist's path to a new therapy.* Boston: Beacon Press.

Frankl, V. E. (1963/1992). *Man's search for meaning: An introduction to logotherapy* (I. Lasch, Trans.). Boston: Beacon Press.

Freedheim, D. K. (Ed.). (1992). *History of psychotherapy a century of change.* Washington, DC: American Psychological Association.

Freud, A. (1937). *The ego and the mechanisms of defence.* The International Psycho-analytical Library, No. 30. London: Hogarth Press, and the Institute of Psycho-analysis.

Freud, A. (1946). *The psychoanalytical treatment of children: Technical lectures and essays.* London: Imago Publishing Company.

Freud, A. (1922–1935). *The writings of Anna Freud: Vol. 1. Introduction to psychoanalysis: Lectures for child analysts and teachers.* New York: International Universities Press.

Freud, A. (1936). *The writings of Anna Freud: Vol. 2. Ego and the mechanisms of defence.* New York: International Universities Press.

Freud, A. (1939–1945). *The writings of Anna Freud: Vol. 3. Infants without families reports on the Hampstead Nurseries by Anna Freud.* New York: International Universities Press.

Freud, A. (1945–1956). *The writings of Anna Freud: Vol. 4. Indications for child analysis and other papers.* New York: International Universities Press.

Freud, A. (1956–1965). *The writings of Anna Freud: Vol. 5. Research at the Hampstead Child-Therapy Clinic and other papers.* New York: International Universities Press.

Freud, A. (1965). *The writings of Anna Freud: Vol. 6. Normality and pathology in childhood: Assessments of development.* New York: International Universities Press.

Freud, A. (1966–1970). *The writings of Anna Freud: Vol. 7. Problems of psychoanalytic training, diagnosis, and the technique of therapy.* New York: International Universities Press.

Freud, A. (1970–1980). *The writings of Anna Freud: Vol. 8. Psychoanalytic psychology of normal development.* New York: International Universities Press.

Freud, S. (1895). Project for a scientific psychology. In J. Strachey (Ed. & Trans.), *The standard edition of the complete psychological works of Sigmund Freud* (Vol. 1, pp. 281–392). London: Hogarth Press.

Freud, S. (1896). Further remarks on the neuro-psychoses of defense. In J. Strachey (Ed. & Trans.), *The standard edition of the complete psychological works of Sigmund Freud* (Vol. 2, pp. 41–61). London: Hogarth Press.

Freud, S. (1900). The interpretation of dreams. In J. Strachey (Ed. & Trans.), *The standard edition of the complete psychological work of Sigmund Freud* (Vols. 4–5, pp. 1–622). London: Hogarth Press.

Freud. S. (1901). The psychopathology of everyday life. In J. Strachey (Ed. & Trans.), *The standard edition of the complete psychological works of Sigmund Freud* (Vol. 6, pp. 1–291). London: Hogarth Press.

Freud, S. (1905/1901). Fragment of an analysis of a case of hysteria. In J. Strachey (Ed. & Trans.), *The standard edition of the complete psychological works of Sigmund Freud* (Vol. 7, pp. 1–122). London: Hogarth Press.

Freud. S. (1905a). Jokes and their relation to the unconscious. In J. Strachey (Ed. & Trans.), *The standard edition of the complete psychological works of Sigmund Freud* (Vol. 8, pp. 1–237). London: Hogarth Press.

Freud, S. (1905b). Three essays on the theory of sexuality. In J. Strachey (Ed. & Trans.), *The standard edition of the complete psychological works of Sigmund Freud* (Vol. 7, pp. 123–231). London: Hogarth Press.

Freud. S. (1908). Character and anal eroticism. In J. Strachey (Ed. & Trans.), *The standard edition of the complete psychological works of Sigmund Freud* (Vol. 9, pp. 167–176). London: Hogarth Press.

Freud, S. (1912–1913). Totem and taboo. In J. Strachey (Ed. & Trans.), *The standard edition of the complete psychological works of Sigmund Freud* (Vol. 13, pp. 1–161). London: Hogarth Press.

Freud, S. (1913). *The Interpretation of dreams* (A. A. Brill, Trans.). New York: The Macmillan Company; London: George Allen and Unwin.

Freud, S. (1914a). On narcissism: An introduction. In J. Strachey (Ed. & Trans.), *The standard edition of the complete psychological works of Sigmund Freud* (Vol. 14, pp. 67–104). London: Hogarth Press.

Freud, S. (1914b). On the history of the psycho-analytic movement. In J. Strachey (Ed. & Trans.), *The standard edition of the complete psychological works of Sigmund Freud* (Vol. 14, pp. 1–66). London: Hogarth Press.

Freud, S. (1916). Some character-types met with in psycho-analytic work. In J. Strachey (Ed. & Trans.), *The standard edition of the complete psychological works of Sigmund Freud* (Vol. 14, pp. 309–336). London: Hogarth Press.

Freud, S. (1920a). Beyond the pleasure principle. In J. Strachey (Ed. & Trans.), *The standard edition of the complete psychological works of Sigmund Freud* (Vol. 18, pp. 1–64). London: Hogarth Press.

Freud. S. (1920b). *A general introduction to psychoanalysis* (G. Stanley Hall, Trans.). New York: Horace Liveright.

Freud, S. (1921). Group psychology and the analysis of the ego. In J. Strachey (Ed. & Trans.), *The standard edition of the complete psychological works of Sigmund Freud* (Vol. 18, pp. 65–144). London: Hogarth Press.

Freud, S. (1923). The ego and the id. In J. Strachey (Ed. & Trans.), *The standard edition of the complete psychological works of Sigmund Freud* (Vol. 19, pp. 1–59). London: Hogarth Press.

Freud, S. (1926). The question of lay analysis. In J. Strachey (Ed. & Trans.), *The standard edition of the complete psychological works of Sigmund Freud* (Vol. 20, pp. 177–250). London: Hogarth Press.

Freud, S. (1927a). The future of an illusion. In J. Strachey (Ed. & Trans.), *The standard edition of the complete psychological works of Sigmund Freud* (Vol. 21, pp. 1–56). London: Hogarth Press.

Freud, S. (1927b). Fetishism. In J. Strachey (Ed. & Trans.), *The standard edition of the complete psychological works of Sigmund Freud* (Vol. 20, pp. 147–158). London: Hogarth Press.

Freud, S. (1930). Civilization and its discontents. In J. Strachey (Ed. & Trans.), *The standard edition of the complete psychological works of Sigmund Freud* (Vol. 21, pp. 1–56). London: Hogarth Press.

Freud, S. (1931). Female sexuality. In J. Strachey (Ed. & Trans.), *The standard edition of the complete psychological works of Sigmund Freud* (Vol. 21, pp. 221–246). London: Hogarth Press.

Freud, S. (1932–1933). New introductory lectures on psycho-analysis. In J. Strachey (Ed. & Trans.), *The standard edition of the complete psychological works of Sigmund Freud* (Vol. 22, pp. 1–182). London: Hogarth Press.

Freud, S. (1937a). Analysis terminable and interminable. In J. Strachey (Ed. & Trans.), *The standard edition of the complete psychological works of Sigmund Freud* (Vol. 23, pp. 209–254). London: Hogarth Press.

Freud, S. (1939). Moses and monotheism: Three essays. In J. Strachey (Ed. & Trans.), *The standard edition of the complete psychological works of Sigmund Freud* (Vol. 23, pp. 1–138). London: Hogarth Press.

Freud, S. (1956/1931). Miscellaneous papers: Libidinal types. In J. Strachey (Ed.), *Collected papers* (Vol. 5, pp. 247–251). London: Hogarth Press.

Freud, S., Ferenczi, S., Brabant-Gerö, E., Falzeder, E., & Giampieri-Deutsch, P. (1993–2000). *The correspondence of Sigmund Freud and Sa?ndor Ferenczi* (3 Vols.). Cambridge, MA: Belknap Press of Harvard University Press.

Frick, W. B. (1997). Interview with John Rowan. *Journal of Humanistic Psychology, 37*(1), 131–156.

Friedman, L. J. (1990). *Menninger: The family and the clinic.* New York: A. A. Knopf.

Fromm, E. (1941). *Escape from freedom.* New York: Farrar & Rinehart.

Fromm, E. (1955). *The sane society.* New York: Holt, Reinhart & Winston.

Fromm, E. (1956). *The art of loving.* New York: Harper.

Fromm, E. (1959). *Sigmund Freud and his mission, an analysis of his personality and influence.* New York: Harper.

Fromm, E. (1968). *The revolution of hope, toward a humanized technology.* New York: Harper & Row.

Fromm-Reichmann, F. (1950). *Principles of intensive psychotherapy.* Chicago: University of Chicago Press.

Fromm-Reichmann, F. (1960). *Principles of intensive psychotherapy.* Chicago: Phoenix Books.

Fürtmuller, C., & Adler, A. (1964). A bibliographical essay. In H. L. Ansbacher & R. R. Ansbacher (Eds.), *Alfred Adler: Superiority and social interest: A collection of later writings.* Evanston, IL: Northwestern University Press.

Furumoto, L. (1979). Mary Whiton Calkins (1863–1930): Fourteenth president of the American Psychological Association. *Journal of the History of the History of Behavioral Sciences, 15*(4), 346–356.

Gardner, H. (1985). *The mind's new science: A history of the cognitive revolution.* New York: Basic Books.

Gardner, S., & Stevens, G. (1992). *Red Vienna and the golden age of psychology: 1918–1938.* New York: Praeger.

Gavin, E. A. (1990). Charlotte M. Bühler (1893–1974). In A. N. O'Connell & F. F. Russo (Eds.), *Women in psychology: A bio-bibliographic sourcebook.* New York: Greenwood Press.

Gavin, E. A. (2000). Charlotte M. Buhler. In A. W. Kazdin (Ed.), *Encyclopedia of Psychology* (Vol. 1, pp. 482–483). Washington, DC: American Psychological Association.

Gay, P. (1988). *Freud: A life for our time.* New York: Norton.

Gelfand, T., & Kerr, J. (Eds.). (1992). *Freud and the history of psychoanalysis.* Hillsdale, NJ: Analytic Press.

Gibson, J. (1979). *The ecological approach to visual perception.* Hillsdale, NJ: Lawrence Erlbaum.

Gifford, S (1997). *The Emmanuel Movement (Boston, 1904–1929): Origins of group treatment and the assault on lay psychotherapy.* Boston: Countway Library of Medicine. Dist by Harvard University Press.

Gifford, S. (2003). Émigré analysts in Boston, 1930–1940. *International Forum of Psychoanalysis, 12*, 1–9.

Gill, M. M. (1961). David Rapaport (1911–1960). *Bulletin of the American Psychoanalytic Association, 17*, 755–759.

Gilles de la Tourette, G. (1891). *Traité clinique et thérapeutique de l'hysterie d'apres l'ensignement de la Salpetriere.* Paris: Librairie Plon, Nourrit et Cie.

Gilligan, C., Brown, L. M., & Rogers, A. G. (1988). *Psyche embedded: A place for body, relationships, and culture in personality theory.* Cambridge, MA: Harvard University, Graduate School of Education, Center for the Study of Gender, Education, and Human Development.

Giorgi, A. (1970). *Psychology as a human science: A Phenomenologically based approach*. New York: Harper & Row.

Giorgi, A. (2006). The psychological phenomenological method. *Journal of Phenomenological Psychology, 37*(2), 284–285.

Goldstein, K. (1939). *The organism, a holistic approach to biology derived from pathological data in man*. New York: American Book Company.

Goldstein, K. (1940). *Human nature in the light of psychopathology*. Cambridge, MA: Harvard University Press.

Goldstein, K. (1941). *Abstract and concrete behavior: An experimental study with special tests*. Evanston, IL: The American Psychological Association.

Goldstein, K. (1942). *Aftereffects of brain injuries in war, their evaluation and treatment: The application of psychologic methods in the clinic*. New York: Grune & Stratton.

Goldstein, K. (1948). *Language and language disturbances: Aphasic symptom complexes and their significance for medicine and theory of language*. New York: Grune & Stratton.

Goldstein, K. (1959). Notes on the development of my concepts. *Journal of Individual Psychology, 15*, 5–14.

Govinda, A. B. (1937). *The psychological attitude of early Buddhist philosophy and its systematic representation according to Abhidhamma tradition*. Patna, India: The University.

Green, E., & Green, A. (1977). *Beyond biofeedback*. New York: Delacorte.

Greenberg, J. (1964). *I never promised you a rose garden*. New York: New American Library.

Gregg, A. (1947). *The place of psychology in an ideal university: The report of the university commission to advise on the future of psychology at Harvard*. Cambridge: Harvard University Press.

Grof, S. (1975). *Realms of the human unconscious: Observations from LSD research*. New York: Viking Press.

Grotjahn, M. (1966). Karl Abraham: The first German psychoanalyst. In F. Alexander, S. Eisenstein, & M. Grotjahn (Eds.), *Psychoanalytic pioneers* (pp. 1–13). New York: Basic Books.

Grunebaum, A. (1984). *The foundations of psychoanalysis: A philosophical critique*. Berkeley, CA: University of California Press.

Guenther, H. V. (1952). *Yuganaddha: The Tantric view of life*. Banaras, India: Chowkhamba.

Gurney, E., Myers, F. W. H., & Podmore, F. (1886). *Phantasms of the living*. London: Rooms of the Society for Psychical Research, Trübner and Company.

Hahnemann, S. (1810). *Organon der rationellen Heikunde*. Dresden,Germany: Arnold.

Hahnemann, S. (1901). *Organon of medicine* (R. E. Dudgeon, Trans.). Philadelphia: Boericke & Tafel.

Hale, N. G. (1971a). *Freud and the Americans: The beginnings of psychoanalysis in the United States, 1876–1917*. New York: Oxford University Press.

Hale, N. G. (1971b). *James Jackson Putnam and psychoanalysis: Letters between Putnam and Sigmund Freud, Ernest Jones, William James, Sandor Ferenczi, and Morton Prince, 1877–1917*. Cambridge, MA: Harvard University Press.

Hale, N. G. (1995). *The rise and crisis of psychoanalysis in America: Freud and the Americans, 1917–1985* (2 Vols.). New York: Oxford University Press.

Haley, J. (1973). *Uncommon therapy; the psychiatric techniques of Milton H. Erickson, M.D.* New York: W. W. Norton.

Hall, N. (1988). *Those women*. Dallas, TX: Spring Publications.

Hanfman, E., Rickers-Ovsiankina, M., & Goldstein, K. (1944). *Case Lunati: Extreme concretization of behavior de to damage of the brain cortex*. Evanston, IL: The American Psychological Association.

Hartmann, H. (1939). Ich-psychologie und anpassungsproblem. [Ego psychology and the problem of adaptation]. *Internationale Zeitschrift für Psychoanalyse, 24*, 62–135; English translation (1958), *Journal of the American Psychoanalytic Association, Monographs 1*. New York: International Universities Press.

Hartmann, H., & Kris, E. (1945). The genetic approach to psychoanalysis. *Psychoanalytic study of the child* (Vol. 1). New York: International Universities Press.

Hartmann, H., Kris, E., & Lowenstein, R. (1946). Comments on the theory of psychic structure. *Psychoanalytic study of the child* (Vol. 2). New York: International Universities Press.

Hartmann, H., Kris, E. & Lowenstein, R. (1949). Notes on the theory of aggression. *Psychoanalytic study of the child* (Vols. 3, 4). New York: International Universities Press.

Hartmann, H., Kris, E., & Lowenstein, R. (1953). The function of theory in psychoanalysis. In R. M. Lowenstein (Ed.), *Drives, affects, and behavior.* New York: International Universities Press.

Haule, J. R. (1986). Pierre Janet and dissociation: The first transference theory and its origins in hypnosis. *American Journal of Clinical Hypnosis, 29*(2), 86–94.

Hawthorne, N. (1850). *The scarlet letter.* Boston: Ticknor, Reed, and Fields.

Haynal, A., & Falzader, E. (Eds.). (1994). *One hundred years of psychoanalysis: Contributions to the history of psychoanalysis.* London: H. Karnac Books.

Heidegger, M. (1962). *Being and time* (J. Macquarrie, Trans.). London: S. C. M. Press.

Hendrick, I. (1934). *Facts and theories in psychoanalysis.* New York: A. A. Knopf.

Henle, M. (1978). Gestalt psychology and Gestalt therapy. *Journal of the History of the Behavioral Sciences, 14*, 23–32.

Hillman, J. (2004). *Archetypal psychology* (3rd ed.). Putnam, CT: Spring Publications.

Hoffman E. (1988). *The right to be human: A biography of Abraham Maslow.* Los Angeles: J. P. Tarcher.

Holt, R. R. (1989). *Freud reappraised.* New York: The Guilford Press.

Homans, G. C. (1941). *English villagers of the thirteenth century.* Cambridge, MA: Harvard University Press.

Homans, G. (1970). The relevance of psychology to the explanation of social phenomena. In R. T. Borger & F. Cioffi (Eds.), *Explanation in the behavioral sciences* (pp. 313–329). Cambridge, MA: Cambridge University Press.

Homans, G. S. (1984). *Coming to my senses: The autobiography of a sociologist.* New Brunswick, NJ: Transaction Books.

Homans, G. C., & Curtis, C. P. (1934). *An introduction to Pareto: His sociology.* New York: A. A. Knopf.

Horney, K. (1937). *The neurotic personality of our time.* New York: W. W. Norton & Company.

Horney, K. (1939). *New ways in psychoanalysis.* New York: W. W. Norton & Company.

Horney, K. (1942). *Self-analysis.* New York: W. W. Norton & Company.

Horney, K. (1950). *Neurosis and human growth: The struggle toward self-realization.* New York: W. W. Norton.

Honorton, C., & Krippner, S. (1969). Hypnosis and ESP performance: A review of the experimental literature. *Journal of the American Society for Psychical Research, 63*, 214–252.

Hornstein, G. A., & Fromm-Reichmann, F. (2000). *To redeem one person is to redeem the world: The life of Frieda Fromm-Reichmann.* New York: Free Press.

Howard, J (1984). *Margaret Mead: A life.* New York: Simon & Schuster.

Hull, C. L. (1933). *Hypnosis and suggestibility, an experimental approach.* New York, London: D. Appleton-Century Company.

Hunt, H. T. (2005). Why psychology is/is not traditional science: The self referential basis of psychological research and theory. *Review of General Psychology, 9*(4), 358–374.

Huxley, A. (1945). *The perennial philosophy.* New York, London: Harper & Brothers.

Huxley, A. (1954). *The doors of perception.* New York: Harper & Brothers.

Jacobi, J. S. (1959). *Complex/archetype/symbol in the psychology of C. G. Jung.* Bollingen series, 57. Princeton, NJ: Princeton University Press.

Jacobi, J. S., & Bash, K. W. (1942). *The psychology of C. G. Jung: An introduction with illustrations.* London: Routledge & Kegan Paul.

Jaffé, A. (1970). *The myth of meaning in the work of C. G. Jung.* London: Hodder & Stoughton.

Jaffé, A. (1979). *C. G. Jung, word and image.* Bollingen Series, 97, 2. Princeton, NJ: Princeton University Press.

Jahoda, M. (1977). *Freud and the dilemmas of psychology.* London: Hogarth Press; New York: Basic Books.

James, W. (1868). Moral medication. Review of Liébeault's Du sommeil des états analogues, considérés surtout au point de vue de l'action du moral sur le physique. *The Nation*, 7(159), 50–52.

James, W. (1884). What is an emotion? *Mind*, 9(34), 188–205.

James, W. (1890a). *The principles of psychology* (2 Vols.). New York: Henry Holt and Company.

James, W. (1890b). The hidden self. *Scribner's Magazine*, 7, 361–73.

James, W. (1893). Person and personality. *Johnson's universal cyclopedia*. In F. H. Burkhardt, F. Bowers, & I. K. Skrupskelis (Eds.). (1975), *Works of William James. Essays in psychology* (pp. 315–321). Cambridge, MA: Harvard University Press.

James, W. (1894). Review of Breuer and Freud's "Preliminary communication on the nature of hysterical phenomenae." *Psychological Review*, 1, 199.

James, W. (1897). *The will to believe*. New York: Henry Holt.

James, W. (1902a). *The varieties of religious experience: A study of human nature*. New York: Longmans, Green, and Company.

James, W. (1902b). Frederick Myers's services to psychology. *Proceedings of the Society for Psychical Research*, 17, 13–23.

Janet, P. (1885). Notes sur quelque phénomènes de somnambulisme. *Bulletins de la Société de Psychologie physiologique*, 2, 70–80.

Janet, P. (1893). *Contribution à l'étude des accidents mentaux chez les hystériques* [The Mental State of Hystericals]. Paris: Rueff et Cie.

Janet, P. (1889a). *L'automatisme psychologique. Essai de psychologie expérimentale sur les formes inférieures de l'activité humaine* [The Automatisme Psychological: Test experimental psychology on the lower forms of human activity]. Paris: Ancienne Librairie Germer Ballière.

Janet, P. (1889b). Névroses et idées fixes [Neurosis and Fixed Ideas and Obsessions] (2 Vols.). Paris: Alcan.

Janet, P. (1903). Les Obsessions et la psychasthénie [The obsessions of Psychasthenia] (2 Vols.). Paris: Alcan.

Janet, P., Paul, E., & Paul, C. (1925). *Psychological healing a historical and clinical study* (2 Vols.). New York: The Macmillan Company.

John, O. P. (1990). The "Big Five" factor taxonomy: Dimensions of personality in the natural language and in questionnaires. In L. A. Pervin (Ed.), *Handbook of personality: Theory and research* (pp. 66–100). New York: Guilford.

Jones, E. (1953). *The life and work of Sigmund Freud: The formative years and the great discoveries, 1856–1900. Vol. 1.* New York: Basic Books.

Jones, E. (1954–1958). *Sigmund Freud: Life and work* (3 Vols.). London: Hogarth Press.

Jones, E. (1959). *Free associations: Memories of a psycho-analyst*. London: Hogarth Press.

Jourard, S. M. (1958a). *Personal adjustment: An approach through the study of healthy personality*. New York: Macmillan.

Jourard, S. M. (1958b). A study of self-disclosure. *Scientific American*, 198(5), 77–82.

Jourard, S. M. (1959). I-Thou relationship versus manipulation in counseling and psychotherapy. *Journal of Individual Psychology*, 15(2), 174–179.

Jourard, S. M. (1964). *The transparent self: Self-disclosure and well-being*. Princeton, NJ: Van Nostrand. (Rev. ed., 1971, New York: Van Nostrand Reinhold).

Jourard, S. M. (Ed.). (1967a). To be or not to be... Existential-psychological perspectives on the self. *University of Florida Monographs, Social Sciences, #34*. Gainesville: University of Florida Press.

Jourard, S. M. (1967b). To be or not to be transparent. In S. M. Jourard (Ed.). To be or not to be... Existential-psychological perspectives on the self. *University of Florida Monographs, Social Sciences, #34* (pp. 27–36). Gainesville: University of Florida Press.

Jourard, S. M. (1967c). Experimenter-subject dialogue: A paradigm for a humanistic science of psychology. In I. F. T. Bugental (Ed.), *Challenges of Humanistic psychology* (pp. 109–116). New York: McGraw-Hill. Reprinted In A. G. Miller (Ed.). (1972). *The social psychology of psychological research* (pp. 14–24). London: The Free Press.

Jourard, S. M. (1971). Some ways of unembodiment and re-embodiment. *Somatics*, 1(1), 3–7.

Jourard, S. M. (1972). The transcending therapist. *Voices, 8*(3), 66–69.

Jourard, S. M. (1974). *Healthy personality: An approach from the viewpoint of humanistic psychology.* New York: The Macmillan Company.

Jourard, S. M., & Kormann, L. A. (1968). Getting to know the experimenter and its effect on psychological test performance. *Journal of Humanistic Psychology, 8*(2), 155–159.

Jourard, S. M., & Secord, P. F. (1953). Body-cathexis and personality. *British Journal of Psychology, 46*(2), 130–138.

Jung, C. G. (1901). *On the psychology and pathology of so-called occult phenomenae.* Medical Dissertation, University of Zurich (*Collected Works, Vol. 1*, 1902).

Jung, C. G. (1904–1907). Studies in word association. In H. Read, M. Fordham, & G. Adler (Eds.), *Experimental researches: Vol. 2, Collected works.* London: Routledge and Kegan Paul.

Jung, C. G. (1907a). *U?ber die psychologie der dementia praecox: Ein versuch* [The psychology of dementia praecox]. Halle a S.: Verlagsbuchhandlung Carl Marhold.

Jung, C. G. (1907b). In H. Read, M. Fordham, & G. Adler (Eds.), *The psychogenesis of mental disease: Vol. 3, Collected works.* London: Routledge & Kegan Paul.

Jung, C. G. (1909). *The psychology of dementia praecox* (F. Peterson, & A. A. Brill, Trans.). *Nervous and Mental Disease Monograph, 3.* New York: The Journal of Nervous and Mental Disease Publication Company. (Original work published 1906)

Jung, C. G. (1912). *Wandlungen und symbole der libido: Beiträge zur entwicklungsgeschichte des denkens* [Transformations and symbols of the libido: Contributions to the development history of thinking]. München: Deutscher Taschenbuch Verlag; Reprinted 1991.

Jung, C. G. (1913). The theory of psychoanalysis. In H. Read, M. Fordham, & G. Adler (Eds.), *Freud and psychoanalysis: Vol. 3, Collected works.* London: Routledge & Kegan Paul.

Jung, C. G. (1916a). *Psychology of the unconscious: A study of the transformations and symbolisms of the libido: A contribution to the history of the evolution of thought.* London: Kegan, Paul, Trench, Trubner.

Jung, C. G. (1916b). *Psychology of the unconscious: A study of the transformations and symbolisms of the libido* (B. Hinkle, Trans.). New York: Moffat, Yard and Company.

Jung, C. G. (1916/1963). Appendix V: *Septem sermones ad mortuos* [Seven sermons to the dead]. Written by Basilides in Alexandria. In A. Jaffé (Ed.). (1963), *Memories, dreams, reflections* (pp. 378–390). New York: Vintage Books.

Jung, C. G. (1921a). *Psychological types* (H. G. Baynes, Trans.). London: Kegan Paul Trench Trubner.

Jung, C. G. (1921b). *Psychological types.* In H. Read, M. Fordham, & G. Adler (Eds.), *Collected works of C. G. Jung, Vol. 6.* London: Routledge & Kegan Paul.

Jung, C. G. (1927). Women in Europe. In *Collected works of C. G. Jung* (Vol. 10, pp. 113–133). London: Routledge & Kegan Paul.

Jung, C. G. (1928a). *Contributions to analytical psychology.* London: Routledge & Kegan Paul.

Jung, C. G. (1928b). *Two essays on analytical psychology* (H. G. & C. F. Baynes, Trans.). New York: Dodd, Mead and Company.

Jung, C. G. (1934). A study in the process of individuation. In H. Read, M. Fordham, & G. Adler (Eds.), *The archetypes and the collective unconscious: Vol. 9.1, Collected works* (pp. 290–354). London: Routledge & Kegan Paul.

Jung, C. G. (1953). *Two essays on analytical psychology.* In R. F. C. Hull (Trans.), *Collected works of C. G. Jung* (Vol. 7). Bollingen Series XX. Princeton NJ: Princeton University Press. (Original works, On the psychology of the unconscious published 1917; The relations between the ego and the unconscious published 1928)

Jung, C. G. (1957–1990). *Collected works of C. G. Jung* (Vols. 1–20). (H. Read, M. Fordham, G. Adler, & W. McGuire, Eds.) (R. F. C. Hull, Trans.). Princeton, NJ: Princeton University Press.

Jung, C. G. (1958). *The undiscovered self.* Boston: Little, Brown.

Jung, C. G. (1959a). *Flying saucers: A modern myth of things seen in the skies.* New York: Harcourt, Brace.

Jung, C. G. (1959b). *Modern Man in search of a soul* (W. Dell & C. F. Baynes, Trans.). London: Routledge & Paul.

Jung, C. G. (1963a). *Memories, dreams, reflections*. A. Jaffé (Recorder and Ed.).(R. & C. Winston, Trans.). New York: Vintage Books.

Jung, C. G. (1963b). *Mysterium conjunctionis: An inquiry into the separation and synthesis of psychic opposites in alchemy*. In H. Read, M. Fordham, G. Adler, & W. McGuire (Eds.) (R. F. C. Hull, Trans.), *Collected works of C. G. Jung* (Vol. 14, 2nd ed., pp. 475–508). Princeton, NJ: Princeton University Press. (Original work published 1955–1956)

Jung, C. G. (1966). The aims of psychotherapy. In H. Read, M. Fordham, G. Adler, & W. McGuire (Eds.) (R. F. C. Hull, Trans.), *Collected works of C. G. Jung* (Vol. 16, pp. 35–52). Princeton, NJ: Princeton University Press. (Original work published 1931)

Jung, C. G. (1968). *Alchemical studies*, Commentary on "The Secret of the Golden Flower." In H. Read, M. Fordham, G. Adler, & W. McGuire (Eds.) (R. F. C. Hull, Trans.), *Collected works of C. G. Jung* (Vol. 13, pp. 1–57). Princeton NJ: Princeton University Press. (Original work published 1929)

Jung, C. G. (1969a). A study in the process of individuation. In H. Read, M. Fordham, G. Adler, & W. McGuire (Eds.) (R. F. C. Hull, Trans.), *Collected works of C. G. Jung* (Vol. 9i, pp. 290–354). Princeton, NJ: Princeton University Press. (Original work published 1950)

Jung, C. G. (1969b/1936). *Psychology and religion: West and east*. In H. Read, M. Fordham, G. Adler, & W. McGuire (Eds.) (R. F. C. Hull, Trans.), *Collected works of C. G. Jung* (Vol. 11, 2nd ed., pp. 529–537). Princeton NJ: Princeton University Press. (Original work published 1936; Shri Ramakrishna Centenary, No. III (C. F. Baynes, Trans.). "Yoga and the west." *Prabuddha Bharata* (Calcutta).

Jung, C. G. (1969c). Foreword to the German edition of D.T Suzuki's *Introduction to Zen Buddhism*. In H. Read, M. Fordham, G. Adler, & W. McGuire (Eds.) (R. F. C. Hull, Trans.), *Psychology and religion: West and east. Collected Works of C. G. Jung* (Vol. 11, 2nd ed., pp. 538–557). Princeton NJ: Princeton University Press. (Original work published 1939)

Jung, C. G. (1969d). Psychological commentary on *The Tibetan book of the dead*. In H. Read, M. Fordham, G. Adler, & W. McGuire (Eds.) (R. F. C. Hull, Trans.), Psychology and religion: West and east. *Collected works of C. G. Jung* (Vol. 11, 2nd ed., pp. 509–528). Princeton NJ: Princeton University Press. (Original work published in German, 1935)

Jung, C. G. (1969e). Psychological commentary on *The Tibetan book of the great liberation*. In H. Read, M. Fordham, G. Adler, & W. McGuire (Eds.), *Psychology and religion: West and east. Collected works of C. G. Jung* (Vol. 11, 2nd ed., pp. 475–508). Princeton NJ: Princeton University Press. (Original work published in English, 1954)

Jung, C. G. (1969f). Answer to Job. In H. Read, M. Fordham, G. Adler, & W. McGuire (Eds.) (R. F. C. Hull, Trans.), *Collected works of C. G. Jung* (Vol. 11, pp. 355–470). Princeton, NJ: Princeton University Press. (Original work published 1952)

Jung, C. G. (1971). *The archetypes and the collective unconscious*. In H. Read, M. Fordham, G. Adler, & W. McGuire (Eds.) (R. F. C. Hull, Trans.), *Collected works of C. G. Jung* (Vol. 9.1). Princeton, NJ: Princeton University Press. (Original work published 1934)

Jung, C. G. (1976). Psychological types. In H. Read, M. Fordham, G. Adler, & W. McGuire (Eds.) (R. F. C. Hull, Trans.), *Collected works of C. G. Jung* (Vol. 6). Princeton, NJ: Princeton University Press. (Original work published 1921)

Jung, C. G. (1989). *Analytical psychology: Notes of the seminar given in 1925* (W. McGuire, Ed.). Princeton, NJ: Princeton University Press. (Original lectures delivered October 15, 1930–March 21, 1934)

Jung, C. G. (2001). *Psychology of the unconscious: A study of the transformations and symbolisms of the libido: A contribution to the history of the evolution of thought*. In W. McGuire (Ed.) (B. Hinkel, Trans.), *Collected works of C. G. Jung* (Supplementary Vol. B). Princeton, NJ: Princeton University.

Jung, C. G. (2008). *Children's dreams: Notes from the seminar given in 1936–1940.* (L. Jung & M. Meyer-Grass, Eds., E. Falzeder & T. Woolfson, Trans.). Princeton, NJ: Princeton University Press. The Philemon Series.

Jung, C. G., & Franz, M.-L. v. (1964). *Man and his symbols.* Garden City, NY: Doubleday.

Kaiser, C. (1995). An interview with Kurt Adler (1905–1997) on his 90th birthday. Adler Institute of Zurich, Adler Institute Homepage. http://ourworld.compuserve.com/homepages/hstein/kurt-90.htm

Kalupahana, D. J. (1987). *The principles of Buddhist psychology.* Albany: State University of New York Press.

Kant, I. (1899). *Dreams of a spirit-seer, illustrated by dreams of metaphysics.* London: S. Sonnenschein & Company; New York: The Macmillan Company.

Kardiner, A., & Linton, R. (1939). *The individual and his society: The psychodynamics of primitive social organization.* New York: Columbia University.

Karpf, F. B. (1932). *American social psychology; its origins, development, and European background.* New York, London: McGraw-Hill Book Company.

Kaufmann, W. (1956). *Existentialism from Dostoevsky to Sartre.* New York: World Publishing Company.

Kerr, J. (1993). *A most dangerous method: The story of Jung, Freud, and Sabina Spielrein.* New York: A. A. Knopf.

Khan, M. M. R. (1974). *The privacy of the self: Papers on psychoanalytic theory and technique.* New York: International Universities Press.

Khan, M. M. R. (1983). *Hidden selves: Between theory and practice in psychoanalysis.* New York: International Universities Press.

Khan, M. M. R. (1988). *When spring comes: Awakenings in clinical psychoanalysis.* London: Chatto and Windus.

Kihlstrom, J. F. (1987). The cognitive unconscious. *Science, 237*(4821), 1445–1452.

Kihlstrom, J. F. (2002). Demand characteristics in the laboratory and the clinic: Conversations and collaborations with subjects and patients. *Prevention & Treatment, 5*(36c) [Special issue honoring Martin T. Orne]. Retrieved 5/20/08 from http://journals.apa.org/prevention/ volume5/pre0050036c.html

Kihlstrom, J. F. (2003). Expecting that a treatment will be given when it won't, and knowing that a treatment is being given when it is. *Prevention & Treatment, 6*(1), 4c. Commentary on F. Benedetti, G. Maggi, L. Lopiano, M. Lanotte, I. Rainero, S. Vighetti, et al. "Open versus hidden medical treatments: The patient's knowledge about a therapy affects therapy outcome." Retrieved 5/20/08 from http://journals.apa.org/prevention/volume6/pre0060004c.html.

Kirsch, T. B. (2000). *The Jungians: A comparative and historical perspective.* London: Routledge.

Kirschenbaum, H. (1979). *On becoming Carl Rogers.* New York: Delacorte Press.

Kircher, T., & David, A. S. (2003). *The self in neuroscience and psychiatry.* London, New York: Cambridge University Press.

Kircher, T., & David, A. S. (2005). The self in neuroscience and psychiatry. *Educational Psychology in Practice, 21*(2), 156–157.

Klein, M. (1932a). *Die psychoanalyse des kindes* [The psycho-analysis of children]. Vienna: Internationaler Psychoanalytischer Verlag; International Psycho-analytical Library, No. 22. London: Hogarth Press.

Klein, M. (1932b). *The psycho-analysis of children* (A. Strachey, Trans.). London: L. & V. Woolf at the Hogarth Press and the Institute of Psycho-analysis.

Klein, M. (1948). *Contributions to psycho-analysis, 1921–1945.* London: Hogarth Press.

Klein, M. (1961). *Narrative of a child analysis: The conduct of the psycho-analysis of children as seen in the treatment of a ten-year-old boy.* London: Hogarth Press and the Institute of Psycho-analysis.

Klein, M. (1963). *Our adult world and other essays.* New York: Basic Books.

Klein, M. (1975a). *The writings of Melanie Klein: Love, guilt and reparation and other works 1921–1945* (Vol. 1, No. 103). The International Psycho-analytical Library. London: Hogarth Press.

Klein, M. (1975b). *The writings of Melanie Klein: The psycho-analysis of children* (Vol. 2, No. 220). The International Psycho-analytical Library. London: Hogarth Press.

Klein, M. (1975c). *The writings of Melanie Klein: The psycho-analysis of children: Envy and gratitude and other works 1946–1963* (Vol. 3, No. 104). The International Psycho-analytical Library. London: Hogarth Press.

Klein, M. (1975d). *The writings of Melanie Klein: Narrative of a child analysis* (Vol. 4, No. 55). The International Psycho-Analytical Library. London: Hogarth Press. (Original work published 1961)

Kluckhohn, C. (1927). *To the foot of the rainbow: A tale of twenty-five hundred miles of wandering on horseback through southwest enchanted land.* New York, London: Century Company.

Kluckhohn, C. (1944). *Navaho witchcraft.* Cambridge, MA: The Museum.

Kluckhohn, C. (1949). *Mirror for man: Relation of anthropology to modern life.* New York: Whittlesey/McGraw-Hill Book Company.

Knapp, R. (1949–1974). *Collected papers. Archives of the History of American Psychology.* Akron, OH: University of Akron.

Koch, S. (Ed.). (1959–1963). *Psychology: A study of a science* (6 Vols.). New York: McGraw-Hill.

Koch, S. (1992). Psychology's Bridgman vs. Bridgman's Bridgman. *Theory & Psychology, 2*(3), 261–290.

Köhler, W. (1929). *Gestalt psychology.* New York: H. Liveright.

Köhler, W., & Winter, E. (1925). *The mentality of apes.* London: K. Paul, Trench, Trubner & Company; New York: Harcourt, Brace & Company. (Original work published in 1917 as *Intelligenzenprüfungen an Anthropoiden; Intelligenzenprüfungen an Menschenaffen,* 1921)

Koffka, K. (1924). *The growth of the mind; an introduction to child psychology.* (R. Morris, Trans.). New York: Harcourt, Brace & Company.

Koffka, K. (1935). *Principles of gestalt psychology.* New York: Harcourt, Brace & Company.

Koltko-Rivera, Mark E. (2006). Rediscovering the later version of Maslow's hierarchy of needs: Self-transcendence and opportunities for theory, research, and unification. *Review of General Psychology, 10*(4), December 2006. pp. 302–317.

Krafft-Ebing, R. v., & Chaddock, C. G. (1892). *Psychopathia sexualis.* Philadelphia: F.A. Davis.

Kreuter, E. A. (2006). *Victim vulnerability: An existential-humanistic interpretation of a single case study.* New York: Nova Science Publishers.

Kripal, J. J (2007). *Esalen: America and the religion of no-religion.* Chicago: University of Chicago Press.

Krippner, S. (1969). The psychedelic state, the hypnotic trance, and the creative act. In C. T. Tart (Ed.), *Altered states of consciousness: A book of readings* (pp. 271–290). New York: Wiley.

Krippner, S. (1978). The interface between parapsychology and humanistic psychology. In M. Ebon (Ed.), *The Signet handbook of parapsychology* (pp. 79–87). New York: New American Library.

Krippner, S. (1999). The varieties of dissociative experience: A transpersonal, postmodern model. *International Journal of Transpersonal Studies, 18,* 81–101.

Krippner, S. (2000). *Varieties of anomalous experience: Examining the scientific evidence* (with E. Cardena & S. J. Lynn). Washington, DC: American Psychological Association.

Krippner, S. (Ed.). (2003). *The psychological effects of war on civilians: An international perspective,* [co-edited with T. McIntyre; Foreword by S. Hobfall; Afterword by J. Achterberg.] Westport, CT: Praeger.

Kris, E. (1952). *Psychoanalytic explorations in art.* New York: International Universities Press.

Kris, E. (1954). Introduction. In M. Bonaparte, A. Freud, & E. Kris (Eds.), *The origins of psychoanalysis: Letters to Wilhelm Fliess, drafts and notes, 1887–1902, by Sigmund Freud.* New York: Basic Books.

Kroeber, A. L., & Kluckhohn, C. (1952). *Culture: A critical review of concepts and definitions.* Cambridge, MA: The Museum.

Kroll, J. (2002). The nine lives of the dynamic unconscious. *Philosophy, Psychiatry and Psychology, 9*(2), 168–169.

Lacan, J. (1968). *The language of the self* (A. Wilden, Trans.). Baltimore, MD: John Hopkins University Press.

Lacan, J. (1977). In J.-A. Miller (Ed.) (A. Sheridan, Trans.), *The seminar, book 11, the four fundamental concepts of psychoanalysis.* New York: W. W. Norton & Company.

Lacan, J. (1988a). In J.-A. Miller (Ed.) (J. Forrester, Trans.), *The seminar of Jacques Lacan: Book 1, Freud's papers on technique, 1953–1954.* New York: W. W. Norton & Company.

Lacan, J. (1988b). In J.-A. Miller (Ed.) (S. Tomaselli, Trans.), *The seminar, book 2, the ego in Freud's theory and in the technique of psychoanalysis, 1954–1955.* New York: W. W. Norton & Company.

Lacan, J. (1992). In J.-A. Miller (Ed.) (D. Porter, Trans.), *The seminar, book 7, the ethics of psychoanalysis, 1959–1960.* New York: W. W. Norton & Company.

Lacan, J. (1993). In J.-A. Miller (Ed.) (R. Grigg, Trans.), *The seminar, book 3, the psychoses.* New York: W. W. Norton & Company.

Lacan, J. (1998). In J.-A. Miller (Ed.) (B. Fink, Trans.), *The seminar, book 20, on feminine sexuality, the limits of love and knowledge.* New York: W. W. Norton & Company.

Lacan, J. (2006). *Ecrits: The first complete edition in English* (B. Fink, Trans.). New York: W.W. Norton & Company.

Lacan, J. (2007). In J.-A. Miller (Ed.) (R. Grigg, Trans.), *The seminar, book 17, the other side of psychoanalysis.* New York: W. W. Norton & Company.

Laing, R. D. (1960). *The divided self.* London: Tavistock Publications.

Laing, R. D. (1961). *Self and others.* London: Tavistock Publications.

Lammers, A. C., Cunningham, A., & Stein, M. (Eds.). (2007). *The Jung-White letters.* New York: Routledge.

Larsen, S., & Larsen, R. (1991). *A fire in the mind: The life of Joseph Campbell.* New York: Doubleday.

Larson, G. J., & Bhattacharya, R. S. (1987). *Samkhya: A dualist tradition in Indian philosophy.* Princeton, NJ: Princeton University Press.

Lasch, C. (1982). *The Freudian left and the theory of Cultural Revolution.* London: University College London.

Lashley, K. S. (1929). *Brain mechanisms and intelligence: A quantitative study of injuries to the brain.* Chicago: University of Chicago Press.

Lashley, K. S. (1935). The mechanism of vision, Part 12: Nervous structures concerned in the acquisition and retention of habits based on reactions to light. *Comparative Psychology Monographs 11,* 43–79.

Lashley, K. S. (1950). In search of the engram. *Society of Experimental Biology, Symposium 4,* 454–482.

Leary, D. (1990). William James on the self and personality: Clearing the ground for subsequent theorists, researchers, and practitioners. In M. G. Johnson & T. B. Henley (Eds.), *Reflections on "The Principles of Psychology": William James after a century* (pp. 101–137). Hillsdale, NJ, England: Lawrence Erlbaum Associates, Inc.

LeClair, R. C. (Ed.). (1966). *The letters of William James and Théodore Flournoy.* Madison, WI: University of Wisconsin Press.

Lee, M. A., & Shlain, B. (1992). *Acid dreams: The complete social history of LSD: The CIA, the sixties, and beyond.* New York: Grove Weidenfeld.

Lewin, K. (1931). The conflict between Aristotelian and Galilean modes of thought in contemporary psychology. *Journal of genetic psychology, 5,* 141–177.

Lewin, K. (1934). *A dynamic theory of personality: Selected papers* (D. K. Adams & K. E. Zener, Trans.). New York, London: McGraw-Hill.

Lewin, K. (1936). *Principles of topological psychology.* New York: McGraw-Hill.

Lilly, J. C. (1972). *Center of the cyclone: An autobiography of inner space.* New York: Julian Press.

Lowry, R. (1971). *The evolution of psychological theory: 1650 to the present.* Chicago: Aldine-Atherton.

Mack, J. E. (1995). *Abduction: Human encounters with aliens.* New York: Ballantine Books.

MacMurray, J. (1939). *The boundaries of science: A study in the philosophy of psychology*. London: Faber and Faber, Ltd.

Maddi, S. R. (1989). *Personality theories: A comparative analysis* (5th ed.). Pacific Grove, CA: Brooks/Cole Publishing Company; Chicago: Dorsey Press.

Madison, B. (Ed.). (1916). *Studies in social and general psychology from the University of Illinois*. Princeton, NJ, Lancaster, PA: Psychological Review Company.

Maidenbaum, A., & Martin, S. A. (Eds.). (1991). *Lingering shadows: Jungians, Freudians, and anti-semitism*. Boston: Shambhala.

Marcuse, H. (1955). *Eros and civilization: A philosophical inquiry into Freud*. New York: Vintage.

Marrow, A. J. (1969). *The practical theorist: The life and work of Kurt Lewin*. New York: Basic Books.

Martin, F. A. (2001). Interview with Adrian van Kaam and Susan Muto, Pittsburgh, Pennsylvania, May 23, 1999. Appendix to *The meaning of humanistic psychology: Interviews with seventy-five living exponents*. Unpublished doctoral dissertation, Saybrook Graduate School and Research Center, San Francisco.

Martinez, T. J., & Taylor, E. I. (1998, Fall/Winter). "Yes, in you the tempest rages": The archetypal significance of America in Jung's own process of individuation. *Spring: A Journal of Archetype and Culture, 64,* 32–56.

Maslow, A. H. (1943). The dynamics of personality organization I & II. *Psychological Review, 50,* 514–39, 541–58.

Maslow, A. H. (1946). Problem centering versus means centering in science. *Philosophy of Science, 13,* 326–331.

Maslow, A. H. (1950). Self-actualizing people: A study of psychological health, *Personality Symposia: Symposium 1 on Values* (pp. 11–34). New York: Grune & Stratton.

Maslow, A. H. (1954). *Motivation and personality*. New York: Harper & Row.

Maslow, A. H. (1966). *The psychology of science: A reconnaissance*. New York: Harper & Row.

Maslow, A. H. (1969). Various meanings of transcendence. *Journal of Transpersonal Psychology, 1*(1), 56–66.

Maslow, A. H. (1971). *The farther reaches of human nature*. New York: Viking Press.

Maslow, A. H., & McKinnon, D. (1951). Personality. In H. Helson (Ed.), *Theoretical foundations of modern psychology*. New York: Van Nostrand.

Maslow, A. H., & Mittelmann, B. (1941). *Principles of abnormal psychology: The dynamics of psychic illness*. New York: Harper & Brothers.

Masson, J. M. (1984). *The assault of truth: Freud's suppression of the seduction theory*. New York: Farrar, Straus and Giroux.

May, R. (1939). *The art of counseling*. New York: Abingdon Press.

May, R. (1940). *The springs of creative living, a study of human nature and God*. New York, Nashville: Abingdon-Cokesbury Press.

May, R. (1950). *The meaning of anxiety*. New York: The Ronald Press Company (Rev. ed. 1977, New York: W. W. Norton).

May, R. (Ed.). (1961). *Existential psychology*. New York: Random House.

May, R. (1967). *Psychology and the human dilemma*. New York: W. W. Norton & Company; Princeton, NJ: Van Nostrand.

May, R. (1969a). *Love and will*. New York: W. W. Norton & Company.

May, R. (1969b). *Existential psychology* (2nd ed.). New York: Random House.

May, R. (1972). *Power and innocence: A search for the sources of violence*. New York: W. W. Norton & Company.

May, R. (1973). *Paulus: Reminiscences of a friendship*. New York: Harper & Row.

May, R. (1975). *The courage to create*. New York: Bantam Books.

May, R. (1981). *Freedom and destiny*. New York: W. W. Norton & Company.

May, R. (1983). *The discovery of being: Writings in existential psychology*. New York: W. W. Norton & Company.

May, R. (1985). *My quest for beauty*. San Francisco: Saybrook.

May, R. (1986). *Politics and innocence*. Dallas, TX: Saybrook Publishers; New York: W. W. Norton & Company.

May, R. (1991). *The cry for myth*. New York: W. W. Norton & Company.

May, R., Angel, E., & Ellenberger, H. F. (Eds.). (1958). *Existence, a new dimension in psychiatry and psychology*. New York: Basic Books.

May, R., & Caliger, L. (1968). *Dreams and symbols*. New York: Basic Books.

May, R., & Schneider, K. J. (1995). *The psychology of existence: An integrative, clinical perspective*. New York: McGraw-Hill.

Mayo, E. (1933). *The human problems of an industrial civilization*. Boston: Graduate School of Business Administration, Harvard University.

Mayo, E. (1945). *The social problems of an industrial civilization*. Boston: Graduate School of Business Administration, Harvard University.

McAdams, D. P. (1995). What do we know when we know a person? *Journal of Personality, 63*(3), 365–396.

McAdams, D. P. (1996). Personality, modernity, and the storied self: A contemporary framework for studying persons. *Psychological Inquiry, 7*(4), 295–321.

McAdams, D. P. (2006a). *The redemptive self: Stories Americans live by*. New York: Oxford University Press.

McAdams, D. P. (2006b). *The person: A new introduction to personality psychology* (4th ed.). Hoboken, NJ: John Wiley & Sons.

McAdams, D. P., Diamond, A., de Saint Aubin, E., & Mansfield, E. (1997). Stories of commitment: The psychological construction of generative lives. *Journal of Personality and Social Psychology, 72*(3), 678–694.

McAdams, D. P., Josselson, R., & Lieblich, A. (2006). *Identity and story: Creating self in narrative*. Washington, DC: American Psychological Association.

McAdams, D. P., & Pals, J. L. (2006). A new big five: Fundamental principles for an integrative science of personality. *American Psychologist, 61*(3), 204–217.

McClelland, D. (Ed.). (1953). *The achievement motive*. New York: Appleton-Century-Crofts.

McGuire, W. (Ed.). (1974). *The Freud-Jung letters: The correspondence between Sigmund Freud and C. G. Jung*. Bollingen Series, 94. Princeton, NJ: Princeton University Press.

McLaughlin, F., Jourard, S. M., & Combs, A. W. (1971). (Eds.). Conversation: Two humanists. *Media & Methods, 8*(4), 24–29.

Mead, M. (Ed.). (1937). *Cooperation and competition among primitive peoples*. New York: McGraw-Hill.

Meier, C. A. (Ed.). (2001). *Atom and archetype: The Pauli/Jung letters, 1932–1958*. Princeton, NJ: Princeton University Press.

Melville, H. (1851). *Moby Dick*. New York: Harper & Brothers.

Merleau-Ponty, M. (1962). *Phenomenology of perception* (C. Smith, Trans.). London: Routledge & Kegan Paul.

Messer, S. B., Sass, L. A., & Woolfolk, R. L. (1988). (Eds.). *Hermeneutics and psychological theory: Interpretive perspectives on personality, psychotherapy, and psychopathology*. New Brunswick, NJ: Rutgers University Press.

Micale, M. S. (1987). Diagnostics discriminations: Jean-Martin Charcot and the nineteenth-century idea of masculine hysterical neurosis. *Dissertation Abstracts*. (UMI No. AAT 8729120)

Micale, M. S. (1990). Charcot and the idea of hysteria in the male: Gender, mental science, and medical diagnostics in late nineteenth-century France. *Medical History 34*, 363–411.

Micale, M. (Ed.). (1993). *Beyond the unconscious: Essays of Henri F. Ellenberger in the history of psychiatry* (F. Dubor & M. S. Micale, Trans.). Princeton, NJ: Princeton University Press.

Mishra, R. S., Patanjali, B. S. M., & Patanjali, B. K. S. I. (1971). *The textbook of Yoga psychology, a new translation and interpretation of Patanjali's yoga sutras for meaningful application in all modern psychologic disciplines*. New York: Julian Press.

Morrow, A. J. (1969). *The practical theorist: The life and work of Kurt Lewin*. New York and London: Basic Books.

Moustakas, C. E. (Ed.). (1956). *The self: Explorations in personal growth.* New York: Harper & Brothers.

Moustakas, C. E., & Jayaswal, S. R. (1974). *The self: Explorations in personal growth.* New York, London: Harper & Row.

Mullahy, P. (1973). *The beginnings of modern American psychiatry: The ideas of Harry Stack Sullivan.* Boston: Houghton Mifflin.

Murchison, C. (Ed.). (1930). *Psychologies of 1930.* Worcester, MA: Clark University Press; London: H. Milford, Oxford University Press.

Murray, H. A. (1948). *Assessment of men: Selection of personnel for the Office of Strategic Services.* New York: Rinehart.

Murray, H. A., & the Workers at the Harvard Psychological Clinic. (1938). *Explorations in personality: A clinical and experimental study of fifty men of college age.* New York: Oxford University Press.

Murphy, G. (1929). *An historical introduction to modern psychology.* London: K. Paul, Trench, Trubner & Company; New York: Harcourt, Brace & Company.

Murphy, G. (1935). *A briefer general psychology.* New York, London: Harper & Row.

Murphy, G. (1947). *Personality: A biosocial approach to origins and structures.* New York: Harper & Brothers.

Murphy, G. (1956). The current impact of Freud on psychology. In L. B. Murphy (Ed.). (1989), *There is more beyond: Selected papers of Gardner Murphy* (pp. 58–74). Jefferson, NC: McFarland & Company.

Murphy, G. (1958). *Human potentialities.* New York: Basic Books.

Murphy, G., & Jensen, F. (1932). *Approaches to personality: Some contemporary conceptions used in psychology with psychiatry.* New York: Coward-McCann.

Murphy, G., Jensen, F., & Levy, J. (1935). *Approaches to personality: Some contemporary conceptions used in psychology and psychiatry.* New York: Coward-McCann, Inc.

Murphy, G., & Likert, R. (1938). *Public opinion and the individual: A psychological study of student attitudes on public questions, with a retest five years later.* New York, London: Harper & Brothers.

Murphy, G., & Murphy, L. (1931). *Experimental social psychology.* New York: Harper.

Murphy, L. (Ed.). (1989). *There is more beyond: Selected papers of Gardner Murphy.* Jefferson, NC: McFarland and Company.

Murphy, L. (1990). *Gardner Murphy: Integrating, expanding, and humanizing psychology.* Jefferson, NC: McFarland.

Murphy, M. (1992). *The future of the body: Explorations into the further evolution of human nature.* Los Angeles: J. P. Tarcher.

Murphy, M., & Donovan, S. (1997). In E. Taylor (Ed.), *The physical and psychological effects of meditation: A review of contemporary research with a comprehensive bibliography, 1931–1996* (2nd ed.). Sausalito, CA: Institute of Noetic Sciences.

Myers, F.W.H. (1886). Human personality in the light of hypnotic suggestion. *Proceedings of the Society for Psychical Research, 4,* 1–24.

Myers, A. T. (1890). International congress of experimental psychology. *Proceedings of the Society for Psychical Research, 6,* 171–182.

Myers, F. W. H. (1903). *Human personality and its survival of bodily death.* New York: Longmans, Green, and Company.

Natterson, J. M. (1966). Karen Horney, 1885–1952. In F. Alexander, S. Eisenstein, & M. Grotjahn (Ed.), *Psychoanalytic pioneers* (pp. 450–451). New York: Basic Books.

Newberg, A. B., & d'Aquili, E. (2000). The neuropsychology of religious and spiritual experience. In J. Andresen & R. K. C. Forman (Eds.), *Cognitive models and spiritual maps: Interdisciplinary explorations of religious experience* (pp. 251–266). Charlottesville, VA: Imprint Academic.

Nichols, L. (2006, June). *The genesis of the Parsons school in sociology: Dialogue versus charisma in the 1949 Carnegie seminar.* Paper presented at the 38th Annual Meeting of Cheiron,

International Society for History in the Behavioral and Social Sciences, Sarah Lawrence College, Bronxville, NY.

Nicholson, I. (1997a). The politics of scientific social reform, 1936–1960: Goodwin Watson and the society for the psychological study of social issues. *Journal of the History of the Behavioral Sciences, 33*, 39–60.

Nicholson, I. (1997b). To "Correlate Psychology and Social Ethics": Gordon Allport and the first course in American personality psychology. *Journal of Personality, 65*(3), 773–742.

Nicholson, I. (2003). *Inventing personality: Gordon Allport and the science of selfhood.* Washington, DC: American Psychological Association.

Nicolas, S., & Murray, D. J. (1999). Théodule Ribot (1839–1916), founder of French psychology: A biographical introduction. *History of Psychology, 2*(4), 277–301.

Nitzschke, B. (1989). Sigmund Freud and Herbert Silberer: Conjectures on the addressee of a letter by Freud written in 1922. *Review of the International History of Psychoanalysis, 2*, 267–77.

Norman, W. T. (1963). Toward an adequate taxonomy of personality attributes: Replicated factor structure in peer nomination personality ratings. *Journal of Abnormal and Social Psychology, 66*, 574–583.

Northridge, W. L. (1924). *Modern theories of the unconscious.* London: Kegan Paul, Trench, Trubner and Company.

Nylan, M. (2001). *The five "Confucian" classics.* New Haven, CT: Yale University Press.

O'Brien, J., & Jureidini, G. (2002a). Dispensing with the dynamic unconscious. *Philosophy, Psychiatry and Psychology, 9*(2), 141–154.

O'Brien, J., & Jureidini, G. (2002b). The last rites of the dynamic unconscious. *Philosophy, Psychiatry and Psychology, 9*(2), 161–194.

Ochorowicz, J. (1887). *De la suggestion mentale.* Paris: Doin.

Ochorowicz, J. (1891). *Mental suggestion* (J. Fitzgerald, Trans.). New York: Humboldt Publishing Company.

Orne, M. T. (2002). On the social psychology of the psychological experiment: With particular reference to demand characteristics and their implications. *Prevention & Treatment, 5*(35), 1–11; originally published 1962, *The American Psychologist, 17*(11), 776–783.

Ornstein, R. E. (1972). *The psychology of consciousness.* New York: Penguin Books.

Ornstein, R. E. (Ed.). (1973). *The nature of human consciousness: A book of readings.* New York: Viking.

Parsons, T. (1937). *The structure of social action.* New York: McGraw-Hill Book Company.

Parsons, T. (1942). Age and sex in the social structure. *American Sociological Review, 7*(5), 604–616.

Parsons, T. (1949). *Essays in sociological theory, pure and applied.* Glencoe, IL: Free Press.

Parsons, T. (1951). *The social system.* Glencoe, IL: Free Press.

Parsons, T., & Shils, E. (1951). *Toward a general theory of action.* Cambridge, MA: Harvard University Press.

Paskauskas, A. (Ed.). (1995/1993). *The complete correspondence of Sigmund Freud and Ernest Jones, 1908–1939.* Cambridge, MA: Belknap Press of Harvard University Press.

Perry, H. S. (1980). Clara Thompson. In B. Sicherman & C. H. Green (Eds.), *Notable American women: The modern period. A biographical dictionary* (pp. 680–683). Cambridge, MA: Belknap Press of Harvard University.

Perry, H. S. (1982). *Psychiatrist of America: The life of Harry Stack Sullivan.* Cambridge, MA: Harvard University Press.

Pert, C. (1997). *Molecules of emotion.* New York: Scribner.

Pfister, O. R. (1915). *The psychoanalytic method.* London: K. Paul, Trench, Trubner.

Piaget, J. (1973). The affective unconscious and the cognitive unconscious. *Journal of the American Psychoanalytic Association, 21*(2), 249–261.

Pietikainen, P. (2007). The Volk and its unconscious: Jung, Hauer and the 'German Revolution.' *Journal of Contemporary History, 35*(4), 523–539.

Pomar, S. L. (1966). Max Eitingon: The organization of psychoanalytic training. In F. Alexander, S. Eisenstein, & M. Grotjahn (Eds.), *Psychoanalytic pioneers* (pp. 51–62). New York: Basic Books.

Popplestone, J. A. (1998). Virginia Staudt Sexton (1916–1997). *History of Psychology, 1*(1), 88–90.

Prescott, H. M. (2000). "What is 'Normal' Adolescent Growth?" A Paper Presented at the History of Childhood in America Conference, August 5–6, 2000, Washington, DC.

Prince, M. (1906). *The dissociation of a personality.* New York: Longmans, Green and Company.

Pumpian-Mindlin, E., Hilgard, E. R., & Kubie, L. S. (1952). *Psychoanalysis as science: The Hixon Lectures on the scientific status of psychoanalysis.* Stanford CA: Stanford University Press.

Purdy, D. M. (1937). The biological psychology of Kurt Goldstein. *Journal of Personality, 5*(4), 21–330.

Putnam, J. J. (1907). Recent experiences in the study and treatment of hysteria at the Massachusetts General Hospital; with remarks on Freud's method of treatment by "psychoanalysis." *Journal of Abnormal Psychology, 1*(1), 26–41.

Putnam, J. J. (1915). *Human motives.* Boston: Little, Brown, and Company.

Quen, J. M., & Carlson, E. T. (1878). (Eds.). *American psychoanalysis: Origins and development: The Adolf Meyer seminars.* New York: Brunner/Mazel.

Quinn, S. (1988). *A mind of her own: The life of Karen Horney.* New York: Addison Wesley.

Ragsdale, S. (nd). Charlotte Malachowski Buhler, Ph.D. (1893–1974). *Women's intellectual contributions to the study of mind and society.* www.webster.edu/~woolflm/charlottebuhler.html.

Rank, O. (1909). *Der mythus von der geburt des helden versuch einer psychologischen mythendeutun* [The myth of the birth of the hero]. Schriften zur Angewandten Seelenkunde, Heft 5. Leipzig: Deuticke.

Rank, O. (1912). *Das inzest-motiv in dichtung und sage: Grundzüge e. psychologie d. dichterischen schaffens* [The incest motif in poetry and saga]. Leipzig: Deuticke.

Rank, O. (1918). *Der künstler: Ansätze zu e. sexual-psychologie* [The artist: Approches to sexual psychology]. Leipzig: International Psychoanalytic, Verlag.

Rank, O. (1924). *Das trauma der geburt und seine bedeutung* für *die psychoanalyse* [The trauma of birth and its significance for psychoanalysis]. Internationale Psychoanalytische Bibliothek. Leipzig: Internationaler Psychoanalytischer Verlag.

Rank, O. (1996). In R. Kramer & R. May (Eds.), *A psychology of difference: The American lectures.* Princeton, NJ: Princeton University Press.

Rapaport, D. (1942). *Emotions and memory.* Baltimore, MD: The Williams & Wilkins Company.

Rapaport, D. (1945). *Diagnostic psychological testing: The theory, statistical evaluation, and diagnostic application of a battery of tests.* Chicago: The Year Book Publishers Inc.

Rapaport, D. (1945–46). *Diagnostic psychological testing* (2 Vols.). Chicago: The Year Book Publishers, Inc.

Rapaport, D. (Ed., & Trans.). (1951). *Organization and pathology of thought, selected sources.* New York: Columbia University Press.

Rapaport, D. (1958). A historical survey of psychoanalytic ego-psychology. *Bulletin of the Philadelphia Association for Psychoanalysis, 8*, 105–120.

Rapaport, D., & Gill, M. M. (1959). The points of view and assumptions of metapsychology. *International Journal of Psycho-analysis, 40*, 1–10.

Rapaport, D., Schaefer, R., & Gill, M. M. (1946). *Manual of diagnostic psychological testing. II. Diagnostic testing of personality and ideational content* (Vol. 3, No. 1). New York: Macy, Josiah Jr. Foundation.

Ray, P. H., & Anderson, S. R. (2000). *The cultural creatives: How 50 million people are changing the world.* New York: Harmony Books.

Reich, W. (1925). Der triebhafte Charakter: Éire psychoanalytische studie zur pathologie des ich [Character-analysis; principles and technique for psychoanalysts in practice and in training]. Leipzig: Internationaler Psychoanalytischer Verlag.

Reich, W. (1933). *Die massenpsychologie des faschimus* [The mass psychology of fascism]. 2 Auflage, Sexpol Verlag.

Reich, W. (1945). *Character-analysis; principles and technique for psychoanalysts in practice and in training* (T. P. Wolfe, Trans., 2nd ed.). New York: Orgone Institute Press.

Reich, W. (1946). *The mass psychology of fascism* (T. P. Wolfe, Trans.). New York: Orgone Institute Press.

Reid, J. C. (2001). *Jung, my mother, and I: The analytic diaries of Catherine Rush Cabot*. Einsiedeln, Switzerland: Daimon Verlag.

Reisman, J. M. (1966). *The development of clinical psychology*. New York: Appleton-Century-Crofts.

Reisman, J. M. (1976). *A history of clinical psychology*. New York: Irvington.

Reisman, J. M. (1991). *A history of clinical psychology* (2nd ed.). New York: Hemisphere Publishing.

Richter, P. (1881). *Etudes cliniques sur l'hystéro-épilepsie ou grande hystérie*. Paris: Delahaye et Lecrosnier.

Ritvo, S. & Ritvo, L. (1966). Ernest Kris, 1900–1957. In F. Alexander, S. Eisenstein, & M. Grotjahn (Eds.), *Psychoanalytic pioneers* (pp. 484–500). New York: Basic Books.

Roazan, P. (1975). *Freud and his followers*. New York: A. A. Knopf.

Robinson, F. (1992). *Love's story told: A life of Henry A. Murray*. Cambridge, MA: Harvard University Press.

Robinson, P. A. (1969). *The Freudian left: Wilhelm Reich, Geza Roheim, Herbert Marcuse*. New York: Harper & Row.

Roe, A. (1961). The psychology of the scientist. *Science, 134,* 456–459.

Roger, W. (2005). *Masud Khan: The myth and the reality*. London: Free Association Books.

Rogers, C. R. (1939a). *The clinical treatment of the problem child*. London: Allen & Unwin.

Rogers, C. R. (1939b). In L. Carmichael (Ed.), *The clinical treatment of the problem child*. Boston: Houghton Mifflin Company.

Rogers, C. R. (1942a). *Counseling and psychotherapy. Newer concepts in practice*. Cambridge, MA: Harvard University Press.

Rogers, C. R. (1942b). In L. Carmichael (Ed.), *Counseling and psychotherapy: Newer concepts in practice*. Boston, New York: Houghton Mifflin Company.

Rogers, C. R. (1951). *Client-centered therapy, its current practice, implications, and theory*. Boston: Houghton Mifflin.

Rogers, C. R. (1959). A theory of therapy, personality, and interpersonal relationships, as developed in the client centered framework. In S. Koch (Ed.), *Psychology: A study of a science* (Vol. 3, pp. 184–257). New York: McGraw-Hill.

Rogers, N. (1980). *Emerging woman: A decade of midlife transitions*. Point Reyes, CA: Personal Press.

Rogers, N. (1993). *The creative connection: Expressive arts as healing*. Palo Alto, CA: Science & Behavior Books.

Rosenthal, R. (1966). *Experimenter effects in behavioral research*. New York: Appleton-Century-Crofts.

Routh, D. K. (1994). *Clinical psychology since 1917: Science, practice, and organization*. New York: Plenum Press.

Routh, D. K. (2004, August). *The challenges of writing a history of international clinical psychology*. Paper presented at the meeting of the International Society of Clinical Psychology in Beijing, China. Retrieved July 11, 2007 from http://htpprints.yorku.ca/archive/ 00000222/01/Beijing.htm

Rowan, J. (1976). *Ordinary ecstasy. Humanistic psychology in action*. London, Boston: Routledge & Kegan Paul.

Rowan, J., & Cooper, M. (Eds.). (1999). *The plural self: Multiplicity in everyday life*. Thousand Oaks, CA: Sage Publications.

Rudhyar, D. (1970). *The astrology of personality: A re-formulation of astrological concepts and ideals in terms of contemporary psychology and philosophy*. New York: Doubleday.

Samuels, A. (1985). *Jung and the post-Jungians*. London: Routledge & Kegan Paul.

Sartre, J.–P. (1956). *Being and nothingness; an essay on phenomenological ontology*. New York: Philosophical Library.

Sartre, J.–P. (1957). *The transcendence of the ego; an existentialist theory of consciousness*. New York: Noonday Press.

Schenk-Danziger, L. (1963). Fundamental ideas and theories in Charlotte Bühler's lifework. *Journal of Humanistic Psychology, 3*(2), 3–9.

Schimmel, A. (1975). *The mystical dimensions of Islam*. Chapel Hill, NC: University of North Carolina Press.

Schlesinger, H. J. (2007). The treatment program at Menninger. *American Imago, 64*(2), 229–240.

Scholtes, M. (1998). *Become Jesus: The diary of a soul touched by God*. Pittsburgh, PA: Dorrance Publications Company.

Shamdasani, S. (1993, Spring). Automatic writing and the discovery of the unconscious. *Journal of Archetype and Culture, 54*, 100–131.

Shamdasani, S. (1994). Encountering Hélène: Théodore Flournoy and the genesis of subliminal psychology. In S. Shamdasani (Ed.), *From India to the planet Mars: A case of multiple personality with imaginary languages* (pp xi–li). Princeton, NJ: Princeton University Press. (Original work published 1899)

Shamdasani, S. (1995). Memories, dreams, omissions. *Journal of Archetype and Culture, 57*, 115–137.

Shamdasani, S. (1998). *Cult Fictions: C. G. Jung and the founding of analytical psychology*. London, New York: Routledge.

Shamdasani, S. (2003). *Jung and the making of modern psychology*. London: Cambridge University Press.

Shane, P. (1999). *The contribution of Laura Perls to the development of Gestalt therapy*. Unpublished Master's Thesis, Saybrook Graduate School and Research Center, San Francisco.

Shane, P. (2002). *Return of the prodigal daughter: Historiography and the relationship between Gestalt psychology and Gestalt therapy*. Unpublished doctoral dissertation, Saybrook Graduate School and Research Center, San Francisco.

Shevrin, H., & Dickman, S. (1980). The cognitive unconscious: A necessary assumption for all psychological theory? *American Psychologist, 35*(5), 421–434.

Sidis, B. (1898). *The psychology of suggestion; a research into the subconscious nature of man and society* (Preface by William James). New York: D. Appleton & Company.

Sidis, B. (1909a). *An experimental study of sleep (from the Physiological Laboratory of the Harvard Medical School and Sidis Laboratory)*. Boston: Badger.

Sidis, B. (1909b). Studies in psychology: The psychotherapeutic value of the hypnoidal state. *Boston Medical and Surgical Journal, 161*, 242–247; 287–292; 323–327; 356–360.

Silberer, H. (1917). *Problems of mysticism and its symbolism* (S. E. Jelliffe, Trans.). New York: Moffat, Yard and Company.

Silberer, H. (1951). A method of eliciting autosymbolic phenomena. In D. Rapaport (Ed.), *Organization and pathology of thought* (pp. 195–207). New York: Columbia University Press.

Silverman, H. (1977). *The human subject in the psychological laboratory*. New York: Pergamon Press.

Simmel, M. L. (Ed.). (1968). *The Reach of the mind: Essays in memory of Kurt Goldstein*. New York: Springer.

Skinner, B. F. (1938). *The behavior of organisms: An experimental analysis*. Upper Saddle River, NJ: Prentice-Hall; New York: Appleton-Century-Crofts.

Smuts, J. C. (1926). *Holism and evolution*. New York, London: Macmillan.

Sorokin, P. A. (1925). *The sociology of revolution*. Philadelphia: J. B. Lippincott Company.

Sorokin, P. A. (1937–1941). *Social and cultural dynamics*. New York: American Book Company.

Sorokin, P. A. (1941). *The crisis of our age: The social and cultural outlook*. New York: E. P. Dutton (2nd Rev. ed., 1992). London: Oneworld.

Sorokin, P. A. (1947). *Society, culture, and personality: Their structure and dynamics, a system of general sociology*. New York: Harper.

Sorokin, P. A. (1950). *Altruistic love: A study of American "good neighbors" and Christian saints.* Boston: Beacon Press.

Sorokin, P. A. (1963). *A long journey: The autobiography of Pitirim A. Sorokin.* New Haven, CT: College and University Press.

Sorokin, P. A. (1975). *Hunger as a factor in human affairs* (E. P. Sorokin, Trans.). Gainesville, FL: University Presses of Florida.

Sorokin, P. A., & Lunden, W. A. (1959). *Power and morality: Who shall guard the guardians?* Boston: P. Sargent.

Spiegelberg, H. (1972). *Phenomenology in psychology and psychiatry: A historical introduction.* Evanston, IL: Northwestern University Press.

Stagner, R. (1937). *Psychology of personality.* New York: McGraw-Hill Book Company.

Stagner, R. (1988). *A history of psychological theories.* New York: Macmillan; London: Collier Macmillan.

Starcher, D. C. (1999). The chakra system of Tantric yoga: *The Sat-Cakra nirupana, interpreted within the context of a growth-oriented depth psychology. Dissertation Abstracts International, B 64/10.* (UMI No. 3110201)

Stefano, G. B., Fricchione, G. L., Slingsby, B. T., & Benson, H. (2001). The placebo effect and relaxation response: Neural processes and their coupling with constitutive nitric oxide. *Brain Research Reviews, 35,* 1–19.

Stein, H. T. (Ed.). (2002–2006). *The collected clinical works of Alfred Adler* (Vols. 1–12). Bellingham, WA: Classical Adlerian Translation Project.

Stein, H. T. (2007). Adler's legacy: Past, present, and future. Ansbacher Lecture. Annual Conference, North American Society for Adlerian Psychology, May 24, 2007. Vancouver, B.C. Adler Home Page. http://ourworld.compuserve.com/homepages/hstein/adlers-legacy.htm

Stern, W., & Spoerl, H. D. (1938). *General psychology from the personalistic standpoint.* New York: The Macmillan Company.

Stevens, S. S. (1951). *Handbook of experimental psychology.* New York: Wiley & Sons.

Stokes, A. (1985). *Ministry after Freud.* New York: Pilgrim Press.

Strange, J. R., & Taylor, E. I. (1972). A theory of integrative levels useful in teaching psychology. Position paper. Department of Psychology, Southern Methodist University, Dallas Texas.

Strunk, O., Jr. (1972). The self-psychology of Mary Whiton Calkins. *Journal of the History of the Behavioral Sciences, 8*(2), 196–203.

Sullivan, H. S., & Mullahy, P. (1947). *Conceptions of modern psychiatry.* William Alanson White Memorial Lectures. Washington, DC: W. A. White Psychiatric Foundation.

Sulloway, F. J. (1979). *Freud, biologist of the mind: Beyond the psychoanalytic legend.* New York: Basic Books.

Sutich, A. (1944). Toward a professional code for psychological consultants. *The Journal of Abnormal and Social Psychology, 39*(3), July 1944. pp. 329–350.

Sutich, A. (1976). *The founding of humanistic and transpersonal psychology: A personal account.* Unpublished doctoral dissertation, Humanistic Psychology Institute, San Francisco.

Swami Akhilananda (1946). *Hindu psychology.* New York: Harper & Brothers.

Swan, W. (2007). *C. G. Jung and active imagination: A case study of Tina Keller,* Saarbrucken, Germany: VDM Verlag.

Szalay, S. (1998). Tributes to Whitmont. *American Homeopath, 4,* 63–67.

Tart, C. T. (1969). *Altered states of consciousness.* New York: Wiley.

Tart, C. T. (1972). States of consciousness and state-specific sciences. *Science, 176*(4040), 1203–1210.

Taylor, E. I. (1983). *William James on exceptional mental states.* New York: Charles Scribner's Sons.

Taylor, E. I. (1985a). Psychotherapy, Harvard, and the American Society for Psychical Research, 1884–1889. *Proceedings of the 28th Annual Convention of the Parapsychological Association.* Tufts University, Medford, Massachusetts, August 15, 319–346.

Taylor, E. I. (1985b). James Jackson Putnam's fateful meeting with Freud: The 1909 Clark University Conference. *Voices: The Art and Science of Psychotherapy, 21*(1), 78–89.

Taylor, E. I. (1988). On the first use of psychoanalysis at the Massachusetts General Hospital, 1903–1908. *Journal of the History of Medicine and Allied Sciences, 43*(4), 447–471.

Taylor, E. I. (1992). The case for a uniquely American Jamesian tradition in psychology. In M. E. Donnelly (Ed.), *Reinterpreting the legacy of William James* (pp. 3–28). Washington, DC: American Psychological Association.

Taylor, E. I. (1999). *Shadow culture: Psychology and spirituality in America.* Washington, DC: Counterpoint.

Taylor, E. I. (2000). "What is man, psychologist, that thou art so unmindful of him?": Henry A. Murray on the historical relation between classical personality theory and humanistic psychology. *Journal of Humanistic Psychology, 40*(3), 29–42.

Taylor, E. I. (2001a). Foreword: The Americanization of Jungian ideas. In W. McGuire (Ed.) (B. Hinkle, Trans.), *Psychology of the unconscious: A study of the transformations and symbolisms of the libido: A contribution to the history of the evolution of thought: Collected works of C. G. Jung, Supplementary Vol. B*, (pp. xvii–xxvi). Princeton, NJ: Princeton University Press.

Taylor, E. I. (2001b, Winter). Positive psychology versus Humanistic psychology: A reply to Prof. Seligman. *Journal of Humanistic Psychology: Special Issue, 41*(1), 13–29.

Taylor, E. I. (2001–2002). The Varieties and its influence. In *William James and the spiritual roots of American pragmatism.* Lectures on the Centenary of James's *Varieties of Religious Experience* for the Swedenborg Society at Harvard.

Taylor, E. I. (2008). William James on pure experience and Samadhi in Samkhya Yoga. In K. R. Rao (Ed.), *Handbook of Indian psychology.* Allahabad, India: Allahabad.

Taylor, E. I. (2008). "Come Hither and Be Measured": On the problematic relation between cognitive psychology and spiritual experience from a Jamesean point of view. Presented as the keynote address to The Conference on Religion and Cognitive Science. Co-sponsored by the Cognitive Science Program at the University of California at Berkeley and the Graduate Theological Union Berkeley, California, January 16, 2008.

Taylor, E. I. (In press). Jung on Swedenborg redivivus. *Jung History,* 4. (Ardmore, PA: Philemon Foundation).

Taylor, E. I. (In press). The Zen doctrine of no-method. *The Humanistic Psychologist.*

Taylor, E. I., Martinez, S., & Martin, F. (Eds.). (2000). *Old Saybrook one: Landmark in the history of humanistic psychology: Commemorative edition.* Cambridge, MA: The Essene Press.

Thompson, C. (1950). *Psychoanalysis: Evolution and development.* New York: Hermitage House.

Tillich, P. (1952). *The courage to be.* New Haven, CT: Yale University Press.

Tillich, P. (1954). *Love, power, and justice.* New York, London: Oxford University Press.

Tissié, P. (1887). *Les aliénés voyageurs; essai médico-psychologique.* Paris, Doin.

Tissié, P. (1890). *Les rêves; physiologie et pathologie.* Paris, Ancienne Librairie German Baillière.

Tomkins, S. S. (1943). *Contemporary psychopathology.* Cambridge, MA: Harvard University Press.

Trotter, W. (1916). *Instincts of the herd in peace and war.* New York: The Macmillan Company.

Ullman, M., & Krippner, S. (1970). *Dream studies and telepathy: An experimental approach.* New York: Parapsychology Foundation.

Ullman, M., & Krippner, S. (1973). *Dream telepathy.* New York: The Macmillan Company.

Van Dijken, K. S., Van der Veer, R., Van IJzendoorn, M. H., & Kuipers, H. J. (1998). Bowlby before Bowlby: The sources of an intellectual departure in psychoanalysis and psychology. *Journal of the History of the Behavioral Sciences, 34*(3), 247–269.

Van Kaam, A. L. (1964). *Religion and personality.* Englewood Cliffs, NJ: Prentice-Hall.

Van Kaam, A. L. (1966a). *Existential foundations of psychology.* Pittsburgh, PA: Duquesne University Press.

Van Kaam, A. L. (1966b). *The art of existential counseling.* Wilkes-Barre, PA: Dimension Books.

Varela, F. J. (1995). The emergent self. In J. Brockman (Ed.), *The third culture: Beyond the scientific revolution* (pp. 210–222). New York: Touchstone.

Varela, F. J., & Bruce, T. (2002). Consciousness in the neurosciences. *Journal of European Psychoanalysis, 14*, 109–122.

Vasile, R. G. (1977). *James Jackson Putnam, from neurology to psychoanalysis a study of the reception and promulgation of Freudian psychoanalytic theory in America, 1895–1918.*Oceanside, NY: Dabor Science Publications.

Vaughan, F. E. (1979). *Awakening intuition.* New York: Anchor Press.

Vaughan, F. E., & Walsh, R. N. (Eds.). (1980). *Beyond ego: Transpersonal dimensions in psychology.* Los Angeles: J. P. Tarcher.

Velmans, M. (1993). A reflexive science of consciousness. In *Experimental and theoretical studies of consciousness* (pp. 81–99). Ciba Foundation; Oxford, England: John Wiley & Sons.

Vich, M. (1988). Some historical sources of the term "transpersonal." *Journal of Transpersonal Psychology, 20*(2), 107–110.

Vidal, F. (2005). Le sujet cérébral: Une esquisse historique et conceptuelle. *Psychiatrie, Sciences Humaines, Neurosciences, 3,* 37–48.

Wade, N. (2005). *Perception and illusion: Historical perspectives.* New York: Springer Science.

Walker, C. E. (Ed.). (1991). *The history of clinical psychology in autobiography.* Pacific Grove, CA: Brooks/Cole Publishing Company.

Wallace, R. K., & Benson, H. (1973). The physiology of meditation. In D. Shapiro, T. X. Barber, L. Dicara, J. Kamiya, N. Miller, & J. Stovya (Eds.). *(1972), Biofeedback and self control* (pp. 353–364). Chicago: Aldine.

Walsh, A. A. (1978). "Mollie Fancher: The Brooklyn enigma." *New Port Magazine, 1,* 2 (Salve Regina College); (1899) *Proceedings of the British Society for Psychical Research, 14,* 396.

Watson, R. L. (1975). *Scientists are human.* New York: Arno Press.

Watts, A. (1957). *The way of Zen.* New York: Pantheon.

Watts, A. (1961). *Psychotherapy east and west.* New York: Pantheon.

Watts, A. (1962). *The joyous cosmology: Adventures in the chemistry of consciousness.* New York: Pantheon.

Weide, T. N. (1973). Vallombrosa: A major transpersonal event. *Journal of Transpersonal Psychology, 5*(2), 205–208.

Wertheimer, M. (1945). *Productive thinking.* New York: Harper & Row.

White, B., Wolf, R., & Taylor, E. I. (1984). *Stanley Cobb: A builder of the modern neurosciences.* Boston: Francis A. Countway Library of Medicine.

Whitmont, E. C. (1969). *The symbolic quest: Basic concepts of analytical psychology.* New York: Putnam.

Whitmont, E. C. (1982). *Return of the goddess.* New York: Crossroad.

Whitmont, E. C., & Perera, S. B. (1989). *Dreams, a portal to the source.* London, New York: Routledge.

Widiger, T. A., & Trull, T. J. (2007). Plate tectonics in the classification of personality disorder: Shifting to a dimensional model. *American Psychologist, 62*(2), 71–83.

Wilber, K. (1975). Psychologia perennis: The spectrum of consciousness. *Journal of Transpersonal Psychology, 7*(2), 105–132.

Wilber, K. (1977). *The spectrum of consciousness.* Wheaton, IL: Theosophical Publication House.

Wilhelm, R., & Baynes, C. F. (1968). *The I Ching, or, book of changes.* London: Routledge & Kegan Paul.

Winnicott, D. W. (1958). *Collected papers: Through paediatrics to psycho-analysis.* London: Tavistock Publications; New York: Basic Books.

Winnicott, D. W. (1975). *Collected papers: Through paediatrics to psycho-analysis.* London: Hogarth Press and the Institute of Psychoanalysis.

Winnicott, D. W. (1992). *Collected papers: Through paediatrics to psycho-analysis.* London: Institute of Psychoanalysis and Karnac Books; New York: Brunner/Mazel.

Winter, D. G., & Barenbaum, N. B. (1999). History of modern personality theory and research. In L. A. Pervin & O. P. John (Eds.), *Handbook of personality: Theory and research* (2nd ed., pp. 3–27). New York: Guilford.

Wolff, W. (1943). *The expression of personality: Experimental depth psychology.* New York, London: Harper & Brothers.

Wolff, W. (1948). *Diagrams of the unconscious: Handwriting and personality in measurement, experiment and analysis.* New York: Grune & Stratton.

Woodworth, R. S. (1918). *Dynamic psychology.* New York: Columbia University Press.

Woody, J. M. (2002). Dispensing with the dynamic unconscious. *Philosophy, Psychiatry and Psychology, 9*(2), 155–157.

Wysong, J., & Rosenfeld, E. (1982). An oral history of Gestalt therapy: Interviews with Laura Perls, Isadore From, Erving Polster, Miriam Polster, Joe Wysong, Edward Rosenfeld. *Gestalt Journal, 1–3.*

Wyss, D. (1966). *Depth psychology: A critical history, development, problems, crises.* New York: W. W. Norton.

Yin, R. K. (2003). *Case study research: Design and methods.* Thousand Oaks, CA: Sage.

Young-Eisendrath, P., & Dawson, T. (Eds.). (1997). *The Cambridge companion to Jung.* Cambridge [Cambridgeshire]: Cambridge University Press.

Zahavi, D. (2005). *Subjectivity and selfhood: Investigating the first person perspective.* Cambridge, MA: MIT Press.

Zaretsky, E. (2004). *Secrets of the Soul: A social and cultural history of psychoanalysis.* New York: Alfred A. Knopf.

Zilboorg, G., & Henry, G. W. (1941). *A history of medical psychology.* New York: W. W. Norton.

Zimmer, H. R. (1952). In J. Campbell (Ed.), *Philosophies of India.* London: Routledge & Kegan Paul.

Zimmer, H. (n.d.). *Two lectures.* Privately printed. Cambridge, MA: Harvard University.

Index

Breinigsville, PA USA
11 February 2010
232324BV00008B/97/P